The Ernest Bloch Professorship
of Music and the Ernest Bloch Lectures
were established at the University of California
in 1962 in order to bring distinguished figures
in music to the Berkeley campus from time to time.
Made possible by the Jacob and Rosa Stern
Musical Fund, the professorship was founded
in memory of Ernest Bloch (1880–1959),
the first beneficiary of the Stern Fund and
Professor of Music at Berkeley
from 1940 to 1952.

THE ERNEST BLOCH PROFESSORS

1964	Ralph Kirkpatrick	1993	Susan McClary
1965–66	Winton Dean	1994–95	Wye J. Allanbrook
1966–67	Roger Sessions	1995	Jonathan Harvey
1968–69	Gerald Abraham	1997	Lydia Goehr
1970–71	Leonard B. Meyer	1998	Izaly Zemtsovsky
1972	Edward T. Cone	1999	David Huron
1975–76	Donald Jay Grout	2002	Roger Parker
1977	Charles Rosen	2003	Steven Stucky
1979–80	William Malm	2005	William Bolcom
1980–81	Alan Tyson	2007	Martha Feldman
1980–81	Andrew Porter	2008	Steve Mackey
1983	Ton De Leeuw	2009	Steven Feld
1983	James Haar	2010	Pedro Memelsdorff
1985	Richard Crawford	2010	Peter Franklin
1986	John Blacking	2011	Fred Lerdahl
1987	Gunther Schuller	2013	George E. Lewis
1989	George Perle	2013	Martin Stokes
1989	László Somfai	2014	Georgina Born

The publisher gratefully acknowledges the generous contribution
to this book provided by the Humanities Visiting Committee
of the University of Chicago and the Gustave Reese Endowment
of the American Musicological Society, funded in part by the
National Endowment for the Humanities and
the Andrew W. Mellon Foundation.

The publisher also acknowledges the generous support of the
Ahmanson Foundation Humanities Endowment Fund of
the University of California Press Foundation.

The Castrato

The Castrato

Reflections on Natures and Kinds

Martha Feldman

UNIVERSITY OF CALIFORNIA PRESS

University of California Press, one of the most distinguished university presses in the United States, enriches lives around the world by advancing scholarship in the humanities, social sciences, and natural sciences. Its activities are supported by the UC Press Foundation and by philanthropic contributions from individuals and institutions. For more information, visit www.ucpress.edu.

University of California Press
Oakland, California

© 2015 by The Regents of the University of California

First paperback printing in 2016

Library of Congress Cataloging-in-Publication Data
Feldman, Martha.
 Th e castrato : reflec tions on natures and kinds / Martha Feldman
 p. cm. — (Ernest Bloch lectures)
Includes bibliographical references and index.
ISBN 978-0-520-27949-0 (cloth) | 978-0-520-29244-4 (pbk. 1.
Castrati. I. Title.
 ML1460.F45 2015
 ML1460.F45'6—dc23   2014011273

24 23 22 21 20 19 18 17 16
10 9 8 7 6 5 4 3 2 1

*like ghosts, like family, like angels,
translucent and in-between*

For additional images and audio-visual materials, see the book's website at http://www.ucpress.edu/go/castrato.

Castraporce'lli, s.m.
Castrapor'ci, s.m.
[che esercita l'arte di castrare] a gelder.
Castra're, to geld, to castrate, to cut. *Castrare [lo 'ntaccare i mattoni e le castagne accio non iscoppino quando si metton nel fuoco per cuocerli]* to cut. *Castrare un libro [levarne qualche cosa]* to castrate a book, to cut off something from it, to castrate some part of it.
Castra'to, s.m. *[castrone]* a wether, a male sheep gelded.
  Castrato [carne di castrato] mutton.
Castra'to, adj. gelded. *Libro castrato,* a castrated book.

GIUSEPPE MARCO ANTONIO BARETTI, *DIZIONARIO DELLE LINGUE ITALIANE, ED INGLESE* (VENICE, 1795)

CASTRATO, A musician, who in his infancy had been deprived of the organs of generation, for the sake of preserving a shrill voice, who sings that part called sophrano. However small the connection may appear between two such different organs, it is a certain fact that the mutilation of the one prevents and hinders in the other that change which is perceptible in mankind, near the advance of manhood, and which, on a sudden, lowers their voice an eighth. There exist in Italy, some inhuman fathers, who sacrificing nature to fortune, give up their children to this operation, for the amusement of voluptuous and cruel persons, who have the barbarity to require the exertion of voice which the unhappy wretches possess.

JEAN-JACQUES ROUSSEAU, *THE COMPLETE DICTIONARY OF MUSIC* (LONDON, [1779])

CONTENTS

Preface xi
*Note on Textual Transcription, Translations, Lexicon,
    and Musical Nomenclature* xxiii

PART ONE. REPRODUCTION

1. Of Strange Births and Comic Kin 3
2. The Man Who Pretended to Be Who He Was: A Tale of Reproduction 40

PART TWO. VOICE

3. Red Hot Voice 79
4. Castrato De Luxe: Blood, Gifts, and Goods 133

PART THREE. HALF-LIGHT

5. Cold Man, Money Man, Big Man Too 177
6. Shadow Voices, Castrato and Non 211

Acknowledgments 263
Abbreviations 267
Notes 269
Bibliography 369
List of Illustrations 401
Index 405

PREFACE

During the centuries bracketed by around 1550 and the late nineteenth century many boys were castrated to be made into full-throated adult sopranos. The last one died in 1922. Nowadays we call these singers castrati (singular: castrato), though most often and more politely in their times they were called *musici, eunuchi, cantori evirati,* or simply *soprani* (musicians, eunuchs, emasculated singers, or sopranos). There was no one sort of castrato but irreducibly many different sorts joined by a few stubborn physiological and social facts. All of them shared the deformation of having been castrated testicularly before puberty, the hormonal effects of which were erratic across the population and the anatomical consequences thus highly variable. There were high sopranos, mezzos, and altos, strident voices and sweet ones, loud and mellow voices, more and less flexible throats, very tall men and very short, well- and ill-proportioned castrati, older ones beset by osteoporosis or melancholy and others not.

What was invariable was the high voice that resulted and that essentially remained so throughout life. Upon reaching maturity the voices of castrati were typically resonant, often strong, and often nimble owing to a combination of physical predisposition and intense, multifaceted musical training through which their bodies were radically disciplined. All this can be variously laid to account for the collective professional success of castrati over the long run, with a number of them also achieving high cultural capital in the form of prestige, fame, wealth, and social mobility. By the late seventeenth century the distinct musical legacy they left had an importance that is hard to overestimate. It is no exaggeration to say that the entire classical foundation of virtuosic solo singing in the West, sacred and secular, culminating in the early nineteenth-century singing associated nowadays with the trio of Rossini, Bellini, and Donizetti, owes its existence to the musical traditions and practices of castrati. It was their lost singing tradition that in the mid-nineteenth century allegedly prompted Rossini to pine nostalgically for their "bel canto."[1]

How and why did this phenomenon, whether at a grand international scale or a local one of family and church, take shape precisely in and around men who lacked the ability to produce offspring through direct bloodlines, which the society that generated them so highly valued? And how did the castrated body represent and embody society symbolically while pressing against its foundational norms and narratives?[2] This book suggests that while the resolute infertility of testicular castration made filiation of wealth problematic, it was strangely but necessarily coupled with many uniquely efficacious forms of cultural exchange in which castrati participated, and in such varied domains as music making, composing, reputation building, networking, power brokering, courting, and estate and legacy building.

To tackle the question of cultural exchange that is central to these essays, I start by noting that in decisions to castrate and in after-the-fact explanations of them, castration for singing was widely framed as a form of sacrifice entailing both renunciation and gain. Many facts and motivations remain obscure and contradictory, yet the evidence so far recovered suffices to suggest, first, that the operation itself—of castrating and of being castrated—was a performative one that involved bloodshed through mortification of the flesh; and second, that there was a consequence. Crudely put, something was given up and something else obtained. What was given up was typical male anatomy, secondary sexual characteristics, normal growth, and, most of all, the ability to make progeny. (Sexual performance, to the extent it was affected, was typically deemed a lesser loss, and sexual orientation, as we think of it, was basically irrelevant.) What was gained was a high, often-exceptional voice, amenable to training beyond what was otherwise usual in a conservatory, church, cathedral school, or private teacher's home, one that would minimally lead to a small-town church career and maximally to elite celebrity status, in some cases meaning a major career with the potential to change a family's fortune (rarely did no musical career result).

At first glance what I call a sacrifice may look like nothing more than a bargain, but a bargain differs from a sacrifice in that it takes place in the exchange mode of compacts and contracts. It involves a transaction in which two parties attempt to balance the transactional equation, at least in principle, with no higher purpose at stake. A sacrifice, by contrast, is only worthy of the name if it involves a sanctification or "sacralization" of something that is renounced in an act directed at a higher being: the man who sacrifices a tuber to a deity in hopes of having a good harvest or who sacrifices a cow in exchange for a healthy family renounces something to a greater authority or makes an offering or pays homage to one. That which is sacrificed can nowise equal the magnanimity and incalculable beneficences returned of life itself because the former is paltry by comparison with the latter, just as the one who sacrifices is small and inconsequential compared with the being or entity to whom the sacrifice is made. Think of Agamemnon, who in most versions of his myth sacrificed his daughter Iphigenia to obtain winds from the gods that would allow his fleet to set sail for Troy and thus save his entire people; or Abraham, who was prepared to sacrifice Isaac as proof of his fear of the Hebrew God. Crucially, exchange in all these instances takes a vertical form at the lower end of which are human beings positioned beneath the one(s) who may (or may not) accept the sacrifice as a form of deference and reverence worthy of a return.

How, then, might we understand castration in a sacrificial idiom given that it was recruited for conflicting, and often self-interested, purposes, prospectively and retrospectively, by the various parties involved, and given that all these purposes were complexly imbricated in a Catholic church that itself made contradictory demands? Canon rule did not in fact permit bodily mutilations except for medical necessity, yet the early modern Church developed a seemingly insatiable desire for high male voices whose existence therefore had to be rationalized (women could not sing in church because of Pauline proscriptions that forbid it; indeed, they could not sing in public at all in the Papal States). Clearly, it was in no small part because of such proscriptions that boys had nominally and a priori to declare their wish to be castrated—the Jesuit Tommaso Tamburini (1591–1675) said outright that a castration could be done only "provided there is no mortal danger to life and that it is not done without the boy's consent."[3] For the same reason boys often explained their castrations a posteriori as sacred donations to God, church, and prince (the last a divine representative of God on earth), and surgeons, parents, teachers, patrons, colleagues, and fans generally followed suit. If boys and their families needed subsistence or good jobs, or simply wanted to improve a family's standing in the world, they were also borrowing available symbolic and discursive repertoires of explanation to justify a practice that had little precedent around 1600 as a social one carried out to create musical careers.

Furthermore, castrations and their explanations were by a certain reckoning speech acts, hence simultaneously discursive and pragmatic, and *perlocutionary* in the sense that the utterances themselves can be thought to have produced the effect of establishing sacredness in the speakers' minds and listeners' understandings.[4] At the same time, the conception of the castration as sacrificial had a *prophylactic* value for the principals involved. The castration may have been illegal, but the claim of sacrifice made it a sacred donation to God and church, something that all in all should do more good than harm and leave no one at fault for defying canonical prohibitions.

The motives of those who participated in castration for singing were more straightforward than those of the church, but their justifications and explanations were often hedged by attempts to satisfy the ecclesiastical authority that both condoned and condemned it. In the face of those contradictions, it's not surprising that surviving accounts are marked by a bewildering diversity of claims, intentions, and registers. For even if sacrificing a son to castration in order to improve one's lot may not be altogether different from sacrificing a tuber or a cow, justifying it had to be carefully hedged and nuanced.

In thinking about the broader context for these practices, it is important to bear in mind that castrations for singing, beginning well before 1600, took place only in Italy, geographic heartland of the one, holy, catholic, and apostolic church. In *The Juice of Life: The Symbolic and Magic Significance of Blood,* Piero Camporesi uses a variety of genres, medical, theological, and mystical, to elucidate the utter centrality of blood in the symbolic universe of late Renaissance and baroque Italy.[5] Blood in Italy was omnipresent as an object of spectacle, a common sight in the public arenas of punishments and executions but also common in the smaller ones of butchery, dissections, and bloodlettings. It mirrored the soul at its most harmonious and salubrious, as typified by beautiful women and plump, ruddy youths. It was also a source of purification and regeneration as concocted in culinary and medicinal recipes. Binding together all these functions was the commonality in the popular imagination of blood as a reminder of Christ's crucifixion, associated positively with salvation and negatively with the horrific suffering of the mortified flesh. In Italy, then, a critical context for ritualizing the bloodshed of humans as a form of sacrifice was the passion of Christ, which human bloodshed symbolically imitated.

Richly for our themes, Christ's blood sacrifice, in Camporesi's analysis, gave rise at the same time to guilt-ridden fantasies about the cruelty of human destroying human. The destruction of God's own son prompted continual symbolic reenactments because in the early modern imagination it dishonors the proper relationship Father/Son (God/Christ), creating a worrisome psychic disturbance that must eventually be confronted. To dramatize the point, Camporesi glosses a passage from Saint Catherine of Siena bewailing the atrocity of the passion of Christ as one committed against the very propagation of the species by doing violence to the originary generative relationship. We are impotent, in other words, and can live only *because* of the blood of another. In Camporesi's words, quoting Catherine's metaphor of Christ's followers as mere grafted, sterile trees, "The Passion of the Cross, in all of its forms, was relived as an act of hateful contempt for the link between the tree-Father and the Son-shoot, as a horrendous outrage to the germinating flesh and blood-sap of the tender, helpless Plant, the paradisiacal Bud. 'Sterile, fruitless trees, without any fruit soever!' Saint Catherine of Siena used to say. 'With his precious blood . . . we are grafted onto the tree of life.'"[6]

The landscape of Catholic Italy has endless sources of identifications with Christ's shedding of blood and no end of need by the faithful to experience it again and again. Some saints and martyrs seem to think of little else. The ubiquity and transformability of blood, manifest in the "obsessive presence of the drama of the Passion in the collective trauma of paradise lost," occasions such mass theaters of gory anatomical display that we might almost conceive castrato performances as objects of intense scopophilia by spectators engrossed in fantasizing back to the bloody bodily modifications that originally produced them.[7]

. . .

In formal terms, castrati are celibates, if celibacy is understood as the permanent state entered into as a result of renouncing (or being constrained to renounce) marriage and generation. They can thus be assimilated to the structural position of second sons who could not marry so typically went into careers in the military or the church (as *cadetti*). But not all celibacy was created equal. By contrast with castrati, noncastrated celibates could have illegitimate offspring, and those offspring in turn could find substantial places within life and death schemes involving baptisms, godparents, lay religious memberships, schooling, marriage, children, parental care, inheritance, funerals, and burials.[8] Alternatively, depending on their status, noncastrates might marry later in life or assume the position of a first son if the son first in line were to die, be deemed unfit, or be disabled or disowned; or they might marry simply because marriage norms had loosened over the course of their lifespan, as happened often in the later eighteenth century. Although uncastrated celibates were thus *likely* to stay that way, they did not all do so,[9] by contrast with castrati who occupied a distinct existential status because they had entered an irrevocable physical state that forevermore annihilated all possibility of biological generation. Unlike the celibacy of *cadetti* and their lower-born counterparts among the poorer and middling classes, the castrato's was a celibacy with no back door. In common parlance, we could say that for the castrato the sacrifice was greater because it was more definitive than for others. It was also publicly legible by virtue of the developmental malformations it caused, at minimum beardlessless and maximally considerable ill proportions—no small matters given the intense preoccupations in Italy with social performance and with family and blood ties. And it set them apart even relative to other singers, since, as we will see, everything about their renunciation and their state was understood to be tantamount to a complete dedication to singing and little else.

Insofar as this totalizing condition marks the castrato, its keenest analytic model might be the brilliant theory of sacrifice by Henri Hubert and Marcel Mauss of 1898, generalized from a dense corpus of Vedic and Hebrew evidence. For Hubert and Mauss sacrifice is a dynamic idiom involving three functions: the *victim* (the one sacrificed), the *sacrificer* (the one actively performing the sacrifice), and the *sacrifier* (the one on whose behalf the sacrifice is carried out).[10] Adapting these to the castrato case, the constellation of functions would include the boy as victim, the surgeon (usually) as sacrificer, and one or more sacrifiers who might include an individual (a ruler, a teacher), an indigent or upwardly mobile family, an institution (a church, cathedral, chapel, court, or great house or palace) or, by extension, an aggregate of persons: operagoers, congregants, or courtiers.[11]

Among the invariable elements of sacrificial acts that Hubert and Mauss induce from their cases is the occurrence of some kind of conflagration or other catastrophic destruction of the victim, who somehow has to be ravaged in a solemn but devastating way. The resulting release of energy effects his transformation from a desecrated state to a sacralized one.[12] The end goal is to sanction the victim so as to authorize him for a special purpose, removing him (or her or it) from ordinary life, sometimes by death, in this case by radical alteration that leads to a kind of rebirth.[13] Thereafter the victim, now improved—at a minimum in order to be suited to safeguard the sacrifier—mediates between sacred and profane worlds.[14] Through his sacrifice he also *substitutes* for the sacrifier, since the latter's own eventual and inevitable end (by loss of power, health, or life) can thereby be deferred.

How might this ravaging be conceived in relation to castrations for singing? Although I argue that the latter were on some level consistently so framed, I hasten to emphasize that sacrifice in the account that follows is in no way invoked to provide a comprehensive *explanation* for the phenomenon, musical or social. Many factors contributed to the virtually unprecedented phenomenon of castrating hundreds or thousands of boys for music. Economic crisis converged with a mass desire for exceptional male sopranos that could fill large spaces with what listeners often described as extraordinarily affecting music. The socioeconomic and political systems were in transition and were thus still hybridized in ways that opened an unusual space for the practice, one that operated in the interstices between a gift economy governed by patron-client relations and an emergent bourgeois economy based in mercantilism and cash exchange. The two had rough correlates to absolutist-style governments on one side and reform-minded governments on the other, though in reality all of these components were variously mixed.[15]

By 1600 creating male trebles via prepubertal castration seems to have been done exclusively and systematically in Italy, where it was widely (if always ambivalently) accepted.[16] The phenomenon was never wholly premodern nor certainly was it ever modern, if what we mean by premodern is something like feudal, preindustrial, and vested in direct revelation and unquestionable authority and what we mean by modern is something that is postfeudal, bureaucratic, industrial, money-centered, empirical, and sensist—all of which are in any case arbitrary when decontextualized. If any of these categories is heuristically useful, we might think of the whole existence of castrati between around 1550 and 1922, when the last of them died, as being structurally caught betwixt and between. The emergence of the phenomenon ran parallel to the decidedly unmedieval practice of patriliny (descent based on direct male lines), which favored a radically vertical form of primogeniture, economically advantageous given widespread economic crisis in the later sixteenth and seventeenth centuries, in contrast to medieval clan-based family systems. The specific realities of patriliny meant that fewer males could marry so that more became celibates of various kinds. At the same time, more lower-class sons were in desperate need of work while the families of others in the middle ranks saw castration as opening up a possibility for upward social and economic mobility. By opting for castration, families, and arguably some boys themselves, saw the chance to take advantage of new forms of clientage to climb the socioeconomic ladder.[17]

In my gloss, then, the very institution of the castrato was invested in the patriarchal character of this system by practical attempts by castrati to participate in it despite "lacking what it takes." What they claimed was not that they were ambiguously sexed, hermaphroditic, or sexually "continuous," as late twentieth-century scholarship often had it, but that they were decidedly male.[18] Maleness was a zone of ambiguity only if we presuppose it as a category of sexual identity in the first place. Understood independently of either sexual orientation or sexual object of choice, maleness is fundamentally a political category more than a social/sexual or biosocial one. Politically castrati compensated for being infertile through a number of strategies, which I delineate in chapters 2 and 4: adoption, often of nephews; extended international friendship networks with patrons, royals, writers, singers, artists, and others; paternal relationships with acquired father figures and sometimes maternal ones (in particular with patrons and with patrons' families, but also with teachers and other colleagues); careful acquisition of goods and money; and careful management of their estates, heirs, and bequests. On rare occasions some even married Protestant women abroad, attempted or "wished" to marry, or were involved in marriage-like living arrangements. They were apt to align themselves with male power, including rulership, if they could sing at court or in important churches or opera houses. In all this we can see them engaging in concrete forms of male social reproduction.

The symbolic and cultural meanings of that maleness are braided together here with empirical evidence in a dialectical rhythm that modulates this book. The former are elaborated in chapter 1, in which I show that explanations of how men came to be castrated are typically framed as sacrifices but also often as iterations of male courage, "necessitated" by, for example, accidents caused by fighting or hunting or playing too hard or by fighting off a terrible illness. Glosses of the castration itself often deemed it a form of masculine courage as well. Within these explanations, a sacrificial notion of bloodshed is implicit, but the explanations also accommodate other, conflicting pressures and interests: the hypocrisy of ecclesiastical prohibitions against castration for singing, the widespread ecclesiastical and broad cultural desire for castrated voices, and the urge on the part of victims and other participants to frame castration in the idioms of renunciation.

We might speak then of a multidirectional sacrificial economy in which explanations for and justifications of castration claim to forestall the ills of accidents and infirmities before the fact (prophylactically), or claim to cure them after the fact (therapeutically). Can such explanatory narratives imply a temporal logic, moving victims from budding male hubris to humility and servitude, and from a kind of mangily ordinary existence to an extraordinary, sacralized one? If anything, changes in the nature of these explanations that come in the wake of economic recovery and the transition to an Enlightenment political and moral regime suggest they can. For as the numbers of castrati declined along with the numbers of other celibates, explanations if anything became even more diversionary and displacing, less ordinary and more sacralizing, once again putting castration not outside maleness but within it.

. . .

The most explicitly symbolic relationship to social reproduction is one I delineate in chapter 1, which concerns the iconographic and discursive associations between the castrato and Pulcinella, the archetypal figure of comedy and transformation. Just one aspect of early modern festivity in which the castrato is implicated, Pulcinella formed with respect to him part of a symbolic totality of high and low. He functioned as an "anti-castrato," a term that helps clarify the encompassing nature of the relationship with its vertical movement, so outwardly improbable.[19] Pulcinella is a cackling male figure with a high voice and womanly physical traits, a womanizer forever plagued by hapless sexual misfires, and an endlessly transformable performer who reproduces himself prolifically in quasi-male form. In various myths of origins, he is birthed by male gods or animals. Satirists sometimes elide the castrato with Pulcinella or other comic figures, critical among them the still-obscure castrato-writer Filippo Balatri (1682–1756), who authored a large amount of prose and poetry in manuscript and is a principal informant for this book.

Most of Balatri's writings are both satirical and autobiographical. They can usefully be read alongside other materials in joking genres, which complement the "real" by exposing that which cannot easily be spoken.[20] Northrop Frye's take on what he calls ironic comedy, including satire, is relevant here, as it understands satire as featuring the abject, often in contexts including pain, victimhood, and even human sacrifice.[21] Not coincidentally, satire as moral criticism mirrors the abuses and follies of society for the purpose of its own self-inspection, serving as a tacit tool of shame exacted through exaggeration, parody, rude double entendres, and cruel laughter. As a prominent literary genre for commenting on castrati, satire makes castrati into instruments par excellence of social criticism.[22]

So if the castrato is Pulcinella's symbolic antitype, it is because both figures are seen as hovering between braggadocio and abjection, passing or passing themselves off as something they are not (a nobleman, a good sexual performer, a brother-in-law or son-in-law, a father *in potentia*). In particular, they participate in a larger social dynamic linked to the festive time of Carnival, which constitutes them in collective psychic terms as Others within a putatively larger social Self that they variously stimulate, antagonize, and enchant but finally allow to return to its status quo.[23] To analyze this dynamic in a symbolic register is in no way incompatible with understanding it in real-time cultural performances, staged or not. That castrati "generate" other men through adaptive strategies in "real" life as well as in symbolic and joking registers is important here, since they cannot do so "normally."[24] What they can do is to play men (at least most of the time) in such genres as opera, oratorio, and cantatas, learn at a master's knee, and form paternal and fraternal relationships. They might be praised for being "inseminated" with song and voice, laughingly said to be pregnant, or claim jokingly that (like Pulcinella) they were born from a god or a rooster's egg. They could also fashion the boys and men who would succeed them musically, professionally, socially, and economically by registering themselves in their throats and minds and even in certain vital statistics or deeds of property. What they could never do was to make the men who would succeed them biologically.[25]

. . .

If the castrato has a low symbolic counterpart in Pulcinella, is there a high symbolic counterpart? In chapter 4 I pursue this question at the uppermost level of sociopolitical organization, proposing that those castrati who attain preeminence through extraordinary musical and social performances come to represent the monarch or the "king's men" not just by virtue of casting but by embodying, projecting, and indeed manipulating royal charisma and diffusing it geographically and temporally from city to city. "Monarch" here is intended in the anthropological sense of a centralization of mystical power within the person of a king, duke, prince, or any number of other titled persons in other political contexts in whom extraordinary power resides in mystifying ways.[26] Offstage castrati may serve as a monarch's brokers, confidantes, courtiers, diplomats, spies, or even ministers. But in such roles, slippery and hard to negotiate, deluxe castrati often found themselves uneasily serving as a ruler's "proxy." For all intents and purposes, they could become his charismatic double; or in the extraordinary case of Farinelli at the royal court of Spain (1737-1759), even participate in a virtual diarchy.[27] On this view the affinities of top castrati with royalty are not incidental. Yet unlocking the interpretative potential of those affinities requires some kind of generalized theory of kingship as a form of social organization. In the pages that follow, the form to which I hew is broadly akin to that advanced by H. M. Hocart, which understands the governmental power of kingship to lie more in its ritual functions than its executive ones. Royal power in this sense *demonstrates* itself *as such* rather than concentrating within itself some objective quality.[28]

Why, then, a castrato for the purpose of instilling the affective dimension of power? Indeed, why singing at all? Like a king, the castrato was a sacralized creature. In adulthood he was regarded as standing outside normal society by virtue of his boyish appearance, high voice, and often-deformed body. Above all else, he commanded an extraordinary vocal technology, as we can infer from scores, anecdotes, and singing treatises. The leading singing treatise of the early modern era was the castrato Pierfrancesco Tosi's *Opinioni de' cantori antichi, e moderni* (1723), which made the components of extraordinary singing clear.[29] They included the ability to mark phrases precisely through accents, articulations, dynamics, and diction, to place the voice accurately, to make perfect transitions between registers, to produce a crystalline trill, to sing bravura passages of distinct kinds securely without losing resonance, to command total control of the breath, to bring to perfection portamento, intonation, and the ever-critical legato, and to sing with the purest of vowels. (Later in the century, executing martellato hammering, arpeggios, and graceful successive leaps were added by the century's other great castrato singing teacher Giambattista Mancini, though different singers specialized in different skills.) The very invisibility and ultimate inscrutability of the voice, specifically one of such special character, made it powerful as a site of exchange. We might thus infer from Tosi and the pedagogical traditions that preceded and succeeded him something like an ideal "monarchical" voice, materially embodied and often complemented in iconography and written descriptions by physical grandeur combined with noble carriage and dignity. Indeed the very technology of singing is itself a kind of affective power to attract, affect, and control, acting as what Alfred Gell describes as an engine of efficacious performance.[30] It is the reason that many castrati were understood as so honoring monarchs through their singing as to merit honorific titles—Ferri, Pellegrini, Farinelli, and Crescentini, for example—functioning in all as highly transactional beings.

Notwithstanding the vast amount still to be learned from scores, treatises, and other writings, they will never wholly make up for the fact that we still lack access to the sound of the castrato's voice, save some early recordings of the last castrato. In a materialist turn, I take up that vexing problem in chapter 3. The effort is fraught with the problems of any radically contingent project whose objects are ultimately unknowable (and, in this case, any conclusions, however tentative, are sure to invite much more skepticism than agreement, as anything to do with singing always does). The problem is a rather physical one—not style per se but the physiology of the vocal apparatus, the physics of the power source, and the behavior of the resonators, plus the resulting acoustic frequencies and the timbres they might produce—a focus, in other words, on physiology and physics as they relate to vocal emission and production. To a limited extent, I concern myself with voice as *kind*— as a type of sound or timbral quality, as line, envelope, spectrum, frequency, or register; as a projectile in space, a kind of heft; as breath or even "touch." The explorations proceed from the technical effort to derive new conclusions or better ones from concrete data via small inferential steps, and by such means to understand some conditions of possibility for castrato voices. If there is payoff in the very struggle into that void, however fitful the process and bracketed the results, above all it lies in the exercise itself, in asking the central unanswerable question of what would happen were we to try with all the faculties and resources we can muster to imagine the very thing that we can never locate, much less experience. What spectrum of possibilities might we hear in our mind's ear?

I hope what emerges is some greater definition of the problem and a greater understanding of the inherent material conditions of a castrato's musical labor and his musical excellence, the very thing that warranted castrations for singing and allowed him to operate in important domains of power and brokerage—a voice not just of volume and peal but one that ideally had finesse, nuance, breath, and line, the kind of control capable of inhabiting his listeners. The ideal voice we might imagine has a lustrous surface, potentially powerful, potentially majestic, potentially brilliant, potentially silvery or metallic, potentially liquid, yet never necessarily any and certainly not all of those things. Perhaps too all those voices had something unique, something not shared by the voices of women or uncastrated men, as observers over a long period of time often remarked.

. . .

Over the later centuries in which castrati were singing, especially from the eighteenth to the nineteenth, there was a big uptick in the number of voice types participating in the singing profession. Tenors, baritones, and basses became major players and the space for female singers became richer and more rewarding than before. At the same time that for castrati narrowed drastically. To rationalize the place for those castrati who still prevailed, a new duality emerged in the 1760s and 1770s, as I describe in chapter 5, marked by a tendency to distinguish flamboyant bravura castrati from Orphic ones, the latter accommodated within the new cult of individual feeling. By this means a whole strain of castrati was cast in the image of the original operatic Orpheuses of Peri and Monteverdi in the early seventeenth century. Purveyors of sympathy, they are continuous with the later eighteenth-century mode of sensibility being cultivated everywhere in Europe, which is incompatible with the perceived betrayal of inner human feeling, human nature, and good parenting that the whole business of castrating boys for singing was seen to entail.[31] Inevitably, though the sentimental makes room for castrati, it also excludes them since Enlightenment morality, which saw nature as sacrosanct, did not look kindly on the whole practice. And inseparably too the castrated man is at odds with an emerging sexual binarism and a new set of representational codes that insists that things seen and heard should be true to nature, and hence that representations on stage not be disjunct from the bodies doing the representing.

This was an eventual death knell to castrati, apart from those who by 1830–50 had retrenched to the churches of central Italy. Berlioz is only one among many who could not suffer the thought of a castrato playing Romeo. Yet we will see that, ironically, the operatic incarnation of Romeo moves from being the property of castrati around the turn of the nineteenth century to being the property of female mezzos who not only take on the role in trousers but carry forward the musical gestures, ethos, and even specific ornaments of their immediate castrato predecessors. Giuditta Pasta is only the most prominent of those new castrato-like mezzos.

More than anything else, it is the enraptured listening of Stendhal that gives eloquent witness to the dying of the castrato vocal tradition, a dying he attributes to a loss of spontaneity caused by a new tendency toward excessively detailed notation of ornaments. And in Stendhal's account it is the contralto Pasta who symbolically heals the wound of that loss. The inheritance, hinted at in 1813 by E. T. A. Hoffmann, has an arc that is resketched in Balzac's *Sarrasine* of 1830, a new reading of which ends this book. The reading does not rest on Lacan or on Barthes, whose *S/Z* came in the late twentieth century to be used as a bible for castrato analysis. Instead its goal is to show that *Sarrasine* constructs a series of cross-continental inheritances, vocal and monetary, that makes legible the fate of these blood sacrifices. In Balzac's Parisian optic, one of their aftereffects is dirty money that founds false lineages yet continues to generate the most sublime singing.

Where did that singing go? It was left to others, to tenors, mezzos, sopranos, baritones, even basses. By the time of Rossini, Donizetti, and Bellini it had been pressed into the rubric of bel canto, taken up by singers who were French by training though often Italian by birth, its origins forgotten or mythicized. Eventually it was betrayed by the new tenors *di forza*, the advent of which was concretized in historical accounts with a high C supposedly delivered in chest in 1837.[32] Exactly what kind of acoustic trace the castrato's singing left in the mid- to late nineteenth and twentieth centuries is impossible to say with assurance, but that its trace was powerful there can be little doubt.

NOTE ON TEXTUAL TRANSCRIPTION, TRANSLATIONS, LEXICON, AND MUSICAL NOMENCLATURE

Translations of texts are mine unless otherwise noted.

Primary sources used in this book include manuscripts and prints, musical and verbal. For some sources I have had to rely on modern editions. I use a much modified version of current Italian principles for transcribing older texts, generally removing elisions that have no semantic purpose while retaining savory idiosyncrasies of language and spelling. Thus "un' buon cantòre!" becomes "un buon cantore!," eliminating both the orthographic elision and accent of the original, but "niun' riconoscente, e niun'che si curì" remains unchanged. I have removed most capitalizations of common nouns but have not generally changed spellings that might reflect older pronunciations or dialects. This approach will not satisfy the demands of modern Italian philology but seemed the most reasonable solution for a nonnative speaker not specialized in Italian philology. Readers wanting to know exactly how original sources appear will have to make direct recourse to them.

Throughout this book I use the term "castrato" to refer to castrated male singers. Even though the term was pejorative, or at a minimum discourteous, in the heyday of the phenomenon and was little used in Italy except in private discourse or satire, it has become the most widely understood term in both lay and scholarly usage.

Pitches are expressed using Helmholtz pitch notation where middle c = c′, an octave above middle c = c″, and so on.

PART ONE

Reproduction

1

Of Strange Births and Comic Kin

Sometimes a project begins with a clue or a hunch from an unexpected quarter. I date the beginning of this one from a time when I began stumbling over a number of unrelated facts, among them a peculiar repertory of explanations for castration, resemblances between various castrato caricatures and feathered comedians, jokes that cast castrati as capons, fears of castrati as strange, grotesque, and overly moneyed, images of castrati as angels, and a myth of origins that assigns the castrato's birth to a rooster's egg. Imagine, then, my fascination when I read this passage from Gabriel Garcia Márquez's story "A Very Old Man with Enormous Wings: A Tale for Children."

> Everyone knew that a flesh-and-blood angel was held captive in Pelayo's house. Against the judgment of the wise neighbor woman, for whom angels in those times were fugitive survivors of a celestial conspiracy, they did not have the heart to club him to death. Pelayo watched over him all afternoon from the kitchen, armed with his bailiff's club, and before going to bed he dragged him out of the mud and locked him up with the hens in the wire chicken coop.... A short time afterward ... [their] child woke up without a fever and with a desire to eat.... when they went out into the courtyard with the first sight of dawn, they found the whole neighborhood in front of the chicken coop having fun with the angel, without the slightest reverence, tossing him things to eat through the openings in the wire as if he weren't a supernatural creature but a circus animal.
> ... The news of the captive angel spread with such rapidity that after a few hours the courtyard had the bustle of a marketplace and they had to call in troops with fixed bayonets to disperse the mob that was about to knock the house down. Elisenda ... then got the idea of fencing in the yard and charging five cents admission to see the angel.[1]

If every idea yearns for an epiphany, this was mine, a promissory note for my odd miscellany. Here a bizarre, ambivalent creature floats down on an earthly dwelling like flotsam from heaven. He terrifies its owners, who cage him with their chickens only to find that he miraculously cures their sick child. The miraculousness of a therapeutic cure is not irrelevant to the history of the castrato. Nor is the fact that far from earning him freedom, the angel becomes more captive than ever, prized as a healer but no less so as an object of rough curiosity by an unruly crowd, and a profitable one at that.

Parts of this story resonate with different animal myths I had encountered while studying early modern festivity in connection with eighteenth-century opera. Such myths are invariably shot through with anthropomorphism, especially between men and fowl, and often they fetishize fowl. In ceremonies, rituals, and displays, fowl repeatedly feature as mediating figures alongside men—from the post-Romans in South Britain, where chickens were part of votive assemblages, to Salento, Italy, where hens are still celebrated for their chthonic powers, to present-day Zaire, where a boy's father would traditionally offer him a meal of turkey after his circumcision, and not least to the Balinese cockfights made famous by Clifford Geertz, which display men's passions in "a medium of feathers, blood, crowds, and money."[2] Though neither fully animal nor human, fowl in these various usages typically live close to humans, to their cults, their social habits, and their fantasies of origin.[3] They are metaphors of human society that move ambiguously between the poles of a stable social self and an alien other. Related myths invoke other domestic animals—notably pigs, which we will encounter anon, likewise endowed with attributes that give them redemptive powers for a larger group and often make them sacrificial spectacles, objects of marketplace commerce, or both.

In these are shades of Garcia's winged old man whose containment and exhibition not only heal but also enable the exchange of money with a gawking crowd. Transformed into the pliable forms of folktales, myths, and popular literature, such are the tales of angels, monsters, and clowns, or what Peter Stallybrass and Allon White call "creatures of the threshold."[4] Such too, I will argue, are the myths of the castrato, which have much to reveal about the long-lived and peculiar European phenomena of producing, exchanging, and patronizing castrated singers. But these mythic forms are also profoundly bound up with the exceptional vocal art of castrati, which engaged the subjective ambivalences of listeners at their nervous, sensory, and psychic core.[5] Small wonder that over time castrati as a group came to be enmeshed in many myths of their own: myths of origin that recounted how they were born and bred, myths of lifestyle that elaborated how they passed their days in primping, courting, and hobnobbing, myths of superhuman vocal powers generated by real vocal feats and often extraordinary physiological traits, which typically included fatty chests, a beardless face, fleshy hands, chest, and neck, and a sometimes outsized height or deformed proportions; and myths of a prodigious sexual allure, associated androgynously with both male and female attractions.[6] One might say that although—or, indeed, because—castrati were often recruited to represent young male lovers and heroes, they were living avatars of mythological modalities of thought and belief.

MATTERS AND FACTS

Who exactly made up this caste of men? Over most of history and in most settings castrated singers were Italians whose testes had been removed before puberty to retain their vocal range into adulthood, after which their voices remained high but went on to mature with the power of adult men. Many, but not all, had been singled out for castration because they showed promise as boy chapel singers. In the shank of the seventeenth century, when the practice of castrating boys was at its peak, the Italian peninsula was suffering from severe economic woes, pestilence, and war, and many families could find no means of subsistence. Parents often hoped that by having their sons castrated, they might improve the prospects of the family, the child, or both, which otherwise could be meager or nil. To castrate one or more sons so that they might eventually land a secure position singing in a Catholic church, at which women were forbidden from singing by Pauline proscriptions, was a reasonable course of action for such families. Families of middle-class station whose material circumstances were less dire often sought to indemnify themselves against declining resources or to improve their social lot, usually singling out younger sons who lay outside inheritance schemes for alternative forms of employment, much like sending a younger son off to the military or the priesthood.[7] Castrations were also mobilized by systems of patronage and cultural production, being urged on by teachers, local chapelmasters, parents or relatives, or agents working for prospecting patrons, princely or non, or for princes themselves.

At first glance, the castration phenomenon may seem like a historical aberration or mere curiosity. But for a long swath of European history, castrated singers stood categorically at the top among musical creator-performers. There were, of course, plenty of journeymen castrati, workaday men who populated minor chapels, some traveling around gigging in small operatic parts or oratorios, or singing cantatas and songs in private homes in their time off. Still, we should understand them, on the whole, as more than "performers" in our modern sense of proficient conveyors of a score. Collectively they formed a prominent musical elite, perhaps *the* elite caste of musician-performers, because their art required special powers of invention, execution, finesse, and nuance, fortified by musical skills that went beyond the standard musicianly competencies of sight-reading and keyboard proficiency to include highly developed skills in figured bass and improvisation on vocal parts as well as advanced skills in counterpoint and composition, which involved writing partimenti and composing works in different genres.[8] It was because of these skill sets that many were consulted on all manner of musical subjects by cognoscenti and doubled as professional composers, impresarios, chapelmasters, and teachers, and why for many composers over about two centuries, including Monteverdi, Cavalli, Vivaldi, J. C. Bach, Handel, Mozart, Haydn, Cimarosa, and the young Rossini, writing for the best castrati was a top goal, and having them on payrolls and playbills was equally important to rulers from Frederick the Great and Maria Teresia to the three French Louis and Catherine the Great.[9]

Enabling this vocal capital were both the conditions of the castrato body and its acculturation in singing. Typically in the period up until the eighteenth century the apprenticeship of a castrato was longer and more concentrated than that for other singers, especially in the stage of development after a boy was castrated but before his first major employment. This was true regardless of where he was trained, whether in a conservatory, cathedral school, or private teacher's home. A rough survey of the seventy or so most famous castrati during the prime years of castrato singing, from the early seventeenth century to the late eighteenth, reveals that about half were known both as singers and as composers with some meaningful output, though the two activities tended to be intertwined, with their compositional emphasis on vocal music, sometimes with orchestral accompaniments and sometimes not. Among castrati who produced a significant corpus of compositions, we can count, in the seventeenth century, Loreto Vittori, Atto Melani, and Francesco Antonio Massimiliano Pistocchi; and in the eighteenth Carlo Broschi (known as Farinelli), Vito Giuseppe Millico, Giusto Ferdinando Tenducci, Giuseppe Aprile, Venanzio Rauzzini, and Girolamo Crescentini.[10]

. . .

The earliest castrati cropped up in Italy during the 1550s in northern parts of the peninsula and the chapels of Rome. By no later than the 1550s there were two at the duke's chapel in Ferrara.[11] The first to appear in the Sistine Chapel (the pope's private chapel, also called the Cappella Pontificia or papal chapel) was a Spaniard named Hernando Bustamante who joined in 1558, though officially the pope did not authorize their recruitment until decades later, in 1589, and the papal bureaucracy did not identify them as such in its registers for another ten years. Other castrato singers at the papel chapel were also Spanish, but, as Corinna Herr shows, high parts in the period were sung by both castrati and falsettists, who overlapped for many decades, both groups including singers of both Spanish and Italian origin. It is very hard to say when choirs in Italy moved toward all-castrato treble sections, and it is not clear that all did so entirely.[12] But there is no doubt that by the early to mid-seventeenth century castrati proliferated in Italy, having moved quickly into church jobs and often thence onto the stage. Although Italy evidently had a monopoly on producing castrati, Germany took an interest in them early on.

Orlando di Lasso corresponded from Bologna about one in 1574. His patron Duke Albrecht V of Bavaria kept castrati in Munich at least briefly in the same period, and by the 1580s they were established there. Not long thereafter, by the early seventeenth century, they had moved further abroad to Württemberg and Vienna.[13] The diaspora coincided with economic distress, caused and compounded by the agonies of natural disaster, plague, and war, which led thousands of desperate families, especially rural ones, to seek any means of livelihood and prompted them to flood Italian cities.

These are some broad outlines of what we know, but I want to claim that the business of having a son castrated is not reducible to a quest for survival or improvement. Always mediating the phenomenon were Catholic religious ideas, often intermixed with rural folk beliefs as well as familial strategies for distributing wealth and functions within a system of primogeniture, none of the strands of which can be disentangled. As John Rosselli insisted, to offer one's son for castration was to make an offering to God and thus a consecration to the church, which also mediated family relations. Legally the church condemned the practice as being against the order of nature and counter to the obligation to be fruitful and multiply. And yet proscriptions do not map onto the symbolic load castration bore. In some sense castration for singing, as a sacrificial offering to the church, was much like joining the priesthood. Accordingly it was freighted with beliefs and obligatory utterances—the two are hard to distinguish—about giving up procreation and typical sexuality in order to gain subsistence for one's family or to improve oneself and one's loved ones, to find salvation, a place in society, the good graces of the Lord, and the good graces of the Lord's shepherds, meaning ecclesiastical authorities and royal patrons who ruled by divine right. Carried out in a kind of indirect symbolic imitation of Christ's passion, such sacrifices were a more than viable alternative in a world where want and famine were rife and where mutilation, whether as physical therapy or punishment or the consequence of harsh labor, disease, and other misfortunes, was commonplace. That virtually all castrati did sing primarily or (more often) exclusively for the church speaks to this issue of castration as sacrifice in the properly Catholic sense. Only starting in the later seventeenth century were some mainly theater and court singers, and even those usually had a home base in a church or princely chapel.

Surgically speaking, all these men had undergone a bilateral herniotomy, or bilateral orchiectomy. The testicles were eliminated by crushing them, squeezing them to cause them to atrophy, or, more commonly, excising them. Much less often the testicles were removed by resection of the entire scrotum, and never was there full oblation. The procedure seems not to have been far removed from that of castrating livestock and other domestic animals, a practice with which many rural people in earlier centuries were familiar, though animals tended to be younger at the age of castration relative to their life-span.[14]

Before surgery began, boys seem typically to have been given opium or had their carotid artery compressed to induce a coma (or a coma-like state), after which they were immersed in milk baths or cold baths as a form of anesthesia before the cut. The vas deferens was severed (as for a vasectomy), and the testicles scored with a two-centimeter incision.[15]

Some understanding about the operation comes from an obscure mid-sixteenth-century German "incisor" (a doctor of the surgical class) named Caspar Stromayr from Lindau am Bodensee on Lake Constance in Bavaria. Stromayr was a meticulous and supremely conscientious expert who performed his craft not to produce castrated boys as singers, but rather as therapy for chronic and acute medical problems. In addition to practicing surgery, he spent many years toiling away on a manuscript, completed in 1559 but not published until 1925, on the radical treatment of hernias and cataracts, replete with 186 hand-colored illustrations, each captioned with a couplet of explanation, including ritualistic prayers. The excision techniques described appear to be versions of what was practiced in Italy, as well as certain corollaries,[16] for example, having the patient sit in a milk bath before the operation and having him lie in a tilted position with the legs above the head (Fig. 1), a forward-looking technique of Stromayr's own invention.

. . .

The direct role of the church is critical to this history, for it was through the church that boys began entering the profession in the latter half of the sixteenth century and through it that the remaining ones exited more than three and a half centuries later. Many castrations were instigated by church schools, churchmen, priests who taught at conservatories, and teachers or parents who worked within the church. The question nonetheless remains: why did the practice develop on a massive scale and why were castrati prized in virtually every corner of Europe? Assuredly, eunuch singers have thrived in other times and places—the courts of the late Ming and early Qing dynasties, the Ottoman empire, and precolonial India, for example—in some cases with similarly exceptional training and status. But in no case do singing eunuchs seem to have moved decisively beyond the paternalistic, hierarchical contexts of courtly patronage to operate as independent professionals in a modern, money-driven marketplace as Italians did throughout western and eastern Europe, especially by the later seventeenth century and increasingly thereafter.[17]

The fact is contradictory, for castrati were not just expressions of symbolic figurations of the old regime but arguably its direct products and important public representatives of old-regime governments. It is no coincidence that the practice of castrating boys for singing arose at a time that overlapped with what Jürgen Habermas has portrayed as the weakening of industrialization and the refeudalization of Europe—a merging of state and society, private and public, that involved an emphasis on representation at the expense of reasoned debate, both of which were endemic to absolutist political practices and both of which set in during the later sixteenth century, when castrati started to emerge, and consumed Italy like wildfire in the seventeenth.[18] It was throughout this precise period and beyond that various castrati stood close to absolutist rulers. They consorted with them, portrayed them, portrayed their generals, heroes, betrothed, siblings, friends, counselors, and confidantes, and even emulated them in real life, whether they were singing to the glory of god and prince, impersonating sovereigns or their children on stage, or singing about love in royal courts or noble households.

As it happens, the most famed castrato of all time, Farinelli (Carlo Broschi [1705–82]), also had the most important royal connections. A portrait made of him at age thirty by his lifelong friend Jacopo Amigoni (1682–1752) depicts him with Euterpe, goddess of harmony, who is about to lay a coronet on his head. The crowning by Euterpe asserts Farinelli's sovereignty over all other singers but also over an entire cultural kingdom (Fig. 2) since Euterpe synecdochically takes the place of M/music, whose realm Farinelli is declared to rule.[19]

Fifteen years later, when the king of Spain made him a knight of the exalted ancient military order of Calatrava, the "crowning" was not just musical or metaphorical. By then Farinelli had already been carrying out extensive state duties in his high-powered role as minister of entertainments and had been a household intimate of two successive pairs of Spanish royal heads of state. He had consorted with numerous crown heads of Europe along the way. To commemorate all that, Corrado Giaquinto pictured him in 1755 majestically attired, wearing the cross of Calatrava with the royals of Spain hovering in the background among the angels—almost as if to declare the castrato de facto king (see Fig. 3).[20]

Like many other castrati, Farinelli, far from separating himself from the old order, took comfort in it, as we will see at various points throughout this book. Yet also like others who gained autonomy in the eighteenth century as professional musicians, he was part and parcel of a new bourgeois order. He had made his fame singing in large commercial theaters attended by thronging publics that included members of the haute bourgeoisie and nobility, servants, dignitaries, middle-class doctors, lawyers, teachers, merchants, military men, and sometimes royals. He had negotiated with agents over contracts. He had traveled alone, which is to say with his own servant, as well as with other singers or superiors. He had also purchased numerous things for himself, including practical items, musical instruments, real estate, horses, and luxury objects, and had been given many luxurious things and lots of cash.[21]

In this and other respects he and other castrati were born on a bed of paradox, residing between the old patronage system and the new order, But famously they were also poised between adulation and fear, approval and censure. They were ridiculed as often as acclaimed, and not unrelatedly were sanctioned by the church, which was dependent on but embarrassed by them, yet disapproved by Roman law.[22]

Whatever cultural ambivalences were in play, the physiological facts that victimized them were dogged. Because castrated boys were deprived before puberty of their major source of testosterone, their larynxes remained supple, small, and undescended in the throat, like a boy's, and the vocal cords that vibrated across the top of the larynx remained correspondingly short. J. S. Jenkins reports, "Under the influence of testicular secretion, the male vocal cords increase in length by 67% in adult men compared with prepubertal boys, whereas in the female the increase is only 24%," a two-thirds increase that castrated boys never underwent, or only slightly if some testosterone figured in the growth process before castration.[23] Depending on the particular inherited body and bodily development, the mature voice might be equally capable of developing sustained legato, excellent agility, and a special capacity for articulation and nuance, or it might specialize in only some of these. Many of the adult bodies that housed the voice had a larger than normal chest, head, jaw, and even nose. Their resonating chambers were thus larger than normal in proportion to the vocal emission equipment (the larynx), so much so that we can suppose that with the right training some castrato voices could deliver a sound of greater punch and more powerful resonance than those typical of trained women and uncastrated men. Most had particular areas of competency or excellence, ranging widely from a special pathos to a riveting virtuosity, with everything in between and many differences of kind. Had you gone to the church of Santa Maria della Pace in Brescia during Lent in 1712, for instance, you could have heard the poignant strains of a male soprano (we don't know who) singing Vivaldi's *Stabat mater*. He embodied the pain of the grieving mother at the cross through the chromatic turns and diminished chords of the "Cuius animam," "her weeping heart, full of anguish and sorrow, pierced by a sword." And had you gone to the royal opera house in Turin during Carnival 1731, you'd have heard a heroic young Farinelli ripping off dazzling coloratura with plunging registral shifts as he sang "Qual guerriero in campo armato" (Like an armed warrior in the field), written by his brother Riccardo Broschi for the opera *Idaspe*.[24]

. . .

If castration could produce the asset of large resonating chambers, it also produced the deficit of real developmental problems. Depriving a boy's growing body of testosterone prevented the epiphyseal plates in the bones from fusing at the joints at the proper time in the growing cycle, causing the limbs of some to grow to great lengths, their ribcages to become larger than normal, and their jaws and other facial bones to extend irregularly. Such erratic development produced abnormal proportions across a great range of variations, as well as medical problems (osteoporosis and melancholia) in middle and old age.[25] Hence the many well-known caricatures of castrati, including many by the Venetian aristocrat and onetime head of the Marciana Library Anton Maria Zanetti, as well as by renowned

Roman artist Pier Leone Ghezzi.[26] Zanetti famously turned Farinelli into a gangly youth ambling with soaring elegance in his "traveling attire." Elsewhere he parodied the height of certain castrati by juxtaposing them with their diminutive leading ladies (Fig. 4) or by placing their images in his album in close proximity to men of typical stature. He arranged Balatri's image atop that of a noncastrate. A later hand comically labeled him "il gran Ballatri" and the figure beneath him "Capon" (evidently a play on the Florentine name Capponi or Cappone) (Fig. 5).[27]

As castrated boys grew up their larynxes remained small and high in the throat, with short, thin vocal cords, and their bodies developed secondary sexual characteristics of women: fatty deposits in their neck, chest, haunches, thighs, and bellies as well as smooth boyish faces. Lack of facial hair was particularly legible as a mark of difference. All this was probably as hard to disguise in flattering, normalizing portraiture as it was easy to caricature. A well-known London mezzotint from 1735, during Handel's time, done by John Faber Jr. (after a painting by George Knapton), showed Farinelli's rival Giovanni Carestini (Il Cusanino, ca. 1704–ca. 1760) in such a way (Fig. 6). Faber's Carestini has the mass of a man but the plump feel of a mature woman whose neck swells continuously into her chest. Bartolomeo Nazari painted a half-length portrait of Farinelli a year earlier, in 1734, at the time of his arrival in London (Fig. 7), giving a fleshy but flatteringly well-proportioned account of the singer's face and arms elongated in a grandeur that extends gracefully out and in front of his torso—though if measured literally, taking into account the foreshortening of the right arm, the arms are longer than average by a good head or two's length, judged in proportion to the subject's own head. Finally, a seated photograph from 1898 of Domenico Mustafà (Fig. 8), chapelmaster of the Sistine Choir, shows the massiveness of his head and fleshiness of his thighs and calves.

Neither caricatures nor portraiture offer any comforting unanimity about castrato development, supporting rather the inference that both the amounts by which testosterone was lowered (likely affected by the age at which castration was done) and the individual physiological response to lowered testosterone levels varied widely across populations of castrated males.[28] In surviving iconography some are given the prettiness of a boy—Marc'Antonio Pasqualini being crowned by Apollo in Andrea Sacchi's painting of 1641, for instance, which overlaps with the very period when Silke Leopold notes castrati began to acquire a new "accent" as high-voiced symbols of youth, notably in Monteverdi's L'incoronazione di Poppea (Venice, 1643).[29] Others were round and fleshy yet smallish and fairly well proportioned (Ghezzi drew the Sistine Chapel director Andrea Adami da Bolsena that way), still others hulking and elephantine, with skeletons that were severely malformed, presumably by the erratic production of testosterone during pubertal and young adult growth, which was how Ghezzi drew Valeriano Pellegrini [ca. 1663–1746]).[30] (See Figs. 9, 10, and 11.) Thus we might be able to generalize about an ideal castrato type, visual and perhaps vocal, for specific periods, places, and repertories, but we cannot easily generalize across genres of representation or life cycles.

LOCATING CASTRATION

Castrations were almost always clouded in social and legal taboos, but obfuscations surrounding talk about them thickened in the late seventeenth century. It seems that once economic privation abated, talk about castration went further underground, pushed by a new kind of morality. By around 1700 explanations were vaguer, even fanciful, expressing the hope to please one's prince, teacher, or other patron, and at least implicitly the wish to be of service to God. Some protagonists produced justifications that kowtowed to the moralizing, rationalizing climate of the eighteenth century, albeit in magical ways that ironically were indirect and anything but rational.

Among other things, there was clearly an unspoken interdiction against naming the surgeon involved, given that only two exceptions have come to light. One surgeon was named by Balatri in two different manuscripts as Accoramboni from Lucca; the other was revealed by a surgeon's son named Tommaso Massi, who was speaking under oath to a London court that was trying to annul a castrato marriage by determining that the husband had been impotent at the time of it.[31] The second makes a precious contribution to a long-puzzling issue. Who carried out these surgeries and why? Massi swears to having assisted his father, Pietro Antonio Massi of "Nurcia" (Norcia), who in 1748 "or thereabouts" castrated the later celebrated Giusto Ferdinando Tenducci (1735–90) on order of the child's father (an order that echoes Balatri's case, as he reports in his prose autobiography; see chapter 2). Finally we begin to veer from fiction into the realm of history. *Norcini* were indeed itinerant surgeons trained in the town of Norcia in southeast Umbria. During both Balatri's and Tenducci's times, the profession of *norcino*-surgeon was a very particular one. *Norcini* specialized in using catheters and ligatures to treat kidney obstructions, cataracts, peritoneal fistulae, and umbilical hernias. David Gentilcore's book on medical charlatanism in early modern Italy shows that *norcini*, though on the fringes of the medical profession, did hold licenses in "minor" surgery and that they were also part of a hereditary profession.[32] Hence Tommaso Massi could declare, "My father brought me up to the Profession of Surgeon which I exercise at Present and used to take me with him to all his Operations that I might practice."[33] The purpose of the hearings was that Tommaso Massi specify the location of the castration, in the village of Monte San Savino, and the procedure his father used, castrating Tenducci "of both parts by making the usual Incisions in the Groin and of having Executed and cut out his Two Testicles and the Spermatick Ducts."[34] Massi's work with his father was thus consistent with what is known of castration and furthermore with the work of performing surgeries on hernias, for which castration was the recommended therapy for males of all ages and classes (it was especially common among hard laborers).

All this helps explain why when boys, parents, patrons, or observers assigned conventional provenances to castrations, the town of Norcia, famed for both surgery and butchery, was common, and why castration by a *norcino* still more so. Habitually *norcini* traveled for surgical work far outside of Norcia. Hence both Norcia and *norcini* were the butt of widespread comic comment in early modern texts. But other accounts, often generic, dissimulating, or confabulating, give other sites of castration: for example, the kingdom of Naples, home of the great conservatories and vocal traditions seated in churches and opera houses, or Bologna, where castrati were often trained in masters' homes. When forced to give reasons for castration, many described them as responses to urgent medical necessity, often with causes that were vaguely worded, like distemper or wounds on the front side. Ferri, who was castrated by age twelve, is described by his maternal nephew as having had an incident while playing with his brother (though administrative books from the church in Orvieto make it clear that the church intervened).[35] In all, surviving explanations, especially from the eighteenth century onward, have functions more diversionary or displacing than documentary.[36]

In 1765–66 and 1770, respectively, the astronomer Joseph de Lalande (1732–1807) and the music historian Charles Burney were each frustrated to find out that castrations took place in a mood of secrecy and taboo. Burney famously tried to discover places where boys were castrated but could learn nothing.

> I was told at Milan that it was at Venice; at Venice, that it was at Bologna; but at Bologna the fact was denied, and I was referred to Florence; from Florence to Rome, and from Rome I was sent to Naples. The operation most certainly is against the law in all these places, as well as against nature; and all the Italians are so much ashamed of it, that in every province they transfer it to some other.[37]

My own luck has been hardly better: I have collected about thirty-five allusions of various kinds to individual castrations of singers over several centuries. In some accounts boys plead for castration, but in most no surgeons, sites, or actual circumstances are given. Many of these allusions, brought to light by John Rosselli, record legal arrangements made by parents or guardians with teachers, conservatories, cathedral schools, or courts, some of which paid for and later benefited from the castrations. Most of the time first sons were excluded because primogeniture was the rule in Italy, hence first sons were heirs, breeders, and eventual legatees, though very poor or very ambitious families sometimes did have first sons castrated, including the family of Handel's principal castrato Senesino (Francesco Bernardi), whose older brother was a castrato, and first son Gaetano Berenstadt (1687–1734), of Tyrolean descent, who ended up caring extensively for his family's needs.[38]

SACRIFICE AND ANIMALITY

One of the hardest problems in trying to untangle this knot is that nominally boys had to give their consent in order to be castrated. If consent was required and castration was ordered by elders, how are we to read petitions by boys in a world in which the very Rousseauean notion of the innocence of childhood was lacking, as was a notion of consent predicated on voluntary acquiescence based upon the power to act unencumbered by external forces? Can any legitimate instances of consent exist? A boy singer for the Duke of Modena, Rinaldo Gherardini, petitioned around 1670 to be castrated so as to "make progress in [the] profession and give much better service both to Our Lord and to Your Highness," adding that he wanted to become a priest since he had two brothers who were already married.[39] His petition framed his hoped-for castration as a gift to God and prince (and implicitly therefore to the Lord's flock), yet, as Rosselli points out, both this petition and another by a Silvestro Prittoni were approved evasively, justified with the phrase "for reasons known to us," barely admitting a deed condoned much less done.[40] And Gerardini's petition has signs that a secretary helped write it.[41] Further compromising the appeal is the boy's admission that he needed to become a celibate (specifically a "priest") because his brothers had married.

More pointed explanations usually implied that the operation had saved a boy's life or saved his family from desperate poverty (though the latter explanations became fewer after the seventeenth century, when the numbers of boys being castrated for singing were dropping and disapproval of the practice was on the rise).[42] Since canon law required medical necessity in order for a male to be castrated, and since it also required the consent of a boy, a goodly number of novices made declarations stating that they needed to forestall the dire consequences of accidents and misfortunes. Typical is the claim that Domenico Bruni (1758–1821) of Frata (now Umbertide, in Umbria) was prescribed castration by doctors following an "accidental physical indisposition," by which means he was said to have "maintained his enchanting soprano voice."[43] In 1707, a French Huguenot lawyer living in Berlin named Charles Ancillon offered a treatise on eunuchism, allegedly inspired by the need to settle the matter of whether castrati could marry, in which he explained such prophylactic and therapeutic uses by quoting the ancients: castration prevented gout according to Hippocrates and Pliny, cured madness for the Sybil priests, and corrected deformities in the children of Troglodytes; for most everybody it also prevented baldness and leprosy. But the more Ancillon specified the castrati in question, the more general his accounts seem to be. With a sweep of the hand he claims that Pasqualini and others used castration to cure "distemper"—an inclusive term that signified disease or disorder and still resonated for Ancillon with its earlier sense of a humoral imbalance.[44] This was the kind of explanation composer/satirist Benedetto Marcello parodied in his *Il Teatro alla moda* of 1720 in recounting the tale of a castrato from an excellent family who had

had to be castrated owing to an infirmity,[45] a sort of hedge that became more prevalent the more castration became taboo.

Striking in nearly all accounts is the thick interlayering of castration as sacrifice and as medical therapy. If we suppose that explanatory tropes were nimbly deployed to safeguard against both legal reprisals and subjective threats to self-preservation, practical, existential, and symbolic, we can see why such broad-spectrum agents were used.[46]

Some explanations are framed in such a way as to suggest that castrations regulated an imaginary relationship between men and beasts by neutralizing threats to manhood. Prevalent among ex post facto justifications from the late seventeenth century onward were falls from trees or horses and bites by wild pigs, wild boars, and (later) even wild swans. Farinelli was imperiled in childhood by an accident that took place while he raced around on a horse, according to his posthumous biographer Giovenale Sacchi.[47] The sixteenth-century humanist Paolo Giovio earlier noted that castrations were often necessitated by the bites of wild pigs (or wild boars, *"cinghiali,"* which pose dangers to hunters and gatherers in parts of rural Italy to this day).[48] Swans, we should remember, were renowned in mythic and lyric traditions for singing while dying. Castrato poet and composer Loreto Vittori (1600–1670) extended the tradition in his 1662 comic-heroic epic *La troia rapita* (The kidnapped pig) by calling his colleagues "musical swans" (*cigni armoniosi*) who wept on the death of their princely Florentine patron (canto 8, stanza 15). At the Vatican, he wrote, they raise their festive voices to make sweet harmonies, though he quickly shaded the scene with the specter of death (8.19): "How many swans have I seen surrounded by laurel, handling Dirce's lyre with a plectrum of gold?" (Quanti Cigni vid'io cinti d'alloro / Trattar con plettro d'or cetra Dircea; 8.24)—that is, how many lauded castrati have sung while dying (like swans), as Dirce did when she was trampled by a bull?[49] Or perhaps: how many, though exceptional in their art, were made to die as progenitors, being thus killed off as men? Vittori's gloss may sound like mere literary fancy but it's noteworthy that in the early twentieth century Franz Haböck was still told by all the castrati he interviewed in Rome that they had been castrated because they had been endangered by the bites of wild pigs or, in one case, a wild swan.[50] First they had been castrated, and then they had to retell their own tales of emasculation in self-castrating forms of obfuscation.

All these late Roman castrati came from poor or working-class village families in Lazio, Umbria, and Le Marche, enclosed in the Papal States until after unification; and all got their starts in provincial chapels, only then advancing to "orphanages" in Rome.[51] Besides residual Galenic notions of medical cures founded in tempering the bodily humors (cold and wet, hot and dry; see Fig. 45) to which they probably still hewed, however roughly,[52] villagers and small-town people of modest means most likely combined such traditional notions syncretically with

Catholic vernacular beliefs and superstitions about how to manage relations between humans and animals. They may well have invoked these syncretic explanations in strategic quests to find urban livelihoods for children who ended up being castrated. And certainly they involved them in after-the-fact explanations about why sons were eligible to sing treble parts.

The conjunction of sacrifice and therapy that marks these stories, by engaging rural superstitions as explanatory strategies, thus betrays what might be understood as a Galenic surplus. The stories resonate with twentieth-century Italian examples that have been studied by ethnographers in which harm by wild animals needs to be checked by acts of human bloodshed.[53] Where bloodshed safeguards human integrity, a logic seems to dictate that should a victim be allowed through inaction to be assimilated to the condition of a beast that has preyed upon it—a literal beast or, in this instance, a beastly dilemma—or should a purported victim be imperiled during a male activity such as hunting, which ought to elevate him over bestial others rather than endangering and lessening him, then the fine line separating humans from animals could break and the boundaries between the civilization of men and the wilderness of beasts be threatened with mayhem.[54] Small wonder that such beliefs have traditionally been marked in rural areas where animals have strong practical and metaphoric links to humans. In the castrato case, simply *asserting* that castration had therapeutic, prophylactic, or propitiatory benefits seems to have had a value all its own, offering a metaphysical realignment to the psychic, subjective disturbance wreaked upon the individual and the larger reproductive order.

Relevant here is that the Italian Peninsula was beset with contradictions regarding reproduction, which it strongly favored yet fiercely limited starting in the 1570s through the rule of primogeniture. Primogeniture introduced a reproductive tyranny into what had already been a patriarchal society, organized around direct father-son bloodlines. Within that context, interrelated claims about castration as sacrifice and therapy should have performed a kind of perlocutionary work where the claims themselves served as a hedge against subjective disintegration—a disintegration not by whatever purportedly necessitated the castration but by castration itself. They accommodated canon law (contradictory in practice, in any case) while giving order to the some of the events that took place around castration, but they also reframed those events as acts of renunciation—of fertility, marriage, and children, above all—that could justify the attainment of something else (health, security, prosperity, protection, longevity, a livelihood for one's family, religious salvation, affinity with God, and religiously inspired, quasi-divine vocal prowess).

Such sacrificial thinking took a bizarre turn in a case unearthed in the early twentieth century from the archives of seventeenth-century Piedmont.[55] A nobleman from a great family discovered his nonnoble wife *in flagrante* and killed her. For the cuckolded father one effect of her sin was evidently having polluted their infant son, whom the father forthwith gave over for castration before anything was known of his voice or talent. We might suppose that in doing so the enraged man banished his own negative alter ego by means that should have helped restore subjective coherence to both father and son and restored the viability of their relationship. In a less psychological interpretation, castrating the infant immediately would also have ensured against the possibility of perpetuating his family line through a child he doubted was his. Once the boy was old enough the father offered him to the Duke of Savoy's chapel, where he went on to serve God and his prince (just as the boy singer for the Duke of Modena said he wished to do). As his life continued, the son had a long but obscure career, never attaining any status higher than that of a minor chapel singer. In fact, despite having kept his noble name, Ottavio Cacherano d'Osasco (which was unusual among castrati), he was omitted from all contemporaneous genealogies of the Osasco lines—an omission that may have had as much to do with the disgrace of his being a paid professional as with his origins or the dark chapter in Osasco history.

Castration in this instance was an intentional obstruction, an elimination converted into a sacrifice a posteriori through an indecently precipitous donation to the church. In many other instances it was a subsistence strategy, in others a strategy that mobilized familial improvements, social and political. In no case can it be separated entirely from appeal and donation to God's grace.

THE LOGIC OF NARRATIVES

If these explanations ameliorated the subjective perils castration posed to males, they also provided them with temporal narratives of ritual passage, from situations that purportedly threatened to make them uncivilized, unmale, or inhuman to ones that guaranteed civilization, humanness, life, and at least a modified form of maleness.

It is ironic that precisely the thing that is certified by explanations for castration is what is typically satirized. Caricatures and parodies often elide castrati with animals, especially roosters, hens, and capons but also horses and pigs—all farm animals that sit at the margins of humans' domestic life and often mirror human conditions and anxieties, though there are resemblances to other animals too, as we will see. In 1731 Ghezzi caricatured the great Bolognese soprano Antonio Maria Bernacchi (1685–1756)—famed for popularizing a showy, instrumental kind of virtuosity—proudly displaying his paunch and plumed headdress, rooster-like, with a sword at his side (Fig. 12). Zanetti showed him in 1735, beplumed again and with a rotondly avian underside being propped up by a dwarfed servant (Fig. 13),[56] and gave similar airs and attire to Nicolini and Senesino, each of whom he drew with one of his a leading ladies (see Fig. 4). (Contrast these with a short tenor whom Zanetti drew with regular features without any swagger, in Fig. 14.)

. . .

The image of a feathered castrato resonates fascinatingly with a burlesque passage from Balatri's satiric autobiography in verse, which I discuss further in chapter 2.[57] Relevant here is that as a teenage boy, in 1698, Balatri was lured away from his hometown of Pisa and the environment of the Tuscan court to the court of Peter the Great in Russia. Upon sending him off, his primary benefactor the Grand Duke of Tuscany, whom both his parents served and who gave the family the modest palace in Pisa in which they lived, elicited a promise that Balatri would keep diaries throughout the sojourn. Now lost, the diaries were the basis for a prose autobiography called "Vita e viaggi di F. B., nativo di Pisa" (originally ten volumes, of which nine survive at the Moscow State Library), on which the verse autobiography "Frutti del mondo," was based. "Frutti del mondo" tells colorfully of his encounter with a great Tartar khan, whom he astounded with his singing when he visited a few months after his arrival in Russia as part of a huge embassy sent by the czar to Astrakhan on the lower Volga. Upon hearing him sing, the khan became so enraptured by the vocal virtuosity of the "ominessa" (femme-man—a made-up word) that he wanted to know what sex he was and where he could get one of his own. In answering, the young Balatri first stumbles in embarrassment but then settles the question of gender by producing a myth of origins for the castrato.

> He started by asking me whether I was male or female, and where from; whether such people are born (or rain down) with a voice and ability to sing. I was all confused about how to answer. If "male," I'm practically lying, if "female," still less do I say what I am, and if "neuter," I would blush. But, screwing up my courage, I finally answer that I'm a man, Tuscan, and that cocks are found in my region who lay eggs, from which sopranos come into the world; that these cocks are called *norcini*, who go on brooding for many days among our people; and that once the capon is made, the eggs are festooned with flattery, caresses, and money.[58]

> Incomincia dal farmi domandare
> se maschio son o femmina e da dove,
> se nasce tale gente (ovvero piove)
> con voce e abilitade per cantare.
>
> Rest'imbrogliato allor per dar risposta.
> Se maschio, dico quasi una bugia.
> Femmina, men che men dirò ch'io sia,
> e dir che son neutral, rossore costa.
>
> Pure, fatto coraggio, al fin rispondo
> che son maschio, Toscano, e che si trova

> galli nelle mie parti che fann' uova,
> dalle quali i soprani son al mondo;
>
> Che li galli si nomano *norcini*,
> ch'a noi le fan covar per molti giorni
> e che, fatt'il cappon, son gli uovi adorni
> da lusinghe, carezze e da quattrini.⁵⁹

The tale jokingly invents a natural order in which reproduction is the work of males, specifically cocks, which have widely symbolized male sexual aggression and procreative power. Here the cocks are called *norcini*, who lay eggs that hatch male sopranos. It is no coincidence that Norcia not only produced traveling surgeons but was (and remains) famous for rearing and fattening pigs, which its butchers were reputed to castrate with particular skill and make into delicious sausages.⁶⁰ Balatri's joke of the *norcino* as castrator reverberates with the writings of earlier satirists.⁶¹ The painter and poet Salvator Rosa (1615–73), for instance, rubbed the faces of his beleaguered countrymen in their political and economic woes—the consequences, he claimed, of corruption, plague, drought, and war—by insinuating that castrated singers ("eunuchi" or "musici") echoed more generalized, varied sexual infamies of the peninsula. He mocked his countrymen as "becchi ... e castrati" (cuckolds and castrati) and "i cornuti e i cantor" (cuckolds and singers). But unlike Rosa's "cantori," who are as barren as Italy's priests and politicians, Balatri's *norcino* is a fertile, brooding cock, a male who produces other males by bestowing perpetuity in a kind of perpetual reproduction rather than ending it.⁶²

Why does the castrato invent a tale that makes infertile males out to be breeders, which is precisely what they cannot be? Why does Balatri make male paternity the butt of a joke that is also part of his alibi?

A clue is embedded in an anonymous mid-seventeenth-century cantata called "Il castrato," preserved in manuscript at Bologna.⁶³ Against his naysayers, the singer of the cantata, or the figure he envoices, boasts that, far from being ill equipped for sex, he's like a tree that grows stronger when pruned, a key that turns but leaves no mark. He is a cannoneer on a great holiday who fires without balls, and though he's hairless at a grown-up age, his love-wounding Cupid's arrows need no hairs for their strings. Blustering on, he breaks from recitative into arioso and then spills into a combative gasconade.⁶⁴

Recitative
E se dice talun ch'io sparo a vuoto, *If someone says that I shoot empty bullets,*

Arioso
gli rispondo *I answer him*
che nel mondo *that in this world,*
per nascite e per feste *for birthdays and holidays*

EXAMPLE 1. Anonymous cantata "Lamento del castrato," excerpt from Bologna, MS Q46, recitative "E se dice talun" through arioso "gli rispondo che nel mondo."

e per piaceri,
sparano senza
palle i bombardieri.

and for pure enjoyment,
cannoneers shoot
without any balls.

The festivities are excuse for showy melismas and dotted-note cannonade. But they are a mere prelude to the round fired off in the last aria:

Aria 3/2
Poco amate delle guancie
son le rose quand'armate
se ne stanno di spine annose,
ché nemica dell'età
fu mai sempre la beltà.

Roses are little loved for their
soft cheeks when they're armed
with big thorns,
for the enemy of age
was always beauty.

Arioso C
Benché sia vecchio Amor, nato col mondo,

Though Cupid, born with the world,
may be old,

EXAMPLE 2. Anonymous cantata "Lamento del castrato," Bologna, MS Q46, excerpt from aria "Poco amate delle guancie" through arioso "ché nemica dell'età."

nel volto ancor non ha pelo nascente,	*with still no hair growing on his face,*
e l'arco omnipotente	*isn't the all-powerful bow*
ond'egli scocca l'amoroso telo	*with which he shoots his amorous target*
ha la corda di nervo e non di pelo?	*made not of hair but a string of sinew?*

The castrato here is all parody and braggadocio, protesting against the very ridicule he would bring upon himself. He is a sacrificial clown because he is abject not just as a result of his primary loss but because he must ritually reiterate that loss, repeatedly exposing and embellishing it publicly for the amusement of others.

There can hardly be any question that whoever wrote the lyrics and music (the same or most probably different authors), they were performed by a castrato whose performance was part of the joke, presumably shared in a private setting that was the natural habitat of cantatas. Doing so, a castrato would thus have extended one aspect of an ancient comic tradition that, like Balatri's cock-hatched castrato, cast certain stage and social actors as sexually exaggerated yet inefficient, deviant, or transgressive. The tradition goes back at least to ancient Greek times, where phallic grotesques appear as base characters before their superiors but also as sexually overdone. In a drawing on a Greek vase, a short, thin, knobby-kneed equerry trots after his master brandishing feathers and a huge beaked nose but with a protruding belly and long, pendulous testicles—a creature whose overtly superior equipment marks him ironically as absurd and inferior (Fig. 15).

PULCINELLA CASTRATO

In early modern Italy the performing prototype of the comic grotesque was Pulcinella, the quintessence of irony, liminality, and Carnival.[65] Not only was Pulcinella unable to maintain clear boundaries between the worlds of humans and beasts, he was also doubly sexed—a man marked by a squealing, high-pitched voice whose randy sexual appetite leads him into endless social misadventures and sexual blunders.[66] In the late seventeenth century, Burnacini was one of innumerable artists who made his figure softly womanish, with a fatty neck, drooping chest, and billowing sleeves, and did not hold back in giving him an immense phallic nose (Fig. 16).

Pulcinella's androgynous sexuality was also echoed in his many animal affinities. He rode on donkeys, danced with cats, and kept regular company with birds. Ever prone to transformations, he could multiply himself in innumerable forms or be killed and return as a dog.[67] Often his scatological ways put him close to pigs. In one anonymous painting from the eighteenth century, the food he's given turns into baby Pulcinellini, whom he births through his anus (Fig. 17). A group of Pulcinella-styled men look on as a mannish midwife clasps her hands in joy.[68]

These animal kinships and sexual ambiguities suggest mysterious, diabolical powers, realized in a vast repertory of mischief and signified by his black mask. Like the castrato, he was a performer, in this case of street tricks, and acted in street plays. Sometimes he was a busker and sometimes an outdoor singer of tales (a *cantimbanco* or *cantastorie*) (Fig. 18).

Among all characters of the commedia dell'arte and Carnival, Pulcinella most thoroughly epitomized the paradoxical but symbiotic dualities of pathos and parody. A mediator on stage, he was infinitely complex and changeable, playing parts from note bearer to spy, servant, ruffian, pastor, idolator, quack, Jew, gypsy, Turk, and even nobleman. Across this boundless range, he was a symbol of cultural exchange, who helped viewers test their own limits but ultimately to ratify their own certainties.

Most strikingly for us, Pulcinella has a high, crowing voice, pitched like a castrato's, and similarly too was linked with male generation. In one of his two main myths of origin he had hatched from an egg, animal or mythological, which in most accounts was propagated or brooded by a male. In one elaborated dramatic narrative, Pulcinella is born portentously from the bowels of Vesuvius and the mouth of the Inferno, having been issued directly from an eggshell that appeared by the will of Pluto at the summit of the volcano with the help of two sorceresses.[69] A drawing by Giandomenico Tiepolo has Pulcinella hatching from the giant egg of a turkey who struts by proudly in the background (Fig. 19).[70]

A particularly bizarre gloss on this male palingenesis, produced in burlesque sonnet form by the seventeenth-century librettist Francesco Melosio, explains Pulcinella's birth as the result of a hen having been impregnated by severed testicles that were cut off and then thrown carelessly in a corner by a boy's own father:

> A guy from Salò castrated one of his sons so he could put his talent to better use, and then threw his testicles aside. There was a broody hen at his house, and I don't know how one of them got up inside her, but indeed she brooded the egg and it hatched in its time.
>
> This is how the Marquis was born, who grew up making it as an ass so as not to betray his birth. And on stages from that time on, anybody who acts like an idiot in our day is called Pulcinella.

> Castrò un suo figlio un dì quel di Salò
> Perché meglio attendesse alla virtù
> Per applicarlo a qualche servitù;
> Ed incauto i testicoli gettò.
>
> Ha in casa una chiocca, ed io non so
> Come di quei coglion si cacciò sù,
> Basta con gli ovi anche ei covato fu,
> Era suo tempo anch'egli pullulò.
>
> Quindi nacque il Marchese il qual così:

> Per non far torto alla natività,
> Cresciuto un coglioncello riuscì.
>
> E in sù le scene da quel tempo in qua,
> Un che faccia il coglione a' nostri dì,
> Pulcinella nominar si fa.[71]

Pulcinella and a phony, vainglorious marquis here are one and the same, their shared origins linked to a castrated male.[72] Note that after the hen's egg hatched, the newborn Pulcinella/castrato gave the slip to the social order of class relations, much as his birth had given the slip to the natural orders of species and gender.[73] He ended up passing himself off as a nobleman, hiding his bestial origins by strutting on the stage like a pompous fool. The "coglioncello" is a tricksterish creature, less man than half human, whose very name, uttered in the final line of the sonnet, betrayed the *pullus* at his origins while conjuring up for those familiar with his exploits his many failed sexual adventures.

Melosio's sonnet thus participates in a narrative complex in which the castrated man and the clown sit at a nexus of maleness and births that are prodigious in kind and number. The sonnet makes Pulcinella's connection to castration patent while tracing it to his kinship with ever-proliferant birds, which elsewhere function as his primary link to the animal world. Pulcinella loves Colombina, named for a dove, and Rondinella, named for a swallow, but his lot is forever thrown in with the symbolically dynamic chicken (*pullus* or *pollo*) from whom he takes his name. His sexuality is riddled with obscene, mercenary allusions to making chicks, brooding with damsels, playing the cock ("facendo il gallo"), and letting himself be castrated should he fail, as he often does. He crows out such traditional birdsongs as the *canario* and *cucurucù*, familiar to Renaissance scholars, and sometimes he sings better than a turtledove—though above all he's an androgynous, or at least ambiguous, mix of the crowing cock and the cackling hen. Above all his transformable nature combines with his many outrages to form part of an expiatory apparatus that wards off the very evils it seems to embody. He is the inverted self, the Other that presses up against, antagonizes, and thereby creates the self. In that sense, Pulcinella is a castrate as much as the singing castrato is a figurative Pulcinella.

This reflexive dynamic is a product of performative time and space. Where Pulcinella was the androgyne clown who challenged the social order outdoors during Carnival—a liminal time that privileged liminal creatures—the castrato ruled the stage indoors during Carnival when the opera season was at its height. The castrated singer could variously embody angels, heroes, or sovereigns yet he was repeatedly the target of comic jabs, ridicule, and other abuses. Like the clown, he allowed viewers to identify with a distorted, malleable body, reminiscent in its sacrificial aspects of the effigy of the murdered man carried about at Carnival—a kind of pagan approximation of Christ. And like the clown, the castrato was both exalted and taunted, even as he finally helped reinforce the patriarchal order that both desired and excluded him.[74]

The threads that join Pulcinella, castrato-like, to an amphibious animal world epitomized by chickens also include a classic reversibility that likewise resonates with a comically abject castrato: Pulcinella, the obscene comic tramp, can sometimes fraternize with aristocrats and even royals, as he does in a remarkable (anonymous) Neapolitan painting from about 1830–40, shown in Figure 20. Wearing the insignia of the golden Neapolitan order of San Gennaro e del Toson, Pulcinella gestures affectionately, one prominent nose to another, toward Ferdinando I of the Two Sicilies. Beside him is Maria Carolina of Austria and to his upper right Carlo III with a beloved hunting dog. He is part of a dialectic of the royal and the clown, perhaps especially well tolerated by the Bourbon regime because its absolutist politics needed to accommodate the popular classes.[75]

But Pulcinella, though often heroic or even angelic, can, like a human castrate, be as vain as a rooster or as gross as an ape. He can behave like a devil or, as here, an agent provocateur, or be the mildest of creatures.

. . .

In light of these relationships, can it be coincidental that in operas and oratorios castrati so often represented society's male elites? Perhaps so, but the castrato in some contexts was as much the hypernormative male, a virtual parody of maleness, as Pulcinella was the nonnormative or hyponormative male.[76] Look again at the immense, puffy Senesino, who premiered so many of Handel's male leads (Alexander the Great, Richard I, Titus Andronicus, and the eponymous Julius Caesar—indeed, the score of Handel's *Giulio Cesare* sits beneath him in the well-known mezzotint by Van Haecken), yet who, in Zanetti's caricature with Faustina Bordoni, delicately extends his wrist to the prima donna (see Fig. 4). The young but regal Farinelli was caricatured in female dress (at age nineteen) by Ghezzi in 1724, but with a hulking head and a mouth and nose almost resembling a pig's (Fig. 43). We might say, then, that whereas Pulcinella's femaleness is his undoing, his phallic mask often ridiculed with cuckold's horns and his inability to be a real man parodied in countless stories, the castrato is often an overdone male who can bleed into femaleness. In some instances he is, as Roger Freitas shows, an attractive boyish figure. Perhaps he is even prototypically so, but he can be turned into an off-kilter, fantastical exaggeration of maleness. In the eighteenth-century coming-of-age stories that made up the *dramma per musica* (commonly known as opera seria), he tends to mature into what we moderns would tend to see as a sexually amphibious creature, with a fleshy bosom, often encased in an armored cuirass that is topped by a soft neck and cheeks and sometimes a helmet.[77] When Pulcinella and the castrati are viewed together, they highlight the cultural confusion—but also the potential for collective psychic reconciliation—characteristic of an encompassing principle that is challenging because contradictory but that also facilitates the social system writ large.

One of Zanetti's little-known images seems to muse on just these relationships (Fig. 21). The castrato Bernacchi stands on a *calle* in Venice, gazing up at a show given by two puppets, one a Pulcinella, the other a damsel (Colombina?), who perform in a night-lit Venetian window. On the image someone has written in pseudo-Venetian dialect the caption "Bernach, who is enjoying Pulcinellina in Piazza San Marco."[78]

MONEY

As a *pullus*, Pulcinella is salable and consumable. He embodies the unsettling powers of money. A series of nineteenth-century German prints held in the Italian theater prints collection at the Getty Research Institute in Los Angeles shows Pulcinella's grouchy old comic relative, the fatherly Pantalone, being attacked by thieves; money appears and disappears in the shape of a chicken before it returns as a dog.[79] Not just beggarly and ravenous, Pulcinella can be, like Pantalone, both haughty and grotesquely greedy. As Domenico Scafoglio and Luigi Lombardi Satriani say of Pulcinella, money is one of the "motors" of his universe and "he defends it like a miser."[80]

In Pulcinella's world money also functions as part of a dynamics of metamorphosis. As such, it gives us purchase on cutting jokes about the commerce in castrati and perhaps even about their own exchanges of money. Gluck's librettist Ranieri de' Calzabigi, in branding the business of castrati a "great traffic in caponizing," in his satiric *poema eroicomico La Lulliade* (1789),[81] echoed numerous earlier observers like De Brosses.[82] And in Handel's time Porpora's librettist Paolo Rolli jeered about the London theaters, where indeed everything depended on having top singers in order to outsell opponents. "You Englishmen complain that castrati are too costly, so that too much money ends up in Italian lands, but if you want to make all this use of them and [still] make savings, it's amazing that for such a profit you still can't castrate there."[83] In another gloss, Rolli elided capons and castrati with competition: "London is already all divided; the parties have no check. Who will want the Haymarket? Who the fruit market? Here they love contention, like their country dances; yet it won't be a battle of roosters but capons."[84] The famed contests of Farinelli and the trumpeter, or of Caffarelli (Gaetano Majorano, 1710–83) and virtually all his fellow leads, come to mind here, like the cockfights gambled on by Balinese men.[85] Contests made castrati into gladiatorial figures capable of defeating their competitors with song but figures whose very ability to do so could become sore points, taken as signs of greed and pomp; or they could make them laughingstocks, like the castrato of the anonymous cantata above, proving their money and status boasts to be as unwarranted as the sexual ones.

Echoed in the pecuniary aspects of these contests is a vast lexical and symbolic universe in Italian language and culture that elaborates the triad of fowl, men, and money—equivalents in Italian to "feathering one's nest" or "building a nest egg." The Tuscan *pollinaio* collects the excrement of chickens, humans, and other animals, which he mixes up to sell as fertilizer, his name marking the chicken's metonymic role in the circulation of waste. Many other words point to humans' industry in fowl: *pollariolo* or *pollarolo, polleria,* and *pollivendolo*. Capons in particular bring more money than hens or cocks because they are tender and fat, worth turning into commodities that will be valuable enough as meat to be given up as breeders.

It is telling in this connection that for various reasons, some of which we have now glimpsed, chickens are decidedly ambivalent creatures. Intimate in their relations with humans, they are assimilated to a negative dimension of humanness by ingesting what is inedible to humans and putting varieties of human carnality on view.[86] But in this mix of negative and positive, they can also be sacred and have remained so in rituals of the Neapolitan region of Campania, which have been provocatively written about by Roberto De Simone. As the capon is a symbolic equivalent to the castrated man, De Simone shows, the chicken is often a symbolic equivalent to death. In modern-day Salento chickens are still lamented in funeral songs, and in Pagani (Salerno) they are venerated in the feast of the Madonna delle Galline (Madonna of the Hens). The feast of the Madonna delle Galline expands on the infernal and subterranean aspect of fowl through a popular legend according to which hens centuries ago scavenged the earth and brought forth an image of the Madonna del Carmine, who had been buried many years before as a result of incursions by the Saracens. Thenceforth the Madonna del Carmine came to be popularly called and accepted by the church as the Madonna delle Galline, and hens, geese, and other fowl have been offered votively to her once a year at the same time as processions take place carrying her effigy.[87] That these are not isolated instances is attested by the fact that in the area around Naples the sudden illness or death of a chicken has traditionally been taken as a sign of the evil eye *(il malocchio)*, and that fowl have frequently been worshiped, scapegoated, sacrificed, and attributed with magical powers such as carrying souls away, bestowing fertility, and transcending sexual boundaries.[88]

THE SACRIFICIAL CYCLE

All these creatures are linked by a dynamic sacrificial cycle of which castration, in the case of the castrato, can be viewed as the initial, if most dramatic, part. After their castrations, or even before, boys were incorporated into a patronage system that separated them from their parents or guardians and put in the latter's place full-time sponsorship by a conservatory or private teacher (or in other cases an institution of the church), who generally provided training, room and board, and all other material needs.⁸⁹ Students were at the mercy of their new caretakers, whose names they often assumed and to whom they turned over any earnings they brought in as boys and part of their earnings as men.⁹⁰ In a very real sense, their new patrons assumed the paternal role previously occupied by parents, as attested by surviving contracts that assign teachers and patrons legal rights in loco parentis.

Whatever the specific case, castration was usually preceded, followed, or otherwise demarcated by a partial renunciation of the natal family. This formed only the central part of a wider series of renunciatory acts that effected the transformation of a young castrato, beginning with "his" petition and the castration itself, continuing with his subsequent loss of sexual development and procreative potential, and culminating in his exclusion from the patrilineal order, at least in the strict sense.

A castrato placed for training in one of the four Neapolitan conservatories experienced the first extension of this renunciatory process. Not insignificantly, the conservatories had begun in the later sixteenth century as charitable homes for poor boys and by about 1630 had effectively become music schools as well as Catholic orphanages.⁹¹ Their training regimens and overall orientation were religious through and through, many of the academic masters and music tutors being priests as well as permanent residents.⁹² A boy who entered the Conservatorio della Pietà dei Turchini, for example, was subjected to an intense entry ritual. It began with confession followed by communion, during which he knelt at the altar beside the rector while carrying over his arm a cassock and surplice, which were later to become his permanent garments. Alongside the other boys there was then a short prayer, a blessing of his clothes, and a *Veni creator spiritus* chanted. Like all sacrificial sequences, these ritual elements prepared the initiate for his transformation as a sacrificial victim by stripping him of his former identity, physically replacing materials on his body that were linked to a former secular existence with new materials that assimilated his outward appearance to those of his peers. Two of the assistants helped him dress, and only then was the most sacred *Ave Maria* sung to the Virgin and the Davidic psalm *Ecce quam bonum* recited, followed by the blessing of the rector.⁹³

As with other students at the Pietà dei Turchini, castrati were subsequently subjected to an austere disciplinary regimen, which included weekly or biweekly confession, rising daily at 6:30 in winter and 4:45 in summer to intone the *Laudate pueri Dominum* while washing and dressing and going to morning mass. There were prayers throughout the day and in the evening an examination of conscience in the chapel. Since cassocks and surplices were color-coded according to the conservatory to which they belonged and all other ornaments forbidden, boys' identities were wholly subsumed into that of the group, a state of affairs that was reinforced through stringent rules for behavior.⁹⁴

Once conservatory life got underway for a castrated boy, he lived permanently among the "eunuchs" with whom he was classed and was subjected to numerous special considerations that collectively marked his group. Most notable were strict rules of containment, which far exceeded those for other boys by proscribing him from eating any meals or spending any nights outside the conservatory walls. But eunuchs also enjoyed privileges and protections unique to their class, including special provisions, extra heating, and other comforts that typically went well beyond those permitted other students.[95] Special treatment was materially justified by the fact that eunuchs were particularly good sources of income owing to their active role in the life of the city's churches and lay religious organizations. If for no other reason it was warranted to guard against threats of malnutrition and illness.[96]

The professional lives of young eunuchs were structured in yet another way that sacralized them, even as it contributed to their being marginalized. Throughout a period lasting about two centuries, one of the eunuchs' principal forms of employment outside the conservatory consisted of maintaining vigils in which they sang over the bodies of dead children in the guise of cherubic angels, "figlioli angiolini."[97] As angel-guardians of the dead, young castrati were assimilated to other androgynous beings of long ancestry, giving them special mimetic flexibility as intercessories with the divine. Students from the Poveri di Gesù Cristo, for example, took part in the so-called *battaglini*, processions with floats representing mysteries of the Virgin and Christ. On the final float, the Immaculate Virgin stood bedecked with lighted candles, praised by a choir of about forty eunuchs in angel garb who were echoed by instruments.[98]

This angelic representational imagery followed eunuchs into their professional lives to become one of the most fertile metaphors applied to them by travelers and natives, and not surprisingly has shaped various modern-day writings as well.[99] An extended testimonial lingers in the pages of the *Historia musica* of 1695 by the Perugian singing master, castrato, and historian Giovanni Andrea Angelini Bontempi (ca. 1624–1705), eponymously also angelic, who exemplified his ideas on the relationship between beautiful singing and a harmonious world order with the "divine singing" of his fellow Perugian Baldassarre Ferri, noting that Ferri's singing had been praised in encomia as "divine and angelic." "The harmony of his voice, being concordant with the harmony of the spheres, [made] inferior the very song of the angels."[100] The Neoplatonic character of Bontempi's praise diminished in eighteenth-century encomia of castrati, but the metaphor of the angels lived on. Observers from Mersenne to Casanova to the demimondaine Sara Goudar repeatedly described the castrato's commanding voice as "angelic" and quasi-feminine, transhuman and thus divine. Even Marie-Antoinette's personal painter Madame Vigée-Lebrun called the sopranists' performance of Allegri's *Miserere* at the Sistine Chapel "truly the music of angels."[101]

. . .

What then of Márquez's angel-man? Not just the stuff of children's tales, he is a mythical archetype, dreaded and gruesome but capable of changing life for the good. He invites ridicule and awe, creates chaos and then order. Strangest of all, he is a commodity *in potentia*. Like the castrato, he embodies what Gary Taylor calls "a contest of kinds," a category confusion caused by boundary creatures, especially those cooped up, fattened, cut, and eaten, whose flesh and blood nourish that of their owners but whose special powers may also threaten to deprive them of the very things that are promised.

Not surprisingly, Balatri's capon is also magical—something the khan declares might as well rain down from heaven (like Márquez's creature) as be born. Metamorphosis and paradox, after all, are divine prerogatives; or, as Casanova wrote of the castrato Salimbeni, "Mutilation had turned him into a monster, but all the qualities that embellished him made him an angel."

Of course the castrato's image as angel is ironic too, since his voice lay at the crux of a tension between the old patronage system and the new economy that commodified his voice. In the eighteenth century, it thus lay specifically between the ancien régime and the emerging nation-state. Paid to represent rulers, castrati became stars who sometimes threatened to usurp sovereignty, and that in a world where absolutist rulers were already under threat and where a castrato might be paid better than the prime minister or virtually become one himself. Balatri, for one, was blunt about the castrato's place in a world of abstract exchange. In his myth of origins the castrato is produced by a cock that sits protectively on his eggs for days, only to have them showered, once hatched, with blandishments that effectively turn into money. In this too the castrato was glossed as a figurative chicken, domesticated by humans but abundantly exchanged in commerce.

Appendix to Chapter 1
Texts and Translations

NO. 1, CANTATA "IL CASTRATO" (LAMENTO)

Music and text: Anonymous

Musical source: Bologna, Museo Internazionale e Biblioteca della Musica, MS Q46

Recording available on I Solisti della Cappella Musicale di San Petronio, directed by Sergio Vartolo with Angelo Mazzotti, countertenor, *Lamenti Barocchi*, vol. 2 (Naxos, Alte Musik, DDD 8.553319; 1995)

Recitative

Quando tal'hor mi discopro amante d'un feminil sembiante,	When from time to time I reveal my love for a feminine countenance,
tal'un si move a riso.	some people are moved to laughter.
E ciascun veder ch'io non ho pelo in viso	And seeing as how I have no hair on my face
mi tien per un inerme ed impotente	they take me to be harmless and impotent
e prende sovente a dir così di me:	and often seize the opportunity to talk this way about me:
"Quest'è l'amante, ohibò! E che giammai far può	"Is this the lover? oh, for shame! How can he ever do it

quando arrivi all'amoroso amplesso	when it comes time for the amorous embrace,
privo delle due parti di se stesso?"	deprived of those two parts of himself?"

Così ciascun si crede	So it is that everyone is convinced
che nel regno d'Amor	that in the kingdom of Love
fabbricar mia fortuna indarno io tenti	I try to make my fortune in vain,
mentre non ho strumenti—	even though I have no tools—
quasi non fosse vero,	almost as if it weren't the case
ch'anco senza sonagli	that even without jingling bells
fa prede fortunate un sparaviere.	a hawk has the good fortune to take his prey.

Aria

Per mia fe non è così.	On my word, it's not like that.
Anzi l'esser non intero	Indeed my not being whole
fa ch'io vaglia tanto più	makes me even more precious
che sta solo nel mezzo la virtù.	since my virtue stands in the middle all by itself.

Recitative

Quando tagliansi i rami di una pianta	When the branches of a plant are pruned away
divien più grosso il tronco;	the stem becomes thicker;
e si vede a tutte l'hore	and one always sees
che levansi i bottoni	that when buds are pruned
perché venga il garofalo maggiore.	because a bigger flower develops.

Su l'amorosa mensa	On the table of love
imbandisco ancor io cibo che basta,	I still set down food that suffices,
nè vorrò haver quella vivanda sciocca	nor do I want to have those useless victuals
che mai non entra in bocca;	that never enter the mouth;
si che vero goder è il goder solo,	for true pleasure is pleasure alone,
onde nulla desio di condur meco	wherefore I have no desire to bring
alle mie congiunzioni	relatives, friends, or witnesses with me
i parenti, gli amici e i testimoni!	to my couplings!
Così non avverrà ch'io mai pavente	Thus I will never fear
che per tal compagnia	that for such company
alcuna gioia mai resti pendente,	any jewel should be left hanging,[1]

nè che i diletti amati	nor that beloved pleasures
sian dal periglio lor contrappesati.	should be outweighed by danger to them.

Aria 3/2

O com'è diletta	Oh how pleasing
e/a bella ritrosa	and wonderfully unusual[2]
oprar una chiave	to turn a key
si piena d'ingegno,	so ingenious
che apre per tutto	that it opens for one and all,
e mai non lascia il segno.	and yet never leaves a mark!
O com'è diletta	Oh how pleasing
a man virginale	to a virginal hand
trattar uno strale	to handle an arrow
che ben sia pieno	that may well be
di dolce veleno.	full of sweet poison.
Se mai fa ferite	Should it ever strike
non v'è chi l'addite	there's no one there to whom it adds
nel gonfio del seno.	by swelling the womb.
O quanto è bel gioco	Oh what a lovely game it is
d'honesta beltà	for an honest beauty[3]
scaldarsi ad un fuoco	to warm itself in a fire
ch'in sè mai non ha	that never has in it
fiamma d'honor nemica.	that flame that is the enemy of honor.
E s'avventura talor la scotta	And if perchance it sometimes burns,
la scottatura non fa venir vescica!	it doesn't make a blister!

Recitative

Ma di sentir già parmi	But I can already hear
che m'otteggi/moteggi più d'un ch'in questa guisa	more than one person jesting that
sempre son fiacche e mal temprate l'armi!	the weapons are always limp and dull!

Aria 3/2

Oh falsa opinione!	Oh what a false view!
E chi potrà giammai	Who could ever have a
aver arma miglior d'uno spadone?	better weapon than a broadsword?[4]

Recitative

Poss'io morir se merito	May I die if such
le piaghe si profonde,	deep wounds are merited,
che tutta vi s'asconde	for a weapon that doesn't finish things off
un'arma che non habbia il finimento.	is completely hidden there.
E se dice talun ch'io sparo a vuoto,	And if someone says that I shoot empty bullets,

Arioso

gli rispondo	I answer him
che nel mondo,	that in this world,
per nascita e per feste	for birthdays and holidays
e per piaceri,	and for pure enjoyment,
sparano senza	cannoneers shoot
palle i bombardieri.	without any balls.

Recitative

Taccia, pur, dunque taccia!	Silence, then, silence!
Nè più vano amator altri mi creda	No longer should others think me a futile lover
perché d'ispido pelo	just because my face isn't covered
io non copro la faccia.	with bristly skin.

Aria 3/2

Poco amate delle guancie	Roses are little loved by
son le rose quand' armate	soft cheeks when they're armed
se ne stanno di spine annose,	with big thorns,
ché nemica dell'età	for the enemy of old age
fu mai sempre la beltà.	was always beauty.

Arioso C

Benché sia vecchio Amor, nato col mondo,	Though Cupid, born with the world, may be old,
nel volto ancor non ha pelo nascente,	with no hair yet growing on his face,
e l'arco omnipotente	isn't the all-powerful bow
ond'egli scocca l'amoroso telo	with which he shoots his amorous target
ha la corda di nervo e non di pelo?	made not of hair but a string of sinew?

NO. 2, "LAMENTO DEI CASTRATI: I MADRIGALI"

Preface by Benedetto Marcello (1686–1739)
Music and text: Benedetto Marcello?
Musical source: Bologna, Museo Internazionale e Biblioteca della Musica, GG 144 (STBB)
Recording available on I Solisti della Cappella Musicale di San Petronio, directed by Sergio Vartolo, *Lamenti Barocchi*, vol. 2 (Naxos, Alte Musik, DDD 8.553319; 1995)

Preface

Il primo madrigale si canta da tenori e bassi
li quali annunziano ai castrati una disgrazia terribilissima.
Questi nel sentir il fatale decreto,
prima di interderne la ragione,
interrompono con note acutissime
per significare la proprietà loro che cercano
Di toccare con la voce gli estremi.
Lusingandosi che questo più alto
il musico ascende tanto sia egli
di maggior prezzo e riputazione.
All'udire poi la ragione evangelica
per la quale devono ardere nel foco eterno
non fanno che strillare "Ahi, ahi!"
quasi che allora si trovassero tra le fiamme
overo in quel punto restassero stesticolati,
alludendosi con le due semibrevi degli "Ahi ahi!"
testicoli appunto ch'hanno perduti.

(The first madrigal is sung by tenors and basses who announce to the castrati a terrible misfortune. In hearing the fatal decree, and before understanding the reason for it, the castrati interrupt with very high notes to show off their ability, wanting to reach the top. For the higher castrato goes, the higher his price and reputation. When they then hear the biblical reason why they must burn in eternal fire, they do nothing but shriek, "Ahi, ahi," almost as if they'd actually found themselves amid the flames, or were at that moment being castrated, alluding with two semibreves of "Ahi, ahi" to the two testicles they have lost.)

Madrigal

No che lassù ne Chori almi e beati non entrano castrati? Perché è scritto in quel loco "Dite dite, che scritto mai?"	Can't castrati join the choir of the blessed up there? Why is it written in that place— "Tell us, tell us, why should it be written?"
Arbor che non fa frutto arda nel foco! "Ahi, ahi!"	A tree that bears no fruit burns in fire! "Ahi, ahi!"

NO. 3, "LAMENTO DELL'IMPOTENTE (PAROLE DEL SIGNOR MELOSI)"

Text by Francesco Melosio; musical setting by Fabrizio Fontana (?) (ca. 1620–95)

Musical source: Bologna, Museo Internazionale e Biblioteca della Musica, Q46

Recording available on I Solisti della Cappella Musicale di San Petronio, directed by Sergio Vartolo, *Lamenti Barocchi*, vol. 2 (Naxos, Alte Musik, DDD 8.553319; 1995)

Tante preghiere e tante all'amata beltà facea mai sempre	So many repeated implorings were made again and again to a beloved beauty
un impotente amante ch'ella stordita un dì li disse alfin di si. Ma a che pro s'à quel sì tutto il restante ostinossi a dir di no? Che non fece e non tentò per accordar su quella dolce nota? Disperato e contento l'otioso instromento con soavi maniere si pose a ricercar tutte le chiavi, ma quel musico folle ogni cadenza sua fe per bemolle.	by an impotent lover that, deafened, one day she finally told him yes. But what good was that "yes" when all the rest insist on saying "no"? For did he not sing or try to tune that sweet note? Desperate and happy, that lazy instrument softly set about seeking out all the keys, but that foolish musico made every one of his cadenzas through B♭.[5]
Nel variar i tasti stancò la destra e la sinistra mano ma tutto fece invano,	In varying the keys[6] he tired his right, then his left hand but all in vain,

e trovò sempre i nervi arridi e guasti.
Alfin tutto anelante
tra nettare e velen, tra gioia e duolo,

non potendo sonar sovra la parte
si pose a cantar solo,
e mostrò nel suo fallo
ch'era nato per cigno e non per gallo.
 "Voi mi tradite, o stelle!
Per favor d'Aura soave la mia nave,
già salvata a tocca il porto, ma
d'entrar io tento invano
ch'à tenermene lontano
fassi remora il timone,
son le calme otiose atre procelle.
 "Voi mi tradite, o stelle!"
Cade al suol già vinta e nuda,
questa cruda, e tremante mi rimira
di coraggio e darmi carco

ma lo stral diventa un arco
quando il prendo per ferire
e mi fuggon di man l'armi rubelle.

 "Voi mi tradite, o stelle!"
Ma perché mi querelo
dell'alte stelle, ahi lasso,
se l'autor del mio mal veggio si basso?
Qual furia dunque o qual crudel demonio
ha di cangiar possanza
in fredda tramontana il mio favonio?

Quel incantesmo strano
fa ch'el Ciclope mio diventi un nano?
Scioglimi il dubbio,

always finding his sinews dry and useless.
Finally, completely out of breath,
between nectar and poison, joy and grief,

unable to play any part,
he started to sing all alone,
and showed in his failure
that he was born a swan and not a cock.
 "You betray me, o stars!"
Favored by a sweet breeze my ship,
already saved, touches the port, but
in vain do I attempt to enter it—
for holding me at bay
the helm delaying,
the idle calm turns into dark storms.
 "You betray me, o stars!"
She falls to the ground; conquered
and bare this cruel, trembling one
gazes up at me and fills me up with courage,

but the dart becomes a bow
when I take it to strike,
and the rebellious weapon flees from my hand.

 "You betray me, o stars!"
But why complain
of the stars above, alas,
if I see the author of my grief down below?
What fury then, or what cruel demon
has the power to change
my west wind into the cold north?

What strange spell
makes my Cyclops become a dwarf?

Solve the riddle,

tu Filosofante Astratto:	you Abstract Philosopher,
Perché la mia potenza	of why my potency
quanté prossima più	falls away
men si riduce all'atto?	the closer it comes!
Nell'alma mia che fa	What is potency in my soul
se potenza non è la volontà?	if not my will?
Ahi, che la natural filosofia	O, natural philosophy
oggi è per me si oscura	is so obscure to me today
ch'io nemmen la capisco	that I don't even comprehend
quando i secreti suoi m'apre Natura!	when Nature opens her secrets up to me!
Dimmi tu di me stesso,	Tell me about myself,
inuntil membro, unfruttuoso parte,	you useless member, fruitless organ,
sei tu forse di sasso	maybe you're made of stone
che gallegiar non puoi	that cannot float
sovra un mar di dolcezza?	on a sea of sweetness?
Ma se tu sei di sasso	But if you're made of stone
Dov'è la tua durezza?	then where's your hardness?
Giuro ch'io non so come	I swear I don't know how
Natura all'huom ti dia	Nature gave you to man
se non hai di virile altro che il nome.	if you've nothing virile but your name.
Hor si che dir bisogna	Now I must say
ch'altro non se dell'huom che la vergogna.	that for a man, you're nothing but his shame.
Se la gravosa testa	If you lack the strength
non hai vigor di sollevar dal suolo	to raise your heavy head from the ground
nonché d'alzarti a volo	or raise yourself in flight,
ben ha poco cervello	then a fellow who wants to call himself a bird
che vuol chiamarsi uccello!	surely has a small brain!
Ma purtroppo lo sei	But, alas, you,
per mia vergogna e rabbia	to my shame and anger,
e sei di quella razza	are of that race
che vuol pascer in pugno	that wants to nosh during fisticuffs
e non in gabbia?	instead of [having them] in a cage![7]
Di qual colpa reo ti senti	What wicked act are you guilty of
che paventi d'una carcere soave	that you should fear a sweet prison
di cui tu sol sei prigioniero e chiave?	of which you alone are both prisoner and key?
Chi sarà che non ti ammiri	Who will not wonder at you

rea cagion delle mie doglie	who are the evil cause of my grievous labors,
se contrasti ai miei desiri	if you oppose my desires
col piegarti alle mie voglie?	by bending to my wishes?
Questa voce dolente	With this dolorous voice,
dalla speme derisa	shattered by derided hope
sparse e non altro, il misero impotente,	and nothing but, did the wretched impotent man,
e dal suo duol conquisto	conquered by his grief,
novo Tantalo strano	finally perish from hunger with food in hand,
di fame alfin perì col cibo in mano?	like a strange new Tantalus.
L'impossibile impresa finse gradir	She pretended to enjoy the unachievable deed
con volto assai giocondo	with quite a cheerful face—
la bella importunata	that importunate beauty—
e per la prima al mondo	and for the first time in the history of the world
si disse all'impossibile *obbligata*!	was heard to say to the great beyond: "much obliged!"

2

The Man Who Pretended to Be Who He Was

A Tale of Reproduction

FATHER MEETS SON

In 1734 a newcomer was given seven arias and a duet to sing in the pasticcio of *Artaserse* staged at London's Haymarket. Most leading men got four or five numbers, but this one was already a legend. That night he debuted as Arbace, the son betrayed by his own father who has not only killed their king but also framed the son for the king's murder in a twisted scheme intended to elevate him to the throne. Midway through the opera, the singer stood in chains while his father made a show of condemning his son to death before the Persian court. Faced with this snarl of regicide and public censure, the son implored his father to watch over his beloved in an aria of sublime cantilena marked by a beating heart accompaniment, sighing appoggiaturas, and sentimental Scotch snaps (Ex. 3).

> Per questo dolce amplesso,
> Per questo estremo addio,
> Serbami, o Padre mio,
> L'idolo amato.
>
> Sol questo all'ombra mia
> Pace e conforto sia
> Nel fier mio fato.[1]

[Oh, my Father! In return for this sweet embrace, this final adieu, preserve my beloved idol for me. May this be the sole peace and comfort for my shade in its harsh fate.]

The text was one Johann Adolph Hasse had set for the Venetian Carnival of 1730 using a revised libretto of Metastasio's *Artaserse*, with Farinelli playing Arbace.

EXAMPLE 3. Johann Adolphe Hasse, "Per questo dolce amplesso," facsimile from *The Favourite Songs in the Opera Call'd Artaxerxes by Sig.r Hasse* (London: Walsh, [1735]), fols. 10r–10v, Newberry Library, Chicago. Reproduced by permission.

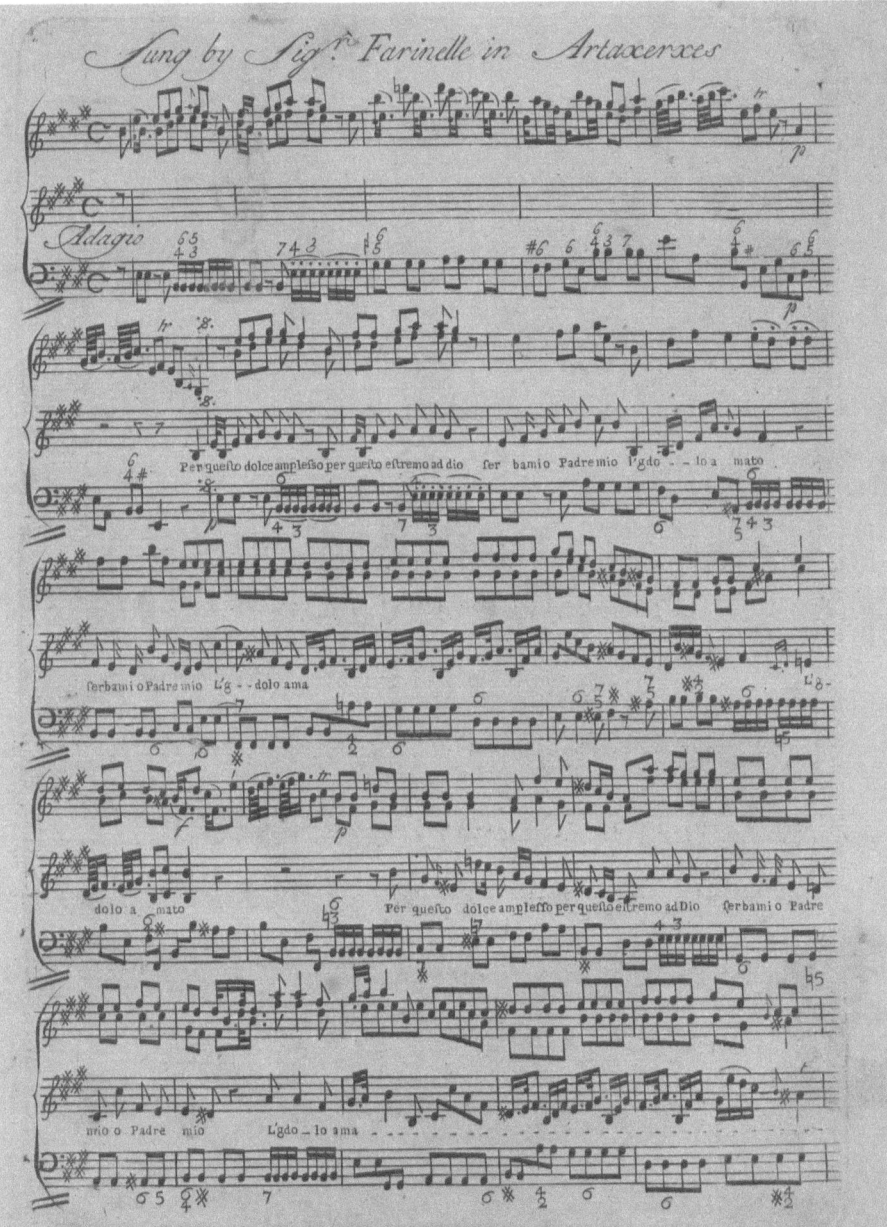

EXAMPLE 3. *(Continued)*

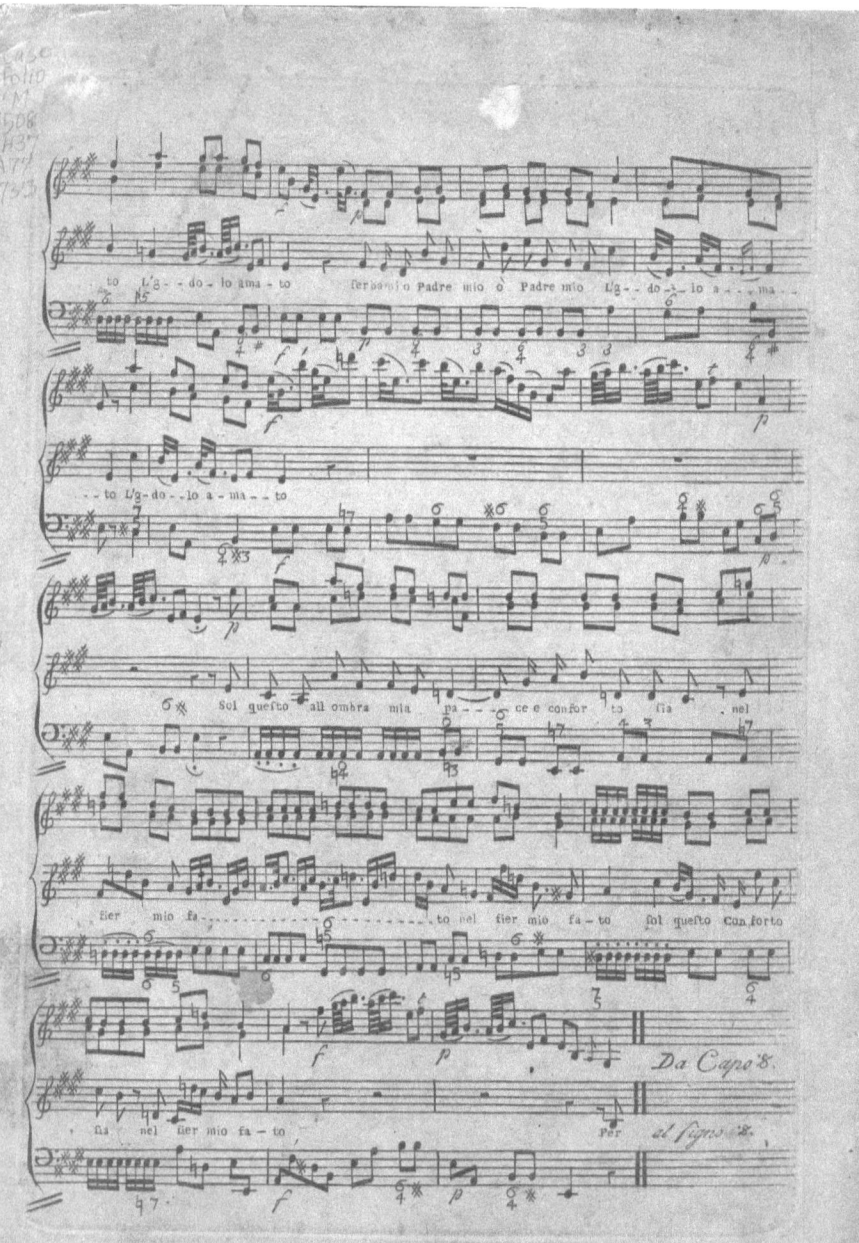

By 1734 Farinelli was already renowned for his pathetic rendition of "Per questo dolce amplesso," which required exquisite breath control, nuance, color, range, and above all the ability to hold the melodic line, phrase after phrase, like a strand of pearls. The aria had to be iconic, to crystallize the climactic turning point in the story when Arbace, betrayed by his father, is about to forsake all patriarchal protection, by suspending the moment and floating it through the galleries and chandeliers. To give wings to song through perfect legato: that was the supreme art of the vocal hero, which none could embody better than the very best of the castrati.[2] Other arias he sang that night displayed his vocal power and agility—in "Son qual nave ch'agitata" (Ex. 18) he metaphorically fought off angry seas with dashing virtuosity—but it was "Per questo dolce amplesso" that turned him into a marvel of transporting emotion, a being who could take your breath away by seeming almost to sing without breathing.[3]

"Per quel dolce amplesso" was soon printed by John Walsh together with other arias of Farinelli's to commemorate the occasion. In later years people circulated the legend that Farinelli's singing that night was so heartbreaking as to rouse even the vain, irascible star who sang the part of his father, Artabano. As Burney told it, "Farinelli ... so softened the obdurate heart of the enraged tyrant, that Senesino, forgetting his stage-character, ran to Farinelli and embraced him in his own."[4] The point was that Senesino, the ill-tempered divo who had held the stage in a series of Handel debuts for a decade and a half and was Farinelli's senior by eighteen years, forgot he was playing a nefarious father and openly showed his own emotion to Farinelli. Mark the emphasis Burney gives the story: not that the father had abandoned his sternness to embrace his son but that Senesino, overcome, had lowered himself to embrace his young rival Farinelli. Or perhaps it was both, for we do not know where in these retellings stage lives and real lives peel apart.

Following up on myths of male reproduction broached in chapter 1, we can begin to ask how being a man and being a castrato converged on the hard ground of lived life. Note that doubts cast on the maleness of the castrato encountered to this point have come from the literary registers of satire, invective, and comedy, the visual genre of caricature, and plays of wit in music and poetry, all of which were to continue through the later eighteenth century. We could add to these registers, genres, and artful forms of sociality a number of others: audience abuse at performances, rowdy jokes, and ridicule "on the street." All posed bona fide challenges to the masculinity of castrati that warrant consideration, but I hope to convince you that the conclusions often drawn—namely, that with a stroke of the knife castrati "ceased to be men," became manmade hermaphrodites, "prima donnas," nonmen, "genderless," or radically ambiguous—largely contradict the evidence.[5] Were such conclusions tenable, there would have been straight-faced assertions that castrati were not perceived as men and were not classifiable as male. Yet during their heyday even their manliness was rarely questioned outside the discursive and generic frameworks of joking, ridicule, invective, satire, and abuse except in some theological or legal contexts and pseudomedical texts.

All this may seem so obvious as to leave us asking what kind of news it is to say that a mutilated man was still a man. That has often been my own question. Certainly neither cross-dressing onstage, nor having sex with other men (about which we know very little), nor having intimate, even amorous male friendships, nor making male-to-male emotional displays, nor even the castrato's sexual morphology marked him as a nonman in any cultural sense. When direct challenges to the gender of castrati were made, they were the backwash of Enlightenment morality—and even then, claims of unmanliness were bracketed since they were rife with tendentious, often casuistic ardor. Such claims began pooling up in the mid- to late eighteenth century, when castrati seemed "unmanly" to many because monstrously uncategorizable. By then, broadcasting disaffection and disapproval of them became a matter of political and existential duty, tightly bound up with the sanctity of nature—hence the marquis d'Argens's gloss of castration in 1747 as a "smothering ... of nature" and Rousseau's claim that parents of castrati were simply "sacrificing nature to fortune."[6]

What *was* understood as exceptional about the castrato's gender can be boiled down to two things: 1) that he was biologically *nongenerative;* and 2) that he had a high singing voice that was *"natural."* However much a castrato was understood as a third kind, sexually continuous, queer, or nonnormative,[7] he can also be recuperated to a socially grounded and historically situated notion of gender through generation and voice. As much as the one was a deprivation, the other was an endowment. By at least 1600 the castrato's "natural" high voice was apprehended in contradistinction to the voice of a falsettist, which was thought high by virtue of a vocal trick, produced by "una voce falsa," singing falsetto thus being a kind of artful fakery, seemingly more or less synonymous with a head voice.[8]

Taken together, being nongenerative and being naturally high-voiced indexed part-womanly men with some feminine physical features and also denoted men who might be poorly equipped to or incapable of having sexual intercourse (something undoubtedly variable among them and surely related to the age at castration). That it indexed men was not in doubt, though within the category "man" lay a wide range of variations. Roger Freitas has persuasively argued that in the seventeenth and early eighteenth centuries adult castrati were often objects of erotic desire for both men and women precisely because they were perceived as boyish figures, avatars of the superstar-as-quintessential-man/child embodied in the 1980s by celebrities such as Michael Jackson and Prince. With roguish literary license, some contemporaries wrote scurrilously or with intentional ambiguity about castrati as "object-choices" or sexual subjects, or they cast them as Siren or femme types. Most notorious in the later eighteenth century is Casanova. In an episode about his infatuation with the young castrato Bellino he insists that Bellino is really a girl with an artificial attachment, though in fact it is the boy he desires, and even more so once her "real" female sex is confirmed but still hidden behind the castrato guise.[9]

PATRIARCHY, PRIMOGENITURE, AND PATRILINY

In this chapter I suggest that the castrato's nonprocreative status has a distinctive place within critical boundaries of patriarchy, and that it is no coincidence that castrating boys for music became a going concern in Italy during the very period when patriliny hardened into a norm.[10] By "patriarchy" I refer here to a wider set of cultural conditions that valorized and accorded male authority, whether in families or (inseparably) political structures; by "patriliny" I refer to descent, including devolution of estates, through the male bloodline of a given family branch. Other kinds of descent did occur in early modern Italy, but since they were less desirable they generally entailed compromises or tensions. Systematizing property devolution through a male line to preserve or increase wealth was the essence of patriliny, even when property devolved, by default or special interest, upon females, cognates, or affines. More particularly, patriliny can be thought of as a specific outgrowth of the widespread practice of primogeniture, which de facto made a first-born male the sole heir of his family's property. And holding property indivisible within thin, vertical male lines kept riches and hence power from straying outside a given bloodline.

If some form of patriarchy had long been the rule, patriliny by contrast took root in a historically precise way only around 1570, as we have glimpsed above.[11] Prior to that time the ideal had been to marry off all or most sons to increase a family's power not just vertically but horizontally, within a wider network of kin, with the goal of fortifying the clan as a whole. With the marrying off of first sons only, a situation arose in which younger sons were typically consigned to military or ecclesiastical careers and thus formally speaking to legal or effective celibacy at the same time as most upper-class daughters entered convents. Both strategies intensified with the severe economic crisis of the seventeenth century, but the practice continued afterward, albeit with increasing tendencies toward diversification and stratification.[12]

What has gone largely unremarked in writings about the castrato phenomenon is that Italy witnessed an amazing coincidence between the consolidation of strongly patrilineal practices and the practice of castrating boys for singing. Furthermore, at a time when castration for singing was becoming a regular Italian practice, Italy was one of the most patrilineal regions in all of Europe. The sound of the singing castrate whose flesh had been mortified to produce him might thus be imagined as the audible approximation of a wailing Christ. Still, it is unlikely that castrations for singing would have been become widespread without the enabling factor of patriliny, within the bounds of which prepubertal castration was regarded by early modern families of various classes as a special case of sacred celibacy.[13] Only when, in the eighteenth century, it became both less necessary as an economic alternative and less amenable as a social practice were there commensurate drops in the population of castrati.[14]

If the situation sounds a bit too tidy—the obligatory becomes desirable and the desirable obligatory—it is offset by plenty of messy ironies and inconsistencies. In the telos of classic eighteenth-century opera seria—the principal form of opera over virtually all of Europe—the leading, usually castrated male protagonist is repeatedly propelled toward marriage, and hence toward reproduction of the social and biological order, the critical anthropological sense in which I use the term "reproduction" in this chapter.[15] Yet had Arbace been an average Milanese aristocrat in the first half of the seventeenth century, he would have stood at best a 50 percent chance of getting the girl to the altar in the end. Had he been a younger son in the later seventeenth century, his life prospects could have been much worse because his living allowance would probably have been severely depressed, like the dowries of Milanese girls.[16] That the institution of patriliny had largely shaved family loyalties down from the strongly corporate groups of the Middle Ages—the cognatic clan—to one principal paternal line comprised of agnatic kin (those of male descent) only compounded the economic misfortunes that pummeled younger generations, aristocratic and non, even as it solved larger economic problems. Nor is that the whole story, for always contravening this otherwise male-descent-oriented world were little exceptions and rebellions by persons who were literally cut out by the system, and who often litigated, contested wills, married on the sly or for love, or made unconventional bequests—an arena in which castrati participated widely by tinkering creatively with the prevailing patrilineal system of affiliation and bequest.

Now if castrated males came mainly from lower- and middle-class backgrounds and few were firstborns, why did it matter that blood and money flowed downward in a patrilineal stream? After all, even if boys who ended up being castrated had *not* been, they probably would not have been able to marry and thus generate legitimate male heirs. Some families of the middle and lower classes instead tried to position sons so they could mimic aristocratic habits. Those who were successful professionally could move up the social ladder to levels where aping aristocratic and even royal ways, on stage and off, was basically required of them. This certainly caused discomfit to many and provoked some derision.[17] But since such singers had wealth to bequeath, they had to find ways to make the patrilineal system work for them, especially as depleted family coffers had often been a major incentive in creating patrilineal modalities in the first place.

Poor families played their part too. According to the Huguenot lawyer Charles Ancillon (1659–1715), the "very famous" castrato uncle of Pauluccio, from a poor family, was the one who actually castrated his nephew when the boy was ten years old, just as he did several other children in the family. Ancillon says he spoke with Pauluccio in his rich quarters in Rome and learned that the uncle had believed Pauluccio "might one Day be a Support to the Family if he was like himself, for then he might get considerable Sums of Money which must flow into that Channel, *since he could have no children of his own to divert the Current.*"[18] The stress here is not just on supporting the natal family as a result of acquiring means but on continuing to do so fully because the castrate lacks other family obligations.

Pauluccio's story as told by Ancillon is one of many that frames castration of singing boys paradoxically as a form of male reproduction, in this instance avuncular (uncle to nephew). Note apropos that the explanations for castrations encountered in chapter 1 fall essentially into three groups, all of them indirectly implicated in generation. One involves a scenario in which castration is a male surrender of blood for the common good of the patriarchal order, framed as an extreme act of devotion to church, prince, or God. A related scenario involves a broader form of exchange in which renunciation of virility—forced by accident or carried out by force of will—enables a boy or his family to overcome such adversities as poverty or infirmity. And a third involves a joking scenario in which males carry out castrations in order to produce other males: the father in Melosio's sonnet who castrates a son from whom Pulcinella is generated; a male creature who fathers (or minimally raises) a castrate (Tiepolo's braggart turkey who generates the castrato-like Pulcinella; Balatri's broody Norcian rooster who lays eggs that hatch male sopranos).

The sacrificial dynamic that links these various scenarios all involve castrations performed on males by other males, or promoted or nurtured by them. In some instances the castrations are instigated by male figures, and in all they're sanctioned by male authority. They are thus linked to the symbolic nexus of the pregnant or birthing male associated with the effectively castrated Pulcinella. In Fig. 17 we saw Pulcinella give birth through his anus to little Pulcinellini who drop onto the floor. As he does so, a community of men assists (both watching and helping), one of them, Pulcinella-like, feeding him gnocchi at his front side and another attending to the expelling orifice around his back. We know here who the essential Pulcinella is—the ur-Pulcinella—because he is the progenitor of all others. (The woman is only an onlooker.) In a companion painting, Pulcinella again plays a parturient, this time birthing babies through his back surrounded by what appears to be a wife, or perhaps an off-duty midwife, and other Pulcinella-esque family members.[19]

Other depictions make him look like he's great with child. In the seventeenth century Francesco Bertelli conjured up a deformed Pulcinella. Instead of having the usual fat man's stomach, he has the slim figure of a young woman whose protruding low-slung belly foretells an imminent birth (Fig. 22).[20]

The attribution of pregnancy was not unknown in satires of castrati, especially in London where satire was the bread and butter of theater life. *An Epistle to John James Heidegger, Esquire, on the Report of Signior Farinelli's Being with Child* of January 1736, in which a satirist asks "Is the soft warbler . . . a wench with Child?" was addressed to the manager of London's Haymarket Theater, where Farinelli was playing at the time. The question was repeated more than once that year.[21] Fielding's 1736 play *Pasquin* has the character of Miss Mayoress remark to her mother, "Yes, Mama, and then we shall see Faribelly, the strange Man-Woman that they say is great with child" (act 2, scene 1)—as if Farinelli were nothing but cheesy popular spectacle and going to see him he were no different from going to see the "fine pictures at Merlin's cave" or lowly "Rope-Dancing" and "Tumbling."[22]

If reproduction in all these tales and representations was a form of male creation, it was always in the face of what was not. As Valeria Finucci points out, it was precisely the lack of generative power that was marked in Pope Sixtus V's famous 1587 brief "Cum frequenter," which proclaimed that "eunuchs, castrati, and *spadones*" (men with damaged sexual organs) could not marry *not* because they lacked the capacity for heterosexual love or some kind of acceptable sexual activity, but rather because they could not generate. The timing of the pope's brief says a lot. It was produced in just the years when eunuchs were starting to replace at least some falsettists in the papal chapel, twelve years before the chapel made admittance of them official, and not long before castrati were to become a widespread presence throughout Italy and soon thereafter throughout Europe. Finucci underscores the coincidence by noting that just around the time when male castrates became pervasive, especially in chapels, the church asserted that they were not "real men," for to be a real man outside the clergy, you had to be able to make the men who would succeed you "generationally": "The ability to perform sexually . . . may have made a man look like one, but the ability to generate . . . alone guaranteed that he was one in the eyes of the legal and ecclesiastical system. . . . Manhood had to be a performance to register on the body of the next generation."[23]

The pope's pronouncement was not consistent with the Aristotelian notion of a generative man, which saw no essential function of the testicles in producing semen, but rather (not surprisingly) conformed with Galenic theory, which understood the testicles to be the site where semen was formed in a final stage of production.[24] If Galen won out on this point, a compensatory cultural system might be thought to have taken root at the same time in which the power of song became a virtual substitute for the power of semen. Bontempi claimed as much when he declared that the virility of Baldassare Ferri's lost semen was immanent in his wondrous singing—singing as if through a kind of phantom vocal phallus. Effectively, perhaps, so did the French theologian Gregorius Sayrus (Gregory Robert Sayer, 1560–1602) when he claimed, à la Aristotle, first, that "the voice is a faculty more precious than virility, since it is through the voice and reasoning that man is distinguished from animals," and second, that therefore "to embellish the voice it is necessary to suppress virility."[25] On such views, Senesino's impassioned embrace of his "son" Farinelli, understood alongside many other accounts of the power of castrato voices to stir feelings, amorous, fraternal, monarchical, and otherwise, was not just a breach of the prescribed hierarchical relationship of father/son, and hence *fuori di carattere*. Rather, it was a breach of the performer's professional boundaries as divo, an overstepping of embodied emotional limits that were deeply sedimented.

PRETENDING HUSBANDS

Ancillon's treatise was first issued in French in 1707 as *Traité des eunuques, dans lequel on explique toutes les différentes sortes d'eunuques, quel rang ils ont tenu, & quel cas on en a fait, &c.* . . . *Par M*** D**** (pseudonymously signed C. d'Ollican), shortly after the practice of castration for singing had reached its numerical apex. Virtually the sole treatise on eunuchism, it was brought out eleven years later as a little duodecimo pocket book under the real name of its author with a title that highlighted the marriage dilemma:

> Eunuchism display'd: describing all the different sorts of eunuchs; the esteem they have met with in the world, and how they came to be made so; wherein principally is examin'd, whether they are capable of marriage, and if they ought to be suffer'd to enter into that state; the whole confirm'd by the authority of civil, canon, and common law, and illustrated with many remarkable cases by way of precedent; also a comparison between Signior Nicolini and the three celebrated eunuchs now at Rome, viz. Pasqualini, Pauluccio, and Jeronimo (or Momo); with several observations on modern eunuchs; occasion'd by a young lady's falling in love with Nicolini, who sung in the opera at the Hay-market, and to whom she had like to have been married.
> [Epigraph: "There are, who in soft Eunuchs place their Bliss, And shun the Scrubbing of a bearded Kiss." Dryden's *Juvenal*.][26]

Ancillon's ostensible discourse on eunuch marriage was driven by other motives. Like many, he pictured famous castrati he had heard and heard about as being so coddled and so showered with "considerable Sums of Money" that they had become "puffed up with a Vanity which is ever peculiar to Eunuchs." Some had even "got it into their Heads, that truly the Ladies were in Love with them, and fondly flattered themselves with mighty Conquests" (v–vi). Nicolini, Handel's first great castrato (see Fig. 4 at bottom), allegedly proposed to the female love object cited on Ancillon's title page and only failed to carry through because her relations squelched the affair (vii); otherwise she might have married someone "absolutely uncapable to answer the End of Marriage" whose aims could "only terminate in sordid interest, downright Money" (viii). The first reference is not, of course, to impotence but to sterility (medical evidence suggests that those castrated at later ages, about eleven to thirteen, were capable of erection; see chapter 1). But the issue is less sterility than avarice.[27] Marriage in Ancillon's titillating account was deemed right when it obeyed God's command to "Increase and Multiply," hence eunuchs were damned to singlehood because "neither naturally nor supernaturally capable to get Children." To take the money of a good family through such a ruse was intolerable.[28]

What to make, then, of the many, wildly diverse eunuch love stories involving both women and men that come down over time? Loreto Vittori (1604–70) alludes to his brazen elopement with a married woman in his own comic-heroic, quasi-autobiographical epic *La troia rapita* (1662) as "un lieve error di giovanil desio" (a slight error of youthful desire; canto 8, stanza 33, line 3);[29] and Atto Melani (1626–1714) evidently made overtures to Hortense Mancini, to whom he was madly attracted, as well as her sisters, all nieces of Cardinal Mazarin, some of whom probably returned the attraction in spirit if not in deed. The sociopolitical stake in the game of castrato attractions is patent. Atto's flirtations with Hortense, even if nothing more, sufficed to have him banished by Louis XIV because the king was persuaded of threats to honor by Hortense's jealous duke of a husband, threats that may have been plausible if we believe a satire written by an intimate of Atto's, which claimed the castrato did have some kind of sex with women. Atto most definitely had sex with men, apparently always as a passive, and thus boyish, partner, notably with Carlo II Duke of Mantua, as Freitas infers from thinly veiled allusions in their correspondence and affirms in general for Atto via a satire that claims he bent over for sex.[30] De Castris had sex with men too.[31] Later in the century Siface (Giovanni Francesco Grossi, 1653–97) ran off with a marquise until her family's hired henchmen caught up with their carriage and did him in.[32] Another, Domenico Cecchi, called Il Cortona (ca. 1650–55 to 1717–18), reportedly wanted to marry a Barbara Voglia, but his petition was flat-out denied by Pope Innocent XI with the much-repeated apocryphal-sounding "Si castra meglio" ("May you castrate yourself better," or "Be castrated better").[33] Filippo Balatri composed quixotic, self-mocking episodes in verse about falling in love with two females—first in Russia with a young English mistress of Peter the Great's named Anna Mons when he was only seventeen, and second with a nun in Pisa, neither of which, according to him, was requited.[34] Farinelli fell in love with a woman at least once and could well have had a youthful tryst with Metastasio, as we will soon see. And Charles Burney's daughter Susanna was mutually enamored with the great star Gasparo Pacchierotti, known for his profound and seductive vocal expressivity.[35]

Clandestine love with a castrato in these varied forms may have been no more than a pinprick on the face of society if kept quiet and not institutionalized, but subjectively it could spell social calamity and a psychic slide into the imaginary monster's den. In those few, extraordinary instances when love with eunuchs led to heterosexual marriage, male and female desire were much stronger than the prospect of sexual performance of the kind that so preoccupies advertisers, (male) consumers, and some scholars today. Moreover, male generative power outweighed both.

It will be useful to look at three instances.[36] Least problematic was the case of Filippo Finazzi (ca. 1706–76), a Bergamasque soprano and composer popular in Venice from the later 1720s onward and in Germany beginning in 1743. Around 1755, while living in retirement at his country estate near Hamburg, Finazzi was being helped to recover from two broken legs by his working-class housekeeper, the widow of a blacksmith who nursed him back to health and with whom he ended up getting romantically involved. He took over her sons' education and, in 1761, wanted to tie the knot, but first he had to obtain special clearance from the Hamburg senate. Friends in high places testified to his character and cultivation (he was also a composer whose opera *Temistocle* had been performed there), so he succeeded with relatively little ado.[37] His ability to get away with the marriage can partly be chalked up to his connections and infirmity, which evidently gained him the necessary sympathy. But most relevant no doubt was that there was little at stake. The couple was older and living in obscurity outside Lutheran Hamburg, in addition to which she was a widow and mother of lower station. In 1746 Finazzi had even converted to Protestantism.

. . .

The two other known castrato marriages, both involving young Protestant women from prominent professional families, were far more vexed. The more sensational, and sensationalized, was the elopement in early 1766 of Giusto Ferdinando Tenducci (ca. 1735–90) with an Irish girl of fifteen named Dora (Dorothea) Maunsell. By the time they met Tenducci had already become a big star in London as the English lover-hero Arbaces in Thomas Arne's hugely popular *Artaxerxes* (1762), and in 1765 he was living and singing in Dublin. Until recently the marriage had been best known through Dora's account of the travails the couple endured in their first year of marriage, published as *A True and Genuine Narrative of Mr. and Mrs. Tenducci in a Letter to a Friend at Bath, Giving a Full Account from Their Marriage in Ireland, to the Present Time*.[38] Recently the veracity of the account has been confirmed in historian Helen Berry's *The Castrato and His Wife*, which contextualizes and greatly expands on it through many new documents and shows that indeed the memoir was almost certainly written by Dora herself. Berry notes that the *True and Genuine Narrative* takes inspiration from the genre of teenage romance fiction, specifically Richardson's epistolary novel *Pamela, or Virtue Rewarded*, hence its plotting.[39] Soon after falling in love with Tenducci, Dora discovers that her father plans to force her into an unwanted marriage, prompting her to elope hastily in order to forestall a loveless union. Marriage to a castrato provokes such furor in her family as to put him in and out of dank, dark jails where he languishes with common felons, and to cause her relatives to abduct her, strip her of freedom, clothing, and company, and expose her to unwanted sexual advances, innuendo, threats of rape, and other abuses in their attempt to have her repudiate Tenducci, all for nearly a year until the family finally relents.

Tenducci's own life was peppered with infatuations and dalliances with women. In a series of Freudian inversions, he boasted to other men about his ability to please women safely, got involved with more than one gentlewoman, and used on his correspondence a personalized wax seal showing a barely dressed woman with a well-muscled man. The Maunsells, who surely thought leaving their daughter alone for singing lessons with a eunuch a safe thing to do, would hardly have found comfort in knowing all that. But their ire was stoked both by Tenducci's sterility, permanent and visible on his body, which made the marriage shameful and its legal status questionable, and by the couple's total flouting of the need for parental consent or even knowledge, exacerbated by the fact that their marriage was performed by a decrepit Catholic priest in an assault on the raw nerve of Irish Protestant/Catholic relations. The prolonged frenzy into which the family descended over the marriage can be accounted by the effects of all these insults on the whole clan. Numerous members of the family, nuclear and extended, colluded to exploit any stratagem that might cause Dora to back down. Her father, being a shrewd, well-to-do barrister in Dublin and well connected legally even in London, drew the whole matter into the realm of British law. When the parents finally caved in (without actually consenting), the couple remarried in a Protestant ceremony in spring 1767. Tenducci moved them to Edinburgh in June 1768. There he played a direct part in new trends toward sensibility by singing ballads for the Edinburgh Musical Society. Dora mysteriously gave birth there to a child—perhaps what Tenducci meant when he called them his "family"[40]—after which the Tenduccis moved to London, where polite London society gave Dora a withering reception but one that was no worse than what they experienced in Italy, to which they moved early in 1771, living clandestinely since legal proscriptions there were fierce. In Florence Dora resided with Tenducci's mother and sister under cover of being a singing student while her husband traveled, but after some months she fled with a young British gentleman whom she married in a Catholic wedding in Rome in April 1772 and again, after their return to England, in a Protestant ceremony in 1773 (a confessional repetition of her two successive marriages with Tenducci). Once Dora left, Tenducci was said to have spoken dolefully about having lost "his Dorothea."[41]

In 1775, in an attempt to erase the stain completely, Dora's new husband initiated complex legal proceedings to have her previous marriage annulled, which ultimately produced the desired outcome with the judgment that it had been a "feigned marriage." The proceedings brought forth some of the most fascinating testimony that has ever surfaced about castration (for the discovery of which we have Berry to thank), since the major issue for the courts was to demonstrate through irrefutable firsthand accounts that Tenducci had indeed been made a eunuch, and hence could not procreate.[42] Berry rightly stresses that the act of eliciting the evidence put the castrato's manhood on trial as much as it did his marriage. In addition to detailed firsthand descriptions of the castration provided by the surgeon's servant and son (see chapter 1), a deposition about Tenducci's body was given by his former roommate Charles Baroe. Baroe recalled that Tenducci always carried with him a red velvet purse containing what he said were his excised testicles, the sack thus substituting for the empty scrotum as if to replace or commemorate its former wholeness but also commemorating a blood sacrifice in keeping with the Roman Catholic fetish for preserving and displaying relics of the bodies of saints. Tenducci's attachment to the red purse corresponds with his other assertions of manhood, not just courting women and marrying one but also his claiming courage in the face of castration surgery, as he reportedly boasted to librettist Nicolo Tassi: "I have heard . . . Ferdinando Tenducci say he submitted to undergo the operation with great courage in order to be cured . . . choosing castration rather than pass his life with such an irksome imperfection which often filled his scrotum with gross humors."[43]

. . .

The third marriage story brings the nexus between castration, reproduction, and manhood into startling discursive focus. The details, concerning Bartolomeo Sorlisi, who from about 1646 onward was much plumed and beribboned at the courts of Bavaria and Dresden, have been carefully researched and elaborated by Mary Frandsen.[44] In 1665 Sorlisi was ennobled by the emperor, and in the succeeding years his rank and privileges continued to rise to the levels of an aristocrat, not entirely unlike the situation of Atto Melani in an overlapping period. Several years before, in about 1661–62, Sorlisi, at age forty-eight, had already acquired some fame and means, and so he set out to do what most castrati in his position did, namely, to buy a feudal estate. In the process he became mutually enamored with the sixteen-year-old stepdaughter of his real estate lawyer. For about two years the couple prevailed on her parents to let them marry until finally the amiable elders entered into a provisional marriage agreement with Sorlisi. They were smart enough to specify that it was valid only if it held up to civil law and ecclesiastical judgment, evidently believing it would not, and pronounced Sorlisi an honorable gentleman without mentioning that he was a eunuch.

Sure enough a storm of legal-theological controversy erupted. Sorlisi petitioned the Leipzig consistory, but in a brazen act of displacement he pretended to act not on his own behalf but on behalf of a close friend. The "friend" was said by Sorlisi to be a knight, a great warrior whom he named, of all things, Titius, conjuring up a Titan through an odd series of linguistic manipulations (Titius being a pseudo-Latinization of the Italian Tiziano, meaning Titus, probably thus signifying the Roman emperor and possibly also evoking the eponymous saint addressed in the epistle of Saint Paul). Titius had suffered battle wounds that had left him infertile, yet he nevertheless wished to marry. The lucky woman was an "aristocrat" to whom Sorlisi gave the sexually charged name of Lucretia, recalling the chaste wife of Roman antiquity who was raped by Sextus Tarquinius.

The equation of the castrato's "injury" with a war wound is not without parallels: Girolamo Crescentini's "wound" was explicitly so equated when he was knighted by Napoleon (Fig. 48, where Crescentini is named "Cavaliere Girolamo Crescentini").[45] I have already suggested that such perilous male activities as hunting, horseback riding, and climbing trees played a compensatory symbolic and pragmatic role in the repertory of explanations used to justify many castrations after the fact, but Sorlisi's account goes further, turning the perils of bloodshed, through a stunning leap of imagination, into a full-blooded medieval romance of derring-do.

> Some years ago . . . in the fierce battle . . . between their Royal Majesties of Denmark and Sweden, a Swedish aristocrat of distinguished lineage whom we shall call Titius [so wir Titium nennen wollen] was hit on both thighs and in his genital organs by a very dangerous canister shot. As a result, he lost the greater portion of his scrotum, as well as one complete testicle, and his other testicle was crushed, so that subsequently in treatment it was completely destroyed, and had to be removed. As a result of this misfortune, Titius became utterly incapable of and unfit for the perpetuation of the human race.[46]

With a meticulousness worthy of an anatomist, Sorlisi went on to describe how Titius sometimes had "an erection of the virile member" and was "not entirely incapable of sexual congress, especially as his virile member had been a little less damaged in the foreskin and the glans."[47] In doing so he also delineated a view of manhood founded in the sacrificial economy of donation and return but veering toward the "bargain" I describe in the preface. Titius became infertile as an adult warrior when his wounds caused him to lose his generative capacity and a part of his sexual function. For that Sorlisi claimed he ought to be compensated with a spousal companion, thus enabling him to achieve a substantial gain on his heavy, selfless, and dangerous investment in manliness.[48]

What it meant to be "Swedish" was evidently to be of fighting stock, manly, Lutheran, and un-Italian. And what it meant to be even quasi-virile (at least as cooked up for theological eyes) was probably not to be any sort of castrated man, given that many Lutheran theologians believed, as Frandsen skillfully shows, that prepubertal castration precluded all sexual function.[49] Yet in Sorlisi's eyes, being quasi-virile because brave clearly meant, or should have meant, being qualified for marriage. He repined that the hoped-for marriage of his alter ego was being protested by some relatives, despite the couple's mutual love and Titius's courteous character, simply because Titius was a foreigner. Peeling through the layer of alibis, we can see that was as much as to say that to be a castrato was to be wrongly seen as some kind of alien—shades of Stallybrass and White's "threshold creature"—and hence alarming no matter how faultless.[50] To that faultlessness Sorlisi directly opposed the perfidy of those who sought to impede the match. Especially guilty was the doctor, who, he claimed, had breached confidence by divulging the condition, thereby (conveniently) forcing the reluctant "Titius" into "many dangerous duels"—unwelcome but decisive ritual reiterations of his manliness, not unlike the iterations made by brave novices (such as Tenducci) who underwent castrations and later had the added injury of having to explain them.

Equally striking, the fictitious mother in Sorlisi's narrative at first opposes the match but is later endeared to it by the couple's mutual devotion and by Titius's honorable disclosure to her of his condition—a stitching together of his medieval romance with the protobourgeois parable disseminated on the baroque stage whereby love leads through virtue to marriage.[51] In fact, a parable of the sort became the basis for the whole rest of Sorlisi's petition, which decked Titius out with virtue but began first contra the marriage, then pro, as Frandsen points out, in the venerable tradition of the *ars disputandi*.

A clearer articulation of the mythical archetype that Wendy Doniger would gloss as "the man who pretended to be who he was" would be hard to imagine (and I thank her for my chapter title).[52] *Pretending to be who he was* meant, among other things, explaining to himself the very thing that Sorlisi was trying to explain to the authorities. In a particularly revealing moment, Sorlisi went beyond Arthurian romance to invoke as justification for Titius's proposed marriage the marriage of King David to Avishai, which took place when he was old and thus "frigid."

COLD PRODIGIES

Now "frigid," far from being an innocuous word in the seventeenth century, is a highly marked one, especially joined as it is here with "maleficatus" (malformed). Frandsen makes the astute observation that the two words appear together in the thirteenth-century decretal *De frigidus et maleficatus, et impotentia coeundi* (Of cold, malformed, and impotent unions).[53] It so happens that they were also deployed by Balatri to characterize himself in the earlier of his two autobiographies, the multivolume Russian manuscript "Vita e viaggi di F. B., nativo di Pisa."[54] The first of its nine surviving volumes, set down in 1725, offers the only native's account I know that both attributes the decision to castrate to the father and describes how a father made the decision. Balatri first boasts about his vocal ability in terms that would have satisfied even the renowned singing master

Pierfrancesco Tosi (1654–1732), whose treatise was published just two years earlier,[55] claiming that his elders—teacher, father, and various friends of his father's—determined that his voice was worthy of castration. "It was established that my voice was of the finest timbre, with a natural trill, a good attack, outstanding fluency in passagework, and a general taste for natural singing." Just after saying so, he makes their infatuation suspect through another Freudian twist:

> The basis for this judgment was urgently arrived at by friends of my father's, crying out "Cut! Cut!" and then, more than all the others, by my singing teacher to advise my father; so that after the many cries of "Cut! Cut!" finally my father joined in too, and sent to Lucca for the surgeon Accoramboni, who was made to come to the house to stay for two months and engage me in a little gracious conversation.[56]

It would seem that the reason the surgeon came to stay at the Balatri residence was that he had been commandeered into the cause of winning the child's confidence and perhaps eliciting his nominal consent.

In trying to interpret these scraps of lore, it is important to recognize that even though Balatri was a preternatural satirist, he generally based his satire on historical particulars. When he does tell tall tales, he lets us in on the fact and generally lets us know why. Unlike the later "Frutti del mondo"—an extraction and generic recasting of the prose autobiography into comical, semifictitious verse—the earlier autobiography hews closer to fact. The difference is worth bearing in mind in reading what he next says in the "Vita e viaggi":

> [All] this chit-chat [with the surgeon] came at such a cost that instead of the doctoral degree that I would one day have been able to obtain, I was given a diploma to pass as a "Frigidus et Maleficatus" [cold and malformed man] for the rest of my life, renouncing forever the sweet name I would one day have heard given me of "Father."[57]

Balatri thus reckons his castration as a form of victimhood. The surgery itself drew an immutable temporal line by ending one life and initiating another. It was a kind of ritual bloodshed and rebirth. And the legacy Balatri ascribes to his father in all this is dark: he capitulated to the pressure of peers, he obstructed his son's education, he bequeathed him a "cold," injured body, and he prevented him from continuing the paternal line and experiencing the rewards of fatherhood. Small wonder that in a long satirical testament of 1738 Balatri declares that for his funeral he wants none of the cadenzas, passaggi, trills, and other ornate singing that he had cultivated throughout his life as a result of his castration and subsequent initiation into the ranks of professional soloists, which he deems unsuited to a stinking corpse and to its passage from earthly to celestial realms. Nor does he want polyphony but only a mass sung in chant "with devotion by four priests":

> Because I was a castrato of some distinction, perhaps a din of voices and instruments will blow in as if it were a wedding, serving no function except for people to say,

"Let's go hear the funeral of so-and-so; hopefully it'll be nice, because all the music of the city will be there." And while I, closed in a coffin, warmed by candle lights and the crowd, start to stink like a carrion, the musicians may go on extending passaggi and trills with cadenzas half an hour long, with listeners applauding and probably not chanting as much as a "Requiem aeternam" for me.[58]

A "Requiem aeternam" delivered as solo chant could hardly have registered more differently than the opulent multivoiced and often theatrical requiems set by Italianate composers of Balatri's time, which sound at least as diverting as they do devotional. Imagine, for example, the disparity between a chanted "Dies irae" sequence and the multimovement, orchestrally accompanied polyphonic settings by Balatri's contemporary Antonio Lotti (1666–1740), whose *Dies irae* setting is lushly melismatic, even on such a stanza as the "Mors stupebit," and disarmingly cheerful in the "Juste Judex."[59]

By the time Balatri wrote the "Testamento" in 1737-38 he had left the Munich court after nearly two decades and retired to a nearby Cistercian monastery. This was after years of singing opera intermittently, starting when he did a bit part in Albinoni's *Aminta* at the Tuscan court in 1703, aged twenty-one, and continuing, after a ten-year hiatus, through the period 1713–27. During most of those years Balatri was employed as a court singer to the Palatine Elector Maximilian Emanuel at Munich where he was first engaged in 1715. In Peter Jacob Horemans's 1733 painting of a concert at the court's summer residence in Schloß Ismaning, Balatri, seated at the harpsichord at the center of a grand scene, peers directly into the viewer's eye from a long bony head placed atop a lanky figure (Fig. 23). Performing a trio sonata with some fellow musicians, he is strikingly *of* the court, both fixture and ornament, as his parents had been at Cosimo's.

During the 1720s he repeatedly shared the Munich stage with famed alto coloraturist Bernacchi, the first international opera star to be identified pointedly with a radically new instrumental style of singing that was disparaged by Tosi in 1723 (cf. Bernacchi's solfeggio exercise in Ex. 8).[60] His own teacher, the castrato Pistocchi, a composer and a great singer in his own right, was rumored to have quipped to him, "I taught you to sing, and you want to play"[61]—a remark that, although probably apocryphal, nevertheless summed up Bernacchi's reputation as the prodigal son among castrato coloraturists. Balatri also remembered with a thrill the time in 1724 when he had performed with the dazzling female coloratura Faustina Bordoni in Vienna, where they sang in *Semiramide in Ascalona* with text by Apostolo Zeno and music by Antonio Caldara, she as the eponymous queen and he as the general.[62]

It's especially poignant that on the spectrum from plain and pious to ornately secular singing that Balatri invokes in his "Testamento," solo coloratura is disowned for falling at the decadent latter extreme.[63] In truth it's less coloratura that offends than the very making of the man who can execute it, and those who would make (or unmake) him. With a Freudian sweep of the hand, Balatri can therefore repudiate his father both socially and musically. The "cold and injured man" of the Moscow text is a humorally distressed one, the phrase referring to his father's having deprived him of the vital male "heat" that made men marriageable because procreative and that ultimately made them men who were meaningful in the patriliny. Insofar as a castrato might be manly, it was mainly through his high, powerful, and often agile voice, the exploitation of which is precisely what Balatri casts off in his satirical will, written about the same time that he joined a monastery.

PRETENDING FATHERS

The castrato's approach to the afterlife formed the last part of a ritual cycle of male reproduction, which in my analysis began with castration and continued with the intense training routine that generally followed it. Parents or guardians who sought to have their boys accepted for training by a private music teacher, school, or conservatory generally placed them in full-time, live-in arrangements that transferred full-time paternal care to teachers and institutions.[64] Such searches were ubiquitous and often urgent. They pepper the huge *epistolario* of Padre Martini, for example, the largest such in all eighteenth-century music, numbering well over six thousand letters, which cover all of Europe and span fifty-four years.[65] On September 27, 1752, a Turinese woman asked Padre Martini to recommend a particular youth to the teacher Nicolò Giovanardi (Giovinardi or Zanardi [1661–1729]) since the boy didn't want to return to his old teacher. Besides, his father wanted him to progress to singing in the theater—another way of saying he wanted him to reach the highest echelons of the profession where the best money was to be made. On October 16, 1765, Carlo Antonio Rossi wrote the padre from Alessandria on behalf of a soprano in his provincial chapel to see whether the boy might be accepted into the household of the Bolognese singing master Lorenzo Gibelli. Gaetano Maria Schiassi sent Martini a letter dated May 6, 1751, with a young court castrato who was going to Bologna from Lisbon in hopes of studying with Bernacchi, acceptance into whose household was a virtual guarantee of strong career prospects.[66] The Martini letters brim with commerce in young eunuchs of the kind, involving placement of them in cathedral schools as boy choristers and students as well as in teachers' homes, both before and (more often) after castration (a private arrangement that was often negotiated through private connections), and touching on numerous strategies to hire them or hire them out.

Finding the best and most highly esteemed instruction following castration was critical, for only thus could the body be shaped into a maximally gainful vehicle for singing, one even hirable without audition.[67] Bontempi's famed account of 1695 describes the severity of a typical day of study at the house of the seventeenth-century composer and teacher Virgilio Mazzocchi (1597–1643), with whom he himself had studied as a boy: three hours of morning classes, counting one hour to practice singing, including divisions; one hour of literary study; and one hour of vocal exercise with the maestro before a mirror—all that prior to the midday meal. Then half an hour of theory, ditto for counterpoint, and another hour of literary study, followed by practice on a keyboard or other instrument and composition of psalms or motets.[68] Nicola Porpora (1686–1768) was famed for the daunting disciplinary routines he inflicted on singing pupils. An anecdote attributed to Porpora's famous student Caffarelli claims the teacher constrained all students to a single page of exercises covering a gamut of different vocal challenges for no less than five years before letting them branch out.[69] To whatever extent this was true, chief among the exercises would have been the passaggio, by which means the transition between the vocal registers was smoothed, for it epitomized the deep and prolonged study necessary in a lifelong struggle for vocal perfection. The Caffarelli anecdote, exaggerated though it may be, underscores the rigor everywhere associated with the high accomplishments of the top schools, which encompassed many other musical skills. Tosi seconds its sentiment in counseling the castrati to whom his singing treatise is chiefly addressed to "study, study more, and never be satisfied with little," for "he who does not aspire to ... the first rank is very close to occupying the second and gradually will come to be satisfied with the lowest."[70]

Some few tenors and more female singers also studied with preeminent private teachers to achieve high mastery, especially as time wore on. Farinelli's frequent casting partner and traveling companion Vittoria Tesi and Mozart's eponymous *Idomeneo* the tenor Anton Raaff were among Bernacchi's live-in students, for example, and other, less renowned teachers specialized in teaching women (e.g., Bennati and Consoni in Bologna), though the prestige of a Bernacchi was generally not to be found among teachers specializing in female singers after the shank of the seventeenth century.[71] Until the mid- to late eighteenth century noncastrated pupils in the houses of teachers as famous as Bernacchi were relatively few in number, for castrati alone were seen as members of a kind of closed guild and they alone had been ritually inducted into a life of total, irreversible dedication to singing and nothing but. They were the ones who had sacrificed their lives to song, and everything about their cultivation reflected that.

Eventually boys grew into men within paternalistic relations of sociability similar to those that had implicated them as adolescents. Many ended up teaching boys in churches, much as they themselves had been taught. Marzio Erculeo, for instance, taught singing to the seminarians at two different church schools in Modena until his death in 1706.[72] Gizzi, like Bernacchi and Porpora, taught live-in boys at his home, among them the famed Egizziello (Gioacchino Conti, often called Gizziello, 1714–61), who took his name. And Francesco Roncaglia (1750–1812) taught boys at the conservatories of Bologna and Naples in the early nineteenth century, as Girolamo Crescentini (1762–1846) did after 1812.[73] As we have seen, for a teacher or institution to assume teaching duties usually meant taking on the full range of paternal duties, which had previously been the province of brothers, uncles, mothers, and fathers, the last two of whom renounced their parental rights contractually.[74]

Important to comprehending these relations is the fact that before the Napoleonic Code there was no official coming-of-age for children. Indeed, as Philippe Ariès claimed some years ago, there was not yet any formal concept of the child as having his or her own essential and implicitly innocent nature; and before Rousseau's ground-shifting *Émile, ou De l'éducation* of 1762 and the many spin-offs it generated, there was no notion of child development in any recognizably systematic sense.[75] One token of the paternalistic old-world system in which castrati were reared is that when they sang for pay as children, they compensated their teachers by contractual agreement by giving them a goodly part of their earnings, then and thereafter. Only if parents or uncles paid for castrations or instruction was there an explicit expectation that they would be repaid, cared for, or otherwise helped down the line (although, owing to the nature of Italian families, they generally were helped anyway).

FAMILIES

Where the waters part is between boy singers placed in relatively familial contexts and those placed in relatively more institutional ones, although there was seemingly a large middle ground between the two. At one pole, for instance, we have the later eighteenth-century castrato Domenico Bruni (1758–1821), who was taught by the musical director of his father's own confraternity, the same man who paid for his castration. At the opposite pole were young victims of the singer Nicola Tricarico (fl. 1685–1727), who with his brother ran some kind of operation collecting children to be castrated for profit, at least to surmise from one father's virtual sale of his eight-year-old to be castrated by them if he showed sufficient promise during training.[76] One might almost wonder whether Zanetti was alluding ironically to this underground commerce in child castration when he depicted Tricarico gesturing wildly with his head concealed behind cape and beard (though he may simply have been registering his role as a singer of *buffo* parts; see Fig. 24).

Reproduction in sum cuts across a variety of patterns from the outset of a castrato's career. Strikingly, all of these patterns participate in old patronage systems, with teachers or institutions as the first in a series of surrogate fathers. In conservatories boys were called "figliuoli,"[77] and in biographies, letters, and apprenticeship and employment contracts they are usually described as surrogate sons to teachers and patrons, much as on stage they were often noble sons such as Arbaces or princely sons such as Achilles or Timantes.

Unless a castrato failed to develop vocally, the intensive training ideally culminated in a permanent church position or a long-term position at court, typically with an emphasis on chapel singing. Either of these secured for the boy a stable place in a larger *famiglia* but also constituted another paternal setting in the cascading familial hierarchy that was the old regime.[78] The highly successful Matteuccio (Matteo Sassano or Sassani, 1667–1737)—one of the very best of all time—was essentially a church singer for whom theater gigs were exceptions. Going off to sing opera could even risk the goodwill of a worthy church patron, at least before the eighteenth century, when releasing church singers to perform in operas or salons became an unavoidable necessity.[79] Once churches were regularly letting musical staff freelance extensively in the secular world, as happened with Caffarelli, Gaetano Guadagni (1729–92), Giuseppe Aprile (1732–1813), Giovanni Tedeschi (Giovanni Filippo Maria Dreyer, "il Tedeschino," ca. 1703–72), Gizzi, and Giulio Maria Cavalletti (Giulietto, 1668–1755), singers still usually stayed on the payrolls of chapels for extended periods or for life.

The career of Cavalletti exemplifies the oscillation between church and theater work. In 1683 Cavalletti was a member of the Congregazione dei Musici of Rome, a collective of musicians, and in 1784 he was also a member of the chapel of Saint Mark's in Venice. Meanwhile, during the 1683–84 season he appeared at the Teatro San Bartolomeo in Naples. A pupil of Giovanni Battista Colonna and possibly Pistocchi in Bologna, he joined the Accademia Filarmonica there in 1688 and the chapel of San Petronio, though he was also listed between 1683 and 1692 as a singer at the church of Santa Maria Maggiore in Rome. In 1696 he again sang in opera, performing Perti's *Penelope la casta* and *Furio Camillo* in Rome. By 1698 and until 1703 he was *virtuoso di camera* to the Duchess of Laurenzano, who gave him leave to sing on the Neapolitan stage, where he played in three of Alessandro Scarlatti's operas at the San Bartolomeo (*La caduta de' Decemviri* of 1697, *Tito Sempronio Gracco* of 1702, and *Tiberio imperatore d'Oriente*, also in 1702). Cavalletti went on singing opera while in the service of the Grand Prince Ferdinando in Florence in 1705–7 (the title role in Gasparini's *Ambleto* and Spiridate in Orlandini's *Artaserse*) until called to Barcelona by Charles III, where he was made Charles's *primo musico di camera*, overseeing opera production and also acting as assistant *maestro de capilla*.[80]

Others who were on private or court payrolls might travel widely, sometimes almost continually, singing at various courts and in private spaces, churches, and theaters. One example was Atto Melani, who was on the payroll of the private Florentine patron Prince Mattias de' Medici, and Siface, who was on the payroll of the court chapel of Francesco II d'Este, Duke of Modena.[81] Through such arrangements they took advantage of permanent appointments embedded within old patronage systems that produced steady income and life benefits, unlike commercial opera or one-off gigs, which could pay better but left singers out on a limb.

In the seventeenth century it was not unusual for a castrato to become a priest. For Andrea Adami da Bolsena, who wrote about the papal chapel in his the *Osservazioni per ben regolare il coro de i cantori della Cappella pontificia* (Rome, 1711), priesthood was inseparable from his extensive work and influence in the churches of Rome, though it was above all his devoted patron of fifty-four years (1686–1740), Cardinal Pietro Ottoboni, who opened doors by treating him like a son. Decades earlier, in 1643, Vittori in middle age was ordained a priest in a large ceremony at the Chiesa Nuova. Giulio Rivani (b. 1614), soprano castrato and older brother by fifteen years of the more famous Antonio Rivani (Ciccolino or Ciecolino, 1629–86), was probably already a priest at the Pistoia cathedral by that time (and from 1644 was maestro di cappella at the Church of San Stefano dei Cavalieri in Pisa, where Balatri later trained). And Tosi took the cloth at age twenty-seven, in 1681.[82]

A few castrati were actual monks, though their situations could be more fluid than one might expect. Mario Agatea (1623 to 1628–1699), an Augustinian monk, composer, instrument maker, and soprano castrato, was nonetheless employed from about 1649 as a singer at the Modenese court of the Este and joined the choir of San Petronio in Bologna in 1660. One of the Melani brothers, Filippo (Francesco Maria or Padre Filippo, 1628–1704), was a castrato soprano and Servite monk who ultimately changed his fate by leaving the order, though not before singing church music in Venice, outside the order.[83] He was later released from his vows but allowed to remain a priest, ostensibly at the insistence of Cardinal Mazarin in France, who wanted him to sing in a secular opera at the French court, a revival of Cavalli's *Serse* (1660) in which he played the role of La Patience. By that time Filippo had already been singing in the service of the Archduke Sigismund of Austria, whom he served from 1657 to 1663. In later years, 1672–1700, he sang for the Grand Duke of Tuscany.

Castrato careers seem to have made the biggest historic shift away from holy life around the early eighteenth century. In all eighteenth-century examples that I know of, those castrati who took vows of monkhood did so either later in life, upon retirement, as did Balatri, Giovanni Battista Minelli (1687? to after 1735), and Egiziello, or else in midcareer (as, for example, Dreyer).[84] For Pellegrini joining a monastery was a kind of Medicare benefit, as he only became a monk when he lost his voice, which reportedly ended his means of earning his livelihood.[85] The papal castrati who took holy orders in the nineteenth century were another matter because the opportunities to sing on a public stage had radically diminished or evaporated by then. Many had little or no history of secular performance, unless they had sung in sacred dramatizations of operas, sacred musical plays, or other entertainments while in training schools, or managed to sing concert pieces in Roman salons or hotels.[86] Moreover, they were pensioned after retiring from the papal chapel.

Few singers, regardless of patronage schemes, wanted to be cut completely loose in the free market, even in the market-driven eighteenth century. One hedge against the potential for free fall presented by free agency and touring was to become nestled in virtual families of colleagues, patrons, and employers.[87] What arguably distinguishes those who hit the opera trail full-time is that they were more apt to acquire multiple successive father figures over the course of a lifetime, together with an accumulating band of "brothers" and sometimes "mothers" and "sisters." They built shifting networks of what we now might call "invented" or "adoptive" families that might include peers, fellow courtiers, patrons, impresarios, poets, painters, literati, and fellow travelers, among others. The same was true for castrati who were traded between different princely courts, for either way, family-styled networks developed in which unspoken rules of relative paternal dominance figured strongly—not that such relationships didn't develop among other kinds of figures who took up positions distant from home or traveled extensively, but for castrati they seem to have had a different valence.

The dynamics of paternalism and the changing vectors of kinship over the course of a castrato's life are brought into dramatic relief by the story of Balatri's early days in Russia. He was sent from Italy to Moscow at about age seventeen, but only after extensive negotiations that took place at the court of Tuscany. As Balatri tells it, the Grand Duke Cosimo III wanted to satisfy the czar and so looked to Filippo's father for the boy's release. The father resisted at first, but the czar's agent—a cousin of Peter the Great from the Golitsyn family—persisted and then succeeded on the condition that Filippo be treated "as a son." In the end it was not really the father who released and sent him abroad, of course, but the grand duke, nor was there any difficulty breaking a three-year contract the father had recently signed with a local singing master at whose home Balatri was living in Florence.[88] In all these ways, the young castrato was caught in a triangulated relationship of authority and submission in which the monarch nominally directed his "requests" to the castrato's father and the two passed down orders to teacher and child.[89] Such a scheme thickened once Balatri arrived in Russia. The czar became Balatri's surrogate patron/parent, though the Golitsyn prince ended up being his immediate father figure, especially after Balatri moved in with him and his wife after having been harassed by *spalniks* in the czar's palace. Balatri was called "son" by both the czar and the Prince and Princess Golitsyn, but only with the Golitsyns did he use the address "father" and "mother." In their time together he gained unheard-of access to the sexually segregated, staunchly Orthodox female quarters of the household, where he spent many an hour by the embroidery frames, and he was even dressed up in drag by the princess and her girls for fun.[90]

Even outside highly conservative Russia of this time, intergenerational relationships were marked by extreme hierarchy and stratification, which echoed the larger structure of the old regime. By contrast, fraternal relationships, including with other singers, could be cooperative, helping rather than hampering singers' new professional function as commodities in the ever-quickening world of capital.

FRIENDS

During the 1720s and 1730s Zanetti memorialized the friendships that marked the life of a cosmopolitan castrato by drawing pictures of them both solo and in pairs as they traveled in and out of the world of Venetian theaters and churches. Some of his caricatures are well known, but in general only in a form that divorces them from their material context, which consists of a large album in the genre of the *album amicorum* (album of friends). There castrati take their place alongside prima donnas, tenors, traveling mates, literati, impresarios, servants, theatergoers, patrons, and other habitués of Venetian society. Pasted onto large folios in groupings of twos, threes, fours, or nines, they offer whimsical commentaries on the mutual affections and hierarchies between their subjects.[91] In Fig. 25, the gangly Farinelli appears in traveling clothes as a first among equals, strolling away from his mostly costumed colleagues: Anna Bagnolesi in a trouser role at right, the castrato Valentini (Valentino Urbani, fl. 1690–1722) looking melodramatic at top left, Pallante menacing at top center, Farinelli's frequent traveling companion and costar Vittoria Tesi at top right. On a comparable page, Bernacchi is judiciously pasted into Zanetti's album near his colleagues Carestini and two female singers, epitomizing castrato extravagance even more than in solo images. Likewise the grand Senesino is shown flanked by members of his London circle, Margherita Durastanti (fl. 1700–1734) at left and his librettist buddy Paolo Rolli (1687–1765) at right (Fig. 26).

In these widened networks, adoptive kin tended to merge with natural ones. The ties were ones of mutual understanding, professional, musical, and personal. Carlo Scalzi (fl. 1718–39), a great soprano, rose to the defense of Margherita Gualandi (La Campioli), one of the day's leading ladies, who was so badly treated during the start of a year-long engagement in Naples that she fled shortly before the opera was to open. The chief offense, seemingly unprecedented, was that the Neapolitans had contracted two prima donnas for the same role. Scalzi submitted an extended letter of testimony in Gualandi's defense.

> The rehearsals began and there was not one aria that suited her. She begged that the arias be changed, but with unheard-of tyranny the German composer [Hasse] would not hear of it; he finally changed three arias, which were worse than the originals. . . . The auditor general, who was already against her because of a letter written to him by Porpora maligning the poor woman, vetoed the impresario's intentions, which were to allow her to insert arias of her own choice. They made her come to rehearsals on foot, and once she had arrived they hurled insults at her to the point of even saying

(as I heard), "Perhaps we'll all eat her up right away" *[Chissà no' nsieme ce la manniamo frisca frisca]*. Those people from the viceroy's court who should have helped her began to persecute her.

Scalzi vociferated on behalf of Gualandi against the slander of the same agent who, to his shame, had contracted her to sing at the same time as another singer was being contracted by another agent for the same role to be sung during the same season. While pleading that she be praised and shown compassion, Scalzi leapt to the defense of a raft of prima donnas who had been mistreated in Naples: "Here they want either beauties or else professional whores, while they speak badly of Faustina, La Merighi, La Tesi, La Vico, and many others who come here.... The city is diabolical in these matters, and it is a point of honor among the noblemen, once they have visited a singer, to say that they have enjoyed her *[sono in obbligo di dire d'averla goduta]*."[92]

Scalzi's letter can be interpreted within wider networks of family, invented and biological. Many castrati worked and traveled with siblings, who often figured in employment and reproductive strategies. When Berenstadt's father died in their hometown of Florence, the singer, who was also a book printer and dealer, moved himself and his sister to Naples in hopes of finding better work and a lower cost of living.[93] Filippo Vismarri got money from the Viennese court to send for his sister so she could marry a court singer. The same was largely true of Aprile, whose brother Raffaello was employed at the Stuttgart court as a violinist during Aprile's years there as a singer, between 1762 and 1769. Balatri's brother Ferrante, a tenor, followed him after their parents died and thereafter he had failed to find church work in Rome. In 1713 the two went to London via France to try Filippo's fortunes, then proceeded the next year to Munich, where the elector of Bavaria—whose wife was Cosimo III's sister and hence a kind of surrogate mother to the two young singers—took them in and where Ferrante got occasional small operatic parts at court. When Balatri took trips away from the Munich court, it was with leave from the elector and with his brother in tow. On one of these trips Ferrante died, to Filippo's great grief. He returned to Munich, where he remained integral to the court *famiglia* until his retirement to the cloister at Schloß Ismaning. And Gluck's first Orpheus, Guadagni, sang in a 1764 imperial court performance of Piccinni's *La buona figliuola* along with his two sisters.[94] All these are echoed by the fraternal and paternal acts that constantly mark castrato relations.

If children were not children in our sense, then, they were sons and daughters in another sense. A good patron extended care to the larger fraternal group because he was head of a wider political family. Guadagni's performance with his sisters would thus have been understood by the emperor's guests as inseparably a gift to them of entertainment and a display by the emperor of such paternal care.[95]

As with Balatri, some of these cases included a weaker brother tagging along with a stronger one on the performance circuit. Senesino's elder castrato brother spent time with him in London, and Farinelli's composer-brother Riccardo Broschi (also older) likewise joined him in London and followed him to Madrid. In such circumstances the patrilineal order was already upset, since younger brothers had surpassed older ones by accumulating greater wealth and prominence by virtue of talent or star quality. Freitas has made a related argument with respect to Atto Melani, the third of eight brothers, all but one long-lived, for whom he created various professional opportunities and for whom he functioned as family "padrone."[96]

. . .

Reinventing the "natural" order was vital to a castrato in the lifelong process of preparing for the afterlife and the disposition of wealth. Farinelli can hardly stand in for all castrati, yet his case may be indicative of the most successful of them. Over his lifetime he acquired several father figures, each about a decade apart: around 1717 the Neapolitan magistrate Farina, from whence his nickname, and his teacher Porpora; in 1727 the Bolognese count Pepoli, who adopted Farinelli as a virtual son, groomed him for high society, and got him and his brother to change their legal residence to Bologna; and from 1737 two successive Spanish kings.[97] The Spaniards snatched Farinelli from the jaws of England to sing away the bouts of melancholy that plagued King Philip V (1700–1746, with a hiatus in 1724), yet in his writings to Pepoli Farinelli, a devout monarchist, never betrayed the slightest disconcertion about Philip's fits of drooling and howling. He acquired remarkable intimacy and influence in the royal household, culminating in his induction by King Ferdinand VI (r. 1746–59) into the knighthood of Calatrava in 1750, as commemorated in various portraits, including the famous group portrait by Amigoni (Fig. 27). Surrounding him in this fraternal scene are Metastasio (at far left), his oldest and best friend, with whom he had debuted thirty years earlier and jointly adopted the lifelong nickname of "twin,"[98] the soprano Teresa Castellini, and Amigoni (at right).

As Daniel Heartz has elaborated, it was Metastasio who sent Castellini from Vienna to Farinelli in Madrid, where she became the supposed object of their joint infatuation, though never without a touch of ironic jealousy on Metastasio's part.[99] "What is the lovely Castellini up to?" he asked.

> Is it really true that my greetings are so dear to her? That she wants to honor me with her adored letters? Oh, if you love me, don't allow my friendship to be put thus to the test. After the lubricious descriptions you've given me of such a lovable person, the violent temptation of one of her letters might precipitate my betraying you in my thoughts, and then I would be inconsolable. Tell her too that as your twin, it's impossible for me not to feel all of the movements of your heart, or at least their

reverberations; that when I hear her name, I'm invaded by a certain tingling sensation that won't let me be, and yet I don't wish it to end; [tell her] that if the Manzanare were not so distant from the Danube I would have come to see whether she would receive me with open arms, as she does my greetings. . . . No, sir. Don't tell her anything. The path is too slippery. It's easier not to take it than to walk there without falling.[100]

Tucked in among Farinelli's pleas for Metastasio's portrait and their exchanges of settings of the poet's pastoral *Canzonetta di Nice*, the letter verifies a long, intimate friendship that belonged to them alone. But always there was the irony and joking: "So you absolutely want my portrait? Oh what a penance! . . . But who can resist the entreaties of a twin brother? At my return from the country I shall undertake this business as a penitence for my sins and try to indulge your longing to be pregnant in such a manner as may prevent a miscarriage."

Now this is a rich joke for our themes of male reproduction, and indeed pregnancy came up more than once. Farinelli, as minister of entertainments, was getting Metastasio to adapt his librettos to Spanish audiences, but Metastasio grumbled about the task several times, saying, "Is there a tyrant from Syracuse or Agrigento who knows how to torment a poor gentleman as you torment me for an opera? And should I not then call you a sea monster! I begin to suspect that you're pregnant, because this is never a masculine longing."[101] Joking about the very thing Farinelli could neither be nor cause, and in terms suggesting the eunuch was more beast than man—that is something we've seen before, and some of the jokes were even more direct. On cutting a libretto to make it fit the Spaniards' attention span, Metastasio wrote, "I've already circumcised the first act of *Alessandro [nell'Indie]*: oh, what butchery! I cut 266 verses and three arias. Dear twin, this thankless job is done only for you. To make oneself a eunuch with one's own hand is a sacrifice with few precedents."[102]

Metastasio alludes to twinning and cutting much as the Aristophanes of Plato's *Symposium* recounts Zeus's efforts to divide and conquer the obstreperousness of the human race by slicing each human being into two halves: twins. Each became so madly, self-destructively desirous of the other that they eventually starved, whereafter, following some bizarre anatomical adjustments made with the help of Apollo, the gods had themselves a race of devoted human beings, tamed by their loving desires. Aristophanes tells of these exploits in order to explain that the ancient nature of attraction is so deeply embedded in persons that the very sex to which they are attracted, whether same or opposite, depends upon which half formerly was implanted in us.[103] "Love collects the halves of our original nature, and tries to make a single thing out of the two parts so as to restore our natural condition. Thus each of us is the matching half of a human being, since we have been severed like flatfish, two coming from one, and each part is always seeking the other half" (191d).

It's hard to imagine that Metastasio could not have been thinking of this account in his numerous elaborations of twinship with Farinelli (or even toying with it), especially as he wants to claim it as a mutual male love and a kind of ideal condition, regardless of what others might say. This is what Plato had Aristophanes declare:

> Those who are split from the male pursue males. While they are boys, since they are a slice off a male, they are fond of men and enjoy lying with men and becoming entwined with them. These are the best of the boys and young men, and at the same time are the most manly in nature. Anyone who says they are shameless is mistaken, for they do this not from shamelessness but from courage, manliness, and masculinity, welcoming what is like themselves. When they become men they are lovers of boys and by nature are not interested in marriage and having children ... they would be satisfied to live all the time with one another without marrying. This is certainly the sort of man who becomes a lover of boys, and as a boy is fond of such lovers, always welcoming a kinsman. Thus whenever a lover of boys, or anyone else, happens to encounter the person who is their other half, they are overcome with amazement at their friendship, intimacy, and love, and do not want to be severed, so to speak, from each other even for a moment. These are the people who spend their entire lives with each other, though they don't know how to say what they want from each other. No one would think this is a mere union of sexual passion, as though that were the reason each enjoys and is so enthusiastic about being with the other. On the contrary, it's clear that there is something else. (191e–192c)[104]

The something else was everything else.

Let us return to the summer of 1747, before Castellini arrived in Madrid, when Metastasio's mood had been plainly loving: your "tender friendship ... makes me so sure of your love that I'd sooner doubt anything else. This would suffice to oblige me to love you—you know from much experience 'that love with nothing loved [in return] forgives loving.'" He adds:

> You are as loveable as you are unique; ... the intimacy with which you speak to me of your affairs, the kindness with which you offer to sort out mine, the tender concern you show for my health, the ... ways you administer to [it] ... your generous concern for my palate and even my nose—add them all together and then tell me if an arithmetician is to be found who would know how to quantify the end result. I don't know how to express myself better than to tell you that I love you as much as Farinelli deserves to be loved.

Metastasio also thought there were snakes in the grass, so he stopped short, declaring, "But let's drop these sweet nothings so no malicious person may ... console their envy of honest, tender, true, and disinterested friendship."[105]

There has been some tiptoeing around the sworn twinship of Farinelli with Metastasio, perhaps because the possibility of a gay history might call up too many essentializing ghosts of papers past. But "gay" is surely all wrong here, a word rife with our categories and not theirs. Evidence gathered by early modern historians makes it look more and more as if same-sex relations among men were almost as prevalent in early modern Italy as what classical historian James Davidson, in his brilliant piece for the *London Review of Books*, "Mr. and Mr. and Mrs. and Mrs.," calls "inter-sex" relations.[106] These relations were differently institutionalized from ours. Guido Ruggiero has gathered literary and archival evidence from the sixteenth century that shows that same-sex relations between noble Italian men were ordinary if not downright prescribed, though they were also much bound up with life cycles. "Renaissance Italians understood sexual identity ... as something that changed throughout stages of youthful experimentation, marriage, adult companionship, and old age."[107] Whether same-sex relations branded a man as being of a "particular" kind or sexual persuasion probably depended on many factors at different times and places, but same-sex male relations were generally tolerated and for young men even ritualized, while older men were expected to take on more intersex ways. If a man's leanings made him out-and-out resistant to marriage and procreation, there were alternatives, of course, especially in the church. And many men had relations with different sexes, marked by varying strategies of publicness and privateness. In this regard Metastasio had his "Romanina," Maria Benti Bulgarelli, his first Didone in 1724 and his mentor in theatrical direction, a married woman with whom he most probably had a love tryst; and in 1733 Farinelli wrote Pepoli about his mad love for a ballerina in language evocative of a Metastasian aria: "Cupido mi tien legato / e Iddio sa quando sarò slegato, / poiché dall'una e l'altra parte, / si soffre, si tace, si pena, / e pure vien gradita tale / dolcissima catena" (She holds me bound and God knows when I'll be unbound; so from every side I suffer, I sulk, I grieve, and yet I welcome such sweet enchainment).[108]

If Metastasio showed himself smitten, passionate, adoring, and nostalgic toward his friend, who probably returned many of the same sentiments, he also made sure we would never know much about it. Or perhaps they did not fully know how to say what they wanted from each other, and no one would ever have thought it "a mere union of sexual passion." Yet their twinship remains rich for what it does not say. What is twinship, above all, but a metaphor for reproduction? The egg splits, the egg has a mate. Two eggs grow in the same womb, infused with the same blood. Brothers meet who were egg mates, friends meet who could have been. Always implied is mutual birth, identity, profound understanding, intimate recognition, deep immersion in the other's loves, jealousies, griefs, vanities, self-deprecations, joys, and guilt. Histories and myths tell repeatedly of such twinships, especially among men: of sworn brotherhoods, pledgings, blood brothers, and other male bondings. The twinship of Farinelli and Metastasio even has a whiff of "separation at birth," the twinship birthed by one theatrical event and marked thereafter by a physical separation that became total during their last fifty years, at the end of which both died in the same year, 1782. Like many mythical twinships, their bond not only withstood the Romaninas and ballerinas but was seemingly stronger than either had ever had with a woman—a bit like "The Two Brothers" tale from *The Brothers Grimm,* which Doniger retells: a princess mistakes her husband's long-lost twin brother for her own husband, who at that moment is also lost, when her husband's twin brother suddenly reappears; but when the latter is forced to bed down with her, he remains strenuously faithful to his twin.[109]

BEQUESTS

Although stories of castrati in liaisons with men are not few, almost none of those partners were principal legatees of wills, the route through which castrati could filiate themselves into future generations by "inseminating" heirs with wealth. For that they turned to natal kin, with exceptions that only prove the rule. In 1746 Farinelli wrote from Spain beseeching Pepoli in Bologna to help secure him a suitable sister-in-law and, through her and his brother, a natural heir.

> I would like it if my possessions could be enjoyed by a person who merits them. Ambition lies far from me, nor does vanity drive my sense of duty. I would like to find a woman who springs neither from the heavens nor the valleys. Your Excellency, with your good heart and true friendship, could find someone suitable. . . . My brother is presently enjoying a good position, given him by the grace of the King of Naples, which earns him [just] under a thousand ducats a year, a nobleman having occupied this position with great esteem before it fell to my brother. My sister is married to another gentleman, who now occupies the post of preceptor in . . . Salerno, which gives him 2,000 ducats a year. Your Excellency may see how *my heart* sits with respect to my relatives.

Having disjoined ambition from wealth, somewhat disingenuously, Farinelli tore into a rather stunning joke.

> I don't claim that I was born from the third rib of Venus or that my father was Neptune. I am Neapolitan and the Duke of Andria held me at the baptismal font. That's enough to give you the idea that I'm the son of a good citizen and a gentleman. It seems to me that up to now I've produced a good deal of honor for myself, my homeland, my family, and my profession. I would hope in light of such reflections that no good daughter would have to speak ill of such a match. . . . I cannot (as you know) marry myself, *so I must think about my blood* and look for a woman who can merit all that God has given me.[110]

Farinelli's opening is a ploy, envoicing and immediately disclaiming a lofty parentage for himself before moving on to say that all his disclaimers were just a preamble to showing that his origins are essentially noble after all, and that he's only made them more so.

Money with no vertical descent by blood: this was the castrato's dilemma. Farinelli's rhetorical contortions nearly invert the originary Christian order of gender. To be born from the rib of Venus is to be sprung semidivine from an ur-woman—a replacement of Adam's rib with Eve's and, metonymically, a replacement of mortal paternal parentage with that of a divine woman—or, if we light upon his second option, a replacement of mortal parentage with the immortally divine Neptune. To say that he is (not) the son of Neptune is probably to point out that he is (not) *actually* the heroic Theseus, whom he had played in 1731 and later staged in Madrid, while using the disclaimer as a springboard for what he is.[111] "I could be the progeny of an ur-goddess, or I could be the son of an ur-god," he seems to say (the latter another case of male generation); "but really, even if I *were* figuratively speaking divine or semidivine it would not matter because I'm literally speaking practically noble—or just as noble as anyone nobly born—and thus no family should think my money wouldn't enrich their blood." And this before he was even knighted.

THE RETURN HOME

Farinelli's effort to transcend his blood didn't turn out as he hoped. Riccardo died ten years after Farinelli wrote Pepoli, still childless. In 1759 Charles III returned from Naples to take the Spanish throne and Farinelli left Spain to start his retirement. He left alone. Among his first stops was Naples, where he went to see his sister and choose a nephew as his heir.[112] The nephew and his then new wife later lived with Farinelli in his villa outside Bologna, where their daughter was born, but they stayed only for one unhappy year. The birth of a grandniece promised only more uterine filiation, a blow Farinelli softened by insisting that his nephew become Matteo Pisani Broschi, taking his surname, as other castrati and celibates often did. In a notarial letter to his niece-in-law, Farinelli protested against presumed charges by his critics that he had received her baby daughter badly, saying to the contrary that he had held her with "cordial affection" at the baptismal font and established a handsome trust for her from which to build her dowry, acts that he called "completely spontaneous . . . of my own will."[113]

. . .

We are indebted to the Rankean enthusiasms of various turn-of-the-century provincial scholars, voiced in the *wie es eigentlich gewesen* spirit, for knowing that most of the castrati who left a significant historical footprint, even those with large feet, ended up returning around the end of their careers to their native patria. In 1797 Giovanni Battista Andreoni died in his native Lucca after creating roles under Pergolesi, Hasse, and Handel. Aprile, though very famous throughout Italy and elsewhere, and especially in Naples, where he was pensioned at the age of fifty-three, nonetheless returned to his hometown of Martina Franca, where he died in

1813 at age eighty-one. Bruni sang all over Europe until age forty-five, but in 1821 he died in Fratta, Umbria (now Umbertide) after some twenty-five years back home. Ferri did the same in 1680 in Perugia. Guadagni drifted back to his native Veneto and died in Padua in 1791. And even one of the very last castrati, the great Domenico Mustafà (1829–1912), after sixty years in Rome and over fifty years in the papal chapel, including a number spent as chapelmaster, died near his home in Montefalco in Umbria, where he had returned in 1902.[114] None of these men could participate in biological generation, but what they could do, like so many other Italians of different stripes, was to re-cement natal bonds when old age approached and death loomed.[115]

Even the very cosmopolitan Giuseppe Millico (1737–1802) showed such tendencies. Millico epitomized the young hero, the emoting son, and the genteel prince in his roles as Orpheus, Farnaspe, Acis, Rinaldo, Paris, Perseus, Megacles, Timantes, Alcestes, and Arbaces. He never made it back to his small town in Puglia but remained in Naples throughout the period of his blindness, which came on at age sixty, until he suddenly died of apoplexy at age sixty-five. Nevertheless, the will he drafted at age fifty-five named as his universal heir his late sister's son, who ended up caring for him throughout his disability,[116] and in the end he requested that lifetime dispersals from his estate be made to relatives in his hometown: his brothers, sisters, nieces, and a nephew.

Those few who bequeathed estates to "adoptive" relations usually left them to young men, sometimes other castrati. Tosi left his estate to a younger castrato, whose legal proxy was a relation of Bernacchi,[117] though at death Tosi had naught but thirteen shirts, three bedside covers, two wigs, fourteen priest's collars, a sword, four breviaries, a pair of pistols, a gold-framed portrait, a wool suit, a gold watch, and some other items of similarly modest value.[118] Bernacchi's rich and famous teacher Pistocchi designated and disinherited more than one young man in his struggle to find a trustworthy heir.[119] His was an unhappy story, but the patrilineal course that devolved property onto a biological nephew was not necessarily happier. Farinelli concentrated all his tremendous wealth on his nephew with whom he got on badly and whose marriage he opposed. He wanted the couple to give him care and companionship in his old age but kept them ignorant of domestic affairs and thought them indolent, unimaginative, and unsophisticated. Visitors came repeatedly to the house, as we know from Burney, Mozart, and numerous others. Nothing could equal those splendid visits, and the toll of low androgen levels became worse with age, as it did for many others of his kind. Eventually he did become much endeared to his little grandniece, who lived with him without her parents from age seven to thirteen, until her granduncle died. In 2006 his remains were found crumpled at her feet in her own tomb, where he had been moved at her behest.[120] Still, he did not want her father to have rights to "disposition, direction, and management" of his inheritance. Of particular concern was that nothing be alienated that had come from royalty and was thus infused with the transcendence of a magnificent gift from a great paternal figure. Farinelli simply made his nephew "first in natural line," giving him only usufruct, while a legal guardian was put in place to try to ensure that nothing be removed from the estate.[121] Though the inventory eventually made was extraordinarily detailed, Farinelli's very long holograph everywhere shows discomfiture with the succession and bequeathal, again insisting that Matteo use the Broschi name, *as if he had been a son* (as Pacchierotti's nephew later did, but happily so).[122]

Were such heavy-handed efforts to make nephews and other boys into surrogate sons the rule among rich castrati? Not all did so, but many, perhaps most, did.[123] Senesino, who was rich, became increasingly paranoid, irrational, and dejected over the course of his life and certainly was all three in his last years in Siena, as his descendant Elisabetta Avanzati recently revealed. He tormented the nephew whom he made his heir along with his nephew's wife.[124] The couple found themselves in the highly uncomfortable but not uncommon position of being both surrogate children and perpetual reminders to the castrato of what he was missing. They were living, breathing reminders of that lack that resulted in affairs poorly arranged for posterity and a deformation of a social and physical order—the same deformation that Farinelli probably intended when he told Burney in 1773 that he was a "despicable creature," when Pauluccio supposedly wept in telling Ancillon that, though he was a man, "si manca qualche cosa" (something is lacking), or when Balatri recounted bitterly how his own father had deprived him of fatherhood (as did Tenducci). These were the unsmiling responses to castration that some betrayed, as against the jokes endlessly made by the English about Monticelli, Farinelli, Senesino, Berenstadt, and Carestini, or the geysers of self-mockery that Balatri continually spewed forth about his own inability to reproduce or perform sexually—charges of which he was a target especially because he was also an "idol" of princes and nobles, an "Orpheus," as he winkingly called himself.[125]

On these matters Balatri is our most comical and most eloquent witness. Lampooning his lack again and again, he is a "castratino," "di gener misto," a "hic et hoc," a "castrone male," a "cappone," a "capponcino"; he even spells out lack as "cast . . . o" and "ermaf. . ."[126] But tellingly, it is in his 220-page will—a literary and satirical yet ingenuous document—that he jokes most seriously, defending his bodily terrain against prurient invasion, even after death, by declaring that he doesn't want "some old woman entertaining herself by inspecting his body to see how sopranos are made."[127] Nor is he about to turn himself into a conceited idiot and let everyone who disdained him in life feed on his funeral and riches in death: "Would you think me so foolish, having been a simple castrato, that I might then want to *turn my ass into a marquis* when it goes to putrefy the earth? I have fed it fodder enough in life without my thinking to distinguish it by embalming it, perfuming it, and flattering it after it's kicked the bucket." No, he plans to shed his worldly ties and die a pauper and a pauper's friend:

> For, having been graced by the blessed sacraments, it suffices to . . . go to a cemetery, or a church, which is the house of God. If a thousand, two thousand candles were enough to send the soul straight to its true center, oh I should fill my mug with my own fisticuffs had I not thought of making such an expenditure. But having considered that two thousand sighs of the poor, sent to God to obtain mercy for me, burn better, *I greatly prefer going to my burial as baron of the piazza than as marquis of the city.*

Recall that in Melosio's sonnet discussed in chapter 1, the marquis and the ass were one, the castrato-like Pulcinella a pompous, strutting fool, hatched from an egg fertilized by castrated testicles. In early modern poetics, the "baron of the piazza" is a three-penny image. Balatri uses it to declare that although he may no longer have any kin in this world, through the stroke of a single bequest to the nameless poor he'll nevertheless acquire a whole family in the afterlife.

> Inasmuch as I . . . have no wife, children, or relatives, one lone friend (and even then, only if he wants to be), few acquaintances (mostly monks), no one who is beholden to me, and no one who cares if I live a hundred years or drop dead tonight, *I wanted to marry some people I don't know, and get from them sons, brothers, relatives, friends, and others myself* . . . and because of that I've resolved to make a testament conforming to what I'll state below.[128]

Balatri's melancholy, like Farinelli's, was surely hormonal and also circumstantial, the latter the inevitable loneliness of an itinerant performing celibate. But here he overcomes it through a utopian fantasy of the afterlife that puts an end to mourning. The cut that elsewhere Balatri dramatized *("taglia, taglia")* for us moderns to read about after his death—we who see it as the ultimate metonym for the castrato, as in *castrato:* he who is *cut,* castrated like a gelded calf or an abridged book; or *the cut* as a thing rather than an action performed—that cut is healed in the fantasies of Balatri's testament.

. . .

To castrate one's son or to be the son who is castrated by his father reverses the primordial scene of Zeus who overthrows (or, in some accounts, castrates) his father, Cronus, in order to steal his power, as Cronus had castrated and killed his father, Uranus; or of Oedipus, who kills his father in order to (unintentionally) marry his mother (the ultimate form of castrating the father postmortem). All of these are myths of disempowerment. The singing castrato can be an Oedipus who retaliates (castrating the castrator) through fame, wealth, social connections, or ironic declarations ("I was given a diploma . . . ") that betray ire and disdain; and, best of all, castrated singers are apt to have listeners.

Given all this, we might wonder whether the twentieth-century apostle of castration theory was onto something when he dreamt of a primeval world in which castration fantasies are an everyday part of family drama. In *Totem and Taboo* Freud stages the originary historical moment when a boy wants to kill his father because of his incestuous love for his mother. This Oedipal urge produces such overwhelming guilt as to generate the beginning of civilization. Such a Freudian scenario would understand the castrated boy as having seen his worst fear realized—the fear of having been castrated by an enraged father (or, phantasmatically, some totemic substitute), who (recasting this now as a universal fantasy) the boy himself had had an urge to kill.

Now allowing that the fantasy is just that, but that in our case the castration is real, the substitution of alternate father figures, combined with the structural displacements from natal family required by prevailing patronage systems and the inaccessibility of the mother, could become intelligible, at least in theory, as characteristic features inseparably of the castrato's psyche and of his kinship system. So too the castrato's kinship relations with other castrati and theater people, as idealized in Amigoni's familial group scene, which we might even understand as some distant realization of Freud's notion that a band of brothers shared the rebellious urge against their father, just as they shared their erotic attachments to one another in and through music.[129]

I am not arguing that we rehabilitate an unreconstructed Oedipal complex to explain the emotions and hybridized kinship structures of castrati nor to explain why castration was taboo, but I'm not sure we can ignore it either. Not only are psychoanalytic concepts always in circulation, furtively or not ("guilt," "suppression," and "repressed desire" floating ever free for us post-Freudians, and often unmarked);[130] they might actually give us some traction on these intractable matters. That said, my own interest is to ground cultural dynamics in history—in this instance, to explore how tales of birth and becoming surrounding castrati relate to patterns of kinship and reproduction, how they manifest in the writings of castrati and in wider discourses of praise and criticism that attach to them, and how the unmanned man circumvents the hierarchical order in ways that speak to the status of that order.

A good place to return to these questions is Sacchi's life of Farinelli, which claims that his natural parents were noble.[131] Sacchi's terms are suspiciously generic, even more than Farinelli's own, but they have the strategic advantage of allowing him to insist that Farinelli's castration was done out of necessity and not for profit: he was "placed under the knife in childhood not to preserve the tenderness of his voice, and thus sell it," Sacchi tells us, "but . . . to preserve a life in grave danger as a result of his boyish liveliness in bounding about on a horse, in consequence of which he was wounded on his front side."[132] Sacchi's biography is thus founded on a double myth of origins, which stems equally from his parentage and from his castration. But it's an obituary in the mode of a saint's life, a *vita*, and as such a moral tale and celebration of the castrato that tells how deftly he reproduced himself in life and will do so in death.

FIGURE 1. Image showing surgical preparation for testicular castration, from Caspar Stromayr's *Practica copiosa*, written in Lindau and completed in 1559, with caption that reads, "Dise Figur ziagt gar Eben / Wie die Kinder sein zu legen" (This figure shows exactly how to lay the children down). The original is extant in Leipzig, Frankfurt am Main, at the Deutsche Nationalbibliothek. Reproduced from *Die Handscrift des Schnitt- und Augenarztes Caspar Stromayr in Linden im Bodensee in der Lindauer Handscrift (P.I. 46) vom 4. Juli 1559*, edited by Walter von Brunn (Berlin: Idra, 1925), plate 8 (p. 267).

FIGURE 2. Jacopo Amigoni. Farinelli crowned by Music (Euterpe), 1735. Amigoni suggests a mythological crowning at a moment when Farinelli was at the height of his vocal and representational powers and was still singing publicly in London. Oil on canvas. 277 × 186 cm. Muzeul National de Arta al României, Bucharest.

FIGURE 3. Corrado Giaquinto, portrait of the singer Farinelli with King Ferdinand VI and Queen Maria Barbara in the background (and with a self-portrait by the artist visible). Farinelli's medal from his knighting into the Order of the Cross of Calatrava is prominent in the painting. Ca. 1755. Museo Internazionale e Biblioteca della Musica, Bologna. Reproduced by kind permission.

FIGURE 4. Anton Maria Zanetti, caricature of two castrati with their prime donne. At top, Senesino (Francesco Bernardi, 1686–1758) with soprano Faustina Bordoni (1697–1781); at bottom, Nicolini (Nicola Grimaldi, 1673–1732) with soprano Lucia Facchinelli, called La Beccheretta. The two drawings are pasted onto the same page of Zanetti's *album amicorum*, an album of collected sketches of friends, acquaintances, and other local characters. Fondazione Giorgio Cini, Venice. Photo by Matteo De Fina.

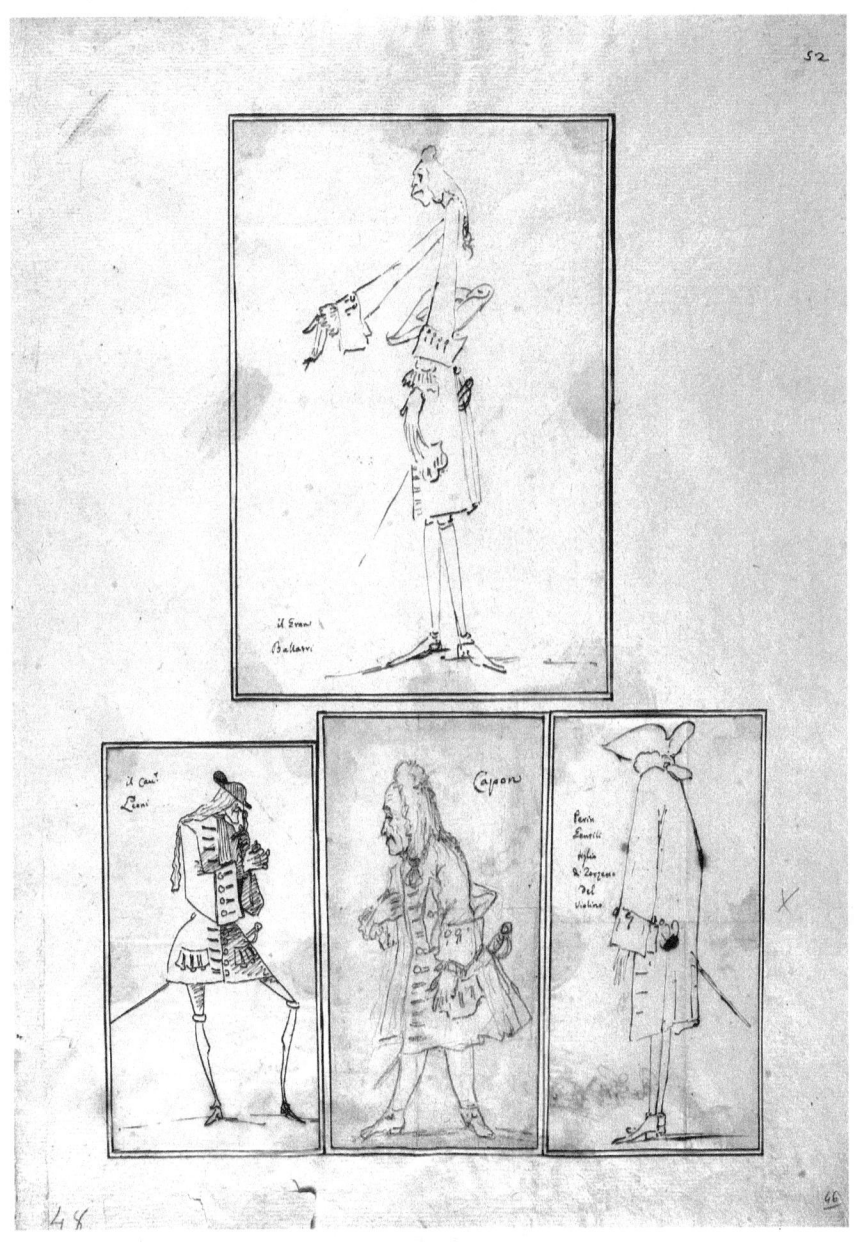

FIGURE 5. In ca. 1730 Anton Maria Zanetti, or a later compiler, captioned his drawing of castrato Filippo Balatri "il gran Ballatri." When it was later arranged in Zanetti's *album amicorum*, Balatri was placed over a drawing of a now unknown man named "Capon." The name could refer to the Florentine family of the Capponi, thus to a "Capon" who was not a castrato. Whatever the case, the juxtaposition was likely meant as a joke punning on both a person and an epithet. Fondazione Giorgio Cini, Venice. Photo by Matteo De Fina.

FIGURE 6. A mezzotint of Giovanni Carestini (Il Cusanello or Cusanino; ca. 1704–ca. 1760), done in London by John Faber Jr. after a painting by George Knapton, 1735. The singer, poochy but handsome, adopts a majestic pose. Royal College of Music, London.

FIGURE 7. Bartolomeo Nazari, oil portrait of a young Farinelli (1705–82), done upon his arrival in London in 1734. The singer shows a combination of masculine nobility, a powerful chest, and fleshy hands and cheeks. Note too the great length of his limbs. Royal College of Music, London.

FIGURE 8. Domenico Mustafà (1829–1912), castrato and chapelmaster *(direttore perpetuo)* of the Cappella Sistina in the Vatican (1878–1902), photographed at age sixty-nine, in 1898. Mustafa's physiognomy was marked by a large square jaw and legs that seem to have been bulky and fleshy. A copy of the photograph is held in the private collection of Luciano Luciani (I-Rluciani) in Fiumicino (Rome), another at the Archivio Moderno della Cappella Pontificia, Rome. Photograph by author from the latter.

FIGURE 9. Andrea Sacchi, oil painting of Marc'Antonio Pasqualini (1614–91) being crowned by Apollo. 1641. Image courtesy of the Metropolitan Museum of Art, New York City. Purchase, Enid A. Haupt Gift and Gwynne Andrews Fund, 1981.

FIGURE 10. Sketch in pen and ink made in 1723 by Pier Leone Ghezzi depicting Andrea Adami da Bolsena (1663–1742), castrato, chronicler, chapelmaster of the Sistine Chapel (1701–14), and author of the *Osservazioni per ben regolare il coro de i cantori della Cappella pontificia* (1711). For fifty-four years (1686–1740) Adami enjoyed the protection of Cardinal Pietro Ottoboni in Rome, at whose palace he was a musician-in-residence. In 1690 he became a member of the Arcadian literary academy. Ghezzi's sketch shows him in direct address looking sweet but a bit skeptical. Biblioteca Apostolica Vaticana, Ottob. Lat. 3114, fol. 120.

FIGURE 11. Pier Leone Ghezzi, caricature of Valeriano Pellegrini (ca. 1663–1743), shown in a drawing of 1728 with a hulking head and large irregular jaw. Biblioteca Apostolica Vaticana, Ottob. Lat. 3116, fol. 162.

FIGURE 12. Pier Leone Ghezzi, sketch of Antonio Bernacchi (1685–1756), drawn in 1731. Bernacchi's round body and proud feathered head are consistent with other sketches of him. Biblioteca Apostolica Vaticana, Ottob. Lat. 3116, fols. 131v–132.

FIGURE 13. Anton Maria Zanetti, caricature of Bernacchi with belly held aloft by a page. Bernacchi is shown in his role as Timantes in the opera *Demofoonte* composed by Schiassi (Venice, Teatro San Giovanni Grisostomo, 1735). Fondazione Giorgio Cini, Venice. Photo by Matteo De Fina.

FIGURE 14. Zanetti's depiction of the tenor Salvatici. He is short but lacks the kind of irregular proportions of most of Zanetti's castrati. Fondazione Giorgio Cini, Venice. Photo by Matteo De Fina.

FIGURE 15. Greek equerry following his master, from an ancient Greek vase. Reproduced in Albrecht Dieterich, *Pulcinella: Pompejanische Wandbilder und römische Satyrspiele* (Leipzig: B. G. Teubner, 1897), from the Hamilton Collection.

FIGURE 16. Lodovico Ottavio Burnacini (1636–1707), *Pulcinella*, watercolor, late seventeenth century. Österreichische Nationalbibliothek, Vienna

FIGURE 17. *Pulcinellata.* Painting by an anonymous eighteenth-century Venetian, showing Pulcinella birthing little Pulcinellini from his anus while being fed through his mouth. Oil on canvas. Present owner uncertain.

FIGURE 18. C. Lindstrom, Pulcinella *cantastorie,* shown singing outdoors in the Largo del Castello (now Palazzo del Municipio) in Naples, pen and ink, circa 1812. Collection Umbert Bowinkel, Naples. Reproduced by kind permission.

FIGURE 19. Giandomenico Tiepolo, drawing of Pulcinella hatching from the egg of a turkey, surrounded by Pulcinella figures. Sepia ink on paper, ca. late eighteenth century to 1800. Private collection, London. Photographic Survey, The Courtauld Institute of Art. Reproduced by kind permission.

FIGURE 20. Pulcinella and the Bourbons, anonymous Neapolitan painting, first half of the nineteenth century. Pucinella motions with his arm and nose in a gesture of affinity with king Ferdinando di Borbone. Private collection of Giuliana Gargiulo, Naples. Reproduced by kind permission.

FIGURE 21. Anton Maria Zanetti, sketch of Bernacchi in street clothes, captioned by a later hand as "Bernach che gode Pullicchinella in Piazza di San Marco" (Bernacchi enjoying a Pulcinella puppet show in Piazza San Marco). Note the immense paunch and the sword at his side, a sign of his having been knighted. Fondazione Giorgio Cini, Venice. Photo by Matteo De Fina.

FIGURE 22. Francesco Bertelli, "Maschera di Pulisinella." Pulcinella's stomach is so enlarged that he more closely resembles a trimly built woman late in pregnancy than a fat man. The motto at the top reads, "Se una botte vi par Puricinella / Vi può ben dar da bere anco a cannella" (If Pulcinella looks to you like a wine barrel / He can certainly offer you a drink from the tap!). From Francesco Bertelli, *Il Carnevale mascherato italiano* (Venice, 1642).

FIGURE 23. Peter Jakob Horemans, *Court Concert at Schloß Ismaning*, summer residence of the elector of Bavaria, Munich, 1733. Filippo Balatri is seated at the keyboard, joined by a flutist, violinist, and viola da gambist, poised to play a trio sonata, or perhaps to accompany an aria. Bayerische Nationalmuseum, Munich, Inv. no. R 7159. Reproduced by kind permission.

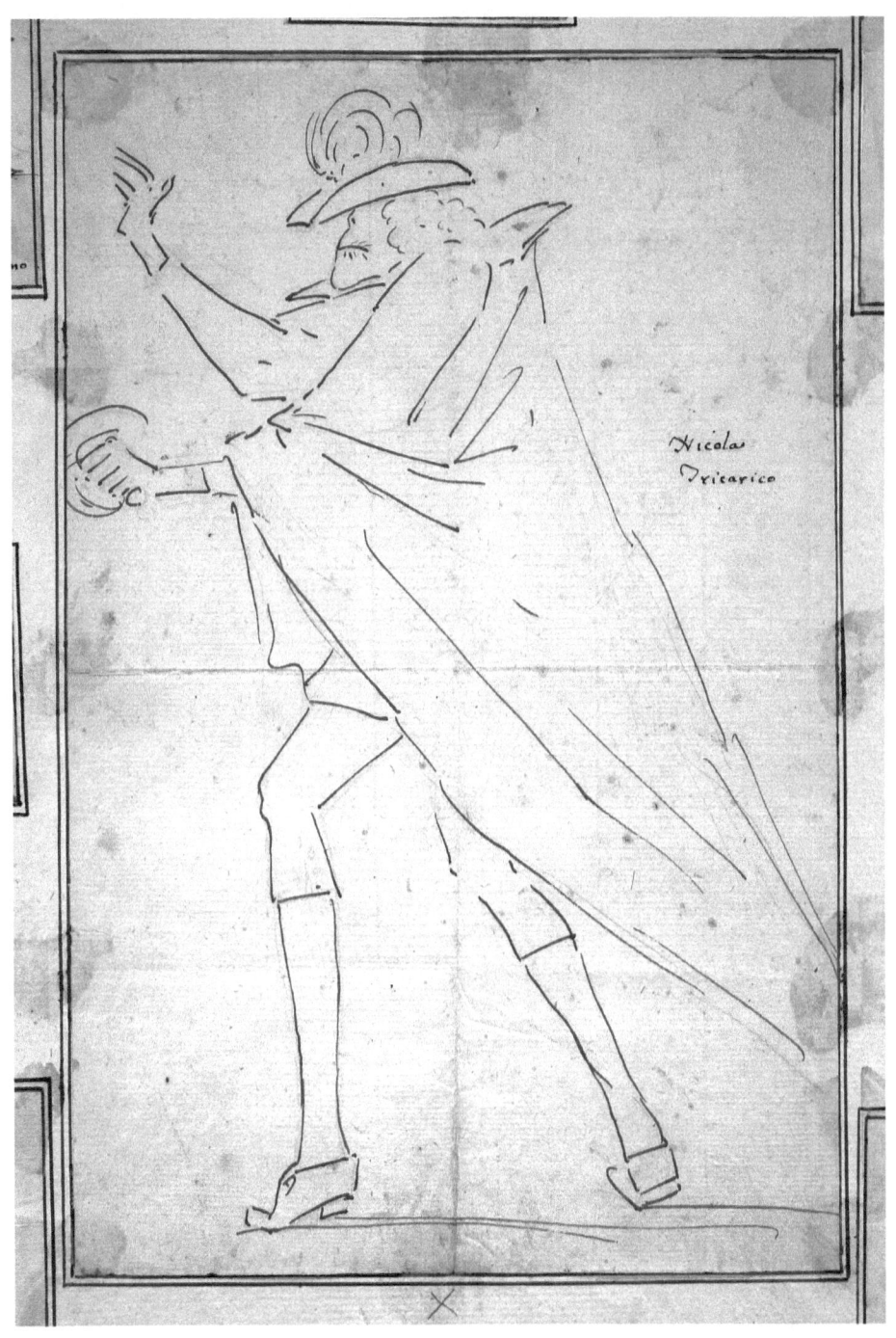

FIGURE 24. Anton Maria Zanetti, sketch of Nicola Tricarico, castrato, comic singer, and apparent trafficker in procuring young boys to be made into eunuch singers, 1720s. Fondazione Giorgio Cini, Venice. Photo by Matteo De Fina.

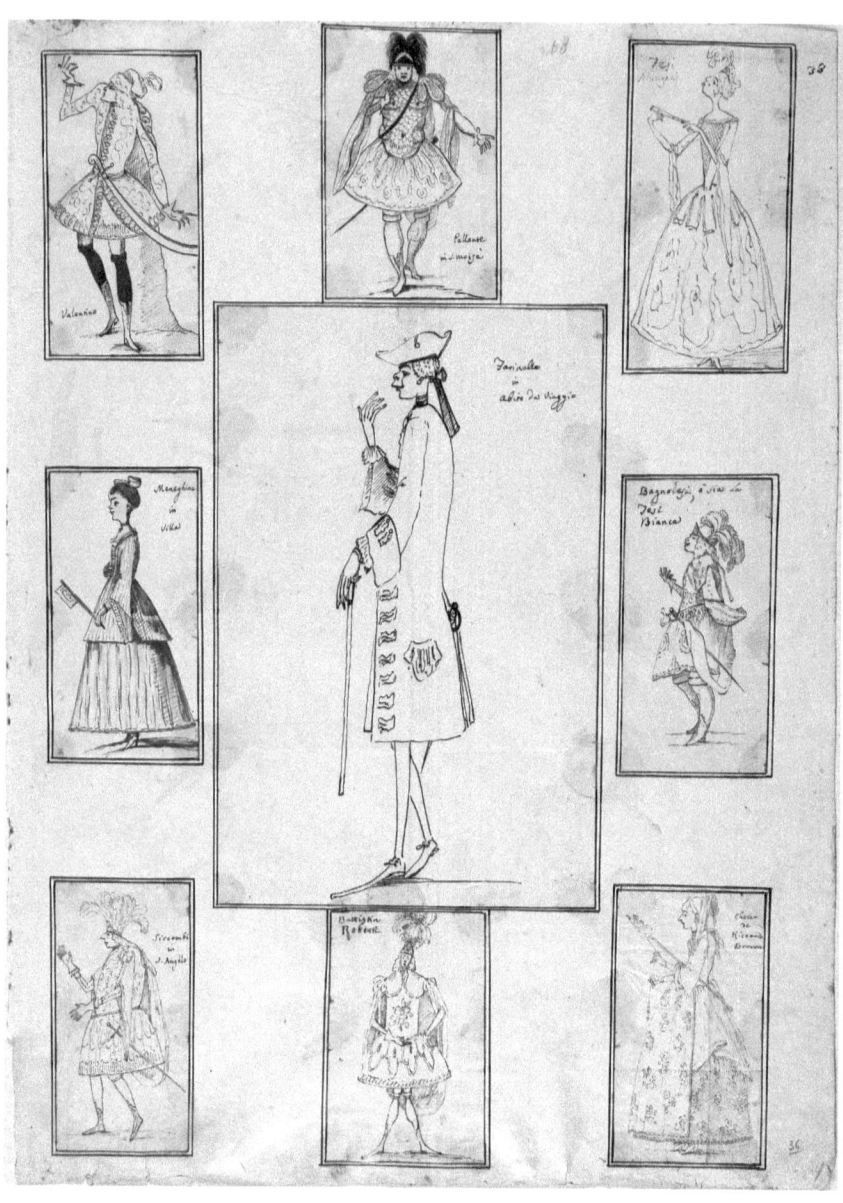

FIGURE 25. Anton Maria Zanetti's 1725 depiction of Farinelli in traveling clothes as pasted into Zanetti's *album amicorum*. In the arrangement of the album the singer circulates among colleagues, notably his costar and frequent traveling companion prima donna Vittoria Tesi at top right. Fondazione Giorgio Cini, Venice. Photo by Matteo De Fina.

FIGURE 26. Anton Maria Zanetti, Senesino shown in Zanetti's *album amicorum* with friends including contralto Margherita Durastanti and poet Paolo Rolli. Fondazione Giorgio Cini, Venice. Photo by Matteo De Fina.

FIGURE 27. Jacopo Amigoni, *Farinelli e i suoi amici*, ca. 1750–52. Oil on canvas. 172.8 × 245.1 cm. From left to right: Metastasio (Imperial poet), Teresa Castellini (soprano), Farinelli, Amigoni, and unidentified boy and dog. National Gallery of Victoria, Felton Bequest.

PART TWO

Voice

3

Red Hot Voice

Most of what we know about castrato voices is how little we know. We presume that some physical constants among them once existed in their full acoustic presence, yet we remain agnostics about how they sounded because they now elude virtually all sensory access. In phenomenal terms we might call their conditions prehistoric, for the visceral, tactile je ne sais quoi of those voices is gone. I'm not talking about anything so slippery as a psychoanalytic Lacanian voice, the voice as an "acoustic mirror" of the listening "subject," the object of a drive, or the uncanny space between mechanism and cause; nor I am talking about old-school notions of musical style. I mean something closer to what Roland Barthes called the *grain* of the voice, something that falls "outside the realm of textuality" and relates on one side to the production of voice and on the other to a "drastic" experience of its performance.[1]

Just as vexing yet barely as much a threshing floor for many writers on voice is the very notion of the voice of *the castrato* as a particular genre of singer. On many accounts the castrato would seem to possess a unitary voice as quality-controlled as cold-packed foodstuffs. Some even argue the point on the grounds of neoclassical aesthetics, presuming the voice of an archetypal castrato cultivated for a transcendent purity and consistency. Of course at some magnitude of classificatory principle, given a minimal gamut of shared physiological and acoustic constants, there is a heuristic utility to grouping voice kinds by qualities. Accordingly we speak of mezzos, lyric tenors, soubrettes, and so on, with varying degrees of historical and musical specificity. But are the voices of castrated male singers amenable to such orders of classification? And when all is said and done, isn't every voice as irreducibly distinct from every other as each human face or each cat's leg?

Moreover by that reckoning if individual castrato voices were differentiated as much as, say, Natalie Dessay from Birgit Nilsson, then what "voice" or subsets of a voice type might we even be trying to conceive or designate? The question should give us pause. It is anterior to any generalizations we might hope to make and a problem to which we will always circle back.[2]

Still, I will claim in what follows that certain robust features of castrato voices do map onto their collective population and perhaps also correlate with distinctive modes of learning and vocal production. On a few of these we have a degree of consensus. Strong resonance, for instance, understood as relative loudness and intensity, with timbral richness. Tessituras higher than usual for men, absolutely. Most likely a certain predisposition toward agility singing, at least among many. It seems reasonable to ask therefore whether somewhere out there there was not a pool of voices with a shared spectrum of possibility, however much it changed over a wide swath of historical time and varied according to such individual variations as processes of growth, maturation, aging, states of sickness and health, and adaptations to the epiphenomena of training, aesthetic expectation, performing conditions, travel conditions, spaces of performance, institutional contexts, and audience types. What I offer here is one attempt to approach those issues. My suggestions will be patchy and highly provisional, but I nevertheless hope to convince you that a pool of voices did share some anatomical conditions and cultural imprinting, and that castrato voices all told may be a bit more knowable than we usually grant.[3]

These matters were already in my mind when I chanced upon the following firsthand description of a performance traceable to Europe shortly before the First World War:

> About 1912, I heard two castratos—soprano and alto—who toured Europe with the Sistine Chapel Choir. They were billed as victims of accidents (an old subterfuge ever since the seventeenth century), but there they were, middle-aged and no longer at the peak of their power, relics from another age. Though I was young, just about the age when a castrato would have his "accident," I vividly remember their voices because of the shock of hearing grown men sing in the stratosphere. Their voices were white, clear, and powerful and had absolutely no resemblance to a woman's voice.[4]

The account comes from Paul Henry Lang, the Hungarian musicologist born in 1901 who migrated to the United States in 1928. Encountering Lang's comment sent me searching for tours, reviews, and anecdotes associated with Roman castrati from the early twentieth century, the last survivors of their dying kind. Franz Haböck mentions that small groups of papal singers toured through Germany and Austria at the beginning of the twentieth century, singing concerts with mixed programs similar to those they did in the hotels of Rome at Christmastime; and a disciple of the "last castrato," Alessandro Moreschi (1858–1922), writes in passing that Moreschi "sang in the churches of all of Italy and even abroad."[5] When exactly either took place, in particular the last, is quite unclear.[6] Other papal singers did outside gigging, at home and abroad, but we will see that the phenomenon of small groups touring under the name of the Sistine Choir probably did not happen until shortly before Moreschi's death.[7]

Whoever those "white, clear, and powerful" voices were, Lang's chronology is problematic at the very least, since by 1912 castrati had suffered almost complete eradication. In 1902 Lorenzo Perosi (1872–1956) took over full time from castrato-director Mustafà, by then a fifty-four-year member of the papal chapel and a devotee of the old ways. In 1903 castrati were banned from the chapel except for those grandfathered in.[8] By early 1904 only two castrati were in any singing voice, and after March 10 of that year Moreschi was the only one alive. As far as we know all the altos in the Sistine Chapel during the nineteenth century were noncastrates. Even if there were incentives at the time for singers to tour (in 1912 financial cuts eviscerated the formerly opulent chapel performances, and in 1914 chapelmaster Perosi's always precarious mental health collapsed with the death of his arch supporter Pope Pius X), it isn't possible that castrati, plural, were among those who did.[9]

If my quest to locate Lang's two castrati has failed, it has produced fascinating detours that partly ground the rest of this chapter. They begin at what we might call castrato voice ground zero, the site of the acoustic remains, which are admittedly scarce: twenty-four gramophone matrices made of Moreschi by the London-based Gramophone and Typewriter Company in 1902 and 1904, some as soloist, some with fellow Vatican choristers.[10] Such unique auditory evidence might well be treated like Homeric fragments, yet the recordings are often dismissed as useless romantic artifacts of the Roman church by a singer said to have been past his prime.[11] Why not imagine them instead as aural palimpsests, the scraped and funneled parchments of an acoustic past, much like fragmentary parchments of Beneventan chant or Notre Dame polyphony? Will Crutchfield has shown how crucial it is to attend to early phonographic recordings that preserve ornamentation practices proximate to Verdi's time and before and has argued passionately for the priority of early recordings to understanding nineteenth-century singing generally. John Potter has shown the value of recorded evidence for understanding the transmission of eighteenth- and nineteenth-century portamento practices into the early twentieth century.[12] In that spirit I marshal Moreschi's recorded voice as a serious part of the evidentiary package for accessing a material, physiological voice, however mediated. What exactly the evidentiary package consists of and whether Moreschi's singing can be understood as a "living sample" of a castrato "vocal vernacular," perhaps a meaningful link in a historical tradition, are the remains that haunt such a project.[13]

The first question is whether the recordings provide enough acoustic material even to infer anything about Moreschi's voice. Their most severe limitation is not the surface noise of cracks and pops but their pre-electrical horn and cutting-stylus technology, which preserves quite a true sound as far as it goes but does not register acoustically the entirety of the vocal resonance. This is because the human instrument, though sometimes high in decibels and large (or loud) in acoustical "size," is low in wattage power (actual output). Early recordings could capture only a part of its resonance, and the part they did capture was that closest to the fundamental frequency.[14]

We know that the harmonic overtones in the voice of a trained "classical" singer are the ones that produce ringing sounds or "resonance," which occur more or less in the range of 2,000–4,000 hertz (vibrational cycles per second) and above, whereas the earliest technology could only record up to about 2,100 hertz, and only very erratically upward of 3,000 hertz.[15] That frequency ceiling eliminates many or most of the upper partials, which in the higher range are especially important to male voices, castrato and non.[16] Generally there were no "retakes," certainly no edits, and dynamic effects had to be registered by modulating the distance between the singer and the horn, typically by having someone move the singer backward on forte notes to prevent overinscribing the grooves, which was hard on technique, especially intonation.[17] Altering their voices in response to the horn, singers experienced a kind of schizophonia. Perhaps the disjunction was not so unlike what modern singers using electronic technology experience when their monitors are set incorrectly, since lacking access to what listeners hear they have to alter their vocal output to adjust to what the monitors tell them is being heard.[18] All this is to say nothing of how modern-day transfers affect study of old recordings, sometimes introducing extraneous noise and removing frequencies as engineers attempt to filter nonmusical surface sounds from old and usually deteriorated originals. The parchment analogy is fitting, for what evidence survives is literally fragmentary, the early recorded voice of 1902–4 not fully apprehensible because not fully present.

EARLY RECORDED SOPRANOS

Hearing what survives with historical ears requires schooling and tolerance, without which it is illegible (nor is it easy to apprehend even for schooled listeners).[19] Still, there is a quantum difference between this provision of evidence and an utter lack of it. To start to distinguish between what recordings do capture, it is useful to develop an aural context by juxtaposing Moreschi's recordings with contemporaneous ones. The piece in Moreschi's recorded repertory that produced the greatest number of recordings by other artists in the shortest period of time is Gounod's *Méditation sur le premier prélude de piano de S. Bach* (1853), known as the Bach-Gounod *Ave Maria*.[20] A favorite with early twentieth-century recording artists, it was the very kind of chestnut Moreschi would have been performing in Roman hotels and salons. At least six recordings of the *Ave Maria* were cut by sopranos in the period 1904 to 1912/16, providing a controlled cluster of recordings that share a single score, one basic recording technology, and one relatively narrow slice of recording history (see table 1 for a sample of five of these).

TABLE 1 Five Recordings of Gounod's *Méditation sur le premier prélude de piano de S. Bach*, 1904–16 (the Bach-Gounod *Ave Maria*)

Singer	Accompanists	Location and date recorded	Key	Length	Production notes
Alessandro Moreschi (1858–1922)	With unidentified pianist and violinist	Vatican Palace, April 11, 1904	G major	3:18	Remastered on *Alessandro Moreschi: The Complete Recordings* (Wadhurst, E. Sussex, England: Opal Records, 1984), program notes by John Wolfson and Elsa Scammell; also on *Alessandro Moreschi, Soprano-Castrato (1858–1922), Complete Gramophone Company Recordings (Roma, 1902–1904), Also Includes Records from the Same Sessions by Other Vatican Artists* (Stutensee: Truesound Transfers, 2004), TT-3040, remastered by Christian Zwarg
Nellie Melba (1861–1931)	With Landon Ronald, piano, and Jan Kubelik, violin	London	G major	2:57	Remastered on *Nellie Melba (1861–1931): The Complete Gramophone Company Recordings, Vol. 1*, track 21 (Naxos Historical, 2002), with notes by Peter Dempsey. Produced by Ward Marston, whose note reads, "I have paid special attention to pitching Melba's voice since even a slight deviation from the proper speed will cause her voice to sound unnatural."
Adelina Patti (1843–1919)	With Landon Ronald, piano, and Marianne Eisler, violin	Craig-y-Nos Castle, Patti's home in Wales, December 1905	F major	2:26	Originally recorded by the Gramophone and Typewriter Company, first published on International Record Collectors' Club (IRCC) 33; on *The Complete Adelina Patti and Victor Maurel*, 2 CDs (Marston 52011-2), CD 1, track 11. The remastering, by Jeffrey Miller and Ward Marston, uses a pitch of 435 Hz in accordance with historical piano tuning (ibid., 17–19).
Emma Eames (1865–1952)	With violoncello obbligato by Josef Hollman	Camden, New Jersey [?], 1906	G major	2:47	Remastering of Victor Records 88016 on *Emma Eames: The Complete Victor Recordings, 1905–11*, 2 CDs ([London]: Romophone, 1993), CD 1, track 15. N.B. Eames made a recording without cello in the previous year.
Eugenia Burzio (1872 or 1879–1922)	With piano and violin accompaniment, unknown performers	Milan, 1912–16	G major	2:58	Columbia on *Eugenia Burzio, Verismo Soprano: Complete Recorded Operatic Repertoire*, produced by Scott Kessler and Ward Marston (Marston 52020-2)

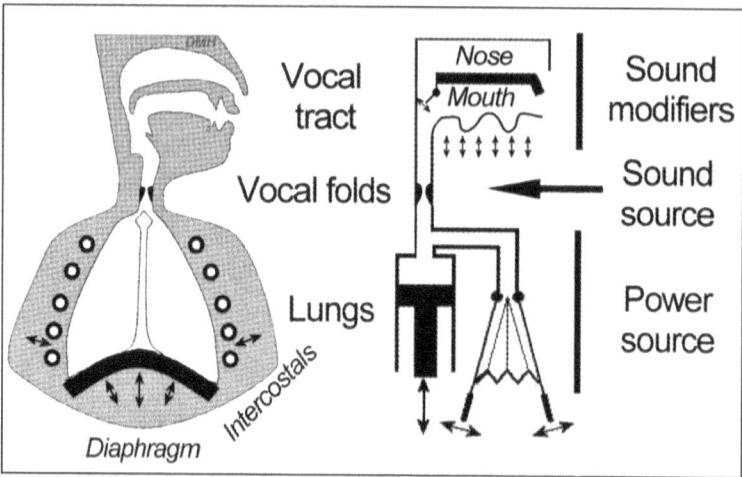

FIGURE 28. The lungs, larynx, and nasopharyngeal tract as drawn by David M. Howard, head of the Audio Lab at the Department of Electronics, University of York, and founding member of the York Centre for Singing Science. The top part shows the resonating cavities, including the nose, face, and vocal tract, where vocal color is shaped. The middle represents the air delivery mechanism of the larynx, where vocal registers are manipulated. The lungs at bottom are the power source from which air is pushed through the larynx (or voice box), topped by the vocal cords, a highly sensitive passage for delivery of air. From Howard's "Acoustics of the Castrato Voice," in Nicholas Clapton, *Moreschi and the Voice of the Castrato* (London: Haus Books, 2008), p. 230. Image courtesy of Haus Books.

In addition to Moreschi's recording of April 11, 1904, the group includes a 1904 recording by Australian Nellie Melba (1861–1931), a 1905 recording by the legendary (though here aged) Adelina Patti (1843–1919), a 1906 recording by American Emma Eames (1865–1952)—like Melba a product of the studio of Mathilde Marchesi—and a 1912–16 recording by the verismo soprano Eugenia Burzio (ca. 1872–1922).[21] Each is unique, yet all differ from modern singers in using relatively lush portamento, some virtually vibratoless white notes, and a relatively focused sound—what Italians call a *filo* (thread or thin stream of breath), marked to quite varying degrees by intermittent guttural effects. All seem to take the chest voice higher than modern sopranos do, and all therefore have more in common with each other in terms of vocal production than they have with the vocal production and stylistic leanings of present-day singers (and probably with most singers up until at least the 1930s; refer to this book's website).

What arguably sets Moreschi apart is his "chest" register, though his voice never sounds "chesty" as the term is used in common parlance. Since the matter of registers is fractious and elusive, let me clarify that I use "register" here to mean the *mechanical production of sound via the larynx or voice box*, which includes the two vocal folds (the everyday term is vocal cords). Sometimes called "mechanisms," registers are importantly bound up with the very source of sound. (See Fig. 28 for a basic map of the vocal anatomy including lungs, larynx, and vocal tract and the book's website for a strobe of the vocal folds shown in slow motion.) Despite different kinds of accounts given over the centuries, most medical, therapeutic, and linguistic writing still widely refers to two mechanisms: "chest" (called by speech pathologists the "modal" or speaking range and by early moderns the "natural voice") and "head" (often called "falsetto" in early writings, albeit with many contingencies, varied referents, and sources of ambiguity). The physical site at which vocal register occurs contrasts with that of vocal "color," which is produced not in the larynx but in the various resonating cavities of the throat, mouth, and face above the larynx by manipulating vowels in various parts of the vocal tract (neck, jaw, tongue, soft palate, cheeks, lips). The differences between register and color thus hinge on the different physical spaces they occupy and the actions they perform, though in practice they are artfully confounded.[22]

Seizing upon our heuristic distinction, note that pedagogues and singers have consistently agreed over time that both male and female voices, high and low, experience a registral shift (a change of laryngeal mechanism) between about e♭ and f♯ above middle c (speaking in terms of A = 440). (A typical default pitch for groups specializing in eighteenth-century music is A = about 415, which brings the pitches named here downward by about a semitone.) The notion of a registral "shift" can be loosely construed as meaning that somewhere in that span the chest voice normally gives out and the head voice has to take over.[23] Explicit assertions about such a shift date back to the early eighteenth century, but they were implicitly recognized much earlier, arguably as early as Jerome of Moravia. Some call this a "transitional" area or "vocal break," while Italians have traditionally referred to it with the more positive term *passaggio*, emphasizing the need to smooth the joint. However characterized, *the area of pitch transition is nearly always the same*, down to octave specificity, for both men and women. It follows that men, who are normally lower-voiced than women, typically have more chest notes available than women have, and women have more head than men.[24]

In 1847 Manuel Garcia the younger produced the "Tableau de la classification des voix" for part 1 of his *Traité complet de l'art du chant* showing where these registral transitions occur in various conventional voice types. His male voices included basso/basse-taille, baritono/baryton, tenore/ténor, and contraltino/haute-contre, and female ones contralto, mezzo-soprano, and soprano—each with a different typical ambitus and (Garcia claimed) a different area of overlap between *poitrine* (chest) and *tête* (head).[25] (See Ex. 4.) Confusingly for us, Garcia called this area of overlap *fausset* (falsetto). By suggesting falsetto as a third register (to my knowledge only Johann Friedrich Agricola had done so earlier, in 1757, with little influence), Garcia broke with the old two-register system, making falsetto/*fausset* not synonymous with head (or a variation upon it in a similar range) but an index of change, in-betweenness, or transition within a single given voice type.[26]

Another confounding aspect of register, and indeed of voice generally, is that empirical claims about what voices are doing physiologically do not rest on hard and fast aural referents. They are notoriously hard to substantiate because the terms used to express them can rarely be harnessed securely to a common listening experience. No matter how I describe what I hear, you may hear something different. Or you may understand in your mind's ear something quite different from what I intended my words to convey about my aural experience. So we are back to the heuristic distinctions delineated above: "chest" and "head" as muscular and mechanical function of the larynx versus color as a function of vocal tract; and perhaps chest as sounding "strong," "rich," "buzzy," or "heavy" compared with head, which sounds "light" and "clear" compared with chest.

. . .

With these caveats in mind, we can make some preliminary observations about our early twentieth-century sopranos. Melba's vocal is emission is quite focused (perhaps in keeping with her fairly metronomic pacing), with an apparent head-dominant mechanism and smoothly joined registers. Patti, the eldest, has a duskier, rather glottal voice, shrill on some high notes and bold, shooting out of the starting block at a tempo of sixty-six beats per minute and galloping up to eighty, as if pressing applause out of a cabaletta.[27] Melba and Patti, like Eames, make smooth transitions at the apparent change of registers. Compared to each other the differences in vocal production are not so obvious, but what is obvious is that Burzio sounds most akin to Moreschi. When she delivers the passage in Ex. 5 she drops on e' into a decidedly veristic chest (m. 9). (Note that Moreschi, Melba, Eames, and Burzio all sing the *Ave Maria* in G major, the traditional and original key, used in Ex. 5, while Patti uses F major, which allows her aged voice to lie a step lower.)

Burzio's low e' is obviously meant to *sound* chesty, whereas Moreschi makes the ascent and descent with no audible change of mechanism. Only when he leaps up to high g" in m. 13 does the registral mechanism sound pronouncedly different.[28] If these inferences are correct, we can probably agree that Moreschi has more chest or "chest-dominant" notes in the half octave from f#' to c" than the women do. Listen to Burzio deliver the sequenced phrases on "Gratia plena, Dominus tecum" from mm. 9 through 12 and compare them with Moreschi doing the same on this

EXAMPLE 4. Manuel Garcia, *Traité complet de l'art du chant en deux parties* (Paris: Mayence, 1847), pt. 1, pp. 22–23, chart of ambitus and registers for different voice types. University of Wisconsin Library, Madison.

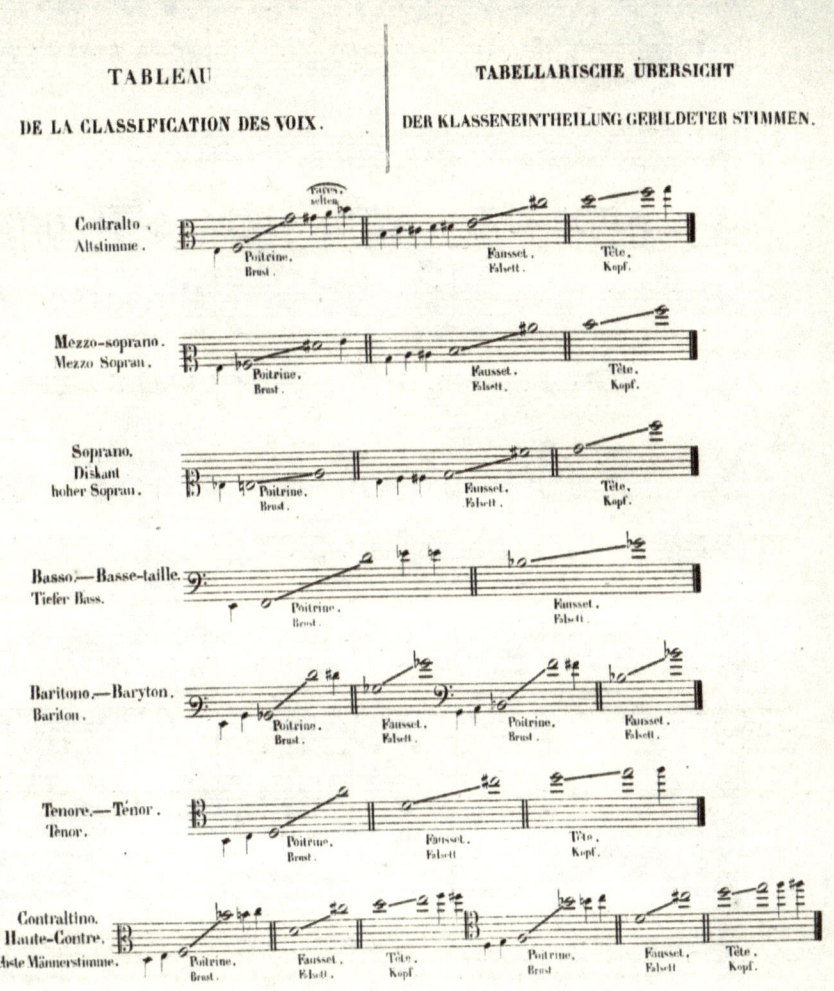

EXAMPLE 5. Charles Gounod, *Méditation sur le premier prélude de piano de S. Bach* (1853), known as the Bach-Gounod *Ave Maria*.

book's website. Burzio seems not to intone a single chest-dominant note until she plunges to the low e' on "gratia," and then not again until the same phrase sounds in sequence, diving back down to d' (m. 11).[29] Patti, who was a master manipulator of register and color, seems to mix more chest into the high notes—perhaps a stylistic desideratum of her older era (see this book's website). But Moreschi alone starts out using one mechanism and continues to do so throughout the first phrase, with no apparent shift to high c" and d".

Since imputing head and chest is a messy, subjective business, there is room to hear things differently. But in one spot the phenomenon sounds indisputable: the stepwise ascent from a" to e" in mm. 15–17 and from a" to d" in mm. 18–19, where Moreschi is the only soprano not to evince a discernable change of mechanism.[30] It seems he had higher-pitched chest-dominant sounds available to him, up to high d" and even e". What we don't know is whether his vocal folds were still supple in his mid-forties. Some castrati undoubtedly developed calcifications on the folds at a relatively early age, causing their voices to drop. According to Johann Joachim Quantz, these singers included Gaetano Orsini, Carestini, and seemingly Manzuoli. When younger, Moreschi had coloratura flexibility, to judge from oral accounts and from what he sang. His repertory included various coloratura-style numbers: the role of the Seraph in Beethoven's *Christus am Ölberge* (sung in 1883), with high b'''s and ossia c#'''s in the Allegro, graceful thirty-second-note gruppetti in the Largo, and generally sustained lines and an expansive range (a piece that famously won him a place in the Sistine Chapel in 1883); the jewel song "Ah, je ris de me voir si belle," from Gounod's *Faust*, at about the same time; the mezzo aria "O mio Fernando" from Donizetti's *La favorita*, with its sudden large registral shifts (performed in 1888); and Rossini's Crucifixus from the *Misse petite solennelle*, which he performed often and recorded in 1902 and again in 1904. If he was already experiencing a hardening of the laryngeal cartilage and hyoid bone in, say, the 1890s, at his approach to age forty, when these evidently affected some castrati, he still combined short folds and a small larynx with a large ribcage and lungs. That would explain how he managed to sing with noted success through 1921, and why Haböck, who heard him in 1914, described him as "quite strong" with a very developed chest.[31]

FURTHER ON THE "REGISTER" CONUNDRUM

Uses of *voce di petto* (chest voice), *voce naturale* (natural voice), and *voce di testa* (head voice) do not make up the whole marshland of naming and hearing registers. In 1723 Tosi speaks of the *voce di petto* as the "voce naturale." For that he had many predecessors, most of them surely unknown because buried in oral tradition. He distinguished *voce di petto* from *voce di testa* by describing the latter as a product of artifice. Some alto castrati of Tosi's time may have sung entirely in a *voce naturale*, although Tosi says all singers in his day—when the pitch universe was fast expanding—needed to have a head extension.[32] By this reckoning *voce* referred not to a given singer's voice or a given voice type overall but rather to different kinds of access to different vocal areas of a given voice. Giulio Caccini, the principal codifier of solo song around 1600, may be thinking along similar lines when he writes in his *Nuove musiche* of 1602 that when sopranos go up high their voices can become insufferable for listeners, especially "in *voci finte*" (literally, feigned voices). Aurally, we don't know precisely what Caccini meant by *voci finte*, and whether it pertained to falsetto singers or to sopranos if and when they accessed a falsetto register. If the former we can probably presume that he was referring to a mechanism that modern physiologists of voice call "second-mode phonation,"[33] but we have even sparser means to attach an audible referent to Caccini's verbal description than we do for Tosi's since Caccini's notational practices and theoretical language are even more distant than Tosi's and the *notated* ranges are considerably more limited.[34]

Accepting the problems above, what probably marks the whole Italian tradition from at least the seventeenth century onward has been some ideal of continuity between registers as a key to singing gracefully (which is not to say an ideal of homogeneity between entire registers or parts thereof). Continuity is made possible by the elegant mechanism of the larynx, carefully built around the cartilages on which the vocal folds rest and move, anemone-like. The principal cartilages of the voice box, namely the cricoid cartilage (the ringed one around the trachea) and thyroid cartilage (the largest and uppermost of the two, including two fused lamina, and on the anterior side of an uncastrated man, the Adam's apple), comprise a single hinged mechanism that articulates smoothly, as seen in footage of a dissected larynx from *Acland's DVD Atlas of Human Anatomy* (see the book's website).[35]

As trained singers blend chest and head to finesse registral shifts along with shifts of color, they actually reshape both the larynx (the sound source) and the vocal cavities that sit adjacent to it (the sound modifiers) in a continuous process.[36] Abandoning the idea of a radical distinction between mechanisms of the larynx and activities in the pharynx, a more complex reality emerges. Crutchfield describes a continual tweaking by individual singers to different "'segments' or 'areas of different response'—groups of tones in which timbre, available volume, ease of vowel formation and/or other subjectively described characteristics are distinct from the corresponding factors in the next segment above or below"—a view that understands the conventional head/chest division as only the most prominent and widely shared of such segments.[37]

THE CASTRATO "CHEST"

With these thoughts in mind, Tosi's views take on new meanings. As the first significant vocal teacher in the history of Western classical singing to publish a treatise on singing (as Sergio Durante has stressed), Tosi spoke pointedly about register in relation to vocal production, conceiving it here (as rendered into English by Galliard in 1743) as a problem of teaching:

> 20. Many Masters put their Scholars to sing the Contr'Alto [*fanno cantare il Contralto a loro discepoli*—make their students sing contralto], not knowing how to help them to the Falsetto [*per non sapere in essi trovar il falsetto*], or to avoid the trouble of finding it.
>
> 21. A diligent Master, knowing that a *Soprano*, without the *Falsetto*, is constrained to sing within the narrow Compass of a few Notes, ought not only to endeavor to help him to it, but also to leave no Means untried, so to unite the feigned and the natural Voice, that they may not be distinguished; for if they do not perfectly unite, the Voice will be of divers Registers, and must consequently lose its Beauty.[38]

How exactly an eighteenth-century singer may have smoothed the joint between registers and how an auditor may have discerned the difference between them remain open questions. But the passage leaves no doubt that for Tosi they were different, hence the need to join them imperceptibly, which preoccupied eighteenth-century singing teachers.

More apposite still is Tosi's ensuing comment that "*the Extent of the full natural Voice terminates generally upon the fourth Space, which is C; or on the fifth Line, which is D; and there the feigned Voice becomes of Use*, as well in going up to the high Notes, as returning to the natural Voice" (23–24)—that is, whether ascending into head (falsetto) or descending to chest (the "natural" voice).[39] Tosi therefore advises teachers to "consider, of what Moment the Correction of this Defect is, which ruins the Scholar if he overlooks it."

The last prompts him to make an aside that is revealing in its very strangeness. "Among the Women, one hears sometimes a *Soprano* entirely *di Petto*"—presumably an alto who sang specialized parts in a limited range, though probably using some blended chest notes at the top—and then adds, "Among the Male Sex it would be a great Rarity, should they preserve it after having past the Age of Puberty." For Tosi, "males" singing past puberty means mostly castrati, like himself, to whom his treatise is essentially addressed. These "natural" male trebles must use "feigned" or head voice once matured in order to fulfill expectations that they execute pitches in the stratospheres *above* their natural span of (middle) c' to c'', d'', or e''. We know about these feigned high pitches from the few examples of written ornamentation that survive.[40] Note, for instance, Porporino's ornamentations for Hasse's "Digli che io son fedele" in Ex. 6, with its several ornamental high a'''s and b'''s and highly elaborate passagework, as compared with Faustina's.

The other main pedagogue of the eighteenth century, Giambattista Mancini, also a castrato, writing half a century after Tosi, addressed a more catholic audience of singers and teachers. Nevertheless, in the first edition of his singing treatise, published in 1774, Mancini identified the registral break of the (male) "soprano" in the same vicinity as Tosi, specifically as low as b'' and as high as e'':

EXAMPLE 6. Hasse's melody line for his aria "Digli che io son fedele" (*Cleofide*, act 1, scene 6; Dresden, 1731) compared with versions with the ornaments supposedly fashioned by soprano Faustina Bordoni (second system) and by the castrato Porporino (third system). Adapted from Hellmuth Christian Wolff, *Originale Gesangsimprovisationen des 16. Bis 18. Jahrhunderts* (Cologne: Arno Volk, 1970), no. 10.

The voice in its natural state is ordinarily divided into two registers, one of which is called the chest, the other the head or falsetto. *I say ordinarily, because there are rare examples in which someone has received from nature the most unusual gift of being able to execute everything in the chest voice.* I am speaking only of the voice in general divided into two registers, as commonly happens.

Every student, whether soprano, contralto, tenor, or bass, can ascertain for himself the difference between these two separate registers. It is enough, if he begins to sing the scale, *for example if he is a soprano*, from sol on the third line [soprano clef] (g′) and, going to c on the fourth space (c″), he will observe that these four notes will be sonorous, *because they belong to the chest*. Should he wish to pass to D (d″), he will produce the note only with pain and fatigue if the vocal organ is not strong and is defective.

This mutation is nothing but the changing of the voice, which has arrived at the end of the first register, and entering the second finds it by necessity more feeble.

This chest voice is not equally forceful and strong in everyone; but to the extent that someone has a relatively more robust or more feeble organ of the chest, that person will have a more or less robust voice. *In many, the natural voice, or chest voice, does not extend beyond B-mi; and many others will be able to ascend as far as E-la-mi.*[41]

. . .

Mancini was taken to task by the German voice teacher Johann Adam Hiller for not recognizing the difference between female and (castrated) male sopranos. "Contrary to Mancini's belief, female voices have, most often, different limits for both registers. For the most part their voices are chest or head voices; with the former it is possible to go lower, and with the latter to go higher. It is therefore not unusual to find female voices which reach up to f‴ or g‴." At stake in his protestations is a cultural gulf: between Mancini's presumption of "soprano" as synonym for the castrato and Hiller's (north German) insistence on a wider world of sopranos, each worthy of being taught and thought about distinctly.[42]

EXAMPLE 7. Sustained note and trill from "Perfido, di a quell'empio tiranno" (mm. 80–92), which Handel wrote as substitution aria for the revised version of *Radamisto*, act 1, scene 6, created for Senesino and performed December 28, 1720, at the King's Theater upon the singer's arrival in London. The part was premiered the previous April 27 with Margherita Durastanti, by then a mezzo-soprano, playing in trousers in the title role.

In light of the above, we can begin to understand a number of comments that, read in ensemble, leave no real doubt that castrati accessed a head voice above b″, c″, or even higher and used the natural chest with ease below that. Charles Burney notes that Giovanni Maria Rubinelli (1753–1829) was a "true and full contralto from C, in the middle of the scale, to the octave above. He sometimes however goes down to G and up to F, but neither the extra low nor the high are very full. *All above C is falset.*" In calling attention to Rubinelli's registral shift and denigrating his head voice, Burney underlines the transition into head above c″. Rubinelli's head voice, he continues, is "so much more feeble and of a different register than the rest, that I was uneasy when he transcended the compass of his natural and real voice."[43]

More famously, Quantz marveled that Senesino, an alto, sang divisions "from the chest."[44] Senesino's voice ranged from about g to e″ in all, a range in which he excelled at fioritura in the Handelian style. Because Handel wrote no fewer than seventeen roles for him, a wealth of pieces exhibit careful crafting for Senesino's voice with unusual emphasis on sustained notes and coloratura in the upper half octave from g′ to c″ (see Ex. 7, from *Radamisto*). But Quantz also praised the chest voices of other castrati. Of Carestini he wrote that he "had extraordinary virtuosity in brilliant passages, which he sang in chest voice, conforming to the principles of the school of Bernacchi and the manner of Farinelli."[45] By the time Quantz heard him, Carestini's voice had dropped from soprano to alto, but Farinelli had extensions well upward and downward, beyond the range of other mortals, and written examples show that his fioritura singing abounded throughout his tessitura.[46] Most surprisingly, the now-lesser-known contralto castrato Orsini, one of Quantz's favorites, was a singer whom Quantz deemed moving and virtuosic in all he sang not least because of his natural chest voice, which he seems to have used almost exclusively, doubtless with unwritten ornamentation since Quantz says he sang touching adagios, which would have required it.

> Gaetano Orsini, one of the greatest singers that ever was, had a beautiful, even, and stirring contralto voice of no small compass; a pure intonation, beautiful trill, [and] an uncommonly charming delivery. In Allegros he articulated passaggi, especially triplets, very beautifully with his chest; and in Adagios, masterfully artful, the direct, moving qualities were so touching that he went right through the heart of the listener, whom he overcame in the highest degree.[47]

· · ·

Quantz's remarks shed light on the passaggio and establish that Orsini made an entire practice of executing virtuosic passagework in the compass of the designated chest or natural voice. In commenting about Carestini also singing "brilliant passages" from the chest, according to *"the principles of the school of Bernacchi and Farinelli"* (emphasis mine), Quantz effectively adds a number of singers to the practice. Recall that Bernacchi's Bolognese school included Mancini, the alto Amadori, soprano Tommaso Guarducci, mezzo Antonio Pasi, plus briefly Farinelli and others, all of whom would have sung in chest up to at least b″ or c″.[48]

Quantz's observations are seconded by twentieth-century papal falsettist Domenico Mancini (1891–1984), who was interviewed about his studies with Moreschi, which began on November 17, 1904, when he was thirteen. He recalled coming "under the spell of [Moreschi's] outstandingly beautiful voice":

> I began my studies with Moreschi by *imitating his voice with my own, since, as it hadn't changed yet, I just sang as he did, in chest voice, passing from there into head voice* [emphasis mine]. But then, at around fourteen, well, my voice became that of a man, and so singing with the falsettists, I began to use the type of head voice which normal adult men have; naturally to sing with it you have to train it, because it's a voice that is made by training and musicianship: you need to be a musician to use it.[49]

Mancini's interview does not specify pitch, but his meaning is legible in light of pedagogical and recorded evidence. As a boy pupil, Mancini could center his tessitura in the natural chest, as his teacher did, but as a postpubertal falsettist he had physiologically lost that ability. To remain a soprano he had to make the chest voice he had lost (about f′/g′ through c″/d″) into a cultivated head above f′/g′) and had to adjust to having a lower region of principal registral shift—in short, to having the "universal passaggio." The crucial point is that the boy Mancini "imitated" Moreschi's singing using his chest voice but the man Mancini could not.

. . .

We should not take leave of this discussion of castrato registers with too fixed a notion. Consider the situation of Bernacchi. By 1736, when he retired from the stage and was devoting himself to teaching, as he did until his death in 1756, he had to prepare most male students (including some tenors) to cover a considerably larger ambitus than he had needed to do when he started his career in order to deal with modern repertory. In 1703, Bernacchi the alto basically needed no more than a tenth to sing the repertory of his time, and hence could do so mostly within chest. By the 1730s the pitch universe for singing had expanded dramatically, as reflected by Bernacchi's own solfeggi for his students. Besides echoing his own rather instrumental style of singing, they show a remarkable upward extension. The partial set of transcriptions from Münster MS Santini 458 available on Robert O. Gjerdingen's website includes, for example, the exercise in Ex. 8, which could never have been sung without extensive use of a head voice no matter how high a castrato's "natural" voice—witness the passagework reaching above high c, including many a'''s in alt starting in m. 6.[50]

REGISTER AND PHYSIOLOGY

Why does it matter whether castrati had more chest available than head? Let's return to the mechanism and proceed to acoustics. In chest voice, the thyroarytenoid muscles of the larynx are tensed, the more so the higher the pitch sung, whereas in head voice they're relaxed since head voice involves a lengthening and thinning out of the vocal folds with the larynx raised up in the throat.[51] At lower pitches the vocal folds vibrate more slowly, just as airwaves move more slowly from a contrabass than from the higher-pitched strings of a violin. Vibrational speed is a matter of the amount of time it takes for the vocal folds to complete a glottal cycle (coming together and separating), many of which in succession form pitches (e.g., 440 hertz equals 440 glottal cycles per second—a process distinct from the "vibrato"). The processes can be seen in a strobe of a man singing in falsetto made at the University of Chicago Medical Center by two ENTs specializing in voice (including professional voice), Dr. Daniel Martin and Dr. Jacquelynne Corey (see this book's website). The folds engage hundreds of times per second, but because the singer uses a falsetto voice they do not make full-body contact with one another. Some breath escapes, hence the "breathy" quality people sometimes (although not always) ascribe to falsetto singing. The "falsetto" voice, as David M. Howard and Damian T. Murphy note, has a high fundamental frequency achieved by restricting the vibrating portions of the vocal folds.[52]

EXAMPLE 8. Anton Maria Bernacchi, solfeggio in B♭ major marked Adagio (mm. 1–42), from D-Mü, Santini MS 458 solfeggio; = Gj 5624. Solfeggi from the manuscript are transcribed on the website of Robert O. Gjerdingen's *Monuments of Solfeggi*.

EXAMPLE 8. *(continued)*

Listeners who are drawn to voices with a rich spectrum of formants (frequency peaks of the vocal sound spectrum) won't hear that at the top of today's highest male voices, great as some are, for countertenors, lacking chest above the "universal passaggio" and producing high notes that are, acoustically speaking, "thinner" than those of trained females, especially those of a spinto or dramatic variety, are vocally almost physiological opposites of castrati in all but range. Unlike countertenors, castrati did have full contact between the folds in high unforced chest. Voice scientists talk about such contact in terms of the "closed quotient" (CQ) of larynx output (Lx), indicating the amount of time in each glottal cycle that the folds are fully closed. "CQ has been found to change with f_o [fundamental frequency] and with singing experience and/or singing training. . . . For adult males, CQ remains relatively constant with f_o but increases with singing training/experience."[53] Intense training and exercise not only add to a singer's natural abilities to maximize CQ but also allow one to sing longer on a single breath, controlling the folds with maximal efficiency such that less breath escapes and more tone is transmitted in output—hence the acoustical difference.[54]

A corollary of the faster vibrations and greater purity of a female soprano's head voice is that it normally produces audible harmonic overtones only up to about 2,000 hertz, as compared with the overtones of chest voice, which can reach 4,000 hertz and higher in a particularly rich timbral spectrum. Female singers enrich and darken sound by blending to varying degrees chest into head, which naturally inclines toward a sine-tone purity because the vowels in head voice have a strong fundamental. Most voice specialists say that female sopranos lack the so-called "singer's formant," a resonance in the 2,500–4,000 hertz region that allows a voice to project over an orchestra (often described as "ring"), clustering in the third, fourth, and fifth formants. Swedish voice specialist Johan Sundberg is definitive about the absence of the singer's formant in women.[55] In recent years he joined an international group that raised the provocative question of that formant in a castrato, noting that all reports of their penetrating quality, combined with their man- (or indeed superman-) sized vocal tract, would point to its existence.[56] If they are right, then we have an irreducible acoustic difference between castrati and all other singers: a singer's formant in the prevalent pitch area of f'/g' through c" to e" achieved without "pushing" the voice.

. . .

Can anyone else sing high in chest without pushing unnaturally hard? To a limited extent, yes. As Moreschi's student Domenico Mancini suggests, a number of boys can, often ascending in chest as far as a" or b" a sixth or seventh above middle c', and not infrequently to c", d", or e" (albeit with highly variable degrees and kinds of acculturation, from the pure trebles of Westminster Cathedral to the chesty ones of the Vienna Boys Choir).[57] Garcia had his own explanation for how this occurs, though the truth for us moderns is probably even more variable than he allowed:

> During childhood, from a young age until the time of puberty, the human voice, identical in girls and boys, evinces a clear-cut distinction between chest, which in the former years extends from c' to g', but strengthened with age, extends further in both directions, and (though rarely) descends to a♯ or b and up to the extremes of c" and c♯". Yet one must add that these notes are the result of violent efforts.
>
> This observation can be verified in child choristers. *Forced to sing from seven to twelve years of age, in vast edifices and often in massive milieus with a formidable voice, they screech without carefully managing use of either their lungs or their throats.* It is then that one hears violently formed sounds above a" up to d♯" in chest, and that one can predict a certain ruination of their voices. (emphasis mine)[58]

Garcia's concern is echoed in modern times by Paul Miles-Kingston, former chorister in the Winchester Cathedral Choir and famous for his boy solo on the recording of Andrew Lloyd Webber's *Requiem*. Miles-Kingston argues against overemphasizing the chest in teaching boys because it is easy to do yet harmful. Young children, he writes,

> naturally develop a fuller sound around middle C because they have often used that range for speaking from their earliest years. It is therefore louder and more developed than their head sounds, making it more projected and immediately usable for performance. Children are very drawn to it for this reason and are often encouraged to develop "chest" sounds as high as top D or even E flat.... Some children also have a predisposition to producing this type of sound if their speaking voices are already chesty.[59]

Without pressing for a monolithic picture of boys' vocal mechanics or proclivities, Miles-Kingston then provisionally assigns the following pitch spans to corresponding registral spans: c′ to e♭′ to "chest"; e′ to b♭″ to "lower-middle"; b♮″ to e♭″ to "upper-middle"; and e♮″ in alt to c‴ in altissimo to "head," mechanical areas that he takes to be similar to those of a female soprano for the obvious reason that "the size and mass of the vocal folds of a child produce a range similar to that of an adult [female] soprano."[60]

> Boys can be treated differently from girls in that the lower- and upper-middle areas can be trained to be heavier in terms of resonance, particularly with boys approaching puberty when their folds begin to gain mass and length as the skeletal structure of the larynx enlarges. This richer tone quality will also enrich the head voice if handled correctly.[61]

As for registers, he notes that there is

> a discernible change in the vocal fold position of boys between B flat and B natural above middle C, as indeed there is in many tenor adult voices in the octave below, hence the notion introduced in the first part of the study about regarding boys as boy *tenors* rather than boy *sopranos*. At this point in the voice, the vocal folds need to be allowed to "thin" and adjust to allow the upper pitches to be produced comfortably.[62]

Miles-Kingston's points concerning the increasing mass and length of vocal folds in the approach to puberty and the tenor-like character of a typical boy are apposite to castrati. Depending on when boys were castrated and how advanced their progress in puberty, their vocal folds may not have been as short upon maturation as those of a young boy, which would also account for the prevalence of alto castrati and of those with a strong downward tenor extension like Pacchierotti.[63] Yet even if that is so, they would still have had the largest number of chest notes of any "normal" high voice type and probably the only formant among sopranos or altos. Add a large ribcage and lungs and you have the makings of a unique voice, still much shaped by the disparity between the size of the chest and the length of the folds and correlated size of larynx, both more flexible, at least at younger ages, than in a man whose growth had been "fed" by average levels of testosterone. Such a singer could gather up a great quantity of highly compressed air in his chest and explode it through his small larynx with its still short and (while in best voice) still supple vocal folds—a highly sensitive delivery vehicle using an air pressure-to-opening ratio probably unequalled by other voice types, least of all again a modern countertenor, who emits less air pressure from the larynx than other voice types because the larynx is not fully closed during adduction of the vocal folds. (Some vocal pedagogy would call this an increase of "subglottal pressure.")[64] Then, on exiting the larynx, the air would flow upward and resonate through a man's vocal tract and nose. We can therefore say that the "subglottal pressure," overtones, singer's formant, and physiology of the castrato all seem, acoustically speaking, closest among modern singers to those of a very high tenor.[65]

Consider these facts in combination with several others. Deprived of testosterone, the larynx of a castrato would not have descended in the throat as it normally does in growing boys, nor would his folds have thickened. Presumably the elaborate laryngeal system of cartilage, bone, hinges, muscles, membranes, and ligaments retained a childlike suppleness and predisposition to flexibility. For many boys testosterone deprivation would have prevented the bones of the ribcage from fusing to the sternum at the usual time in the growing cycle; those of some may have continued growing, creating an overdeveloped chest cavity resembling keel or pigeon chest.

Pediatric endocrinologist Robert Rosenfield notes that in men who have grown without the benefit of typical testosterone levels, the cartilage of the sternum will remain softer than usual, hence pliant, and unobstructed by the ribs, which may never fully fuse.[66] That insight changes the way we might look at Zanetti's famous caricature of Bernacchi, blowing an immense cadenza over the bell tower at Saint Mark's and landing it with a cadential trill on the doge's palace (image and details in Figs. 29 a, b, and c). The power needed to carry off the feat is maximized by another anomaly seen above: the great protruding jaw that develops when the mandible and/or maxilla fails to fuse properly, thereby making a great resonating chamber for the large supply of air. Although Ghezzi's sketches are less cartoonish than Zanetti's, they illustrate prodigious jaws just as clearly. The jaw of papal singer Memmo (Mommo) in Fig. 30 calls to mind a number of others: Pellegrini's in Fig. 11, Berenstadt's in Fig. 44, and Balatri's in Fig. 23, the last important because it is a court painting with no interest in exaggerating the singer's anatomy.

If you were to take a big-voiced tenor like Placido Domingo singing at the top of his range or a modern Rossinian tenor like Lawrence Brownlee, you could approach vocally some of these variables. The phenomenon was explored in the 2006 BBC program *Handel and the Castrati*, hosted by Nicholas Clapton, which featured a new electronic reconstruction of the castrato voice by David M. Howard. The reconstruction synthesized the voice of a young boy singer with that of a fearless young adult tenor named Darren Abrahams, who sings Handel's "Ombra mai fu" in a boy's octave using all chest, to ear-splitting effect. But there is a simpler

FIGURE 29. a. Anton Maria Zanetti, caricature in pen and ink from 1723 of Antonio Bernacchi singing a long and highly instrumental cadenza, made up almost entirely of sixteenth notes, on the word "apri," imperative of the infinitive "aprire" (to open). The image proclaims that Bernacchi can sail a cadenza over the bell tower at Piazza San Marco and land a trill on the doge's palace, all in a single breath. The drawing was made the same year that Bernacchi sang in *Mitridate, re di Ponto* at the Teatro San Giovanni Grisostomo in Venice, with music by the abbot Giovanni Maria Cappelli. Fondazione Giorgio Cini, Venice. Photos by Matteo De Fina.

b. Detail of the ascent of the cadenza.

c. Detail of the trill landing on the Doge's palace.

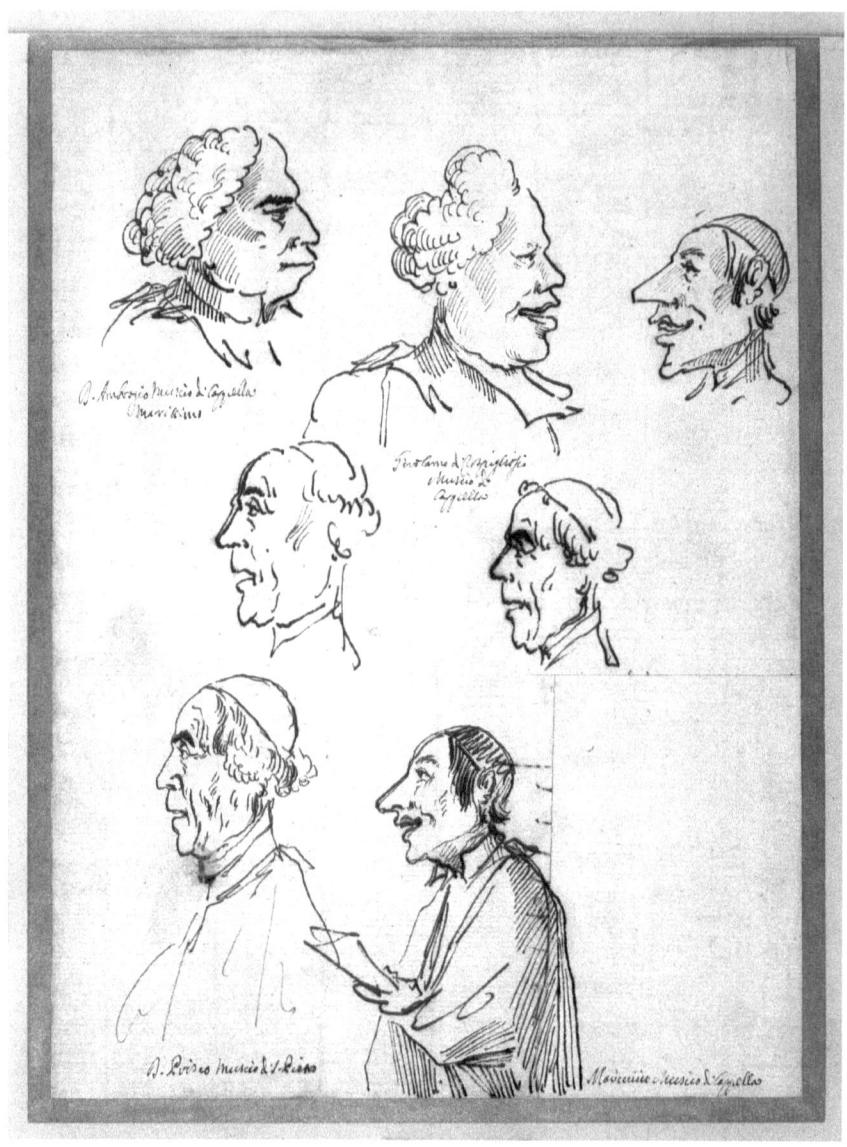

FIGURE 30. Pier Leone Ghezzi's sketch sheet, ca. 1715–17 (probably 1716). Top center: papal soprano/contralto "Mommo" (Antonio Girolamo Bigelli, also called Girolamo di Rospiglioso). Top and bottom right: papal tenor "Mariuccio" (Mario Pippi). Middle center (2) and bottom left: Cappella Giulia bass Giulia Prisco (Perrini). Note the contrast of the massive protruding jawline of Mommo with the regular features of the tenor and bass. The image forms part of the Collection of the Duke of Devonshire, Chatsworth, England, cat. no. 642B (314). © Devonshire Collection, Chatsworth. Reproduced by permission of Chatsworth Settlement Trustees.

physiological observation to be made about the castrato chest. Even a Wagnerian Heldentenor or an Italianate *tenore robusto* or *tenore spinto* has to "push" the voice against its natural tendency in order to ascend above f′ or g′ with much chest in the voice (and how far any have ever succeeded remains a matter of controversy, as Marco Beghelli argues).[67] By contrast, if all or most castrati retained the boy's chest notes on achieving adulthood, including those whose chests were of normal size, then all had a relatively large chest-to-larynx size ratio, which mitigated the need to push the chest voice even for those without an enlarged thorax. Add to this that chest singing requires less airflow than head and that castrati were trained with an intensity beyond anything imaginable nowadays and you have an extraordinary set of vocal conditions, with highly fast, efficient glottal cycles plus the potential for great breath control, power, accuracy, and often flexibility. The closest physiological cousins today at the upper vocal crust of all populations, past and present, would be muscular but flexible tenors, plus mezzos and dramatic sopranos.

TIMBRE AND AMPLITUDE

Imagine the effect of such mechanical factors on timbre. Farinelli, Carestini, Caffarelli, Senesino, and Manzuoli, among others, all attracted the epithets "brilliant," "voluminous," "powerful," and "thundering" for their volume and doubtless the richness of their voices. Many spoke of Farinelli's brilliant sound, Vincenzio Martinelli saying his voice was as big as his "semigigantesca statura" (an oblique reference to his height). Carestini began his career as "a powerful and clear soprano," with a range of b to c‴; Burney said that after his voice dropped, he was remembered for having "the fullest, finest, and deepest counter-tenor that has perhaps ever been heard."[68] Metastasio deprecated Caffarelli's Viennese performances of 1749, reporting to Farinelli that some considered his voice "intensely but falsely strident" ("molta ma falsa stridula"),[69] yet had his voice not been extremely powerful he could never have reigned over the notoriously large and noisy Teatro San Carlo in Naples as he did from 1737 to 1753. Burney confirms as much by noting that Handel planned Caffarelli's air "Voglio che sia" (*Faramondo*, 1738) for a "voice of great volume."[70] About Senesino's delivery of the aria "L'onor severo" from Giovanni Bononcini's revision of *Astarto* (King's Theatre, November 19, 1720), Burney wrote, "The divisions, though now very common, must have had a great effect, as rolled and thundered by the powerful voice and articulate execution of this singer."[71]

In the first half of the eighteenth century, to be a polished singer of power and majesty was to be a singing star, especially for male sopranos. Burney often makes the equation. Revealing in physico-acoustic terms is that loud, ringing voices ("squillante," as present-day Italians would say) were often also called "sweet" or "mellow."[72] The list of singers who attracted both groups of epithets cuts across cultural-metaphoric expanses of time, place, and language. Among "sweet" singers in the seventeenth century were Ferri and Siface and in the eighteenth Farinelli, Martini, Monticelli, Senesino, Caffarelli, Manzuoli, Guarducci, Pacchierotti, and Marianino. To hear Mancini tell it, though Ferri's voice was reputed to be sweet and flexible, it could be made "proud, serious, and tender at will." In 1687, after hearing Siface's messa di voce, John Evelyn effused that "his holding out & delicatenesse in extending & loosing a note with that incomparable softnesse & sweetenesse, was admirable."[73] The attribution of sweetness accords with the findings of Louise K. Stein, who has been studying scores written for him along with other evidence.[74] Siface's mastery of the messa di voce would have included control and power. It recalls his phenomenal success in impersonating the courageous Syphax, whom he played in Minato and Cavalli's *Scipione affricano* (1664) at the very large Teatro SS. Giovanni e Paolo (five tiers high with about 145 boxes), and which earned him his moniker.[75]

Sweet singers abound in the eighteenth century, often in a dyad with power. Burney repeatedly said this of Farinelli, writing that he was "gifted with a voice of such uncommon power, sweetness, extent, and agility" that he "enchanted and astonished his hearers by the force, extent, and mellifluous tones of the mere organ." When he called Manzuoli the "most powerful and voluminous soprano that had been heard ... since the time of Farinelli," it must have been because of his combination of "native strength and sweetness."[76] Quantz said Senesino's vigorous alto was "clear, equal, and sweet," a comment echoed by Mrs. Pendarves.[77]

Although later in the century sweetness was doubtless still often a companion of power, power by then had become a kind of silent partner. Performances still took place in big churches and theaters, often with even larger orchestras than before,[78] yet in 1753 the Baron Friedrich Melchior von Grimm (1723–1807) could call the booming voice of Caffarelli simply "angelic"—an epithet that conventionally presupposed sweetness. Pacchierotti was unfailingly revered for sweetness and nuance. Lord Mount-Edgcumbe called his voice "sweet and round," suggesting the full spectrum of overtones produced by a voice with good ring and chest production, both of which, by all accounts, Pacchierotti—whose lower extension astounded—had in spades.[79] Hence Susan Burney's gloss, which comes close to Lord Edgcumbe's but touches the heart of new trends in sensibility that shrank from imputing power: "His Voice was so clear, so full, so sweet."[80] And in the nineteenth century, the German critic Georg Ludwig Peter Sievers (1775?–1828) could attribute the sweetness of Mariano Astolfi (Marianino), absent the power he had previously had, to his older age, with what Sievers said was no less power to move the heart.

> No singer ever made such a deep and spiritual impression on me as Mariani [sic].... The melting sweetness of his notes (I do not say "voice," because he no longer has that in great volume), the expression with which he sings, his artistic training ... all moved me to tears.... This singer (he must be close to fifty) still has a fair range: I heard him take the high C with great ease a number of times, and at the bottom of his compass he sings down to a B-flat and A.[81]

HEAVY METAL

Complicating this descriptive repertory is another set of metaphors clustered around the sounds and surfaces of metal. In talk about castrati, "metallic," "golden," or "silvery" voices were seemingly indivisible from powerful ones. A Florentine critic wrote in 1772 that the castrato Michele Angiolo Neri was developing "a voice of silver"—Neri whose teacher was that most "voluminous" of all singers from the later eighteenth century, Manzuoli.[82] Schopenhauer invoked the power/metal dyad explicitly for Girolamo Crescentini (1762–1846), saying his voice was "supernaturally beautiful," with a "silver purity" and yet "indescribable power."[83]

If silver indexed purity, then the metaphor might imply exceptional vocal efficiency and clarity, as many castrati were said to have had. But something more particular seems to be at issue, closer to the Italian word "metallo." Sonically it means timbre, but "una voce di metallo" means specifically a voice of substance or body, as Balatri claimed he had in his youth (see chapter 2). "Metallo" evokes strong air currents with consequent resonance or "ring" produced by a rich overtone spectrum, ring hinging here on the timbral color(s) of the voice and the vowel formants that Howard and Murphy discuss.

But "ring" is semantically contingent. The Italian infinitive "squillare" means to ring or peal, while its present participle "squillante" means "shrill"—something like "stridulo" (strident or shrill, or even screeching), as Metastasio said of Caffarelli.[84] Again, however, things become both more complex and more interesting if we follow the path of literal usages. A Roman alto wrote in his diary about a pontifical mass in which he heard Moreschi as soloist, saying he had a "voice of gold, not just rare but unique."[85] This was unqualified praise, like Habóck's for Moreschi, which adopts the metaphor of crystal to index both substance and perfect clarity.

> If one wants to describe the sensuous impression of a voice, one says, of course, that the organ has a golden or a silvery sound, that it seems warm or cold. Moreschi's voice can only be compared with the clarity and purity of crystal. The absolute evenness and even coloring [i.e., timbral unity] of his sound, which was singularly powerful, bright [or ringing—*hell*], transparent, sweet, and yet other than both a woman's vocal sound and also a boy's. The complete effortlessness [*Mühelosigkeit*] with which, because of his apparently inexhaustible powers of vocalizing with controlled breathing [*beherrschten Stimmgebung*, translatable as "air supply"], one almost physically empathizes with him all aroused in me an overwhelming impression of the most extraordinary wind instrument ever given life by human breath. . . . When his voice rose above the choir in a crescendo . . . it overpowered the accompanying boy sopranos as a searchlight outshines a candle.[86]

Habóck's "crystal" calls to mind Pietro Verri's comment that Luigi Marchesi's trill was "di granite" (see chapter 5), as opposed to the more broadly cast praise by

Burney of Senesino's adagio aria "Spartite o pensieri" as releasing "his whole volume of voice in all its purity and force."[87] It may be no coincidence that Haböck goes on to rhapsodize about Moreschi's "matchless messa di voce" and allude to his "metallic speaking voice."[88]

Why this tumble of metaphoric densities? Repeatedly the voice of the castrato suggests a power that overcomes the listener's senses and descriptive apparatus, and yet confusingly synesthetic usages of "metallic" have long been applied to large noncastrated voices as well. In *Grove* we read about the "metallic ring" in the top notes of tenor Jan Peerce, the "metallic, penetrating timbre" of tenor Giovanni Dimitrescu, and the "large, rich metallic timbre" of mezzo Rita Gorr; or we might think of Desmond Shawe-Taylor's description of Danish tenor Lauritz Melchior as having a "lusty high C [that] always rang thrillingly,"[89] or imagine a *tenore robusto* like Domingo or Pavarotti (i.e., a *spinto*, or "pushed," voice) or a silver-toned tenor like Jussi Bjoerling. All these are midrange voices, but other references are to the likes of Adelina Patti, Henriette Sontag, and Joan Sutherland. What all share, castrato and non, is the ability to force the vocal folds tightly together under a great deal of subglottal air pressure. On this book's website listen to the ring in the voices of Bjoerling and Nilsson, two of the biggest, most brilliantly metallic of recorded singers, in the duet "In questa reggia" from *Turandot*, recorded in 1959.

. . .

We might wonder whether some boys singled out for castration had already "showed their *metal*" in this sense. Reminiscent of Balatri's boast about his adolescent *voce di metallo* is Garcia's explanation of children's timbre: "The head voice begins on c♯″, at d″, or at e♭″ and rises, becoming round, sweet, and silvery; it extends up to g‴ or a‴."[90] If a sweet, silvery voice is indeed the kind that castration sought to arrest before puberty, we might hope that spectrographic analysis would show its ring, but precisely such analysis is not possible for Moreschi's recordings because the formants of the ring—those we presume to have been there—never registered on the recordings, nor can the voice be isolated except in a single monophonic chant that covers the range of a fourth. Just as problematic is the anecdoctal evidence for Moreschi and other castrati, for "metallic" and its lexical cousins are always metaphorical bandits, ready to plunder your meanings or mine, to flatter the referent or not. The *OED* defines "metallic" as sonically resembling that which is "produced by a metal object when struck; sharp and ringing; [and] (esp. of a voice or a cry) harsh and unmusical." Yet it lists among its examples the epic purity evoked by the metaphorically extravagant Thomas Carlyle in the phrase "Among clear metallic heroes, and white, high stainless beauties" and the high, echoing, metallic ringing of cicadas in Steinbeck's *The Pearl*. It also gives a flattering nod to a "silvery" sound as having "a clear gentle metallic resonance ... , melodious" of the kind conjured in Lord Byron's "The silvery bell rang" or Charles Kingsley's "In his ears one silvery voice was ringing."[91]

However contradictory these metaphorical leanings, they can hardly be ignored in the repertory of anecdotes about castrati, who were so often perceived synaesthetically as large or round yet sweet, brilliant, or shiny, and with the dense feel of metal. We might imagine listening to chest at high range in any singer—the combination is exciting.[92]

...

The sound I hope is coming into focus, though manmade and highly variable, nevertheless produced some physiological constants, transhistorical in kind even if culturally contingent because much varied across the population. How much each factor acted upon any one voice can never be answered by more than speculation, hunch, or probability, mostly because of the acoustic lack but also because lines of tradition have moved forward unevenly over time, continuing within some pedagogical traditions and repertories, being intermixed with newer developments in others, and rejected outright by still others.

One thing we can date rather definitively is a break in traditions of male operatic singing soon after the last operatic castrati left the stage for good. Its famously ostentatious and mythical beginning occurred when the French tenor Gilbert-Louis Duprez ostensibly took his chest voice up to a high c" in a Paris performance of Rossini's *Guillaume Tell,* on April 17, 1837. The moment marks symbolically the advent of a heavier, more muscular, and more declamatory way of singing, appropriate to Verdi, Wagner, or the verismo composers of the late nineteenth and early twentieth centuries, but not to Rossini, or most of Bellini and Donizetti, much less their predecessors at the height of castrato singing.

Whether or not we call the latter "bel canto" is often more a matter of the superiority I claim for my method over yours—something more like vocal theology than history.[93] That the term has long postdated the practice as an aftereffect, a kind of nostalgia for bygone times or simply a crude codification of them, is embodied in the very fact that it came to be pressed into use as a substantive noun. Yet the idea of beautiful singing had long been not a *thing* but a practice, especially of teaching and doing.[94] Some early uses are indicative: the title page of Nicola Vaccai's *12 ariette per camera in chiave di violino per l'insegnamento del bel canto italiano* (12 chamber ariettas in violin tuning for teaching Italian bel canto), printed by Ricordi in 1839, for instance, and a letter of recommendation written by Rossini in 1849. The latter, heretofore unknown, though short, is telling because it is precisely about being qualified to *teach* beautiful singing because able to *do* it:

> I am pleased to attest that Mr. J. P. Goldberg, member of the Musical Academy of Vienna, who sang in Italy in the capacity of *primo basso assoluto, is capable of*

teaching bel canto, of which he gave proof beyond a doubt by having taught artists who became distinguished in the Italian theater.
Sincerely,
Gioacchino Rossini
November 22, 1849
Florence[95]

Rossini's letter precedes by nine years the first reference to bel canto widely cited, when Rossini is said to have repined for the castrati with the phrase, "Alas for us, we have lost our bel canto."[96] But usages of close relation crop up a good deal earlier, with similar offhandedness. In 1814 Antonio Benelli referred to "le bellezze del canto," and in 1824 Andrea Costa wrote of the "bell'Arte del Canto," calling the Italian language "la più adattata al bel canto."[97]

Given this pedagogical genealogy it's not surprising that another cluster of variants comes from the castrato Crescentini, who taught singing during his 1806–12 residency in Napoleon's Paris and again in the conservatories of Bologna (from 1817) and Naples (from 1824), and who counted among his pupils Rossini's wife Isabella Colbran. In 1840 Crescentini referred in a dedicatory preface to Francesco Florimo's book on singing as the "bell'arte di canto" and to the author's "bel metodo di canto." (Florimo's own text uses similar variants.)[98] Crescentini's dicta on good singing, included in his collection of *vocalizzi* (see Fig. 51), can be read retrospectively from the perspective of various bel canto glosses since the it outlines the essential elements of *le bellezze del canto*: expressive control of nuance through *accento*, color, and sensitivity to text and characterization; flexibility of voice; the ability to ornament; purity and sweetness of tone; perfect intonation; clarity of diction; and the perfect joining of the vocal registers—all in broad accord with the teachings of Tosi and Mancini.[99]

Tosi and Mancini themselves wrote in the wake of the seventeenth-century preference for male chest singing, which generally endured until the early to mid-eighteenth century. By the third quarter of the eighteenth century and even before, chest singing overlapped with and was being superseded by a new penchant for high notes that accompanied a considerable expansion upward of the normative range. The ambitus of a ninth or tenth typical in music of Caccini's time had expanded to two octaves and more, and the general tessitura (the lie of the voice) rose accordingly. The trend had already seen significant development by the era of Alessandro Scarlatti about 1680, and developed further with early Handel, when the normal compass reached as much as a twelfth, continuing outward to the two-octave span with Jommelli and Mozart.[100] Some castrati, like Egiziello who sang for Handel up to high c''', two octaves above middle c, must have emphasized the head, though the practice was attacked by elements of the older generation who prized the purity of the "voce naturale."

With this enlarged mid-eighteenth-century range came a public that clamored for virtuosic *passaggi*, despite the protests of old-timers and new reformers. Meta-

EXAMPLE 9. Christoph Willibald Gluck, aria "Contro il destin, che fremo" from *Antigono* (Rome, 1756), part of Demetrio written for Ferdinando Mazzanti, mm. 16–49.

stasio, for instance, began inveighing against singers who sounded like piccolos, violins, and cicadas, grumbling to Farinelli in 1756 that the castrato Ferdinando Mazzanti (ca. 1725–1805?) was "a great violinist in falsetto." Mazzanti had a range that went regularly up to d′′′ and a very high lie of his tessitura, at the high end of which he performed fancy figurations, all of which are on display in his aria "Contro il destin, che freme" from Gluck's *Antigono* (Ex. 9).[101]

Metastasio later objected that generally singers, instead of "working to make their voices firm, robust, and sonorous," were studying to make them "light and flexible," cautioning, "A voice that is threadbare and weakened . . . by arpeggios, trills, and leaps *[volate]* can cause the pleasure . . . of marvels . . . but never the kind of pleasure instantaneously produced by the vigorous physical impression of a clear, firm, and robust voice that moves *[scuote]* the organs of our hearing."[102] The word I translate as "threadbare" *(sminuzzata)* is revelatory. It implies a sound that is acoustically shaved down or thinned out, a less resonant voice, probably not very blended and less rich in overtones than the voices loved by Metastasio and the composers of his youth, such as Bononcini, Handel, Vivaldi, Vinci, Pergolesi, and Leo.

Even Mancini continued to valorize the unforced "voce naturale" in the 1770s, while teaching "voce di testa" and "voce di petto" in fairly equal measure, unlike Tosi's predecessors, whose cultivation may not have been so explicit.[103] By the eighteenth century, as castrati produced ever more elaborate coloratura, especially in the second quarter of the century, head voice became a necessity, as Tosi declares outright for notes a ninth above middle c.[104] All this heralds a new age of the head voice, even for those already mutilated, and it certainly marks the indisputable arrival of an age that, for singers castrated and not, accorded equal stature to multiple registers.

MESSA DI VOCE AND SMOOTHING THE PASSAGGIO

Mancini uses "falsetto" interchangeably with and as a stand-in for "voce di testa" (article 4, "Della voce di petto, e di testa, o sia falsetto?"). We have seen that only one pedagogue in the eighteenth century agitated to apply "falsetto" to a "mixed," presumably blended middle register, namely the Berliner Agricola, in his annotated translation of Tosi into German of 1757. The later Italians Mancini and Vincenzo Manfredini surely did not know the translation but would have ignored the suggestion anyway, and only with Garcia was falsetto placed between head and chest, for his own reasons (Ex. 4).

Important for our story is that the pedagogical eruption of terminology, led by an expansion of vocal compass, underlies ever-increasing pressures on vocal registers, as voices of different physiological training and capacity entered the profession. Yet it's reasonable to suppose that already before the eighteenth century unwritten embellishments moved into pitch ranges, hence registers, that exceeded the hard and fast, fixed notational text and required sweeping breath control and command of pitch space. Here Bontempi writes of Baldassare Ferri:

> In addition to the clarity of his voice, the felicity of his passaggi, the beating of his trills, the agility with which he arrives sweetly at whatever pitch he wishes, after the extension of a very long and beautiful passaggio in a single measure, he had no need to take another breath. He began, without inhaling, a very long and beautiful trill, and from that passed to another passaggio longer and more vigorous than the first, without any movement whatsoever of his face, of his mouth, of his body, as immobile as a statue. The descent with a trill from half-step to half-step without any insecurity, and with a voice lightly reinforced from the high octave of a''' [a twelfth above middle c] to the a

below middle C... —an operation which, if not entirely impossible, was nevertheless of the greatest difficulty for any other worthy singer—was nothing to Ferri, since from this he passed without taking a breath to other trills, passaggi, and marvels of the art.

Dryly Bontempi added that such a thing is "not often heard or practiced."[105]

In the eighteenth century, the art of a Ferri was becoming more systematized, codified, written out, and perhaps explicitly inculcated, and was newly being written about as vocal practice. A single vocal technique was routinely taught to mitigate registral shifts and fortify virtually every other aspect of singing: the messa di voce, that gradual swelling and diminishing of a single held note that Evelyn remarked in Siface. Designed to smooth the joining of the registers and "cover" it, the messa di voce was an ever more intense focal point of a singer's training, even for those castrati who had as many as thirteen or more chest notes available.[106]

Tosi, like most others, enjoined its use for steadying the voice. Mancini deferred specific discussion of it until article 9, building up to it with chapters on registers, intonation, economy and support of breath, legato, and steadying the voice ("fermare la voce") because he focused on using it with sophisticated musical nuance. By contrast, primers and advanced treatises, solfeggi and *vocalizzi* almost invariably promoted it as the first of all singing exercises, as shown in its most rudimentary form in Tenducci's popular manual (see Ex. 10).[107] In 1810 Anna Maria Pellegrini Celoni also explained messa di voce as promoting sweetness of sound.[108] All in all, it was both a means to an end and the end itself, both the means and effect of a great artist.[109]

Well into Garcia's time, perfecting the messa di voce was not only the most effective way to smooth the passaggio but was used to perfect the voice in many other ways.[110] Singers typically practiced the messa di voce by beginning with pitches in or just under the passaggio, initiating a note with a lightly muscled quasi-head tone, swelling to a full-breathed adducted chest, and diminishing back to a quasi-head in order to adjust perfectly every smallest increment of resonance, transition, volume, color, and so forth. You can hear examples on this book's website as sung by Eugène de Creus and Marilyn Horne; and examples abound in the early twentieth century, by such singers as Sigrid Onégin, Rosa Ponselle, Ernestine Schumann-Heink, and Anna Nezhdanova. Practiced for many hours a week, the messa di voce was the ne plus ultra of eighteenth-century and earlier nineteenth-century singing manuals.[111] In 1810, the instruction manual of tenor Domenico Corri (1746–1825), a student of Porpora's who made a teaching career in London, pictured the messa di voce visually in his *Singer's Preceptor* as "the soul of music," showing how it was to be practiced on successive ascending semitones (Ex. 11).

When Handel rewrote the part of *Radamisto* for Senesino's much-anticipated debut in London in December of 1720, he left us a good example of the castrato's

EXAMPLE 10. First exercise from *Instruction of Mr. Tenducci to His Scholars* ([London]: Longman and Broderip, 1785), p. 1, showing the messa di voce to be practiced by beginning students. Image courtesy of Harvard College Library.

ability to deliver a perfect messa di voce. The aria substituted for Senesino in act 1, scene 6, "Perfido, di a quell'empio tiranno," included a sustained bb'' of three measures, after which he began to trill on the same tone, continuing for another three measures before tumbling through six measures of figuration to a "low" bb' (Ex. 7). The previous April Margherita Durastanti's aria in the same position, "Ferite, uccidete, oh numi del ciel!," had included "only" a four-measure sostenuto (mm. 75–78).[112] Whether women were sufficiently trained in the early eighteenth century to equal the gymnastic feats of top castrati or had sufficient lung capacity to do so—indeed, whether any singers did—is unclear (cf. again Ex. 6). In the late eighteenth century those castrati who survived on stage were still doing elaborate passagework and other vocal feats. Many scores written for Luigi Marchesi attest to that, as do transcriptions made by Czech composer Václav Pichl of different ornaments Marchesi sang on a single melody line on four different nights (see Ex. 12). But by that time a great deal of evidence shows that the most athletic and flexible female singers were too, notably Marchesi's rival Nancy Storace (cf. chapter 5 and

EXAMPLE 11. Demonstration of a soprano singing a messa di voce, followed by exercises for practicing it. From Domenico Corri, *The Singer's Preceptor* (1810; London: Chappell & Co., 1811), p. 14. Corri, a London-based tenor and voice teacher, was the last pupil of Nicola Porpora, who had earlier taught Farinelli, Caffarelli, and Salimbeni. Newberry Library, Chicago.

Ex. 23). There was an upping the ante of levels of difficulty as the century wore on, and no doubt a transformation that came about as women increasingly trained with castrati and learned from their singing techniques.

The messa di voce was in any case not simply an aid to agility singing but also to adagio, spianato, or decorated singing and other practices, including crescendos and diminuendos, all of which required particularly good breath control. Key to singing "on the breath," the messa di voce was also prerequisite to executing a perfect legato, as Crescentini wrote. You can hear the continued effect of such practice on breath and dynamic control and focused air flow on this book's website in tenor Tito Schipa's 1913 recording of Puccini's "E lucevan le stelle," with a phenomenally graduated diminuendo extending to a long-held pianississimo of a kind he delivered at the immense Teatro Colón in Buenos Aires but is rarely if ever heard in opera houses today.

PORTAMENTO

Whether castrati aimed to achieve a consistent timbre and weight throughout the entire ambitus or simply to smooth actual shifts in register remains an open question. Crutchfield infers from his studies of early vocal recordings that while attempts to smooth the passaggio were universal, there was little effort to disguise the register of the voice, whether in head or chest, even among female singers (and likewise in male singers who did not use a forced chest), and even within the very first generation of vocal recording artists born in the 1830s and 1840s who were chronologically closest to castrati.[113] Head and chest were sites of difference, head presumed to move more nimbly and sound lighter than chest.[114] Perfecting the messa di voce allowed singers to master expressive transitions between notes of different registers, which in turn was indivisible from the practice of portamento—what Mancini called "a correct and limpid graduation," "almost imperceptibly gliding between intervening pitches."[115] John Potter has similarly demonstrated, through recourse to notational, verbal, and recorded evidence, that from at least the eighteenth through the early- to mid-twentieth centuries singers utilized pervasively something related to what we think of as portamento by connecting notes in different registers or areas of vocal response.[116] "Portamento" had a more generalized meaning than it does now, suggesting bearing or carriage (as in "come si porta qualcuno"), more like *comportamento,* with affinities to notions of behavior disseminated in conduct books.[117] By means of portamento, a continuous subtle adjustment of volume, timbre, and vowels promoted elegant nuance and smooth movement through floating lines of melody.

As early as 1620 Francesco Rognoni gave an exercise with trills made on every eighth note of a dotted-note scale, which seems to have served to develop portamento in support of legato singing (Ex. 13). Two centuries later, in the wake of ever

EXAMPLE 12. Four different sets of ornaments on the aria "Cara negli occhi tuoi" from Zingarelli's opera *Pirro, re di Epiro* (Milan, 1792), sung on different nights by the castrato Luigi Marchesi. The ornaments were transcribed by Czech composer Václav Pichl. Adapted from Will Crutchfield, "Voices," in *Performance Practice: Music after 1600*, edited by Howard Mayer Brown and Stanley Sadie (New York: Norton, 1989), 303–4.

EXAMPLE 12. *(continued)*

more detailed notational habits, Corri provided amateur singers with numerous written-out examples of portamento, akin to what Garcia, in his own versions, supplied as exercises de rigueur under the rubric of the *port de voix* (Ex. 14).

Just one of many instances of written-in portamenti in Corri's 1810 tutor and anthology compilations shows amateurs where to use portamento in singing. No professional singer would have needed to be shown. Like the messa di voce and the appoggiatura, portamento was fundamentally an unwritten way of ensuring "fluidity in nuance and dynamics,"[118] which Corri's anthologies supplied to aid amateurs and aspiring professionals. Try singing Corri's version of Haydn's song "She Never Told Her Love" with and without the written-in portamenti (Ex. 15). With them, Haydn's modestly leap-filled melody takes wing with a balletic grace, lifting off and landing on softly pillowed surfaces; without them the tune will likely sound foursquare and wooden.[119]

There were specific names for the movements of sliding upward or downward with all the intervening pitches fully joined: *scivolo* (slide) and *strascino* (drag).[120] Both Tosi and Mancini largely disapproved of using them pervasively, wanting portamento to be a subtle affair, sparing in Tosi's case, and not spanning more than a fourth. A Paduan physician and naturalist Antonio Vallisnieri wrote a satiric sonnet pretending to pan Farinelli for his *passaggio scivolato*.

> To take a painful asthmatic breath
> and mask passaggi on this and that;
> to run out of breath after four arias;
>
> an uncertain trill and Neapolitan taste;
> passaggi neither *battuto* nor *strascinato*:
> tell me if that is not Farinelli?[121]

EXAMPLE 13. Exercises for practicing how to carry the voice ("portar la voce"), from Francesco Rognoni's *Selva di vari passaggi* (Milan, 1620), fol. 1r.

EXAMPLE 14. Manuel Garcia Jr.'s exercises for practicing *port de voix* (portamento), from his *Traité complet de l'art du chant en deux parties* (Paris: E. Troupenas et Cie. 1847), p. 32. Digital Collections and Archives, Tufts University.

EXAMPLE 15. Portamenti notated for singing Haydn's canzonetta "She Never Told Her Love," as given by Domenico Corri in his *Volume Second of Corri's Singing Preceptor consisting of English, Scotch, Italian & French Songs, Duets &c &c. Embellished with Cadenzes [sic], Graces & Other Ornaments, and with an Accompaniment for the Piano Forte. Being a Continuation as a Fifth Volume of the Well Known Publication Entitled Corri's Work Dedicated to the Queen* (London: Silvester and Longman, [1810–11]), p. 34. Newberry Library, Chicago.

Evidence suggests that in the nineteenth century portamento became increasingly extravagant, perhaps closer to Moreschi's to judge from numerous early recordings and from the bad name it eventually acquired among modernists, until it was no longer amenable at all. This lavishness is adumbrated in a few attempts to notate the ornaments and nuances made by castrati in the early nineteenth century. Portamento indications proliferate in Garcia's edition of Crescentini's insertion aria "Ombra adorata, aspetta" (see excerpt in Ex. 29) and in his version of Giambattista Velluti's performance of Morlacchi's aria "Caro suono lusinghier" from *Tebaldo ed Isolina,* where it is notated at intervals as large as the octave and ninth (see Ex. 16). It is anachronistic to call this abuse or excess, because it was still cherished in Moreschi's time and practiced by most, even though the stylization of portamento changed over time and place. A veristic portamento could hardly have been like a Handelian one or like a bel canto-type sung by Velluti, yet the basic practice and term remained in place.

Prima facie, the history of vibrato might be thought to run parallel to that of portamento, but until the second half of the twentieth century, or at least no earlier than the 1920s or 1930s, this is evidently untrue in the sense in which modern singers understand vibrato. Most early twentieth-century singers used an audible vibrato only intermittently, as an ornament, as did string players. Jascha Heifetz famously made a violinistic specialty out of "chilling" white notes that crescendoed from what David Schoenbaum has described as "zero to glass-shattering intensity, with all intervening degrees."[122] In the present context, Schoenbaum's description is jolting. Given the vibrato in Moreschi's *Ave Maria,* which, although intermittent at first, is often lush and plentiful, we can hardly apply to his singing Lang's comment that the Sistine castrati he heard had "white" voices of straight tone and "cold neutrality," a hearing that can only manifest Lang's own psychic horror of the encounter.[123]

HIGH NOTES

However much the relationship of Moreschi's voice to earlier castrati remains a cipher, it's intriguing that above d" it borders on a glassiness familiar from the near "pure head" sound of some older coloratura singers such as Amelita Galli-Curci, Luisa Tetrazzini, or even the lighter-voiced Lily Pons. Perhaps we have a clue about why from a proximate source. In 1922 the great French soprano Emma Calvé (1858–1942) wrote in her autography *My Life* about venturing over to hear the Sistine Chapel choir in late summer 1891 during her time off from rehearsing the part of Suzel in Mascagni's *L'amico Fritz* (premiered October 31, 1891). There she became enchanted with the voice of its castrato-director, the towering Domenico Mustafà (1829–1912), and asked him by and by she if she could take lessons with him.

EXAMPLE 16. Portamenti in Garcia's edition of Morlacchi's romanza from *Tebaldo ed Isolina* as sung by Giambattista Velluti and printed in Garcia's *Traité complet de l'art du chant en deux parties* (Paris, 1847), 103. Digital Collections and Archives, Tufts University.

He had an exquisite high tenor voice, truly angelic, neither masculine nor yet feminine in type—deep, subtle, poignant in its vibrant intensity.... He had certain curious notes which he called his fourth voice—strange, sexless tones, superhuman, uncanny! At our first lesson ... the first question I asked was how I might learn to sing those heavenly tones.[124]

So far so good, but listen to his answer: "It's quite easy ... You have only to practice with your mouth tight shut for two hours a day. At the end of ten years, you may possibly be able to do something with them." Though reportedly the feat ended up requiring from her a mere three years of hard labor, she says she succeeded in making these special notes part of her own registral/timbral palette.[125]

What was this "fourth voice"? Calvé glosses it as "heavenly" and genders Mustafà's voice as something amphibious—"angelic, neither masculine nor yet feminine." She decisively connects both her hearing of them and her learning to sing them with a castrato. In a later work, her diary *Sous tous les ciels j'ai chanté . . . Souvenirs*—published in 1940, when she was eighty-two, though presumably written much earlier—she calls them "flute tones" and notes that their "thinness" (or tenuousness, "tenuité"), "lightness, and pretty tone" "let her go up very high," to d′′′, e′′′, and f′′′, with "great sweetness," adding that they recall the thin sound of violin harmonics that Lilli Lehmann talks about in a chapter from her 1902 vocal treatise on very high singing.[126]

Now "flute tones" could not have been unique to Mustafà, or to castrati in general. In fact, mechanically speaking, if we understand flute tones strictly as notes that are pure head or close to pure head beginning in the octave two octaves above middle c, it's quite possible that he never used them at all. I wonder if he may have produced high, "otherworldly" sounding notes that were *perceptible* as flute tones, or facsimiles thereof, without recourse to a special technique.[127] Perhaps at age sixty-two, when he taught Calvé, he found them vocally useful; or perhaps they were fitting in a setting where romantic religious repertoire was sung in a the tradition of Roman chapels, a tradition to which we largely lack direct aural access.

Regardless, Calvé's description is precise enough to make fairly clear the mechanism of what she learned. Anyone can produce such tones, at least clumsily, by humming high up on the consonant *m*, which causes an involuntary depression of the soft palate in the back recesses of the mouth. (Try this, and view this book's website, where you can see a video overlay from *The Singer's Voice* by Robert Caldwell and Joan Wall of an MRI taken of a soprano who sings the *m* sound with a visibly lowered soft palate. The singer's mouth is closed, so the airflow fails to escape from her mouth and instead exits from her nose.)[128] The resulting sound resembles a water glass rubbed with a finger (something certainly thought "otherworldly" by George Crumb and other composers).[129] Sometimes referred to as "suprafalsetto" or as "whistle tone," the sound emerges through a very thin use of the vocal folds and is sometimes used by singers as a special effect. On this book's website you can hear Patricia Barber singing suprafalsetto as a special effect in a setting of Maya Angelou's "Mourning Grace." As Angelou's poem asks from the grave, "Will you have the grace to mourn for me?" the voice rises scalewise from e♭′ to f′′ and again on the next octave from e♭′′ to f′′′, transitioning to fluted notes on the long closed vowel *ē* of *me*—an otherworldly vowel that is amenable to being sung in very high tones, as Lilli Lehmann points out (and all singers know)—and continues in a fluted vocalise to a♭′′′.[130]

Calvé uses flute tones in Félicien David's "Charmant oiseau" (from *La perle du Brésil*), with programmatic effect.[131] She first imitates the flute part in a richly mixed head voice and then continues at higher pitch in a suprafalsetto—presumably Mustafà's "fourth voice." A bit later the "fourth voice" returns in arpeggios that take her up as high as c′′′ (see the book's website). In truth, then, the masterful Calvé, at the time of the recording sixty-two as Mustafà had been when he taught her, was not really scaling such great heights but creating the effect of doing so while letting the flute take the highest pitches a third or sixth above her. Yet her high c′′′'s are unmistakably fluted.[132]

Having probably had in older age the thinner, flexible vocal folds of a castrato and having sung primarily in chapel settings, Mustafà likely never had to take weight off the voice by softening his vocal muscles to make high ethereal sounds—something a large-voiced prima donna singing verismo roles, with no prior training in suprafalsetto, would have had to work hard to do.[133] Hence my conjecture that he did not teach Calvé to repeat mechanically what he was doing but instead gave her a way to imitate it, adapting his technique to her own instrument to create the effect. Further, in *My Life* she gives a hyperbolic description of her reaction to his advice that she spend ten years humming with her mouth shut tight for two hours a day.[134]

> That was hardly encouraging!
> "A thousand thanks!" I exclaimed. "At that rate, I will never learn! It takes too much patience!"
> Nevertheless with the tenacity which is a fundamental part of my character, I set to work. My first efforts were pitiful. My mother assured me that they sounded like the miauling of a sick cat! At the end of two years, however, I began to make use of my newly acquired skill; but it was not until the third year of study that I obtained a complete mastery of the difficult art.
> These special notes, which I have used since then with great success, are rarely found in the ordinary run of voices. I have tried repeatedly to develop them in my pupils; but, in spite of hard work and close application, I have never found one pupil who has been able to imitate them.[135]

Imitate indeed. Much as Calvé tried to get her pupils to imitate her flute notes (and as Moreschi made the falsettist Domenico Mancini imitate him), the account reinforces the idea that Mustafà had Calvé imitate his "fourth tones." The comparison of a castrato voice to a flute, though mechanically dubious, is not totally unknown in writings about castrati either. Ancillon said of Mommo (also known as Jeronimo or Momo) that his voice was "so soft, and ravishingly mellow, that nothing can better represent it than the Flute-stops of some Organs," which he sometimes imagined were "not unlike the gentle Fallings of Water" he had often heard in Italy.[136] The sound in his ear may have been akin to Marin Mersenne's "eunuch flute," used to characterize a mirliton (otherwise, membranophone), a seemingly toylike device, like a kazoo, that causes a very fine membrane to vibrate and combine with the sound of a player's voice.[137] And in the last years of the castrati, Enrico Panzacchi implied that a solo soprano castrato at Saint Peter's whom he had heard in the 1880s—probably Giovanni Cesari (1843–1904)—had a very light phonation in the upper register, with relaxed, almost effortless production above the unforced chest:

> Imagine a voice that combines the sweetness of the flute and the lively mellifluousness of the human larynx, a voice that rises, light and spontaneous, as a skylark flies through the air when it's inebriated by the sun; and then when it seems that this voice must be poised on the highest vertices of the ultra-high range, takes further flight, and rises and rises, always with equal lightness, equally spontaneous, without the least expression of force, without the slightest indication of artifice, of searching about, of effort.[138]

If Moreschi's pitches are not "flute tones," some top notes in a light head voice sound rather flutelike in comparison with Patti's and Melba's head tones, which project much more strongly than his. Moreschi's upper register sounds pure, light, and lightly blended compared to his chest, yet the contrast was likely acceptable, perhaps even taken for granted, in the tradition that preceded him (see this book's website for an example).[139] Keeping the voice open and pure meant allowing for its natural registral differences—strength in the lower register and lightness and agility in the upper—and ensuring that the vocal apparatus remained unconstrained.[140]

LAST NOTES

So do Moreschi's recordings give us any acoustical purchase on a now lost bel canto castrato sound, however mediated by history and technology? Does a residue survive? Heard through a glass darkly, I think so, though it has taken me many years to take the recordings seriously. Certainly if we consider a number of other artists from the era of early recording, their connection to eighteenth- and early nineteenth-century singing traditions seems patent from their fine shadings of color, expressive nuance, clear vocal production and diction, and legato singing, "on the breath"—singers such as Tito Schipa, Bidú Sayão, Mattia Battistini, and Lucrezia Bori, to name a few.[141] Singers of the early twentieth century might even be very roughly divided into those whose training handed down a bel canto remainder and those whose training followed more the modern methods and styles associated with Verdian declamatory style. How it was possible for such a genealogy to have endured, however transformed, is a matter suggested as recently as 1987 by Lucie Manén in her book on bel canto teaching, which reports that she learned to sing from a pupil of the famed Pauline Viardot. Viardot was the famous mid-nineteenth-century singer and teacher who was sister to both Maria Malibran and Manuel Garcia the younger and daughter of Garcia the elder, Rossini's first Almaviva in 1816. Just five years earlier Garcia the elder had studied in Naples with tenor Giovanni Ansani, whose own voice was beloved by composers in the late eighteenth century for its mix of sweetness and power.[142] Manén's genealogy may be willful or imaginary, reaching back two hundred years over a mere five generations, but can we discount the notion that some DNA of vocal production might be documented if only we had better means of tracking it? If we peer through our binoculars from the other end, similar questions emerge. Crescentini was taught by Lorenzo Gibelli of the Bolognese school developed by Bernacchi, whose own legacy extended back to Pistocchi; and Crescentini, in turn, taught singers in Bologna, Paris, and Naples, including the Rossinian Colbran, as noted above.[143] Up through about the 1930s to 1950s other such genealogies of teachers and students may have existed, with apparent traceable connections if not continuous lines of dissemination, which can be grossly differentiated from genealogies of the "voce di forza" made famous by Duprez. The golden-voiced tenor Beniamino Gigli, who reigned supreme at the Metropolitan in the 1920s, demonstrates these distinct lineages with comical concision in the 1936 film *Du bist mein Gluck,* when he caricatures the vocal production of a German singing pupil who pushes too hard on his larynx (see this book's website).[144]

Gigli was much vaunted in the 1920s for the flexible chiaroscuro of his voice, its darkening and lightening vocal color, and for always leaving a good deal of voice in reserve.[145] Castrati of Moreschi's milieu were all central Italian and taught by local chapelmasters, most of them (Moreschi, Ritarossi, Cesari, and Vissani) by Gaetano Capocci, organist at San Giovanni in Laterano and composer of solo religious music whose teaching may have owed something to such a tradition. Certainly Moreschi's inheritance, if it is that, is mixed with verismo: lavish portamenti that turn into acciaccaturas (crushed notes) and notes rapidly approached from an octave below; scooping glissandi, glottal attacks, chesty white sound, *h* sounds in some legato phrases, little sobs, and in general "a tear in every note," as put by Lillie de Hegermann-Lindencrone (1844–1928)—originally Lillie Greenough of Cambridge, Massachusetts, and later known as the singer Lillie Moulton, who trained under Garcia and after marrying spent time in Rome as the wife of a Danish diplomat.[146] All these mannerisms were used by other singers of the time, but especially those who specialized in Mascagni, Puccini, and other veristic composers, whose music was highly fashionable in Moreschi's Rome.[147] What we may have in Moreschi, then, is a highly mediated yet valuable fragment of the past, with faint echoes of a more distant mode of singing but clearer evidence of a bygone vocal physiology.

. . .

Calvé adds a phrase I've neglected until now: those "fourth tones" she heard in Mustafà were "strange, sexless . . . , superhuman, uncanny!" "Fourth tones" in this gloss become something like "third kinds," notes that exceed the usual registral triptych conventionally described for human voices, much as humans can exceed or defy a "typical" sexual dyad. Fourth tones are strange and other. White and cool like Calvé's flute tones, they lie for her beyond nature and sex, beyond earth, beyond knowing. Her description of the "exquisite . . . voice" of Mustafà as "truly angelic, neither masculine nor . . . feminine," has a familiar ring. Mrs. Hegermann-Lindencrone went often to hear vocal performances at the Sistine Chapel and elsewhere: "I sit entranced, listening in the deepening twilight to the heavenly strains of Palestrina, Pergolesi and Marcello. Sometimes the soloists sing Gounod's 'Ave Maria' and Rossini's 'Stabat Mater.' . . . A choir of men and boys accompanies them in 'The Inflammatus' [sic], *where the high notes of M[oreschi]'s tearful voice are almost supernatural.*"[148] Hearing Moreschi often, in concerts probably organized by Capocci at the home of her friend Mrs. Charles Bristed (Grace) of New York, she remarked (here the fuller context of the quote above):

> The Pope's singers are the great attraction . . . her *salon* is the only place outside of the churches where one can hear them. . . . The famous Moresca, who sings at the Laterano, is a full-faced soprano of some forty winters. He has a tear in each note and a sigh in each breath. He sang the Jewel Song in [Gounod's] "Faust," which seemed horribly out of place. Especially when he asks (in the hand-glass) if he is really Marguerita, one feels tempted to ask "Macchè" [certainly not!] for him.

Hegermann-Lindencrone's alternating fascination and distress in the face of Moreschi's singing resonates, with far less violence, with Paul Henry Lang's. What "shocked" him when he heard those "grown men sing in the stratosphere" was not just that their voices "had absolutely no resemblance to a woman's voice" but that they were "white, clear, and powerful." In Lang's memory their voices were white as death, conjuring up a psychic, Freudian death, a dysphonic aura marked by an overpoweringly frigid lack of emotion. He shows his hand just prior to mentioning the concert at which he purportedly heard them:

> One of the cardinal rules of the instruction [of castrati] is that for several years the pupil was not permitted to sing any music with a text. The teachers did not want him to be distracted by emotions from his primary task of faultless singing. . . . Obviously the castrato was considered a sort of virtuoso instrumentalist of the larynx, rather than a singer in the sense we understand the term; he was an infallible singing machine. . . .

It is significant that whenever a castrato was praised, it was the marvelous flexibility and accuracy of his voice that were held up for admiration—that is, his extraordinary technique; the sensuous beauty of the voice and the power of emotional communication that we expect from a singer were seldom mentioned. The castrato was in fact an *outré* countertenor; thus his voice had a quality fundamentally different from those of the women who are substituted for him today. The cold neutrality and lack of color of his voice were intensified by the demand, expressed by Tartini among others, that he sing without vibrato.[149]

. . .

What really could Lang have heard? After the pope officially banned further castrati from entering his chapel, along with much of the solo music that they had participated in singing throughout the previous century—standbys like Rossini's *Crucifixus* from the *Misse solennelle* and solo church music by the likes of Capocci—Moreschi went on singing there until his thirty-year tenure was completed in 1913. Until shortly before his death in 1922 he sang in other papal churches in Rome. The only other castrato to have sung anywhere near as late was Vincenzo Sebastianelli (1851–1919), whom De Angelis described as having a very high voice but poor intonation,[150] but there is no evidence of his having toured at this late date either.

In November 2006, when I first went looking in Rome for twentieth-century castrati who might have drifted into traveling choirs, I was led to the home of Luciano Luciani, a papal singer and friend to some of the families of papal singers from the last few centuries. He has assembled an important archival collection of Sistine Chapel materials from the late nineteenth and twentieth centuries and reorganized other materials now held at the modern archives of the Cappella Musicale Pontificia "Sistina" on via Monte della Farina. At his home are scores, diaries, photographs, newspaper clippings, letters, treasured objects, and even recordings, which have contributed substantially to volumes 6 and 7 of Giancarlo Rostirolla's series Storia della cappella musicale pontificia.

Among the treasures of his collection are original posters from performances given by a Roman vocal quartet (SATB), the Quartetto Vocale Romano, that toured extensively in 1919, always presented as singers from the Sistine Chapel and displayed in choir robes. Among other places, they sang at Notre Dame Cathedral in Paris on June 20, in Grand Rapids, Michigan, presented by the Business Girls' Cooperative, on October 1, and in the All-Star Concerts series in Des Moines, Iowa, on November 6. The soprano and alto were close to Moreschi, with whom they were well acquainted as younger colleagues. On this book's website you can listen to them sing an excerpt from Capocci's "Cor meum, et caro mea," a Communion text sung with organ accompaniment for a recording made in the United States in 1919 as part of the Lyric Record series of the Lyraphone Company—a very rare recording, a copy of which was given to Luciani by the then ninety-three-year-old son of the alto.¹⁵¹

It is amazing to hear elements of Moreschi's vocal production transmitted clear as a bell in the singing of the soprano, and to hear the strength of the alto's upper register. What surprised me on first hearing the recording was that neither the alto nor the soprano is a castrato, as you can see plainly in Fig. 31. Nor was the quartet officially *of* the Cappella Sistina, though it was consistently billed that way by promoters. New York's *Sun Times* made a direct query to the Vatican about the quartet's status vis-à-vis the Cappella Sistina and followed up on September 6, 1919, with a piece titled "Both Choirs Lack Vatican Sanction":

> Careful investigation by THE SUN yesterday revealed that neither of the rival musical organizations contending for public favor in concerts to be given in Carnegie Hall on Sunday and Tuesday nights, September 14 and September 16, has as yet the official sanction of the Vatican. Both "The Vatican Choirs," a chorus of sixty or seventy voices, and the "Quartet of Soloists from the Sistine Choir" come with high recommendations as to their musical ability from distinguished persons in Rome to distinguished persons here, and men familiar with the Roman choirs say that both, in their respective fields, are a notable accession for American concert audiences.¹⁵²
>
> The "Vatican Choirs" have been advertising their concert as "the only official body of Vatican singers." The "quartet" has been describing itself as "the only real and legitimate quartet of soloists from the Sistine Choir." The managers of each concert yesterday exchanged sharp statements. Each admits that the other may be producing a very creditable musical performance but objects violently to the mutual assertion that each is exclusively of the Vatican.
>
> . . .
>
> The quartet, consisting of Alessandro Gabrielli, Ezio Cecchini, Luigi Gentili and Augusto Dos Santos, which is to sing on Sunday night, September 14, carries a letter from Lorenzo Perosi, perpetual director of the Cappella of St. Peter in the Vatican, asserting that they have "for years and years sung in the Sistine Chapel, meeting with general satisfaction." Men familiar with the choirs at Rome assert, however, that these men have been soloists brought in on gala occasions to augment the regular Sistine Choir.¹⁵³

Also on September 6, *Musical America* carried a feature titled "Managers Seeking Light on Visit of the Roman Singers," which extended the war of words and documents alongside a large picture of Ernest Bloch, who had just won the 1919 Chamber Music Competition.¹⁵⁴

. . .

Haböck writes that the voice of the falsettist Alessandro Gabrielli, a singer in the Quartetto Vocale Romano whom he encountered on his last visit to Rome in 1914, was "powerful, full, and well balanced." He also notes that all of the castrati employed at the Sistine Chapel were sopranos and that the altos were all falsettists

FIGURE 31. Poster announcing a performance by the Quartetto Vocale Romano Gabrielli-Gentili, Grand Rapids, Michigan, October 1, 1919. Presented by the Business Girls' Co-operative Club. Image of poster in the private collection of Luciano Luciani, Fiumicino (Rome).

(which was probably true through most or all of the nineteenth century; Gabrielli was a soprano in the chapel only from the 1920s, and he joined officially in 1935).[155]

Perhaps Paul Henry Lang recalled what he thought he had heard or what he wished he had heard. Clearly he also set down what he feared in both the recollection and the wish: the uncanny whiteness, the indefinable gender, and a cold instrumentality that preceded language. But between what he wrote and what he heard there is a large gap. His account has thus become no more than an odd footnote in my files, yet it's a peculiarly precious one because it prompts a provocative question: How might we imagine the castrato's voice in the mind's ear from mere palimpsests?

4

Castrato De Luxe

Blood, Gifts, and Goods

BRAVURA, COMPETITION, STRUGGLE

Sometime during the 1720s the starry image of the castrato became entwined with the sound of a fiery allegro. Not that fiery allegros were new at the time, but they had not been written through with agility figuration, often instrumental in kind, nor had the public imagination been so singularly held in their thrall. Most of the castrati from that period who loom largest in memory were renowned for such singing: Bernacchi, Senesino, Carestini, Farinelli, and Caffarelli. The capacity endured in a number of later castrati. Aprile and Marchesi were expert in it, as were Crescentini and Velluti in the nineteenth century, though the instrumental style had largely fallen out of favor after the 1770s at the latest. Not all preferred agility singing or were preferred in it, nor was it the acme of the art for many connoisseurs. But for legions of listeners in the shank of the eighteenth century, it was the thing that bathed the castrato in stardust.

Bound up with the agility craze was a kind of vocal potlatch, promoted by steeply rising numbers of commercial theaters with attendant increases in demands for professional singers. Corri summed up the situation in a one-paragraph history of singing that prefaced his *Singer's Preceptor*. Singing was brought to an apogee with "the shake, turn, divisions, variations, cadences, &c &c," of recent times, which in turn had "given rise to bravura singing" and "a kind of contest amongst professors in the vocal art."[1] Corri dates a correlation between bravura singing and competition to the modern period when his own teacher, Porpora, was producing a number of Europe's most famous singers. Coincident with that period are records of legendary vocal feats and contests, notably Farinelli's: his youthful contest with a trumpeter as reported by Burney; his superhuman instrumental passaggi in Giacomelli's bird aria "Quell'usignolo," unmatchable for precision, endurance, and breath control; his heart-stopping messe di voce and coloratura in "Son qual nave"; and his explosions through two and a half octaves of martial passaggi and dazzling registral shifts, pitched like a warrior's blows on the battlefield in the role of the lover-prince Darius in his brother's "Qual guerriero in campo armato," immortalized by one encomiast as his "canto guerriero" (see Ex. 17).[2]

Of course bravura singing was not the only measure of victory and defeat. Competition was always frothing in the wake of virtuosity, whether bravura or pathetic, adorned or unadorned. Competition was a gauntlet the singer threw down to himself, to other singers, to obbligato instrumentalists, to listeners and their memories of past performances—a present performance as provocation to past ones (his own or others') intended to fulfill or exceed listeners' desires to be moved, amazed, or surprised. To sing as a virtuoso was to produce a reaction and expect a riposte, as each vocal spectacle tried to up the ante on countless rivals and predecessors, killing off some of the competition but also inciting feats more extraordinary than the last.[3] The repertory of feats seems to have been ever expanding, whether in sostenuti, long-breathed legato melodies, decorative arabesques, rocketing arpeggios, or vaulting leaps—the more the better. People said that that early master of the instrumental variety of bravura, Bernacchi, once when trading rounds of ornamented stanzas with the young Farinelli, even managed to best him by unexpectedly delivering a stanza of perfectly unadorned cantilena—or so wrote a Bolognese compatriot who portrayed him as a master competitor who could win his battles even when he'd met his match.[4]

As the technological stakes of singing rose toward the middle decades of the century—when many composed-out arias became lengthier and more filled with coloratura than they had ever been—numerous listeners who might once have yearned to be moved to tears seem to have become fixated with a kind of mouth-agape awe on sheer bravura, as if watching a man contend with devilish figures, leaps, runs, and roulades was not much different from gawking at cockfights or horseraces.

In *Opera and Sovereignty*, I argued that an important part of the job of an eighteenth-century composer was to script interaction between performers and audiences for spaces where only the most gladiatorial singers could command the attention of the crowd—large, often distracting places of entertainment or worship.[5] On this view, scores were not just intentional objects, nor were they just records of performances, presentation objects, or souvenirs, as the case may be, but rather they were templates for audience/performer interactions. In the case of agility arias and others with highly ornamented notation, they were scripts for great face-offs, made with a blackened graphic bravura that might be ascribed to the performer as easily as the scriptwriter. Witness Farinelli's own manuscript copy

EXAMPLE 17. Riccardo Broschi's aria "Qual guerriero in campo armato," written for Farinelli. Transcribed from D-Hs, MS ND VI 1078(2), pp. 80–87.

EXAMPLE 17. *(continued)*

EXAMPLE 17. *(continued)*

EXAMPLE 17. *(continued)*

of "Son qual nave ch'agitata," which was composed by his brother, Riccardo Broschi, but hubristically presented by Farinelli in 1753 to the Viennese Habsburgs with some of his own massive decorations and cadenzas rubricated in red ink along with five other arias that had made him a superstar (Ex. 18a and b).[6]

At midcentury, when the manuscript was dedicated, a composer was still a relatively low (and low-paid) man in the face of a virtuoso, especially a eunuch whose life was made for little else. In that sense we might assimilate the early to mid-eighteenth-century opera composer to Foucault's "author function," for, rather than being a hero in his own right, he occupied a domain of workmanly activity.[7] For the likes of a Farinelli, having a composer construct and record his pyrotechnics was a bit like having his own playwright double as his backroom dresser, someone who custom fit him for his opulent onstage exploits and made sure the props were neatly stored in the dressing room after the show. The hierarchy took a long time to change, although in time the composer became a more highly paid and more prestigious player, in part by becoming a more precise scriptwriter, producing ever longer and more detailed passaggi in longer and longer arias well after the 1750s, when reformers started vociferating against them. During the years 1770–73, when Mozart was in Italy writing bravura arias, entrance arias, and some big pathetic arias, his singers were doing astonishingly drawn-out passage-work (most of which he wrote out himself)—seven-, ten-, and twelve-minute arias instead of Handel's four- to five-minute ones—as were his contemporaries Mysliveček, Di Maio, Guglielmi, and the older Jommelli. Already by 1757 Agricola had remarked on how many more kinds of trills were being written down since Tosi's time.[8] By the 1760s to '70s, the pathetic and sensible had overtaken a big share of the market, enough that we might say that the reformers won out in the end. But technical virtuosity endured into the later eighteenth and nineteenth centuries, by some measures even increasing, now with a more variable, less mechanical surface.[9]

Until about the 1750s the top-drawer treble prodigies were mostly castrati, albeit with some famous exceptions (in particular Faustina Bordoni, Francesca Cuzzoni, and Vittoria Tesi). The 1750s saw the appearance of the astounding *virtuosa* and professionally independent prima donna Caterina Gabrielli (1730–96), a student of Porpora's who was fully the vocal, economic, and social equal of the very best of them, and the likes of Lucrezia Agujari (1741–83) and Anna de Amicis (ca. 1733–1813) shortly thereafter. Gabrielli's appearance coincided with both the peak of the bravura craze and the reformist counterreaction to it, the first salvo launched by Francesco Algarotti in 1755 (anonymously at first, in the debut edition of his *Saggio sopra l'opera*). Algarotti's treatise was more or less coincident with the early years of reform overseen by Niccolò Jommelli in Stuttgart, to which the composer moved in 1753 when his Francophile opera *Fetonte* was staged. The opera's emphasis on obbligato recitative, orchestral color, and ensembles was

EXAMPLE 18. Riccardo Broschi, excerpts from "Son qual nave" as included in Farinelli's presentation manuscript with his own ornaments rubricated, A-Wn MS 19111, dedicated to one of the Habsburg monarchs (addressee uncertain), either the Empress Maria Theresia or the Emperor Francis of Lorraine. Österreichische Nationalbibliothek, Vienna. Reproduced by permission.
a. Illuminated title page of the aria, one of six in the manuscript

EXAMPLE 18. *(continued)* b. Farinelli's final cadenza on the reprise of the A section

EXAMPLE 18b. *(continued)*

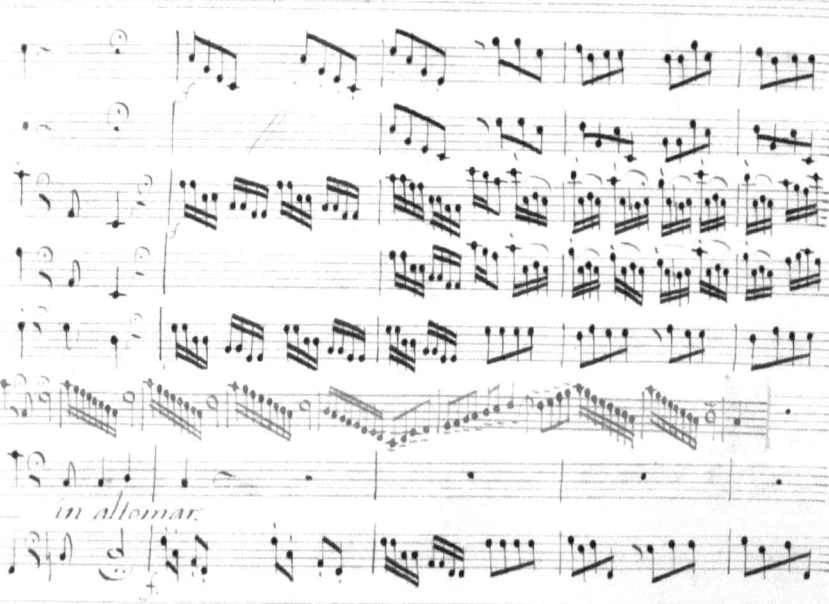

followed by the Parma reform project launched in 1759 by Tommaso Traetta, and by Gluck and Calzabigi's Viennese *Orfeo ed Euridice* (1762). The last ricocheted across Europe with rebounding effects that eventually helped change the nature of virtuosity by tipping the balance from a showy vocality to carefully differentiated musical languages of sentiment while also helping to tip the balance of power from singers to composers.

None of this means that castrati of the mid-seventeenth century could not carry off extravagantly arabesque-style virtuosity and long passage-work. It was hardly de rigueur that composers of the time write out detailed embellishments, and Ferri, Siface, and Matteuccio (Matteo Sassano, 1667–1737), to name three, were all famed for elaborately ornamental passage-work.[10] Embellishment was largely an art of performerly expressivity. In the later seventeenth century especially there were examples of arias amenable to scalar or instrumental figuration and other kinds of written-out ornamental figures and passage-work, especially for bellicose characters or warring situations. Herr discusses a number of examples from Noris and Legrenzi's *Totila* (Venice 1677) and Beregan and Legrenzi's *Il Giustino* (Venice 1683), many for castrati and many with trumpet obbligato.[11] Another written-out topos in the pre-Bernacchian era comes from the tradition of birdsong, which as far back as medieval song and sixteenth-century madrigals and chansons often had an instrumental nature; indeed, it had a direct instrumental counterpart in the seventeenth-century violin music of Marini, Walther, and especially Biber (notably his *Sonata violino solo representative* of ca. 1669).[12] It's clear in those cases how passaggi were executed, whereas undecorated ones invited new embellishments.[13]

. . .

A number of witnesses comment on the ubiquity and newness of mechanistic coloratura in the early to mid-eighteenth century. Tosi speaks of modern passaggi as a necessary evil, without "the power to touch the Soul," while conceding that they were important to winning listeners' "admiration."[14] Others explain that some singers became dependent on their written-out form. Caffarelli reputedly could not sing one night because he'd lost his cadenzas—quite possibly a tall tale but indicative of a scenario that was surely not isolated, though perhaps it was more common among uncastrated singers. Ironically, it seems we should take Metastasio seriously when he has the leading lady of his *intermezzo comico*, interpolated between the acts of his first opera, *Didone abbandonata*, tearing her hair out because she can't find an aria modern enough to have all the baubles written out for her: "This is *too difficult* because it's by an old composer," she cries. "No tremolos, no trills, no appoggiaturas. It's the very opposite of the modern school, which prettifies every word with passaggi."[15] What was "too difficult" for the prima donna in Metastasio's account was having to sing an unadorned melody, or moreover trying to embellish it without a dresser.

Did prescriptive virtuosity become self-perpetuating in eighteenth-century training, one technological "breakthrough" begetting another in a new technology of speeding runs and figures? The notion seems implicit in Burney's claim that, compared with all previous singers, Farinelli was like the racehorse Flying Childers (1714–41), who, undefeated throughout his career, epitomized the organic production of speed and the sensory addiction to it of his admirers.[16] If singers later in the century truly exceeded Farinelli, as Burney implied, they evidently had no technological equals among racehorses.

The rest of this chapter deals not with these musical facts per se, but with the reflexive relationship between deluxe singing and the perception, creation, and self-creation of certain top castrati as figures of luxury. What miraculous throat could sing the likes of "Qual guerriero"? What nobility of nature could translate the extremes of fury and pride into such powerful magic? How could Farinelli, that young eunuch, have bounded like a child at play over octaves, tenths, and twelfths, one after another, as if he were wired with springs, careening through running sixteenths, descending *volés* and spiccati, and relentless trills? What extraordinary bravado could unleash such singing?[17] But also, in the end, how was such a figure, peach-faced, infertile, gangly, and not of high birth, to be managed and manage himself in a deluxe world that implicated singing in nuanced transactions between gifts, goods, blood, and cash?

MAKING FAME

Farinelli is the exemplum of managing these dilemmas well. By age twenty-five he was a wealthy superstar who was fighting off rumors that he was addicted to gambling, which may well have been true.[18] Like others of his ilk, he graduated from having played female roles intermittently for several years early in his career (1722–25) to playing one hero, prince, and lover type after another, even if theatrically he was all Farinelli—Farinelli as the devoted lover (Medoro and Farnaspe), the conqueror (Quintus Maximus and Theseus), the loyal general (Aetius), and the son of unimpeachable innocence and devotion.[19] As lover/heroes, his onstage struggles to reconcile his love for a woman with love for his father, patria, or ruler (or all three, especially in his most famous role as Arbaces) connected his rising star with the realm of nobility and royalty. In this we could say that Farinelli paradigmatically extends the earlier status of the castrato as charismatic stage star. And indeed it is from the agonism of the operatic battlefield that our eighteenth-century hero rides to ever-greater fame and glory.

One eventual outcome of this trajectory might be to rise high enough to retreat from public view and into the king's or cardinal's private salon, as Farinelli did in 1737 by retiring from London public life into the inner sanctum of the court at Madrid (though not without invoking the ire of the British).[20] For always accompanying the transition from the public arena to the private luxury dwelling were shifts between two exchange modalities that can be glossed as giving-and-receiving and selling-and-buying. With entry into the space of private patronage, an eighteenth-century star castrato, who largely conducted business and contracted services within a cash nexus, had to renounce that modality, in principle if not in fact. Unlike payments for operatic performances or ad hoc church solos, which depended on legal contracts made by singers acting as free professional agents (or agents acting for them), payment for private services took place mostly in what Natalie Zemon Davis calls the "gift register,"[21] where exchange was decidedly asymmetrical in kind: song in return for fine gifts or silk purses. The castrato in this elite inner world could ascend to truly mythical renown only by giving and reciprocating with vocal skill, magnetism, and star quality. Endowed with sumptuous goods and great means he could become a man of luxe, though in the process he also faced an eminently early modern challenge—namely, of using what he received to transform himself in an attempt to surpass his very blood.

In the baldest terms this was also the problem of a newly emergent cult of celebrity, which coalesced in the early eighteenth century during the waning decades of the old regime, a cult that brought extraordinary beings into the public eye but made them ambivalent objects of public attention and exchange with the rich and powerful. Nowadays celebrity cults can be marked in much the same way.[22] But the question for a castrated man was whether he, of all beings, belonged among the rich and powerful, even if he had special powers to personify them.[23]

. . .

Imagine a castrato who hobnobs at the very highest level of social organization of the world around him, the world of monarchy, which is paradigmatic for this kind of exchange. His onstage representations and his approximations of the monarchical order offstage help consolidate the order that creates him. Yet in representing the king's realm he tears at its very fabric, for he gives the lie to the claim that an absolutist monarch is really what the term would claim—a *mon*arch, or mono-arch (that is, single archon or ruler). He serves as a representational substitute for the king and his domain by impersonating, metonymically, the king's war hero, his general, his ideal citizen, his son or future son-in-law, the prince or noble as torn lover, and sometimes even the ruler himself.

Virtually all theories of kingship agree about the role of substitution in ensuring the vitality of the monarchical function. In *Twinned Beings: Kings and Effigies in Southern Sudan, East India, and Renaissance France*, Burkhard Schnepel extends through three comparative case studies the classic argument that the twinning of the monarch—cleaving the role in two or shadowing it through an inverted or lesser double—is an inherent provision of kingship. (Nor are all his cases non-Western; one concerns early modern France.) The role of double might be filled by someone with more or less equal authority, but in any case he is a counterpart with a distinct function: he might be a high priest, co-ruler, or deity, or he might be a lowbrow, often parodistic imitator, classically the king's jester or fool. The role might, I would argue, be occupied by a substitute who temporarily assumes, within specific frames of experience, what Max Weber calls the charismatic form of power.[24] Any study of monarchy as such requires exacting study of these distinctions. But for present purposes, we can note that the metaphysics and pragmatics of monarchy require substitutions to fulfill the function and generally warrant the stability of royal power both spatially and temporally.[25]

The problem with substitutions is that they always risk usurping the ruler, betraying his true *non*-mono condition, whether we are talking about a larger world of cultural circulation or the theatrical frame. In our case, substitution risked displacing power onto the performer by draining charisma out of the monarch or the representational figure of monarchy. Nevertheless, in that one sense we can, I believe, view the castrato's role as consistent with the paradox of absolute rule itself, wherein power pretends to be monolithic but in reality is always split—typically with the ruler's (mixed) blessing—between rulers and others (siblings, elders, juniors, servants, generals, confidantes), even when the monarchical function is not explicitly "twinned." Were an absolute ruler not to sanction such divisions of power, how would he fulfill his duties save by personally conquering his every opponent on every battlefield? Effectively, the real form of absolute monarchy and its cognates—perhaps of all systems of power—is heteronomy, a diversification and division of the functions of power rather than their concentration in one supreme authority.

It is within and because of that function, I want to claim, that a star castrato could participate in a kind of virtual diarchy. He played the other half of rule, imitating or representing monarchy in performance but also embodying as proxy its affective and technological powers.[26] Of course I use the term "diarchy" loosely and suggestively here to point up a figurative division between bodies that stand on different sides of a power nexus in an ever-shifting and context-dependent system. For it seems to me that it was precisely because of that functional division, to which the otherness of the bravura castrato is integral, that he could assume a charismatic role that eighteenth-century sovereigns generally could not.

. . .

In 1723, just when Farinelli was starting to flourish along with such contemporaries as Bernacchi, Carestini, and Senesino, Tosi in his comments on executing passaggi ("divisions" in Galliard's English translation) gave an indirect explanation for one way in which castrati secured their charismatic powers by means of "admiration" and "applause." Passaggi, he explains, can be performed in one of two main ways, either *battuto* or *scivolato*, "marked" or "gliding," and the two differ fundamentally.[27] Wryly he declares that the *passaggio scivolato*, because of its slowness, should be called a *passo* rather than a passaggio (more like a "grace," as Galliard calls it, or even a "slur" rather than a division[28]—recall Vallisnieri's sonnet, which jokes deprecatingly that Farinelli's singing made "passi scivolati," as if to say that they were overly frivolous and trite).

The *passaggio battuto* is much harder to execute than a *passaggio scivolato*, and thus demands much more practice. In training routines for it, the teacher had to ensure very light motion of the voice and equality of placement, each note being moderately distinct from its neighbor (neither too joined nor too separated), no matter how fast the execution or how hard the leaps, no matter whether loud and soft notes were intermixed or whether there were trills. Marked agility could be found in descending passages or ascending ones, and Tosi noted that not all castrati could pull it off.[29] To sing a *passaggio battuto* required speed, but speed posed risks: not of singing too softly or lightly per se but of losing vocal *resonance*, the maintenance of which during passage-work was itself a virtuosic feat.[30] The whole beauty of the passaggio, said Tosi, "consists in being perfectly in tune, even, crystalline, equal, distinct, and quick." Even good students could not always achieve these standards and avoid the pitfalls. Reinforcing the point, Mancini, though generous enough to insist in 1777 that poor voices could usually be made good through good instruction and application, nevertheless qualified the point when it came to every aspect of agility singing. "One should not pretend to be able, even through study, to help ill-suited voices acquire the ornaments of singing—that is to say the trill and the mordent—and finally to [conceive] *gruppetti* or other ornaments, because such voices utterly lack all aptitude for them."[31]

Taken for granted, if not explicit, in these comments is that imperative to achieving good agility singing is excellent use of the breath: hence the many warnings by teachers against breathing during passage-work unless a phrase has ended.[32]

As compared with Tosi, Mancini moved away from simply discussing passaggi to talking about "agility" singing. For the purposes of printed pedagogy he broke agility singing down into finer and more nuanced types than Tosi had done while urging teachers to customize—or, rather, continue the tradition of customizing—solfeggio exercises for individual students. All students, regardless of inherent ability, were to maintain focus on breath control, portamento, intonation, purity of vowels, and legato. Among the particular kinds of agility that Mancini discussed were the *volatina*, ascending and descending, simple and doubled (*semplice* and *raddoppiata*); the *scaletta*, for which he gave an example of direct chromaticism (think of the end of "Casta diva"); the mordent; the *scivolo* and *strascino* (very roughly slide and downward slide, both also found in Tosi); and the *martellato*, a hammering of repeated notes said to have been perfected by certain castrati and female sopranos, including Agostino Fontana, Antonio Pasi, Faustina Bordoni, and Caterina Visconti (La Visconti); the *arpeggiato;* and lastly the *sbalzar* or leap, which had to be executed with special grace and portamento to prevent it from sounding like opera buffa.[33]

Equally indispensable, and relatedly so, was the ability to trill without which Tosi claimed no singer could succeed and about which Mancini rhapsodized in 1774, "Oh Trill! Sustenance, life, and beauty of singing!" ("Oh Trillo! Sostegno, decoro e vita del canto!").[34] The trill was impossible to execute without a wide range of other abilities. Quantz repeatedly praised the ability to trill among his favorite castrati: Senesino and Farinelli each had a "schönen Trillo," as did Gaetano Orsini.[35] Bontempi said the same of Ferri, and Verri said so of Marchesi.[36] Although the skill largely died out by the later nineteenth century, we can still hear robust examples of it in some early recordings—besides those of Nellie Melba and Emma Eames, the recordings of Callas's teacher Spanish coloraturist Elvira de Hidalgo (1891–1980), and those of the American phenomenon Rosa Ponselle (1897–1981), some of whose 1934–37 radio broadcasts Callas could have heard as a young teenager before returning to Greece from America in 1937 (though she said she had not).[37]

. . .

Now to mark every note of a coloratura passage in this way not only requires great skill but also heightens the effect of a brilliant, "rocketing virtuosity."[38] Some early sound recordings may still give purchase on it, particularly those of dramatic coloraturists who sang in the old way, on the legato, with something close to what we can surmise was a castrato's strong subglottal air pressure combined with flexibility. Ponselle, Callas, and Sigrid Onégin are all examples of singers with powerful voices yet great elasticity, frank, unobstructed resonance, pure vowels, clear diction, and evenness of tone. In Ponselle's 1936 radio performance of "Bel raggio lusinghier" from Rossini's *Semiramide* of 1823, an aria rich with *canto fiorito*, the coloratura is sometimes lightly marked, sometimes more so, and sometimes goes into staccato. (You can listen to an excerpt of the recording on this book's website.) Whichever kind she is using, the choice sounds clear and the brilliance lies in the evenness and equality of her expressive notes as well as a continual commitment to the overall musical line.

That this kind of coloratura was produced by an indelible impression made on the body is palpable in the legendary 1958 concert Callas gave in Paris, where she sang Rossini's "Una voce poco fa" from *Il barbiere di Siviglia* (1816) with alternately marked and gliding coloratura. Just how akin her differentiations of passaggi are to what Tosi had in mind we will never know, but it nonetheless seems worth noting that Callas learned this kind of singing from de Hidalgo and polished it under the mentorship of Tullio Serafin, who also mentored Ponselle. When thinking about these relationships, we should bear in mind that de Hidalgo was a pupil of Melchiorre Vidal (1837–1911), who at the turn of the century taught coloratura in the manner of his contemporary Mathilde Marchesi. In 1845–47 Marchesi had in turn been a pupil of Manuel Garcia Jr., whose method she taught in her Paris studio during the later years of the nineteenth century. Will Crutchfield points out that Marchesi's pupils—Melba, Eames, and Calvé among them—stand out among early recording artists for their unusual ability to deliver a full-bodied trill.[39] Their trills extend a technical connection to a pedagogical past that in their own time had become tenuous and was becoming ever closer to extinct. It seems all the more significant, then, that Calvé, as we saw in chapter 3, was also a student of the castrato Domenico Mustafà around 1890; and that reaching backward in Mathilde Marchesi's pedagogical genealogy is a strain that runs, now in reverse chronological order, from Garcia the younger back through Rossini and Colbran to Crescentini.[40]

None of this gets us out of having to adjust mentally for a hundred years of vocal difference between the time of early recordings and the present, nor of having to presume another hundred years of difference between the period of early recordings and the singing of the late operatic castrati Marchesi, Crescentini, Velluti, and their contemporaries (to say nothing of castrato singing a hundred years earlier by the likes of Ferri, Siface, Matteuccio, Pistocchi, and Nicolini). To reiterate what may well be the most obvious rupture: there is a distinct shift in vocal production in the so-called bel canto period marked in legend by Duprez's top C in chest, continued with the ascendency of the dramatic declamatory style of middle to late Verdi, and exaggerated by the rugged verismo vocality demanded by Mascagni, Puccini, and Leoncavallo in the late nineteenth and early twentieth centuries. Did Callas inherit from her teachers (and they from theirs) a much-changed but still surviving (in part revived) strain of the vocal practice that predates Verdi—a practice promoted by the revival of the bel canto repertory by Serafin, however mediated by the influence of later repertories and newer ways of singing? However elusive the answer, it does seem so. Especially considering the rigorous training routines to which Callas was subjected in Athens during World War Two under de Hidalgo, when she was a mere teenager, it seems in short that a castrato-like coloratura was etched into the physicality of her practice. In her Paris performance of "Una voce poco fa," you can hear the crisp distinctions she makes between different types of passaggi: *coloratura battuta* at one moment, bravura staccato at another, and *coloratura scivolata* later on (see this book's website for examples).[41]

CAFFARELLI AS ROYAL DOUBLE

If the trill was nearly dead in big opera houses after Ponselle, from the seventeenth through the early nineteenth centuries (at least) it was still what Richard Wistreich has called "a precise marker of "[bodily], aesthetic, and social difference." The same might be said of exacting kinds of passage-work and breath control more broadly.[42] The singer who could master all this was extraordinary indeed, capable of enchanting with a technology that lay beyond normal human or even singerly reach.

But performing extraordinarily while standing in as proxy for the top of the social order has always been a double-edged sword and was especially so in an era when the human exemplum of extraordinariness, the monarch, was subject to increasing skepticism. How worrisomely easy might it be for viewers to displace their attentions from rulers to divos or divas, and for a star to feel like a king? The swashbuckling Siface, enamored with his own power, finished badly when the brothers of a marquise from the Marsili family ended his affair with their sister by having him dealt a murderous blow. Before then he seems to have dazzled and bedeviled by turns, enthralling the Paris court but causing the Modenese agent to write home to Siface's princely patron that he was a "gran fantastico" "like all great virtuosos" (something like an eccentric dreamer, or a real adventurer). He also caused John Evelyn in England to report that his astounding messe di voce attracted what Evelyn thought a rather undevout crowd that assembled, gaping, to hear him in the king's chapel, after which he disaffected the French ambassador's court with demands for money.[43]

In the eighteenth century the contradictions of enchanting and alienating were infamously associated with Caffarelli, a great adept in the art of bravura. After he had established himself internationally, he sang for Handel at the King's Theatre in 1737–38. By then, Italian opera in London was in deep trouble, and Caffarelli had the impossible job of trying to satisfy an apathetic public in the wake of Farinelli's recent decampment to Spain and Senesino's return to Italy. All this militated against the success of Caffarelli's work with Handel, whose last-ditch effort to save the opera included serving up the comic hybrid *Serse*, which combined belly laughs with opera-seria-styled affect and virtuosity.

The pompous Caffarelli played the title role and got some amazing arias, including the big bravura number in act 2, "Se bramate d'amar chi vi sdegna," in which he rages against his unrequiting love object Romilda, whom he's forced to advise that only proud disdain pays off in matters of love. In the course of the aria Caffarelli/Serse had to devolve repeatedly from brilliant divisions into slow faltering passages as he questions his own bravado while counseling Romilda—a progression that in hindsight might strike us as a metaphor for the failing institution of Italian opera that Caffarelli been brought to London to help save. With each effort he annihilates his own self-interest, disintegrating into dolorous, wandering adagios of distracted self-address that wobble, half stuttering, past deceptive cadences through diminished chords and secondary dominants, suspensions, and feckless chromatic inflections as he asks himself how one can possibly disdain one's own beloved, only to answer pathetically, "I know not" (see Ex. 19).

EXAMPLE 19. George Frideric Handel, short score of "Se bramate, d'amar chi vi sdegna," from *Serse* (London, King's Theatre, April, 15, 1738), with bravura falling into faltering self-address, mm. 9–59. Sung by Caffarelli in the eponymous lead role.

EXAMPLE 19. *(continued)*

EXAMPLE 19. *(continued)*

Se bramate d'amar chi vi sdegna	Should you yearn to love he who disdains you,
Vuò sdegnarvi. Ma come? Non so.	you have to scorn him. But how? I know not.
La vostra ira crudel me l'insegna!	Your cruel rage is teaching me how!
Tento farlo, e quest'alma non può.	I try to do so, but this soul cannot.

. . .

In the same opera Caffarelli made his entrance with a number that was to become ever after the single most renowned of all Handel's arias, "Ombra mai fu." Like much of *Serse*, the aria recalls Bononcini's in *Xerxes*, as Harold Powers showed, but boiled down into a thoroughly Handelian reduction.[44] The aria is often interpreted as a piece of comedy because of its brief text—a love song addressed to a plane tree: "Ombra mai fu / di vegetabile / cara ed amabile / soave più" (Never was the dear, loveable shade of a tree so sweet). But many eighteenth-century listeners would have recognized Xerxes emerging in this moment from the deserts of Asia Minor in a great thirst, knowing of his cultic veneration of the plane tree. Pausanias in his *Description of Greece* (4.34.4) says that the "breadth of the tree gives the impression of a small cave" and that "from it the drinking water flows to Corone." Aelian, a showy raconteur of the bizarre, seemingly establishes the tradition that Xerxes's devotion is to be laughed at.[45] Singers never seem to hear it that way, and there's reason to think they're right as concerns Handel's rendition, for it has every mark of a majestic piece in the simple, elegiac mode of a *largo spianato*, a style as crucial to the toolkit of a Caffarelli as bravura, and something he expected to provide (see Ex. 20).[46]

Deceptively simple on the outside, the aria demands superb skills in messa di voce, breath control, legato, placement, and steadying the voice (*fermare* or *mettere bene la voce*)—all told what Winifred Faix Brown calls the ability to "keep a melodic line off the ground for an entire musical paragraph."[47] As such, it has tested the mettle of one singer after another throughout the centuries. Like other parts of Serse's role, it would never have been given to an out-and-out comic character (like the bass Elviro in the same opera) because it's a vehicle for luxury performance. It was Caffarelli's honor to be able to grace it and be graced with it, and it was to the honor of Handel's listeners and colleagues to partake of Caffarelli's graces, however disinterested they had become in Italian opera.

But succeeding in the role of a deluxe castrato was a tricky business. It called not only for great vocal skill and magnetism but also a feel for luxurious modes of exchange, an ability to get others to see oneself as a deft and marvelous "intertwining of art and nature" (and already in the 1730s there were many who were wont to see castrati as monstrous spectacles of social engineering).[48] By 1738 Caffarelli was

EXAMPLE 20. George Frideric Handel, short score of "Ombra mai fu," sung by Caffarelli in the opera *Serse* (London, King's Theatre, April, 15, 1738).

reputed to be the ne plus ultra of enfants terribles, prone to scrapes and outbursts. He was loved by his party of fans at home in Naples and reportedly endeared the Pistoian nobility during the early 1730s, but elsewhere he behaved like such a beast as to make people, including Farinelli, infuriated or disgusted.[49] More than once he pulled stunts on stage, mimicking fellow singers or mugging at audiences, and more than once he got into duels. In Vienna he was so insolent about skipping rehearsals that he ended up dueling with the poet-director Migliavacca and only desisted in a blaze of gallantry when the prima donna moved in gravely to intervene. Judgments of his singing followed suit. Some in Vienna "exalted him to the heavens," Grimm in Paris found his singing perfectly enchanting, and Burney wrote that his teacher Porpora, who abhorred him personally, went around saying he was the best singer in Italy.[50] Against all this we read intermittent complaints that he sounded strident or (to quote Metastasio) that "in all he sings there is a ridiculous tone of lamentation that can turn the most cheerful allegro sour."[51]

Like Serse's "Se bramate," a "sour allegro" smacks of bravura gone wrong. No lowly plebeian can afford to go wrong, whereas a kingly figure—a supreme threshold creature—thrives on the privilege. Whether Caffarelli's "caprices" (as Burney called them) were musical as well as personal, they were certainly not incidental to his being but signs of his enormity, however problematic. They were figurations of a frighteningly multifaceted, ambiguous, and unpredictable character that stirred ambivalence in others because it implied the wild power of an outsider who formed a totality unto himself. As the king has his fool and the angel needs the devil—or as the kings of Metastasio's librettos and Plutarch's *Lives* are rife with contradictions and contrasts, including gross negativity in personal actions and realms—Caffarelli's character, personal and vocal, formed in the public imaginary an ensemble of good and bad.[52] We might say of Caffarelli and certain other star castrati what Bataille said of the sovereign in his brilliant study of social and political economies, *La part maudite:* that he constituted "the creature par excellence of the miracle," signaling through his insolent mix of grandeur and buffoonery a miraculous surplus and "supreme autonomy from subordination."[53] What he could do to us was of a piece with what he had, how it was given and received, used, saved, wasted, redistributed—whether kept with painstaking care or alienated with abandon.

THE TRANSACTIONAL CASTRATO

Caffarelli also engaged an economy of luxury, at once material and affective. We're again reminded of the myth of origins that Balatri told the khan of Astrakhan when asked to sing for him, wherein castrated males are hatched from cocks' eggs and later deluged with flattery, caresses, and coins. Balatri recounts the telling as if he were letting us in on some hilarious scam, conjured up on the fly. Yet he implies a temporal progression that echoes real life: between being hatched and later showered with riches, the sterile hatchling becomes a professional soprano. Throughout his life he's presumably been complicit in various transactions involving tokens of adulation, even erotic attraction, and purses of gold, mobilized by his gifts of song. Transactions of the kind tumble out of Balatri's tales in close succession, especially in the verse of "Frutti del mondo": the arias he sings for the khan for hours on end inspire reciprocation with a Tartar suit of gold, which he later dons to impress Louis XIV, which gains him entrée into the king's Parisian court and thereafter into the upper echelons of London society—all this in a ceaseless flow of goods and song. But stirred into the mix is also money, which circulates in a cash nexus that glares in the cold light of day only to flicker, moth-like, back into the duskier world of gifts.

Farinelli was the reigning expert at modulating the rhythms of these movements. In 1732 he got an audience with the emperor and told him, all atremble, that it was the most fortunate moment in his life (this recounted by Burney). After Farinelli sang magnificently, "as god wished," the emperor exclaimed in Neapolitan, "Voi siete Napoliello" (You're a Neapolitan), and Farinelli made him laugh with a riposte that echoed the emperor's facility with dialect by declaring in *napoletano,* "I am indeed one of those true pasta-eaters." When they met again the emperor asked him about a rumor that he'd lost money to a bad creditor, and again

Farinelli broke up the room by answering that since he had earned the money with his trills, he had reason to hope they would bring him more in future.[54] His talent for gracious banter was of a piece with gifts, for one was so graced when in the "graces" of others.[55] The same letter in which Farinelli joked about his lucrative trills closed by enumerating ritualistically each and every gift he had received after singing for members of the court: a "highly polished and charming" silver chocolate service given "as a gift" from Inviato of Genoa along with a purse of a hundred new Hungarian coins that might foot the bill for many gold medals, a very lovely gold box from Signora Serra, a superb Parisian gold box from Count Martinez, a very heavy box of English gold from the prince of Cardona, from Count Chinxi a watch of gold from England "lovely enough to eat" . . . and on it went. Some presents had money tucked inside, and to others Farinelli himself assigned a cash value ("a gilded plaster cast from England worth eighty louis d'or"; "a silver traveling service worth one thousand florins").[56] All this was a mere prelude to what he brought in at his first benefit concert in London, in 1735, on a single night, but there he was in public, not at court, and "gifts"—some of them immense, especially the one from the Prince of Wales—were openly given in the form of cash.[57] Small wonder that when previously the English had (repeatedly) tried to get Farinelli to come their shores, he had put his Neapolitan foot down until the remuneration offered was huge, and once there he complained to Pepoli that guineas flew so fast he could have bought much Bolognese land with what it cost him to live in London, even though he wasted nothing.[58]

Yet with all that, with the English competing rabidly to outdo each other in gift giving and buying precious souvenirs of him—things like the duke of Leeds' copies of operas and arias and his commission of the now-famous portrait by Bartolomeo Nazari (Fig. 7)—the English were also plaguing the singer with satires of all kinds and accusations of being an avaricious coxcomb. For the purposes of their new booming celebrity media industry, Farinelli was Caesar, Saint George, and Callas rolled into one, so much so that they fell all over each other swooning and trying to make him their own even as some of them mocked him. In the face of this, Farinelli—who had again written home with ritual precision to enumerate their lavish praise and gifts and who was later to inventory and bequeath his own riches with extraordinary care—was already explaining to Pepoli his determination to change his professional identity, for no professional work, with all the money grubbing, celebrating, and defiling it entailed, could befit one who had risen to such stature and at last sought only autonomy.[59]

Some of these dilemmas might characterize a few prima donnas and tenors of Farinelli's time, but none were so extensively made by things and cash, or gave cash and things such a glow in return. Yet always gnawing away was the issue of whether a castrato could fully deserve or assimilate such riches or fully enter the ranks of givers, even those he outstripped in wealth and fame. As Georg Simmel notes in his classic *Philosophy of Money* (1900), money is something to which outsiders cannot afford to be inattentive.[60] The case of castrati is fitting and also unique. Stripped of procreative powers in a patrilineal world, they were often consumed with acquisitions and bequests. Senesino was less rich than Farinelli, but he was still very rich and totally preoccupied by his riches. The paranoia of his old age made him tortured over the bequest of his estate to his nephew and his nephew's wife, and he meticulously recorded his every purchase and gift received in the diaries he kept in London, where for years he took Handel's public by storm and made a great fortune.[61]

GIFTS

In the ever-more money-driven world in which castrati circulated, what sort of complicity exists between the production of a luxury castrato and the dynamics of the gift? In Seneca's classical account of the gift from the first century B.C., *De beneficiis* (On benefits), gifts involve three parts: giving, receiving, and reciprocating. Reciprocation is critical because the gift is a transaction that occurs between parties who become mutually obliged. It is that part of gift giving that is multidirectional and dynamic. If a gift is to work, its receiver must make a return volley, a reciprocal gesture that is likely to produce further giving, receiving, and reciprocating in a *perpetuum mobile* of social transaction. Or as Derrida had it, a gift is a "giving in time," something given to a receiver that must eventually be reciprocated (even though Derrida's gift always already implies a debt that negates the giving in the first place).[62] In the case of a castrato, such a *perpetuum mobile* could be more or less tumultuous by a wide margin. Legions of little-known chapel singers across Catholic Europe found subsistence livings in churches, avoiding, *faute de mieux*, the hypertransactional life of stars. But when castrati were launched to the rocky precipices of class stations well above their hereditary status, a perilous incommensurability of exchange was inevitable, since the hard stuff of gifts and money could never be received unproblematically for the softly evanescent stuff of voice and song.[63]

Troublesomely too, even if a castrato's exchange patterns with the rich and powerful were not unlike the obsequious ones of *valets de chambres* or courtiers, his musical offerings—alluring, caressing, overpowering at their best—could suck the very aura out of sovereignty and funnel it into himself. Curtseying and bowing were deferential performances, but singing arias was emotionally charged and concentrated in a unique physicality. It was exhausting and audacious. After Farinelli reached Madrid, where he was brought to sing away the psychotic melancholy of King Philip V, he portrayed his labors to Pepoli by invoking bodily consumption and expulsion: "Every evening, I drink eight or nine arias into my body."[64] By enveloping the king in song to regulate and calm his soul, the singer was able to replace his psychotic deliriums with ecstatic transports. Swallowing note after note and spewing them out in return for protection, gifts, and cash, Farinelli was a veritable blazon of old-regime transactional modes, though he paid a price to become his own master in the confines of the court.[65]

Unlike Farinelli, the Sifaces, Senesinos, and Caffarellis often fielded these landmines badly; or, in a different interpretation, they fielded them as bad, imperious boys, confounding gifts with cash in ways that sometimes overstepped class lines and made them painfully obvious. A court official in early seventeenth-century Parma defined the problem when he wrote about the impending visit of Loreto Vittori, the composer, soprano, and renowned poet (and thus superior in status to a mere singer or composer), saying that as a person "of the first rank" Vittori should be rewarded with gifts, not money. In the 1680s, Siface—of lowlier stock but a great celebrity—wanted quite the opposite, doubloons and not gifts of ices ("sorbetti"), as he reportedly announced to the French ambassador's man in Rome.[66]

Then there was the astonishing case of Senesino. In 1739–40, after his return to Italy, contract negotiations to hire him for Naples ended in an awkward compromise between these extremes and put his insolence in an ugly light. The evidence, unearthed by William C. Holmes, comes from the Florentine archives of the Albizzi family and specifically the documents of the impresario Luca Casimiro degli Albizzi, who brokered the deal. Ironically, Senesino, then fifty-two years old, was hell-bent against impersonating the wily, authoritarian Ulysses (he wanted to play the young lover), yet he was convinced that he could represent himself by dictating authoritatively the terms of negotiations, including the casting of his role, the amount of his remuneration, and the casting of the rest of the company—all this in the face of a king. He wanted as much money as he had gotten at Naples in 1716, when he was twenty-nine, but at that time, of the nine hundred doubloons he had received, two hundred had not been formally included in the royal contract but had come as a "gift from the ladies."[67] Thinking it improper "to ask that much of his Majesty," Albizzi advised Senesino to appeal instead to the generosity of the king. What was needed was that he show himself contented with gifts and, above all else, that he acknowledge the immutable asymmetry of the exchange. The king's munificence was to be returned with obsequies, deference, loyalty, and unentailed services, like performances at court. But Senesino had his agents go on "bargaining" with those of the king—a kind of folly Farinelli never would have committed—until two hundred doubloons were at last added to the seven hundred proposed. Again the additional sum was reframed as a gift, if not, in this instance, as one from "the ladies." Only this time when Senesino arrived at the royal palace expecting to pay his respects by singing "privately" for the king, he was not received. The embarrassed impresario wrote a colleague about the affair, proffering an immediate counterexample: La Tesi had recently had him tell the Duke of Modena that she didn't care about the "fee" she was to receive from him. According to Albizzi, she declared she would sing for the duke for a mere ribbon, which was what Albizzi called "honorable" in dealing with a sovereign.[68]

According to many, Caffarelli was of Senesino's ilk when it came to matters of money. A story that reportedly still circulated in Paris a hundred years after Caffarelli had left there in 1753, or was cobbled together by its author Castil-Blaze to describe his Parisian reputation,[69] told how the singer had been sent a gold snuffbox from Louis XV, delivered via a distinguished courtier—presumably a reciprocation for having sung at court or an inducement to return the favor by doing so. As legend had it, Caffarelli rebuffed the gesture, showing the courtier his stash of thirty other gold snuffboxes, all fancier than what he had just been offered. And worse, when the courtier protested that his king customarily gave precisely such boxes to no less than foreign ambassadors, Caffarelli reportedly answered, "Then let the ambassadors sing."[70]

Whether such legends carried grains of truth,[71] Caffarelli had to beat a hasty retreat from France because he had exceeded the bounds of courtesy allowed even a brash, newly made man of luxe in an age of new money and modernizing state bureaucracies—a man who had never had to repeat the humiliation of playing a female part, which he did only at his Roman debut at age sixteen (a rite of passage most castrati tried to endure as briefly as possible), and even though he had long been master of his own image, playing male heroes and princes for the previous twenty-five years, including various monarchs (Theseus, Pyrrhus, Cyrus, Artaxerxes, Syphax, and Nero).[72] In May 1734, when the profligate Spanish Bourbons celebrated the queen mother's birthday just after recapturing Naples from the Austrian Habsburgs, they turned to Caffarelli to impersonate the Syrian prince in Metastasio and Pergolesi's *Adriano in Siria*.[73] Caffarelli was such a celebrity by then that every last aria in Metastasio's libretto had to be replaced in order to accommodate him. That is not legend. Rewriting the text made it possible to give Caffarelli the longest, most lyrical arias in the opera and to sing solo arias alone on stage at the ends of both acts 1 and 2, the first enhanced with obbligato oboe and the second with astounding coloratura and a double orchestra.[74]

By means of these extravagances, Caffarelli staged his supremacy to the royal majesties as they in turn staged theirs before their new Neapolitan subjects by staging him.[75]

SACRED DOUBLES

I have suggested that one consequence of exchange with a deluxe castrato was that he might virtually become the royal figure or hero he represented. But by what cultural logic was a eunuch needed for the purpose?[76] Freitas has proposed, as we have seen, that castrati tended to be perceived as boyish figures of erotic appeal. The prototype had a notable endurance, at least if we take seriously the representations still being made by costumers and scenographers in the later eighteenth century. Witness Leonardo Marini's drawings for the royal theater of Turin, one of which, from 1774, shows the Grand Mogul Mahomet in Cigna and Pugnani's *Tamas Kouli-Kan* (Fig. 32) as a boyish figure, despite the oriental power attributed to Mahomet and the power attributed to the voice of Manzuoli, who portrayed him. Another from 1772 shows the heroic Mycenaean prince Eurystheus (Euristeo), played by Giuseppe Aprile in Zeno and Mysliveček's *Antigona* looking even more tender. Both singers were effectively boy-kings, staged in Turin at a time when categorical differences between manly men and childlike boys were starting to express themselves in complaints about just such disjunctures in representation.[77]

If the castrato as erotic boy was an enduring object of attention, he was arguably just one embodiment of the larger charismatic role that castrated boys and men assumed in dividing and redistributing a monarchical function. On this view castrati were mutually entangled with royalty by virtue of impersonating the royal body or occupying the royal sphere, making it immediate, intimate, empathic, charming, and palpable. But to reemphasize an earlier point, they could only do so because kingship is inherently divisible. Ernst Kantorowicz brilliantly showed that in medieval Europe the traditionalist power of kings depended specifically on a division between the eternal *office* of kingship as a figment of the realm and the mortal *person* inhabiting it. The division provided a solution to the never-ending and universal problem of royal continuity, of how to ensure that the death of a royal figure not spell the death of kingship. Assurances of royal perpetuity in turn answered two principal dilemmas: one temporal (what if the king dies?), the other spatial (how can the king be manifest throughout the realm?).[78] Kantorowicz elaborated his case specifically for medieval France, but the problem of continuity, a temporal problem with inseparably spatial implications, is structurally central to all kingships, Western and non-Western, in any of its particular forms. And if continuity is solved through division, then what kind of division does the eunuch singer signify in re-presenting royalty?

Can we think, furthermore, of the deluxe castrato as providing one kind of division among many possible ones in the face of the impending demise of kingship—not a formal division but a mediatized one, as an integral part of the media of representation deployed by kingship and its cognates? On such a view, the utility of dividing and displacing royal mystique by that most rationalizing, moralizing of centuries would have been realized by deepening the emotional imprint of royalty and of royal circles of power. Particular eunuch singers might thus have become virtual sacred doubles by embodying the "voice" and animus of royalty. Most importantly, the very figure of the castrato could have symbolically become so. In the economy of functions that Bataille called "the accursed share" of sovereignty, we would thus regard the castrato as the abject Other onto whom a part of sovereignty was placed. He would be a sacrificial being—critically so in within the sociopolitical fabric of Europe in that he helped defer the very sacrifice of kingship as an institution.

The castrato's doubling can also be understood within a classical view of monarchy, which understands the monarch as boundary figure. In the dynamic described by Hubert and Mauss, monarchs are often outsiders who have shed blood in sacrifice or have had others do so on their behalf; or, in myths of origins, their forebears may have done so. Hubert and Mauss show that this outsider status is invariably sacred, understanding the term in a way that is more continuous with the everyday than it is in modern-day conceptions.[79] In contemplating these relations and affinities, I have advocated that we rethink the many declarations by castrati saying that they had sacrificed themselves for God and princes, along with the fact that princes sought out both the sacrifices and the enunciations of them as such. If we accept that what confronts us is not only a defense against the paradoxical illegality of castration for singing, that it is rather both a symbolic sacrifice and a fully embodied one that entails a radical transformation of being, then it becomes clearer in what specific respects the castrato can perform a function that a monarch cannot: how a castrato might give affective and technological force to the feelings of love, loyalty, divided loyalty, friendship, and love of state ascribed to monarchs in the narratives that castrati enacted on stage (and might even approach offstage) while giving monarchy a mythical and universal grandeur and the legs to travel throughout the monarch's realm.

What, then, of the castrato as the monarch's cultural twin? Like the warrior and the conqueror, the foreigner or the madman—often the king's progenitors and familiars—the castrato bears physical marks of difference, which affirm his transcendence of a middle ground. His outsider status can be a liability, but it is also the basis for affinity.[80] These relationships were expressed theatrically and diffused in music, theatrical and non (and of course all music was in a sense "theatrical"). Relevant too is that they were also ratified in the honorific forms of printed sonnets, portraits, and dedications and by titles given by special order, titles that were sometimes bestowed by rulers or ruling groups for exceptional service. In 1623–24, at age twenty-three, for instance, Vittori was made cavaliere in the Milizia di Gesù Cristo by Pope Urban VIII. In 1660 Atto Melani was made gentleman of the chamber at the court of Louis XIV.[81] Valeriano Pellegrini in 1709 was knighted by the elector Palatine of Dusseldorf after he carried off some very tough music as Gheroldo in Steffani's *Tassilone* (1709), including more than one high b".[82] Ghezzi made him look like a homely abbot later in life when he had fallen on hard times, but he did not, and would not, have failed to include the inscription "Cavaliere" (cf. Fig. 11).

Other titles were given as lifetime "achievement" or "service" awards, equivalent to the gold watch that corporate venality has now made virtually extinct. Such titles were still infused symbolically such that they aligned their recipients with nobility offstage. Ferri, Nicolini, and Guadagni (Gluck's Orfeo) were each made knights (cavalieri) of St. Mark's in Venice, a distinction that fell upon a castrato only once every several decades.[83] And Matteuccio returned to Naples from his travels abroad a marquis. When Bruni retired in the late eighteenth century he joined the nobles in his hometown of Fratta as a town council member and later became gonfaloniere (effectively mayor), though he had to overcome some small-town realpolitik in the process since normally that position was strictly reserved for nobles. All this is to say nothing of Farinelli's induction by the king of Spain into the exalted order of Calatrava, a vicissitude unmatched as an event in castrato history and one that saw vocal and social prowess consolidating an elite place at the top of society. (Amigoni depicted him thus more than once, the first such portrait being done around 1750–52.)[84]

Having a title bestowed had no real resemblance to buying one, as was so common in the hard-up seventeenth century, and it was much more prestigious than simply being named a *virtuoso di corte*. Such titles could not be legally devolved, but symbolically they were loaded with the hereditary implications of belonging to a noble class of feudal ancestry, including the rights to bear arms, obligations to serve one's ruler militarily, and even participate in exclusive forms of rule. They implied proximity to rulers of great vassalage. They also had attention-grabbing and up-pulling social force that was profoundly constitutive for those who bore them, even when the titles were largely symbolic. What Matteo Pisani Broschi inherited from his uncle, after all—whatever limitations were placed on his inheritance—was the estate of *Cavaliere* Don Carlo Broschi detto il Farinelli, which is one reason star-studded castrati made a change of surname prerequisite to a legatee's inheritance. Even if the title endured only for the natural life of its bearer, it accorded permanent stature to the persons and things surrounding it in the eyes of observers.[85]

Before Farinelli's time, shrewd exchange was probably never practiced better than it was by Atto Melani, though some of his exchanges were marred by audacity or outright offenses. Melani became indispensable to the queen of France while quite young. Freitas shows that his circulation among monarchs demanded a facility with gift idioms in order for them to obtain and retain him and in order for his primary patron to have him eventually returned. By rights it was the latter, with whom exchange of the castrato originated—in this case Prince Mattias de' Medici—who had primary dibs on his employee/client. Mattias's loaning of Melani to Mazarin, who had requested Melani's services for the French court, certainly benefited Mattias, but it was also a sacrifice on his part. By reminding Mazarin of that, he upped the value of his gift to the French.[86]

> My eagerness to serve His Most Christian Majesty and Your Eminence is so great that, although many considerations inhibit me from sending my castrato Atto to France, ... having refused this to many great princes, ... I am nonetheless pleased

that he should come serve His Majesty. . . . I concede him . . . for the period of time you've asked of me, hoping that afterward you'll do me the favor of sending him back to me and not detaining him further . . . so that he'll be able to serve me in a work that I have already decided to have performed.[87]

. . .

Much as the status of a castrato might be concretized with titles, his functions could be concretized with assignments that involved him in confidences and delicate missions. Filippo Vismarri (before 1635–1706?) performed diplomatic missions in the 1660s for the Count of Neuhaus; Tosi and Domenico Cecchi (Il Cortona, ca. 1650–55 to 1717–18) carried out delicate assignments for Joseph I; and De Castris (ca. 1650–1724) in the early eighteenth century played the hopeless role of intermediary between Cosimo III, Grand Duke of Tuscany, and his estranged son until the whole thing blew up and led to his exile from Florence to Rome, where he continued to carry out diplomatic missions for the Grand Duke.[88] These positions and actions paled by comparison with Farinelli's, but Melani's in the previous century were equally flamboyant, if transitory and sometimes shady (he accepted favors from different princes left and right, and in 1667 he claimed chief responsibility for the election of Cardinal Giulio Rospigliosi as Pope Clement IX).[89]

We might call castrati in these exceptional positions "king's doubles," yet they are not doubles of any single type but rather figures whose functions float and change. They represent, embody, transfer, and transport the monarchical image and function. They do so in various forms, positive and negative, but always encompassed within the totality that is monarchy. Indeed they are kindred spirits to monarchs precisely because they are ambiguous in function, extensible to different domains, and sacrificial in serving as substitutes for the one on whose behalf the sacrifice is made.

THE EMBODIED VOICE

In the eighteenth century, many claimed that heroic, "monarchical" voices were legible not just in gestures and stances but as indices on such bodily parts as faces, brows, jaws, chests, arms, and legs. Burney routinely memorialized the voices of star-studded castrati along with their physical excellences, signs that multiplied their exceptionality. Carestini's profile was "majestic" (Fig. 6), Marchesi's full of "grandeur and dignity." Guarducci, by contrast, had no such added value. That he sang "divisions from the chest" bore witness to his power and stature, but since no physical or gestural greatness accompanied them—no visible vessel to carry the voice—he remained a perceptual cipher (and, indeed, no portrait of him seems to survive): "Guarducci," Burney writes, "tall and awkward," "inanimate," and "in countenance ill-favoured and morbid," was, however, "one of the most correct singers I ever heard." Perforce, his career was an exercise in compensating for "prejudice," which "ran high against him on his first arrival in London."[90] By contrast, when Quantz wrote in one and the same breath that Senesino's action was "natural and noble," his figure "majestic," and that he "sang divisions from the chest," he assimilated the singer's body to the overall physical and metaphysical systems of royalty.[91] In Vanderbank's oil painting of Senesino in the role of Bertarido, heir to the Lombard throne (Fig. 33), the singer is about to deliver "Dove sei" in act 1, scene 6 of Handel's *Rodelinda*, which opened at the Royal Academy of Music on February 13, 1725. He is searching for his lost wife, who has fallen into the hands of the usurper, his body elegantly poised with an almost come-hither air of *sprezzatura* as if a vocal performance were imminent.

Senesino was represented as the inner essence of kingship, almost more real as a phantasmic reembodiment of a king than a king himself. Reembodiments of the kind recurred again and again. Even the noblemen in small Perugia in the Papal States, when they signed Giuseppe Aprile to appear in the reopening of their theater in 1778, enfolded his vocal reputation with their millennia-long imperial myth of foundation that asserted that the city had been founded by the emperor Augustus, placing the emperor's bust before a tribune that read "Aprilem memorant."[92]

All of these were immortalizing gestures. They could be as offhanded as the description by the *Gazzetta di Napoli* of Nicolini's voice as "otherworldly" ("più che terrena," 1730) or as permanent as Crudeli's poetic ascription to Farinelli of a magically Orphic voice and the valor of Jason. Streams of encomiastic sonnets and odes, prose in the form of treatises, memoirs, histories, and diaries, commemorative scores in print and manuscript, and majestic portraits were produced as honorific gestures, but they were other things as well: durable objectifications of honor as well as media by which others could reinterpret and interiorize magnificence. When the immortalizing gesture came in the form of an unmistakably royal painting, such as Giaquinto's of Farinelli or Flipart's of Scalzi (Figs. 3 and 34), it could commemorate to varying degrees the real man or the stage man, or both at once, though in either case setting the honor permanently on canvas was itself a regalizing event.[93]

THE REGAL RETURN: A CODA

A castrato who became regal by singing and courting fame hoped finally to reward himself with chattel, a domicile or two, and some fine dispersions. The last was a kind of final crowning, for if a man's dwelling is his kingdom, then a castrato whose kingdom was properly established and transferred could take his regality to the grave, as almost every castrato of great renown tried to do. Pacchierotti retired to the sumptuous Paduan villa previously lived in by Pietro Bembo, Renaissance dean of Italian letters, where he studied literature and surrounded himself with

British furniture and books (including complete editions of Corneille and Metastasio), fine old manuscripts, a remarkable collection of paintings, coins, coats of arms, statuary, and other notables, and where he received many notable visitors including Goldoni, Stendhal, and Rossini.[94] Rauzzini lived out his days as a gentleman, moving between his deluxe town house at Bath and his country estate, Perrymead (Fig. 35), where his visitors included Haydn.

Senesino, like most, retired back home, but he painstakingly re-created every element of an eighteenth-century English gentleman's house on his Sienese estate. And Rivani, Arnaboldi, and Caffarelli all bought noble lands that came with titles.[95] Caffarelli's was a dukedom purchased along with a title, though he went one better on his city house by erecting a stone inscription over the entryway by means of which he elided himself with a deity: "As Amphion [god of music] built Thebes, so I built this house, 1754" (Fig. 36)—and that the year after he presumably hastened out of France.[96] The inscription concretized the astounding supremacy he had in the theater, and it complemented the neoclassical way he had himself painted, as documented in a later engraving (Fig. 37).

For these self-made potentates, a deluxe dwelling was far more than a mark of prestige measured by brute things, for above all it organized, displayed, and commemorated a lifetime of deluxe exchanges. To comprehend this exchange dimension, we should recall that in the era in which castrati thrived, the quality of being regal was indivisible from the *regalo* (gift). In 1531 Sir Thomas Elyot spoke to this very relationship when he wrote, "For what purpose was it ordeyned, that Christen kynges ... shulde in an open and stately place, before al theyr subiectes, *receiue* their crown and other regalities"[97]—this at a time when the etymological and practical alliances between regalness, regalia, and regaling were still palpable and when regality implied an extended jurisdiction and a giving and receiving carried out between rulers and subjects that differentiated those *with* jurisdiction from those *subject* to it. In this dynamic sense, regalness was attested through a nexus of exchange that took place between persons, whether of similar or markedly different status. In Chambers's *Cyclopedia* of 1728–38 the description of "regale" conveyed this reciprocal movement: "The enjoyment of the fruits of the see is called the *temporal regale*, that of presenting the benefices, the *spiritual regale*." In defining the regal function as split into a temporal receiving and a spiritual giving, Chambers explained how French kings (regals) could have the exclusive right both "of enjoying the revenues of vacant bishoprics and abbacies, and of regaling others with them in the form of benefices."[98] He disclosed the dynamic of giving and receiving that was traditionally inherent in the regal condition, the exclusive right, in a sense, to have it both ways: to both benefit from revenues (benefices) and to benefit from regaling them (as benefices) at their will.[99]

It is that multiple sense of regality, now lost to our modern imaginations, with which illustrious castrati were complicit. The Bolognese household of Farinelli can be taken as exemplary here, not only because Farinelli was the exemplum of his kind but also because such a wealth of archival information about his household survives. Notably, the house was filled with the legacy of royal family but not with natural kin. At only one time in his twenty years at the house did a few nuclear family members live there, and that only for one unhappy year. Much sunnier were Farinelli's last five years, when his grandniece lived there without her parents until Farinelli died.

The gemstones in these archives are a very long holograph will and a huge posthumous legal inventory compiled on Farinelli's orders by his nephew and two executors.[100] The inventory shows the house to have been an effective autobiography in space, chronicling a life mapped through careful collection, preservation, and arrangements of things that reflected how his relationships had constituted his singularly luxurious stature.

Its exceedingly cosmopolitan focus was portraiture, to which the eminences who made the pilgrimage to the Farinelli villa between 1763 and 1782 were treated (see Fig. 38).[101] Portraiture dominated in the great hall, which was peopled with Amigoni's portraits of King Ferdinand VI and Queen Maria Barbara of Spain, along with portraits of their predecessors Philip V and Elisabetta Farnese, who had saved Farinelli from the travails of public self-exhibition, satire, money grubbing, and bad air that he had suffered for nearly three years in England. Maria Barbara was further commemorated in portraiture throughout the villa, for she had left him her entire collection of musical scores and three of her harpsichords.[102] Other portraiture in the great hall completed a panopticon of European royalty: Emperor Karl VI and his wife Elisabeth Christine, Maria Teresia and her consort Francis I, Pope Benedict XIV (monarch of the Papal States), Carlo III and Maria Amalia of Spain, Louis XV, the Duke and Duchess of Parma, the king and queen of Sardinia, and the boy king Ferdinand IV of Naples and the Two Sicilies.[103]

When visitors moved from the great hall to its antechambers, they were greeted by Amigoni's oils of Farinelli with Music being crowned by Fame (Fig. 2) and his group portrait of Farinelli and friends (Fig. 27), Giaquinto's royal portrait of Farinelli (Fig. 3), and an extensive gallery of still lifes, genre paintings, battle and maritime scenes, an armed soldier on a white horse, and portrayals of mythical fables and great personages, including the same Darius whom Farinelli had famously played in *Idaspe* when he sang Riccardo Broschi's "Qual guerriero in campo armato."[104]

The house had critical meanings for the eventual transfer of Farinelli's patrimony, but his control over destiny turned out to be limited by the wantonness or sheer uncouthness of his heirs. As in the case of Senesino's estate, many treasures in Farinelli's, including the richest ones, were liquidated for cash within a decade of his death, and the losses worsened with the Napoleonic invasions. The villa itself withstood numerous indignities as it was turned into a candy factory and later allowed to degrade until after the Second World War it was finally razed to the ground (see Fig. 38 for its prior state). Unable to benefit from the protections afforded by natural sons and other males in the patrilineal system, the patrimony of castrati was passed on in their role as uncles who were uneasy about bequests to nephews they often barely knew, who had sometimes become feckless with the knowledge that large inheritances awaited them. Without the social grooming and concern needed to care for the bequests, the estates often dissolved in posthumous family squabbles or were alienated through sales. Not unlike the voices of their founding owners, the estates have now largely turned to dust.

FIGURE 32. Leonardo Marini, drawing of Maometto Gran Mogul (the Grand Mogul Mahomet), conceived at Turin for primo soprano castrato Giovanni Manzuoli, who played the role in *Tamas Kouli-Kan* (Turin, Regio Teatro, 1772). By permission from the Ministero dei Beni e delle Attività Culturali e del Turismo, Direzione Regionale per i Beni Culturali e Paesaggistici del Piemonte–Biblioteca Reale di Torino.

FIGURE 33. Portrait of Senesino by John Vanderbank showing the singer as Bertarido wearing a "Hungarian" costume in Handel's *Rodelinda* (King's Theatre, 1725), about to sing "Dove sei" in act 1, scene 6. A note on the back, written by its original owner, James Harris (1746–1820), attests that the portrait was originally commissioned by Richard Willoughby, Esq. of Knoyle. Collection of James Carleton Harris the 7th Earl of Malmesbury. Reproduced by kind permission.

FIGURE 34. Charles Joseph Flipart, portrait of Carlo Scalzi (Signor "Sirbace"), who is given a decidedly royal expression and bearing as he points to his regalia, which includes a theatrical crown with great ostrich plume and a sheet of music. 1737. Oil on canvas, 18 ½ × 14 inches. Wadsworth Athenaeum Museum of Art, Hartford, CT. The Ella Gallup Sumner and Mary Catlin Sumner Collection Fund, 1938. No. 177. Reproduced by permission.

FIGURE 35. James Hutchinson, portrait of Venanzio Rauzzini with his dog Turk, ca. 1795. © Holbourne Museum of Art, Bath (A 169). Reproduced by permission.

FIGURE 36. Portal over the front of the house of Caffarelli (Gaetano Majorano, 1703–83), bearing the inscription "AMPHYON THEBAS EGO DOMUM ANNO MDCCLIV" (As Amphion built Thebes, so I built this House. 1754). The building, known as Palazzo Majorana, still stands at via Carlo de Cesare 15, Naples. The portal is made of volcanic rock native to the area. The house has a pointed arch and upper cornice that function as a balcony for the *piano nobile,* inside of which is a great staircase with cross vaulting. Photograph by Matteo Piscitelli, Naples. Reproduced by permission.

FIGURE 37. Caffarelli in neoclassical garb, after a painting by Stich. Engraved by G. Stuppi. Lithograph, 7 × 9 inches. Civica Raccolta delle Stampe Achille Bertarelli, Castello Sforzesco, Milano. Reproduced by permission.

FIGURE 38. Farinelli villa, photograph (now lost) from the very late nineteenth century or first half of the twentieth century, presumably before it was turned into a candy factory. Reproduced from Corrado Ricci, *Figure e figuri del mondo teatrale* (Milan: Treves, 1920), plate between pp. 136 and 137.

FIGURE 39. Anton Maria Zanetti, drawing of Andrea Pacini (ca. 1690–1764), turtle-like, seen from the underside of a shell. Elsewhere Zanetti drew Pacini plumed and fat, not unlike his drawings of Bernacchi. Fondazione Giorgio Cini, Venice. Photo by Matteo De Fina.

FIGURE 40. Anton Maria Zanetti, drawing of Castorino, looking simian. Fondazione Giorgio Cini, Venice. Photo by Matteo De Fina.

FIGURE 41. Zanetti's drawing of the castrato Nicolini (Nicola Grimaldi), who points, in a separate drawing, to the alligator-like Cavaliere Filippi di San Angelo, as arranged in Zanetti's *album amicorum*. Fondazione Giorgio Cini, Venice. Photo by Matteo De Fina.

FIGURE 42. Pier Leone Ghezzi's drawing of Domenico Annibali, armadillo-like, ca. 1730. Bibilioteca Apostolica Vaticana, Ottob. Lat. 3116, fol. 149.

FIGURE 43. Pier Leone Ghezzi's drawing of Farinelli at age nineteen, depicted in the female dress of the character Berenice, a role he played in Leonardo Vinci's *Farnace* at the Teatro Alibert (or "delle Dame") in Rome, 1724. Ghezzi gives him a porcine profile. The 1724 season was the last in which he played a female part. The Pierpont Morgan Library, New York. 1985–87. Gift of Mr. Janos Scholz.

FIGURE 44. Pier Leone Ghezzi's pen and ink drawing of contralto Gaetano Berenstadt, May 17, 1725. Bibilioteca Apostolica Vaticana, Ottob. Lat. 3115, fol. 140.

FIGURE 45. Engraved woodcut by the alchemist Leonhard Thurneysser, published in his *Quinta essentia* (Leipzig, 1574), showing humors in relation to the human body. Munich, Bayerische Staatsbibliothek. Reproduced by permission.

FIGURE 46. John Nixon, caricature of Luigi Marchesi, depicted in a concert performance in London. London, National Portrait Gallery, No. 5179. Reproduced by permission.

FIGURE 47. Pier Leone Ghezzi's sketch of the papal castrato Farfallino of Urbino (Giacinto Fontana, fl. 1712–35), January 20, 1723. Presumably the diminutive "Farfallino" referred to the singer's small stature, and perhaps to the fact that he specialized in playing female roles in the Papal States. By the 1770s Alessandro Verri might have suggested he was the kind of castrato who flirted with Roman abbots, but in his own time he was a vaunted high-voiced soprano of considerable musical powers, as Biancamaria Brumana has shown. Biblioteca Apostolica Vaticana, Ottob. Lat. 3114, fol. 113.

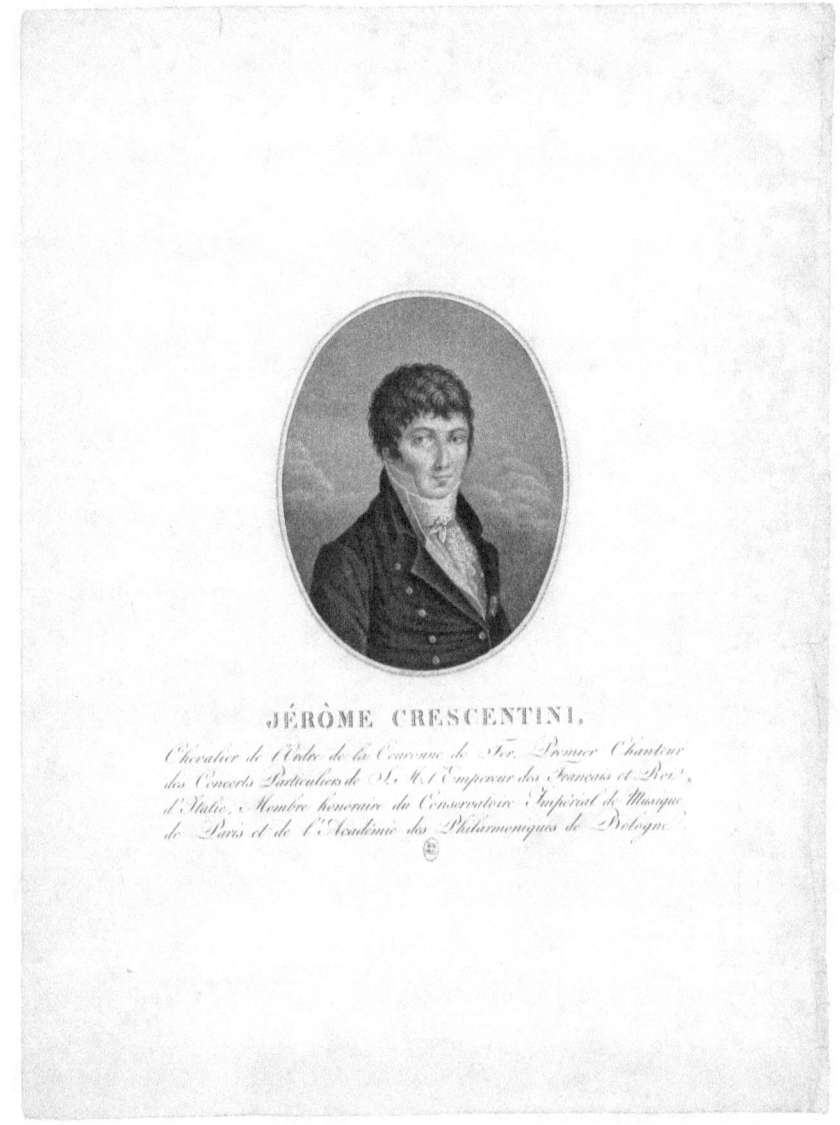

FIGURE 48. Girolamo Crescentini (1762–1846), Cavaliere dell'Ordine di Croce di Ferro. Engraved portrait made ca. 1810–11, after Crescentini was inducted by Napoleon into the knighthood as Chevalier du Chemin Fer. Paris, Bibliothèque Nationale de France, Richelieu Musique, Fonds estampes, Crescentini 002.

FIGURE 49. Giuditta Pasta (1797-1865) as Romeo in Zingarelli's *Giulietta e Romeo* (Paris: C Motte, ca. 1821 or after), lithograph. Paris, Bibliothèque Nationale de France, Richelieu Musique, Fonds du conservatoire, Pasta G. 002.

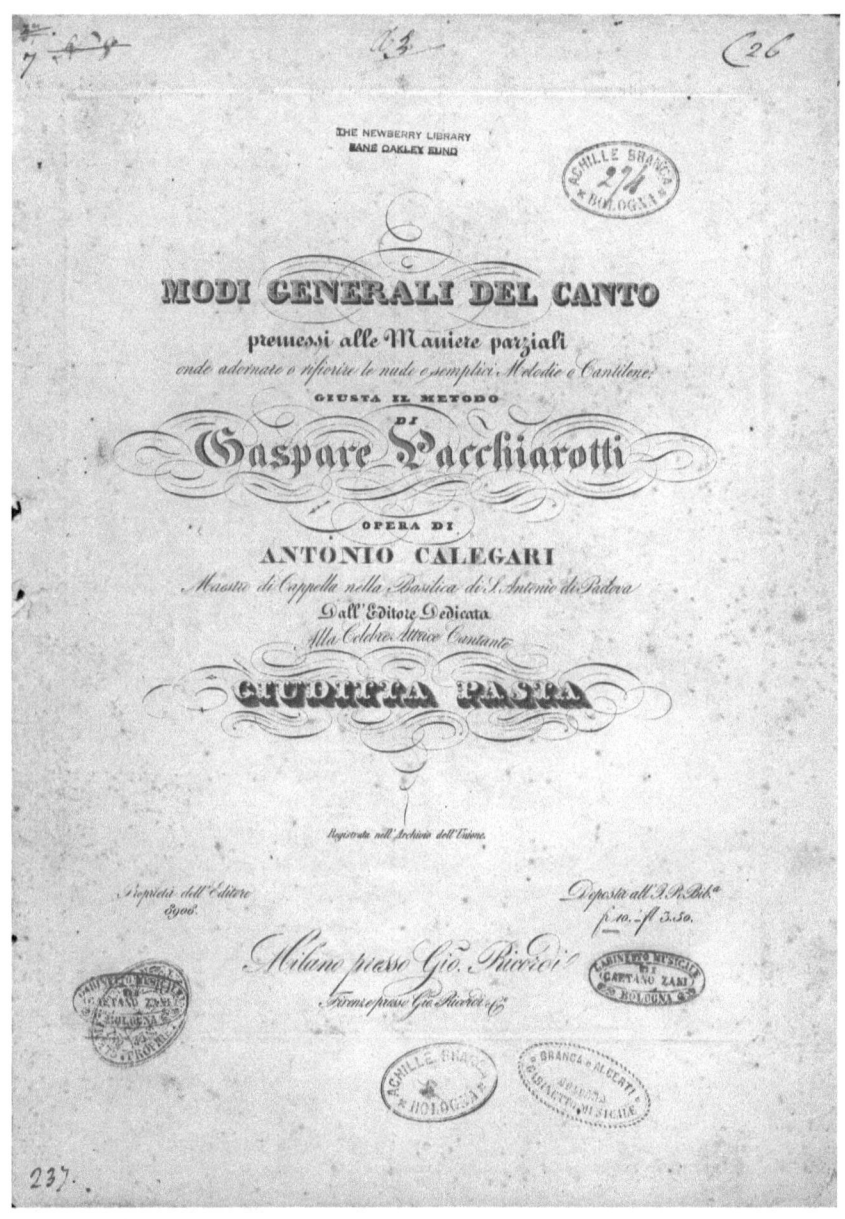

FIGURE 50. *Modi generali del canto, premessi alle maniere parziali onde adornare e rifiorire le nude o semplici melodie o cantilene, giusta il metodo di Gaspare Pacchierotti, opera di Antonio Calegari, Maestro di Cappella nella Basilica di S. Antonio di Padova, dall'editore dedicata alla celebre attrice cantante Giuditta Pasta.* Milan: Ricordi, [n.d.]. Newberry Library, Chicago. Reproduced by permission.

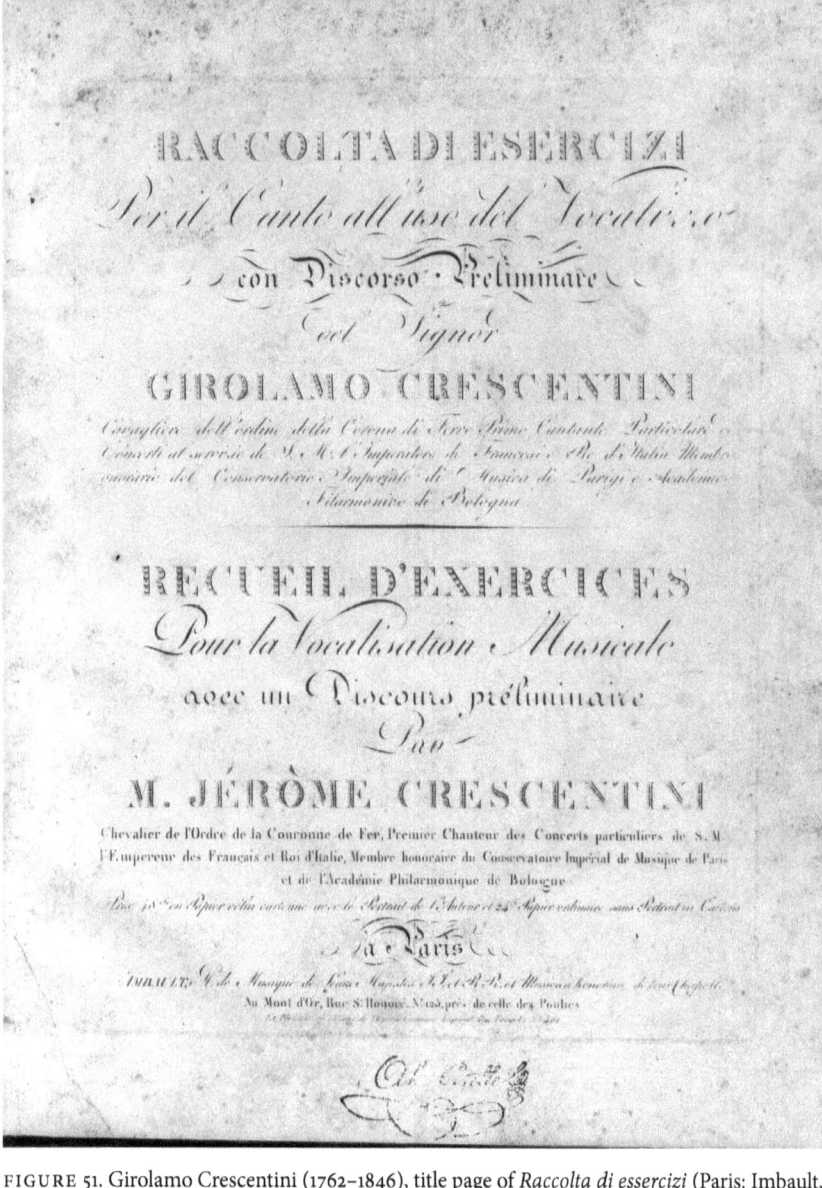

FIGURE 51. Girolamo Crescentini (1762–1846), title page of *Raccolta di essercizi* (Paris: Imbault, [ca. 1810]). Crescentini was court singer and teacher for Napoleon from 1806 to 1812 and published his *Raccolta di essercizi* as instruction in singing bel canto around 1811. The book starts with a lengthy dual-language preface in French and Italian and continues with advanced exercises for pupils.

FIGURE 52. Anne-Louis Girodet de Roussy-Trioson (1767–1824), *The Sleep of Endymion*, 1793. The painting is mentioned in Balzac's *Sarrasine*, where it hangs fictitiously in the salon of the Lanty family and absorbs the attention of the narrator's female auditor. Nowadays it is housed in the Louvre in Paris. © RMN-Grand Palais / Art Resource, New York. Reproduced by permission.

FIGURE 53. Alfred Edward Chalon, watercolor of the last major stage star among castrati Giambattista Velluti, who retired from the stage in 1830. Dated 1826, the image shows Velluti as the knight Armando in Giacomo Meyerbeer, *Il crociato in Egitto* (1825), staged in London in 1826, for which he was given a goatee to masculinize and contemporize him. Opera Rara Archive, opera-rara.com. Reproduced by permission.

PART THREE

Half-light

5

Cold Man, Money Man, Big Man Too

DENUNCIATIONS

The great art of singing, descended largely from castrati, had, by the later eighteenth century, become clouded with charges of aristocratic luxury, vanity, and decadence, charges that were inseparable from critiques of castration itself. In the 1780s the marquis Francesco Albergati Capacelli, a Bolognese playwright, penned a strident denunciation on both fronts:

> I owe ... a public pronouncement to Truth. In speaking against castrati, I do not ... deny any one of them the merits of culture, honesty, and civility that are found in few of them, but are nevertheless found. I inveigh against their profession, their state, and the unworthy principle of maintaining, feeding, fomenting, cherishing, and rewarding it.
>
> Only Italy has the pride of producing and cultivating such fine fruit; and only France has that of abhorring and refusing it. In point of fact, everyone is saved from knowing the *man* in these people; and, the rare *prizes* among ... them indeed create such a strong illusion that here and there one manages to forget their monstrosity. ...
>
> But the time has come to stop sacrificing these wretched victims. Is it not enough that a throat and the [lure of] luxury should expose the lives of so many people to such calamities ... that people should nevertheless want to reduce men to vile, disgusting monsters simply to tickle their ears with a little aria?[1]

So much for the luxurious singing of the Farinellis, Caffarellis, and Rauzzinis.

Or not? Mozart wrote his famously virtuosic motet *Exsultate, jubilate* (KV165/158a) for Rauzzini not long beforehand, in January 1773. And in 1774 the singing treatise of the castrato Mancini treated agility with more space and a good deal less ambivalence than Tosi had done fifty years earlier, in a text that dutifully warned fathers about castrating any but their most gifted sons.[2] These and many other examples show that Albergati's remonstrations were delivered in the teeth of the still-wide popularity of castrati on stage and in church, especially in Italy but also in London and elsewhere, much of it generated by their command over coloratura and the capacity for nuance in the newish idioms of the pathetic and sensible. Attacking them in the inflated preface printed with his comedy *Il ciarlator maldicente* (The badmouthing chatterbox), the playwright climbed up on a moral hobbyhorse to target the depravities of his age and suggest that their very existence betrayed that new Enlightenment divinity, Nature.[3] The play included a foppish castrato with the ridiculous name of Meneguccio Sfrontati detto lo Scarpinello, probably a reference to Tassoni's 1621 mock-heroic epic *La secchia rapita,* in which a blind singer of tales named Menecuccio is chased away by laughter.[4] By the 1780s, denunciations of the kind had become commonplace, even de rigueur. They were the liberal cries to preserve Nature by condemning any cruel perversions that might threaten disfigure Her, where Nature was a cipher of deeper-seated stakes because metaphysically prior. Albergati went on, "After such barbarity has made these miserable men vile and deformed, destined for denatured song, a . . . dreadful education, the study of nothing but singing, the frequent burden of conversing with others of like kind—[after all that], then caresses, ignorant applause, [and] the gold of madmen and squanderers add to making them ever more audacious and wicked."[5]

Caresses, adulation, money. This unholy trinity had often attached to castrati in earlier decades, but there was a new lug and tow to Albergati's words. It was not just that they were cultural misfits, but that they were morally inferior as evinced by their impudence and decadence and by their boorish, dissolute fans. Castrati had become abhorrent because sexually misaligned yet still recruited to fit into a new sexual order. Hence Albergati's dictum in the play that the castrato Scarpinello be played either by a real castrato or by a young actor speaking in falsetto, *"but never by a woman dressed like a man."*[6] Acting the part of the wrong sex was now only one degree removed from being (like a castrato) denatured, vile, and deformed. In the new order, Claudius would have to be played by Claudio and Claudia by Claudia. Though in practice no consistency on the matter was to exist or even be much demanded for decades to come, the impulse to typify sexual difference by representing ideal, contrasting sexual categories was coming of age. It held on stage and off. And it was of a piece with new bourgeois notions that wanted clear-cut dimorphic sexual morphologies, which gave new moral sanction to intersex marriage and proscribed same-sex relations, and which elevated the status of parenthood and the nuclear family.[7] The subtext in all such reorientations (not always so "sub") was a new quest for "truth to" Nature, the latter figured through a promiscuous set of signs deployed to make things seem what they allegedly were, or were supposed to be.

Albergati gave expression to feelings that had been brewing for a long time. In Handel's London, Italian opera and castrati had never truly *not* been foreign, profligate, irrational, squandering, feminizing, and corrupting, no matter how attractive they were to many, and the French had never had them in public spaces at all.[8] The philosopher, musician, and historian Charles de Blainville, who heard castrati in Italy during the 1740s, gave early warning that they were intolerable to new Enlightenment ideologies of human integrity and chalked the evil up to their parents: "It is known to everyone that these poor Fellows did not *cease to be men* with their own Consent," we read, "but merely thro' the Avarice of their Parents, who reduced them to that Condition, at an Age so tender."[9] A senator in Voltaire's *Candide* of 1759 scoffs about "swooning with pleasure if you want or can at the sight of a eunuch chirruping the roles of Caesar and Cato."[10] His own word for "eunuch" was "châtré," designating an emasculated animal. Arnulphe d'Aumont used the same word as a synonym for "eunuch" in his *Encyclopédie* article "Eunuque."[11] In this atmosphere Rousseau, that architect of new family values (and pretending bulldozer of the old-style paterfamilias), was constrained to denounce castrati vociferously in his 1767 *Dictionnaire de musique*, which cried that in Italy there are

> fathers so cruel as to sacrifice nature to fortune, and . . . submit their children to this operation, that they may gratify the pleasure of the voluptuous and the inhuman; who do not hesitate to make others unhappy that they may produce them pleasure. Let us leave to the good women of great cities, the modest laugh, the disdainful air, and those just pleasantries, of which these wretches are the eternal objects; but let us endeavour to make the voice of modesty and humanity heard, which cries out against this infamous practice; and let those princes who seek to encourage it, for once blush at a custom that is so injurious to the preservation of mankind.[12]

The French had of course long cultivated their own tradition of high lyric tragedy for which they used high tenors with falsetto extensions, called *haute-contres*, and were constitutionally opposed to castrati, even if they had been alternately sidling up to and blustering against Italian opera and castrati ever since the mid-seventeenth century. Italian and other European resistance was more compromised. In 1748 Pope Benedict XIV was pressed to consider banning castrati in church but was too politically savvy to do so and instead simply reinforced prohibitions against amputating body parts except for medical necessity.[13] There were whispers of change elsewhere on the peninsula. Such a prominent friend to castrati as Padre Martini, who networked continually throughout the middle decades of the century to place them in schools, chapels, and even theaters, filling hundreds of manuscript letters with recommendations, noted in 1750 that the Franciscans in Rome had not taken any castrati for a long time with "very just motives."[14] Others were more outspoken. The Christian moralist Giovanni Antonio Bianchi (Arcadian name: "Lauriso Tragiense") in 1753 lambasted those soft, depraved "semimale singers with female voices," maligning them with that worst of all epithets, "luxuries."[15] By the time Algarotti's famous *Saggio sopra l'opera* (Essay on opera) appeared in 1755 and 1763—after various Italian translations of Rousseau and other philosophes had been streaming out and after the widespread publication and translation throughout Europe of Cesare Beccaria's *Crimes and Punishments* (1764), which denounced torture and the death penalty—to protest against castration was to pledge allegiance to an irrefutable new social program. In Milan the poet and librettist Giuseppe Parini, who was central to the Milanese group centered around the opera-loving intellectual powerhouse Pietro Verri, who published the periodical *Il Caffè*, declared that the malevolence of castrating fathers was even more unnatural than the state of their sons. "You Italian Father [Italo Genitore]: . . . it's not error but vice that pushes you into this horrid business," he cried in his lengthy ode "L'evirazione" (Castration), only later more delicately renamed "La Musica."[16] Countless expats and visitors to Italy likewise felt compelled to register their indignation. The coquettish social climber Sara Goudar declared in 1774 upon seeing L'Amadori (Giovanni Tedeschi) play Ulysses's son Telemachus, "Je n'aime point les Eunuques" (though she added cheekily that perhaps it was because she was a woman).[17] The Marquis de Sade reacted more violently. The next year he sat through a Florentine production of *Perseus and Andromeda* in horror, above all because of the "half-man" onstage from whose "large, fatty, somewhat ill-formed body" came a "high, clear voice" (the man was Giuseppe Millico, one of Gluck's favorites).[18]

That de Sade should have imputed monstrosity to others may seem ironic, but the temperature of the time was such that Millico's performance of sensibility had to fit in, aurally and morally, with his public display of voice and body. In a particularly shrill complaint the Englishman John Moore elaborated on the covenant between performances sensible and moral by ill-suited bodies when he wondered who these "wretched castratos" were, with their "artificial trills. Is not the horrid practice which is encouraged by this manner of supplying the place of female singers a greater outrage on religion and morality, than can be produced by the evils which their prohibition is intended to prevent?"[19]

For the cosmopolitan intelligentsia of the time, castration had a specific political valence, signifying the depravity of the old regime at a time when, as Philippe Ariès has claimed (rightly, I think), no stable notion of the privileged child of innocence yet existed.[20] Incipient signs of its arrival were on the way, signs that the child was beginning to acquire its own nature. And because Nature was sacrosanct—denoting something prior, given, and untouched by humankind—it was not to be maimed but rather, in the metaphor of the time, nurtured and allowed to grow, not "developmentally," as the science of the 1830s would have it, but according to its proper "natural" course. If the *axioma* trumps its own *explanans,* the fact that it doesn't need saying is precisely the point. At work were not just inroads made by a new bourgeois familial and sexual outlook but an overhaul in the whole subjective order. Lorraine Daston and Katharine Park have shown that the enchantments of wonders and spectacles that marked public life during the old regime were being seen by the mid-eighteenth century as dodgy and politically motivated. The imagination that had once permitted wonders to flourish became prey to suspicions of unreason or pathology, and fantasy became the mark of lapses in self-knowledge or personhood.[21]

COLD, BAD, AND UGLY: BEASTLY STEREOTYPES

As the lifeblood of the castrato's employ, wonders and other marvelous spectacles, once they were attacked, had the net effect of moving castrati ever more out of their festive worlds. Where prior to the mid-eighteenth century castrati were often treated with a kind of rough but endearing laughter—manifest during the seventeenth century in ribald cantatas by the likes of Francesco Melosio and the lewd satires of a Salvatore Rosa, and during the earlier eighteenth century in the self-mockery of Balatri, the bawdy verse epistles of Paolo Rolli, and the sometimes bizarre but largely amiable caricatures of Zanetti and Ghezzi—by the mid-eighteenth century they were denounced with a new moralizing sobriety.[22] Consider on the earlier side of this divide the affectionate humor that infuses Zanetti's depictions of the castrato Andrea Pacini as a turtle (Fig. 39) and Castorino (player of tyrants) as an ape (Fig. 40); Nicolini pointing in Zanetti's album to a nobleman dressed as an alligator (Fig. 41); or, no less kindly, Ghezzi's depiction of Annibali looking like an armadillo (Fig. 42) and a rather porcine Farinelli dressed in drag during his first season in Rome (Fig. 43).[23]

All this contrasts with the later eighteenth century, when castrati were no longer a laughing matter. Visual satires by then had grown somewhat attenuated on the Continent, many surviving ones emerging from the tradition of English engravings. Meanwhile verbal satires turned deadly serious or assimilated their subjects not just to roosters, capons, and chicks, to which they were often likened before the mid-eighteenth century, but to a monstrous slew of beasts conjured up to epitomize Nature gone astray.

A wicked English prose satire published anonymously in early 1778, *The Remarkable Trial of the Queen of Quavers*, is a case in point. It attributes the infatuation with English opera (dubbed the "quavering itch") to "an imp," here meaning a devil or evil spirit.[24] Assuming, in the bizarre allegory of the satire, the shape of a fly, the creature slides through the ear and gets into the pineal gland, where "it dries out the ethereal spirit, which is the essence of the soul, and produces ... a total alienation of mind."[25] Through this Cartesian misadventure a veritable menagerie of bestial devotees to opera is produced whose affinities with castrati cause them to despoil the social order once dismembered by their barbaric progenitors. "The box of Pandora did not contain a more pernicious calamity: It is the fierce Medea that cuts and dismembers children ["the Castrati," a footnote reads];

and the barbarous Circe, by whom human creatures are metamorphosed into brutes. Hence those who are afflicted with this disease [of castration] are so apt to whinny like colts, croak like frogs, bellow like bulls, roar like lions, squeak like pigs, and most commonly bray like asses."[26] At stake was not just the welfare of children or the morality of parents but above all the "safety of the nation." The Queen of Quavers and her associates the castrati were guilty of threatening the "glory" of the "mighty Empire" through the deadly sins of pride, avarice, lust, and impertinence.[27] They have made a bargain with the devil, we read, and are "liable to an action for usury."[28]

Ian Woodfield has shown that in real life the eponymous queen (elsewhere in the text called Polly Farmer) was Mary Ann Yates, who managed the King's Theatre—the exclusive venue for Italian opera for much of the 1770s—along with two other real-life protagonists, "Dicky Blunderall" and "Goody Crooks" (the latter a prominent novelist and playwright named Frances Brooke). The trial of the title is a mock affair staged on the moon to signify madness, but much of the satire turns on battles that were actually taking place at the time between theater managements, particularly, Woodfield shows, between Brooke (the satire's anonymous author) and David Garrick, actor and manager of Drury Lane, which was home to spoken theater; for Brooke held a blistering grudge against Garrick for his having once turned down a play of hers,[29] an offense for which she had also retaliated with ad hominem mockery in a recent novel.

If *The Remarkable Trial of the Queen of Quavers* is the work of losing bidders in an attempt to take over the King's Theatre, it displaces some of its bile and the brunt of its symbolic load onto the castrati, those wantonly extravagant, piggishly "loathsome" creatures such as Miccio (Giuseppe Millico) and Wrong Call Ye (Francesco Roncaglia) "who cannot live upon a clear income of three thousand pounds."[30] The prosecutor for the Crown makes this explicit in delivering the opening arguments by summoning various animals as tools of verbal abuse while assimilating the directors and opera addicts to eunuchs.

> It is in consequence of this amazing depravity of taste that seven exotic animals yclep'd[31] castrati were lately imported from the Continent, at such a most enormous expence.—Such filthy lumps of mortality as the wilds of Africa never produced!—They have the look of a crocodile, the grin of an ape, the legs of a peacock, the paunch of a cow, the shape of an elephant, the brains of a goose, the throat of a pig, and the tail of a mouse: to crown the whole, if you sit but a few moments in their company, you will be sure of having your nostrils perfumed in a strange manner; for they have continually about them the odoriferous effluvia of onion and garlic.... Indeed it is not possible to conceive a more nauseous and odious creature than a Castrato.[32]

Like other invectives, *The Remarkable Trial of the Queen of Quavers* takes greed and rapaciousness as a figment of the body grotesque, adored by the gawking devotees of Italian opera: "Contrary to the system of Plato, who places the summum bonum in *regular* beauty," it declares, they "stick to deformity, and distortions of nature." Connections between animality and money now are constitutive, destroying the self and the body social. The castrato, that "outlaw of nature," "the monster of monsters," as Claudian had it, "is neither man nor woman but something between the human species and the brute creation, like a monkey." Hence the bestial character and "imbruted" "mental powers" of his fans form in totality a social monster that needs too much money and costs too much money.[33]

Charges of money mongering cannot be pried apart from fears of the in-betweenness of men who grew irregularly compared with others and therefore failed to conform to "normal" men in shape and size. The long limbs, great height, barrel chests, and large jaws variously given individual castrati in early eighteenth-century caricatures by Zanetti, Ghezzi, William Hogarth, and Marco Ricci (cf. Figs. 5 and 30) were irregularities that mediated public perception and interactions. Pellegrini and Berenstadt were given distended, protruding lips to go with their oversized jawlines, and enlarged lips were also drawn with devastating results on Scalzi, the papal sopranos Menicuccio (Domenico Ricci) and Raffaellino, the operatic star Domenico Annibali (Fig. 42), and Farinelli (Figs. 2, 7, 25, and 43), in contrast to the regularity seen in tenors (e.g. Fig. 14).[34] Some portraits betray irregularities, while others (for instance, Flipart's regal depiction of Scalzi in Fig. 34) smooth them out. But caricatures are physically sites of different kinds of exposure, even when they overdo abnormalities (e.g., Ghezzi's Berenstadt, with its great head and bizarre lips and chin yet bookish, kindly aspect, shown in Fig. 44), revealing chinks in the social armor with corresponding increases in verbal critiques.[35]

. . .

How did changes in cultural values and subjective mechanisms turn men from idols and eminences into monsters, from inspiring amused pleasure to demanding unsmiling moral judgment? Toughening critiques of castrati from the latter half of the eighteenth century follow the general trajectory of an increasingly binary sexual regime that tracks reform-minded views of the human body as immutable and sacrosanct. The developments are imbricated in pressures on the collective psyche, which was moving toward a more two-sided and strenuously contentious form. Intensifying resistance to castrati is one warrant of a line being drawn in the later eighteenth century in a changing ideal of the self to which the castrato is consistently opposed. As Sander Gilman would have it in *Difference and Pathology*, the Other in this line-drawing operation is always immanent within the Self. Presuming castrati to be implicated in such an operation, we should note that they had not always been rattling so violently at the inner psychic door. Before the mid-eighteenth century negative feelings about castrati had generally been more moderate, even dormant, allowing a caste of castrated men to be accommodated to self and society with relative ease. Serious trouble began only once a new Self was awakening, not in the collective dreamland of an easygoing early modern psyche but in the growing nightmare of a more modern Self- and Other-policing one. In that new psychic landscape, the perceived line between Self and Other was starting to shift, to be drawn more oppositionally, as the Other hardened into Gilman's notion of a "stereotype," something hideous and frightening that causes the Self to seek a reordering by ousting those it fears, making recourse to its own inherently recurrently protean, line-shifting, self-cleansing tendencies. The castrato was turning ever more into a "counterweight" to the Self, a quality that in a psychoanalytic view is intrinsic to all mental representations but is exaggerated in this instance, as the relatively good (or at least tolerable) castrato ossified into the bad Other.[36]

The paradigm speaks to a dialectic between the individual and the social that maps onto changing historical views of castrati in the later eighteenth century. The "beastly" in them, at best problematic and ambivalent, went from being fun to being a sign of pollution and thus a source of anxiety. Castrati who were big, fat, or otherwise distorted became tripping cords for feelings of repulsion and fear. Those castrated men who were in no way obviously deformed had to be dissected for signs of ills hidden beneath their surface. In 1791 a Venetian *filarmonico* named Innocenzo Della Lena jumped through hoops to find physical fault with Luigi Marchesi, for, as he put it, despite outer appearances that Marchesi was handsome and regular in his features, "Nature will not give up her rights."[37]

SIGNS OF COLDNESS

Accompanying this shift were changed understandings of coldness, which had earlier been charged with humoral significance and later with meanings of sensibility, or both. The early modern castrato, who is wondrous for singing though humorally "cold"—*like a woman* in Galenic terms, which understood women to be cold and moist, full of phlegm[38]—comes to be thought of as "cold" because incapable of human "warmth" and thus unable to move the heart. (See Fig. 45, a woodcut that shows schematically the cold vs. hot / wet vs. dry Galenic schema in an anatomical diagram by Leonhard Thurneysser from 1574.)

Roughly parallel to this transition was a gradual decline in humoral, and specifically Galenic, ways of thinking. Owsei Temkin, in his history of Galenic philosophy, traces the erratic course of this decline, starting in the highest academic circles of the Renaissance and continuing in medical and popular circles of the nineteenth century. Meticulous anatomical dissections carried out by Vesalius in the early sixteenth century posed challenges to Galen's pathological theories. They disproved, for instance, Galen's claim that idiopathic epilepsy was caused by an accumulation of a cold and viscous humor in the ventricles of the brain, which no anatomical dissection could discover. The ripple effects of such deductions and the empirical urges that had underwritten them tested Galen's belief that a psychic spirit was elaborated in the blood. To counter such a notion, William Harvey offered compelling mechanical explanations in the early seventeenth century for the circulation of the blood. Also around that time naturalist philosophers began challenging the notion of the soul as the *form* of the body. And by the mid-eighteenth century vitalist philosophies positing the operations of a vital life force vied with both mechanical paradigms and Galenic ones. With all this and more, Galen began looking more like Aristotle than not, and his attributions of hot and cold qualities started looking more subjective than objective. Humoral thinking continued to underpin medicine for a long time, especially in popular and folk domains, or what one might call the popular imaginary, and even to some extent in practical science.[39] Though Galen's cures continued to dominate much of the work of surgeons, doctors, and pharmacists and the beliefs of most patients, for whom they were good precisely because traditional, not least in Italy, the scientific and philosophical reign of Galenism was coming to an end.[40]

Now if the castrato's life course ran generally alongside that of humoral thinking, what precisely had been his humoral profile and what was it becoming? In 1581 a medical detractor pronounced that castrated men humorally fell midway between men and women, too cold and too moist to have the wit, energy, and bravery of men and even worse off than women because humorally out of balance. The spokesman was a Spanish doctor named Juan Huarte, who was so simplistic in his humoral views as to repeat an ancient tale that they were incapable of pronouncing r's.[41] Huarte's simplifications and excesses aside, attributing cold humors to castrated men was customary. We saw this above in the case of Sorlisi's mid-seventeenth-century marriage, which invoked theological charges of his being "ill-made and cold"; and likewise in Balatri's lament of 1725 over having been made "cold and ill-formed" by his father. Unlike Huarte's censorious ascriptions of coldness, however, Sorlisi and Balatri used "coldness" principally to denote a condition of being biologically nongenerative. This was something the Huguenot lawyer Charles Ancillon claimed directly in 1707 when he wrote, on the pretext of protesting Nicolini's proposal of marriage to a woman, that eunuchs were of a "cold and frigid Temperament," that is, incapable of generation.[42]

What changed around the mid-eighteenth century is that traditional attributions of coldness became charged with a newly negative and newly affective meaning, as they became mixed up in widespread critiques of both social norms and virtuosic singing. Most such critiques attached to castrati, but they were also used against the ultra-famous freelancing female coloratura Caterina Gabrielli. Where coloratura singing had once been a thing of wonder, it was now damned by outspoken cognoscenti for being instrumental and unfeeling. For Metastasio, coloratura signaled an inhuman failure of music to give genuine expression to words, which was tantamount to a betrayal of nature; or, as he said, "Singers nowadays ... think themselves better the more they stray from human nature. Their archetypes are nightingales, piccolos, crickets, and cicadas, not persons and their emotions."[43] He specifically lamented the state of castrato singing in letters exchanged with, of all people, the castrato-tutor Bernacchi;[44] and in 1762 he associated the problem as well with Gabrielli, then performing in his midst at the Viennese court, reframing it in the physico-sentimental terms of hot versus cold: "If the wondrous Gabrielli doesn't have a melisma thirty measures long and doesn't go up to high e *in alt* [e'''], the spectators freeze. She could warm them more by singing to the heart, but to do so she would have to find a new method."[45]

Warm singing had fluidity of motion, hence Metastasio's cold instrumental singers were "*inanimate* nightingales,"[46] "marvelous players of the throat who, having completely forgotten their humanity, aspire to nothing but the glory of violins, ... disdaining all the paths that lead directly to the hearts of spectators."[47] In 1764 the main object of his discontent was again the "modern" singing of castrati, whose feats had something inhuman about them. "Our excellent singers are ashamed to compare themselves to men, from whom they take the name." Angling to seduce spectators' ears at the expense of their hearts, "they yearn only to vie with radiator grills, whistles, and violins."[48]

The feeling that a new coldness had come into modern singing was easily imputed to the inhumanness of castrati and absorbed into new antimechanistic, provitalist, prosentimental strains. But as I have begun to suggest, it was also part and parcel of a growing political critique of aristocracy and luxury. In 1771 the Italian theater architect Francesco Milizia articulated the relationship in a damning equation that made instrumental bravura, specifically of castrati, equal to the bejeweled fashion plates of the French aristocracy: "Most castrati ... split the voice *[squartare la voce]*, leap from note to note, shake, and make arpeggios. And with passaggi, trills, caprices, and arpeggios and little broken-up bits *[spezzature]* [they] make music florid and choked with ornament, and disfigure any beauty. In this guise ... their arias resemble the ladies of France."[49]

Milizia pointed in the direction of one of the ills decried by Della Lena in his diatribe on the wildly popular Marchesi, whom he called an "insensate machine" or "pole," "totally devoid of action or expression adapted to manifest properly its sentiments."[50] (Cf. Fig. 46, John Nixon's caricature of Marchesi, who shows his prideful nature with his chin up and out and his head held high while singing in a London concert in 1789.)

Della Lena was not alone. In 1789 a German correspondent in Venice compared Marchesi with the great Gasparo Pacchierotti (both of whom he had heard both privately and publicly) "in order," he said, "to give some idea of the excellency of Pacchierotti." He began his review by calling Marchesi "a true favorite of nature" who combined "a most advantageous, captivating figure [with] the finest voice that can be imagined, a clear intonation, and ... an unsurpassable fire," one whose principal failing was to "hurry" him frequently into "excesses." Furthermore, he went on, "in what concerns the recitative, which most tries the art of the singer," Marchesi was "far behind his rival Pacchierotti ... [who is] the reverse of all I have said of Marchesi: a hideous figure, insupportable features of face, a nasal voice (which however is uncommonly pliable) and extravagant action, which are peculiar to all such long and meager bodies. But his singing melts in a moment every bad impression into tenderness and melancholy, whether we will or not. To his inexhaustible variations of melody, he unites the severest conscientiousness toward harmony; and I have never once heard him trespass against it, even in the most adventurous flights."[51]

Resistance to Marchesi's singing style was already anticipated by the Verri brothers, who contrasted him with both the young Pacchierotti and Pacchierotti's slightly older kindred spirit Giuseppe Millico. In 1769 Millico had played Gluck's Orfeo in *Le feste d'Apollo* at the court of Parma, in 1770 he was the Paris of Gluck and Calzabigi's five-act reform opera *Paride ed Elena* at the Burgtheater in Vienna, and in 1772 he again played the character of Orpheus, this time in London.[52] From Rome Alessandro wrote his brother Pietro during Carnival in 1777 to say that there was nothing any good in the theaters there save Millico, who "sings with great expression."[53] To vouchsafe his powers as a new man of sensibility and expressive depth, he reported that Millico had earlier gone to Paris and met Rousseau, who beamed hypocritically when he learned he was a castrato and asked him to sing. Alessandro wanted his brother Pietro to believe Rousseau had been "astonished and transported" by Millico, even though the singer had had to accompany himself on the philosopher's "horribly out of tune harpsichord"; and that he was especially swept away by Millico's singing of stanzas from the epic romances of Ariosto and Tasso, for which the castrato had allegedly invented a special expressive declamation so fine that Rousseau told him, "If Tasso had heard them sung he would have written a new poem for him."[54] Millico on this account incarnates the new ideal of Italianate singing that runs inherently counter to the awkward simplicity of Rousseau's opéra comique style and abreast the rhapsodic melody of epic recitation.

That Millico was a Pacchierotti prototype for Alessandro Verri is clear from his account of Pacchierotti's moving performance in a Roman salon. Perhaps it helped that he could testify that Pacchierotti was also a "manly" eunuch who had once beaten a Neapolitan nobleman in a duel after being struck by him with his walking stick "out of jealousy."[55]

In the same season, Pietro Verri, famed as a sensist literato, was hearing Pacchierotti in Milan, and he too was a fan. But what is most revealing is the contrast Pietro draws, by turns laudatory and damning, between Pacchierotti and the young Marchesi after hearing Marchesi's La Scala performances of 1780.

> [Marchesi's singing] is very beautiful, resonant, and even throughout his range, and I can find no singer with whom to compare him. He's faultless in intonation, does things of great difficulty, and commands his voice as one would a violin. He's also able to make a crystalline trill [*un trillo granito*, in the sense of being highly secure and perhaps also acoustically gleaming] and to raise up the trill up by six or seven notes in a row without interruption, as one does on a bowed instrument, sliding the hand on the string. He supports [*sostiene*] his voice and fills the theater, vast as it is. And to all this one should add that his beautiful voice is passionate, tender, and compassionate in a way I've found in no other singer. He has everything.

But then comes the devastating exception:

> The only thing he lacks, I think, is *feeling*, the kind that knows how to touch your soul.

And why?

> At the loveliest part of a tender piece, after he's already ventured a sweet beginning, Marchesini makes you do a violent spin and takes you out of yourself with some bizarre, cheerful caprice, thus dampening your nascent sensibility. If he should ever seduce your heart, he will become a perfect enchanter [*incantatore*], but until now he's a marvelous piece of non sense, all bits and pieces.[56]

ORFEI AND VIRTUOSI

It was these very oppositions—sensible/pathetic versus ostentatious/bizarre—that lurked in Rousseau's condemnations of castration and castrati. The ideals of "modesty and humanity" invoked in his case against castration would have found broad if not universal sympathies with the likes of Metastasio and later Susan Burney, daughter of Charles, who championed Pacchierotti's combination of sensitivity and passion. Rousseau's contradictory claim that castrati sang without "warmth and passion" would have rung bells with Pietro Verri, Della Lena, and our German reviewer, all of whom were unmoved by Marchesi's displays of wondrous extravagance and missed in him an ardor in singing and acting, which was tantamount to truth in representation.[57]

Two lines were being drawn in the sand. One, which we might call the Orfeo line, started with Gluck's first Orpheus, singing actor and alto castrato Gaetano Guadagni (Vienna 1762), trained in London by Italian actors and influenced by David Garrick; continued with Millico in the 1760s-'70s; included Tenducci, who sang the part in 1771 in a much-embellished *Orfeo ed Euridice* in Florence's Teatro del Cocomero, shortly after he had learned to sing Scottish songs with sensibility for the Edinburgh Musical Society in 1768–69;[58] and peaked in the performances of Pacchierotti, who held the stage from 1770 through the early 1790s, when he was Marchesi's principal competition. All except Marchesi were famed Orpheuses in various redactions of Gluck's opera.[59] The other line—we might call it the flamboyant line—had its principal exponent in Marchesi, though others, like Rauzzini and to some extent Aprile, could be grouped with him.[60] The divide is admittedly rough and far from unbridgeable, nor does it lack historical precedents in the earliest staged theatrical singing of castrati in the first decade of the seventeenth century and afterward. But it is at a minimum a useful heuristic, echoing the impressions of contemporaneous listeners, which clustered antagonistically along opposed axes grounded in genealogies of performance. When Millico played Paris, lover of Helen of Troy, in Vienna in 1770, he had been preceded there by Guadagni's Orfeo only eight years earlier. Millico's calling card, like Guadagni's, was expressivity and cantabile, often lyrical and parlante by turns. You can hear these qualities in the beginning of the most famous of his arias, "O del mio dolce ardore," from Gluck's *Paride ed Elena*, which he performed at Vienna's Burgtheater on November 3, 1770. It was sung by the young Paris/Millico at the moment when he stood with his fellow Trojan sailors on the shores on Sparta offering sacrifices to their goddess Venus, and broke into an intensely yearning address to his beloved.

O del mio dolce ardor	Oh desired object
Bramato oggetto,	of my sweet passion,
L'aura che tu respiri,	the breeze you breathe
Alfin respiro.	at last I breathe.
Ovunque il guardo io giro,	Wherever I turn my gaze
Le tue vaghe sembianze	your beautiful face
Amore in me dipinge:	paints love for me.
Il mio pensier si finge	My thoughts conjure up
Le più liete speranze;	the happiest hopes;
E nel desio che così m'empie il petto	and in the longing that thus fills my breast
Cerco te, chiamo te, spero e sospiro.	I seek you, I call for you, I hope and I sigh!

The aria, still a standby for young singers, trades on the beating heart of the accompaniment, the repeated melody notes that carry the first verse, the yearning, prescient echoes of the oboe, the quasi–ad libitum passage toward the end, and a soaring and plunging lyricism throughout (Ex. 21). It adumbrates the reformist agenda advocated in 1772 by the Neapolitan Antonio Planelli, who called for parlante singing, with few notes, a limited range, and touching melody, as part of a general plea for emotion in opera that went by the name of the "pathetic."[61] In Planelli's ideal, opera would move from being a *genere sonabile* to being a *genere cantabile*—from being an "instrumental," aestheticizing genre to being a singing, expressive one, which the noble "pathetic" would embody. It can be no coincidence that Gluck and Calzabigi called on Millico, whose adopted town was Naples, for both *Le feste d'Apollo*, in which he played Orpheus, and in the following year *Paride ed Elena*; nor that in 1774 Pacchierotti performed the Italian version of Gluck's Orfeo at the court theater in Naples.[62]

In fact, it was Millico who, in a long preface to a printed score of his opera *La pietà d'amore* of 1782, pledged his allegiance as singer-composer to both Gluck and Planelli by advocating simple, direct declamation and a unifying overture. Millico admitted that in his own opera he had included passaggi ("gorgheggi") and word repetitions, but he protested that he had done so to preserve the "brilliance" of certain singers who had "studied to resemble warbling birds more than [to sing] frank melodies that touch the heart" and "move to tears." The preface is pure Gluckian doctrine, shot through with reformist buzzwords and apologies for concessions to Italians' taste for virtuosic display. Midway through, it shifts the narrative through a coy sleight of hand to turn Millico from narrator to protagonist, from composer and proselytizer to the most moving of singers. Wistfully as he moves along he starts to recall that in 1769 everyone at Parma wept when he sang the diminished-seventh- and linear diminished-fourth-filled recitative that precedes "Che farò senza Euridice." This is the one in which Orpheus loses Eurydice a second time after his fateful backward glance in Hades (act 3, scene 1), and which Gluck ended with chokingly blank cries of grief (Ex. 22).

ORFEO:
Smanio, fremo, deliro... ah! mio tesoro...
(si volta con impeto e la guarda)

EURIDICE:
Giusti Dei, ch'avenne! Io manco. Io moro. *(more)*
(Alzandosi con forza e tornando a cadere)

ORFEO:
Ahimè! Dove trascorsi? Ove mi spinse
un delirio d'amor? *(Le s'accosta con fretta)* Sposa!... Euridice! *(la scuote)*
Euridice!... Consorte! Ah più non vive;
la chiamo in van. Misero me! La perdo,
e di nuovo, e per sempre: o legge, o morte!
O ricordo crudel! Non ho soccorso,
non m'avanza consiglio. Io veggo solo,
o fiera vista! Il luttuoso aspetto
dell'orrido mio stato:
saziati, sorte rea! Son disperato.[63]

EXAMPLE 21. Christoph Willibald Gluck, *Paride ed Elena* (Vienna, Burgtheater, November 3, 1770), "O del mio dolce ardor," mm. 1–23, as sung by Vito Giuseppe Millico.

EXAMPLE 21. *(continued)*

EXAMPLE 22. Gluck, *Orfeo ed Euridice* (Vienna, Burgtheater, October 5, 1762), recitative, "Smanio, fremo e deliro," act 3, scene 1, revised version staged for the wedding festivities of the royal infante Don Ferdinando and the Archduchess infante Maria Amalia as *Le feste d'Apollo* (Parma, Royal Court Theater, August 1769); part of Orfeo as sung by Vito Giuseppe Millico.

EXAMPLE 22. (continued)

ORFEO:

I am mad . . . I rave . . . I tremble . . . Oh, my treasure!

EURIDICE:

Great gods, what's happening to me? I am fainting, I am dying. *(dying)*
(Getting up forcefully and falling back down)

ORFEO:

Alas! Where have I gone astray? To what has this
delirium of love pushed me? *(He quickly approaches her)* My wife! Eurydice!
(He shakes her)
Eurydice! My consort! Ah, she is no longer living;
I cry out in vain! Wretched me! I lose her,
again and forever! Oh bitter law! Oh death!
O cruel remembrance! I have no succor!
How to carry on? I see only,
O ferocious sight! The mournful look
Of my horrid state!
May you be satisfied, Cruel Fate! I am desperate!

Millico attributes his ability to elicit tears in this climactic scene to his varying timbres. "The singer" (note the third person) "succeeded in coloring his voice so well that it made all the listeners weep."[64] Vocal chiaroscuro of the kind was a subtle affair but perhaps not quite as elusive as sometimes now thought. In the mid-1770s both Mancini and Manfredini were both clear about manipulating vowels to achieve varied colors, and even in the early 1730s Riccardo Broschi indicated vocal coloration in a score (albeit without noting how it was to be produced; cf. Ex. 18b).[65]

If "O del mio dolce ardore" embodies the new sense and sensibility of castrati in a Gluckian mold, then where do we find the Marchesian *non*sensibility, "all bits and pieces," of Verri's or Della Lena's descriptions? Not necessarily at the notational surface of any given aria or aria type, for it seems that most, and perhaps nearly all, operatic castrati could sing at least some florid passages of the agility and pathetic types. Where they surely differed widely was in their proclivities and delivery—phrasing, timbral coloring, accentuation, and so forth, as well as the extent and kind of acrobatic ability—all which would have been inseparable from their particular styles of ornamentation. In that seems to lie the divide between a Marchesi and a Millico or a Pacchierotti, a divide listeners and critics wedged still further apart by clustering singers into opposing camps.[66]

Textual evidence of Marchesi's singing style is not completely lacking. In chapter 3 we saw that in 1791 the composer Václav Pichl wrote down four different sets of ornaments that Marchesi sang for Zingarelli's aria "Cara negli occhi tuoi" from the opera *Pirro, re di Epiro* in Venice (Ex. 12). The four versions show an extravagance that practically leaps off the page. The still-famous *Prima la musica, poi le parole*, Antonio Salieri's 1786 send-up of opera seria, actually included a spoof of Marchesi that incorporated excerpts from Sarti's *Giulio Sabino*, the lead of which Marchesi had played in Vienna to great acclaim the previous year. In "Là tu vedrai chi sono," in which Sabino assures his family that he will return from exile, Salieri had Nancy Storace parody Marchesi/Sabino's pomp in an opening Andante maestoso. From there he had her flexible throat go on imitating Marchesi's extravagant agility singing, with characteristically castrato-like registral shifts and hyperflexible arpeggiated coloratura (Ex. 23).[67]

. . .

In the divide between agility and pathetic singing, one aria became a flash point, namely Sacchini's lovely "Se cerca, se dice," originally composed in 1763 for a production in Padua on the famed text from Metastasio's *L'olimpiade*.[68] It was sung there by castrato Filippo Elisi (ca. 1720–24 to ca. 1772–75), who was particularly known for his expressivity and elegance in the pathetic and had participated in the operatic reforms at Parma and elsewhere, playing Hippolytus in Traetta's *Ippolito ed Aricia* (1759), with libretto by Frugoni after Pellegrin and Rameau. Modest and musical Susan Burney was transported by the pathos conveyed when Pacchierotti sang it on a visit to London in 1780. Afterward she scribbled in her letter-journal,

> What he enchanted me in was the *Se Cerca se dice* & preceding recitative 'Misero! Che veggo! Ah! L'oppresso il dolor'—He sings now the whole scene as Sacchini composed it for Millico—& Most divine it is—Marchetti indeed when she sung it at the Pantheon gave me no idea of it . . . And Pacchierotti *so* sung it!—I who never heard Millico in it, can conceive nothing more exquisitely pathetic.[69]

In her understanding, Millico adumbrated Pacchierotti's pathetic. During the performance of the recitative that precedes "Se cerca, se dice," "Misero me! Che veggo," she "absolutely melted—and cried *as [. . . she had] at the first serious opera [. . . she] heard, when Guadagni performed Orfeo*." "I never heard anything more touching, nor shall I ever recollect it without emotion. 'Ah no, sì gran duolo non darla per me' [Ah no, such great grief for me] yet resounds in my Ears— yet I hear . . . [Pacchierotti's] sweet voice!" "It was felt by the audience wonderful . . . "—three ellipses follow as she braces herself for a gasp of protest—"No, not 'wonderfully,' since it was felt only as it *ought* to be."[70] Not, that is, in a state of dumbfounded awe, which might conjure up the marvel-studded world of an earlier age, but rather with the sympathetic disorientation that should be felt in a world where the reverberations of listeners' emotions were meant to match the poignant outpourings onstage.[71] On the effects of Pacchierotti's performance she continues,

EXAMPLE 23. Aria by Giuseppe Sarti, "Là tu vedrai," mm. 24–71, on text by Pietro Giovannini; inserted into Antonio Salieri, *Prima la musica, poi le parole* (Vienna, Schönbrunn Orangerie, February 7, 1786). Sung by Nancy Storace in imitation of Luigi Marchesi.

EXAMPLE 23. *(continued)*

Such a Murmur spread, especially from that corner of the Pitt where My Father sat, of whispered bravos as I scarce ever heard—& the moment, nay even *before* the song was quite done there was a burst of vehement applause, which affected me in a *new* way—indeed I felt sensations very exquisitely delightful.[72]

Those "sensations," a song "felt only as it ought to be," her impetuous stops and sighs, her ellipses—all these were the expression of a sensible soul. And "Se cerca, se dice," that text that had long been set and sung as a singer's benchmark for affecting delivery, now counted more highly than ever as something naturally, inwardly moving but also multidirectional in its triggers and effects. Burney was affected by the singing but also moved by the emotion of the audience; the ethical prompt ought to occasion an aesthetic response.

Sacchini's aria was later revised by Cimarosa for Marchesi. But Della Lena was unmoved, declaring that Venice was disappointed because Marchesi's *L'olimpiade* was cold, the opposite of Pacchierotti's, which just the year before (1792) had accustomed Venetians to a manner that was sweet and touching ("dolce commovente"), that "had softened and swelled one's heart" ("intenerito, e dilettato il cuore"). By comparison, Marchesi's performance was all emotionless, soulless languor, especially in his rendering of "Se cerca, se dice," for which Pacchierotti was so lovingly remembered.[73] The aria was memorialized as Marchesi's in a rendition of Sacchini's revised by Cimarosa, in which form it starts with a larghetto that steps right out of a Mozartean tenor idyll like Don Ottavio's "Dalla sua pace" or Tamino's "Dies Bildnis," opening with a falling diminished fourth already into m. 3 and immediately thereafter a shift to the key of flat VI and a series of falling chromaticisms. (See Ex. 24.) More generous than Della Lena, the German reviewer claimed that "Se cerca, se dice" showed that in London Marchesi had learned to sing with greater "sentiment and emotion" than before, but he added that he was still "far behind his rival" Pacchierotti in the greatest of all arts: recitative.[74] Pietro Verri would have agreed.

Haydn himself made the most of Pacchierotti's recitative through his ravishing cantata "Arianna a Naxos," originally written for a teenage soprano at Esterháza around 1789 but revised and made famous in London in 1791, when the composer adapted it for Pacchierotti and accompanied him several times from the keyboard at the Pantheon. The performance met with immense acclaim, not least for its culminating recitatives,[75] which in harmonic and declamatory terms were among Haydn's most dramatic. Nothing epitomizes the dialect of the pathetic more than Ariadne's second extended recitative, where she looks portentously for her beloved Theseus on the shores of Naxos, only to see him sailing away (Ex. 25).

Che miro? Oh stelle!	What do I see? Oh heavens!
Misera me! Quest' è l'argivo legno!	Woe is me! That is an Argive ship!
Greci son quelli! Teseo!	They are Greeks! Theseus!
Ei sulla prora!	He at the prow!
Ah, m'inganassi almen . . . ?	Ah, couldn't I be mistaken . . . ?
no, non m'inganno. Ei fugge,	But no, it's no mistake. He's fleeing,
ei qui mi lascia in abbandono.	He's leaving me here abandoned.
Più speranza non v'è, tradita io sono.	There is no longer any hope, I'm betrayed.
Teseo, Teseo! m'ascolta, Teseo!	Theseus, Theseus! Listen to me, Theseus!
Ma oimè, vaneggio!	But alas, I'm dreaming!
I flutti e il vento lo involano	The waves and the winds are taking him
per sempre agli occhi miei.	From my eyes forever.

Trembling, she falters, stumbling on prose-like enjambments and feeling herself expiring with grief.

There is more at stake in the sensible/flamboyant divide than may first meet the eye. To accept a "smothering" of Nature of the kind to which d'Argens, Rousseau

EXAMPLE 24. Antonio Sacchini / Domenico Cimarosa, *Se cerca se dice sung by Sig.r Marchesi, in the opera Olimpiade composed by Sig.rs. Sacchini & Cimarosa* (London: Longman and Broderip, 1788), pages 1–2 of 11.

EXAMPLE 24. *(continued)*

EXAMPLE 25. Second recitative from Franz Joseph Haydn, "Arianna a Nasso" (Hob.XXVIb:2), mm. 188–222, cantata sung by Gasparo Pacchierotti with Haydn at the keyboard, London 1790.

EXAMPLE 25. *(continued)*

(differently), and many others objected presupposed an a priori political order. It presupposed an order prior to any given affective state in which a human might actually find him- or herself. D'Argens challenges such presuppositions on distinctly political grounds when he writes that those who approve a smothering of Nature have thereby "been so assiduous to approve everything done by a Sovereign, that they have, with an unconcernedness peculiar to Courtiers, applauded the very barbarities which have depriv'd them of their own Children."[76] There is an ontological correlate that we have seen developing in later eighteenth-century demands for subjective self-control, which extend to authorial control. When Della Lena insists we should all emend singers by forbidding them to alter in the slightest a composer's score, he co-opts the position of a musically absolutist sovereign like Frederick the Great. Control of the performing human could not take place outside criteria of politically motivated Self-and-Other control, nor of control over the power immanent in authorship. Rather it took place alongside each of them.[77]

NATURE AND THE DIMORPHISM OF THINGS IN PLACE

By the 1790s these filiations can be traced in different solutions to the problem of how to salvage the very pinnacle of European singing, the foundation of what Rossini in the next century famously sighed for with the nostalgic words "our bel canto." One temporary solution, I'm suggesting, was to convert the castrato into the supreme Orphic voice of sensibility and pathos of operatic origins; another was to update and ratify his inimitable technical bravura. But everywhere black crepe was starting to fall. Della Lena did the math, adding up the best and worst singers of his time, which is to say the most moving and the coldest. Two of the three worst and just one of the four best were castrati.[78]

The numbers were not on their side, for castrati had become irreversible signs of things out of place. No longer just altered or "mutilated" men, or partially male only in the registers and media of jokes, satires, and caricatures, by the later eighteenth century they were sternly, categorically half men or even nonmen. The disparity between their persons and the persons they represented was starting to become unbearable, since in the new way of thinking maleness could not be represented by emasculated men.[79]

Englishmen were particularly fearful of castrati, but they were also fearful of Italian men generally, with their "degenerate" clothes, manners, and sexual mores. By 1770 a term had crystallized to refer to an Englishman who returned home from Italy more feminine than when he left: "macaroni." In Robert Hitchcock's 1773 play *The Macaroni [sic]*, the protagonist is told by a friend, "You make such large advances to the feminine gender, that in time 'twill be difficult to tell to which sex you belong." Implied was effeminacy but also homosexuality, both of which were unacceptable in a world where appearances, actions, and duties—the inner body indivisibly with its outer look and performance—were supposed to be brought into harmony, bounded and closed within newly rigidifying categories that ensured that men were men and women women. Even Italians started disparaging the less bounded sexuality that the English feared in them. Alessandro Verri fulminated over the attentions the Roman abbots gave castrati during Carnival in 1773, when outdoor life seemed to be all about horse races and pretty young castrati dressed like princesses, who flung themselves at hoards of abbots the same way they "flung" themselves all over Italy, imitating the "charms of ... languid-eyed divas." A specialist in female roles like the high-voiced, small, boyish, and rather feminine Giacinto Fontana (1692–1739), known as Farfallino, was widely valued for his excellence as a high soprano in the 1720s and '30s, but he would have been repugnant as a representational and social type in the phantasmatic schemata of Verri's time.[80] (See Ghezzi's depiction of him in Fig. 47.) "Antinoi" for the besotted Roman abbots, Verri huffed, alluding to the emperor's love for the young Antinous but pluralizing the name as if the young castrati were boy toys.[81] In the early nineteenth century, an anticlerical Roman sonneteer put it bluntly in the local tradition of bawdy political pasquinades: "Will Rome suffer that some mutilated singer ... should pretend to be a woman for the amusement [a spasso] of its prelates? ... If the Romans want to be good at castrating, let them ... castrate their cardinals so the Collegio won't have balls."[82]

Blaming the clergy, and especially the abbots who populated the theaters, for the whole phenomenon of castration, notwithstanding how easy it was to do in Rome, was of a piece with reformist incursions on church power during the Enlightenment, which included the removal of what had come to be thought of as abuses such as landed estates and tax exemptions. But these were just the official, outer face of reform. Achieving a one-to-one correspondence between the actor and the part acted became a matter of solidarity with a new political cause on behalf of nature. To insist on it was to insist on an almost tyrannical fidelity to a presumed truth behind appearances, to seek truth through an identity between things and their appearances. The endgame was to defeat the old world body, at play with itself and others, and replace it with a new, more bounded, less porous, and more predictable body that could serve as a warrant of truth to nature. The unstable body was what Blainville, like Voltaire and Albergati, could least bear on the Italian stage:

> It is a Thing monstrously incongruous . . . to see the Personage of a Junius Brutus, of a Mutius Scevola, or a Manlius Torquatus, or some other brave austere Roman in the Time of the Republic, represented by so ludicrous an actor as a *Castratus,* a half man, almost without Gesture, without Fire capable to express the great and noble Passions of the Soul, and what is worse, with a shrill, squeaking Voice, more capable to personate the Character of a Woman than that of a Heroe.[83]

The castrato became what Della Lena called a "fallen mast of truth and illusion." He was a bundle of incongruities, incapable of dominating the viewer's fantasy in the service of "Truth."[84]

Eventually castrati as a mainstream phenomenon were swept away in the undertow of Enlightenment morality. It's certainly true, as John Rosselli notes, that they became extinct at the same time that religious institutions became less numerous and less populated. The decline in the number of religious institutions followed economic recovery in Italy, but the relationship between the two phenomena is not entirely causal. If castrati became fewer in number just when monks, nuns, and ecclesiastical clerics did, it's also because the world of absolute power in which all such figures had thrived was choking on challenges to its patronage systems and its very ideological, perceptual, and cosmological premises. Intolerant views of castrati ran parallel to suspicions of absolute power. They were voiced within a vacuum of knowledge, power, and moral certainty that left open to question numerous rules and mores about what it meant to be human. Thus it is no coincidence that the castrato arose with the ascent of an absolutist political order (understood in its broadest sense) and fell under its collapse. Perhaps he was even a contradiction that, not unlike that order, was accompanied by an increase in state bureaucracy, an increase in contracts and abstract exchange, a weakening of the ruling class, and new possibilities for independent agents in a world where money could be earned and deployed to create new statuses by new professionals using new social networks. To understand him fundamentally, at all times, as a contradiction *of* his times gives us some purchase on why increasing complaints about the luxuries, money, and social mobility of prominent castrati—characteristics that had never been excluded from discourses about them—intersected with critiques of their deformations and sexuality in the eighteenth century. Indeed, as I elaborate in the next chapter, anxieties about money were still, perhaps still *more,* the axis at which castrati figured in the nineteenth century.

Then too, when the castrato first came into being, the human body in Europe was still a relatively open site, permeable and reproducible (even if various cultural attempts to define and delimit it were already underway). Like the Pucinellas who multiplied themselves in twos and fours in country scenes and urban squares, who became others through division, the castrato essentially had one foot in a cosmos in which the body could be pressed into new shapes and functions even as he planted his other foot in a world where the body thrived in more bounded terrain. To mutilate your student, your son, or your political subject for his sake and the sake of a larger social-political-religious order probably caused less heart pounding and palm sweating in the first few centuries of the castrato's existence than it would for us today. No doubt the more delimited place assigned the body in the later eighteenth century was causing more and more anxiety about mutilation. The paradox of the castrato is that he never fully became part of the new order, even if in another sense he was always part of it and a beacon of its newly consolidating form.

. . .

Our most valued informant, Filippo Balatri, already had much to say about these contradictions in 1738, when, in his quasi-literary last will and testament, he satirically but not unseriously bewailed his physical state and his body's destiny after death. In this remarkable text, as we glimpsed in chapter 2, death is a kind of unmasking of the body grotesque, consumed by worms, reeking and rotting away. Over many pages Balatri repeatedly stages himself as a monstrous object of spectacle. In one scene he imagines what would happen if he were to die in Italy. He turns his body into a fetid corpse attended by a nun who trades horrors over it with a fussing, gossipy curiosity seeker.[85]

> *Sister:* I wouldn't know what to tell you, except that he's a foreigner, who came not long ago to stay in this city. Oh, how ugly he is, my Agatha, I tremble for fear of dreaming about him.
>
> *Agatha:* I was thinking about that too, Sister, and to tell you truly I repented of my own curiosity . . . , since I share your fear.
>
> *Sister:* Dear Agatha, I could spend three days not eating, he turns my stomach so much! . . .

Agatha: ... Blessed Sister, don't you see that he has no beard yet, nor any sign of having had one? The illness must have been long and painful ...

Sister: He has no beard because he's a castrato; nothing but dry figs.

Agatha: Oh, he was a castrato? Well, if that's the case, he will have left a lot of money. Does anyone know who he left it to?[86]

Money without blood relations: we have seen that structurally this was a particular dilemma for the castrato. But note that the cycle of disgust-desire that marks Balatri's scene has three prongs. It is mobilized because he has money, but also because he is a foreigner and because he is grotesquely malformed. In this metacommentary on the self, money is key. Elaborating the dilemma further, he makes recourse to a life-and-death parable of the pig, a domestic animal that, like the chickens to whom castrati were often likened, lives near humans, and that for humans is similarly and relatedly among the most ambivalent of creatures.[87]

> Were I a stubborn sort, I'd have cut the figure of a pig. The pig, so long as it lives, is deemed a vile animal; every hole is fine for the pig. All the garbage is given to the pig. Is there anyone who caresses it or keeps it close at hand? But as soon as it's dead, everybody runs to the larder and from its skin on in, there's not the minutest part that isn't prized. It's praised, it's tasted, it's the delight of everyone, because one can eat it.[88]

Balatri's identification with the pig echoes traditional cultural uses of pigs as mediators of money. But the pig also expresses Balatri's abjection. His terms, startlingly modern, give a precise form to Julia Kristeva's psychoanalytics of the abject, as sketched in her *Powers of Horror*:

> There looms, with abjection, one of those violent, dark revolts of being, directed against a threat that seems to emanate from an exorbitant outside or inside, ejected beyond the scope of the possible, the tolerable, the thinkable. It lies there, quite close, but it cannot be assimilated. It beseeches, worries, fascinates desire, which nevertheless does not let itself be seduced. Apprehensive, desire turns aside; sickened, it rejects. A certainty ... of which it is proud holds on to it. But simultaneously ... that impetus, that spasm, that leap is drawn toward an elsewhere as tempting as it is condemned. Unflaggingly, like an inescapable boomerang, a vortex of summons and repulsion places the one haunted by it *literally beside itself*.[89]

This account of the self in a battle of desire/disgust, approach/avoidance, with a threat both inside and outside itself that undoes the self by putting it "literally beside itself" and forces it to hang on to itself (through that "certainty ... of which it is proud"), can be read for our purposes as an account of Enlightenment subjectivity in the face of the castrato. Kristeva defines food loathing as the most *elemental* stimulus of this sensation, initiated in a cycle of revulsion-rejection-desire and of then becoming the other. The *ultimate stimulus* of feelings of abjection are concentrated in the corpse—in death in its most material but also phantasmatic form. "The corpse," she writes, "shows me what I permanently thrust aside in order to live." It shows a kind of disintegration of the subject in the face of abjection but also the possibility of reintegration. By this logic, Balatri's own corpse shows us the stimulus of the cycle that is manifest in that desire mixed with envy, the increased heartbeat, spasms in the belly, what Kristeva calls "sight-clouding dizziness." It may help us understand why such ambivalent desire is so terribly extreme, an "exorbitant outside or inside," and the fear it causes so great. Why else would that proudest and most desired of beings, Farinelli, have been so canny as to tell Charles Burney, in the 1770s, that he was a "despicable being"—a phrase that articulates the dynamics of abjection as residing both in the self, where revulsion-desire begins, and in the other/beholder who first perceives abjection as a state outside himself but in the end must acknowledge it as his own.[90]

In time, ideologies that favored natural growth were to exact the steep price of a certain cultural normalization. What was good for me became good for you, so that, king or no king, we would all know what was good for us. To discover what that "good" was required collective agreements about "intrinsic plausibility," the collective presumption that certain things were true, creditable, and right on purely inherent grounds. Such thinking was bound to be bad for the survival of the (implausible) castrato, who had thrived on things *not* being perfectly produced by nature's course and *not* being just what they seemed. Indeed, castrati quickly came to stand for the very opposite of an Enlightenment program, so that increasingly all he could seem like was a castrated man, either an emperor with no clothes or a monster in emperor's clothes.

6

Shadow Voices, Castrato and Non

On January 21, 1792, Louis XVI was killed off and many of his entailments eradicated from public life. Two eunuchs from the royal chapel who faithfully accompanied the king to his meditation and attended the last mass of the royal family were among them. After the king was decapitated, the two had to scurry away, bits of debris from the volcanoes of horror and exultation of that time.[1]

The number and stature of castrati had always been paltry in France compared with elsewhere: about sixty over the course of a century and a half, all confined to the Chapelle Royale.[2] All the more reason to see the king's last castrati as an index of the end of the old regime. In hindsight their rapid exodus after the king's execution betokens the fate then befalling castrati everywhere in Europe. Not coincidentally, under Napoleonic rules of occupation, which went into effect in each Italian city-state immediately after his troops invaded between 1796 and 1799, castrati were banned from the stage as immoral, unmanly, and altogether antifamilial.[3]

The real paradoxes only emerged a few years later. On May 18, 1804, Napoleon proclaimed himself emperor, and on December 2 he was crowned by Pope Pius VII as "Emperor of the French," giving the old political order one of its many last hurrahs. Earlier that year, during a trip to Vienna, Napoleon had heard the castrato Girolamo Crescentini sing the part of Romeo in Niccolò Zingarelli's *Giulietta e Romeo*. Crescentini premiered the part at La Scala eight years earlier opposite soprano Josephina Grassini and had subsequently sung it to enormous acclaim in productions in Reggio Emilia, Venice, Vienna, and Lisbon.[4] Napoleon was ravished. Shortly afterward he was plotting for Crescentini to come reside at his court, which the singer at first resisted but finally, under duress, did do in 1806. On

March 9, 1809, the first full-dress performance of *Giulietta e Romeo* was staged at Napoleon's Théâtre des Tuileries.[5] The title page of the libretto, printed in Italian and French, highlighted the auratic presence of their imperial majesties at the performance of the work:

> Romeo e Giulietta,/ dramma in musica in tre atti./ Romeo e Juliette,/ drame en musique/ en trios actes./ Represanté au Theatre des Tuileries, en presence/ de leurs majestés imperials et royals./ Paris,/ Imprimerie de Fain,/ 1809.[6]

By this time Crescentini was more famous in France than any previous castrato in French history, and soon after he was made a Knight of the Order of the Iron Cross (Chevalier de l'ordre de la Couronne de fer) in a move Stendhal characterized as the only blunder of civic administration in Napoleon's career (Fig. 48).[7]

What are we to make of Napoleon's proscriptions against castrati in Italy and his subsequent infatuation with one? The former extended and codified the bourgeois moral critique of them produced throughout Europe during the mid- to late eighteenth century that was a subject of the previous chapter. Proscriptions fixed into law what had previously been expressed as fear, disgust, or outrage. Insofar as such feelings had existed over the course of the previous two hundred years, they participated in the dynamic of a sacrificial economy in which the castrato functioned as an exceptional being, as singer and boundary crosser. In the absence of continued vigorous production of castrati, the early nineteenth century found itself heir to a vocal tradition of unprecedented expressive and technical power yet disinherited of those to whom that tradition had belonged. The situation led to a number of different adaptations in different cultural institutions and political regimes, but Napoleon's personal elevation of Crescentini into iconic, transformative status once again made the castrato the site of an engulfing slippage, one that in this instance accompanied Napoleon's plunge back into absolutist monarchical authority.

What follows makes no attempt to indicate the full range of solutions, differently manifested, that this dilemma involved at different geographic sites and times. Instead it offers various threads of evidence, most literary or musical, which index in ensemble some of what was lost, reframed, or replaced. One thread touches on the shift from castrato singing to the singing of castrato stage roles and vocal parts by female mezzo sopranos; another on memories of castrato singing, of one castrato in particular, that persisted for decades, indirectly, beyond Crescentini's departure from France in 1812. I emphasize France as the locus of a startlingly new and powerful reinvention of the castrato inheritance for several reasons: because France was a vigorous actor in the cultural transfer and translation of opera, because it was the site of a major shift in the central locus of singing, and because the castrato legacy had no more canny reception than in the decade from 1820 to 1830 at the hands of Stendhal and Balzac.[8]

BELOVED SHADES

Jean Starobinski has lined up a shrewd parade of witnesses to Crescentini's Paris Romeo in an essay included in *Enchantment: The Seductress in Opera*.[9] The journalist-painter Étienne-Jean Delécluze, a good friend of Stendhal's, remembered a performance from 1811 at which "the galleries of the imperial theater were filled with women of the court and princesses both foreign and French. Generals and chamberlains, dressed in the richest clothes, stood behind the ladies. In the orchestra stalls were all the commanding officers. Foreign ambassadors were seated in boxes according to the importance of the nation they represented, as were the kings of Naples, Holland, Westphalia, Bavaria, and Württemburg, among others." "There was nothing more imposing to be seen than the respectful terror that the sight of Napoleon inspired in all these spectators of such different rank, condition, and probably opinions as well." All of them were surrounded with a "luxury and sparkle that highlighted in such a lively way the serious incertitude of their bodies," held so that they might at will gaze "obliquely toward their master," who was "attentive to the performance." Never had Delécluze seen or heard anything comparable to the beauty of the singing, especially that of Crescentini, who had

> made a prodigious impression on all the spectators.... When Crescentini (Romeo) fell down dead after kissing his beloved, a movement of curiosity mixed with emotion spread throughout the orchestra stall from which there rose up a stifled sigh. But calm was soon restored and all eyes turned nervously and curiously toward the master who made a solemn sign of the hand and departed.

Napoleon's exit thus marked the very crux of the drama—Romeo's swooning collapse to his death toward the end of act 3, scene 1.

The scene takes place in the Capulet funeral vault, evocatively lit in a neoclassical style, with dark, shaded steps ascending to Juliet's tomb. Just after entering, Romeo finds Juliet dead (so he believes). His Montague comrades lament her "ombra adorabile" (loveable soul) until, stirring from the numbness of grief, Romeo brushes them away with an Orphic recitative "Non più compagni: andate" (No more, my friends, begone)—a gesture of pathos, rich with orchestral and harmonic coloring reminiscent of "Basta, basta, o compagni" from Gluck and Calzabigi's *Orfeo ed Euridice* (Vienna, 1762), sung in famously feelingful ways as subsequently revised for several of Crescentini's vocal ancestors (as delineated in Chapter 5 above).[10] Afterward, the opera having progressed to about midway through the scene, Romeo begins his last solo *scena* with the lyrical cavatina "Idolo del mio cor" (Ex. 26). He will end it with the aria "Ombra adorata, aspetta," just before Juliet awakens and Romeo takes his last breath in her arms, in a melodramatic departure from Shakespeare.[11] (See text and translation following.)[12]

EXAMPLE 26. Nicola Zingarelli, "Idolo del mio cor," recitative transcribed from Zingarelli's *Giulietta e Romeo* (Milan, La Scala, 1796), Milan, Biblioteca Nazionale Braidense, Ricordi collection.

ANDANTE SOSTENUTO, 3/8, F MAJOR (CAVATINA)

Idolo del mio cor,	Idol of my heart,
deh, vedi il pianto mio,	oh, look at my tears,
i gemiti, il dolor	the moans, the grief
del tuo fedel.	of your faithful one.

RECITATIVE, 4/4, F MAJOR

Ma che vale il mio duol? Mia bella speme,	But what use is my grief? My lovely hope,
Io ti sento. Mi chiami a seguirti fra l'ombre, ebben m'aspetta.	I hear you. You call me to follow you among the shades, so wait.
Ti seguirò. Se a te compagno in vita non mi volle la sorte,	I will follow you. If fate does not allow me to accompany you in life,
teco m'unisca almen pietosa morte.	may I at least be united with you in merciful death.
(cava un'ampolla, e beve il veleno)	*(he pulls out an ampulla and drinks poison)*

ANDANTE SOSTENUTO, 44, D MAJOR

Tranquillo io son. Fra poco teco sarò, mia vita. Accogli intanto,	I am calm. In a short time I will be one with you, my Life. My Hope, my Soul,
mia speme, anima mia, questo ch'io per te verso ultimo pianto.	may you welcome this final lament that I pour forth for you.

RONDÒ, ANDANTE SOSTENUTO, 44, D MAJOR

Ombra adorata, aspetta!	Beloved shade, wait!
Teco sarò indiviso.	I will be inseparable from you.
Nel fortunato Eliso	In blissful Paradise
avrò contento il cor!	my heart will be content!
Là fra i fedeli amanti,	There among the faithful lovers
ci appresta Amor diletti.	the delights of Love await us.
Godremo i dolci istanti	We will enjoy sweet moments
de' più innocenti affetti,	of the most innocent feelings,
e l'Eco a noi d'intorno	and the Echo all around us
risuonerà d'amor.	will resound with love.

With the F-major recitative "Ma che vale il mio duol?" (But what use is my grief?), Romeo hears Juliet's voice in his mind's ear calling him to follow her among "the shades" of an idyllic underworld. He stops pleading for Juliet's pity, drinks poison, and, thus becalmed, delivers a brief second recitative, "Tranquillo io son" (Ex. 27), now in the distant minor-third-related key of D major, as he prepares himself for a plaintive outpouring of joy over their imminent reunion in the afterworld. The much-anticipated aria initiates the progress of a romantic love-death by the most famous lovebirds in history, if still in a neoclassical Orphic mood in which innocence and fidelity are rewarded by the triumphant echoes of love in Elysium, that mythical land of dead heroes.

This was the very moment Delécluze remembered as the one when Napoleon made his departure. It marked the crux of the drama, just after the rondò, as Juliet awakens and Romeo dies, before her death from grief at Romeo's death. For the French court it also marked the moment Napoleon's castrato fell dead, without whom he evidently did not care about bearing imperial witness to the rest of the drama. Perhaps, as Starobinski thinks, Napoleon left not only because by then he had heard his favorite aria, but above all because he had caught "the attention of the audience," perceiving the "powerful effect produced by his protégé," who was effectively "an extension of his own power."[13] The observations of Empress Josephine's lady-in-waiting Mademoiselle D'Avrillon (ghostwritten by Charles-Maxime de Villemarest), though omitted from Starobinksi's account, confirm his view: "From

EXAMPLE 27. Nicola Zingarelli, "Tranquillo io son," recitative transcribed from Zingarelli's *Giulietta e Romeo* (Milan, La Scala, 1796), Milan, Biblioteca Nazionale Braidense, Ricordi collection.

the box where I was, I could see perfectly with my lorgnette the face of His Majesty. While Crescentini was singing the famous *Ombra adorata, aspetta* it was, without exaggeration, radiant with pleasure. The Emperor shifted on his seat, spoke frequently to the senior officers of the Empire who surrounded him, and seemingly wanted to make them share the admiration he felt."[14]

"OMBRA ADORATA, ASPETTA"

Just who or what was the Crescentini who held Delécluze, Napoleon, Madame D'Avrillon/Villemarest, and all the court and court visitors in his thrall (to say nothing of audiences across Europe)? A reviewer from the *Allgemeine musikalische Zeitung* described Crescentini's vocality after hearing the same Viennese performance that Napoleon had.

> The celebrated castrato Crescentini ... took the stage anew on April 28 in *Giulietta e Romeo*. Since he has made a sensation, we expand upon it in a detailed description. ...
>
> Crescentini is without doubt one of the best singers currently alive in Europe. His voice, which he uses with wise discretion, is incredibly pleasing, round, full, and flexible. His style is elevated and aesthetically perfect, without being in the slightest overloaded. Particularly beautiful and singular is the pure soaring ever higher of his enchanting voice, for which at a certain point he rises up with a continuous crescendo until he goes higher still and then sustains the note for several beats with full, ringing vigor. Since Crescentini sings in a perfectly correct way and joins to these musical gifts a pleasing action, sometimes very passionate, one can easily excuse a slight lack of low notes.[15]

A further idea of his singing can be gained by combining additional accounts with a small gleaning from the heaps of surviving manuscripts, prints, and instrumental arrangements of "Ombra adorata, aspetta," an aria that took Europe by storm throughout the first half of the nineteenth century.[16] Its prehistory is germane. Crescentini first appeared as Romeo on February 3, 1796, in the La Scala debut of Nicolò Zingarelli's *Giulietta e Romeo*. The opera was entirely by Zingarelli, but by the time it was produced in Reggio Emilia on April 30 of that year, Crescentini, presumably feeling he could make something better of the scene, had already composed his own insertion aria on "Ombra adorata, aspetta" to sing in place of Zingarelli's (see keyboard reduction in Ex. 28).[17]

Bear in mind that as the aria erupts at the fulcrum of the opera, Romeo's soul is growing lighter and lighter with its release from life. At its fixed objective core, Crescentini's aria is very plain, using a small tessitura and rhythmic range and moving within a narrow harmonic compass. One might think of it as an elaboration on strophes, repeating the small quatrain in successive variations in the form of ABA' + coda, in the middle of which the aria barely deflects to the dominant for

EXAMPLE 28. Girolamo Crescentini, short score of "Ombra adorata, aspetta / Rondeau / inserito nel dramma serio di / Giulietta, e Romeo / del Sig. Girolamo Crescentini / in Reggio la Fiera dell'anno / 1796." Transcribed from I-Vc, Correr, busta 8.2, now in the holdings of the Conservatorio B. Marcello, Venice.

EXAMPLE 28. (continued)

EXAMPLE 28. *(continued)*

the second strophe before returning to further variations upon the first. It contrasts sharply with the complex aria Zingarelli wrote for the premiere, which it replaced, and especially with the rangier, composerly two-tempo rondò that Zingarelli composed as an apparent alternative to his own first setting.[18]

Crescentini's aria is such stuff as a singer's dreams are made on—a quasi-romanza fashioned for the finest and most evanescent of nuances and for a spontaneity of expression and improvisation capable of carrying the singer to the heights of fame (which it did, ultimately taking him to Paris to the tune of thirty thousand francs).[19] Its triumph was both immediate and long-lived such that almost all surviving versions of the aria are that of Crescentini.

Andrea Malnati has traced the dramaturgical and textual history of the aria in its original north Italian contexts. He shows that its success prompted Zingarelli to gnaw away disconcertedly at his own setting, eventually composing no fewer than four different versions of "Ombra adorata," none of which ever became widely known. Crescentini's was the one audiences expected and got to hear for many decades from spring 1796 onward, and even into the latter half of the nineteenth century, with only the rarest of exceptions, though there are many more attributions of it to Zingarelli than to Crescentini (notwithstanding the fact that many credible sources believed the aria to be Crescentini's, as we will see).[20] Just one instance of this ascription tradition is the clutch of printed versions with keyboard accompaniment issued roughly between 1823 and 1834 in London and Dublin, which ascribed authorship of "Ombra adorata" to Zingarelli, as composer of the opera, as did most manuscript copies. Ironically, Zingarelli benefited from these misattributions through the great success and uncommon longevity of the opera, which was performed in full until 1837 and whose third act was staged until at least 1841.[21] For decades salon singers had to have their own redactions of Crescentini's "Ombra adorata," from the music rooms of duchies in Sweden, Denmark, and Germany to noble and princely houses in Dubrovnik, Berna, and Kastély (Hungary) to the houses of amateur music buyers throughout Europe, most of whom got their versions from the print shops of London, Paris, Dublin, Florence, and Naples or from music dealers far and wide. Prints were often linked through their titles to specific singers well known in the British Isles—notably the bravura soprano

Angelica Catalani, who never sang the aria on a large London stage, and the phenomenal mezzo Giuditta Pasta, who sang in six different productions of the opera between 1824 and 1837 in London alone and dominated the role of Romeo with appearances throughout Europe from 1821 through 1841 (see her engraved portrait as Romeo in a Paris print from the earlier end of this span, Fig. 49).[22]

· · ·

What to make of the place of the castrato tradition in this riotous history, which overlaps with the time when castrati were in steep decline and would soon disappear from the stage? In the most authoritative and influential singing treatise in nineteenth-century Europe, Manuel Garcia the younger's *Traité complet du l'art de chant* of 1847, the entire scena is given as an exemplum of elegant theatricality achieved through a vocal finesse vested in expressive shaping and ornamentation, including attacks, swells, sighs, subtle gasps, runs, and the like.[23] Garcia prints the aria juxtaposed alongside a highly decorated, annotated version of Francesco Morlacchi's romanza "Caro suono lusinghier" from *Tebaldo ed Isolina* as sung by the castrato Giambattista Velluti,[24] but with an important difference: in attributing the writing of the latter to Morlacchi and its performance to Velluti, Garcia split the creative goods between composer and performer. With "Ombra adorata" he may at first glance appear to give both to Crescentini with a rubric that reads, "Air pour mezzo soprano composé par CRESCENTINI et intercallé dans le Romeo et Giulietta de ZINGARELLI" (Aria for mezzo soprano composed by Crescentini and inserted in Zingarelli's *Giulietta et Romeo*),[25] much as pianist and composer Filippo Rolla subtitled his manuscript of the aria "Rondò cantata [sic] da Girolamo Crescentini e di sua composizione" (Rondo sung by Girolamo Crescentini and composed by him).[26] (For Garcia's edition, see Ex. 29.)

But the performative trace in Garcia's "Ombra adorata" is actually much harder to pin down than the compositional one, and much harder to mark out than it is in his edition of Morlacchi/Velluti's romanza. Just *which* Crescentini Garcia's top voice represents we will never really know, for what we get in Garcia is a performing singer writ down in a kind of musical pseudodocument, as if the score might be a real transcription of a given performance delivered on a certain night, or perhaps sung on most nights, or a performance conjured up through brushstrokes of an ideal performance (partly remembered, partly reimagined?). Why Garcia might veer into notational yarn spinning, if he did, is not hard to understand. He knew intimately the ornamental styles of the best living singers, not least those of Pasta and Malibran, and was able to utilize his refined insider knowledge to convey to advanced students what could be made of the aria. What he decidedly does not claim to represent in his edition of "Ombra adorata" is what Crescentini *sang*, saying rather, "Here's the aria by Crescentini the composer (which, incidentally, Crescentini the singer made famous)"—unlike his edition of the Morlacchi

EXAMPLE 29. Niccolò Zingarelli's recitative and Girolamo Crescentini's "Ombra adorata, aspetta," with ornaments, from the edition in Manual Garcia Jr., *Traité complet de l'art du chant en deux parties*, part 2 of 2 (Paris: Troupenas, 1847).

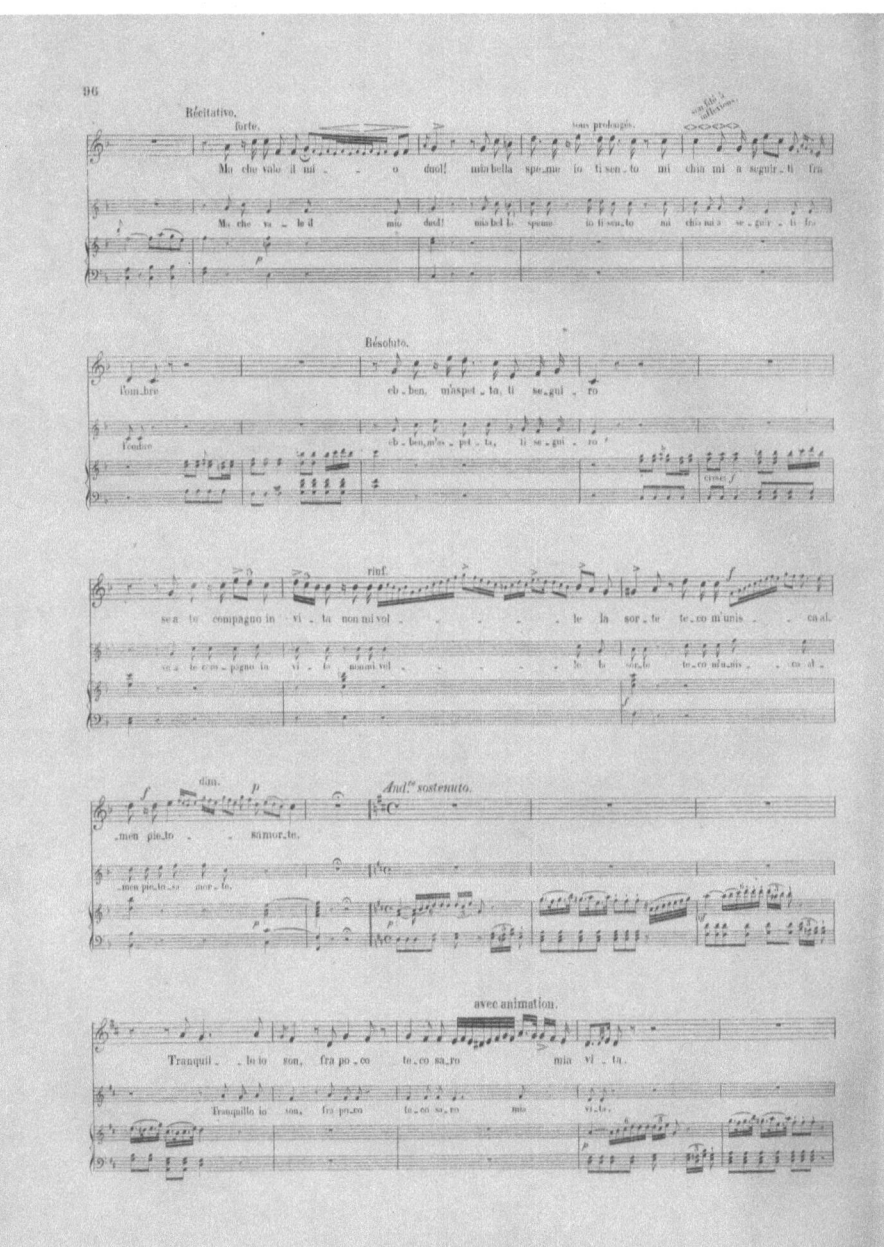

EXAMPLE 29. *(continued)*

EXAMPLE 29. *(continued)*

romanza, which he designates a "remarkable example" of "the manner of the past century, taken from Velluti."[27]

If Garcia's work is not our direct trace of a performance by Crescentini—whose aria had by then turned into an expressive staple of two generations of performers and listeners but who, as a species, had effectively died out by Garcia's time—then what is? A few strands from the skein of scores that allege to record actual performances are suggestive. Crescentini's Viennese triumphs are arguably memorialized in two sources. Both are for two violins, a singing principal and an accompanying second, and both come from the time and place where Napoleon heard Crescentini sing *Giulietta e Romeo* on April 28, 1804. One is a set of variations in G major on the A section of "Ombra adorata, aspetta," the melody that sets the first quatrain of text. It was composed by violinist Giacomo Conti (1754–1805), who died in Vienna the following year.[28] The other, infinitely more revealing, is by violinist Heinrich Eppinger, whose score of "Ombra adorata" purports to record directly Crescentini's ornaments with the phrase "colli ornamenti come la cantava il Signor Crescentini" (with ornaments as Crescentini sang the aria).[29] (The accompanying second violin part is lost, but with no loss of information about Crescentini's performance.) Whether Eppinger's score transcribes a given performance or approximates several different ones, its intent and proximity to Crescentini in the moment of his encounter with Napoleon are clear and make his notations highly credible.

Indeed for anyone who thinks about the art of great singing, encountering Crescentini via Eppinger is like hearing a Chopin nocturne when previously you had only known the tune. Compare the melody lines of Crescentini's notated original, Eppinger's notation of Crescentini's singing of it, and Conti's theme based on the aria (Ex. 30). (In the example Conti's melody is transposed down a fourth from its original key of G major to allow for a more direct comparison.) Filled with gruppetti, trills, arpeggios, portamenti, wide leaps, and rising and falling scales, Eppinger's score conjures up a brilliant, convincing portrait of Crescentini's reputedly graceful and spontaneous ornamentational art. It goes so far as to provide some very particular articulations: mordents (m. 5 and 54), descending sixty-fourth-note glissandi in passages of a kind Tosi called "scivolati" (sliding; m. 11) and others "battuti" (i.e., marked; m. 37, for example, which is actually designated *marcato*), turns that sigh behind the beats (mm. 27), delicate linear chromaticisms (m. 30), roulades (m. 40), accented articulations (m. 53), and great registral leaps of up to two octaves (m. 41), a feat for which castrati were famous. All this conforms to Will Crutchfield's authoritative summary of the variety that an early nineteenth-century singer was expected to bring to bear on a performance, ranging from small-scale decorations (e.g., appoggiaturas, acciaccaturas, and passing notes) to free elaborations upon melodic repetitions, fioriture introduced over chordal accompaniments, and new variations on existing melismatic patterns.[30]

EXAMPLE 30. Three melody lines for Crescentini's "Ombra adorata, aspetta!"
a. Crescentini's original as given in Ex. 28.
b. Heinrich Eppinger's notation of Crescentini's singing of it for violin: "Ombra adorata, aspetta colli ornamenti come la cantava il Sig.r Crescentini . . . ," undated manuscript, probably 1804, I-Mc, Noseda, P 5.23.
c. Conti's theme based on Crescentini's aria, from *Variations pour deux violons sur l'air Ombra adorata aspetta de l'opéra Giuletta e Romeo, composées par J. Conti* (Vienna: J. Cappi [1809–11?]), here transposed down a fourth to D major from its original key of G major.

EXAMPLE 30. (continued)

EXAMPLE 30. *(continued)*

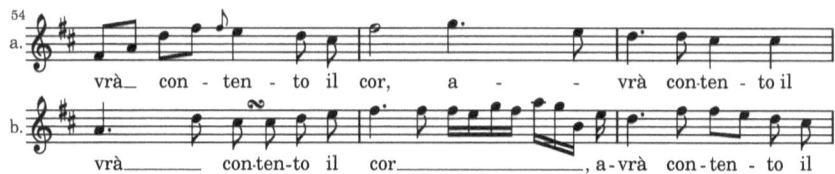

Compared with Eppinger's transcription, Conti's theme (Ex. 30c) has a value limited to whatever slim inferences about Crescentini's performance of the A section we might draw out. (The succeeding variations are banally conventional and don't relate directly to the cantilena of the aria.) Of most interest are Conti's ornaments on the last line of the opening strophe, "Avrò contento il cor" (My heart will be content), which closes the A section, and eventually the aria as a whole, with a blissful encomium on death. Nearly identical to the ornaments given by Eppinger at mm. 7 and 17–18, Conti's provide early clues to the biography of the aria. In both versions descending gruppetti give *accento* to Romeo's imagined contentment at his imminent joining with his beloved in death, straightforwardly so at first and more elaborately at the verse's second occurrence where gruppetti open into a decorated prolongation that is basically identical in both versions. Singing with the soul of Romeo as Crescentini's voice embodied it, the Eppinger version documented a brilliant age of vocal performance that was eventually to pass out of ear, mind, and memory.

LISTENING TO "LA BONNE ÉCOLE"

Stendhal's *Vie de Rossini* (1824) attended to that very line in his rhapsodic chapter on Pasta, who sang publicly between 1816 and 1841. There he claimed that the spirit of dedicated amateur listeners ("dilettantes"), among whom he counted himself, could be so "genuinely delicate" as to act as a kind of "microscope that allows them to see clearly the slightest *nuances* of singing."[31] For him Pasta not only transmitted nuance but also created ones of which even the composer never dreamt. The sublime shadings of *accento* on "Avrò contento nel cor" that she surrendered when she sang the role as a trouser mezzo exemplified for him this creativity by animating and quickening the love that urges Romeo to his death. Indeed music, as articulated in Stendhal's philosophical essay on love, *De l'amour* (1822), was part of a "crystallization" process in which the distant beloved assumes qualities of ideal beauty in the imagination of her lover. A person will fall into a love reverie by listening to music sooner than by any other means because the experience of musical beauty erotically transforms the love object into an adored creature of virtue and of extraordinary value for the one who listens (and here, for Stendhal, we can read vocal music). Sublime music therefore has incalculable worth, perfect music being akin to perfect love in giving more intense pleasure than anything else on earth.[32]

All this may bring to mind Susan Burney's rhapsodic engagement with Pacchierotti's singing—not surprisingly, for Pasta carried forward precisely what Stendhal called "le grand siècle," meaning the eighteenth. Her affiliation with that century was effectively asserted by the music publishing magnate Ricordi in a print called *Modi generali del canto premessi alle maniere parziale onde adornare o rifiorire le nude o semplici melodie o cantilene giusta il metodo di Gasparo Pacchierotti* (General ways of singing based on the preliminary methods for adorning and embellishing the bare and simple melodies and songs according to the method of Gaspare Pacchierotti), which ratified the vocal genealogy by dedicating the print to her (see Fig. 50).

Now Stendhal was as great a defender of the school from which Pasta came as any nineteenth-century amateur, and he insisted that it was the same school as that of her castrato predecessors and contemporaries Crescentini and Velluti.[33] Usually he called this "la bonne école" (said twice in connection with Pasta), though other times he spoke of "l'ancienne école" or referred to the tradition of "le beau chant" or "le grand siècle," which he sometimes elided with the phrase "le beau ideale." Among the practitioners of the tradition named in the *Vie* are a number of eighteenth- to early nineteenth-century singers, including five female sopranos (Caterina Gabrielli, Anna de Amicis, Luigia Todi, Brigida Banti, and Giuditta Pasta), three tenors (Giovanni Ansani, Matteo Babbini, and Giacomo David), and no less than nine castrati (Pistocchi, Bernacchi, Farinelli, Aprile, Millico, Pacchierotti, Marchesi, Crescentini, and Velluti). Stendhal is consistent in delineating the tradition, notwithstanding the fact that the *Vie* is filled with reversals and doubts on many points and at many junctures—a text that reads as a polyphony, or cacophony, which Benjamin Walton aptly describes as "the clamour of running arguments with old adversaries, the phrases of other contemporary critics, the oscillation between extravagant praise and exploration of significant doubts, the mixing together of biography . . . , anecdotes, digressions, contradictions, aesthetics, and semi-scientific theory."[34] Indeed one reason Stendhal's text does not easily satisfy the traditional needs of music histories is because in the end it is not chiefly concerned with works and texts, Rossini's or anyone else's, but with acts—music as heard, works as performed, and above all sung melodies—hence the utter centrality of singers to the text, which consists less in conventional argumentation than in a loose accumulation of musings, inspirations, and emotional outbursts, which are the very acts and art of Stendhal's criticism.

Let me hazard a Stendhalian digression and suggest that Stendhal's very particular singling out of a climactic verse about the bliss of dying, which is at the same time about a kind of dying musically, is consonant with his unapologetic love for singing and his lament over the loss of good singing, underpinned by his philosophy of love. Music, or rather vocal music, is sheer sensual pleasure. In this Stendhal is (as he professed) a friend of the "idéologues" Pierre Jean George Cabanis and Antoine Louis Claude Destrutt de Tracy, who gave primacy to melody because it was material and hence a primary sensational cause. It predisposed peoples to passion and melancholy, manifesting itself in the asemantic realm of such untexted melodic figures as arabesques and roulades.[35] In Stendhal's personal philosophy, this sensual pleasure is also a lifeline to hope in the often dreadful journey of life, and thus a kind of unfulfilled romantic longing. Like other arts, but even more so, music is the vehicle through which humans may glimpse happiness or, at another stage of remove, may *dream* of a glimpse of happiness that may *almost* give hope. The dual capacities here of music to give pleasure and provide solace are indivisible. Thus too for Stendhal it was misguided to be overly serious about music. It was not just a pedantic, joy-killing habit but wrong because music could only act as a conduit to hope when encountered with epicurean delight. Music in Stendhal's world should be a way to daydream, a plaything approached in the most intense, passionate, and committed way.

We are back to his obsessions with the great singers of "la bonne école," and, contrariwise, to the supposed loss—the dying or dying out, to extend the castrato theme—of spontaneous singing, which for him was the dissipation of an increasing infatuation with composers. Before one of his various attacks on Rossini's new method of writing in ornamentation, especially for agility singing, Stendhal gushes forth in an erotically paratactic delirium of bel canto prose.

> The nuances [of the old school] in holding the voice *[tenues la voix]*, the singing of portamento, the art of tempering the voice to make it rise equally on every note of legato singing, the art of taking a new breath in an imperceptible manner and without breaking the long vocal period of the aria [i.e., a whole strophe or A section] at one time used to comprise the most difficult and necessary part of execution.[36]

For Stendhal such nuances were possible because "la bonne école" valued spontaneity, improvisation, originality, and the native qualities of each individual voice, including its timbre *(metallo)* and its distinct registers. This made possible the deliciously "seductive flexibility" of the castrato Velluti, who warrants a small chapter and more in the *Vie* as proof against Rossini's misguided textuality and who was seemingly a good deal more ornate a singer than Crescentini.[37] It explains why Stendhal is fixated on the ruination of singing by the growing practice of specifying the ornamentation, to be repeated verbatim from a score by one singer after another from a fixed written text, which could only make singers into acrobats and automatons who had no bodily dominion over their shadings and embellishments because it was impossible to make them their own.[38]

. . .

Now for Stendhal in the early 1820s to dwell on a school he claims is vanishing while focusing on a sung verse about euphoric death is to fixate on the very thing that is, like the castrato himself, receding from his grasp. Such death is complexly layered. As Starobinski stresses, although the Orphic Romeo may go happily to the underworld, seeming simply to obey the instruction, or *message*, of his lover's call, "it's the *voice* of the lover that creates this enchanting call by declaring his complete submission"—the *medium*. Thus the real power to seduce, even in death, belongs to voice alone.[39] (Note especially the echoes and resounding in Ex. 28, mm. 39–47, which for Stendhal could come to life only by virtue of how they are sung.)

But speaking of medium, we have another source of seduction. If Crescentini's voice was what Stendhal understood as the most appropriate for expressing a lovers' call and response—from the beloved, presumed to be dead, to the singing lover—surely it was so not least because his voice was a liminal, in-between one that mediated between presence and absence, self and other, exterior and interior life, and at last life and death. Diderot glossed the problem in his *Paradox of the Actor*. The voice of such an actor, he wrote, is brought to life as he climbs through the top of a huge wicker mannequin to inhabit the soul of the author from within. Inhabiting another's soul, he moves its limbs in a way that terrifies all who watch, with a feigning effect that was for Diderot not unlike the effect made by children when they "frighten each other by lifting their short little jackets over their heads, dancing about and imitating as best they can the hoarse, lugubrious voice of the phantom they pretend to be."[40] Here there is no hoarse phantom, only the ghostly presence of an old regime past. In the drama of the opera not only was this phantom body about to die; it might also be thought to have inhabited, in Crescentini's time, a kind of gap between cause and effects, between the musical sound and its inscrutable source, in short, the gap of the uncanny, now, in the nineteenth century, when castrato voices were on the brink of extinction, more troubling than ever.

To know where those voices had gone by 1821–23, when the *Vie* was drafted, after many years during which its author shuttled often between Italy and Paris, Stendhal is crucial. In the first decades of the nineteenth century, mezzos in trouser roles were taking over what had formerly been castrato parts and were simultaneously taking over the castrato functions of high-voiced lover and—for a time, at least—they took over much of the sound in opera houses of a shaded, multi-timbredness of voice.[41] Tenors were encroaching too.[42] Velluti was the last surviving castrato who was a major stage star, hanging on by the skin of his teeth until his retirement in 1830. That year, to which I will return, represents a significant moment of demarcation: in France it was the year of Stendhal's *The Red and the Black,* of Balzac's famous novella *Sarrasine* on a castrato episode, and of the July Revolution, which ended the Bourbon Restoration and initiated the July Monarchy dominated by the haute bourgeoisie of bankers, financiers, merchants, and industrialists. It was also the year of Berlioz's *Symphonie fantastique* and, across the Alps in Venice, of Bellini's *I Capuleti ed i Montecchi* on the Romeo and Juliet tale, both of which relate to my story here.

Although Stendhal's musical facts are often self-contradictory, borrowed, or simply wrong and must therefore be corrected or read with many grains of salt,[43] his existential philosophy of listening and his perceptions of singers illuminate, among other things, the extinction of the operatic castrato, which Crescentini's Romeo presages and Velluti's astounding singing career limns out. To elaborate on the imminent death of this art, Stendhal invokes an exiled Neapolitan friend—in real life, paradoxically, Pasta's professional coach and close friend the chevalier Alexandre Micheroux, for whom her performance as Romeo, reminiscent vocally of a castrato's, induces a deep longing for the moonlit nights of his homeland. Note that it is the moment of listening to Pasta, shared by Stendhal and Micheroux, that induces this nostalgia, which extends what earlier in the *Vie* Stendhal calls "a glimpse of happiness," the capacity of music to make "happiness visible, even if as a dream, by giving hope."[44] Importantly Micheroux's monologue as conveyed by Stendhal begins just after the two have heard Pasta sing "Ombra adorata, aspetta," when Micheroux is gripped by feelings of loss. The text needs to be quoted in full because it wants to re-create the sensation the music is said to cause.

> The fluctuations of sound in that sublime voice remind me of the sensation of tender joy that I sometimes found during the pure nights of our unhappy homeland, when the flickering stars shine out of a deep blue sky, when one can see the clear moon on the banks of the Mergellina of that enchanting country that I will no longer see. The isle of Capri used to float in the distance in the midst of streams of silver on a sea softly agitated by the refreshing midnight breeze. Imperceptibly a diaphanous mist would come to steal the nighttime moon, and its light would seem, in those moments, softer and more tender; the quality of nature would have something more touching in it, the soul would be attentive. Soon the moon would rise again, purer and more brilliant than ever, our shores bathed in its lively, pure light. And the countryside too would reappear in all the radiance of its beauty. Well, the voice of Madame Pasta, with its changes of *registers,* gives me the sensation of that light, more touching and

tender in that it covers itself up one moment to reappear quickly a thousand times more brilliant.⁴⁵

Going to sleep at sunset, when the moon would disappear behind Posillipo, our heart would seem to submit naturally to a sweet melancholy. I don't know what kind of seriousness would seize us then; our soul would seem to be in harmony with the evening and its tranquil sadness. That was the feeling just now, though with a more rapid movement, when Madame Pasta declaimed:

Ultimo pianto!

It's the same feeling that seizes me, but in a more lasting way, on the first cold days of September, followed by a light mist on the trees, which announces the approach of winter and the death of the beauties of nature.

The dying of autumn, the death of nature. Pasta's registral shifts are as melancholic and changeable as bel canto itself, as fleeting as a day lily or the perfume of a rose on an evening stroll. The last words Romeo declaims before singing "Ombra adorata, aspetta" are "Ultimo pianto!" (My final lament), an ecstatic herald of the impending love-death that Stendhal calls Romeo's "sublime praise of suicide."⁴⁶

As Pasta's teacher, Micheroux wanted avidly to safeguard her subtleties. On October 21–22, 1826, he wrote her in Naples on the verge of her debut there to warn her about operatic conditions he feared would cover up this subtlety. Were she, for instance, to debut as a fury such as Medea or Semiramide, the typically noisy Neapolitan opera orchestra would not be discouraged from its usual bad habit of drowning out singers and would thus destroy all possibility that listeners might hear her nuanced middle register:

> Your voice, in the mezzo notes, is almost always veiled *[velata]*. This frailty is not only a precious quality but indispensable to obtaining a magical effect in the inflections of a sadly *affettuosa* expression, or in those of an expression I will call mysterious, for example in "mi chiami a seguirti fra l'ombre" [you call me to follow you among the shades—from the F-major recitative in Romeo's final scena].
>
> To obtain this effect, however, the orchestra must not make noise since the voice should not have to push. Otherwise that veil, that somberness of the voice, produces a confusion of sound, which is deprived of fluctuation.⁴⁷

One printed castrato aria comes especially close to capturing these nuances notationally: Garcia's edition of Velluti's singing of the romanza "Caro suono lusinghier." When Tebaldo hears the harp of Isolina offstage a direction reads, "Here two timbres are necessary, a clear one for the b″ and a covered one for the grace-note passage" (end of second system). As the singer delivers lush passaggi on the words "the sounds of love," a direction tells him to execute it with "supple movements of the throat" (see excerpt in Ex. 16).⁴⁸ Other annotations read "hopeless," "shuddered with joy," "the pharynx narrowed," "the sound softened," "light exhalation," "note and syllable light," "melancholic voice, expand the voice over all the notes," "physiognomy smiling, impetus of the soul," "sound imitating echo, muffled," "breath after portamento," "smiling mouth," "noisy exhalation," and "leave the sound with an exclamation." Only an art that was dying—especially one founded in performative knowledge that exceeded words and had been passed on from student to teacher and from performer to performer, through demonstration, imitation, repetition, and rehearsal—would require such a lather of explanation.

• • •

We have access to various prints and scribbles that attempt to record the nuances Pasta sang in the second recitative, "Tranquillo io son," and the aria "Ombra adorata, aspetta." From these, for the sake of comparison and because of their importance to the theme of blissful dying, I focus now on the verse "Avrò contento il cor." Pasta's approach is even more filled with leaps than Crescentini's, in keeping with Stendhal's and Micheroux's evocations of her castrato-like fluctuations of register and timbre, but they sit in a performative tradition of which Crescentini was a critical part and, in this case, which he initiated.

Two sources make this particularly clear. One is an arrangement of the aria for piano and flute by Anton Diabelli and Johann Jean Sedlatzek. Published in London in 1832, it is nestled in an album of their Italian aria arrangements under the supertitle *Souvenir à Pasta, et Rubini*.[49] Sedlatzek's flute, as carrier of the melody, plays a Crescentini-esque first iteration of "Avrò contento il cor" (Ex. 31a) against Diabelli's piano. The flute then plays more leap-filled Pasta-like elaboration, well up in the instrument's stratosphere, the second time around (Ex. 31b). When "Avrò contento il cor" returns after the B section, it echoes Crescentini's sixteenth-note gruppetti but with the Pasta-styled variant that each gruppetto ends with a lightening-quick leap up a sixth (Ex. 31c). The contours of the soaring octave leap on "cor," which Eppinger and Conti record Crescentini as having made, remain fundamentally unaltered (compare Ex. 30, line b, m. 51, which the flute mimics and extends in Ex. 31c).

The title of Diabelli and Sedlatzek's arrangements captures the memorializing nature of the albums, which are auditory "souvenirs," strewn with little trinkets, mementos, and novelties of the singers they celebrate. Quite different is the expressed object of an 1834 London edition of "Ombra adorata" for voice and keyboard printed by Chappell. Announcing that "the whole of Madame Pasta's ornaments, &c. are added in small lines above the original," the Chappell print makes a marketing claim to reproducing Pasta's ornaments literally, a claim it affects to realize by providing decorations to the main vocal line plus variants for selected passages (see title page, Ex. 32a). A significant point of commonality among all the embellishments of "Avrò contento il cor" seen thus far is that of course they grow increasingly complex and nuanced over the course of the aria (Ex. 32a–c). Again

EXAMPLE 31. *Souvenir à Pasta, et Rubini* (London: Wessel & Co, 1832), no. 5, "Ombra adorata aspetta," Cavatina de l'opera *Romeo et Giulietta, de Zingarelli,* arranged by Anton Diabelli and Johann Jean Sedlatzek, excerpts from pp. 2, 3, and 5. Louise Hanson-Dyer Music Library, The University of Melbourne.
a. Upbeat to m. 10 to downbeat m. 12

b. Mm. 18–24 (downbeat)

EXAMPLE 31. *(continued)* c. m. 53 to the end

Pasta's are versions of Crescentini's, but they are inflected by her proclivity for bounding quickly across vocal registers, perhaps even in an exaggeration of castrato vocality. The first iteration is like Crescentini's per Eppinger and Conti (compare Ex. 30, systems b and c at m. 11, with Ex. 32a) yet already evinces Pasta's signature vaulting and plunging, which intensifies in further iterations and variations. Chappell's print also agrees with Diabelli and Sedlatzek's "souvenir": the fast-bounding leap on the first iteration of "Avrò contento il cor" (beats 3 and 4 in Ex. 31 compared with Ex. 32a) culminates in pervasive leaps in the iteration that follows the B section (Ex. 32b), producing the momentum needed to sail through Crescentini's iterations of "il cor" (heart) (Ex. 32b, m. 56).

By 1834 Crescentini had long been a memory in the shadow of Pasta. Yet wittingly or not, the Chappell editor memorializes Pasta memorializing Crescentini, or her inheritance of him, variously branding all the occurrences of the climactic verse with Crescentini's trademark, which so struck the minds of Conti, Eppinger, Diabelli, Sedlatzek, Micheroux, Stendhal, the Chappell arranger, and, as we will see, E. T. A. Hoffmann and Balzac, as they had Napoleon's.

As indices of the "bonne école," Pasta's nuances had, for Stendhal, an élan that could not be notated—not her beautiful portamento, as he said, nor her rare powers of invention, nor most definitely her uncommon ability to sing soprano and contralto equally well, with a voice of more than one timbre, or what Stendhal noted the Italians called "several *registers*" or "physiognomies" placed on different parts of the scale.[50] In his view some top singers from the previous century had used this ability (which might otherwise have been a disadvantage) to great effect, notably Luigia Todi and the great Pacchierotti. He argued that such a voice was more expressive than an all-silvery one, unchanging timbrally throughout the extension, since the former could make veiled, covered sounds in impassioned moments and, alternating between nearly opposed head and chest, produce swift expressive shifts of color.[51] It hardly seems coincidental that Pasta, master of registers and registral leaps, should also have been aligned with the bel canto of the castrati.

. . .

The tangible footprints borne by Crescentini's "Ombra adorata" and carried forward with innumerable alterations are something toward which I can only gesture here. Those we have glimpsed suggest the existence of a distinct tradition, available to be plied by outstanding professional singers but also by amateurs who could take it up as a kind of material trace. A British Library copy of an early Birchall issue from about 1823–24, rather speciously titled "as sung by Madame Catalani," has added to it some anonymous handwritten ornaments. The addition to "Avrò contento il cor" at m. 11 (Ex. 33) is just like the one in Eppinger, Conti, Diabelli/Sedlatzek, Pasta/Chappell, and Garcia, sources that range from around 1804 to 1847.[52]

EXAMPLE 32. *Tranquillo io son Recitative—Ombra adorata, aspetta! The Celebrated Air sung by Madame Pasta in the Opera Romeo e Giulietta composed by Zingarelli. The whole of Madame Pasta's ornaments, &c. are added in small lines above the original* (London: S. Chappell, 1834). British Library, London.
a. mm. 1–12

b. mm. 20-24 (downbeat)

c. mm. 19-24

EXAMPLE 33. Facsimile from print of Crescentini's aria *Tranquillo io son / Ombra adorato* [sic] *aspetta . . . sung by Madame Catalani . . .* (London: Robert Birchall, [ca. 1824]), mm. 10–12. Note that ornaments have been written into the British Library copy by an unidentified hand. British Library, London.

We can't know for certain why these very similar passages circulated in so many sources.[53] In the case of Ex. 33, a teacher or amateur singer could well have given voice to a memory that was still being transmitted in performances in 1823–24 without those who performed it necessarily being aware of its origin. Pasta herself, who in the summer of 1817 played the role of Giulietta at Brescia opposite Crescentini's longtime partner Grassini in the latter's newly adopted role of Romeo, seems to have been taught by Grassini, whom Haydn's biographer Giuseppe Carpani in turn regarded as the last real beauty of eighteenth-century singing. Thus Pasta may well have learned the part of Romeo much as Crescentini performed it.[54] But there is a quality, too, of Crescentini's version being "in the air" in the theaters and salons of the 1810s, '20s, and '30s, and perhaps even later.

To be sure, those scores that attempt or purport to record singers have a status very different from those that a singer (often amateur) annotates for him- or herself. In the case of this aria, though, exceptions generally seem to prove the rule, representing variations upon a prior, perhaps prototypical embellishment-qua-improvisation. We are brought around to what E. T. A. Hoffmann wrote in his short story "Ombra adorata" of 1813, in the *Kreisleriana:* "As the genius of Italian melody dictates, certain embellishments were allowed for, both in the recitative and in the aria. But is it not a blessing that the way in which the composer and singer Crescentini performed and embellished the aria himself *has been handed down, as though by tradition? No one would now introduce inappropriate flourishes, at least not without being rebuked.*"[55]

Hoffmann is admittedly closer temporally to Crescentini's era in France than are various scores I adduce here, yet he is more distant culturally and geographically. Nonetheless, his view is revelatory in that he identifies in Crescentini's rendition of the aria a "tradition" "handed down" from which other singers evidently cannot depart at will. As for Garcia's score, if it memorializes Crescentini in bygone moments, it gestures in much the same direction as Stendhal's *Vie de Rossini*, whereas Crescentini, along with Velluti and Pasta, epitomizes spontaneity and originality conveyed through those shades of expression that emanated "from the inspiration of talent and the soul" yet is also, like them, the prompt for nostalgia. Prospectively and retrospectively, both at once, we could go on and on listening to scribbled whispers—by singers, guitarists, harpists, pianists, violinists, flutists, arrangers, editors, transcribers, students, writers, all of whose renditions of "Ombra adorata" doubtless in some way commemorated Crescentini knowingly or not, even as most by the 1820s and 1830s explicitly commemorated another singer.

Stendhal aims to account for this phenomenon when he writes that no composer on earth

> could ever manage to note down exactly the infinitely small elements that make for perfection in the singing of this aria by Crescentini—infinitely small elements that change moreover according to the singer's voice at that moment and the amount of enthusiasm and illusion working through him. One day he might feel like executing the ornaments gently and with *morbidezza* [softness]; another day it is *gorgheggi* [flashier ornaments, literally "warbles"] full of force and energy that come to him as he goes onstage. To attain perfection, the singer must yield to the inspiration of the moment.[56]

Here Stendhal clarifies something that has eluded the mindset of a strongly textualist tradition: namely, that expression and ornamentation were traditionally indivisible, that ornamentation was the full body given to an expressive feeling. Thus Stendhal said that each and every time Crescentini performed "Ombra adorata" he "would give his voice and all its inflections a vague, faraway coloring of happiness . . . ; for it would seem to him, *at the precise moment that he was singing it*, that this was the very feeling an impassioned lover who is about to reunite with the woman he loves should have."[57] Just as he imbibed the poison, he pressed out spontaneously the romantic love-death limned in the scene.

Romantic seduction, longing, and dying, but also dying off, become one.

. . .

In a book of vocalises intended for study by advanced singers, *Raccolta di esercizi per il canto all'uso del vocalizzo con discorso preliminare del signor Girolamo*

Crescentini, published by Imbault in Paris around 1810–11, Crescentini himself delineated the requirements of a spontaneous, chiaroscuro bel canto in his dual-language Italian/French preface (see title page in Fig. 51).[58] Singers were to use his exercises to overcome every difficulty by practicing "tournures différentes, et d'embellissemens peu usités" (various turns and little-used embellishments), above all learning how to conserve and support the breath (3). They were also to learn the difficult but crucial art of *legare*, of tying note to note to form a continuous melodic line (hence even those notes separated by rests, marked by staccato, and such), and of *portare*, of carrying the voice smoothly yet without dragging it (2–3). To achieve this, students learned to execute his *vocalizzi* (vocalises), those untexted melodies that were of high difficulty—much more so than so-called *solfeggi or solfèges*, which were more elementary untexted tunes. They were to master the *vocalizzi* so as to sing them with expression, using coloring, flexibility, and exact attention to the *accento*, the last variously produced through attacks, vibrato, trills, gruppetti, and so forth, whichever were most needed for the poetry in the aria at hand. All this required physical and spiritual ("moral") talents, for, as Crescentini wrote,

> Music makes known the heart and spirit of whoever professes it. Hence, because the singer may need to execute a religious, amorous, or agitated piece [in Italian, "un pezzo religioso, amoroso, allegro agitato ec., ec."; in French, "un morceau tendre, religieux, gai, expressif, ou passionné"], it's necessary that he have a sensible, susceptible heart, a penetrating mind, and good judgment [in Italian, "un cuore sensibile, suscettibile, mente penetrativa(,) giustezza di ragionamento"; in French, "le coeur sensible, l'esprit pénétrant et un raisonnement juste"].

. . .

Crescentini's remained a grammatical art in which *sense* and expression were intimately bound up with *syntax* since singing for him was a kind of eighteenth-century "imitation of discourse." Words added to vocalises, combined with rigorous study and many natural gifts, could bring the whole to perfection, above all through *accento*, a word that suggested in a broad stroke the rhythmic-cum-expressive force that a singer would give to words and gestures. This aesthetic presupposed elegance, the mystery of the alluring refinement, the enchantment of a vocal maquillage. Hence Crescentini declared himself against anything so grainy as the sound of a singer's breath. In this aesthetic universe ornaments were anything but mere artifice or superfluity, much less filler or noise, as some may think. Their entire function was to give wings to expression, to give it mobility and flight: "A volatina, a gruppetto, a trill, made at the appropriate moment," he wrote, "augments the flexibility, nuance, and *accento*."[59]

One way that "Ombra adorata" surely condensed this rarified vocality for its contemporaries was through its phenomenal character, its character as metasong, singing within the sung whole of the opera as Carolyn Abbate has sketched it.[60] The aria comes into being when there is nothing left to Romeo but song itself, passionately invoked at the end of his last recitative as "mio ultimo *pianto*"—a stock metaphor for song or lament laden here with its sense of weeping ("the last song I will sing" means here "the last time I will ever have to weep"). That the aria bursts into being *as* song, that it points wholly toward the beloved object for whom it is performed as song—and only at once remove for those who watch him perform it for her—and that it is has no other raison d'être, all these are prefigured in the very syntax of Foppa's verse: "Questo ch'io *per te* verso ultimo pianto," meaning "this final lament that I pour forth for you," but with emphasis on the verb "verso" (from "versare"—"This [that I for you pour forth] final lament"). With this cleaving of subject and verb, "io" from "verso," Romeo's recitative brackets but thus draws attention to the interruptive "per te"—"toward (or 'for') you." The heft of the aria is wholly *toward* the beloved object, who is addressed directly and for whom body and voice will be sacrificed in the love-death. As if such obsession can bear nothing but the single key, voice is largely carried along in D major.

What then of Garcia's score? Perhaps what it records is how voluptuous ornaments animated the song and how inflections of resonance, color, *accento*, and breath shaded its expression, as he indicates through many verbal directions: "exultation," "with power and warmth," "stretching out the voice," "mezza voce" (half voice), "voce piena" (full voice), "half breath," "rinforzato," "full and sonorous voice." Caught up in a similar interplay of colors, lines, and planes, Stendhal's "listener" gives way to a dizzying subjugation, which he claims opens an inner ear onto oneself. Music is a tripping cord of memory that produces self-reflection. Yet a single ornament, performed without fervor, could break the spell that requires and rewards the kind of subjugation that alone can mobilize this self-reflective process: the ultimate romantic ploy.

. . .

As Starobinski points out, Berlioz, for one, found little in the aria of what its adorers had found so much of. "Ombra adorata," though "graceful, elegant, and very well executed overall," with some pretty flute parts in dialogue with the vocal line, was to Berlioz essentially a trivial bore in which everything was "sunny." And in any case, he cried, "Where in God's name is it written that Juliet's lover should appear lacking any of the attributes of *manhood*? . . . His despair at the moment of exile, his dark and terrible resignation upon learning of Juliet's death, his delirious convulsions after drinking the poison: do all these passions ordinarily take root in the soul of a eunuch?"[61] Berlioz, like many of his time, could tolerate only the most clearly demarcated instances of sex and gender; nor could he tolerate theatrical representation that was or that appeared to be disjunct from real life as he understood it. In his world view, there would hardly have been a role that a eunuch could have sung.

ONCE MORE *SARRASINE*

There is a certain poetic justice in Berlioz, the Frenchman, singling out Crescentini's immensely famous aria to decry the figure of the eunuch-lover. Frenchmen had been castigating castrati for a long time (even though the royal chapel had had plenty of them for a century and a half). The rogue-diplomat Ange Goudar in 1777 satirized castrato singing teachers as home wreckers preying upon fashionable Frenchwomen; and in their opera *Tarare* (Paris, 1787) Beaumarchais and Salieri staged a married, squealing castrato named Calpigi—a figure of old-regime debauchery in Hedy Law's gloss.[62] By the second half of the eighteenth century, Frenchmen were also mocking castrati as lovers (which had long been an Italian and English sport). Their voices were not just theatrically anathema but superfluous in a country filled with high tenors. Traditionally these were the *haute-contres* of French *tragédie en musique* and *opera comique*, sometimes called *tenorini* in the new nineteenth century, which in the case of the legendary Giovanni Battista Rubini (1794–1854) meant ascending all the way up to f″ (a fourth above the top of today's high tenors). This was the backdrop when Napoleon brought Crescentini to the (by then) imperial French court.[63]

. . .

Berlioz's contemporary Balzac (1799–1850) also staged a performance of "Ombra adorata" in his 1837 novella *Massimilla Doni*. The setting is the banks of the lagoon in a moonlit Venice, the motivation love, and the singer a tenor trained according to the "wise methods" of Crescentini and Velluti. Balzac's tale is in turn indebted, as Starobinski points out, to E. T. A. Hoffmann's "Ombra adorata," both of them engaging with the aria's simplicity and lack of artifice to develop romantic tales about sublimated and narcissistically over-the-top love.[64]

No "Ombra adorata" appears in Balzac's *Sarrasine*, but the novella is entirely prompted by the castrato's legacy. Completed in November of 1830, it was written at a moment when older Frenchmen still harbored memories of Crescentini, whom Alfred de Vigny recalled in 1835 as having had a "seraphic voice coming from a worn and wrinkled face"[65]—shades of Gabriel Garcia Marquez's "Very Old Man with Enormous Wings," who is reckoned as an angelic figure of mediation in chapter 1 of this book. In *Sarrasine* the old castrato floats through a sparkling Parisian mansion as a remnant of a long-lost world, an ethereal old man as weightless as a seraph and as wrinkled as death. The present is not *his* world, but it is he who provides for it and who causes the male narrator to tell his companion the tale-within-a-tale that makes up the core of the novella, set in the mid-eighteenth century.[66]

Much ink has been spilled on this little book, mainly of a quasi-Lacanian kind concerned with gender and voice, which dominated castrato studies in the 1990s, especially owing to Roland Barthes's brilliant reading in *S/Z* (1974).[67] His semiotic analysis turns on the novella's inner torso wherein the sculptor Sarrasine is fatally obsessed with a *travesti* opera singer named La Zambinella. Their relation produces Barthes's central theme of an "axis of castration," which connects the castrated man with a castrating androgyne, hence S slash Z. In this analysis the castrato's Lacanian phallus can only be, semiotically and psychically speaking, ambiguous in being a lack. The ambiguity of the androgyne is nerve-racking to his observers, an instance of traumatically thwarted desire in which the desire itself is sexually ambiguous, as expressed not only in the inner plot but in the outer limbs of *Sarrasine* by the effects of his ghostly presence.

Barthes's analysis has produced ex post facto a kind of psychoanalytic roadmap of the castrato, a figure who for some virtually condenses the central project of psychoanalysis. Those enthusiasts who have made of it a small industry suggest that sex in the castrato absents the hollowed-out body and settles in the voice, causing erotic ecstasy (Lacan's *jouissance*) in listeners for whom it becomes the object of an immoderate desire. The first plank was laid down by Lacanian psychoanalyst Michel Poizat in *The Angel's Cry: Beyond the Pleasure Principle in Opera*, published in English in 1992, which begins its inquiry with the effects of operatic singing on modern-day listeners but ultimately turns to the long-gone castrato as an "angel" whose virility is "displaced into his voice." Poizat's move makes the castrato key to understanding the very power of voice, since his being—beyond sex, beyond words, and beyond sense (in Lacan's language, *hors-sexe, hors-parole, hors-sens*)—is produced in an "alchemy" that leaves it without sexual demarcation.[68]

It is not irrelevant here that the very objects Lacan added to Freud's list of drives, voice and gaze, are "love objects par excellence—not in the sense that we fall in love with a voice or a gaze, but rather in the sense that they are a *medium*, a catalyst that sets off love," as Renata Salecl and Slavoj Žižek put it.[69] Stendhal would have agreed, even though their viewpoint rests upon a variation on psychoanalysis that maps awkwardly onto his at best. For them the voice as medium occupies a troubled space between its lever or mechanism and the effects it produces in those who experience it, what Mladen Dolar calls the "the space of a breach, a missing link, a gap in the causal nexus."[70] So what happens when the occupant of that troubled space becomes categorically intolerable? Crescentini's Romeo might be thought to pry open the question, coming at the apex of castrato vocality and on the verge of its fall (something that was even more true of Velluti). His was the voice that functioned as a medium of love but one that had finally to end in an exalted love-death. And that love-death in turn opens a historical precipice.

All this invites us to approach the familiar interpretations of *Sarrasine* by rethinking the historical situation in which the castrato exists in 1830. Barthes's rightly acclaimed and widely rehearsed book-length reading exceeds Saussure's structuralist linguistics by introducing a notion of "codes" that throws it open to overlapping variations on meaning and overall makes possible an open, pluralistic site of analysis. The most important of Barthes's five codes for present purposes is surely the "symbolic" code whose meanings extend through metonymic devices into the fields of rhetoric, sexuality, and economy. The narrator in this code can transgress what is taboo—and sexually castration is the overwhelming form of transgression. All in all it is what doubtless prompts Barthes to make *Sarrasine* the focus of his analysis.

Let me intervene by redirecting our attention to a set of overlapping genealogies of past and present that cannot easily be seen in Barthes's terms. Balzac's reimagining of the castrato phenomenon through a temporal merging of past and present places in psychic relief the conditions of a society that had undergone frequent dramatic changes since the mid-eighteenth century and that, in 1830, was rapidly evolving toward bourgeoisification in which the castrato, as memory, representation, and human being, is violently out of place. To trace this progress we should begin with the inner tale. The unwashed French sculptor Sarrasine goes to Rome as a young man, where he falls madly in love with the beautiful Zambinella.[71] His obsession lasts but a short time, coming quickly to a head when she reveals, in a desperate *Crying Game* moment, that she is a he. Choked with fury, Sarrasine draws his sword to destroy the cause of his anguish but is immediately killed by thugs who have been dispatched by the singer's patron/protector, a powerful Roman cardinal.

That killing initiates a genealogy—or, better, a double genealogy—that offers a first clue to what will be at stake (see p. 253). The hit men make off with Sarrasine's sculpture of La Zambinella, which Sarrasine had molded in clay from fantasy in a kind of Pygmalian-esque fervor. At the time of these imaginary incidents, in 1758, castrati still held the stage, especially in Rome, when in the fiction of the novella the singer is twenty and the sculptor twenty-two. The cardinal has the clay mold copied in rich marble. In that form the singer's effigy is discovered in a Roman museum by the same family who are hosting the ritzy present-tense party in Paris, the Count and Countess de Lanty. The year Balzac assigns to this discovery is a momentous one: 1791. Under the Lantys' sponsorship, the genealogy of artworks continues. From the marble sculpture, it is said that they commissioned a painting by Vien, which in turn inspired Girodet's picture of a frontal, moonstruck Endymion—a tight compression, since in reality Girodet's painting was completed in November 1791 during his exile in Italy, and wasn't exhibited in Paris until 1793. And why Endymion? Endymion the sensualist sleeps eternally to keep his youthful beauty (Fig. 52);[72] the castrato is gelded to retain forever the pristine beauty of his boyhood voice.

The four images (two sculptures, one clay and one marble, and two paintings, by Vien and Girodet) form a lineage, but the Adonis exists in the narrative present, being brought out at a moment when he catches the attention of the narrator's female auditor. Hanging at the Lantys' mansion, lounging on the pelt of a lion, Adonis personifies languorously forbidden eros. The female auditor is much affected by the sight of the lion skin. A hypersymbol of male sexuality, it lies at the

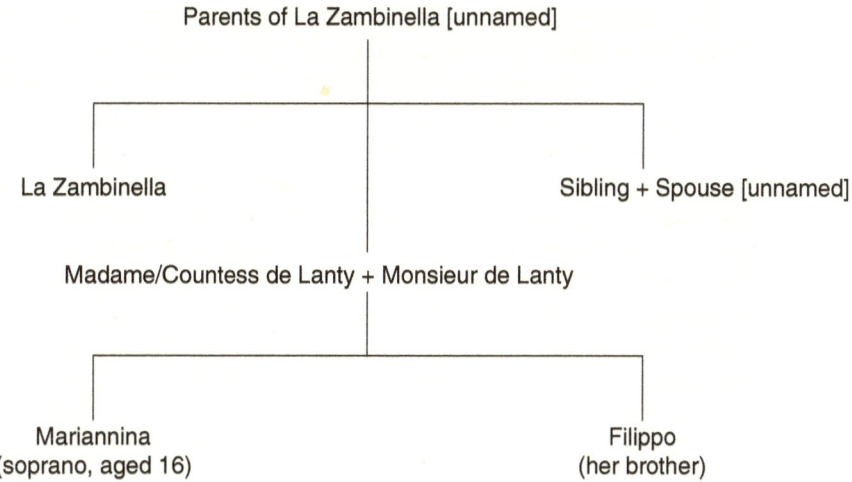

rawest far side of the sensual, otherworldly imaginary from which the psychic dreamland of the moonbeamed Endymion and the clay mold of Zambinella descend. The skin of the lion lies in the gap between that inside and its own outside, torn off by a presumed masculine power. Mythologically Adonis conjures sex, incestuous births, and bloodshed, and the lion pelt associates him with a hubristically perilous form of hunting. Recall that in myth he was killed by the wild boar Ares.[73] In one account, his lover Aphrodite rushed to the spot where Adonis had been wounded and there sprinkled his blood with nectar from which scarlet anemone flowers sprang up. Other accounts give roses, which are ascribed to Aphrodite's sacrifice: as she hastened to her wounded lover she trod upon a bush of white roses whose thorns tore her tender flesh, staining them red. Adonis myths are saturated with the transformative medium of blood, marked by a mobile sexuality and by radical transformation of the self (sometimes he himself changes himself into a red flower).

But it is not only that blood-tinged beauty connects the vertiginous spiral of Adonis variants. Rather it is this: that just as Adonis and his like are associated with beauty, cultic adoration, and bloodshed, so the blood that was discharged through Zambinella's body returns mysteriously in the form of bloodlines that have social status but also stain their descendants with illicit histories that involve further genealogies. With bloodshed comes the horror of a castrato, who disturbs lineage through his inability to generate yet also through the excessive money he produces. Lacking proper bloodlines, he can only generate false lineages, symbolized by copies and fakes that lead, in Lacanian (or Diderotian) mechanisms, to uncanny effects that exist in a troubled gap of the voice (Lacan's "object-voice").

In that sense the evocation of Adonis can be thought key to *Sarrasine*, appearing as it does at the novella's point of maximum tension when the end is nigh. And in the end the wrinkled old man and the young eunuch Zambinella will of course turn out to be one and the same person. Both he and his facsimile, the latter as found and copied by the Lantys, mark the outer ends of the story's chronology, in the middle of which falls the highly symbolic year of 1791, when the Lantys are said to have discovered the clay mold from which all the copies were made. A further series of feints and appearances follows: the person discovered that year is a castrato, yes, but it is also Madame Lanty's uncle (see p. 255)—hence the parallel genealogies, of images and kin, which disturb but describe all too well the lineage of the castrato, fraught with mysterious origins, compounded in visions, copies, and imitations, and shadowed by dreadful new money.[74]

And so we are back to men who pretend to be who they are, or who sometimes pretend briefly to be something other than what they are, only to shed their disguises and emerge as themselves. In 1830 there is a terror of dodgy men, indeed a terror that nearly all men are dodgy. The Lantys' salon, after all, is an haute bourgeoisie one in which the old castrato is laden with luxury goods. He signifies the commodification of a human being who has been exchanged as capital and has produced it. As we have seen earlier in this book, he was interposed at the wide point of transition between an old feudal world and the modern one dominated by bourgeois capital. *Sarrasine* can be read for many things, but it is certainly about the castrato as an index of old times versus new, about the defeat of the Bourbon Restoration only to be replaced with men of money, of their transformations and appearances (and disappearances). Thus for my story, it is also, at last, an exploration of the psycho-historical conditions of one stage in the castrato's long demise.

All of this is exposed at the site of laughter (reminiscent of the jokes and satires we have encountered earlier), which punctuates Balzac's text at several points. The feverish Sarrasine espies La Zambinella's fellow singers lined up at the wings of the stage laughing at the "castrated" man for falling madly in love with a man he thinks is a woman and causing mad blood to stir in Sarrasine's veins, even though he is ignorant of why they are laughing. La Zambinella had occasionally played a "she" offstage too, but only by night (he protests), *to make his friends laugh*.[75] Sarrasine laughs in his turn when La Zambinella invokes Good Friday in an effort to dissuade him from doing violence to her (him?)—Sarrasine a Frenchman of Baron d'Holbach's persuasion, atheistic, in other words, and not about to be thrown off course by superstitious Catholic scruples harbored by this lowborn, God-fearing singer. At the Lantys' house, when La Zambinella is ninety-two years old yet seems "at once a hundred . . . and twenty-two,"[76] his sudden strange appearance within the crowd—a repulsive, dizzying, self-undoing sight—causes "stifled laughter" in the woman to whom his story is about to be told.

GENEALOGY OF PAINTINGS and STATUES
of the castrato La Zambinella in Balzac's *Sarrasine* (1830)

La Zambinella (castrato, aged 20) **meets Sarrasine** (sculptor, aged 22), **1758**

↓

Clay statue of La Zambinella by Sarrasine, 1758
(cold; a Pygmalion's love)

↓

Anonymous copy in marble of Sarrasine's clay statue,
commissioned by Zambinella's patron Card. Cicognara **[circa 1759?]**;
housed in the Albani Museum and seen by the Lanty's in **1791**

↓

Painting of the anonymous marble statue by Joseph-Marie Vien (1716–1809):
Fictitious, dated to 1791; subject called "Adonis"
commissioned by the Lanty family after seeing the marble
copy of the statue of Zambinella at the Albani Museum

↓

Painting of Endymion by Anne-Louis Girodet de Roussy-Trioson (1767–824):
1793, based on Vien
said by the narrator to resemble an unnamed painting of Adonis,
lying with a lion skin, at the Lanty mansion

Laughter in these various moments and guises always erupts at the borders of the self, when the self comes face to face with the foreign or the strange and the boundaries of the ego are uncertain. Never unmixed with fear, this kind of laughter is the unnerving site at which the self determines its limits and hence something of its identity. Because much is at stake, it is often a violent, even cruel laughter—La Zambinella making Sarrasine the butt of his friends' mirth, or Sarrasine laughing in the face of La Zambinella's terror of being hurt. Still, in Balzac it's never entirely clear who's on top, who's inside or outside, who's nature and who's culture, who's savage and wild or, to the contrary, who a mere artifice of civilization. The general grounds and figurations of antitheses are there, but not their resolutions. Nor, consequently, is it clear which alternative is necessarily good and which bad.

The story evolves as an ongoing series of critical and moral crisscrossings and ends with an ongoing tug-of-war between something we might call—not unproblematically—civilization and its opposites.

As an old man, La Zambinella himself radically represents artifice and, more lately, symbolizes its supposed decay.[77] He is referred to as that famously monstrous "creature for which the human language had no name, a form without substance, a being without life, or a life without action," his thighs the thighs of death, like "two bones crossed on a tombstone." A gaudy creature, he embodies old-regime decadence, having been turned in old age into a nineteenth-century piece of "phantasmagoria." He is the hyperexpression of civilization, with his "fabulous," "tasteless" diamond, his "blonde wig whose innumerable curls [give] evidence of an extraordinary pretension," "gold ornaments hanging from his ears," "rings whose fine stones glitter on his bony fingers," and a "watch chain that shimmers like the brilliants of a choker around a woman's neck." Like a Japanese idol, his skin glistens red and white. His manners have retained the coquettishness of a young woman—a gruesome echo of the literary tradition of *vecchia innamorata* (the old woman in love) immortalized in Boccaccio.[78]

The problem for those around his half-dead state is that La Zambinella is disarmingly machine-like but also boundary inhabiting. "It was a man," we read, but really it is an *it*, a neutered being with a feminine, diminutive name and chthonic powers that connect him more to the dead than the living.[79] For his onlookers he is not just the curious shade of a (mis)remembered past, but phantasmagorical because a facsimile of what he was, a being from another world who ought properly to be dead and thereby challenges the living.

Quite opposed to the hypercivilized Zambinella, Sarrasine is a wild man who comes from big money. His father, a lawyer in provincial Franche-Comté (in its original meaning, "free country"), amassed "a professional's fortune, which at that time in the provinces was considered to be colossal."[80] He hoped to make a magistrate of his son, but the child was moody, blasphemous, even violent. As a boy he caused blood to be shed not out of necessity, but because his own bad nature incited him to it. "When a fight broke out between him and a friend, the battle rarely ended without bloodshed. If he was the weaker of the two, he would bite." His name, Sarrasine, means Saracen, recalling heathens and tyrants of literary and operatic fame. Hence he goes east, following contemporaneous cultural geographies made from the optic of western Europeans, according to which his destiny headed off in the direction of an oriental wilderness. Yet Sarrasine's progress only as far as Italy was not nearly east enough in Orientalist terms to accommodate his brute nature, for Italians regarded him as uncouth and anathema to their kind (in one scene he even appears to be masturbating in his opera box).

We learn all this as an implicit contrast to La Zambinella, who has shed blood only perforce, and has made money in consequence, a good deal of it in fact, on his own, not from any inheritance. Unlike Sarrasine, he is as gentle as a kitten and as cultivated as a geisha in spring. A foreigner with respect to the text's French locus of reference, he has by 1830 seemingly long since retired westward, in Paris, where he provides for a family that gathers within its walls the *crème* of bourgeois French society.

Such oppositions are written into *Sarrasine* through and through and are continually inverted and otherwise complicated. At the outset of the novella, the narrator spatializes them by characterizing in cool but vivid tones the decadent bacchanalias of whirling, glittering partiers on one side and on the other the apprehensions of death expressed in trees barely whitened by the death-dealing moon. Between these melodramatic opposites stand the agonies of recent French history and the battered French ego, the artifice, corruption, and deceptions of La Zambinella figuring the dreams and fears of a postrevolutionary, post-Restoration society trying to (re)integrate in the face of an aristocratic class despoiled of and respoiled by its riches and an upstart nouveau-riche class busy making new money. Some earlier components of this dilemma I dealt with in chapters on the "castrato de luxe" and then the "cold and monied man" that the castrato increasingly became. But the history that leads up to the Paris of 1830 makes the dilemma more acute and more ironic. Corruption is a disease of high society that smells and feels like death. Old Zambinella himself produces chills[81] and strikes fear in the hearts of others, which in turn expresses itself in endless talk about money. Money is the lifeblood of the Lanty family, who live on the income of a generatively dead man who was never reproductive except—and prodigiously—in an alienated form, no longer even a cultural one as used to be the case (Pistocchi generating Bernacchi generating Farinelli and so on in a paternalistic pedagogical tradition). On one of his rare appearances, an observer refers to him in hushed tones as a "tête genoise," which he defines as "a man ... with an enormous lifetime capital ... whose family's income doubtless depends on his good health."[82] A working man, in other words, but in his case much more mysteriously wealthy than most. The guests speculate about this. The family might be counterfeiters or crooks, the old man a killer or a confidence man who "kills men's fortunes" (which one partier declares can be even worse than killing a man).

Though there are blood ties, they are suspect. Some unnamed sibling apparently produced a nepotic heir on whom the old man seems to have settled handsome sums in return for assiduous care. Would that Senesino and Farinelli had met such happy returns when they tried to extend bequests to nephews they barely knew. But, unlike them, La Zambinella (he's never given any but this feminine name) has lived far beyond his time, so long as to produce nothing but feelings of horror. Reproachfully, the young marquise who listens to the story tells the narrator afterward, "You have given me a disgust for life and for human passions that will last a long time."[83] Her disgust is not really because the old man is monstrous, but because of the monstrosity of this money, won by others' lust for a lifestyle that includes luxury singing that is complicit with counterfeit, deceit, illusion, and filth. "Paris is a very hospitable place," she adds. "It accepts everything, shameful fortunes and bloodstained fortunes."[84]

That is the pretext on which the novella is built. "Monsieur de Lanty hasn't owned this house for very long, has he?" one guest comments. And the other, "Oh yes. Maréchal sold it to him nearly ten years ago." Ten years ago . . . not even long enough to qualify him as a newcomer in the old world. And yet Parisian socialites relish these parties with whispering curiosity over a polyglot family that seems to speak every language, all with gypsy-like ease, who come from nowhere, from who knows what business—piracy, bank robbing, freebooting. Money for these new Parisians is a way of valuing and devaluing, associating and dissociating, where music forms a part as a kind of distinction in Bourdieu's sense.[85] As elusive as its owners, and no more reputable, the Lanty wealth can justify a covert (and banal?) evil and displace morals. "'Even if it's the devil,'" a young politician says, "'they give a marvelous party.' 'Even if the Count de Lanty had robbed a bank, I'd marry his daughter any time!'" cries a philosopher. For as our narrator says, in the Paris of 1830, "even bloodstained or filthy money betrays nothing and stands for everything."

What you have is who you are, a crass formula in which "social problems are solved like algebraic equations" and family trees are judged by what they cost.[86] It was the kind of formula Stendhal's Julien Sorel comprehended well.

. . .

But things are not so simple after all. Despite this cold calculus, anxiety drips from every sous and every title, for in the end euphoria and dysphoria lie within the self. This is what the castrato's lost voice proves. It reemerges in the person of La Zambinella's beautiful grand-niece, who at age sixteen is already a fantastic singer and alone is able to coax the old ghost from his lair. Marianina "puts into the shade the partial talents of Malibran, Sontag, and Fodor," in whom "one dominant quality has always excluded over-all perfection,"[87] while she, by contrast, "was able to bring to the same level *purity of sound, sensibility, rightness of movement and pitch, soul and science, correctness and feeling.*" "This girl was the embodiment of that secret poetry, the common bond among all the arts, which always eludes those who search for it. Sweet and modest, educated and witty, no one could eclipse Marianina, save her mother."[88] She is the fictional vocal and even genetic heir of the castrato.

Her lineage, we might suppose, rests on unobstructed sound, expressivity, nuance, legato, and intonation, elements encountered repeatedly in eighteenth- and early nineteenth-century writings about singing that are embodied in Crescentini and traced out in his descendants. Marianina descends from those Italian voices that "plunged" Sarrasine into a delicious and dangerous ecstasy when he first went to the opera in Rome in 1758, an ecstasy that "made his "soul [pass] through his eyes and ears" and "hear through every pore." She applies the cherished tradition to a new repertory, singing at the very beginning of the novella "the cavatina" from Rossini's *Tancredi* of 1813, unnamed but of course "Tu che accendi questo core" followed by the cabaletta "Di tanti palpiti." The words and music of the cabaletta, a huge favorite throughout Europe, are a Narcissus-like play on the invertibility of lover and loved, "mi rivedrai . . . ti rivedrò" (you will see me, I will see you).

Tu che accendi questo core,	You who inflame this heart,
Tu che desti il valor mio,	who spurred me to valor,
alma gloria, dolce amore,	glorious soul, sweet love,
secondate il bel desio;	requite [or match] my desire;
cada un empio traditore,	may an evil traitor fall,
coronate il mio valor.	may you crown my valor.
Di tanti palpiti,	For such throbs,
di tante pene	for such pain
da te mio bene,	I beg forgiveness
spero mercè	from you, my love.
Mi rivedrai . . .	You will see me again . . .
ti rivedrò . . .	I will see you again . . .
ne' tuoi bei rai	I will feed
mi pascerò.	on your lovely eyes.

This play on subject and object is of course a quintessential romantic preoccupation. Subjects who were truly, spiritually free were supposed to be (like Sarrasine?) distant from earthly objects. To be commodified was to be stripped of being a person, divorced from social origins and subjective associations; to be a subject was not to be alienated from them. The rift suggests that the continued attraction/repulsion around the monied, object-encrusted castrato, who might invade a person's inner core and induce ecstatic states of euphoria and, still worse, longing for the other, even longing for a castrato himself, could be the crux of those widespread feelings of moral and sensible repugnance, which made society so desperately need to eliminate him.

In Edmond Michotte's pamphlet *An Evening at Rossini's in Beau-Sejour (Passy) 1858* Rossini explicitly acknowledges the vocal connection and implicitly the existential one: "In my youth it was my good fortune to hear some of those fellows. I have never forgotten them. The purity, the miraculous flexibility of those voices, and, above all their profoundly penetrating *accent* [that word again]—all that moved and fascinated me more than I can tell you." He added that in 1813 he had written the role of Armando in *Aureliano in Palmira* for Velluti, "one of the last but not the least."[89]

Rossini's encounter with the "last," in 1813, was famously problematic, ending in some kind of falling out, if apparently a less bad one than reputed by the vagaries of Rossini historiography.[90] Afterward, while roles previously taken by castrati were being given over to mezzos or tenors, Velluti's career went on at full strength as he continued to be widely revered and imitated. His gender was less easily accommodated than his voice alone, however. In an eerie watercolor by Edward Alfred Chalon he is painted with a moustache, playing the knight Armando in Meyerbeer's *Mose in Egitto* in 1824, illuminated from beneath by footlights in ghostly, livid tones (Fig. 53).[91]

By about 1830 Velluti's long stage career was over though, and decades later his kind were objects of nostalgia. In 1866 Rossini could famously sigh, "Those mutilated boys, who could follow no other career but that of singing, were the founders of the *cantar che nell'anima si sente*, and the horrid decadence of Italian bel canto originated with their suppression."[92]

Or near suppression. The narrator of *Sarrasine* tries to console his companion by countering her fears with the suggestion that he has given her a "fine example of the progress made by civilization," since "they no longer create these unfortunate creatures." Of course he is not completely right, and we can count the ways: Domenico Mustafà from rural Umbria, castrated about 1844 and taken to Rome; Pasquale Meniconi, a rural Umbrian, castrated about 1847; Giuseppe Ritarossi, from Lazio, and Giosafat Anselmo Vissani, from Le Marche, both castrated about 1852; Giovanni Cesari, from the mountains of Lazio, castrated about 1855; and still after Rossini's quip Vincenzo Sebastianelli from Castellone, in Lazio, castrated about 1863 (and still illiterate in 1881); Domenico Salvatori from Lazio, castrated in about 1867 and still at the Cappella Giulia after 1907; and Alessandro Moreschi, from Monte Compatri in rural Lazio, probably castrated in 1869, still in the papal chapel in 1913, and singing in other papal basilicas (notably the Cappella Giulia) until 1921, before he died in 1922.[93]

Perhaps it is fitting though that it was really on the international stage that these creatures received their death-dealing blow, or at least the one that blew them back from whence they came, to Italy's churches and soon after to those of papal Rome. All those named above were Vatican singers. The mechanical view of the world that was encroaching on London and Paris in the 1820s, the view that brought the steam engine, the photograph, and the telegraph, wanted no part of them. It was Rossini again, who returned to Paris from Italy in early September 1830 after the July Revolution, two months before Balzac composed *Sarrasine*, who wrote in

1866 of music as an art with "its only basis in ideal and feeling," whereas "art" in his day were "directed exclusively toward *steam,* rapine, and the barricades"— Rossini who famously told Wagner that the decay of Italian theaters in the early nineteenth century was attributable to "the disappearance of the *castrati.*"[94] Prima facie castrati were not eradicated because they betrayed nature but because Europe had learned (it thought) how to be more humane to children and how to align gender with sex in neat polarities—to make men like men and women like women; and consequently because Europe had lost its tolerance for disjunctions between appearance and embodiment on stage. But mechanism also knew the difference. How ironic that when Johann Nepomuk Maelzel, inventor of the metronome and an infamously meretricious peddler of his inventions, developed the first of his mechanical instruments, an automaton made up of flutes, trumpets, drums, triangle, cymbals, and strings, he had it play melodies by Haydn, Mozart, and Crescentini. Yet when the anti-Rossinian composer Henri-Montan Berton asked Maelzel whether he could make a mechanical singer that could perform roulades, he replied that he could do so easily enough but that it would be impossible to make another Crescentini.[95]

ACKNOWLEDGMENTS

This book evolved from the Ernest Bloch Lectures Series, given in the Department of Music at the University of California at Berkeley in fall 2007. I cannot imagine a more exciting invitation for a musicologist or a more humbling one. Throughout the months when I delivered the talks, I was often struck by the kinship between the transitive origins of the emerging book and the nature of its subject. A castrato was first and foremost a singing performer who had to engage the attention of his public. In my case, delivering these talks gave me the chance to produce an entire book, knowing that a brilliant audience would be acting as a kind of credibility serum on first delivery. That invigorated everything about the writing process, even when I feared I could not keep them interested over the course of six talks. For entrusting me with that challenge and for their generous hospitality, I am inexpressibly grateful to my hosts and colleagues, Ben Brinner, Louise George Clubb, Christy Dana, James Q. Davies, Daniel Heartz, the late Joe Kerman, Davitt Moroney, Tony Newcomb, Mary Ann Smart, Richard Taruskin, James Turner, Kate van Orden, and Bonnie Wade. I offer very special thanks to Kate, now at Harvard. She went well out of her way to charm the time there and to engage me and my spouse, Patricia Barber, who held a Townsend Fellowship in the Humanities during that time.

My students at Berkeley have already moved on to great things. I remember our seminar and conference with fond pleasure, not least our breaks at Caffe Strada. Thank you Rebekah Ahrendt, Emily Frey, Jonathan Rhodes Lee, Rachel Li, Camille Peters, Ulrike Peterson, Laura Protano-Biggs, and Emily Richmond Pollack.

Research and writing for this book was supported by year-long fellowships from the American Council of Learned Societies, the John Simon Guggenheim

Memorial Foundation, and in part the Franke Institute for the Humanities. At prior stages, when I was first thinking and writing about castrati, my work was supported by the Getty Research Institute and the National Endowment for the Humanities. This project would not have been possible without generous funding from all these entities.

The Humanities Visiting Committee of the University of Chicago provided substantial financial support toward final research and publication costs. The Gustave Reese Endowment of the American Musicological Society, funded in part by the National Endowment for the Humanities and the Andrew W. Mellon Foundation, provided a generous publication subvention. Deans of the Humanities Division at the University of Chicago Janel Mueller, Danielle Allen, and Martha Roth, and Chairs of the Department Music Thomas Christensen and Bob Kendrick all liberally supported the leaves of absence I had in order to research and write the book. My sincere thanks go to them all.

From 2006 to 2008 I studied voice first with Drew Minter and then with Winifred Faix Brown in connection with this project. I would have been at sea trying to write parts of it without their help in understanding some of the complexities of singing. My respect for singing, my love of it, and my affection and respect for them deepened throughout the process. My thanks to Drew for countless exchanges about singing and recordings, and to the incomparable Will Crutchfield, who repeatedly shared materials and expertise with me. Both became co-conspirators whom I could not do without. I take full responsibility for the brushstrokes of a neophyte that remain. I also thank Roger Freitas and Richard Wistreich for enlightening conversations about singing and castrati.

My thanks to three ENTs, Drs. Avi Lotan, Jacquelynne Corey, and Daniel Martin, the last two specializing in professional voice, for helping me to understand some physiological aspects of this project, and pediatric endocrinologists Dr. Donald Zimmerman and especially Robert Rosenfield for their help with endocrinological aspects.

A special thanks to my good friends Maria Di Salvo, Professore Ordinario of Slavic Studies at the University of Milan, Natalia (Natasha) Solovieva, now retired head of the Gnessin State Music College, Moscow, Gyorgy Ivanovich, cellist and now retired faculty member of the Gnessin State Music College, and Donald and Svetlana Chae. You know how indispensable your help has been. I would also like to thank the head of original manuscripts at the Russian State Library, Molchanov Victor Federovitch, for allowing me to examine the original manuscript of Balatri's "Vita e viaggi." Thanks also to Professor Daniel Schlafly Jr. and to Christine Wunnike for helpfully corresponding with me about Balatri.

My editor Mary Francis brought to this project her intelligence, wisdom, resourcefulness, and deep reserves of patience. For expert, patient work, fond thanks also to project manager Cindy Fulton and copy editor Sharron Wood.

A very special thank you to my all-time favorite book designer Jeff Clark of Quemadura. Thank you, Jeff, for the vision, integrity, generosity, calm, and hilarity.

Chapter 1 had early incarnations at a Clark Library conference on baroque authority, the annual meeting of the American Musicological Society in Atlanta, the Department of Music at Yale University, the Center for Music Information in Belgrade, and the Music History/Theory Workshop at the University of Chicago. Chapter 2 was developed as the Edward J. Dent Lecture for the annual conference of the Royal Musical Association meeting in Glasgow and was later given at the annual meeting of the American Musicological Society in Houston and at Vassar College. Chapter 3 was revised for the annual meeting of the AMS in Nashville, the Peabody Conservatory, the National Early Music Association conference at the University of York, and the conference on Performing Voices held at the American Academy of Rome. Chapter 4 was delivered to the Mediterranean Studies Workshop at the University of Chicago, the Department of Music at the University of Pennsylvania, the Department of Music at Cornell University, the Dipartimento di scienze musicologiche e paleografico-filologiche at the Università degli Studi di Pavia, Cremona, and the Department of Music at Yale University. Parts of chapter 6 were given at the State University of New York at Stony Brook and the whole was discussed by the marvelous fellows group at the Franke Institute for the Humanities at the University of Chicago. I am grateful to all these audiences in helping me shape and reshape chapters of this book, especially to Julie Chu, Xinyu Dong, Berthold Hoeckner, Hoyt Long, and Paola Iovene.

Stanford University Press granted permission to reproduce parts of "Strange Births and Surprising Kin: The Castrato's Tale," in *Italy's Eighteenth Century: Gender and Culture in the Age of the Grand Tour* (2009), and Oxford University Press likewise to use parts of "Denaturing the Castrato," published in *Opera Quarterly* in 2008/2009.

Thanks to Jim Chandler for taking an avid interest in the framing of this book and for deepening my understandings of its cultural meanings both as coteacher of the seminar "Composing Humans, 1760–1840" and as director of the Franke Institute for the Humanities.

My deep thanks for comments on parts of the book to my aunt Johanna Reiss and my stepdaughter Emily Bauman.

To my friends Raine Daston, Sergio Durante, Philip Gossett, and Hedy Law, each of whom read various parts of this book and gave me precious feedback, a big thank you. For valuable input thanks too to the anonymous reader for the Press.

Matt Hess and Pete Smucker in the Department of Music at the University of Chicago worked heroically with me on permissions and images.

A number of research assistants facilitated this project over the years: Andrew Greenwood, Anabel Maler, Meredith Moretz, Jessica Peritz, Richard Plotnik,

Martha Sprigge, Peter Shultz, and Pete Smucker. Siel Agugliaro provided indispensable assistance in Milan.

The musical examples were expertly set by Peter Shultz.

Jenn Dunlap, project cataloguer at the Newberry, came forward at a critical moment to create the bibliography.

The index was created by Martin L. White.

To the staff at the Jean Gray Hargrove Music Library at Berkeley, Manuel Erviti, Cheryl Griffith-Peel, Angela Arnold, and Allison Rhea, and the staff in the Department of Music, in particular Melissa Hacker, Kathleen Karn, and Cuco Daglia: thank you for your bottomless energy and goodwill.

This book is for Patricia, whose spirit, musicality, and genius give me endless reserves of inspiration. It is also for our great friends Jonny Glassman and Jimmy Kern, with whom we share our anniversary, and for our loving families of friends and relatives.

ABBREVIATIONS

A-Wkm   Vienna, Kunsthistorisches Museum
A-Wn   Vienna, Österreiches Nationalbibliothek, Musiksammlung
D-Hs   Hamburg, Staats- und Universitätsbibliothek Carl von Ossietzky, Musikabteilung
D-Mb   Munich, Bayerische Staatsbibliothek
D-MÜs   Münster, Santini-Bibliothek
ECCO   Eighteenth-Century Collections Online (Gale Group, 2003)
F-Pn   Paris, Bibliothèque Nationale de France
GB-Lb   London, British Library
GH   Charles Burney, *A General History of Music*, vol. 4 of 4 (1789)
G-Mbs   Munich, Bayerische Staatsbibliothek
GMO   *Grove Music Online*. Oxford Music Online, www.oxfordmusiconline.com
I-Bas   Bologna, Archivio di Stato
I-Bc   Bologna, Museo Internazionale e Biblioteca della Musica di Bologna (N.B.: siglum formerly that of the Biblioteca del Conservatorio Padre Martini, now Bl, with many former music holdings now at I-Bc)
I-Bl   Conservatorio Statale di Musica G. B. Martini, Biblioteca
I-Mb   Milan, Biblioteca Nazionale Braidense
I-Mc   Milan, Conservatorio di Musica Giuseppe Verdi, Biblioteca
I-Rama Roma, Accademia Nazionale di S. Cecilia, Bibliomediateca (holdings formerly at I-Rsc, Roma, Accademia Nazionale di S. Cecilia, Biblioteca)
I-Rcap* Rome, Cappella Musicale Pontificia Sistina, archivio moderno

* The abbreviation I-Rcap is not an RISM siglum. The modern archive of the Sistine Chapel is not included in RISM as of this writing.

I-Rluciani	Fiumicino (Rome), Collezione privata Luciano Luciani
I-Rvat	Vatican City, Biblioteca Apostolica Vaticana
I-Vc	Venice, Conservatorio di Musica Benedetto Marcello, Biblioteca (includes music holdings formerly at I-Vmc)
I-Vgc	Venice, Biblioteca dell'Istituto di Lettere, Musica e Teatro della Fondazione Giorgio Cini, Biblioteca, Isola di San Giorgio Maggiore
I-Vmc	Venice, Museo Civico Correr, Biblioteca d'Arte e Storia Veneziana
OED	*Oxford English Dictionary*
RILM	Répertoire international de littérature musicale
RISM	Répertoire international des sources musicale
RUS-Mrg	Moscow, Russian State Library (Rossijskaja Gosudarstvennaja biblioteka)
US-BEm	Berkeley, CA, Jean Gray Hargrove Music Library, University of California at Berkeley
US-Cn	Chicago, Newberry Library
US-Cu	Chicago, Special Collections Research Center, Joseph Regenstein Library, University of Chicago
US-Eu	Evanston, IL, Northwestern University Libraries
US-Nn	New York, New York Public Library of the Performing Arts
US-Np	New York, New York Public Library
US-Wfh	Howard University, Founder's Library, Washington, D.C.

NOTES

PREFACE

1. The term "bel canto" largely dates from after the last of the great castrati had left the operatic stage, though it circulated in less reified terminological variants earlier on. Rossini already used the term in 1848 (see chapter 3). For still earlier usages, see Sergio Durante, "Condizioni materiali et trasmissione del sapere nelle scuole di canto a Bologna a metà Settecento," in *Atti del XIV congresso della Società Internazionale di Musicologia, Bologna, 1987: Trasmissione e recezione delle forme di cultura musicale*, edited by Angelo Pompilio et al., 3 vols. (Turin: Edizioni di Torino, 1990), 2: 175–89; Durante, "'Dal dire al fare ... ' Ossia osservazioni sull'esecuzione musicale in rapporto al 'Lessico italiano del canto,'" *Musica e storia* 10, no. 1 (2002): 139–50; and the electronic resource Sergio Durante, Leonello Grasso Capiroli, and Roberta Ziosi, *Lessico italiano del canto* (Naples: Liguori, 2014). See further the exhibition catalog *Arte e musica all'Ospedaletto: Schede d'archivio sull'attività musicale degli ospedali dei derelitti e dei mendicanti di Venezia (sec. XVI–XVIII)* ([Venice]: Stamperia di Venezia, 1978); and chapter 3 below.

2. In foregrounding this question I am in broad sympathy with Valeria Finucci, *The Manly Masquerade: Masculinity, Paternity, and Castration in the Italian Renaissance* (Durham, NC: Duke University Press, 2003), chapter 6.

3. Quote from Tommaso Tamburini, *Expedita juris divini, naturalis et ecclesiastici expedita moralis explication*, 3 parts (Venice, 1692), cited in Anthony Milner, "The Sacred Capons," *Musical Times* 114, no. 1561 (March 1973): 250–52, at 252; and see John Rosselli, "The Castrati as a Professional Group and as a Social Phenomenon, 1550–1850," *Acta musicologica* 60 (1988): 143–79.

4. John Searle, *Speech Acts: An Essay in the Philosophy of Language* (Cambridge: Cambridge University Press, 1969), 25.

5. Piero Camporesi, in *The Juice of Life: The Symbolic and Magic Significance of Blood*, translated by Robert R. Barr (New York: Continuum, 1995), originally published as *Il sugo della vita: Simbolismo e magia del sangue* (Milan: Mondadori, 1988), esp. chapter 3, "The Glorious Blood."

6. Camporesi, *The Juice of Life*, 65; quotation from *Le lettere di S. Caterina di Siena, ridotte a miglior lezione, e in ordine nuovo disposto*, 6 vols., annotated by Niccolò Tommaseo, edited by Piero Mischiattelli (Florence: Marzocco, 1939–47), 2: 23. A brilliant book on the symbolic relationship between bloodshed and man/animal relations and avoidances, using evidence from French butchery in abattoirs, is Noëlie Vialles's *Animal to Edible*, translated by J. A. Underwood, Éditions de la Maison des sciences de l'homme (Cambridge: Cambridge University Press, 1994), originally published as *Le sang et la chair: Les abattoirs des pays l'Adour* (Paris: Fondation de la Maison des sciences de l'homme, 1987).

7. Camporesi, *Juice of Life*, 66.

8. An example is the daughter of literato Cardinal Pietro Bembo, Helena, who did all these things, including marrying a distinguished nobleman.

9. Research developing these questions has taken place in history, sociology, and anthropology throughout the twentieth century and beyond. See, e.g., Alessandro Costanzo, "Intorno alla questione della mascolinità dei nati," *Rivista Internazionale di Scienze Sociali*, series 3, vol. 6 (43), no. 2 (March 1935): 171–81; Franco Savorgnan, "La mortalità infantile dei primogeniti e dei cadetti," *Razza e civiltà* 5-7 (1942): 221–39; Savorgnan, "Il diritto di primogenitura e la sua influenza sulla vitalità delle aristocrazie," *Genus* 6, no. 8, "Atti della terza riunione scientifica della Società italiana di sociologia—Roma 2-3 Ottobre 1942," part 1 (1943–49): 170–80; Carlo A. Corsini, "Note in margine ad una pubblicazione di demografia sociale, *Genus* 30, no. 1/4 (1974): 261–68; Anna Maria Rao, "Esercito e società a Napoli nelle riforme del secondo Settecento," *Studi storici* 28, no. 3 (July—September 1987): 623–77; Cristina Papa, "Famiglia, residenza, patrimonio: Quali modelli?" *La ricerca folklorica* 27, "Forme di famiglia: Ricerche per un Atlante italiano," part 2 (April 1993): 13–33; and Cinzia Cremonini, ed., *Titolati, cadetti e parvenus: Il caso lombardo tra Antico regime e Rivoluzione francese* (Rome: Bulzoni, 1999).

10. "*We give the name 'sacrifier' to the subject to whom the benefits of sacrifice thus accrue, or who undergoes its effects.*" Henri Hubert and Marcel Mauss, *Sacrifice: Its Nature and Functions*, translated by W. D. Halls (Chicago: University of Chicago Press, 1964), 10; originally published as "Essai sur la nature et la fonction du sacrifice," *L'Année sociologique* (1898): 29–138. The word "sacrifier" is an English coinage that Halls uses to render Hubert and Mauss's "sacrifiant."

11. We could take variable sets thereof to comprise *sacrifiers* (plural), although then we might soon be dealing at various levels of remove from a principal or principals and at various temporal and geographic distances from the act.

12. I use the male pronoun here and elsewhere to index the "victim" because my argument specifically treats male victims. In other contexts, sacrificial victims have at least as often been "shes" or "its."

13. Hubert and Mauss, *Sacrifice*, 19–20, chapter 2 and passim.

14. Ibid., 95–99.

15. The ambiguity yet pervasiveness of the absolutist style of government across different kinds of polities is described well in Perry Anderson, *Lineages of the Absolutist State*

(1974; London: Verso, 1979). I hew to something like this in my *Opera and Sovereignty: Transforming Myths in Eighteenth-Century Italy* (Chicago: University of Chicago Press, 2007). For Italy the work of Franco Venturi is essential. Good starting points are *La caduta dell'Antico Regime: Corso di storia moderna per l'anno accademico, 1980–81* (Turin: Tirreni, 1981), and, for the period of transition, *Italy and the Enlightenment: Studies in a Cosmopolitan Century*, edited by Stuart Woolf and translated by Susan Corsi (London: Longman, 1972).

16. It is difficult to determine whether or to what degree high-voiced men who had been castrated as youths for medical reasons may have been used as singers. The fact that castrati often claimed they had undergone the operation for medical reasons has complicated the historiographical problem. In any case, already in the latter half of the sixteenth century an agent for Duke Guglielmo Gonzaga of Mantua suggested that boys be castrated for the duke; see Richard Sherr, "Guglielmo Gonzaga and the Castrati," *Renaissance Quarterly* 33, no. 1 (Spring 1980): 33–56, esp. 36. Giuseppe Gerbino evaluates the problem in "The Quest for the Soprano Voice: Castrati in Sixteenth-Century Italy," *Studi musicali* 32, no. 2 (2004): 303–57 (and see chapter 1 of this volume).

17. Examples would include the Melani brothers, especially the famed Atto Melani (see Roger Freitas, *Portrait of a Castrato: Politics, Patronage, and Music in the Life of Atto Melani* [Cambridge: Cambridge University Press, 2009]); and likely the Broschi family, which had Farinelli (Carlo Broschi) castrated (see Sandro Cappelletto, *La voce perduta: Vita di Farinelli, evirato cantore* [Turin: Edizioni di Torino, 1995]).

18. Michel Poizat, in *The Angel's Cry: Beyond the Pleasure Principle in Opera*, translated by Arthur Denner (1986; Ithaca, NY: Cornell University Press, 1992), was among the first to spin the castrato this way, in the shadow of Roland Barthes's *S/Z: An Essay*, translated by Richard Miller, preface by Richard Howard (New York: Hill and Wang, 1974), with text of Balzac's *Sarrasine*. See also, for example, Joseph R. Roach, *The Player's Passion: Studies in the Science of Acting* (Ann Arbor: University of Michigan Press, 1993); Birthe Schwarz, "Das Spiel mit den Geschlechterrollen: Kastraten und Primadonnen im Musiktheater des 18. Jahrhunderts," in *Gender Studies und Musik: Geschlechterrollen und ihre Bedeutung für die Musikwissenschaft*, edited by Stefan Fragner, Jan Hemming, and Beate Kutschke (Regensburg: Con Brio, 1998), 75–84; and Julia Liebscher, "Das Kastratentum im Diskurs von Thomas Laqueurs 'One-Sex-Model,'" in *Frauen- und Männerbilder in der Musik: Festschrift für Eva Rieger zum 60. Geburtstag*, edited by Freia Hoffmann, Jane Bowers, and Ruth Heckmann (Oldenburg: Bibliotheks- und Informationssystem der Universität Oldenberg, 2000), 47–51. I briefly analyze the influence of Barthes as well as Bakhtin and Foucault on late twentieth-century critical thinking apropos of studies of castrato performance in my "Castrato Acts," in *The Oxford Handbook of Opera*, edited by Helen M. Greenwald (New York: Oxford University Press, 2014), pp. 395–418.

19. I thank the anonymous reviewer of this book for offering up the felicitous term "anti-castrato."

20. Various thinkers have considered deeply the stakes in jokes, satires, and comic inversions in ways I cannot do here. Freud claimed jokes allowed things to be said that were otherwise socially suppressed or forbidden. Foundational are his *Jokes and Their Relation to the Unconscious*, translated and edited by James Strachey (1905; New York: W.W. Norton, 1960), and "Humor," *International Journal of Psychoanalysis* 9 (1928): 1–6. Before Freud's

major study of humor was issued Bergson was arguing in *Le rire* of 1900 that laughter allowed a release of tension but also exposed the mechanical and automatic in human habits. See Henri-Louis Bergson, *Laughter: An Essay on the Meaning of the Comic*, translated by Cloudesley Brereton and Fred Rothwell (1911; Los Angeles: Consortium Books, 1999; repr. ed. New York: Dover Publications, 2005). Important recently is Anca Parvulescu, *Laughter: Notes on a Passion* (Cambridge, MA: MIT Press, 2010).

21. Northrup Frye, *Anatomy of Criticism: Four Essays* (Princeton, NJ: Princeton University Press, 1957), 45–48. Frye thinks of abused buffoonish characters as "comic counterparts of the tragic hero as artist" (45).

22. Note that Frye's ironic comedy is "less an attack on a virtuous society by a malignant individual than a symptom of that society's own viciousness." Ibid., 48.

23. For further on this notion of festivity see Feldman, *Opera and Sovereignty*, chapter 4.

24. The situation eased in the eighteenth century and dramatically so in the early nineteenth century as the number of castrati decreased along with the number of clerics and other "celibates."

25. Cf. Valeria Finucci, "Introduction: Genealogical Pleasures, Genealogical Disruptions," in *Generation and Degeneration: Tropes of Reproduction in Literature and History from Antiquity through Early Modern Europe*, edited by Valeria Finucci and Kevin Brownlee (Durham, NC: Duke University Press, 2001), 1–14, esp. 1–2.

26. "King" and "kingship" are thus placeholders for any monarch(y) regardless of the term used to name them and regardless of their specific organizational features. It is not that specific names are unimportant (they are), but rather that the wider usage in this instance underscores the *kind* of rule that monarchy is tout court.

27. For Farinelli's own viewpoint, see his letters in *La solitudine amica: Lettere al conte Sicinio Pepoli,* edited by Carlo Vitali with Roberto Pagano and Francesca Boris (Palermo: Sellerio, 2000).

28. Cf. A.M. Hocart, *Kings and Councillors: An Essay in the Comparative Anatomy of Human Society*, edited and with an introduction by Rodney Needham and foreword by E. E. Evans-Pritchard (1936; Chicago: University of Chicago Press, 1970). Such a viewpoint also accords roughly with Benedict Anderson's analysis of Javanese kingship ("The Idea of Power in Javanese Culture," in Benedict Anderson, *Language and Power: Exploring Political Cultures in Indonesia* [Ithaca, NY: Cornell University Press, 1990], 17–77), and Clifford Geertz's of Balinese kingship (*Negara: The Theatre State in Nineteenth-Century Bali* [Princeton, NJ: Princeton University Press, 1980], and see Geertz, "Centers, Kings, and Charisma: Reflections on the Symbolics of Power," in *Local Knowledge: Further Essays in Interpretive Anthropology* [New York: Basic Books, 1983], 121–46): the king may be weak in absolute political terms, but the *status* of kingship is nevertheless strongly represented and made more so by a monarch who comes from outside the ordinary. Geertz in particular stresses the role of charisma in concentrating power, which can only be effected by diffusing it through various media and in various places. For the monarch, proxies with real affective power are indispensable to power and persuasion all told because no monarch can spread power alone, much less make it felt.

29. Pierfrancesco Tosi, *Opinioni de' cantori antichi, e moderni, o sieno Osservazioni sopra il canto figurato* (Bologna: Lelio dalla Volpe, 1723).

30. Alfred Gell, *Art and Agency: An Anthropological Theory* (Oxford: Clarendon Press, 1998).

31. Cf. James Chandler, *An Archaeology of Sympathy: The Sentimental Mode in Literature and Cinema* (Chicago: University of Chicago Press, 2013).

32. Others have written about the historiographical and interpretive problem of that high C. See Marco Beghelli, "Il *do di petto*: Dissacrazione di un mito," *Il saggiatore musicale* 3, no. 1 (1996): 105–49; and James Q. Davies, *Romantic Anatomies of Performance* (Berkeley: University of California Press, 2014), 180.

CHAPTER 1. OF STRANGE BIRTHS AND COMIC KIN

1. Gabriel Garcia Márquez, "A Very Old Man with Enormous Wings: A Tale for Children," translated by Gregory Rabassa, in *Fictions*, edited by Joseph F. Trimmer and C. Wade Jennings (San Diego: Harcourt Brace Jovanovich, 1985), 410–11. I am grateful to Emily Bauman for urging me to read the story and for her brilliant insights on its interpretation.

2. Quote from Clifford Geertz, "Deep Play: Notes on the Balinese Cockfight," in *The Interpretation of Cultures: Selected Essays* (New York: Basic Books, 1973), 412–53, on p. 444. On post-Roman peoples of Uley in South Britain, see Ann Woodward, Peter Leach, et al., *The Uley Shrines: Excavation of a Ritual Complex on West Hill, Uley, Gloucestershire, 1977–79* (London: English Heritage with the British Museum Press, 1993), 266, col. 1, where they were part of a votive assemblage; and Don Brothwell, "Interpreting the Immature Chicagon Bones from the Romano-British Ritual Complex on West Hill, Uley," *International Journal of Osteoarchaeology* 7 (1997): 330–32. In the rural zone of the Bena Luluwa [Lulua] of the Democratic Republic of the Congo (formerly Zaire) in Central Africa, a proliferation of edible and commercial chickens traditionally expressed a multiplicity of relations to humans' life cycles, sexual habits, ethics, aesthetics, and physical attributes (especially in eggs) through numerous linguistic and ritual uses, including magical ones; see Badibanga Kantshama and Diambila Luboya, "La Poule chez les Beena Luluwa: Analyse linguistique et anthropologique," *Journal des africanistes* 56, no. 1 (1986): 113–28. Among these, a boy's father would give him a "cock of circumcision" to eat when he was to be circumcised, at age seven. At the Benin court of southwest Nigeria, brass cocks were traditionally deified on the ancestral altars of the mothers of the Oba kings; see Joseph Nevadomsky, "Brass Cocks and Wooden Hens in Benin Art," *Bäßler-Archiv*, new series, 35 (1987): 221–47. And in Seram, eastern Indonesia, chickens have articulated human relations and values through numerous taboos, as Valerio Valeri shows in *The Forest of Taboos: Hunting, Morality, and Identity among the Huaulu of the Moluccas* (Madison: University of Wisconsin Press, 1999), 213–26.

3. Susan Orlean's essay "The It Bird: The Return of the Backyard Chicken," *The New Yorker*, September 28, 2009, pp. 26–31, is a wonderful account of the renewed place of chickens in North American society. Inspired by watching the TV documentary *The Natural History of the Chicken* to get her own, Orlean writes, "Chickens seem to be a perfect convergence of the economic, environmental, gastronomic, and emotional matters of the moment, plus in the past few years, they have undergone an image rehabilitation so astonishing that it should be studied by marketing consultants" (26).

4. Peter Stallybrass and Allon White, *The Politics and Poetics of Transgression* (Ithaca, NY: Cornell University Press, 1986).

5. John Rosselli, "The Castrati as a Professional Group and as a Social Phenomenon, 1550–1850," *Acta musicologica* 60 (1988): 143–79, offers the best historical introduction to the castrati; a shorter, slightly revised version of the article appears in his *Singers of Italian Opera: The History of a Profession* (Cambridge: Cambridge University Press, 1992), chapter 2. I quote below from the former. On a broader scale, see Franz Haböck, *Die Kastraten und ihre Gesangskunst: Eine gesangsphysiologische, kultur- und musikhistorische Studien* (Stuttgart: Deutsche Verlags-Anstalt, 1927). Other monographs include Gino Monaldi, *Cantanti evirati del teatro italiano* (Rome: Ausonia, 1920); Anton Giulio Bragaglia, *Degli "evirati cantori": Contributo alla storia del teatro* (Florence: Sansoni Antiquariato, 1959); and Hans Fritz, *Kastratengesang: Hormonelle, konstitionelle und pädagogische Aspekte* (Tutzing: Hans Schneider, 1994). The best recent treatment is Roger Freitas's splendid *Portrait of a Castrato: Politics, Patronage, and Music in the Life of Atto Melani* (Cambridge: Cambridge University Press, 2009). Corinna Herr, *Gesang gegen die "Ordnung der Natur": Kastraten und Falsettisten in der Musikgeschichte*, foreword by Kai Wessel (Kassel: Bärenreiter, 2013), came to light after I had already written and revised my book; I take it into account where possible but it did not inform the creation of mine. Popular works on the castrato, often anecdotal and sketchy on historical particulars, include Angus Heriot, *The Castrati in Opera* (London: Calder and Boyars, 1956); Patrick Barbier, *The World of the Castrati: The History of an Extraordinary Operatic Phenomenon*, translated by Margaret Crosland (1989; London: Souvenir Press, 1996); Hubert Ortkemper, *Engel wider Willen: Die Welt der Kastraten* (Berlin: Henschel Verlag, 1993); and Sylvie Mamy, *Les grands castrats napolitains à Venise au XVIIIe siècle*, Collection Musique, musicologie (Liège: Mardaga, 1994).

6. The tangle of misinformation about the castrato's sexuality is large. F. D'Amico wrote that they could have sexual intercourse ("Evirato," in *Enciclopedia dello spettacolo* [Rome: Unione Editoriale, 1954–65], 4: cols. 1719–23) while Rosselli, "The Castrati as a Professional Group," 145, accepted the opposite view, common to medical opinion of the 1930s, citing Peter Browe, S.J., *Zur Geschichte der Entmannung: Eine Religions- und Rechtsgeschichtliche Studie* (Breslau: Verlag Müller & Seiffert, 1936), 7–11. Gary Taylor's *Castration: An Abbreviated History of Western Manhood* (New York: Routledge, 2000) clarifies the situation, noting that if castrated testicularly after puberty, "eunuchs are often sexually active, and capable of erections" (16 and see p. 121). An illuminating analysis of the whole morass, given the limits of available evidence, appears in Freitas, *Portrait of a Castrato*, chapter 4, "The Sexuality of the Castrato." Charles Ancillon [C. d'Ollincan], *Traité des eunuques . . .* (Berlin [?], 1707); in English as *Eunuchism Display'd*, translated by Robert Samber (London: Printed for E. Curll, 1718), which is explored further in chapter 2, had historiographical impact but was clearly a titillating popular text with scholarly pretensions and certain serious subject matter. A modern edition of the 1707 French edition has appeared as Charles Ancillon, *Traité des eunuques*, edited and introduced by Michela Gardini (Paris: L'Harmattan, 2007). See also a century later Benedetto Mojon, *Dissertazione sugli effetti della castratura nel corpo umano* (Milan: Giovanni Pirotta, 1822). All in all, it is clear that the sexual capabilities of castrated men varied as much as their considerable developmental differences in physiological makeup, in keeping with differing physical responses to lowered testosterone and other variables, but also that their sexual functioning, strictly speaking, was on the whole lower than that of uncastrated men. It did not include ejaculation of semen.

Stories abounded of women falling in love with castrati. See, for example, the evidence of the great mid-seventeenth-century composer Barbara Strozzi, in Ellen Rosand, "Barbara

Strozzi, *virtuosissima cantatrice:* The Composer's Voice," *Journal of the American Musicological Society* 31 (1978): 251–52, and the trysts and marriages discussed in chapter 2 below, especially on Tenducci's affair and marriage as recounted by Helen Berry, *The Castrato and His Wife* (Oxford: Oxford University Press, 2011), esp. chapter 4.

7. Typical of the middle-class type was the Melani family in the mid-seventeenth century; see Freitas, *Portrait of a Castrato.* Castrati, being generally younger sons, fall into the broad category of *cadetti.* Cognate with the English "cadet," the term has a much wider embrace in Italian history and language, referring to younger or "junior" sons; see Renata Ago, "Ecclesiastical Careers and the Destiny of Cadets," *Continuity and Change* 7 (1992): 271–82.

8. Conversely, it stands to reason that some young musicians may have been castrated but gone on to work only as composers, but almost no specific examples have come to light. Gianni Race argues that Pergolesi was a castrato, albeit on dubious grounds; in "La biografia: Nuovi elementi per la biografia pergolesiana," in *Pergolesi,* edited by Francesco Degrada, Roberto De Simone, Dario Della Porta, and Gianni Race (Naples: Sergio Civita, 1986), 97–102.

On partimenti as the basis of eighteenth-century composition, see Robert O. Gjerdingen's ground-breaking *Music in the Galant Style* (New York: Oxford University Press, 2007); and Giorgio Sanguinetti, *The Art of Partimento: History, Theory, and Practice* (New York: Oxford University Press, 2012). Gjerdingen, together with an international group of scholars, has also been collecting and transcribing solfeggi, melodic/vocal studies usually made by teachers of singing, sometimes with accompanying bass parts; see http://faculty-web.at.northwestern.edu/music/gjerdingen/index.htm, and, for the solfeggi, http://faculty-web.at.northwestern.edu/music/gjerdingen/Solfeggi/collections/index.htm. Scores and in some cases QuickTime audio files are currently available on the site for three castrati, Bernacchi, Farinelli, and Giuseppe Aprile (many other composers of solfeggi were not singers). The site also gives teachers in Naples by their affiliations with one of the four Neapolitan conservatories: http://faculty-web.at.northwestern.edu/music/gjerdingen/WhoWasWho/index.htm.

9. Padre Martini, a great eminence and one of Mozart's teachers, sought out advice about his own motet from famed performer and singing teacher Antonio Bernacchi, from whom he received extensive criticisms—this despite the fact that Bernacchi, who, as far as we know, composed solfeggi only for his students (short textless compositions consisting of vocal lines and thoroughbass accompaniment), protested that he was unqualified to comment on counterpoint and harmony. Martini's letters have a number of other examples of castrati as consultants. See Anne Schnoebelen, *Padre Martini's Collection of Letters in the Civico Museo Bibliografico Musicale in Bologna: An Annotated Index* (New York: Pendragon, 1979), and recent transcriptions of letters in Giovanni Battista Martini et al., eds., *Epistolario Giovanni Battista Martini e Girolamo Chiti (1745–1759): 472 lettere del Museo Internazionale e Biblioteca della Musica di Bologna* (Rome: IBIMUS, 2010). Some ten thousand letters, the core of them by Padre Martini, have been digitized for online use by the Museo Internazionale e Biblioteca della Musica di Bologna (which has absorbed what was formerly the Civico Museo Bibliografico di Bologna), and are available at http://badigit.comune.bologna.it/cmbm/scripts/lettere/search.asp.

10. Only in the later eighteenth century did their numbers drop steeply. By the 1830s castrati were mostly confined to major churches in central Italy. The last known one, Alessandro Moreschi, was still singing at the papal chapel in 1913 and sang elsewhere in Rome

through 1921. It's highly unlikely that any castrati were still singing in the provinces in the late nineteenth and early twentieth centuries since everything known about them in the period suggests they were recruited by Vatican personnel and castrated in Rome-- seemingly their only destination in the period (hence, too, it is highly unlikely that Moreschi was not the last).

11. Anthony Newcomb, *The Madrigal at Ferrara, 1579–1797*, 2 vols. (Princeton, NJ: Princeton University Press, 1980), 1: 30–31. An inquiry the duke made in 1556 was casual enough that it seems they were likely there earlier. The Duke of Mantua was looking for castrati slightly later; see Iain Fenlon, *Music and Patronage in Sixteenth-Century Mantua*, 2 vols. (Cambridge: Cambridge University Press, 1980), 1: 110.

12. The evidence on the Sistine Chapel in Rome and the Bayerische Hofkapelle in Munich is reviewed and expanded in Herr, *Gesang gegen die "Ordnung der Natur,"* esp. 50–60 for Rome and 70–93 for Munich. For the period up to 1601 Herr counts only five castrati who can be definitively identified in the Sistine Chapel, which at that time did not record distinctions between falsettists and eunuch singers; one is cited in Richard Sherr, "Competence and Incompetence in the Papal Choir in the Age of Palestrina," *Early Music* 22, no. 4 (1994): 606–29; a later version is in *Palestrina e l'Europa: Atti del III Convegno Internazionale di Studi (Palestrina, 6–9 ottobre 1994)*, edited by Giancarlo Rostirolla, Stefania Soldati, and Elena Zomparelli ([Rome]: Fondazione Giovanni Pierluigi da Palestrina, 2006), 115–46. An earlier account of castrati at the papal chapel is Enrico Celani, *I cantori della cappella pontificia nei secoli XVI à XVIII* (Turin: Bocca, 1909), though documentation there is sporadic; more briefly, see Anthony Milner, "The Sacred Capons," *Musical Times* 114, no. 1561 (1973): 250–52; and recently the important series Storia della cappella musicale pontificia, which includes Claudio Annibaldi, *La cappella musicale pontificia nel Seicento*, vol. 4 (Palestrina [Rome]: Fondazione Giovanni Pierluigi da Palestrina, 2011); Leopold M. Kantner and Angela Pachovsky, *La cappella musicale pontificia nell'Ottocento*, vol. 6 (Rome: Hortus Musicus, 1998); and Salvatore De Salvo Fattor, *La cappella musicale pontificia nel Novecento*, vol. 7 (Palestrina [Rome]: Fondazione Giovanni Pierluigi da Palestrina, 2005). Volumes on other centuries will be forthcoming.

13. The best overall analysis of castrati in the latter half of sixteenth-century Italy is Giuseppe Gerbino's "The Quest for the Soprano Voice: Castrati in Renaissance Italy," *Studi musicali* 33, no. 2 (2004): 303–57, whose thesis that most castrati in Italy at first were Spanish is, however, persuasively challenged by Herr, *Gesang gegen die "Ordnung der Natur,"* 51–52. See too Richard Sherr, "Guglielmo Gonzaga and the Castrati," *Renaissance Quarterly* 33, no. 1 (Spring 1980): 33–56.

Until 1588 high-voiced singers at the papal chapel were all listed as sopranos, but thereafter castrated singers began to be distinguished as "eunuchi" or, in one case, "soprano castrato."

14. A basic blueprint for the surgery as performed today on children in cases of medical necessity appears in Michael Edwards, "Hernia: Inguinal Child Herniotomy, A Pantogen Operation Script," WikiSurgery: The Free Surgical Encyclopedia, http://wikisurgery.com (accessed September 22, 2009).

15. Paolo Zacchia gives methods for testicular castration in his *Questiones medicolegales in quibus omnes eae materiae medicae, quae ad legales facultates videntur pertinere, proponuntur, pertractantur, resoluuntur*, 6 vols. (Rome: Sumptibus Andreae Brugiotti apud

Iacobum Mascardum, 1621-34), vol. 3, part 1, "De impotentia coeundi, & generandi." Many subsequent editions followed, through 1789. See also Joseph Bajada, *Sexual Impotence: The Contribution of Paolo Zacchia, 1584-1650* (Rome: Ed. Pontificia Universitaria Gregoriana, 1988), 51 and passim.

16. The work is discussed in relation to castration for singing by urologist Meyer M. Melicow with Stanford Pulrang, "Castrati Choir and Opera Singers, *Urology* 3 (1974): 744-64.

17. See, for example, Lynn A. Struve, ed. and trans., *Voices from the Ming-Qing Cataclysm: China in Tigers' Jaws* (New Haven, CT: Yale University Press, 1993); David M. Robinson, *Bandits, Eunuchs, and the Son of Heaven: Rebellion and the Economy of Violence in Mid-Ming China* (Honolulu: University of Hawai'i Press, 2001); Robinson, ed., *Culture, Courtiers, and Competition: The Ming Court (1368-1644)* (Cambridge, MA: Harvard University Asia Center with Harvard University Press, 2008); Vinod Behl, "The Eunuchs," in *Men of the Global South: A Reader*, edited by Adam Jones (London: Zed Books, 2006); Laura Engelstein, *Castration and the Heavenly Kingdom: A Russian Folktale* (Ithaca, NY: Cornell University Press, 1999); Shaun Tougher, *The Eunuch in Byzantine History and Society* (London: Routledge, 2008); Neil K. Moran, "Byzantine Castrati," *Plainsong and Medieval Music* 11 (2002): 99-112. On a related phenomenon in the Ottoman Empire, of effeminate boy dancers and singers, see Dorit Kelbe, "Effeminate Professional Musicians in Sources of Ottoman-Turkish Court Poetry and Music of the Eighteenth and Nineteenth Centuries," *Music in Art* 30 (2005): 97-116. An Indian hijra's autobiography has been published by A. Revathi, The *Truth about Me: A Hijra Life Story*, translated from Tamil by V. Geetha Rēvati (New Delhi: Penguin Books, 2010). More broadly, see Piotr O. Scholz, *Eunuchs and Castrati: A Cultural History*, translated by John A. Broadwin and Shelley L. Frisch (Princeton, NJ: Markus Wiener Publishers, 2001).

18. The "refeudalization of Europe" by absolutist practices of the early modern period comes from Jürgen Habermas, *The Structural Transformation of the Public Sphere: An Inquiry into a Category of Bourgeois Society*, 2nd ed., translated by Thomas Burger with Frederick Lawrence (Cambridge, MA: MIT Press, 1991). The concept of the "refeudalization of Europe" has elicited such major responses as Robert C. Holub, *Jürgen Habermas: Critic in the Public Sphere* (New York: Routledge, 1991), and John P. McCormick, *Weber, Habermas, and Transformations of the European State: Constitutional, Social, and Supranational Democracy* (Cambridge: Cambridge University Press, 2007), among many others.

19. See Franca Trinchieri Camiz, "The Castrato Singer: From Informal to Formal Portraiture," *Artibus et Historiae: An Art Anthology* 18, no. 9 (1988): 171-86, and Camiz, "Putti, eunuchi, bella cantatrice: L'iconographie des chanteurs en Italie," *Musique, images, instruments: Revue française d'organologie et d'iconolographie musicale* 2 (1996): 9-16.

20. Cf. other portraits of castrati in chapter 4, notably that of Carlo Scalzi in Fig. 34.

21. See chapters 2 and (esp.) 4 of this volume.

22. See Milner, "The Sacred Capons," 250-51; Rosselli, "The Castrati as a Professional Group," 151; and Finucci, *The Manly Masquerade: Masculinity, Paternity, and Castration in the Italian Renaissance* (Durham, NC: Duke University Press, 2003), chapter 6.

23. Quoted from the abstract for J.S. Jenkins, "The Lost Voice: A History of the Castrato," *Journal of Pediatric Endicrinological Metabolism* 13, supplement 6 (2000): 1503-8.

24. Vivaldi's *Stabat mater* is recorded by David Daniels, countertenor, with Europa Galante directed by Fabio Biondi (New York: Virgin Classics, 2002), label no. 45474, track 11; modern ed. of the score in Antonio Vivaldi, *Stabat Mater, inno per contralto, due violini, viola e basso: RV 621* [in F minor], edited by Paul Everett (Milan: Ricordi, 1998). "Qual guerriero" is recorded on *Arias for Farinelli*, by mezzo soprano Vivica Genaux with the Akademie für Alte Musik Berlin conducted by René Jacobs, track 6 (copies of which proliferate on YouTube). A modern edition of the score is in *Arie per Carlo Broschi Farinelli*, edited by Luigi Verdi and Maria Pia Jacoboni, with a preface by Carlo Vitali (Rome: Bardi, 2007), 73–87.

25. The best study I know on the topic is Maria Giovanna Belcastro et al., "Hyperostosis Frontalis Interna (HFI) and Castration: The Case of the Famous Singer Farinelli (1705–1782)," *Journal of Anatomy* 219 (2011): 632–37, which is based on anatomical and biological study of Farinelli's remains following an exhumation in July 2006. Despite the poor state of preservation, the authors are able to deduce that the singer's height was about six feet three inches; that his epiphyseal lines were still visible upon his death at about age seventy-eight, connecting his height with disorders caused by castration; and that in old age he had osteoporosis and severe hyperostosis frontalis interna (HFI), a symmetrical thickening of the frontal part of the skull, which is only known to occur in men with hormonal disorders related to androgen deficiency.

26. For reproductions and discussion of works by Zanetti and Ghezzi mentioned throughout this book, see Antonio Bettagno, *Caricature di Anton Maria Zanetti* (Venice: Neri Pozza, 1996), with an introduction by Giuseppe Fiocco; and Giancarlo Rostirolla, with Stefano La Via and Anna Lo Bianco, *Il "mondo novo" musicale di Pier Leone Ghezzi* (Milan: Skira; Rome: Accademia Nazionale di Santa Cecilia, 2001). On depictions more broadly of Renaissance men with plumes, in swaggering postures and with stiff protruding weapons, see Finucci, *The Manly Masquerade*, esp. 4.

27. The arrangements of the images in Zanetti's book are explained in the exhibition catalog *Tiepolo: Ironia e comico*, edited by Adriano Mariuz and Giuseppe Pavanello (Venice: Marsilio with the Fondazione Giorgio Cini, 2004), esp. plates 5–7, 9–11, and 13. I am grateful to Gilberto Pizzamiglio for giving me a copy of the book.

28. The causal relationship between the age of castration and degree of developmental alteration is supported by the research of M. Hatzinger, D. Vöge, M. Stastny, F. Moll, and M. Sohn, "Castrati Singers: All for Fame," *Journal of Sexual Medicine* 9, no. 9 (September 2012): 2233–37, which notes that the effects of castration on physical development were "erratic" and greatly depended on the timing of the operation, and that boys operated on before about age ten tended to develop more feminine features and little or no sex drive.

29. Silke Leopold, "Mannsbilder—Weibsbilder: Händels Personendarstellung im Kontext höfischer Sitten," *Händel-Jahrbuch* 49 (2003): 263–82, at 280. Rosselli, "The Castrati as a Professional Group," has fascinating things to say about Sacchi's portrait of Pasqualini, which has the singer crowned by a well-endowed Apollo but draped seemingly in Dionysus's leopard skin, in an apparent allusion to the fate of Dionysus's follower Marsyas, shown flayed just behind Apollo (170 n. 100).

30. On Valeriano Pellegrini, see Colin Timms, *Polymath of the Baroque: Agostini Steffani and His Music* (Oxford: Oxford University Press, 2003), 65 and 98.

31. The references by Balatri appear in his autobiography, virtually unknown to musicologists, "Vita e viaggi di F.B., nativo di Pisa," RUS-Mrg MS F.218, no. 1247 (1–9), vol. 1,

p. 15; and in his satirical "Testamento, o sia ultima volontà, di F. B., nativo Alfeo," G-Mbs, cod. It. 329, fol. 9. The former dates from 1725-32, the latter from 1737-38. The testimony of Tomasso Massi was uncovered by Berry, *The Castrato and His Wife;* deposition transcribed on 286-89. Berry's account of Massi's testimony is the most recent and vivid to date and unique in not just naming the surgeon but also describing the procedure and circumstances of a castration.

32. David Gentilcore, *Medical Charlatanism in Early Modern Italy* (New York: Oxford University Press, 2006), esp. 181-89. On late medieval ancestors of early modern *norcini,* see Katharine Park, "Stones, Bones, and Hernias: Specialists in Fourteenth- and Fifteenth-Century Italy," in *Medicine from the Black Death to the French Disease,* edited by Roger French et al. (Aldershot: Ashgate, 1998), 110-30. Tommaso Garzoni, in La *piazza universale de tutte le professioni del mondo,* rev. ed. (Venice: Gio. Battista Somasco, 1587), 841, notes in Discorso 132, titled "De' Castradori. Et de' bracherari," that castrators "son comunemente i Norsini" and calls a Norsino ultimately nothing but "un medico da testicoli" (a doctor of testicles).

A sixteenth-century comic poem by Francesco Berni alludes to the castrators of Norcia; see Berni's "Capitolo di Gradasso (al Cardinale Ippolito de' Medici)" (1532), no. 50, in Francesco Berni, *Poesie e prose,* edited by Ezio Chiòrboli (Geneva: Leo S. Olschki, 1934), 125-28. Gradasso was Berrattai Gradasso, Ippolito's dwarf, who came from Norcia. Lines 46-48 read, "Suo padre già faceva i porci eunuchi; E lui fé dottorar nel berrettaio. Per non tenerlo in frasca come i bruchi." The famous Neapolitan castrato Caffarelli was said to have been castrated *at* Norcia by a surgeon originally from Lucca, according to his will, on which see Eugenio Faustini-Fasini, "Gli astri maggiori del napoletano: Gaetano Majorano detto 'Caffarelli,'" *Note d'archivio per la storia musicale* 15 (1938): 121-28, 157-70, 258-70; also cited in Filippo Balatri, *"Frutti del mondo": L'autobiografia di Filippo Balatri,* edited by Karl Vossler (Milan: Remo Sandron, 1924), 70 n. 1. Cf. Giacopo Angelo Nelli (1676-1770): "Si chiama quel norcin castraporcelli, che fece l'operazione a quel musico," from the play *Le serve al forno* (act 2, scene 2) in *Commedie di Jacopo Angelo Nelli,* 3 vols., edited by Alcibiade Moretti, Biblioteca di scrittori italiani (Bologna: Nicola Zanichelli, 1883-99), vol. 2 (1889), p. 45.

33. Berry, *The Castrato and His Wife,* 287.

34. Ibid., 287-88. On p. 286 the operation is referred to as an "amputation of both his Testicles and the Spermatick Ducts." It was assisted by a servant and Tommaso, who also did daily postoperative care of the wounds.

35. See Monica Baiocco, "Su Baldassare Ferri, cantante evirato del Seicento," *Esercizi, musica e spettacolo,* new series 6, no. 15 (1996): 19-46, at 26.

36. Although there is no doubt that parents often acted in coordination with teachers, patrons, conservatories, princes, or relatives, concrete documentation of specific cases is very limited. Benedetto Marcello's reference in *Il teatro alla moda,* edited by Giacomo Alessandro Caula (1720; Turin: Giacomo A. Caula, n.d.), 32, is a parody. Charles Ancillon, *Eunuchism Display'd,* cleaves to ancient humoral theory in accordance with which castration is assigned therapeutic prophylactic value (63-65); originally published in French as *Traité des eunuques* (Berlin, 1707), signed pseudonymously by C. D'Ollincan in the dedicatory epistle. Haböck, *Die Kastraten,* interviewed late papal castrati who cited bites by wild swans and pigs as reasons for castration (197, 202-3); something of the kind was claimed by the humanist Paolo Giovio. On Ferri, see Horace Bushnell Bowman, "The Castrati Singers and Their Music" (PhD diss., Indiana University, 1951), 39. Farinelli was castrated, according to his

eighteenth-century biographer Giovenale Sacchi, because of an injury sustained during horseback riding; *Vita del Cavaliere Don Carlo Broschi detto il Farinello*, edited by Alessandro Abbate (1784; Naples: Pagano, 1994). The castrato Sorlisi invented an alias whom he claimed was castrated after having been valiantly wounded in battle, as Mary E. Frandsen elaborates in "Eunuchi conjugium: The Marriage of a Castrato in Early Modern Germany," *Early Music History: Studies in Medieval and Early Modern Music* 24 (2005): 53–124; see further in chapter 2 below. Other accounts appear in Cristina Pampaloni, "Giovani castrati nell'Assisi del Settecento," *Musica/Realtà* 8 (1987): 133–53; Rosselli, "The Castrati as a Professional Group," 153–55; and Nicola Lucarelli, *Domenico Bruni (1758–1821): Biografia di un cantante evirato* (Città di Castello: Grafiche 2GF and Comune di Umbertide, 1992), 14.

Lists of Neapolitan conservatory boys for two of the four major conservatories are given in Salvatore Di Giacomo, *Il conservatorio di Sant'Onofrio a Capuana e quello di S.M. della Pietà dei Turchini* (Milan: Remo Sandron, 1924), 104–14 and 207–17. See also the classic Francesco Florimo, *La scuola musicale di Napoli e i suoi conservatorii, con uno sguardo sulla storia della musica in Italia*, 4 vols. in 3 (Naples: Stabilimento tip. V. Morano, 1883), and, for a broader treatment, Rosa Cafiero, "Conservatories and the Neapolitan School: A European Model at the End of the Eighteenth Century?," in *Musical Education in Europe (1770–1914): Compositional, Institutional, and Political Challenges*, 2 vols., edited by Michael Fend and Michel Noiray (Berlin: Berliner Wissenschafts-Verlag, 2005), 1: 15–29.

37. A rather generic account of what people generally took to be true is given by Joseph Jérôme Le Français de Lalande, *Voyage d'un français en Italie, fait dans les années 1765 & 1766*, 8 vols., revised and expanded (Yverdon, 1769–90), 6: 218–19, who reports that castrati were mostly made in Naples. He seems to have been repeating the speculations others made on the grounds that so many were trained there. Charles Burney, *An Eighteenth-Century Musical Tour in France and Italy*, edited by Percy A. Scholes (1773; London: Oxford University Press, 1959), 247, is more reliable.

38. See Elisabeth Avanzati, "The Unpublished Senesino," in the catalog of the exhibition *Handel and the Castrati: The Story behind the 18th-Century Superstar Singers, 19 March–1 October 2006* (London: Handel House Museum, 2006), 5–9, based on documents in the private Bernardi Family Archive, the Archivio di Stato di Siena, the Siena Cathedral, and the Siena Public Library; and Lowell E. Lindgren, "An Intellectual Florentine Castrato at the End of the Medicean Era," in *"Lo stupor dell'invenzione": Firenze e la nascita dell'opera, Atti del Convegno Internazionale di Studi, Firenze, 5–6 ottobre, 2000*, edited by Piero Gargiulo (Florence: Leo S. Olschki, 2001), 139–64, at 140–41.

39. The document in question, and others concerning castration, was discovered by Rosselli, "The Castrati as a Professional Group," 151 n. 35, 154, and 154 n. 47.

40. Rosselli, "The Castrati as a Professional Group," 154 n. 37, and C.A. Vianello, *Teatri, spettacoli, musiche a Milano nei secoli scorsi* (Milan, 1941), cited in Rosselli, "The Castrati as a Professional Group," 155 n. 50, who notes a case from 1783 of an eleven-year-old boy who got his father and teacher off of five years of hard labor by insisting that he had begged to be castrated.

41. Rosselli, "The Castrati as a Professional Group," 154 n. 47.

42. Farinelli, from bourgeois stock, was more typical of the eighteenth century. On bourgeois sons being made into castrati, see Rosselli, "The Castrati as a Professional Group," 156 and 156 n. 52. On the poverty of castrated boys at Assisi, see also Pampaloni, "Giovani castrati nell'Assisi," 137–42, and 143 n. 41. Ancillon talks about the misfortune and poor

parents of the castrato singer Paoluccio, ostensibly operated on by his castrato uncle (*Eunuchism Display'd*, 39). See also Benedetto Mojon, *Dissertazione sugli effetti della castratura;* Fritz, *Kastratengesang;* and Lucarelli, *Domenico Bruni.*

43. Giovanni Battista Rossi Scotti, *Della vita e delle opere del cavalier Francesco Morlacchi* (Perugia: V. Bartelli, 1860), xlvi–xlvii.

44. Ancillon, *Eunuchism Display'd,* 40. A very smart contextualization of Ancillon's treatise in its English translation and reception appears in Berry, *A Castrato and His Wife,* 137–42.

45. Marcello, *Il teatro alla moda* (1720), 23.

46. Bontempi's allusion to a laudatory collection of writings published by Baldassare Ferri's nephew upon the singer's death, *Il pianto de' cigni in morte della fenice de' musici* (Perugia, 1680), may be relevant here. Bontempi conjures multiple meanings of "Ferri/ferri" when he says that Ferri's singing had its "origin from a 'ferro'" (a father named Ferri/Ferro, but perhaps also an iron) and with a "ferro" "again . . . reached its end" (i.e., with his encomiast Antonio Ferri). ("Che havendo l'harmonia havuto principio dal ferro, nella morte di Baldassare Ferri, col ferro ancora habbia havuto il suo fine"; *Historia musica, nella quale si ha piena cognitione della teorica, e della pratica antica della musica harmonica; secondo la dottrina de'greci . . .* [Perugia: Costantini, 1695], 111). Besides the relatives invoked, could Bontempi have been playing with "ferro" as in surgical tool, in the sense of being "sotti i ferri" (under the knife), or "ferro" as sword, i.e., as the means by which Baldassare had acquired such powers of singing as could allow him to exceed usual human possibility and thus sing for many sovereigns—braving castration, in other words, and then being empowered by it? ("Quasi eccedeva il possibile della humanità. Onde ha meritato di servire prima tre Re di Polonia, e poi due Imperadori; d'esser creato Cavaliere di S. Marco da' Venetiani; d'esser mandato a prendere con nave particolare da Christina Regina di Svetia"; *Historia musica,* 110). If so, then Bontempi's comment would suggest at once emasculation and virility (the latter associated with possession of the sword), since it recalls in the same breath Ferri's being knighted as Cavaliere di S. Marco. On the 1680 collection of encomia and for a facsimile of it, see Biancamaria Brumana, *"Il pianto de' cigni in morte della fenice de' musici": Poesie per Baldassare Ferri e nuove ipotesi sulla carriera del cantante,* Appendici al Bollettino della Deputazione di storia patria per l'Umbria 29 (2010).

47. Sacchi, *Vita del Cavaliere Don Carlo Broschi detto Il Farinello:* "Apparisce che egli non fu sottoposto al taglio nella puerizia per conservare la mollezza della voce, e così venderla a maggior presso; ma bensì conservare la vita in grave pericolo corso per la sua fanciullesca vivacità, saltando sopra un cavallo, onde cadde, e fu anche offeso nella fronte. Ben la famiglia era povera" (33).

48. Cited in Rosselli, "The Castrati as a Professional Group," 155.

49. Loreto Vittori, *La troia rapita, poema giocoso del cavaliere Loreto Vittori da spoleto dedicato al Serenissimo Fran. Duca di Toscana Ferdinando II* (Macerata: Per li Grifei, e Giuseppe Piccini, 1662), fol. 5r, also refers to swans (8.27), and so does his sonnet dedicated to castrato Domenico Andreoni.

50. Haböck based his information on interviews with castrati from the Sistine Chapel made in 1914 (*Die Kastraten,* 197, 202–3).

51. Information about when various castrati of the period were brought to Rome is compiled in the biographies contained in the series Storia della cappella musicale pontificia

under the general editorship of Giancarlo Rostirolla and the Fondazione Giovanni da Palestrina. See Kantner and Pachovsky, *La cappella musicale pontificia nell'Ottocento*, and De Salvo Fattor, *La cappella musicale pontificia nel Novecento*. The Papal States (Umbria and Le Marche) were incorporated into the Kingdom of Italy in 1860; Lazio fell with Rome in 1870.

52. See Owsei Temkin, *Galenism: Rise and Decline of a Medical Philosophy* (Ithaca, NY: Pergamon Press, 1973). Much attention to Galen in writing on castrati has turned on Thomas Laqueur's analysis of Galen's one-sex model, in *Making Sex: Body and Gender from the Greeks to Freud* (Cambridge, MA: Harvard University Press, 1990), which produced a torrent of responses. A mild but informative one regarding early modern sources is Winfried Schleiner, "Early Modern Controversies about the One-Sex Model," *Renaissance Quarterly* 53, no. 1 (Spring 2001): 180–91.

53. Ernesto De Martino, *Sud e magia* (Milan: Feltrinelli, 1959).

54. Two classic studies are Mary Douglas, *Purity and Danger: An Analysis of Concepts of Pollution and Taboo* (1966; London: Routledge, 2002), and Edmund Leach, *Social Anthropology* (Oxford: Oxford University Press, 1982). See also Valeri, *Forest of Taboos*, which grounds pervasive consequences of taboo in a negative philosophical dialectics. Ernesto De Martino's *Morte e pianto rituale nel mondo antico: Dal lamento pagano al pianto di Maria* (Turin: Edizioni Scientifiche Einaudi, 1958), on mourning rituals in Lucania (now Basilicata), and De Martino, *La terra del rimorso* (Milan: Il Saggiatore, 1961), on tarantella rituals in Puglia, are fundamental philosophically grounded ethnographic studies. Each explores ways of dealing with existential crises of presence by means of rituals that ultimately lead to subjective reintegration within the social order; and presence (Heidegger's *Dasein*) in each instance declares itself in the face of subjective perils even as the means to overcome them may themselves include perilous behaviors. Not by coincidence both sites of research involved preindustrialized societies. For an appraisal of Ernesto De Martino's place in Italian anthropology and ethnomusicology, see Tullia Magrini, "The Contribution of Ernest De Martino to the Anthropology of Italian Music," *Yearbook of Traditional Music* 26 (1994): 66-80. Cultural phenomena in Magrini's appraisal of De Martino are "instruments that are essential to controlling and overcoming situations of crisis," functioning to express and communicate them in "a coherent form that is tolerable for both the individual and the community," regardless of whether the situations that are ritually dealt with actually took place according to standards of factual truth.

55. Gaudenzio Claretta, "Un nobile piemontese musico al principio del XVII," *Estratto dalla* Nuova rivista *(pubblicazione settimanale di Scienze, Lettere ed Arti)* (Turin: Angelo Baglione, 1883).

56. There survive a number of similar images that circulated internationally, of which various copies were made. See, for example, Marco Ricci's drawings, including one of Bernacchi, based on Zanetti's original, in the Smith Collection at Windsor Castle; reproduced in Giuseppe Maria Pilo, ed., *Marco Ricci: catalogo della mostra . . . con un saggio di Rodolfo Pallucchini, sui caratteri di Marco Ricci, Bassano del Grappa, Palazzo Sturm, 1 settembre–10 novembre 1963* (Venice: Alfieri, [1963]); and see Annalisa Scarpa Sonino, *Marco Ricci* (Milan: Berenice, 1991).

57. "Frutti del mondo esperimentati da F. B. nativo dell'Alfea, in Toscana," 2 vols., G-Mbs, cod. It. 39, vol. 1, fols. 36v–37. "Frutti del mondo" was published in the radically abridged modern edition *"Frutti del mondo": L'autobiografia di Filippo Balatri*, edited by

Vossler. Vossler's edition includes about half of the original two volumes of manuscript and threads together the extensive excised portions with the editor's own paraphrases. I cite from the Munich manuscript and also make recourse to Balatri's earlier "autobiography" in prose, "Vita e viaggi," from which the "Frutti del mondo" was condensed and versified by Balatri. Musicologists have heretofore utilized the Vossler edition of the "Frutti del mondo," in-depth treatment of Balatri thus far being limited to work by Slavicists. Important writings include Daniel L. Schlafly Jr., "Filippo Balatri in Peter the Great's Russia," *Jahrbüchen für Geschichte ostereuropas* 45 (1997): 18–98; Schlafly, "A Muscovite Boiarynia Faces Peter the Great's Reforms: Dar'ia Golitsyna between Two Worlds," *Canadian-American Slavic Studies* 31 (1997): 249–68; and especially Maria Di Salvo, "*Vita e viaggi* di Filippo Balatri (preliminari all'edizione del testo)," *Russica romana* 6 (1999): 37–57, whose complete critical edition of Balatri's prose autobiography will soon be in press. A well-done trade biography of Balatri, glossing the "Vita e viaggi," by German novelist and radio journalist Christine Wunnicke has appeared as *Die Nachtigall des Zaren: Das Leben des Filippo Balatri* (Munich: Claassen, 2001). Wunnicke corresponded with me helpfully about her research, as have Professors Schlafly and especially Di Salvo. Earlier Russian sources on Balatri are listed in Di Salvo, "*Vita e viaggi*," nn. 5, 6, 9, and 11.

58. Note that I give poetry translated for its content in prose form. Poetry cited from musical sources is given in verse lines in the translations.

59. Balatri, "Frutti del mondo," 1, fols. 35v-36.

60. Balatri's tale again draws on the traditional ascription of castrators to Norcia. In reality, castrations were seemingly performed all over Italy (see Rosselli, "The Castrati as a Professional Group," and Monaldi, *Cantanti evirati celebri*, 15 and 68), but Norcia was the provenance of most itinerant surgeons who performed castrations, as Gentilcore shows (*Medical Charlatanism*, 181–88, esp. 184–85).

61. E.g., Salvator Rosa, *Satire, odi e lettere*, illustrated by Giosuè Carducci (Florence: G. Barbèra, 1860); Rosa, *Satire, liriche, lettere*, edited by Anton Maria Salvini et al. (Milan: Sonzogno, 1892), 41.

62. There are also many such jokes later on. See, e.g., Paolo Rolli on the "cockfights" of Carlo Scalzi and Carestini, cited in Otto Erich Deutsch, *Handel: A Documentary Biography* (1955; New York: Da Capo Press, 1974), 341.

63. The anonymous cantata *Lamento del castrato*, from I-Bc, MS Q 46, has been recorded by the Cappella Musicale di S. Petronio, directed by Sergio Vartolo, on *Lamenti barocchi*, vol. 2 (Munich: Naxos, distributed by MVD Music and Video Distribution, 1996), publisher's no. 8.553319, track 7. I am very grateful to Vartolo for sending me copies of the manuscript of this cantata and the cantata "L'impotente," with text by Francesco Melosio and music by Fabrizio Fontana (recorded on ibid., track 4).

64. The cantata can be heard at www.youtube.com/watch?v=RvZzc8s1Ipo.

65. On Pulcinella, see, most importantly, the monumental, inspired work of Domenico Scafoglio and M. Luigi Lombardi Satriani, *Pulcinella: Il mito e la storia* (Milan: Leonardo, 1990). A concise essayistic version of their thesis was extrapolated for the 1000 Lire series as Domenico Scafoglio, *Pulcinella*, Napoli Tascabile 30, edited by Romualdo Marrone (Rome: Tascabili Economici Newton, 1996). Among many fascinating images pictured in Scafoglio and Lombardi Satriani's *Pulcinella* are eighteenth- and nineteenth-century drawings from Greek gems and herms showing creatures who are half human and half fowl with

exaggerated phalluses, often comic in style (e.g., plates 152–54). See also the collection of essays edited by Franco Carmelo Greco, *Pulcinella: Una maschera tra gli specchi* (Naples: Edizioni Scientifiche Italiane, 1990).

One could look to other archetypal figures associated with the commedia dell'arte for affinities with the castrato, in particular Harlequin, but I have regarded Pulcinella as having the highest comparative value since he was the supreme instantiation of the archetype and shares with the castrato a strong association with Naples.

66. On literary elaborations of Pulcinella's castrato-like voice, see Scafoglio and Lombardi Satriani, *Pulcinella*, 426–31.

67. In an anonymous eighteenth-century drawing, a Carnival chariot shows Pulcinella along with his own transformations into half-human Pulcinellini and Pulcinella-asses, pulling their Pulcinella-masters like rickshaw drivers (ibid., plate 34).

68. In another painting from the same group Pulcinella gives birth through his back. See the discussion and reproduction in ibid., 233, from a chapter on Pulcinella as a hermaphrodite, part 7, chap. 7, 219-36 and plates 20 and 21, and in Franco Carmelo Greco, ed., *Pulcinella, maschera del mondo: Pulcinella e le arti dal Cinquecento al Novecento* (Naples: Electa Napoli, 1990), 266.

69. The original source is an anonymous Neapolitan comedy called *Gl'incanti delle Maghe per la nascita di Pulcinella dalle viscere del Monte Vesuvio* (Naples, 1802; reprinted 1824 and 1861). The myth has its genesis in much earlier traditions, however; cf. Scafoglio and Lombardi Satriani, *Pulcinella*, 23–24.

70. See Adriano Mariuz, *Giandomenico Tiepolo*, preface by Antonio Morassi (Venice: Alfieri, 1971), plate 31; Marcia E. Vetrocq, *Domenico Tiepolo's Punchinello Drawings*, with introduction by Adelheid M. Gealt (Bloomington: Indiana University Art Museum, 1979), catalog entry on p. 138; and, most recently, *Tiepolo*, edited by Mariuz and Pavanello, where the drawing is reproduced as plate 125 (p. 190) and discussed in Gealt's essay "Divertimenti per li regazzi" (pp. 181–210), on 184. Gealt puts the series "Divertimenti per li Regazzi" into a continuous narrative sequence. Since our Fig. 19 comes first in the series (the constituent drawings of which are numbered but not titled) and is followed by other Pulcinella births, she understands it to represent the birth of Pulcinella's grandfather; see "Divertimenti per li regazzi" in *Tiepolo*, edited by Mariuz and Pavanello, 191; and Adelheid M. Gealt, "The Telling Line: Domenico Tiepolo as a Draftsman/Narrator," in *Domenico Tiepolo, Master Draftsman*, curated by Adelheid M. Gealt and George Knox, catalog of an exhibition held at Castello di Udine, September 14–December 31, 1996, and at Indiana University Art Museum, Bloomington, Indiana, January 15–March 9, 1997 (Bloomington: Indiana University Press, 1996), 62–104. Gealt also speculates on the implied lineage of Pulcinella's birth from an egg in connection with Leda's egg, Castor and Pollux, and Tiepolo's own depiction of an eagle birthed from an egg. Viewed in the context of the Pulcinella myth as spun out in literature and theater, Pulcinella's birth from a turkey's egg also looks like a depiction of one of his two main myths of origin, as I argue here, while other drawings in the series showing Pulcinella's birth and childhood look like mythical variants. Cf. Scafoglio and Lombardi Satriani, *Pulcinella*, 23–28 on Pulcinella's symbolic relationships to the egg.

In another drawing in the Tiepolo series, known in English as *Punchinello with the Ostriches*, dated ca. 1800 (Allen Memorial Art Museum at Oberlin College, Oberlin, Ohio, no. 811), Pulcinella plays with two great ostriches.

71. Francesco Melosio, *Poesie e prose di Francesco Melosio da città della Pieve, aggiuntovi in questa nova impressione altre spiritose, erudite, e bizarre compositioni dello stesso auttore, consacrate all'Illustriss. & Eccellentiss. Sig. Gio: Alberto di Ferschen* (Venice, 1695), 324. "Chiocca" is a variant of "chioccia." As Stefano Castelvecchi pointed out to me, lines 5–7 might also be translated, "And I don't know how she threw herself on them, but this one was also brooded from eggs." In other editions line 8 reads, "Ed a suo tempo anch'egli pullulò." Cf. the anonymous poetry quoted in Heriot, *The Castrati in Opera*, 56.

72. Sometimes the marquis is elided with Harlequin, including by Balatri. Ángel Medina writes about the Spanish counterpart to the Italian history I trace out here, interconnecting singing castrati, capons, and comic characters; see *Los atributos del capón: Imagen histórica de los cantores castrados en España* (Madrid: Instituto Complutense de Ciencias Musicales, 2001), esp. chapters 5 through 9. My thanks to Drew Edward Davies for the reference.

73. Such slippages make sense given the symbolism of the egg. Historically it has probably been the world's most widespread, versatile, and polyvalent symbol of reproduction, as well as a symbol of birth, fertility, and wealth long linked in the West with rebirth in connection with Passover and the Resurrection. See Jean Chevalier and Alain Gheerbrant, *The Penguin Dictionary of Symbols*, translated by John Buchanan-Brown (2nd ed. 1982; London: Penguin, 1996), 337–41.

74. For my analysis here I am much in debt here to Scafoglio's brilliant work not just on Pulcinella but relatedly on symbolic meanings surrounding the famine in southern Italy during 1764, in *La maschera della cuccagna: Spreco, rivolta e sacrificio nel carnevale napoletano del 1764* (Naples: Guida, 1994); cf. my *Opera and Sovereignty: Transforming Myths in Eighteenth-Century Italy* (Chicago: University of Chicago Press, 2007), 202–3 and 224. Reports of heckling and other kinds of abuse in eighteenth-century Italian theaters are notorious, not least those that staged opera seria, which included countless performances by castrati. See *Opera and Sovereignty*, esp. chapters 1 and 4.

75. On the painting see *Pulcinella, maschera del mondo*, 207–9. For more on the dialectical argument regarding the relationship between strong-arm old-regime governments and popular festivity, particularly in Rome and Naples, see my *Opera and Sovereignty*, chapters 4 and 5.

76. This matter has occasioned much confusion. See my "Castrato Acts" in *The Oxford Handbook of Opera*, edited by Helen M. Greenwald (New York: Oxford University Press, 2014). Finucci's stance is characteristic in claiming that the castrato's is not a "body-in-excess, like a woman's, but a body lacking" (*The Manly Masquerade*, 275)—an implicitly Lacanian view. I'm indebted here to Martin Stokes's thinking about the hypernormative singing of Turkish male pop singers. See "The Tearful Public Sphere: Turkey's 'Sun of Art,' Zeki Mürin," in *Music and Gender: Perspectives from the Mediterranean*, edited by Tullia Magrini (Chicago: University of Chicago Press, 2003), 307–28.

77. Cf. my *Opera and Sovereignty*, 253–55 and 364–67.

78. See William L. Barcham, "Il teatro della moda," in *Tiepolo*, edited by Mariuz and Pavanello, 80 and plate 5.

79. Special Collections, Research Library, Getty Research Institute, Getty Center, Los Angeles, "Italian Theater Collection," collection of manuscripts, prints, broadsides, and photographs under shelf number 2003.M.33** (OCLC record number 80964324).

80. Scafoglio, *Pulcinella* in 1000 Lire series, 22. On Pulcinella as robber and robbed, see Scafoglio and Lombardi Satriani, *Pulcinella*, chapter 8, 237–54, and on his relationship to poverty and money, chapter 10, 277–88.

81. Ranieri de' Calzabigi, *La ragione dei "buffoni"* (La Lulliade *di Ranieri de' Calzabigi*), edited by Gabriele Muresu (Rome: Bulzoni, 1977); and Bragaglia, *Degli "evirati cantori,"* 72.

82. Bragaglia, *Degli "evirati cantori,"* 70.

83. From his *Marziale in Albion*, quoted in ibid., 55.

84. Cited in Bragaglia, *Degli "evirati cantori,"* 72, from an autograph of Rolli's in Siena, Biblioteca degli Intronati. Satires about Atto Melani include the capon and the rooster as well, along with rich allusions to money and sex, wonderfully treated in Freitas, *Portrait of a Castrato*, 103–6 and transcribed on 352–57.

85. See Geertz, "Deep Play."

86. For a brilliant analysis of this phenomenon with respect to the pig in German culture, see Jud Newborn, "'Work Makes Free': The Hidden Cultural Meaning of the Holocaust," 4 vols., PhD diss., vol. 1, chapters 2 and 3.

87. See Roberto De Simone, Annabella Rossi, et al., *Carnevale si chiamava Vincenzo: Rituali di carnevale in Campania* (Roma: De Luca Editore, 1977), 185–208, on elisions between sexuality, chickens, Carnival, and Pulcinella in modern-day Campania, and 186–87 on the Festa della Madonna delle Galline. My thanks to Luisa Del Giudice for the lead.

88. A similar belief prevailed in India during cholera epidemics. See Sir James George Frazer, *The Golden Bough*, abridged ed. (1922; New York: Macmillan, 1963), 654.

89. See Rosselli, "L'apprendistato del cantante italiano: Rapporti contrattuali fra allievi e insegnanti dal Cinquecento al Novecento," *Rivista italiana di musicologia* 23 (1988): 157–81; and Rosselli, "The Castrati as a Professional Group," 159.

90. In addition to Rosselli, "The Castrati as a Professional Group," 159, see especially Sergio Durante, "The Opera Singer," in *Opera Production and Its Resources*, The History of Italian Opera, edited by Lorenzo Bianconi and Giorgio Pestelli, part 2, *Systems*, vol. 4, translated by Lydia G. Cochrane (Chicago: University of Chicago Press, 1998), 345–417, and see Haböck, *Die Kastraten*, 110–15.

91. Di Giacomo, *Il conservatorio*; cf. Michael F. Robinson, *Naples and Neapolitan Opera* (Oxford: Clarendon Press, 1972), 14.

92. Santa Maria di Loreto, for instance, was headed by a rector. Working under him were (in descending order) a vice-rector, a manager, several prefects, a steward (who handled meals), several chaplains, and a sacristan. See Michael F. Robinson, "The Governor's Minutes of the Conservatory S. Maria di Loreto, Naples," *RMA Research Chronicle* 10, no. 1 (1972): 1–97. See also Rosselli, "The Castrato as a Professional Group," 159–60.

93. Florimo details this entry ritual precisely for the Conservatorio della Pietà de' Turchini in Florimo, *La scuola musicale di Napoli e i suoi conservatori* 3: 8–9.

94. Ibid.

95. Di Giacomo, *Il conservatorio*, 90–100; and Charles Burney on the Sant'Onofrio, who wrote, "There are in this college sixteen young *castrati* and these lye up stairs, by themselves, in warmer apartments than the other boys, for fear of colds, which might not only render their delicate voices unfit for exercise at present, but hazard the entire loss of them for ever." *The Present State of Music in France and Italy* (London: T. Becket and Co., 1773), 338. (See

also Barbier, *The World of the Castrati,* 44–45, who cites documents from Santa Maria di Loreto, Poveri di Gesù Cristo, and San Loreto.)

96. The matter of containment is especially clear in later eighteenth- and early nineteenth-century images of the castrato's social life, such as found in the memoirs of Goldoni and Casanova and in Balzac's *Sarrasine.*

97. See Di Giacomo, *Il conservatorio,* 67–69, 95, 168, 179, who also explains that the youngest children played angels as well, all of them dressed in white: "I figlioli piccoli, i bambini, erano alla lor volta destinati a rappresentare *turbe* o *cori* d'angioli a publiche feste, a spettacoli sacri, ad accompagnamenti mortuarii, a processioni in onore di santi" (69); "Per gli *angiolilli* in funzione si usava tela *cambraia.* Fino agli ultimi anni del Conservatorio que' figlioli ebbero sottana bianca, e zimarra e mantelletta grige" (168, from the section "La stoffa per i vestiti del figlioli"). Robinson, "The Governor's Minutes," says the boys of S. Maria di Loreto were mostly dressed in white; Burney in 1770 adds that they wore a black sash (2 and 60).

98. Barbier, *The World of the Castrati,* 50.

99. Preface to Francesco Albergati Capacelli, *Il ciarlator maldicente* in *Scelta di commedie e novelle morali del marchese Albergati Capacelli,* 2 vols., edited by Antonio Ravelli (London: Giuseppe Cooper, [1794?]), 2: iv–ix; Xavier Cervantes, "'Tuneful Monsters': The Castrati and the London Operatic Public, 1667–1737," *Restoration and Eighteenth-Century Theatre Research,* 2nd ser., 13 (1998): 1–24. Jean-Loop Charvet explores the angel theme with respect to French high tenors and castrati in "Hautes-contre et castrats: La voix des anges, la voix du coeur," *Litterature classique* 12 (1990): 305–21. Michel Poizat gives a Lacanian gloss in *The Angel's Cry: Beyond the Pleasure Principle in Opera,* translated by Arthur Denner (1986; Ithaca, NY: Cornell University Press, 1992). See also Richard Somerset-Ward, *Angels and Monsters: Male and Female Sopranos in the Story of Opera, 1600–1900* (New Haven, CT: Yale University Press, 2004), esp. chapters 3–4; and Herr, *Gesang gegen die "Ordnung der Natur,"* 68–72.

100. Bontempi, *Historia musica,* 110–11.

101. Elisabeth Vigée Lebrun, *Souvenirs,* 2 vols., edited by Claudine Herrmann (Paris: Des Femmes, 1984), 1: 176: "Le matin du vendredi saint, j'allai, à la chapelle Sixtine, entendre le fameux *Miserere* d'Allegri, chanté par des soprani sans aucun instrument. C'était vraiment la musique des anges."

APPENDIX TO CHAPTER 1

1. The literal meaning of "resti pendente" [o]is "should remain a ball," another pun on the singer's missing testicles.

2. The word "e" is unclear in the calligraphy of the original manuscript. It may well be the letter "a," in which case the line could be translated as "to a timid beauty."

3. The line might best be rendered "of honest beauty," particularly as the earlier line contains the phrase "to a timid beauty" (see n. 2 above).

4. "Spadone" is a pun, since it's also the legal term, used in papal decrees, for a mutilated, hence nonreproductive, man.

5. The pun on B♭ recalls the notation of the flat, which was called "soft" in early notational conventional (be-molle) because of its softly rounded shape.

6. The term I translate as "the keys," "i tasti," is a double entendre meaning both "the keys" and "the touch." The infinitive verb form "tastare" means "to feel" (as with "a pulse"), "to test" (as in the ground or the lay of the land), or "to feel one's way." It also means "to feel about" and was used thus in connection with feeling the notes on an instrument in playing improvisationally in preludes, intonations, ricercars, toccatas, and fantasias from the fifteenth century onward, much as with the verb "toccare" (to touch). The same was true in French; cf. Francois Couperin's *L'Art de toucher le Clavecin* (Paris, 1716).

7. Or "that wants to graze in battle and not in a cage."

CHAPTER 2. THE MAN WHO PRETENDED TO BE WHO HE WAS: A TALE OF REPRODUCTION

1. I silently modify and punctuate the text given in the facsimile edition Johann Adolf Hasse, *The Favourite Songs in the opera Call'd Artaxerxes*, Bibliotheca musica Bononiensis, Sect. 4, no. 209 (London: Walsh, 1735; Bologna: Arnaldo Forni, 1980), 10r–10v.

2. See Sandro Cappelletto, *La voce perduta: Vita di Farinelli, cantore evirato* (Turin: Edizioni di Torino, 1995), 65–66, on Farinelli as singer of this aria and the moment when it occurs in *Artaserse* as epitomizing the stoicism of Metastasian poetics.

The first stanza of Metastasio's unaltered text reads: "Per quel paterno amplesso/ Per questo estremo addio/ Conservami te stesso, / Placami l'idol mio, / Difendimi il mio Re" (Through this paternal embrace, through this last farewell, may you placate my beloved and defend for me my king). "King" here refers to Artaserse, who is still prince at this point but who, in the wake of the murder of his father, King Xerxes, will take the throne at the end of the opera. *Artaserse* was premiered in a setting by Leonardo Vinci (1696–1730) in Rome's Teatro delle Dame during Carnival 1730, on February 4, with Giovanni Carestini in the eponymous role, and only two weeks later was performed in Venice, in a setting by Johann Adolphe Hasse (1699–1783) with textual revisions by Giovanni Boldini. On "Per questo dolce amplesso" and these initial settings of *Artaserse*, see Daniel Heartz, *Music in European Capitals: The Galant Style, 1720–1780* (New York: Norton, 2003), 92–99 (on Vinci's at Rome) and 309–17 (on Hasse's in Venice). The latter stacked up Farinelli against Carestini.

3. The aria is recorded, at a fast pace, by Vivica Genaux, *Arias for Farinelli* (Arles: Harmonia Mundi France, 2002), track 10. Nazari's portrait of Farinelli was done at just about this time (see Fig. 7).

4. *The Fashionable Tell-tale, Containing a Great Variety of Curious and Interesting Anecdotes of Emperors, Kings, Queens, Statesmen, Prelates, Divines, Generals, Admirals, Captains, Physicians, Poets, and Players*, vol. 2, 2nd ed. ([London]: R. Baldwin, in Paternoster-Row, 1778); quote on 53, complete anecdote on 52–53.

5. The phrase "ceased to be men" comes from Mario Bellucci La Salandra, "Vito Giuseppe Millico (Il terlizzese): Sopranista e compositore melodrammatico del Settecento (da nuovi documenti)," *Archivio storico pugliese* 3 (1950): 201–27, on 203. It resonates with a mid-twentieth-century modernist view that places men and women in sharp and unbreachable opposition, a view that was already anticipated with liberal Enlightenment views of the eighteenth century, for instance the Marquis Jean Baptiste de Boyer d'Argens, who in his *New Memoirs Establishing a True Knowledge of Mankind, by Discovering the Affections of the Heart, and the Operations of the Understanding*, 2 vols. (London: Printed for D. Brown, R. Hett, and A. Mil-

lar, 1747), writes of the courtiers of Queen Stratonice in ancient Syria, who "voluntarily ceased to be men" in order to gain her favor (2: 43–44). Some writers understand castrati as man-made hermaphrodites or "prima donnas" (Valeria Finucci, *The Manly Masquerade: Masculinity, Paternity, and Castration in the Italian Renaissance* [Durham, NC: Duke University Press, 2003], 227; Paul J. Moses, *The Psychology of the Castrato Voice* [Basel: Folia Phoniatrica, 1960], 206 and passim), while others claim that cross-dressing, which applies to both sexes, was gender-neutral (see, e.g., Dorothy Keyser, "Cross-Sexual Casting in Baroque Opera: Musical and Theatrical Conventions," *Opera Quarterly* 5 [1988]: 46–57, esp. 47). More often, especially since the 1990s, cross-dressing practices have been taken as a sign of both continuity between early modern sexes and the ambiguity of the castrato's sex; see my take on these trends in "Castrato Acts," in *The Oxford Handbook on Opera*, edited by Helen M. Greenwald pp. 395–418 (New York: Oxford University Press, 2014). Roger Freitas offers an important critique of the entire problem in "The Eroticism of Emasculation: Confronting the Baroque Body of the Castrato," *Journal of Musicology* 20 (2003): 196–249, esp. 196–202, and the best treatment of it in Freitas, *Portrait of a Castrato: Politics, Patronage, and Music in the Life of Atto Melani* (Cambridge: Cambridge University Press, 2009), chapter 4, "The Sexuality of the Castrato." None of the above takes up the question in Barthes's terms, for which see Carolyn Abbate, "Opera; or the Envoicing of Women," in *Musicology and Difference: Gender and Sexuality in Music Scholarship*, edited by Ruth A. Solie (Berkeley: University of California Press, 1993), 231–34, and passingly chapter 6 below.

Felicia Miller calls on the hermaphrodite in a more ironic spirit while offering a critique of the film *Farinelli* (Gérard Corbiau, 1994); "Farinelli's Electronic Hermaphrodite and the Contralto Tradition," in *The Work of Opera: Genre, Nationhood, and Sexual Difference*, edited by Richard Dellamora and Daniel Fischlin (New York: Columbia University Press, 1997), 73–92. As Ann Rosalind Jones and Peter Stallybrass point out, the distinction between hermaphrodite and eunuch was hard to draw for a Renaissance figure such as the surgeon Ambroise Paré (ca. 1510–90), who, in his *Of Monsters and Prodigies* and elsewhere, placed hermaphrodites and eunuchs firmly along a male/female continuum characteristic of the "lability of the whole gendering process." See also Jones and Stallybrass, "Fetishizing Gender: Constructing the Hermaphrodite in Renaissance Europe," in *Body Guards: The Cultural Politics of Gender Ambiguity*, edited by Julia Epstein and Kristina Straub (New York: Routledge, 1991), 80–111, esp. 83.

6. There are exceptions. Already in 1575 the Spanish doctor Juan Huarte (ca. 1533–ca.1592) wrote in his treatise *Examen de ingenios, para las sciencias, donde se muestra la differencia de habilidades que ay en los hombres, y el genero de letras que a cada vno responde en particular* . . . (Baeca: Iuan Baptista de Montoya, 1575) a negative critique of eunuchs (it was long and widely reprinted and translated through much of the seventeenth century); see Giuseppe Gerbino, "The Quest for the Soprano Voice: Castrati in Renaissance Italy," *Studi musicali* 33, no. 2 (2004): 303–57. Yet until about the mid-eighteenth century, when to cause or submit to castration inspired a rallying cry in favor of nature, acceptance remained quite widespread.

An obvious tension is between nature as the product of an enlightened human vision and nature as the creation of God. The number of writings about this issue is vast, but see recently Dan Edelstein, *The Terror of Natural Right: Republicanism, the Cult of Nature, and the French Revolution* (Chicago: University of Chicago Press, 2009).

7. Important on the issue is Emily Wilbourne, "The Queer History of the Castrato," in *Oxford Handbook on Queerness and Music*, edited by Fred Maus and Sheila Whiteley (forthcoming).

8. On the issue of the "natural soprano," traced from the sixteenth century, see Corinna Herr, *Gesang gegen die "Ordnung der Natur": Kastraten und Falsettisten in der Musikgeschichte*, foreword by Kai Wessel (Kassel: Bärenreiter, 2013), 40–46 and passim.

9. Casanova, *Histoire de ma vie*, 3 vols., edited by Gerard Lahouati and Marie-Françoise Luna, with Furio Lucchichenti and Helmut Watzlawick, Bibliothèque de la Pléiade, 132 (Paris: Gallimard, 2013), vol. 2, chapters 1–2; in English as *History of My Life*, translated by Willard R. Trask (Baltimore, MD: Johns Hopkins University Press, 1966), based on the Brockhaus manuscript.

10. In this, and the argument that follows from it, I am largely in agreement with the views of Reinhard Strohm, who writes, "The patriarchal character of [Farinelli's] thought has not been recognized by those who elaborated on the theme [of his reproduction]. It shows that even Farinelli was a victim: the very claim that a castrato was anything other than a man was dictated by a patriarchal ideology obsessed with male procreation and inheritance." Reinhard Strohm, "Who Is Farinelli?," liner notes for the recording *Arias for Farinelli*, with Vivica Genaux, soprano, and the Akademie für Alte Musik, directed by René Jacobs (Arles: Harmonia Mundi, 2002), HMC 901778, p. 23. In this and chapter 5 I attempt to elaborate the "very claim" expressed by Strohm (23). Wendy Heller, "Varieties of Masculinity: Trajectories of the Castrato from the Seventeenth Century," *British Journal for Eighteenth-Century Studies* 28 (2005): 307–21, reaches conclusions that are similar to mine here, though they are arrived at differently.

11. I am indebted here to the synthetic essay of Gianna Pomata, "Family and Gender," in *Early Modern Italy*, edited by John A. Marino (Oxford: Oxford University Press, 2002), 69–86, and to more detailed studies related to the ascendency of patriliny, including Dante E. Zanetti, *La demografia del patriziato milanese nei secoli XVII, XVIII, XIX*, with appendix by Franco Arese Lucini, Annales cisalpines d'histoire sociale, 2nd ser., no. 2 (Pavia: Università, 1972), and Francis William Kent, *Household and Lineage in Renaissance Florence: The Family Life of the Capponi, Ginori, and Ruscellai* (Princeton, NJ: Princeton University Press, 1977).

12. For the later period see Cinzia Cremonini, ed., *Titolati, cadetti e parvenus: Il caso lombardo tra Antico regime e Rivoluzione francese* (Rome: Bulzoni, 1999), esp. Cremonini's introduction (pp. 7–23); and Anna Brugnoli, "Ritratto di un libertino del '700: Il cavaliere Giovanni Verri (1745–1818)," 169–220, in *Titolati, cadetti e parvenus*, on the youngest brother of Pietro and Alessandro Verri.

13. Cf. John Rosselli, "The Castrati as a Professional Group, and as a Social Phenomenon, 1550–1850," *Acta musicologica* 60 (1988): 143–79, which draws on Pietro Stella, "Strategie familiari e celibato sacro in Italia tra '600 e '700," *Salesianum* 41 (1979): 73–109. "Celibacy" in this usage is not, of course, an indicator of actual sexual practice.

14. There has been no thoroughgoing attempt at demographic analysis of the castrato phenomenon, and indeed such an analysis would be extremely challenging. John Rosselli speculated about numbers on the order of several hundred over the period 1630–1750, which strikes me as low ("The Castrati as a Professional Group," 133). Sergio Durante did a study of 531 singers active in or tied to Bologna between 1670 and 1770, where in that single

center a quarter were castrati; see "Condizioni materiali e trasmissione del sapere nelle scuole di canto a Bologna a metà Settecento," in *Atti del XIV congresso della Società Internazionale di Musicologia, Bologna, 1987: Trasmissione e recezione delle forme di cultura musicale*, edited by Angelo Pompilio et al., 3 vols. (Turin: Edizioni di Torino, 1990), 2: 175–89, esp. 176 and 186.

15. See further my *Opera and Sovereignty: Transforming Myths in Eighteenth-Century Italy* (Chicago: University of Chicago Press, 2007), esp. chapter 6, "Myths of Sovereignty."

16. See Zanetti, *La demografia del patriziato milanese*, chapter 3, esp. 71–72 and 83–84; see also 59–60 on the contrast between the seventeenth and early nineteenth centuries; Robert L. Kendrick, *Celestial Sirens: Nuns and Their Music in Early Modern Milan* (Oxford: Oxford University Press, 1996); and Pomata, "Family and Gender," 83. The female side of this story is developed by Francesca Medioli, "Lo spazio del chiostro: Clausura, costrizione e protezione nel XVII secolo," in *Tempi e spazi di vita femminile*, edited by Silvana Seidel Menchi, Anne Jacobsen Schutte, and Thomas Kuehn (Bologna: Il Mulino, 1999), 355–76, in English as "The Dimensions of the Cloister: Enclosure, Constraint, and Protection in Seventeenth-Century Italy," in *Time, Space, and Women's Lives in Early Modern Europe*, Sixteenth-Century Essays and Studies no. 57 (Kirksville, MO: Truman State University Press, 2001), 165–80; and, especially for the earlier period, Gabriella Zarri, "Gender, Religious Institutions, and Social Discipline: The Reform of the Regulars," in Judith C. Brown and Robert C. Davis, *Gender and Society in Renaissance Italy* (London: Longman, 1988), 193–212. Important on marriage is Michela De Giorgio and Christiane Klapisch-Zuber, eds., *Storia del matrimonio* (Bari: Laterza, 1996), and, on Venice specifically, Volker Hunecke, "Matrimonio e demografia del patriziato veneziano (secc. XVII–XVIII)," *Studi veneziani* 15 (1991): 269–319.

17. Important examples include Atto Melani, Ferri, and Farinelli. See Freitas, *Portrait of a Castrato*, 70–71, and further in chapter 3; Monica Baiocco, "Su Baldassare Ferri, cantante evirato nel Seicento," *Esercizi, musica e spettacolo* new series 6, no. 15 (1996): 19–46; and Cappelletto, *La voce perduta*.

18. Charles Ancillon, *Eunuchism Display'd*, translated by Robert Samber (London: Printed for E. Curll, 1718), 39; emphasis mine. Alas, what we know of Pauluccio essentially comes from Ancillon, who is not necessarily a trustworthy witness. See, however, Lowell E. Lindgren, "An Intellectual Florentine Castrato at the End of the Medicean Era," in *"Lo stupor dell'invenzione": Firenze e la nascita dell'opera, Atti del Convegno Internazionale di Studi, Firenze, 5–6 ottobre, 2000*, edited by Piero Gargiulo (Florence: Leo S. Olschki, 2001), 139–64, at 150, a discussion of Berenstadt's description in a letter of February 3, 1720, to diplomat Giuseppe Riva of a "Don Paolino," who appears to be Pauluccio.

19. Reproduced in Domenico Scafoglio and M. Luigi Lombardi Satriani, *Pulcinella: Il mito e la storia* (Milan: Leonardo, 1990), plate 20.

20. Reprinted in Lina Padoan Urban, ed., *Il carnevale veneziano nelle maschere incise da Francesco Bertelli* (Milan: Il Polifilo, 1986), image as plate 3.

21. Thomas McGeary, "Verse Epistles on Italian Opera Singers, 1724–1736," *RMA Research Chronicle* 33 (2000): 29–88, at 44–46.

22. Fielding's play was published in London for J. Watts at the Printing-Office in Wild-Court near Lincoln's-Inn Fields, 1736, with the subtitle "A dramatick satire on the times." See also Metastasio's joke to Farinelli about being his being "pregnant" (n. 101 below).

23. Valeria Finucci, "Introduction: Genealogical Pleasures, Genealogical Disruptions," in *Generation and Degeneration: Tropes of Reproduction in Literature and History from Antiquity to Early Modern Europe*, edited by Valeria Finucci and Kevin Brownlee (Durham, NC: Duke University Press, 2001), 1.

The characterization of castrati as reproducers of other castrati is not unknown outside France. Hedy Law points out that the playwright Marie-Joseph Blaise de Chénier wrote, "Desperate and confused by their impotence," they had "the sole pleasure of producing other eunuchs." From "Aux auteurs de la chronique de Paris," dated January 18, 1790, reprinted in Chénier's *Charles IX, ou L'école des rois, tragédie* (Paris: P. Fr. Didot jeune, 1790), 247; cited in Hedy Law, "An Italian Castrato, His Wife, and His Hero Named Nonsense," unpublished lecture, School of Music, University of British Columbia, May 2, 2012, Vancouver, B.C.

24. Augustine later wrote that women did not generate, but only conceived. The distinction is explained in Thomas Laqueur, *Making Sex: Body and Gender from the Greeks to Freud* (Cambridge, MA: Harvard University Press, 1990), 30 and passim.

25. For Bontempi see chapter 1 above. Sayre translated from Patrick Barbier, *Histoire des castrates*, 127, translated as *The World of the Castrati: The History of an Extraordinary Operatic Phenomenon* by Margaret Crosland (London: Souvenir Press, 1996), 122; from Gregorius Sayrus, O.S.B., *Clavis regia sacerdotum casuum conscientiae, sive Theologiae moralis thesauri locos omnes aperiens*, 2 vols. in 1 (Venice: B. Baretium, 1607). Note too Zaccaria Pasqualigo, who in 1641 wrote that a boy's throat was worth more to him than his testicles; discussed in Peter Browe, S.J., *Zur Geschichte der Entmannung: Eine Religions- und Rechtsgeschichtliche Studie* (Breslau: Verlag Müller & Seiffert, 1936), 99–117.

26. Translated by Robert Samber (London: E. Curll, 1718). The 1718 edition, 273 pages in length, was later reissued as *Italian love: or, eunuchism displayed. Describing all the different kinds of eunuchs; shewing the esteem they have met with in the world, . . . Also a comparison between some celebrated modern Italian eunuchs, . . . Occasioned by a young lady's falling in love with one, who sung in the Opera at the Hay-Market, and to whom she had like to be married. Written by a person of honour* (London: E. Curll, 1740; and London: J. Reason, 1758). On Curll see Paul Baines and Pat Rogers, *Edmund Curll, Bookseller* (Oxford: Clarendon, 2007), esp. 114, 117.

27. See the results of a survey of urologic surgeons by uropathologist Meyer M. Melicow, "Castrati Singers and the Lost 'Cords,'" *Bulletin of the New York Academy of Medicine* 59 (1983): 744–64, at 749–54. Melicow reports, "Bilateral subcapsular evacuation of the stringy seminiferous tubules probably resulted in sterility, but potency was not always eliminated. Numerous cells elaborating testosterone line the interior of the capsule of the testis and, if they survived and functioned, then it was possible for some castrati singers to have had heterosexual relationships" (54). As to the survey, he adds,

> There were some differences in opinion among the urologists as to the efficacy in producing eunuchs through procedures other than bilateral orchiectomy, such as bilateral vasectomy, vasostomy, and vasotomy, which apparently were performed in some cases. The two latter terms were sometimes used interchangeably, but the three terms are not synonymous. Vasectomy means excision of part or all of the vas deferens. Vasotomy means cutting into or across

the vas. Vasostomy means cutting into and making an opening (a stoma) in the vas. Bilateral vasectomy, destroying tubes and blood vessels, i.e., the cords, properly performed prepubertally, should result in sterility and impotentia. Following bilateral vasostomy or vasotomy, atrophy of the genital tracts does not always follow because there can be healing and recanalization. Thus, fertility and potency are not necessarily prevented. (54)

28. Ancillon, *Eunuchism Display'd*, 231.

29. Loreto Vittori, *La troia rapita, poema giocoso del cavaliere Loreto Vittori da spoleto dedicato al Serenissimo Fran. Duca di Toscana Ferdinando II* (Macerata: Per li Grifei, e Giuseppe Piccini, 1662). The title means "The Kidnapped Pig." The poem recounts the war between Rieti and Cantalice in the time of Pope Eugene IV (1383–1447), generically following the contours of Alessandro Tassoni's *poema eroica* titled *La secchia rapita* (The rape of the bucket), first written in 1611 and published in Paris in 1622 (in English see *La secchia rapita; or The Rape of the Bucket, a Heroi-comical Poem in Twelve Cantos*, 2 vols., translated by James Atkinson [London: J. M. Richardson, Cornhill, 1825]). "Troia" in Vittori's title denotes the female pig, sometimes vulgarly used to mean prostitute. Thus the title could be translated as "The Kidnapped or Abducted Whore" (pig and whore can be interchangeable as punning synonyms). A summary of Vittori's poem is given in Carl August Rau, *Loreto Vittori: Beiträge zur historisch-kritischen Würdigung seines Lebens, Wirkens und Schaffens* (Munich: Verlag für Moderne Musik, 1913), 95–100. Both Tassoni's and Vittori's poems have an ancient ancestry in the *Batrachomyomachia* (Βατραχομυομαχία, The Battle of the Frogs and Mice, referred to by Tassoni in canto 5, stanza 23). Authorship of the *Batrachomyomachia* is uncertain, with attribution dates varying from the fifth to ninth centuries B.C. in Greece. On Vittori see Bianca Maria Antolini, "La carriera di cantante e compositore di Loreto Vittori," *Studi musicali* 7 (1978): 141–88; and John Whenham, "Vittori [Vittorij], Loreto [Victorius, Lauretus; Rovitti, Olerto]," *GMO,* and Thomas D. Dunn with Martin Morell, eds., *Loreto Vittori: La Galatea,* Recent Researches in the Music of the Baroque Era (Madison, WI: A-R Editions, 2002), vii–viii, and xii n. 20 on *La troia rapita;* and Frederick Hammond, *Music and Spectacle in Baroque Rome: Barberini Patronage under Urban VIII* (New Haven, CT: Yale University Press, 1994), 175–77.

30. See Freitas, *Portrait of a Castrato,* 104–6. The correspondence is from 1653. As Freitas says, though the satirist can hardly be taken literally, he does play with going gossip about Atto, confirmable from other quarters, when writing, "È di già publica fama / che il giocar non vi dispiaccia / e de giochi sol vi piaccia / calabrache con la dama. / Meritate per tal brama / già che a Dama non vincete / e a calar primiero sete / nelle chiappe lo staffile." Freitas gives these lines two different translations, the less literal of which is bawdier and more pointed: "It's already common knowledge that you don't mind gambling, and of all the games, you only enjoy dropping your pants with a lady. Since you do not master the lady and are the first to lose your erection, you deserve, for that kind of passion, the dick in your butt" (105).

31. Freitas, *Portrait of a Castrato,* 127–28. De Castris had an affair with Grand Prince Ferdinando de' Medici.

32. Carlo Nardini, *Il musico Siface e l'ambasciatore di Francia a Roma nel 1683* (Florence: Coppini e Bocconi, 1891).

33. Anton Giulio Bragaglia, *Degli "evirati cantori": Contributo alla storia del teatro* (Florence: Sansoni Antiquariato, 1959), 34. A number of other cases of women pursuing castrati in marriage and falling in love with them are reported, e.g., in Angus Heriot, *The Castrati in Opera* (London: Calder and Boyars, 1956), but Heriot cites few sources and not all can be substantiated. On the capacity of castrati for intercourse, see Freitas, *Portrait of a Castrato*, 132–41. Cortona's story is not included in Francesco Ravagli, *Il Cortona, Domenico Cecchi* (Città di Castello: Scipione Lapi, 1896).

34. The episodes are recounted in Filippo Balatri, "Frutti del mondo, esperimentati da. F. B. nativo dell'Alfea, in Toscana," 2 vols. G-Mbs, cod. It. 39, 1: 61–69v and 2: 3–34, respectively.

35. Susanna's feelings were expressed in a letter-journal to her sister Frances (Fanny). The manuscripts, in GB-Lb, MS Egerton 3691 2692 (Barrett Collection), vols. 2, 3 (ff. 177, 196), have recently been published in an electronic edition as *The Journals and Letters of Susan Burney: Music and Society in Late Eighteenth-Century England*, edited by Philip Olleson (Farnham, Surrey, England: Ashgate, 2012). Stephen Willier makes important use of them in "Gasparo Pacchierotti in London: The 1779–80 Season in Susanna Burney's 'Letter Journal,'" *Studi musicali* 29 (2000): 251–91, as do Curtis Price, Judith Milhous, and Robert D. Hume, *Italian Opera in Late Eighteenth-Century London* (Oxford: Clarendon Press, 1995). Linda Kelly's *Susanna, the Captain, and the Castrato: Scenes from the Burney Salon, 1779–1780* (London: Starhaven, 2004) is semi-fictionalized.

36. I do not take up two other marriages here: that of a hapless "castratino" whom Duke Guglielmo Gonzaga tried to recruit in 1586 without success because the former was being prosecuted for having married, as was his parish priest, on which see Richard Sherr, "Guglielmo Gonzaga and the Castrati," *Renaissance Quarterly* 33, no. 1 (1980): 33–56, at 55–56; and that of Alessandro Moreschi (1858–1922), whose marriage is dealt with in Martha Feldman with Martina Piperno, "Moreschi and Fellini: Delineating the Vernacular Castrato in Post-Unification Italy," *voiceXchange* 5, no. 1 (2011): 1–34. Too little is known about the former, and the latter falls in a period that is historically too different to be usefully treated here. The comment supposedly voiced by Susan Burney, that she thought Pacchierotti was suggesting to her that "he wished to marry" as given in Kelly, *Susanna, the Captain, and the Castrato*, 69, does not appear in Susan Burney's letters.

37. See Ernst Ludwig Gerber, *Historisch-biographisches Lexikon der Tonkünstler (1790–1792) und Neues historisch-biographisches Lexikon der Tonkünstler (1812–1814)*, 4 vols., reprint edition, edited by Othmar Wessely (Graz: Akademische Druck- u. Verlagsanstalt, 1966–77), 1: 410; J. F. Schütze, *Hamburgische Theater-Geschichte* (Hamburg: Treder, 1794), 193–207 (passim) and 193 ff; Josef Sittard, *Geschichte des Musik- und Concertwesens in Hamburg vom 14. Jahrhundert bis auf die Gegenwart* (Altona and Leipzig: A. C. Reher, 1890), 75, which includes a brief biographical sketch; and James L. Jackman, "Finazzi, Filippo," *GMO*.

38. Dora Maunsell Tenducci, *A True and Genuine Narrative of Mr. and Mrs. Tenducci, in a Letter to a Friend at Bath, Giving a Full Account, from Their Marriage in Ireland, to the Present Time* (London: Printed for J. Pridden, 1768). A famous oil portrait (30″ × 25″) of Tenducci holding a score was done by Thomas Gainsborough in ca. 1773–75. It was sold by Christie's for €2,193,000 at an auction of the collection of Yves St. Laurent and Pierre Bergé held on February 23–25, 2009. See www.christies.com/LotFinder/lot_details.aspx?intObjectID=5157394.

39. Helen Berry, *The Castrato and His Wife* (Oxford: Oxford University Press, 2011). My thanks to Professor Berry for allowing me to read the book in manuscript before its publication and for lively, informative conversations about it.

40. On the implications of Tenducci's time with the Edinburgh Musical Society, see Andrew Greenwood, "Musical Ideas of Sympathy, Sensibility, and Improvement in the Scottish Enlightenment," PhD diss., University of Chicago, 2012, chapter 4.

41. Berry, *A Castrato and His Wife*, 192 and n. 104. Berry also reports that the *Public Ledger or Daily Register of Commerce* wrote that Tenducci was "inconsolable for the loss of his wife" and "determined, like his vocal predecessor Orpheus, to pursue his Eurydice to the shades below, rather than not recover her" (191)—a bit of journalistic spin given the lack of evidence that Tenducci was trying to recover her. In this period Tenducci famously played Orpheus to great acclaim in a revision of Gluck's *Orfeo ed Euridice* (Florence, 1771), as Tenducci himself asserted in his preface to the pasticcio on Gluck's *Orpheus and Eurydice, a Musical Drama, in Imitation of the Ancient Greek Theatrical Feasts, as Performed at the King's Theatre in the Haymarket* (London: J. Jarvis, 1785).

42. A collection of documents from the annulment trial is included in *Trials for Adultery, or, The History of Divorces: Being Select Trials at Doctors Commons, for Adultery, Fornication, Cruelty, Impotence, &c. from the Year 1760, to the Present Time, Including the Whole of the Evidence on Each Cause: Together with the Letters &c. That Have Been Intercepted between the Amorous Parties* (London: Printed for S. Bladon, 1779–81), vol. 6, "Dorothea Kingsman against Ferdinando Tenducci. Libel given October, 1775," pp. 1–50; reprint ed. [Buffalo, NY]: William S. Hein & Co., [2007]; electronic resource at www.heinonline.org. I am grateful to Berry for the reference. One should heed her warning, however, that the collection in *Trials for Adultery* was cleaned up for the 1779–81 publication; some documents are changed from their original manuscript forms, and the collection does not include those depositions given in Florence, which Berry unearthed along with those from the London trial (*A Castrato and His Wife*, 284–85). The trial played the impotency card strongly (*Trials for Adultery*, 5). On p. 1 Tenducci is said to have been castrated at age nine; on p. 7 a man's deposition claims that he heard Tenducci say he was castrated at age seven or eight. Either, if true, would have made him particularly impotent (cf. chapter 1), but other evidence suggests the age was closer to eleven. According to Dorothea's father, she requested passage home from Naples in a letter of apology sent in early 1773 (32–33). Various depositions also refer to the fact of Tenducci being a eunuch for public singing and for hire. All such remarks were driven by the court's efforts to prove that Tenducci was sterile.

43. Quoted in Berry, *A Castrato and His Wife*, 219 (translation lightly adapted).

44. Mary E. Frandsen, "Eunuchi conjugium: The Marriage of a Castrato in Early Modern Germany," *Early Music History: Studies in Medieval and Early Modern Music* 24 (2005): 53–124.

45. "Biographische Notizen ausgezeichnetster italienischer Gesangleherer der neuern und neuesten Zeit nach Originalquellen mitgetheilt und gelegentlich mit Anmerkungen begleitet com Mailänder Correspondenten," *Allgemeine musikalische Zeitung* 38 (September 20, 1837), cols. 613–17 [at 616]).

46. Quoted from Frandsen, "Eunuchi conjugium," 67.

47. Ibid.

48. In a story that is surely apocryphal, Giambattista Velluti's mother allegedly exclaimed regarding the birth of a son instead of a daughter that her husband dreamed of making their son a "valiant captain," declaring (in a pun on his name), "This will be the first iron velvet!" ("Sarà questo il primo Velluto di ferro!"); from the anecdotal Cornelio Parolari, "Giambattista Velluti, ultimo dei sopranisti sulle liriche scene," *Rivista musicale italiana* 39 (1932): 263–98, at 274.

49. See "sex reassignment surgery" on the medical site www.uptodate.com.

50. Wilbourne would call this being seen as queer ("The Queer History of the Castrato," in *Oxford Handbook on Queerness and Music*).

51. Frandsen notes that instead of mentioning the papal brief "Cum frequenter" (a nasty, invective piece of prose), Sorlisi invoked true love, affection, intimacy, and mutual aid to argue for the marriage on grounds of "divine and natural law." This is consistent with emergent notions of bourgeois love that were already in the air and were certainly the stuff of the new commercial opera.

52. Wendy Doniger, *The Woman Who Pretended to Be Who She Was: Myths of Self-Imitation* (New York: Oxford University Press, 2005).

53. Frandsen, "Eunuchi conjugium," 82. Cf. also Angus McLaren, *Impotence: A Cultural History* (Chicago: University of Chicago Press, 2007), chapter 2, esp. 32.

54. RUS-Mrg, MS F. 218, no. 1247 (1–9), vol. 1, p. 15 (librarian's pagination).

55. Pierfrancesco Tosi, *Opinioni de' cantori antichi e moderni* (Bologna: Lelio dalla Volpe, 1723); reprint ed., Monuments of Music and Music Literature in Facsimile, 2nd series, Music Literature, no. 133 (New York: Broude Brothers, 1968).

56. "La voce fu trovata d'un buonissimo metallo, il trillo naturale e ben battuto, agilità ben grande nei passaggi, e gusto naturale nel cantare, onde che di più potea bramarsi per farne un buon cantore! Tutte le dette cose cominciorno a sollecitare gl'mmici di mio padre a dirgli *taglia, taglia* (et il maestro poi più di tutti di essi) a consigliarlo onde doppo le molte *taglia, taglia* disse anch'egli; e spedito a Lucca per il Cerusico Accoramboni, il fè venire in Casa, per restare per due mesi a tenermi un pochetto di gratissima conversazzione." Balatri, "Vita e viaggi" (1725), 1: 14–15.

57. "Fu sì cara quella Conversazzioncina, che invece della Laurea Dottorale (ch'avrei possuto un dì ottonere) mi diè la Patente di passar per un de *frigidis et maleficiatis,* per tutt'il restante della vita mia, rinunziando per sempre al dolce nome che m'avrei sentito dar un giorno di Signor Padre." Ibid., 1: 15.

58. "Non voglio musica, ma una messa in cantofermo; e cantata con divozzione da numero quattro sacerdoti."

> Per esser io stato musico di qualche poca di distinzione, forse misi verrà a far un frastuno di voci e strumenti come se fosse un sposalizzio, e che non serve ch'a dire, andiamo a sentire l'esequie del tale; caspita saranno belle, poiché vi è tutta la musica della città; et intanto che io, racchiuso in quella cassa, scaldato dai lumi e dal concorso, comincio a puzzare come una carogna, vadino i musici stendendo passaggi e trilli con cadenze di mezz'ora, e l'uditorio ascoltando et applaudendo, senza forse dirmi alcun di loro Riposa in Pace. (Balatri, "Testamento," fols. 20–20v)

59. Not much has been written about Lotti's sacred music, but see David Carter Madock, "A Study of the *Stile Antico* in the Masses and Motets of Antonio Lotti as Contained in the Codice Marciano Italiano IV, Venice," PhD diss., Catholic University of America, 1996. On the various settings of the requiem masses by Johann Adophe Hasse, see Walther Müller, *Johann Adolphe Hasse als Kirchenkomponist: Ein Beitrag zur Geschichte der neapolitanischen Kirchenmusik mit thematischen Katalog der liturgischen Kirchenmusik J. A. Hasses*, Publikationen der Internationalen Musikgesellschaft, Beihefte, series 2, vol. 9 (Leipzig: Breitkopf & Härtel, 1911), 79–104; Hans Joachim Marx, Wiebke Holberg, and Roland Dieter Schmidt-Hensel, *Die Hasse-Handschriften der Staats- und Universitätsbibliothek Hamburg: Katalog anlässlich des 300. Geburtstages von Johann Adolf Hasse (1699–1783)* (Hamburg, forthcoming); and the electronic Hasse catalog of the Universität Hamburg Staats- und Universitätsbibliothek at www.sub.uni-hamburg.de/bibliotheken/sammlungen/sondersammlungen/musiksammlung/hasse-katalog.html, where two complete requiems by Hasse are housed.

60. For context relevant to the genre in which Tosi wrote his treatise, however, see Sergio Durante, "Strutture mentali e vocabolario di un cantore antico/moderno: Preliminari per una lettura delle fonti didattiche settecentesche," in *Alessandro Scarlatti und seine Zeit*, edited by Max Lütolf (Bern: Haupt, 1995), 38–54, who argues that his impetus was not merely conservative, as is generally thought, but that he was a rationalist and that his intervention by means of a published singing treatise actually marks him as a transgressor of unspoken codes against revealing something equivalent to the secrets of an artistic guild—hence that he was at least as much a *moderno* as an *antico*. See also Durante, "Condizioni materiali," and Durante, "Theorie und Praxis der Gesangsschulen zur Zeit Händels: Bemerkungen zu Tosis 'Opinioni de' cantori antichi e moderni,'" in *Händel auf dem Theater: Bericht über die Symposien der Internationalen Händel-Akademie, Karlsruhe, 1986 und 1987*, edited by Hans Joachim Marx (Laaber: Laaber, 1988), 59–72.

61. Attribution of the remark to Pistocchi comes from Francesco Algarotti, *Saggio sopra l'opera in musica* (Livorno: Marco Coltellini, 1763): "Tristo a me io t'ho insegnato a cantare, e tu vuoi suonare, rimproverava Pistocco a Bernacchi, che si può tenere come il caposcuola, il Marini della moderna licenza" (46). A variant appears in the anonymous 1755 version of Algarotti's essay published by G. Pasquali in Venice, where the two parties are unnamed (p. 19). See Francesco Algarotti, *Saggio sopra l'opera in musica: Le edizioni del 1755 e del 1763*, edited by Annalisa Bini (Lucca: Libreria Musicale Italiana, 1989), translated into English as *An Essay on the Opera Written in Italian by Count Algarotti* (London, 1767), 57, and cf. Ludovico Frati, "Antonio Bernacchi e la sua scuola di canto," *Rivista musicale italiana* 29 (1922): 473–91. Charles Burney, in *A General History of Music, from the Earliest Ages to the Present Period*, 4 vols. (London, 1776–89), 4: 54–57, 114, and 164, counts Pistocchi as one of the five greatest male singers of the seventeenth century (4: 80), and Tosi, who was his pupil, held him up as the best singer of all time.

62. The full title of the libretto is *Semiramide in Ascalona. Dramma per musica da rappresentarsi nel giardino dell'imperial favorita festeggiandosi il felicissimo giorno natalizio della sac. ces. e catt. real maestà di Elisabetta Cristina imperadrice regnante per comando della sac. ces. e catt. real maestà di Carlo 6. imperadore de' romani, sempre augusto l'anno 1725. La poesia è del sig. Apostolo Zeno . . . . La musica è del sig. Antonio Caldara* ([Vienna]: Gio. Pietro v. Ghelen, Stampatore di Corte di S.M.C. e C., [1725]) (digital copy at the

Biblioteca Nazionale Braidense, Milan). Faustina had performed at the court of Munich in 1723. I am grateful to Maria Di Salvo for leading me to this information. The libretto is not in Claudio Sartori, *I libretti italiani a stampa dalle origini al 1800: Catalogo analitico con 16 indici* (Cuneo: Bertola & Locatelli, 1990).

63. Vincenzio Martinelli and Francesco Algarotti both accused Bernacchi, in a mid-eighteenth-century reformist spirit, of "sacrificing expression to execution and singing in adopting an instrumental style." Martinelli's remarks, in his *Lettere familiari e critiche* (London, 1758), 358–561, are particularly back-biting, as if Bernacchi were to blame for a whole generation of mechanical virtuosi who arose in his wake. (Cf. Anne Schnoebelen, "Bernacchi, Antonio," *GMO*.)

That Balatri himself was a coloratura is evident from both his writings and from surviving scores of the operas in which he sang, though his coloratura passages exhibit none of the virtuosity of singers like Bernacchi and Farinelli. All those for Munich are preserved in G-Mbs. In the spring of 1714 Balatri sang the part of Romualdo opposite Anastasia Robinson in the pasticcio *Ernelinda* (London, Haymarket, 1713); Burney, *A General History of Music* 4: 250.

64. Cristina Pampaloni, "Giovani castrati nell'Assisi del Settecento," *Musica/Realtà* 8 (1987): 133–53.

65. Padre Martini's letters have recently become available online at the site of the Museo Internazionale e Biblioteca della Musica di Bologna, http://badigit.comune.bologna.it/cmbm/scripts/lettere/search.asp, where they are now searchable. They are cataloged in Anne Schnoebelen, *Padre Martini's Collection of Letters in the Civico Museo Bibliografico Musicale in Bologna: An Annotated Index* (New York: Pendragon, 1979).

66. The first of these was written on September 27, 1752, by Teresa Bolognini Fontana to introduce a youth named Giacomo Calcina, asking Padre Martini to recommend him to Giovanardi and saying he had previously studied in Bologna with Mazzoni, to whom he did not want to go back; she asks the padre to listen to him and keep an eye out for him (Schnoebelen no. 769). The letter from Rossi (Schnoebelen no. 4483) makes it clear that the aspiring soprano thought Gibelli might accept him into his house since he used to keep Michele Patrazzi there and has asked Rossi to see if Martini would act as intermediary. Schiassi (Schnoebelen no. 4997) says he is giving his letter to a court musician who will be coming to study with Bernacchi. On the importance of acceptance into Bernacchi's household, see Durante, "Condizioni materiali," 2: 177.

67. There is every reason to believe that the intense training routine that was customary in quality circles was more forgiving to the health of the vocal mechanism than is often the case with modern-day practices. Early modern practices emphasized use of a free-floating glottis in all vocal production and prepared the student extensively with exercises and simple melodies before proceeding to work on challenging divisions, leaps, and other such difficulties. No concept of or interest in "pushing" the voice existed, and there were numerous warnings about singing with the voice caught in the throat or the nose. Again, see further in chapter 3.

68. Giovanni Andrea Angelini Bontempi, *Historia musica* (Perugia: Constantini, 1695; facsimile reprint Bologna: Forni, 1971), 170. Mazzocchi had a music school at San Pietro in Rome; see Wolfgang Witzenmann, "Mazzocchi, Virgilio," *GMO*. Like Pacchierotti's nephew and others, Bontempi also recounts regular outdoor excursions to echoing hills or walls to hear the voice in "playback" and thus correct its faults.

69. See Eugenio Faustini-Fasini, "Gli astri maggiori del bel canto napoletano: Gaetano Majorano detto 'Caffarelli'" *Note d'archivio per la storia musicale* 15 (1938): 121–28, 157–70, 258–70. According to Edmond Michotte, the renowned contralto Marietta Alboni (1826–1894) said virtually the same thing in 1858, seconding Rossini's description of his inculcation as a singer: "For three years, my teacher kept me at a single page, which I still have, and which includes by itself all the types of scholastic exercises for holding, agility, etc." (113).

70. The quotes come from two places in the chapter entitled "Osservazioni per chi studia" of Tosi's *Opinioni de' cantori antichi, e moderni*. The first reads, "Chi non aspira ad occupare il primo luogo già comincia a cedere il secondo, e a poco a poco si contenta dell' ultimo" (p. 56); the second, "Studiare, e poi studiare, e non compiacersi per poco" (p. 54).

71. On Bennati and Consoni, see Durante, "Condizioni materiali." Beth L. Glixon treats the prestige and salaries of female singers in mid-seventeenth-century Venice relative to castrati in "Private Lives of Public Women: Prima Donnas in Mid-Seventeenth-Century Venice," *Music & Letters* 76 (1995): 509–31. Further such evidence appears in Beth L. Glixon and Jonathan Glixon, *Inventing the Business of Opera: The Impresario and His World in Seventeenth-Century Venice*, AMS Studies in Music (New York: Oxford University Press, 2006), passim.

72. The Congregazione della Beata Vergine and the San Carlo.

73. Erculeo is an excellent example of the type. Born in Otricoli near Terni in 1623, he spent his whole life as a writer, teacher, composer, and singer, all in church. Among the high points of his career was studying music at the Collegio Germanico in Rome. In 1638, at age fifteen, he sang as a soprano—most probably already castrato—in the court chapel of Duke Francesco I d'Este at Modena, where he continued to serve as a singer until the chapel was disbanded in 1662. He also wrote the text of an oratorio, *Il battesimo di San Valeriano martire*, for the Feast of Saint Cecilia (possibly in 1665). According to Argia Bertini and J. Victor Crowther, "Erculeo [Ercoleo, Erculei], Marzio," *GMO*, once the Modenese chapel was dissolved he petitioned the regent duchess to be reinstated at court as a "musico ecclesiastico di SAS," which she did, though on a much-reduced stipend. Erculeo fell from favor at court in 1674 with the accession of Duke Francesco II, after which he spent his remaining life teaching singing to seminarians at the schools of the Congregazione della Beata Vergine and the San Carlo, where the (later) renowned composer Antonio Maria Pacchioni was one of his pupils. In the 1680s he wrote three books, all attributable to his work as a singing teacher and performer of Gregorian chant and each of which he published in Modena: *Primi elementi di musica* (1683), *Il canto ecclesiastico* (1686), and *Cantus omnis ecclesiasticus* (1688).

74. Usually mothers' brothers filled in for deceased or otherwise absent fathers. We are again indebted to John Rosselli, whose research greatly widened the scope of our understanding here. See in particular his "L'apprendistato del cantante italiano: Rapporti contrattuali fra allievi e insegnanti dal Cinquecento al Novecento," *Rivista italiana di musicologia* 23 (1988): 157–81, and *Singers of Italian Opera: The History of a Profession* (Cambridge: Cambridge University Press, 1992), chapter 2 and passim. Within institutional contexts, the institution in question (e.g., conservatory, cathedral school, court chapel) filled the paternal function.

75. *Émile* was first published in The Hague in 1762 by Jean Néaulme but was banned in Paris and Geneva because of a section that tied faith to reason rather than rule. The point

about the lack of a developmental model at the time was stressed by Ian Hacking in his graduate seminar "Making Up People," given at the University of Chicago in the spring of 2007.

76. Rosselli, *Singers of Italian Opera*, 37–39.

77. Salvatore Di Giacomo, *Il conservatorio di Sant'Onofrio a Capuana e quello di S.M. della Pietà dei Turchini* (Milan: Remo Sandron, 1924).

78. Rosselli, *Singers of Italian Opera*, 42 and passim, who points out that in baroque Rome performing opera and oratorio was more continuous with church work than it was in, say, the commercial and mercantile environment of eighteenth-century Venice.

79. According to Rosselli, clerical castrati at first did not want opera jobs because of this (*Singers of Italian Opera*, 43).

80. Though a soprano, Cavalletti was capable of singing alto parts. In 1720, late in his career, he joined the imperial chapel in Vienna as a tenor. When pensioned in 1723 he returned to Rome. Penna, in the "Catalogo degli aggregati della Accademia Filarmonica di Bologna," which is ascribed to Padre Martini (reprint ed. as Giambattista Martini, *Catalogo degli aggregati della Accademia Filarmonica di Bologna*, Pubblicazioni dell'Accademia filarmonica di Bologna, Monumenti, 1 [Bologna, 1973]), calls him "one of the most famous singers of his time in church and theater" (item no. 273). Cf. Carlo Vitali with Juliane Riepe, "Cavalletti, Giulio Maria [Giulietto]," *GMO*.

81. Melani was in the service of Prince Mattias de' Medici from 1641, at age fifteen. The prince sent him to Rome and Paris, from which he had substantial difficulties retrieving him. Siface was in the service of Francesco II d'Este, Duke of Modena, from 1679 until his death in 1697, but he traveled widely during those years to Venice, Rome, Paris, London, Naples, and Florence, among other places.

82. Before 1679, when Filippo Vismarri (1635–1706?) fled the plague in Vienna, he must have taken holy orders, since from 1679 onward he is always referred to with the title "Don." It was prior to that, in 1660, that he had sung at court in Leopold I's *Il sagrificio d'Abramo* and in his own *Orontea* and in the 1660s that he acted as a sometime political agent for Count Humbert Cernín of Neuhaus; see Filippo Vismarri et al., *Cantatas*, edited by Lawrence Bennett, The Italian Cantata in the Seventeenth Century, vol. 16 (New York: Garland, 1985); and William C. Holmes, "Yet Another Orontea: Further Rapport between Venice and Vienna," *Venezia e il melodramma nel Seicento*, edited by Maria Teresa Muraro (Florence: Olschki, 1976), 199–225.

83. See Glixon and Glixon, *Inventing the Business of Opera*, 195n; and Freitas, *Portrait of a Castrato*, 293–96. Filippo Melani was one of four sons whom their father, Domenico Melani, a bell ringer at Pistoia, had castrated (see Freitas, *Portrait of a Castrato*, 24–32, on why this was probably so, and 21 for a genealogy of the family.

84. Dreyer (ca. 1703–72), a composer and impresario as well as a singer, sang in Wrocław (at that time Breslau), Prague, Moscow, St. Petersburg, Dresden, and Vienna before returning to Italy and joining the order of the Servants of Mary in Florence in 1737. He became a novice in 1738 and by early 1739 was maestro di cappella for the order in their church of SS Annunziata. See John Walter Hill, "Dreyer, Giovanni Filippo Maria ['Il Tedeschino']," *GMO*. The Bologna contralto Giovanni Battista Minelli—the original Demetrio in Metastasio's first opera for Vienna (set by Caldara)—was said to have become a monk after retirement, around 1736 (Dennis Libby, "Minelli, Giovanni Battista," *GMO*). See also Rosselli, *Singers of Italian*

Opera, 35–36. Burney described Egizziello's midcareer retreat to a monastery as prompted by catastrophe: "He was one of a constellation of great singers which the King of Portugal had assembled together in 1755. And narrowly escaping with his life during the earthquake which happened at Lisbon that year he was impressed with such a religious turn by the tremendous calamity, that he retreated to a monastery, where he ended his days." Charles Burney, *A General History of Music* 4: 395. Others speculated that his retreat was because of ill health.

85. See Gabriella Biagi Ravenni, "'Molti in Lucca si applicavano alla professione della musica': Storie di formazione e di emigrazione nella patria di Luigi Boccherini," *Chigiana: Rassegna annuale di studi musicologici* 43 (1993): 69–109; and Winton Dean, "Andreoni, Giovanni Battista," *GMO*. Andrea Pacini, called il Lucchesino (ca. 1690–1764), evidently became a priest later in life and often took part in the annual celebration of San Croce in Lucca (Winton Dean, "Pacini, Andrea ['Il Lucchesini']," *GMO*). On Pellegrini see Winton Dean and John Rosselli, "Pellegrini, Valeriano," *GMO*.

86. Some nineteenth-century papal castrati were priests as well. See Leopold M. Kantner and Angela Pachovsky, *La cappella musicale pontificia nell'Ottocento,* Storia di cappella musicale pontificia, vol. 6 (Rome: Hortus Musicus, 1998), on the soprano Don Mariano Padroni (1774–1847), called the "Gran Professore" of the Cappella Sistina (pp. 171–72), and Don Evangelista Rocchini (1827–61) (p. 181). The papal soprano Don Giovanni Battista Uccelli (1740–1825) was also a priest, but whether he was a castrato is unclear (p. 188).

87. Cf. Carlo Vitali in Carlo Broschi Farinelli, *La solitudine amica: Lettere al conte Sicinio Pepoli,* edited by Carlo Vitali with Roberto Pagano and Francesca Boris (Palermo: Sellerio, 2000), 49–55, who argues similarly, particularly for father-son relations, and Vitali, "Da 'schiavottiello' a 'fedele amico': Lettere (1731–1749) di Carlo Broschi Farinelli al conte Sicinio Pepoli," *Rivista musicale italiana* 26 (1992): 1–36.

88. "Vita e viaggi," 1: 20, 1: 24–30, and 3: 62v; and see Di Salvo, "*Vita e viaggi* di Filippo Balatri," 42 and passim.

89. The pattern is described in crystallized form in "Frutti del Mondo," where Balatri glosses the contractual negotiations: "My father is a man of the pen, and is protected/by his sovereign.... / I was already made into a mixed gender, / that is a soprano, and was quite young. / I apply myself to singing in the most human style, / doing so with industry and a good vocation. / My patron sets his eyes on me / and thinks about putting me in the hands of the said prince. / So he has him listen to me and then says that if all the czar wants is to hear the singing/ of Italian castrati, / one of them will satisfy him as well as two" ("Mio padre è un uom' di penna, ed è protetto/dal suo sovran, gradito, e assai benvisto; / Io reso son di già del gener misto, / idest soprano, e sono giovinetto, / M'applico al canto per il stil piu umano, / il fò con studio e buona vocazzione. / Pon gl'occhi sovr'amme il mio padrone, / e pensa darmi al detto prence in mano; / Onde fa ch' li m'ascolti, e dice poi, / s'il zar non brama che d'udire il canto / dei musici d'Italia, tantettanto / può satisfarsi in uno come in doi"; "Frutti del mondo," 1: 9v).

90. "Vita e viaggi," 3: 147v–49r; cf. Daniel L. Schlafly Jr., "A Muscovite Boiaryarina Faces Peter the Great's Reforms: Dar'ia Golitsyna between Two Worlds," *Canadian-American Slavic Studies* 31 (1997): 249–68. Only the *boyarina* (princess), and not the other women, knew that Balatri was a castrato.

91. Alessandro Martoni of the Istituto di Storia dell'Arte, Fondazione Giorgio Cini, informs me that the institute is currently completing a new catalog of Zanetti's whole album (private correspondence, August 6, 2012).

92. The story is told by William C. Holmes, *Opera Observed: Views of a Florentine Impresario in the Early Eighteenth Century* (Chicago: University of Chicago Press, 1993), 114–16, who assembled the relevant archival evidence. I modify slightly Holmes's translations. The leading ladies mentioned include Faustina Bordoni, Vittoria Tesi, and Diana Vico.

93. On the vicissitudes of Berenstadt's career and his major sideline in the book trade, see Lowell E. Lindgren, "La carriera di Gaetano Berenstadt, contralto evirato (ca. 1690–1735)," *Rivista italiana di musicologia* 19 (1984): 36–112; and Maria Augusta Morelli Timpanaro, "Su Gaetano Berenstadt, contralto (Firenze, 1687–1734), e i suoi amici," *Studi italiani* 9 (1997): 147–211. On Berenstadt as book dealer and even publisher, see pp. 175, 182, and passim.

94. For Vismarri, see Lawrence E. Bennett, "Vismarri [Vismari], Filippo," *GMO*. On Aprile's tenure at Stuttgart, see Joseph Sittard, *Zur geschichte der Musik und des Theaters am Württembergischen Hofe, nach Originalquellen*, 2 vols. in 1 (Stuttgart: W. Kohlhammer, 1890–91), 53 (on Schubart's very high opinion of him), 73, 99, 103, 113–14, 118, 179, and 194. Balatri talks about his brother throughout his autobiographies; cf. Di Salvo, "*Vita e viaggi* di Filippo Balatri (preliminary all'edizione del testo)," *Russica romana* 6 (1999): 37–57, as well as her critical edition of the manuscript, forthcoming, and idem, "The 'Italian' Nemetskaia Sloboda," in *Personality and Place in Russian Culture: Essays in Memory of Lindsey Hughes*, edited by Simon Dixon (London: Modern Humanities Research Association for the UCL School of Slavonic and East European Studies, 2010), 96–109.

The 1764 performance of *La buona figliuola* with Guadagni and his sisters took place at the Teatro Privilegiato (Sartori, *I libretti italiani*, 1: 442).

95. Similar urges may have been even stronger in the previous century. A network in Pistoia, while unusually thick, could be typical: Antonio Rivani trained at Pistoia under castrato Felice Cancellieri (1603–48) along with several Melani brothers. Antonio's brother Giulio Rivani, also a castrato and priest, sang with him at the cathedral, as did various Melani; and Antonio was cast in Jacopo Melani's *La vedova, ossia, Amor vuol inganno* (composed 1662, first performed 1680; libretto by Giovanni Andrea Moniglia) with his sister-in-law and yet another Rivani, possibly a nephew. See Freitas, *Portrait of a Castrato*, 30–31 and passim.

96. Freitas, *Portrait of a Castrato*, 290–301.

97. It was no more usual for a castrato than any other Italian to move from one town to another. Most returned home at the end of their careers, no matter how small and remote the town or how long the career, though there were decidedly exceptions.

98. As Daniel Heartz points out, Metastasio (depicted at back left) looks detached here because he was painted in from a reference portrait, which Farinelli coaxed from him with difficulty; "Farinelli and Metastasio: Rival Twins of Public Favour," *Early Music* 12 (1984): 358–66, at 361. On 359–60 Heartz details Farinelli's request for the portrait of his "caro gemello." It arrived with Metastasio's response only in 1749 (359–60). Heartz writes, "Metastasio's reluctance to have his portrait painted reflects an innate reticence and caution that is quite the opposite of the extroversion of Farinelli, who sat, one suspects gladly, for several of the greatest painters of the time" (359). On the group portrait he writes, "Flanking her is the Abbate Metastasio in clerical garb, his right hand bearing a quill and resting on a laurel wreath, under which the artist has placed a bas-relief on some heroic subject; this likeness

must have been painted after the lost portrait that arrived in Madrid from Vienna in 1749" (361).

99. Heartz, "Farinelli and Metastasio."

100. Che fa la bella Castellini? È poi vero che le sieno sì cari i miei saluti? che voglia onorarmi de' suoi desiderabili caratteri? Ah, se mi amate, non permettete che sia messa a così gran cimento la mia amicizia. Dopo le lubriche descrizioni che voi mi avete fatte di così amabile persona, la violenta tentazione d'una sua lettera potrebbe precipitarmi sino a farvi qualche infedeltà mentale, e ne sarei poi inconsolabile. Ditele per altro che, come gemello, io non posso non risentire almen di ribalzo tutti i moti del vostro cuore: che, quando ascolto il suo nome, mi si mette addosso un certo formicolio che non lascia d'incomodarmi e pure non desidero che finisca: che, se il Manzanare non fosse così distante dal Danubio, io sarei venuto a vedere s'ella riceverebbe me a braccia aperte come fa i miei saluti: e ditele ... [ellipses in original] Signor no. Non le dite nulla. La strada è troppo sdrucciolevole: è più facile non entrarvi che camminarvi senza cadere. (September 6, 1749, Pietro Metastasio, *Tutte le opere*, 5 vols., edited by Bruno Brunelli [Milan: Mondadori, 1943-54)], 3: 424-25, letter no. 325)

Burney translates the passage, "Tell her however that as a twin, I can only receive the emotions of your heart at the rebound; that when I hear your name, I feel a certain tingling sensation that incommodes me, and yet I have no wish that it be discontinued"; Charles Burney, *Memoirs of the Life and Writings of the Abate Metastasio, in Which Are Incorporated Translations of His Principal Letters*, 3 vols. (London, 1796), 1: 289. But Metastasio consistently uses second-person plural pronouns for Farinelli and third-person singular pronouns for Castellini. His meaning is "when I hear *her* name" (italics mine), an extension of the ironic scenario already in progress.

101. September 15, 1750 (letter no. 409), Metastasio, *Tutte le opere*, 3: 565. Cf. jokes from England that Farinelli was pregnant (Fielding called him "Faribelly). A good account of women's attraction to various castrati in London and the threats it caused to a binary sexual regime is given in Berry, *The Castrato and His Wife*, chapter 4, "Fancying Tenducci."

102. "Ho già circonciso il primo atto dell'Alessandro: oh che macello! Nel ho tagliato 266 versi e tre arie. Caro gemello, questo mestiere ingratissimo non si fa che per voi. Il farsi eunuco di propria mano è sacrifizio che ha pochi esempi"; letter no. 706 of December 15, 1753, Metastasio, *Tutte le opere*, 3: 878.

103. "The women who are a section of the woman do not care for men, but have female attachments; the female companions are of this sort. But they who are a section of the male follow the male, and while they are young, being slices of the original man, they have affection for men and embrace them."

104. Cited from *The Symposium and the Phaedrus: Plato's Erotic Dialogues*, translated with introduction and commentaries by William S. Cobb (Albany: State University of New York Press, 1993). I am indebted to Hedy Law for suggesting that I consider this passage in connection with Metastasio's glosses on twinning.

105. Cf. Franco Venturi, "Cesare Beccaria and Legal Reform," in Venturi, *Italy and the Enlightenment: Studies in a Cosmopolitan Century*, edited by Stuart Woolf and translated by Susan Corsi (London: Longman, 1972), 154-64, at 155.

106. James Davidson, "Mr. and Mr. and Mrs. and Mrs.," *London Review of Books*, June 2, 2005.

107. Guido Ruggiero, *Machiavelli in Love: Sex, Self, and Society in the Italian Renaissance* (Baltimore, MD: Johns Hopkins University Press, 2007). See also Ruggiero, *The Boundaries of Eros: Sex Crime and Sexuality in Renaissance Venice* (New York: Oxford University Press, 1985), and Ruggiero, *Binding Passions: Tales of Magic, Marriage, and Power from the End of the Renaissance* (New York: Oxford University Press, 1993). On similar issues concerning same-sex relations elsewhere in early modern Europe, see Alan Bray, *Homosexuality in Renaissance England* (London: Gay Men's Press, 1982) (also available electronically in a later edition from New York: Columbia University Press, 1995, with a new afterword by the author); Bray, *The Friend* (Chicago: University of Chicago Press, 2003); Philip Carter, *Men and the Emergence of Polite Society, 1660–1800* (Harlow: Longman, 2001); Jeffrey Merrick and Bryant T. Ragan Jr., eds., *Homosexuality in Early Modern France: A Documentary Collection* (New York: Oxford University Press, 2001); Kenneth Borris and George Rousseau, eds., *The Sciences of Homosexuality in Early Modern Europe* (London: Routledge, 2008); and indispensably James Davidson, *The Greeks and Greek Love: A Radical Reappraisal of Homosexuality in Ancient Greece* (London: Weidenfeld & Nicolson, 2007), published in the United States as *The Greeks and Greek Love: A Bold New Exploration of the Ancient World* (New York: Random House, 2007).

108. Farinelli, *La solitudine amica*, 124. Here I set the passage up in verse lines to underscore its poetic nature, though of course Farinelli cast it in prose.

109. Needless to say, Doniger's nuanced analysis draws attention to other elements too, in particular the significance of loyalty as signified through the twin brother's placing of a double-edged sword between himself and his brother's wife; *The Woman Who Pretended to Be Who She Was*, 61–62.

110. *La solitudine amica*, letter 55 (September 8, 1740), pp. 163–64 (italics mine).

> Vorrei che la robba mia potesse goderla persona che lo merita. L'ambizione da me sta molto lontana, né vanità trasporta il mio dovere. Vorrei trovare una signora né che sia esposta alle stelle, né tampoco alle valli. Potrebbe Vostra Eccellenza col suo bel cuore e vera amicizia trovarne cosa a proposito; sopra tutto, che ci sia ancora qualche epulenza. Mio fratello presentemente gode un buon officio, datogli dalla benignità del Re di Napoli, che ci rende sotto mille ducati l'anno, avendo esercitato questo impiego un Cavallier di molta stima prima che cadesse a mio fratello. La mia sorella sia maritata con un altro galant'uomo, che ora esercita la carica di percettore nella provincia di Salerno, che gli dà 2000 docati l'anno: veda Vostra Eccellenza quando ha fatto il mio core per i miei parenti. Io non dico esser nato dalla terza costa di Venere, né tampoco aver per padre Nettuno. Son napolitano; il Duca d'Andria mi tenne al fonte, questo basta per dar saggio d'esser un figlio di buon cittadino e galantuomo. Mi pare che io fin al presente d'aver prodotto molto onore a me stesso, alla mia patria, alla mia famiglia, ed alla mia professione. Spererei a tale riflessioni che nessuna buona figlia dovrebbe sputare a questo incontro: . . . Io non posso (come sa) maritarmi, dunque devo penzare al mio sangue e cercare una donna che possa meritare tutto quello che Iddio mi ha dato.

111. The suggestion was made to me by James Davidson, who thought Farinelli might coyly be referring to himself as a modern Theseus, the Athenian founding hero. Farinelli in fact played Theseus in Riccardo Broschi's *Arianna e Teseo* at Milan's Regio Ducal Teatro in August 1731. The inventory of his house in Bologna lists a copy of Giovanni Battista Mele's opera *Arianna e Teseo* (Cappelletto, *La voce perduta*, 213, no. 77). Mele was a Neapolitan composer active in Madrid from 1735 to 1752 from whom Farinelli himself commissioned stage works for the court; see Hanns-Bertold Dietz, "Mele [Melle], Giovanni Battista [Juan Bautista]," *GMO*. He also had scores of settings of the same by the Neapolitan composer Giuseppe Di Maio (Cappelletto, *La voce perduta*, 213, no. 89) and the Bolognese Antonio Mazzoni (ibid., 215, no. 205).

112. The chosen nephew was the second born, as the first had died.

113. "Questa [inserted: nuova dimostrazione, che presenta il mio affetto] tutta spontanea della mia sola volontà," etc.; I-Bas, Notarile, Lorenzo Gambarini, 22 Genn. 1769-23 Dic. 1770, no. 20, letter to Anna Gatteschi, dated September 12, 1769.

114. On Aprile as student see Joseph Vella Bondin, "Who was Girolamo Abos?," *Sunday Times* (Malta), March 17, 1996, and as teacher see Sylvie Mamy, "Tradizione pedagogica del canto a Napoli: Giuseppe Aprile," in *Musicisti nati in Puglia ed emigrazione musicale tra Seicento e Settecento: Atti del Convegno Internazionale di Studi, Lecce, 6-8 dicembre 1985*, edited by Detty Bozzi e Luisa Cosi (Rome: Edizioni Torre d'Orfeo, 1988), 281-311. The most extensive anecdotes are related by the Irish tenor Michael Kelly, in *Reminiscences . . . of the King's Theatre and Theatre Royal Drury Lane* (New York: Da Capo Press, 1968); on Caffarelli retiring to Calabria, 60-61; on Aprile as Kelly's teacher, 73-93: "I was overwhelmed with melancholy at leaving my kind, liberal, and great master. He was a man of the most honourable and independent mind I have ever met, and considered an excellent scholar. He took great pains to explain Metastasio, and other Italian poets to me, and particularly inculcated a love of truth, and a horror of committing a mean action. I may truly say, with Nicodeme in the French play, 'Le maître qui prit soin de former ma jeunesse, ne m'a jamais appris a faire une bassese'" (92). Mozart wrote of his relationship with Aprile; *Mozart: Briefe und Aufzeichnungen, Gestamtausgabe*, edited by Wilhelm A. Bauer and Otto Erich Deutsch with Ulrich Konrad, Internationalen Stiftung Mozarteum Salzburg (Kassel: Bärenreiter, 1962-2005), 3: 280, line 28 (from Mozart in Vienna to his father in Salzburg on July 12, 1783). And see Anthony Pryer, "Mozart's Operatic Audition. The Milan Concert, 12 March 1770: A Reappraisal and Revision," *Eighteenth-Century Music* 1 (2004): 265-88. On Mustafà see Alberto De Angelis, *Domenico Mustafà: La Cappella Sistina e la società musicale romana* (Bologna: Zanichelli, 1926), 183-86.

115. This is not to mention the many who returned to larger hometowns, e.g., Berenstadt and Giovanni Manzuoli (1720-82) to Florence; Bernacchi to Bologna; Senesino to Siena; Nicolini to Naples; Giovanni Maria Rubinelli (1753-1829) to Brescia; Luigi Marchesi (1755-1829) to Milan; and Cavalletti to Rome. The patterns also highlight the fact that castrati came from all parts of Italy. The least represented regions appear to be Abruzzo, Basilicata, Calabria, Liguria, and Piedmont, but this may be because we have demographic information only for the more successful castrati and limited information thus far in general.

116. His estate included "beni stabili e mobili esistenti tanto nella città e territorio di Terlizzi, mia patria, che in Napoli, ed in qualunque altro luogo, cioè case, casini, e territori di qualunque sorte, capitali di denari impiegati, contanti, gioie, argenti, mobile d'ogni sorta,

ecc., ecc." The will is excerpted in Bellucci La Salandra, "Vito Giuseppe Millico," 214–17, quote on 215.

117. Rosselli, "The Castrati as a Professional Group," 178.

118. The will includes such items as two mattresses, three bedside and seat cushions valued at sixty Bolognese lire, two wigs valued at fifty-five, a portrait (subject unspecified) in a gold frame valued at sixty, a gold watch valued at sixty, and a small amount of money in different currencies, plus fourteen priest's collars valued at 2.2, some additional suits, a sword, four breviaries, and a pair of pistols; I-Bas, Notarile, Ufficio del Registro (notaio Roffeni Gioacchino), 5/11, vol. 29, fols. 151r–153r, inventario e dimissione, August 2, 1732, per Pierfrancesco Tosi. The will was originally located by Rosselli, "The Castrati as a Professional Group," 171, n. 104 who notes that the whole was valued at 892.2 Bolognese lire.

119. Rosselli, "The Castrati as a Professional Group," 177–78.

120. A touching photograph is included in Maria Giovanna Belcastro et al., "Hyperostosis Frontalis Interna (HFI) and Castration: The Case of the Famous Singer Farinelli (1705–1782)," *Journal of Anatomy* 219 (2011): 632–37, at 633 col. 1.

121. The best overall account of Farinelli's will and his relations in old age appears in Cappelletto, *La voce perduta,* 124–43.

122. See the nephew's biography of his uncle: Giuseppe Cecchini Pacchierotti, *Cenni biografici intorno a Gaspare Pacchierotti: Ai cultori ed amatori della musica vocale* (Padova: Seminario, 1844), which Stephen Willier, scholar of Pacchierotti, was kind enough to share with me. His biography of Pacchierotti, nearing completion at this writing, will be a very useful source on the singer.

123. Like Pacchierotti, Nicolini was on excellent terms with his natural relations, making his principal bequests to his much-loved family: his sisters and their husbands and children, male and female, with some special bequests to his brother-in-law, the composer Nicola Fago; see Eugenio Faustini-Fasini, "Gli astri maggiori del 'bel canto' napoletano: Il Cav. Nicola Grimaldi detto 'Nicolini,'" *Note d'archivio per la storia musicale* 12 (1935): 297–316, who reproduces Nicolini's will on 311–14 and much of a postmortem inventory on 314–16, and Stephen Shearon, "Latin Sacred Music and Nicola Fago: The Career and Sources of an Early Eighteenth-Century Neapolitan *Maestro di cappella*," PhD diss., University of North Carolina at Chapel Hill, 1992, 50–66, 72–76. I thank Professor Shearon for his helpful correspondence concerning Nicolini and Fago and for sharing with me his unpublished transcription of the memoirs of Bonifacio Pecorone.

124. Elisabetta Avanzati, "The Unpublished Senesino," in the catalog of the exhibition *Handel and the Castrati: The Story behind the 18th-Century Superstar Singers, 19 March–1 October 2006* (London: Handel House Museum, 2006), 5–9.

125. Balatri, "Vita e viaggi," 2: 96v. I do not share Herr's sense that Balatri's account of his feelings cannot be substantiated by those of any other castrati (*Gesang gegen die "Ordnung der Natur,"* 373).

126. Farinelli was parodied a good bit in London for his "lack." In addition to the satirical epistle and Fielding's *Pasquin,* discussed above, there was another Fielding play, *The Historical Register for the year 1736 [as it is acted at the New Theatre in the Hay-Market],* published in 1737, in which a group of ladies swoons over Farinelli's performance of the previous night and puns on his assets and deficits (p. 11; act 2, scene 1). One lady remarks to the others, "Sure he is the Charmingest Creature," to which another answers, "He's

everything one could wish," and a third quips, "Almost everything one could wish." See Daniel Heartz, "Farinelli Revisited," *Early Music* 18, no. 3 (August 1990): 441. An anonymous engraving published in London in 1737 spoofed Monticelli, who was portrayed surrounded by animals and being fondled by a curious woman who inspects the genitalia beneath his garments. The music he holds open to the viewer bears the text "La colpa mia non è" (It's not my fault), which Xavier Cervantes and Thomas McGeary have shown to be an aria of Monticelli's. They have also shown that the figure portrayed is not Farinelli, as previously thought, but Monticelli; see "From Farinelli to Monticelli: An Opera Satire of 1742 Re-examined," *Burlington Magazine* 141, no. 1154 (May 1999): 287–89.

Sara Goudar jokingly pretends to relate a conversation between Tenducci and his wife on learning she was pregnant, which ends by the castrato stressing that he can't give what he doesn't have: "Cara Consorte, lui-dit le Soprano, questa non me l'aspettavo. Nulladimeno ajouta-t-il, si vede oggi tante cose straordinarie ne' Matrimonj, che si puol vedere anche questa. Tuttavia, ajoute-t-il, se partorirete un maschio, che sia Eunuco, l'adotterò per mio figlio. Elle acoucha d'un mâle qui n'étoit pas Eunuque. Fedelissima Sposa, lui-dit alors le musicien, voi vedete bene, che non è mio, perché non posso dare a un altro quel che io non ho." From Sara Goudar, *Supplement au supplement de la musique et de la danse ou lettres de M.r G. . . . a Milord Pembroke* ([Venice], 1774), 40. The joke suggests that generation can only occur between like kinds. Earlier she writes, "C'est ce même Tenducci qui s'engagea dans l'himen sans en avoir la valeur. Il devint Epoux par l'endroit que les hommes cessent de l'être. Si les Eunuques se marioient, il y auroit un double viude dans la propagation; car outre qu'ils n'auroient point d'enfans, ils empécheroient les femmes d'en voir" (ibid., 39–40).

127. "Circa quanto riguarda il corpo, io non voglio . . . esser lavato e maneggiato da donne, come si costuma nel paese in cui al presente mi trovo, et in caso ch'io morissi; poiché oltre l'indecenza che vi vedo, non vuò che si vadino divertendo in esaminare il come sia fatti i soprani" (Balatri, "Testamento," fol. 16).

128. "Comeche . . . io non ho moglie, figli, parenti, ho un sol amico (e anche s'il vuol essere), pochi conoscenti (tutti di cappello), niun riconoscente, e niun che si curì ch'io viva cent'anni o crepi stasera, così *voluto sposare alcuni che non conosco, e trarne figli, fratelli, parenti, amici, et altri me stessi (conforme è l'obbligo che ne stringe tutti)* e che perciò ho resoluto testare conforme dirò inseguito." Balatri, "Testamento," fols. 14v–15 (emphasis mine in original and translation).

129. A boy described by Freud who is pathologically attached to a totem animal has a fowl as his totemic object. His attachment takes the form of a love/hate relationship, and he is also obsessed with the sexual life of the hens and cocks that live in his midst. See Sigmund Freud, *Totem and Taboo: Some Points of Agreement between the Mental Lives of Savages and Neurotics*, translated by James Strachey (New York: W. W. Norton, 1950), esp. 164–92. An engaging critical history of castration and castration theories is Gary Taylor, *Castration: An Abbreviated History of Western Manhood* (New York: Routledge, 2000).

130. See, for example, Katherine Bergeron, "The Castrato as History," *Cambridge Opera Journal* 8 (1996): 167–84, for its tacit analysis of Freudianism in Corbiau's 1994 film *Farinelli;* and Michel Poizat, *The Angel's Cry: Beyond the Pleasure Principle in Opera*, translated by Arthur Denner (1986; Ithaca, NY: Cornell University Press, 1992), for a nontacit Lacanian view.

131. "Nacque . . . da Salvatore Broscho, e Caterina Barese Napolitani, e della qualità della sua schiatta non plebea, ma nobile, e generosa." Giovanale Sacchi, *Vita del Cavaliere*

Don Carlo Broschi detto Il Farinello, edited by Alessandro Abbate (1784; Naples: Pagano, 1994), 33.

132. "Al taglio nella puerizia per conservare la mollezza della voce, e così venderla a maggior prezzo; ma bensì conservare la vita in un grave pericolo corso per la sua fanciullesca vivacità, saltando sopra un cavallo, onde cadde, e fu anche offeso nella fronte." Ibid., 33.

CHAPTER 3. RED HOT VOICE

1. Roland Barthes, "The Grain of the Voice," in Barthes, *Image—Music—Text,* essays selected and translated by Stephen Heath (New York: Hill & Wang, 1977), chapter 12. Michelle Duncan uses the phrase "outside the realm of textuality" in relation to a "discursive system" in "The Operatic Scandal of the Singing Body: Voice, Presence, Performativity," *Cambridge Opera Journal* 16 (2004): 283–306, at 284, whereas I use it nondiscursively. The term "drastic" was revived by Carolyn Abbate, "Music—Drastic or Gnostic?," *Critical Inquiry* 30 (2004): 505–36, following Vladimir Jankélévitch, *Music and the Ineffable,* translated by Carolyn Abbate (Princeton, NJ: Princeton University Press, 2003). Abbate's essay has generated a number of responses both critical (e.g., Karol Berger, "Musicology According to Don Giovanni, or: Should We Get Drastic?," *Journal of Musicology* 22 [2005]: 290–301) and celebratory and certainly has breathed life into discourse around performance in musicology.

2. Castrati and their contemporaries often referred to voice types. Antonio Rivani (1629–86) said that Atto Melani no longer had a "voce di soprano, né di contralto, né di mezzo soprano" (in Sara Mamone, *Serenissimi fratelli principi impresari: Notizie di spettacolo nei carteggi medicei: Carteggi di Giovan Carlo de' Medici e di Desiderio Montemagni suo segretario, 1628–1664* [Florence: Le lettere, 2003], 347, cited in Roger Freitas, *Portrait of a Castrato: Politics, Patronage, and Music in the Life of Atto Melani* [Cambridge: Cambridge University Press, 2009], 155 n. 26), though we should probably take such designations as indexing traditional cleffings for different ambituses, without presuming much about the mode of vocal production within each ambitus. Some accounts distinguish among voices in ways that implicitly disclaim typologies. Charles Ancillon, in *Eunuchism Display'd,* translated by Robert Samber (London: Printed for E. Curll, 1718), for example, pronounced about the voices of three castrati, "In short, they are above Description, and no one can possibly entertain any Notion of them but those who have had the Pleasure to hear them, for though they were all excellent in their kind, yet neither of them had the least Semblance with each other" (30). Pedagogue and castrato Giambattista Mancini suggested that all students' voices were different. See *Pensieri, e riflessioni prattiche sopra il canto figurato* (Vienna: Ghelen, 1774), 33, 77, 179–80; published in an enlarged edition as *Riflessioni pratiche sul canto figurato* (Milan: Giuseppe Galeazzo, 1777); in English translation as *Practical Reflections on Figured Singing: The Editions of 1774 and 1777 Compared,* translated and edited by Edward V. Foreman, Master-works on Singing, vol. 7 (Champaign, IL: Pro Musica Press, 1967).

Contemporary observers put little stock in the capacity of notation to reveal much about voices. As Burney said of Farinelli's embellishments, "We shall now be able to form but an imperfect idea, even if they had been preserved in writing, as mere notes would only shew his invention and science, without enabling us to discover that expression and neatness which rendered his execution so perfect and surprising," *A General History of Music, from the Earliest Ages to the Present Period*, 4 vols. (London, 1776-89), 4: 381. Mancini says something similar (*Riflessioni pratiche sul canto figurato*, 381).

3. Cf. the opinionated agnosticism of Winton Dean, *Handel and the Opera Seria* (Berkeley: University of California Press, 1969), 206-14; and Dean, "Die Aufführung von heroischen männlichen Rollen in Händels Opern," in *Fragen der Aufführungspraxis und Interpretation Händelscher Werke in Vergangenheit und Gegenwart*, edited by Walther Siegmund-Schultze (Halle [Saale]: Martin-Luther-Universität Halle-Wittenberg, 1980), 32-37.

In the second half of the twentieth century Donington was most open to considering the particularity of castrato voices, though his motivation was at least in good part to keep the sex of the singer when filling roles; see his *The Interpretation of Early Music*, rev. ed. (1963; New York: Norton, 1992), 523-24; and Donington, *A Performer's Guide to Baroque Music* (London: Faber, 1973), 73-74. See also the rich Robert Anthony Buning, "Alessandro Moreschi and the Castrato Voice," MA thesis, Boston University, School of Music of the School of the Arts, September 1990), 37-38 and passim (hereafter "Moreschi and the Castrato Voice").

4. Paul Henry Lang, "Performance Practice and the Voice," in *Musicology and Performance*, edited by Alfred Mann and George J. Buelow (New Haven, CT: Yale University Press, 1997), 185-98; quote on 196-97.

5. Alessandro Gabrielli was a kind of disciple of Moreschi's, having been a boy soprano soloist beside him at the Cappella Giulia in Rome. See Alessandro Gabrielli, "Ricordi d'un falsettista (continuazione)," *Rassegna dorica: Cultura e cronaca musicale* 13, no. 5 (May 1942): 58-61, at 60; and Gabrielli, "Riassunto delle conversazioni sulla storia delle cappelle musicali romane (Cappella Giulia, Cappella Sistina, Cappella Libertiana, Cappella Lateranense, contabelle cronologiche di cantori e maestri)," *Rassegna dorica: Cultura e cronaca musicale* 9 (1937-38): 255. Gabrielli omits Moreschi in the account of castrati that appears in his "Il canto dei falsettisti romani," originally published in *Musica* (February 1918) and republished (Rome: Officina Poligrafica Italiana, 1918), strikingly so on 10-11, but other Roman sources of the primo Novecento do so too, e.g., Gino Monaldi, *Cantanti evirati del teatro italiano* (Rome: Ausonia, 1920). See also Elsa Scammell's contribution to the Listserv Opera-L on *Opera-L Archives*, where she speaks of David Howell's knowledge of Gabrielli's study and recordings in the thread "The Counter Tenor Phenomenon." Cf. http://listserv.bccls.org/cgi-bin/wa?A2=ind0111B&L=OPERA-L&P=R9920&m=120987 (November 11, 2001). Howell notes that Gabrielli sounds "exactly" like Moreschi. Though I would not say "exactly," the resemblance of both Gabrielli and Domenico Mancini to Moreschi is quite remarkable. Franz Haböck also wrote about tours that included castrati in *Die Kastraten und ihre Gesangskunst: Eine gesangsphysiologische, kultur- und musikhistorische Studien* (Berlin: Deutsche Verlags-Anstalt Stuttgart, 1927), 204, noting that those who toured, performing motets and madrigals for four, six, and more voices, were not the best and received only "moderately warm receptions" despite their famous origins.

6. Buning, "Moreschi and the Castrato Voice," is an outstanding study of Moreschi and larger questions related to castrato voices considered from physiological, acoustic, medical, and musical perspectives. Critical and perspicacious in its approach to evidence and primary and secondary literatures, this little read work has been of great help to me. For a

biography of Moreschi and further musical insights, see Nicholas Clapton et al., *Moreschi and the Voice of the Castrato* (London: Haus Books, 2008), a lightly revised edition of Clapton, *Moreschi: The Last Castrato* (London: Haus Books, 2004), the former containing new essays by other authors.

Moreschi is sometimes said to have repeated his 1883 Roman performance of the part of the Seraph in Beethoven's oratorio *Christus am Ölberge* (Christ on the Mount of Olives) in Lyon in 1901, though the claim is unsubstantiated.

7. Born in the Lazian hilltop town of Monte Compatri, Moreschi was admitted to the papal chapel in 1883 as a full participant and was pensioned after the standard thirty-year contract, in 1913. That was long after recruitment of castrati was banned in 1902 and boys were introduced to sing alongside soprano falsettists in 1905. Moreschi continued singing in Roman churches until shortly before his death in 1922.

8. Those who remained in 1903 included the excellent soprano Giovanni Cesari (1843–1904), who sang until his death on March 10; soprano Domenico Salvatori (1855–1909), who took on the post of secretary in 1902 and retired in 1907; and soprano Vincenzo Sebastianelli (1851–1919), secretary from 1904, retired in 1909, and emeritus by 1912. Recently deceased at the time was Giuseppe Ritarossi (1841–1902), a choral-level singer who was active until 1901. Domenico Mustafà (1829–1912), virtuoso soprano, composer, and director from 1881, left Rome definitively in 1902 after fifty-four years in the chapel. His letter of resignation (not his first), delivered in December 1902, was officially accepted in January 1903; see Salvatore De Salvo Fattor, *La cappella musicale pontificia nel Novecento*, Storia della cappella musicale pontificia, vol. 7, edited by Giancarlo Rostirolla (Rome: Fondazione Giovanni Pierluigi da Palestrina, 2005), 16; complete text reproduced in Arcangelo Paglialunga, *Lorenzo Perosi* (Rome: Paoline, 1952), 210 ff. For brief biographies of castrated members of the Sistine Chapel in the period, see Leopold M. Kantner and Angela Pachovsky, *La cappella musicale pontificia nell'Ottocento*, Storia della cappella musicale pontificia, vol. 6 (Rome: Hortus Musicus, 1998), sect. V, 137–90; and De Salvo Fattor, *La cappella musicale pontificia nel Novecento*, 205–25.

Even in the mid-1890s negative press was battering the chapel's performances, at least in part because of partisans of the austere Cecilianist program, which opposed the use of castrati and was making itself felt. Chief among the partisans was the rabid Cecilianist Perosi, who was made codirector of the chapel in 1898 with Mustafà.

9. Perosi suffered from "gravi disturbi neurologici" (De Salvo Fattor, *La cappella musicale pontificia nel Novecento*, 206). Mario Rinaldi, *Lorenzo Perosi* (Rome: De Santis, 1967), 225–27, elaborates on the effect in this period of Pius's death and the onset of war on Perosi's mental health. On decrees that preceded and followed various additional difficulties in the institution, see De Salvo Fattor, *La cappella musicale pontificia nel Novecento*, esp. 14–17.

10. The original 78s, exceedingly rare, are remastered on *Alessandro Moreschi, The Last Castrato, Complete Vatican Recordings* (Opal CD 9823), with production notes by John Wolfson and liner notes by Elsa Scammell. The rest were thought lost (Robert Bauer, *The New Catalogue of Historical Records, 1898–1908/09*, 2nd ed. [London: Sidgwick and Jackson, 1947]), but an additional seven recordings with Moreschi and Sistine choir members have come to light and been remastered together with those previously known on the CD *Alessandro Moreschi, Soprano-castrato (1858–1922), Complete Gramophone Company Recordings (Roma, 1902–1904)* (Stutensee: Truesound Transfers, 2004), TT-3040, remastered by

Christian Zwarg from source material provided by Michael E. Gunrem, Michael Seil, Axel Weggen, and Christian Zwarg, which also includes some recordings from the same sessions by other Vatican artists. In all, nine numbers on the Truesound Transfers disk are not included on the Opal remastering, including seven choral works or choral works with soloists (nos. 3, 5, 6, 7, 13, 18, and 19), plus one for solo tenor—a recording in Italian of Bizet's "Je crois entendre encore" from *Les pêcheurs du perles* (as "Mi par d'udir ancora"), sung by Primo Vitti—and one for the Vatican brass band (no. 26). (Capocci's "Laudamus te," included on the Opal recording, is not on the Truesound Transfers recording.) Zwarg notes that castrati other than Moreschi may occasionally be heard, including possibly in 1902 Giovanni Cesari and in 1902 or 1904 Domenico Salvatori, singling out especially "La cruda nemica mia," a four-voice madrigal by Palestrina sung one on a part, and Mozart's *Ave verum* (the latter through inadvertent highlighting of particular choral voices by the recording horn). Cf. Clapton et al., *Moreschi and the Voice*, 211 and 213, who speculates similarly that the alto on "La cruda nemica mia" is Salvatori and possibly on Calzanera's *Oremus pro pontefice* as well. A cautionary note, however: Moreschi's influence may make it hard to discern castrati in other high voices, particularly lacking the presence of many upper partials in the recordings.

The 1902 sessions were recorded on March 3–5 by Fred Gaisberg and the 1904 sessions on April 11 by William Sinkler Darby. The remarkable story that led to Moreschi being recorded by the G&T Company is told in Jerrold Northrup Moore, *A Voice in Time: The Gramophone of Fred Gaisberg, 1873–1951* (London: Hamilton, 1976), 66–70; Clapton et al., *Moreschi and the Voice*, 166–70, 177–79; and Buning, "Moreschi and the Castrato Voice," 12–18 and passim, among others. The recordings are an object of study by Jörg Wilhelm Walter Derksen (Magisterarbeit, Friedrich-Wilhelm-Universität Bonn, 1995); see his "Der römische Sopranist Alessandro Moreschi: Ein Sängerleben zwischen der Tradierung einer Künstlervita und den Wirklichkeiten neuer Medien nach 1900," in *Professionalismus in der Musik: Arbeitstagung in der Verbindung mit dem Heinrich-Schütz-Haus Bad Köstritz vom 22. bis 25. August 1996*, edited by Christian Kaden and Volker Kalisch (Essen: Die blaue Eule, 1999), 123–31; see also Joe K. Law, "Alessandro Moreschi Reconsidered: A Castrato on Records," *Opera Quarterly* 2, no. 2 (Summer 1984): 1–12.

11. The opinion of Roger Freitas, who calls them "the generally execrable recordings by Alessandro Moreschi" ("The Eroticism of Emasculation: Confronting the Baroque Body of the Castrato," *Journal of Musicology* 20 [2003]: 196–249, at 235 n. 111), is fairly representative. Robert Donington differently called Moreschi's a "voice of massive weight and silky power," adding, "It outsoars any countertenor both in range and in dynamic force" and has in it "the strength of a powerful man, in the tessitura of a woman." Donington, *A Performer's Guide to Baroque Music*, 74; see also pp. 73 and 75.

12. Will Crutchfield, "Vocal Ornamentation in Verdi: The Phonographic Evidence," *19th-Century Music* 7 (1983): 3–54; Crutchfield, "Vocal Performance in the Nineteenth Century," in *The Cambridge History of Performance*, edited by Colin Lawson and Robin Stilwell (Cambridge: Cambridge University Press, 2012), 610–42; and John Potter, "Beggar at the Door: The Rise and Fall of Portamento in Singing," *Music & Letters* 87 (2006): 523–50.

13. Buning, "Moreschi and the Castrato Voice," 4; and Crutchfield, "Vocal Performance in the Nineteenth Century."

14. See especially David M. Howard, "Acoustics of the Castrato Voice," in Clapton et al., *Moreschi and the Voice*, 227–58; and for other and greater details, David M. Howard and

Damian T. Murphy, *Voice Science, Acoustics, and Recording* (San Diego: Plural Publishing, 2008); and David M. Howard and Jamie Angus, *Acoustics and Psychoacoustics* (Amsterdam: Focal Press, 2006). An excellent older account of the technology is found in H.C. Bryson, *The Gramophone Record* (London: E. Benn, 1935), which explains that "the normal vocal power of the human voice is only about ten millionths of a watt, and one of the most difficult problems of the early recorders was how to capture a sufficient part of this infinitesimally small amount of energy great enough to energize the diaphragm and cutting stylus." A study by Scott Petersen, "What Are We Listening To? An Analysis of Early Sound Recordings and Early Recording Technology," unpublished seminar paper, Eastman School of Music, University of Rochester, May 2006, tested different kinds of musical sounds using a horn and showed that not only are some partials eliminated altogether but others are delayed through a funneling effect that causes a blurring of frequencies. Petersen is currently assistant director of Yale University's Music and Multimedia Technology Lab. My thanks to Roger Freitas for putting me on to this research paper, carried out for a seminar of his, and to Petersen for sharing it with me.

On vocal production a reliable, albeit quite technical, source is Ingo R. Titze, *Principles of Voice Production* (1994; Iowa City: National Center for Voice and Speech, 2000).

15. "The number of times per second (or other unit of time) that a cycle of disturbances is exactly repeated. For example, if a string is vibrating in its fundamental mode, one cycle could be thought of as starting from the mid-position, moving to a maximum displacement in one direction, moving back to zero, moving to a maximum displacement in the other direction and finally back to zero. The time taken to complete this cycle is the period and the inverse of this quantity is the frequency. When the unit of time is the second, the unit of frequency is the hertz (abbreviated Hz), which is identical to the obsolete cycle per second (c.p.s.)." Clive Greated, "Frequency" *GMO*. See also Charles Taylor with Murray Campbell, "Sound," *GMO*, esp. §4, "Human Response and Physical Measurement."

Clapton suggests that this loss of harmonic overtones should have been less of an issue for a castrato than for other sopranos of the recording era because the castrato could sing notes in chest register up to c″ or d″; *Moreschi and the Voice*, 201–2 (emphasis mine).

16. Additionally, singers were often asked to place their heads very near a recording horn, so near as to feel themselves virtually inside it. Caruso caricatured himself in the act of singing for a recording, with his head inside a recording horn. Evidence about how often this was done is mixed.

17. I am very grateful to Ward Marston, producer, recording engineer, and owner of the Marston label, which produces modern transfers of early recordings, for corresponding with me about this issue (private communication, October 20, 2013). See also H. Courtney Bryson, *The Gramophone Record* (London: E. Benn, 1935), 46. The descriptions of the experience by Australian soprano Nellie Melba (1861–1931) are invaluable; see Nellie Melba, *Melodies and Memories* (1926; Freeport, NY: Books for Libraries Press, 1970), 250–54, esp. 252–53.

18. I adopt the term "schizophonia" from R. Murray Schafer, *The New Soundscape: A Handbook for the Modern Music Teacher* (Toronto: Don Mills, 1969), 43–47: "Schizophonic. It's a word I invented. You know that *phono* pertains to sound. The Greek prefix *schizo* means split or separated. I was thinking of Barbara's wonder at how a voice or music could originate in one place and be heard in a completely different place miles away.... We have

split the sound from the makers of the sound [via recording technology]. This dissociation I call schizophonia." Elsewhere Schafer defines it as "the cutting free of sound from its natural origins" (46).

19. As Crutchfield writes, one must "not only learn to listen through surface noise and imagine the frequencies uncaught by the recording horn, but also to concentrate on the music-making in the face of much [that may sound] rough, inexpert, and haphazard," quickly adding that after some progress, "the old performers sound expert where we sound rough and haphazard" (Crutchfield, "Vocal Ornamentation in Verdi," 3).

20. Moreschi's recording of it has been analyzed before but not to this end, at least not in print.

21. *Nellie Melba (1861–1931): The Complete Gramophone Company Recordings, Vol. 1*, track 21 (Naxos Historical, 2002), Landon Ronald, Herman Bemberg, piano, Landon Ronald, conductor, produced by Ward Marston, recorded March 1904; *The Complete Adelina Patti and Victor Maurel*, 2 CDs (Swarthmore, PA: Marston, 1998), with Landon Ronald, piano and Marianne Eisler, violin, produced by Ward Marston and Scott Kessler (CD 1, track 11), recorded 1905; Emma Eames with Josef Hollman, cello, *The Complete Victor Recordings* (1901–11) (London: Romophone, 1993), CD 1, track no. 15, recorded 1906; *Eugenia Burzio, Verismo Soprano: Complete Recorded Operatic Repertoire*, 2 CDs, produced by Scott Kessler and Ward Marston ([Swarthmore, PA]: Marston, 1999), CD 2, track 21.

22. No such agreement can be found in historical sources on the voice, which use jargon to describe vocal phenomena with little stability or consensus. It may be pointless to quibble with their doing so because they accommodate diverse historical realities, and indeed cleansing that diversity would be death to any grounded cultural approach. But without a provisional language and conceptual apparatus on which to hang shared perceptions, we would be consigned to the infinite purgatory of the armchair, with no aural referents for communicating and no way to gauge our impressions against a given past.

In the *OED*, "register" as it pertains to voice (as opposed to the organ or other instruments) is defined under 9b as "the range of a voice or instrument; *spec.* the particular range of tones which can be produced in the same way and with the same quality."

23. Pitch levels were not standard for a long time, and not officially so until 1939. This means that in the acoustic reality of heard sound, "developed voices can usually produce quite a variety of timbres while using the phonatory mechanism in ways that we would group under the category of 'chest voice' or 'head voice'" (Crutchfield, private communication, November 2006).

24. Voice breaks in transsexuals before, during, and after the change would be an important control here. Studying the desired break across the board in LGBTQQIAAP populations (Lesbian, Gay, Bisexual, Transgendered, Queer, Questioning, Intersex, Asexual, Allies and Pansexual, as from the Urban Dictionary website) would also make for interesting studies on sheer grounds of vocal physiology. My guess is that tessituras, as with all populations, would be easy to manipulate, registers more difficult, and registral breaks virtually impossible outside hormone therapy.

25. Part 1 was first published in 1840 but without the "Tableau de la classification des voix," which was added to part 1 when parts 1 and 2 were published together in 1847.

26. In Garcia the largest area of overlap between head and falsetto within any voice type, a minor sixth, occurs in the contraltino, followed by the tenor, whose head and falsetto

overlap by a perfect fifth. Drew Minter was the first to bring that to my attention (personal communication, May 1996).

27. This is according to Crutchfield's readings of Fernando De Lucia's 1906 recording of Alfredo's aria from *La Traviata* and fragments from a live Metropolitan Opera performance of Verdi's *Ernani* from 1903 ("Vocal Performance in the Nineteenth Century," 619–20). The practice of playing with rhythm, tempi, and phrasing, including speeding up tempi, was clearly prevalent at the time.

28. Whether he was simply unable to create a more blended sound on the high note or didn't care to, and whether it sounds thin because of the recording technology, has been a matter of some contention. Freitas criticizes Moreschi for "flipping" "with noticeable awkwardness from chest to head right around c''—the problem for Freitas being the flip, not its pitch ("The Eroticism of Emasculation," 235 n. 111). See, on the other hand, Joe K. Law, "Alessandro Moreschi Reconsidered: A Castrato on Records," *Opera Quarterly* 2 (1984): 1–12; Clapton et al., *Moreschi and the Voice*; and Buning, "Moreschi and the Castrato Voice," all of whom hear it rather differently.

29. Jessica Peritz, my research assistant and a singer, hears this as horizontal "spread."

30. I am generally in accord here with Buning, "Moreschi and the Castrato Voice," 325–65 (with the exception of his example 26, an analysis of registers in Moreschi's "Ave Maria" recording, on 343–44, which I find uncharacteristically impressionistic).

31. John Rosselli's paraphrase is "powerful and like a wind instrument in its crystalline clarity and purity, with a matchless *messa di voce*, but . . . never . . . a good trill or coloratura" ("Alessandro Moreschi," GMO).

32. *Opinioni de' cantori antichi, e moderni, o sieno Osservazioni sopra il canto figurato* (Bologna: Lelio dalla Volpe, 1723), esp. 13–16.

33. Giulio Caccini, *Le nuove musiche* (Florence: Marescotti, 1601), 6. Note the physiological description of falsetto mechanics, as distinct from "head," delineated in V. E. Negus, Owen Jander, and Peter Giles, "Falsetto," in GMO:

> The stroboscope reveals that, during fundamental phonation (i.e. first-mode, ordinary, basic or chest-register), the vocal processes of the arytenoid cartilages stay open. When second-mode phonation is employed, they take on a firm adduction, in that the mass of the folds corresponding to the inner part of the thyro-arytenoid muscle remains motionless. The vibrating length of available folds is reduced, because the arytenoid cartilages are now together and prevent the posterior third of the folds from undulating. Moreover, as with light-toned, higher-pitched first-mode, in second-mode the vocal folds of the skilled singer are seen to have assumed a thinner and more stretched character, particularly for higher notes.

Note the fundamental difference between a soprano (male or female) singing without falsetto versus a falsetto soprano. The former has thinned, stretched vocal folds but the inner part of the thyro-arytenoid muscle is not motionless, whereas in falsetto it is, hence the less than full contact the folds make during phonation in the latter. Alas, this does not provide an answer to the vexing historical question of what, precisely, Tosi or Caccini meant.

34. Foreman suggests: 1) that Caccini may well *not* have meant by *voci finte* falsetto voices, a term whose existence he notes in Maffei in 1562 and in Zacconi in 1592; and 2) that

Caccini may have avoided the term *falsettista* because he was basically writing about "normal" voices. See Giovanni Camillo Maffei's *Delle lettere . . . da Solofro . . . dove tra gli bellissimi pensieri di filosofia, e di medicina v'è un discorso della voce e del modo d'apparare di cantar di garganta, senza maestro,* 2 vols. (Naples: Raymundo Amato, 1562), 26; and Lodovico Zacconi, *Prattica di musica utile e necesssario si al compositore per comporre i canti suoi regolatamente, si anco al cantare per assicurarsi in tutte le cose cantabili,* 4 vols. (Venice: Girolamo Polo, 1592), book 1, chapters 58–80 (reprint ed. Bibliotheca musica Bononiensis, sezione 2, nos. 1–2 [Bologni: Forni, 1967]). Foreman's study of vocal treatises lead him to agree that the alto castrato may not have been blending registers in the seventeenth century, and perhaps not even in the early eighteenth (*The Art of Bel Canto*, 103–4 and n. 42; and see 113). Maffei and Zacconi both speak of separate registers (chest and falsetto), albeit without mentioning anything akin to blending the two. Buning likewise argues convincingly that a bipartite concept of register existed at least as far back as the Middle Ages. "Moreschi and the Castrato Voice," 335–40. By contrast, Corinna Herr comes close to suggesting that falsetto singers had effective parity with castrato singers throughout the heyday of castrati, in line with her tendency to understand "falsetto" in primary texts less as a reference to a physiological register than to voice type or the register that a certain voice type employed (*Gesang gegen die "Ordnung der Natur": Kastraten und Falsettisten in der Musikgeschichte* [Kassel: Bärenreiter, 2013]). The alternative would be to understand register more as a mechanism to which certain voice types may have special access through a particular vocal "process." Admittedly, though, the distinctions can be subtle in primary texts and the status of "falsetto" *("le voci finte"* or *"la voce falsa")* can be quite confounding.

For Galliard, translating Tosi's *Observations on the Florid Song, or Sentiments on the Ancient and Modern Singers* (1723; London: J. Wilcox, 1743), "register" is "a term taken from the different Stops of an Organ" (23 n). Whether this was really the case, it's noteworthy that the usages given in the *OED* for the organ precede by a long stretch of time usages applied to voice.

35. These exquisitely made dissections, filmed in three dimensions and beautifully narrated, give a tour of the anatomical components that contribute to the vocal process; Robert D. Acland, *Acland's DVD Atlas of Human Anatomy,* 6 vols. (Philadelphia: Lippincott Williams & Wilkins, 2004), vol. 4, "The Head and Neck, Part 1."

36. An excellent introduction to sound in voice production is Johan Sundberg, "Where Does Sound Come From?," in *The Cambridge Companion to Singing,* edited by John Potter (Cambridge: Cambridge University Press, 2000), 231–43, 263.

37. Crutchfield adds that practitioners who have concentrated on the question tend to agree that "in all voices, these changes come twice per octave, and that the boundaries are always in the pitch-class groups that in the age of A = 440 have the names E, F, F♯ and B♭, B, C" (private communication, October 18, 2008). Although the place and nature of such adjustments are particular to individual singers and to what is sung, there are significant overlaps between singers' experiences. (For instance, most sopranos describe a significant "break" in the area of high a‴ to b♭‴, the soprano's so-called *secondo passaggio.*) Relatedly, some practitioners speak in such terms as "blended head voice" or "chest-dominant sound" instead of "chest" or "head" alone, terms that I adopt here.

38. Quoted from *Observations on the Florid Song*, 23, from sections 20 and 21. "Molti Maestri fanno cantare il Contralto a loro discepoli per non sapere in essi trovar il falsetto, o

per isfuggire la fatica di cercarlo. Un diligente istruttore sapendo, che un soprano senza falsetto bisogna, che canti fra l'angustie di poche folde non solamente procura d'acquistarglielo, ma non lascia modo intentato acciò lo unisca alla voce di petto in forma, che non si distingua l'uno dall'altra, che se l'unione non è perfetta, la voce sarà di più registri, e conseguentemente perderà la sua bellezza" (Tosi, *Osservazioni*, 14).

39. Tosi notes that "the Difficulty consists in uniting them" ("la difficoltà consiste dell'unione"); *Observations*, 24.

40. Will Crutchfield, "Early Vocal Ornamentation," Appendix 5 in Gioacchino Rossini, *Il barbiere di Siviglia: Almaviva, o sia, L'inutile precauzione: Commedia in due atti; libretto by Cesare Sterbini after Pierre-Augustin Caron de Beaumarchais*, edited by Patricia B. Brauner (Kassel: Bärenreiter, 2008), 361–420, discusses high notes (higher than written in the score) in final cadenzas and singer-introduced fermatas, which persisted among some singers in the early nineteenth century (esp. 420–22). He also discusses this topic in his remarkable "The Final Cadenza," a chapter in a book he is writing on early nineteenth-century vocal performance practice that he kindly allowed me to read.

41. Mancini, *Practical Reflections*, 20; from article 4, "Of the Voice of the Chest and Head, or Falsetto" (emphases mine):

> La voce, per costituzione sua naturale, ordinariamente è divisa in due registri, che chiamansi, l'uno di petto, l'altro di testa, o sia falsetto. Ho detto ordinariamente, perché si dà anche qualche raro esempio, che qualcheduno riceve dalla natura il singolarissimo dono di poter eseguir tutto colla sola voce di petto. Di questo dono non parlo. Parlo solo della voce in generale divisa in due registri, come comunemente succede.
>
> Ogni scolare, sia egli soprano, sia contralto, sia tenore, sia basso, può da per se con tutta facilità conoscerne la differenza di questi due separati registri. Basta, che cominci a cantare la scala, per esempio se è Soprano, del *sol* posto nel terzo rigo, e seguitando sino al C-*sol-fa-ut* del quarto spazio, osserverà che queste quattro voci saranno sonore, e le dirà con forza, chiarezza, e senza pena, perché provenienti del petto; se poi vorrà passare al *D-la-sol-re*, se l'organo non è valido, ed è difettoso, lo dirà con pena, e fatica.
>
> Ora questa mutazione non è altro che il cambiamento della voce, la quale arrivata al termine del primo registro, entrando nel secondo si trova per necessità più debole.
>
> Questa voce di petto non è in tutti ugualmente valida, e forte; ma come ognuno avrà più robusto, o più debole l'organo del petto, avrà così più o meno gagliarda la voce. A molti la voce naturale, o sia di petto non assiste che per arrivare con stento al *B-mi;* ed a tanti altri riuscirà di salire di petto all' *E-la-mi*. (Quoted from the first edition, *Pensieri, e riflessioni pratiche sopra il canto figurato* [Vienna: Ghelen, 1774], 43–44)

Cf. also article 8, "Of the Union of the Two Registers, Portamento of the Voice, and of the Appoggiatura," paragraph 7.

42. Johann Adam Hiller, *Treatise on Vocal Performance and Ornamentation by Johann Adam Hiller,* translated and edited by Suzanne J. Beicken (Cambridge: Cambridge University Press, 2001), originally published as *Anweisung zum musikalisch-zierlichen Gesange*

(1780), 54, sect. 8. Mancini designated the pitches of the registral break less specifically in the 1777 version of the treatise, perhaps in response to Manfredini's fussing over temperaments (mean-tone and equal). But he actually moved the top note upward by a whole tone to e″. Castrati seem to have been particularly able practitioners of navigating between registers, from a combination of training and physiological predisposition.

43. Burney, *A General History of Music,* 4: 525, which continues by saying that in addition to other admirable qualities (dignity, drama, grandeur, diction, his ability to employ a variety of embellishments), Rubinelli's "chest is so strong, and his intonation so perfect, that I have seldom heard him sing out of tune. His voice is more clear and certain in a theater where it has room to expand, than in a room" (4: 525–26).

44. "In der höhe überstiegt er selten das zwengestrichene f. Seine Art zu singen war meisterhaft, und sein Vortrag vollstandig.... Das Allegro sang er mit vielem Feuer, und wußte er die laufenden Passagien, mit der Brust, in einer ziemlichen Geschwindigkeit, auf eine angenehme Art heraus zu stoßen." In Willi Kahl, *Selbstbiographien deutscher Musiker des 18. Jahrhunderts* (Cologne: Staufen-Verlag, 1948; The Netherlands: Frits Knuf, 1972), 213, reprinted from "Herrn Johann Joachim Quantzens Lebenslauf, von ihm selbst entworfen," originally published in Friedrich Wilhelm Marpurg, *Historisch-kritische Beyträge zur Aufnahme der Musik,* vol. 1, st. 5 (Berlin: Schütz, 1755), 197–250.

45. Kahl, *Selbstbiographien,* reprinted from "Quantzens Lebenslauf," 234–35. Cf. Angus Heriot, *The Castrati in Opera* (London: Calder and Boyars, 1956), 111. Since Handel's fioritura for Senesino regularly reaches f′ (above which he no doubt improvised some fleeting notes), it seems that either Senesino had a very high and flexible chest in "our" sense of the term, or that Quantz was using the term "chest" *(Brust)* as synonymous with the "natural" voice in a sense for which we lack an aural referent. Senesino must also have had great command over joining the registers.

46. For numerous examples see Franz Haböck, *Die Gesangskunst der Kastraten, Erster Notenband: A, Die Kunst des Cavaliere Carlo Broschi Farinelli. B, Farinellis berühmte Arien* (Vienna: Universal, 1923), as well as *Arie per Carlo Broschi Farinelli,* edited by Luigi Verdi and Maria Pia Jacoboni (Bologna: Associazione Clavicembalistica Bolognese, 2007); and see Robert Freeman, "Farinello and His Repertory," in *Studies in Renaissance and Baroque Music in Honor of Arthur Mendel,* edited by Robert Marshall (Kassel: Bärenreiter, 1974), 301–30.

47. "Gaetano Orsini, einer der größten Sänger, die jemals gewesen, hatte eine schöne, egale, und rührende Contraltstimme, von einem nicht geringen Umfange; eine reine Intonation, schönen Trillo, und ungemein reizenden Vortrag. Im Allegro articulierte er die Passagien, besonders die Triolen, mit der Brust, sehr schön; und im Adagio mußte er, auf eine meisterhafte Art, das Schmeichelnde und Rührende so anzuwenden, daßer sich dadurch der Herzen der Zuhörer, im höchsten Grade bemeisterte." Quoted in Kahl, *Selbstbiographien deutscher Musiker,* 218 (numbering from Marpurg); "Herrn Johann Joachim Quantzens Lebenslauf," 125.

48. Sergio Durante, "Condizioni materiali e trasmissione del sapere nelle scuole di canto a Bologna a metà Settecento," in *Atti del XIV congresso della Società Internazionale di Musicologia, Bologna, 1987: Trasmissione e recezione delle forme di cultura musicale,* edited by Angelo Pompilio et al. (Turin: Edizioni di Torino, 1990), 2: 175–89.

49. The interview forms part of the very rare recording of Mancini in the series *Le voci di Roma,* TIMA CLUB no. 37 (Rome, 1981). It is partly translated on the Simone Bartolini Official Web Site, web.tiscali.it/simone_bartolini/Intervista_Mancini_en.htm (accessed

December 23, 2012). Mancini said that Perosi "got it into his head" that since he sang in Moreschi's manner he must have been "one of those 'pure' voices," i.e., a castrato. Mancini's recordings show him to have been a masterful singer and very much after the manner of Moreschi, who apparently made him imitate him. The recordings I know are of Mozart's *Ave verum* and Armando Antonelli's *Benedicta et venerabilis* with the Solistes de la Chapelle Sixtine, Domenico Mancini soprano, Eugenio Travaglia contralto, Armando Fantozzi tenor, Augusto Dos Santos bass; Maëstro Antonelli organ accompaniment (SEMS, 1936; 78 RPM 12-inch recording, SEMS: 1111; matrix nos. XX VAT 117, XX VAT 179; side nos. M6-94418, M6-94419) and Antonelli's *O salutaris hostia* (France: SEMS, 1936), Solistes de la Chapelle Sixtine, Mancini, Fantozzi and Dos Santos, Antonelli organ (SEMS: 1110; matrix nos. XX VAT 163, side no. M6-94414), all at US-Nn.

50. Ex. 8 comes from MS D-MÜs, SANT Hs 458, "Solfeggi a Soprano | di Antonio Bernacchi | Celebre Maestro della Scuola Bolognese | estratti dal suo Originale ora in Copenhagen presso il Cavalier Brondstead | [at bottom] Collezione Musicale di Fortunato Santini Via dell'Anima N. 50," no. 3 in D minor. The collection is a nineteenth-century copy Santini made of thirty-two solfeggi in fifty-eight folios. According to RISM, it is identical to D-MÜs, SANT Hs 459. See http://faculty-web.at.northwestern.edu/music/gjerdingen/Solfeggi/collections/Bernacchi/index.htm.

51. Simplified diagrams are given on the website for the Lions Voice Clinic. The thyroarytenoid muscles shorten the folds by pulling the arytenoid muscles (at the back end) toward the thyroid muscles (at the front end), causing pitch to drop as they vibrate at a slower rate. The cricoarytenoid muscles do the opposite by pulling out and lengthening the folds. They cause the thyroid cartilage to move downward and forward on its hinge as the folds tighten up, vibrating more quickly as pitch goes up. Think of the strings on a harp or a piano. Various stroboscopies online show the vocal folds stretching and lengthening as singers ascend in pitch, for example at www.voicedoctor.net/media/video/normalfemale/large/ascending.mov (accessed January 15, 2010). See also Johan Sundberg, *The Science of the Singing Voice* (DeKalb: Northern Illinois University Press, 1987), and Sundberg, "Where Does Sound Come From?," 231–47, 263.

52. Howard and Murphy, *Voice Science*, 182. They explain that in falsetto singing, "A significant portion of each vocal fold is held firmly so that it cannot vibrate, thereby reducing the mass of the vibrating portion. The contact area is therefore also reduced" (43). Drs. Corey and Martin commented that the Chicago-based tenor Harold Olivey, who graciously allowed himself to be the subject of the strobe, made relatively fuller contact than most men singing in falsetto.

53. Ibid., 44.

54. Ibid.

55. Johan Sundberg, "Level and Centre Frequency of the Singer's Formant," *Journal of Voice* 15 (2001): 176–86.

56. Johan Sundberg, Marianne Troven, and Bernhard Richter, "Sopranos with a Singer's Formant? Historical, Physiological, and Acoustical Aspects of Castrato Singing," *Speech, Music, and Hearing, KTH, CSC Computer Science and Communication, Stockholm, Sweden TMH-QPSR, KTH* 49 (2007): 1–6, esp. p. 5. For the same reason they criticize the reconstruction of a castrato's voice made at IRCAM for Corbiau's film *Farinelli* (1994),

which morphed a countertenor with a female soprano, hence the salient strong partials between 2.5 and 3 kilohertz, as shown by mean long-term average spectral analysis (LTAS) (3, col. 1).

57. Ann-Christine Mecke, Johan Sundberg, and Bernhard Richter, "A Virtual Castrato?," *Logopedics, Phonatrics, Vocology* 35 (2010): 138–43, studied the notion that castrated boys combined an adult male vocal tract with a boy's vocal folds. Predicating their study on the idea that the singer's formant would have been present in castrati since it is linked with the resonance of a wide pharynx in adult males, they synthesized these conditions on manipulated recordings and played them for expert panelists to see how they compared with sounds the panelists "imagined" castrati to have made. Cf. Ann-Christine Mecke's study *Mutantenstadl: Der Stimmwechsel und die deutsche Chorpraxis im 18. und 19. Jahrhundert* (Berlin: Wissenschaftlicher Verlag Berlin, 2007), in which she wonders whether the larynx of a mature castrato was not actually larger than that of both boys and women (in which case the presence of a singer's formant in castrati would be especially salient as a distinguishing factor). My conversations with Dr. Robert Rosenfield suggest that this might only be possible in the case of a castrato castrated very close to puberty.

58. Manuel Garcia, *Traité complet de l'art du chant en deux parties* [first part originally published in 1840] (Paris: Eugène Duverger, 1847), 17; facsimile reprint in *Chant: Les grandes méthodes romantiques de chant*, vol. 4, edited by Jeanne Roudet, Méthodes et traités, series 2, France, 1800–1860 (Courlay: Fuzeau, 2005), vol. 4.

59. Paul Miles-Kingston, "Training Boys to Sing," MA thesis, York University, Music, 2008, 37. My thanks to Felicity Laurence (composer, children's choral director, and lecturer in music education, International Center for Music Studies, Newcastle University) for putting me onto Miles-Kingston's thesis and to Mr. Miles-Kingston for sharing it with me.

60. Ibid., 54. See additionally, "It is the use of too much weight without placement in this upper-middle area that frequently compromises the voice production of children, leading to a debilitating effect on head voice access."

61. Ibid.

62. Ibid. Musicologist and bass Richard Wistreich recalls having hit a high c in chest as a boy (private communication).

63. Meredydd Harries, Sarah Hawkins, Jeremy Hacking, and Ieuan Hughes, "Changes in the Male Voice at Puberty: Vocal Fold Length and Its Relationship to the Fundamental Frequency of the Voice," *Journal of Laryngology and Otology* 112 (1998): 451–54, report vocal folds of about 12 to 15 millimeters in length for boys, 13 to 18 millimeters for grown women, and 18 to 23 millimeters for grown men. The figures vary somewhat among sources but the ratios are fairly consistent.

64. Drew Minter has pictured the castrato's vocal emission as mechanically akin to that of a large, taut balloon breaking through its small tied-off end ("Castrated Voice," seminar session at University of Chicago, Department of Music, May 7, 2006). Cf. William Vennard, *Singing: The Mechanism and the Technic* (New York: Carl Fischer, 1968), 88 at no. 318 and 120 at no. 444; Richard Miller, *The Structure of Singing: System and Art in Vocal Technique* (Belmont, CA: Schirmer/The Wadsworth Group, 1996), 21–23 and passim; and John Potter, *Tenor: History of a Voice* (New Haven, CT: Yale University Press, 2009), 32.

65. As Giambattista Mancini put it, "The strength of the voice depends . . . on the quantity of air expressed from the lungs; depending on how ample these are, the tone . . . , born

from expressing air from the thorax, may be great" (*Practical Reflections*, article 3). The phrase "a tenor singing impossibly high" is quoted from the BBC Four production *Handel and the Castrati*, written and produced by Francesca Kemp, hosted by Nicholas Clapton, and featuring York University professor of electronics David Howard et al. (aired July 5, 2006). See also Potter, *Tenor*, chapter 2. On "subglottal pressure" see William Vennard, *Singing*, 88 at no. 318 and 120 at no. 444; and Miller, *The Structure of Singing*, 21–23 and passim.)

66. "The epiphyseal cartilage at the ends of the ribs (abreast of the sternum) would not calcify ('close') until relatively late in life. This would allow extra growth of the rib cage. And the relative softness of cartilage would have allowed the rib cage to expand even more with the 'voice training' that these men would have had: essentially, a castrato would have exercised his rib cage the way a marathon runner exercises his legs. Furthermore, since cartilage is much more flexible and elastic than bone, it has a 'springiness' that would be expected to have added power to their chest voice" (Robert Rosenfield, private communication, October 7, 2013). He also noted the "poor musculature" of testosterone-deprived men while emphasizing that doctors cannot normally observe the natural history of testosterone deprivation because their role is to intervene clinically in its course (private communication, September 4, 2013).

67. Marco Beghelli, "Il 'do di petto': Dissacrazione di un mito," *Il saggiatore musicale* 3, no. 1 (1996): 117–40, at 108; and Beghelli, "Per fedeltà di una nota," *Il saggiatore musicale* 8 (2001): 295–316. More recently Beghelli and Raffaele Talmelli, *Ermafrodite armoniche: Il contralto nell'Ottocento* (Varese: Zecchini, 2011), use old recordings and vocal analysis to explore nineteenth-century contraltos who took over castrato parts (e.g., Giuditta Pasta).

68. Burney, *A General History of Music*, 4: 369–70.

69. Metastasio, *Tutte le opere*, 5 vols., edited by Bruno Brunelli (Milan: Mondadori, 1954), 3: 395, letter no. 313 of May 28, 1749.

70. See Burney, *A General History of Music*, 4: 422. Similarly Burney commented on Manzuoli's "native strength," calling his "the most powerful and voluminous soprano that had been heard . . . since the time of Farinelli" (ibid., 485).

71. Ibid., 270. He also refers to Senesino's "articulate and voluminous voice" (311) and writes that Handel's "Agitato da fiere tempeste" produced a great effect when "thundered by such a voice" (327).

72. Sweetness and mellowness were not considered mutually exclusive. Cf. ibid., 216, on Catherine Tofts.

73. John Evelyn, *The Diary of John Evelyn*, 2 vols., edited by William Bray (London: George Bell & Sons, 1895), 2: 276 (he is called Cifaccio or Ciffacia in different editions of Evelyn's text).

74. Louise K. Stein, "Siface (Giovanni Francesco Grossi), a Castrato, Voice and Virility," paper delivered at the American Musicological Society, San Francisco, November 10–13, 2011.

75. Beth L. Glixon and Jonathan E. Glixon, *Inventing the Business of Opera: The Impresario and His World in Seventeenth-Century Venice*, AMS Studies in Music (New York: Oxford University Press, 2006), 22, offer statistics on the size of the theater.

76. Burney, *A General History of Music*, 4: 379 on Farinelli (and see also Burney's *The Present State of Music in France and Italy*, 209, on his "strength, sweetness and compass"). In 1735 John Corry, agent for the Earl of Essex, spoke of Farinelli's "fine Gurgle . . . so exceed-

ingly sweet"; quoted in Thomas McGeary, "Farinelli's Progress to Albion: The Recruitment and Reception of Opera's 'Blazing Star,'" *British Journal for Eighteenth-Century Studies* 28 (2005): 350 and n. 107, from a manuscript letter in the British Library. On Manzuoli, see Burney, *A General History of Music*, 4: 485, praising his performances in Milan in 1771.

By no means were all castrato voices deemed both sweet and powerful. Burney said Venanzio Rauzzini's voice was "sweet," though also "too feeble" because he spent too much time composing (ibid., 501). Nor were Guarducci's and Monticelli's voices called powerful, though both were "sweet" (ibid., 491, on Guarducci's "clear, sweet, and flexible" voice, described as having much less power than Manzuoli's; and ibid., 446, on Monticelli's "clear and sweet" voice). The voice of Andrea Martini (1761-1819), one of three singers who bore the moniker Senesino, was thought sweet, flexible, and *not* powerful, hence his specialization in female roles (Heriot, *The Castrati in Opera*, 160).

77. Winton Dean, "Senesino [Bernardi, Francesco]," *GMO*.

78. John Spitzer and Neal Zaslaw, *The Birth of the Orchestra: History of an Institution, 1650-1815* (New York: Oxford University Press, 2004).

79. Similarly, castrato voices were often praised for the bel canto ideal of "purity." In 1813 Rossini said a combination of such things about the soprano Giovanni Battista Velluti after fashioning for him the role of Arsace in *Aureliano in Palmira*, according to Stendhal, *Vie de Rossini suivie des Notes d'un dilettante*, edited by Henri Prunières (Paris: E. Champion, 1922), chapter 21. See chapter 6 below.

80. London, British Library, MS Egerton 3691, 2692, Barrett Collection [Letters of Susan Burney], in a letter of 1780 in which she effuses to her sister Fanny (Frances) after hearing Pacchierotti's performance in Bertoni's *La finta principe;* published electronically in *The Journals and Letters of Susan Burney: Music and Society in Late Eighteenth-Century England*, edited by Philip Olleson (Farnham, Surrey, England: Ashgate, 2012), 156, "journal letter" of May 6, 1780, which refers to "Giardini's benefit at the Hanover Square Rooms" (153 n. 1). The quoted material describes Pacchierotti's second aria, which is untitled and comes from an unidentified Paisiello opera; also quoted in Linda Kelly, *Susanna, the Captain, and the Castrato: Scenes from the Burney Salon, 1779-1780* (London: Starhaven, 2004), 78.

81. Georg Ludwig Peter Sievers, commented upon in F. S. Kandler, "Sur l'état actuel de la musique à Rome," *Revue musicale* 3 (1828): 49-102: "*Astolfi*, dont la voix *d'alto* délicieuse a perdu de son lustre par l'âge, joint à un volume de voix borné à dix notes, la plus grande flexibilité et la pureté la plus délicate. Il montre à quel point le sentiment et l'art peuvent supléer à la nature. Astolfi jouit d'une estime générale à Rome, comme compositeur et comme professeur de chant" (59-60). Astolfi (1790-1854) was a choirmaster at the basilica church of San Lorenzo in Damaso, Rome.

82. Neri was born in Pisa around 1755 and probably died in Florence after 1797; see Robert Lamar Weaver, "Neri, Michele Angiolo," *GMO*. Neri was a student of Giovanni Manzuoli, who in 1771 had just come out of retirement to sing in Hasse's *Ruggiero* and Mozart's *Ascanio in Alba* in Milan and whose own voice Burney praised in response to a London season in which he sang in J. C. Bach's *Adriano in Siria* as "the most powerful ... and voluminous that had been heard since the time of Farinelli" (Burney, *A General History of Music*, 4: 485). By 1771 Manzuoli, who had never been especially flexible, was an alto.

83. Arthur Schopenhauer, *Reisetagebücher aus den Jahren 1803-1804*, edited by Charlotte von Gwinner (Leipzig: F. A. Brockhaus, 1723), 268. Not all to whom these metaphors

attached were cited for power. Burney said Giuseppe Ricciarelli (fl. 1722–66) had a "clear, flexible and silver-toned voice" (*A General History of Music*, 4: 464); and Francesco Redi, in a treatise on snakes, called the voice of Antonio Rivani (Il Ciecolino) "silvery" (*Osservazioni intorno alle vipere* [Florence: All'Insegna della stella, 1664], 38, noted in Freitas, *Portrait of a Castrato*, 283).

84. Cf. James Jorden's review of the Met's new production of *Tosca*: "Baritone George Gagnidze . . . oozed a disquieting creepy quality, and his metallic voice achieved an effective snarl" ("Tosca as Torture," *New York Post*, September 23, 2009).

85. "Vi era la messa pontificale e in quel momento il celebre Soprano della Cappella Sistina, Prof. Alessandro Moreschi, cantava con quella sua voce d'oro, più unica che rara"; quoted from the diaries of Luigi Gentili, held in the private archive of Luciano Luciani, Fiumicino (Rome). Luciani kindly shared with me this and other items cited below, but without the date.

86. Haböck, *Die Kastraten*, 207.

87. Burney, *A General History of Music*, 4: 317. The aria is from Handel's *Admeto* (1727).

88. Haböck, *Die Kastraten*, 207. Cf. Horace Walpole (1717–97), on encountering Senesino's chaise in Siena, who wrote, "We thought it a fat old woman; but it spoke in a shrill little pipe, and proved itself to be Senesini." Horace Walpole, *The Letters of Horace Walpole, Earl of Orford: Including Numerous Letters Now First Published from the Original Manuscript*, 6 vols., edited by John Wright (London: Richard Bentley, 1840), 1: 37.

89. Martin Bernheimer/R, "Peerce, Jan [Perelmuth, Jacob Pincus]," *GMO*; Viorel Cosma, "Dimitrescu, Giovanni [Ioan]," *GMO*; Harold Rosenthal, "Gorr, Rita [Geirnaert, Marguerite]," *GMO*, revised by Alan Blyth; Desmond Shawe-Taylor, "Melchior, Lauritz [Lebrecht Hommel]," *GMO*.

90. Garcia, *Traité complet de l'art du chant*, 7.

91. Thomas Carlyle, *Critical and Miscellaneous Essays: Collected and Republished*, vol. 1 (London: Chapman & Hall, 1857), 161, and John Steinbeck, *The Pearl, with Drawings by Jose Clemente Orozco* (New York: Viking Press, 1947), 6, 91. Cf. *Jazz: The Magazine* 12 (1992): 67, on a vibraphonist: "Eerily metallic, his vibraphone sustains atmospheric passages." Uses of "silvery" come from Lord Byron, *Don Juan* 15.61, and Charles Kingsley's *Hypatia: Or New Foes with an Old Face*, 6th ed. (Boston: Crosby, Nichols, and Co., 1857), 130. See also *OED*, "silvery," 3a and b.

92. Consider too the likelihood that by the era when these combined factors became an ideal, theaters were large enough and numerous enough to make such voices a virtual prerequisite for top-drawer or even middling singers, many of whom spent time scuttling between big commercial theaters and (sometimes cavernous) churches. On loudness and the desiderata of singing for castrati in churches, see Corinna Herr, "'Ad altro modo si canta nelle Chiese & nelle Capelle publiche': Zur Ästhetik des Kirchengesangs," in *Singstimmen: Ästhetik, Geschlecht, Vokaprofil*, edited by Anno Mungen, Stephan Mösch, and Saskia Woyke, forthcoming, which the author kindly shared with me before publication; and Herr, *Gesang gegen die "Ordnung der Natur."*

93. As Philip A. Duey writes in his book on the teaching of bel canto in its "golden age," "It is not uncommon to find teachers today who claim their method is that of *bel canto* . . . but when pressed for explanation [. . . a teacher] adds many words but throws little light upon the subject"; *Bel Canto in Its Golden Age: A Study of Its Teaching Concepts* (New York: King's

Crown Press, 1951), 3. A workable explanation of "bel canto" is given by Foreman, *The Art of Bel Canto*, vi–xxii and passim, and an incisive one in Will Crutchfield, "The Bel Canto Connection," *Opera News* (July 1997): 30–35 and 51. I am using "bel canto" as a placeholder for that paragon of singing that was largely based on the practice of castrati from the seventeenth through the early nineteenth centuries, which, by the time of Rossini's retirement in the mid-nineteenth century, had already become a golden memory of a lost era. I touch here only very lightly on some of the debates and disparities surrounding its usage.

94. See the keyword "bel canto" in the *Lessico italiano del canto* by Sergio Durante, Leonella Grasso Caprioli, and Roberta Ziosi (Naples: Liguori, 2014), electronic edition. Bernardo Mengozzi refers to D. Baderali in the edition of his singing treatise of 1825. Sergio Durante has very generously shared with me his knowledge and various references to bel canto (private communication, November 15, 2013). He suggests, with good reason and evidence, that later definitions are both more generic and even mythographical in nature, whereas earlier ones are grammatical variations of the parts "bel" and canto" (as above). See his article "Singers," in *Opera Production and Its Resources* (Chicago: University of Chicago Press, 1988), on 403–5.

95. "Mi compiacio certificare che il Sig. J. P. Goldberg, Socio dell' Accademia Musicale di Vienna, che cantò in Italia in qualità di Primo Basso Assoluto, è capace d'istruire nel bel canto, e ne diede prove non dubbie col aver ammaestrato artisti che si resero singolari nel Teatro Italiano. Gioacchino Rossini. In Fede del 22 Novembre 1849. Firenze" (emphasis in translation mine). The letter was kindly shared with me by Philip Gossett. In 2007 the autograph of it was held in a private American collection, but its current whereabouts appear to be unknown (Philip Gossett, private communication, December 30, 2009). The singer in question was Joseph Pasquale Goldberg (1825–90), a violinist, composer, and bass singer who was not yet twenty-five at the time.

96. The most reliable source is Edmond Michotte, *Richard Wagner's Visit to Rossini (Paris 1860) and An Evening at Rossini's in Beau-Sejour (Passy) 1858*, translated and annotated, with an introduction and appendix, by Herbert Weinstock (Chicago: University of Chicago Press, 1968), 73–74, paraphrasing Rossini's remarks to Wagner in a visit he made to Rossini in 1860; and 109–10, paraphrasing Rossini's remarks to Michotte in a visit Michotte made to Rossini in 1858 (both originally published by Michotte in 1906). Michotte took detailed notes on these visits; see Weinstock's preface to *Richard Wagner's Visit to Rossini*, v–x.

97. Antonio Peregrino (Pellegrino) Benelli, *Regole per il canto figurato, o siano Precetti ragionati per apprendere i principi di musica, con esercizi, lezioni et infine solfeggi, per imparare a cantare*, 2nd ed. (1814; Dresden: Arnoldische Buchhandlung, 1819), 16; and G. Andrea Costa, *Considerations on the Art of Singing in General and Particularly on Several Errors into which Singers Are Liable to Fall, Also on the Three Styles of Singing Prevalent in Europe, -viz. the Popular, the Sacred, and the Theatrical and on the Four Fundamental Bases of Singing, viz.: the Nature of the Vocal Organs—The Art of Employing Those Organs—Music- and Genius, to Which Are Added Some Opinions on the Elemental Instruction of the Art, . . .* (London: G. Schulze, 1824). The volume by Costa is rare. A later edition, published as Andrea Costa, *Analytical Considerations on the Art of Singing, Containing an Account of the Various Styles of Singing Prevalent in the Principal Countries of Europe, Classed under the Heads of Sacred, Popular, and Theatrical* (London: Sherwood, Gilbert, and Piper, 1838), is less so. See Duey, *Bel Canto in Its Golden Age*, chapter 2, "Definition of Terms."

98. For Crescentini's remarks see Francesco Florimo, *Breve metodo di canto* (Naples: Girard [ca. 1840]), 1, 2, 4, 6, and 7, a rare volume that Florimo says he made for and dedicated to Crescentini.

99. Facsimile reprint in *Chant: Les grandes méthodes romantiques de chant*, vol. 2; English translation of preface as "Girolamo Crescentini: Preliminary Discourse by the Author," in Foreman, *The Art of Bel Canto*, 406–11.

100. The history is well summarized in Rodolfo Celletti, *A History of Bel Canto*, translated by Frederick Fuller (Oxford: Clarendon Press, 1991).

101. "Contro il destin, che freme" was sung by the character of Demetrio, written for Mazzanti by Gluck in *Antigono* (Rome, 1756), act 1, scene 13. See *Antigono: Rom 1756 / Christoph Willibald Gluck; dramma per musica in drei Akten von Pietro Metastasio*, edited by Irene Brandenburg (Kassel: Bärenreiter, 2007), series 3, vol. 20, 148–75, and on Mazzanti, xii–xiii. The letter from Metastasio to Farinelli is from December 8, 1756, in *Tutte le opere*, 3: 1153 (no. 984); "Il primo soprano è il signor Mazzanti, gran suonatore di violino in falsetto." See also Fabrizio Della Seta, "Il relator sincero (Cronache teatrali romane, 1736–1756)," *Studi musicali* 9 (1980): 73–116, on some mid-eighteenth-century letters about disputes over opera in Rome that involve Ferdinando Mazzanti. One of February 19, 1753, calls him "uno de bravi Cantanti dell'Europa," adding, "e Roma gli farebbe maggior onore, se avesse un poco più di azione, e desse ogni sera eguale soddisfazione" (105). Another of January 8, 1756, refers to arias "abellite da Lui con tali grazie, e col suo natural falsetto" (112); see also complaints that Mazzanti was not being allowed to stand out enough, cited in Gluck, *Antigono*, edited by Brandenburg, x–xi. On Mazzanti, see Dennis Libby, "Mazzanti, Ferdinando," *GMO*.

102. Full letter in Metastasio, *Tutte le opere*, 3: 1151–55, as well as April 5, 1770, in ibid., 4: 813–19 (no. 1851); and see Charles Burney, *The Present State of Music in France and Italy, or, the Journal of a Tour through Those Countries, Undertaken to Collect Materials . . .* ([London]: T. Becket and Co., 1771), 281–82, who said that when he heard Mazzanti in 1771, the singer made "ample amends for want of force in his voice, which is now but a thread" (282). This was fifteen years after Metastasio's comment.

103. There is nothing of the kind, for instance, in Ludovico Zacconi's elaborate *Prattica di musica utile si al compositore per comporre i canti suoi regolatamente, si anco al cantore per assicurarsi in tutte le cose cantabili* (Venice, 1592; reprint edition Bologna: Forni, 1967), vol. 1.

104. Tosi, *Opinioni de i cantori antichi, e moderni*, 14. For a comparison of Mancini with Tosi, see Sergio Durante, "Strutture mentali e vocabolario di un cantore antico/moderno: Preliminari per una lettura delle fonti didattiche settecentesche," in *Alessandro Scarlatti und seine Zeit*, edited by Max Lütolf (Bern: Paul Haupt, 1995), 38–54, esp. at 47–51.

105. I quote from the translation in Foreman, *The Art of Bel Canto*, 432.

106. Cf. Manfredini, "Those persons who have more than twelve or thirteen notes in the chest [are . . .] rare" (Foreman, *The Art of Bel Canto*, 104).

107. A book of solfeggi ascribed to the castrato Giuseppe Aprile, *The Modern Italian Method of Singing, with a Variety of Progressive Examples and Thirty-Six Solfeggi by Sigr. S. G. Aprile* (London: R. Birchall, [ca. 1795]), includes virtually the same preface as Tenducci's; see Foreman, *The Art of Bel Canto*, 424–27, for the persuasive theory that the volume was assembled by the Irish tenor Michael Kelly, a student of Aprile's; and see Foreman's edition of the book, *Masterworks on Singing*, vol. 5 (Minneapolis: Pro Musica Press, 2001).

108. Anna Maria Pellegrini Celoni (ca. 1780–1835), *Grammatica, o siano, Regole per ben cantare,* Opera 6 (Rome: P. Piale, 1810; Leipzig: Peters, 1810); in translation as *Grammar, or, Rules for Singing Well,* edited and translated by Edward V. Foreman, Masterworks on Singing, vol. 4 (Minneapolis: Pro Musica Press, 2001), based on the second edition (Rome: Francesco Bourlie, 1817).

109. This also according to his student Anton Raaff; see Martini letters at www.bibliotecamusica.it/cmbm/scripts/lettere/search.asp. John Potter clarifies the interlocking nature of messa di voce as exercise and as stylistic technique in "Vocal Performance in the 'Long Eighteenth Century,'" in *The Cambridge History of Performance,* 506–26, esp. 514.

110. However, note that, as Ellen T. Harris points out, seventeenth-century writers as far back as Caccini describe the practice without naming it ("Messa di voce," *GMO*).

111. David Daniels told me he sings messe di voce at the beginning of every practice session (private communication, November 24, 2007).

112. This comes from the second version, act 1, scene 6. Durastanti's aria, "Ferite, uccidete, oh numi del ciel!," is given in Handel, *Radamisto* (Leipzig: Handel Society, [1875]), act 1, scene 6, with the sostenuto on mm. 75–78. The revision was nicely analyzed by Feng-Shu Lee in my 2003 seminar on the castrato.

113. Crutchfield, "Vocal Performance in the Nineteenth Century," 614.

114. On this point see Richard Wistreich, "Reconstructing Pre-Romantic Singing Technique," in *The Cambridge Companion to Singing,* edited by John Potter (Cambridge: Cambridge University Press, 2000), 178–91, 258–61.

115. Mancini, *Pensieri, e riflessioni prattiche,* "On Agility Singing," 130–47. Cf. Ellen T. Harris with Owen Jander, "Singing," in *Grove Music Online:*

> Portamento ... was considered an essential element of good singing until about the beginning of the 20th century: that is, singers connected notes "almost imperceptibly" by gliding through the intervening pitches. The abuse of this technique at the end of the 19th century and the beginning of the 20th led to its abandonment, but the practice encouraged by Garcia in 1894 of hitting each note "purely" has no basis in earlier history.... Singers not only connected notes, but approached initial notes from as far as a 3rd or 4th below the notated pitch (cercar della nota). A consistent notation for the portamento and *cercar della nota* was never developed, in part because the practice was so normative that notation would have been redundant. Thus our record of this practice is largely limited to written treatises on singing and descriptions of voices, but early recordings also document its regular use.

Cf. Will Crutchfield, "Verdi Performance: Restoring the Color," *High Fidelity/Musical America* 33, no. 6 (1983): 64–66, 100–101.

116. Potter, "Beggar at the Door."

117. Cf. Crutchfield, "Vocal Performance in the Nineteenth Century," 640.

118. Foreman, *The Art of Bel Canto,* 128.

119. *Domenico Corri's Treatises on Singing: A Select Collection of the Most Admired Songs, Duetts, &c. and The Singer's Preceptor: A Four Volume Anthology,* edited with introductions by Richard Maunder (New York: Garland, 1993–95), is a facsimile of the British Library copy. Vol. 3 contains *The Singer's Preceptor* and a collection of songs, many of which have

portamento notated, including Par's "Da che vidi un pastorello," Portogallo's "Frenar vorrei le lagrime," Andreozzi's "Oh quell'anima che sdegna," and Par's "Donne l'amore." Other collections also show written-in portamento, notably the Elizabeth Augusta Wrightson Collection of Italian Printed Arias, with ornamentation added by hand, ca. 1810–40, Northwestern University Music Library (US-En), MSS 617.

120. A good account of the *strascino* appears in Potter, "Vocal Performance in the 'Long Eighteenth Century,'" 512.

121. "Con asmatica pena prender fiato / E i passi mascherar di questo, e quello, / Cantar quattr'arie, e poi restar sfiatato. / Incerto trillo, e gusto Napoliello, / passaggio non battuto, e strascinato, / Ditemi, non è questo Farinello?" From Antonio Vallisneri, *Epistolario, 1714–1729*, edited by Dario Generali (Florence: Olschki, 2005), 1682, no. 1464; from a letter to Umbertino Landi, Piacenza, Biblioteca Comunale Passerini, Landi, *Copia di lettere*, MS Pallastrelli no. 100, fols. 224r–224v, MS copy. My thanks to Paula Findlen for sharing this with me.

122. David Schoenbaum, "Jascha Heifetz at 100: Both Thrilling and Chilling," *New York Times*, December 23, 2001. Schoenbaum describes "the efficiency of the left hand moving horizontally on the fingerboard; the vibrato ranging from zero to glass-shattering intensity, with all intervening degrees."

123. Lang, "Performance Practice," 196. In Italian "voci bianche" is generally shorthand for boys' voices. With reference to castrati it implies voices of grown-up boys. Certainly insofar as the sound of a castrato was really "white" (i.e., straight-toned) it was not because castrati lacked the strength or training to sing with vibrato, which is true of boys if not pushed hard to do so, but not true of grown men and women.

124. Quoted from Emma Calvé, *My Life*, translated by Rosamond Gilder (New York: D. Appleton, 1922; repr. New York: Arno Press, 1977), 64.

125. Crutchfield, private communication, about Lily Pons.

126. Emma Calvé, *Sous tous les ciels j'ai chanté . . . Souvenirs* (Paris: Librairie Plon, 1940), 55, where she calls them "petites notes flûtées enseignées par Mustapha"). The entry is dated April 30, 1888, though the premiere of *L'amico Fritz* was on October 31, 1891. Cf. Lilli Lehmann, *How to Sing*, translated by Richard Aldrich, rev. ed. translated by Clara Willenbücher (1902; New York: Macmillan, 1924; repr. ed. New York: Dover, 1993), 65–69, translation of *Meine Gesangskunst*, 3rd ed. (Berlin, 1922), originally published in 1902. Lehmann tells the following anecdote relating to the closed mouth: "In Berlin, in the part of Matilde in 'Wilhelm Tell,' I frequently played a joke on the audience by holding, in a cadenza, the high e flat with mixed voice *(voix mixte)*, then once more decreasing the already diminished breath, I slowly closed the mouth and so in a shut-off space let the uninterrupted tone resound. I remember how the audience in the parquet suddenly looked about, thinking it had heard an echo which my tone resembled precisely" (67).

The issue of female "falsetto" singing, or the use of a fourth tone (a whistle tone or *soprafalsetto*), has been the subject of controversy among voice teachers and listeners but not speech pathologists, who understand falsetto as a fundamental element of all voices. A reasonable summary of the problem is given in the article "Falsetto," in the section "Female falsetto," on *Wikipedia* (accessed January 17, 2010).

127. Richard Wigmore's article "Singing," in A *Performer's Guide to Music of the Classical Period*, edited by Anthony Burton (London: Associated Board of the Royal Schools of

Music, 2002), 75–89, suggests that certain late-eighteenth-century female sopranos reached very high notes by means of a "falsetto extension" such as one hears on recordings by Calvé (78). Burney complained that at the Franciscan church in Naples the soprano "forced the high notes in a false direction, till they penetrated the very brain of every hearer"—a complaint that suggests a voice that cognoscenti nowadays would think insufficiently blended (Burney, *The Present State of Music in France and Italy,* 304–5). In the same year (1771) he also complained, "All the *Musici* in the churches at present are made up of the refuse of the opera houses, and it is very rare to meet with a tolerable voice upon the establishment in any church throughout Italy" (303–4).

128. From Robert Caldwell and Joan Wall, *The Singer's Voice: Complete Set,* 5 DVDs (Redmond, WA: Caldwell Publishing, 1991–93). During the clip, the narrator remarks, "The singer pronounces the consonant *m* as in 'Mary.' Notice the soft palate is lowered, allowing air into the nasal cavities. And since the lips are sealed, air can only come out through the nose."

129. Drew Minter, private communication, April 2007. One thinks of George Crumb's otherworldly water glasses in *Songs, Drones, and Refrains of Death* (1968) for baritone, electric instruments, and percussion, *Black Angels (Images I): Thirteen Images from the Dark Land* for electric string quartet (1970), and *Dream Sequence (Images II)* (1976) for violin, cello, piano, percussion (one player), and off-stage glass harmonica (two players). Note also the water glass scene in Federico Fellini's *E la nave va* (1982), in which a group of older men play Schubert's *Impromptu hongroise.* Seth Brodsky tells me about water glasses in Luigi Nono's opera *Prometeo* (1981–83, rev. 1984) and Christopher Rouse's *Infernal Machine* (1981), among a number of others.

Practicing with the mouth shut on the consonant *m* requires a great deal of relaxation and a specific isolation of muscular effort to do well. Humming in a high range is considered good practice for reducing tension, since the voice cannot ascend at a certain point without muscular freedom because phonation will choke off and the hum will stop.

130. "One should think of an *ä*, and in the highest range even an *ä* and *ē* with *ōō*, and thereby produce a position of the tongue and soft palate that makes the path clear for the introduction of the breath into the cavities of the head" (Lehmann, *How to Sing,* 65 and 67). Cf. Tosi: "Whoever would be curious to discover the feigned Voice of one who has the Art to disguise it, let him take Notice, that the Artist sounds the Vowel *i,* or *e,* with more Strength and less Fatigue than the Vowel *a,* on the high Notes. The *Voce di Testa* has a great Volubility, more of the high than the lower Notes, and has a quick Shake, but subject to be lost for want of Strength" (Galliard translation of Tosi, *Observations,* 24–25). ("Chi fosse curioso di scoprire il falsetto in chi lo sa nascondere badi, che chiunque se ne serve esprime su gli acuti la vocale *i* con più vigore, e meno fatica dell'*a.* La voce di testa è facile al moto, possiede le folde superiori più che le inferiori, ha il trillo pronto, ma è soggetta a perdersi per non aver forza, che la regga"; *Osservazioni,* 14–15.)

131. On Emma Calvé, *The Complete 1902 G&T, 1920 Pathé, and "Mapleson Cylinder" Recordings,* 2 CDs (Marston, 1998), CD 1, track 15 (2334, 2343), 0276. This is a hill-and-dale recording made by Pathé in Paris in 1920.

132. Compare this with a recording of the same sung by the stratospherically high French coloratura Mado Robin (1918–60), who delivers the *air* at a higher pitch but actually uses a less fluted sound, seemingly produced in the middle of the head instead of high up in the masque—a *voix mixte* even at an unbelievably high a'''' a major sixth above high c'''; on

Mado Robin, Lebendige Vergangenheit series (Austro Mechana Historic Recordings, 2005), 89614, track 4 (especially 4'25"–5'09").

133. Perhaps in 1830–31 Mendelssohn heard other castrati make such ethereal high tones when he wrote home about the very high singing at the Sistine Chapel. On December 1, 1830, Mendelssohn wrote to Carl Friedrich Zelter in Berlin about the Sistine voices in general, and on June 16, 1831, he wrote him again about a very high soprano. Alberto De Angelis, *Domenico Mustafà: La Cappella Sistina e la società musicale romana* (Bologna: Zanichelli, 1926), 21 and 23, respectively.

134. Cf. Elizabeth Wood, "On the Sapphonic Voice," in *Music, Culture, and Society: A Reader*, edited by Derek B. Scott (New York: Oxford University Press, 2000).

135. Calvé, *My Life* (1922), 64–65; Calvé's *Sous tous les ciels* is a later autobiography. Victor Girard, who wrote the liner notes for the Marston reissue, calls *My Life* "almost totally anecdotal" and the second "replete with factual errors." But Calvé's anecdote about her studies with Mustafà corresponds well not just with her biography but with her singing as well. I disagree with Girard's charge that the upper third of the range in Calvé's "Charmant oiseau" evinces "the only noticeable deterioration" in her voice, "some notes of which she touches very gingerly." At sixty-two, when she recorded it, she achieved a delivery that was both artful and authoritative in its full presence and excellent intonation while also being highly attentive to the text and genre.

136. Ancillon, *Eunuchism Disply'd*, 31.

137. Martin Kirnbauer, "Eunuch Flutes: Source Studies on a Still-forgotten Instrument," in *Festschrift Rainer Weber*, edited by Eszter Fontana (Halle an der Saale: Janos Stekovics, 1999), 73–78.

138. Enrico Panzacchi, in a *racconto* titled "Cantores," in Panzacchi, *I miei racconti*, 1st ed. (Milan: Treves, 1889); modern edition as *Racconti*, edited by Valeria Giannantonio (Chieti Scalo: Vecchio Faggio, 1993), 113–17. There is much confusion in the literature, even as far back as Gabrielli, "Ricordi d'un falsettista (continuazione)," 58, who believed the singer referred to Panzacchi as a falsettist. According to Dr. Rosenfield it is possible for a male who is castrated after already starting on his way toward puberty but not having yet reached it to grow a "light beard" or peach fuzz (private communication, September 30, 2013).

139. On the issues broached here, see J. Q. Davies, *Romantic Anatomies of Performance* (Berkeley: University of California Press, 2014), chapter 5, and Crutchfield, "Vocal Performance in the Nineteenth Century."

140. In 1928 Franz Sales Kandler raved about the perfect vocalizations and "clear and light" singing ("le sue inflessioni chiare e leggiere") of the Sistine soprano Vincenzo Ferri in his "Sur l'état actuel de la musique à Rome," 49–102, at 60.

141. See, in particular, Will Crutchfield, "Verdi Performance"; "Vocal Ornamentation in Verdi"; "The Bel Canto Connection"; "The 19th Century: Voices," in *Performance Practice, 2: Music after 1600*, edited by Howard Mayer Brown and Stanley Sadie (London: Macmillan, 1989), 424–58; and "Some Thoughts on Reconstructing Singing Styles of the Past," *Journal of the Conductors' Guild* 10, nos. 3–4 (1989): 111–20.

142. Lucie Manén, *Bel Canto, the Teaching of the Classical Italian Song-Schools, Its Restoration and Decline* (Oxford: Oxford University Press, 1987), 2–3.

143. Cf. Sergio Durante, "Theorie und Praxis der Gesangsschulen zur Zeit Händels: Bemerkungen zu Tosis 'Opinioni de' cantori antichi e moderni,'" in *Händel auf dem Theater:*

Bericht über die Symposien der Internationalen Händel-Akademie, Karlsruhe, 1986 und 1987, edited by Hans Joachim Marx (Laaber: Laaber, 1988), 59–72; and Durante, "Condizioni materiali."

144. This 35mm film was directed by Karl Heinz Martin, written by Lotte Neumann and Walter Wassermann, and produced by Bavarian Film, with the sound mix by Tobis-Klangfilm. On the pushed-down larynx and its place in a nineteenth-century history of embodied performance, see Davies, *Romantic Anatomies of Performance*, chapter 5, "In Search of Voice: Nourrit's *Voix Mixte*, Donzelli's Bari-Tenor," which he kindly allowed me to read in advance of publication.

145. On this point see J. B. Steane, *The Grand Tradition: Seventy Years of Singing on Record*, 2nd ed. (Portland, OR: Amadeus Press, 1993), 51, 174, and passim.

146. Lillie de Hegermann-Lindencrone, *The Sunny Side of Diplomatic Life, 1875–1912* (New York: Harper & Brothers, 1914), 118–19 (dated Rome, 1883). Moreschi was at most twenty-five at the time, not forty.

147. Garcia's "coup de la glotte" is explained in *Traité complet de l'art du chant*, 25. The *h* attack is marked out there in his transcription of the castrato Crescentini's performance of "Idolo del mio cor" (the opening cavatina from act 3, scene 1 Zingarelli's *Giulietta e Romeo* of 1796) with the performance attacks indicated on p. 95, at mm. 6, 12, etc.

148. Hegermann-Lindencrone, *The Sunny Side of Diplomatic Life*, 117 (entry dated Rome, Holy Week, 1881).

149. Lang, "Performance Practice," 196.

150. De Angelis, *Mustafà*, 175, Appendix, document no. 3, "Elenco dei Cantori ammessi nella Cappella Sistina dal 1795 al 1897," n. 17; Kantner and Pachovsky, *La cappella pontificia nel Ottocento*, 183–84.

151. See *Encyclopedia of Recorded Sound*, 2nd ed., 2 vols., edited by Frank W. Hoffmann, technical editor Howard Ferstler (New York: Routledge, 2005), which notes that the Lyraphone Company of America produced three labels, of which Lyric Records was apparently the second, and that in 1919 the president, M. J. Samuels, "announced that the visiting Sistine Chapel Quartette (from the Sistine Choir of the Vatican) would record for Lyric Records" (1: 639). Quite knowledgeable about the series is a collector named Glenn Longwell. He maintained information about labels and phonographs on majesticrecord.com as of 2010, but in 2013 it was no longer accessible.

152. The heads read, "Organizations Seeking Public Favor Bring High Praise from Rome, However," "Each Has Papal Claim," and "Rival Bands of Singers Have Been Received by Prominent Clergymen."

153. "Both Choirs Lack Vatican Sanction," *Sun Times*, September 6, 1919.

154. *Musical America*, September 6, 1919, 1 and 3. By 1919 more than one choir made up of singers from the chapel was circulating abroad. The widest notoriety was probably gained by a choir led by musicologist and composer Raffaele Casimiri, director of the Cappella di San Giovanni in Laterano in Rome. In April 1919 he founded the Società Polifonica Romana using singers from different Roman choirs, which he took on tour in Europe, Canada, and America. In America he promoted the group under the name "The Vatican Choir." See De Salvo Fattor, *La cappella musicale pontificia nel Novecento*, 29. An advance story about the Casimiri choir also appeared in *Cables* [undated, August 1919?]: "Pope Grants Permission for Tour of Vatican Choristers" (subtitle: "Seventy Singers to Come to this Country for 78

Concerts. Trying to Secure Permission for 15 Years. James Slevin Finally Successful. Sail Next Month. Tour Opens Here in September").

155. Haböck, *Die Kastraten*, 202.

CHAPTER 4. CASTRATO DE LUXE: BLOOD, GIFTS, AND GOODS

1. Corri, *The Singer's Preceptor* (1810), in *Domenico Corri's Treatises on Singing: A Select Collection of the Most Admired Songs, Duetts, &c. and The Singer's Preceptor: A Four-Volume Anthology*, 4 vols., edited with introductions by Richard Maunder (New York: Garland, 1993–95), 3: 2.

2. Charles Burney recounts the tale of Farinelli's contest with the trumpeter in *The Present State of Music in France and Italy: or, The Journal of a Tour through Those Countries, Undertaken to Collect Materials for a General History of Music* (London: printed for T. Becket and Co., 1771), 205–6. Reinhard Strohm notes that the numerous clef changes with which "Qual guerriero" was notated in one manuscript were "superfluous" in strict notational terms but served to show Farinelli's "enormous range (g—c''')"; see Strohm, "Who Is Farinelli?," liner notes to *Arias for Farinelli*, Vivica Genaux with the Akademie für Alte Musik Berlin, dir. René Jacobs (Arles: Harmonia Mundi, HMC 901778, 2002), p. 25. Farinelli's arias are available in modern edition in *Carlo Broschi Farinelli: Gesangskunst der Kastraten. I. Notenband*, edited by Franz Haböck (Vienna: Universal, 1923), with several also in *Arie per Carlo Broschi Farinelli*, edited by Luigi Verdi and Maria Pia Jacoboni with Carlo Vitali (Rome: Bardi, 2007). Several technically remarkable performances of Russian soprano Julia Lezhneva singing "Son qual nave" are available on YouTube.

3. Cf. Lorraine Daston and Katharine Park, *Wonders and the Order of Nature, 1150–1750* (New York: Zone Books, 1998), esp. the preface, 9–11, and "Introduction: At the Limit," 12–20, which explains their attempt to recuperate "wonder" as a passion and an object in terms grounded in pre-Enlightenment ways of thinking.

4. The story comes from a Bolognese dialect sonnet, "In favore del musico Bernacchi e contro il Farinello" (In favor of the castrato Bernacchi and against Farinelli), which alleges that as a virtuoso Bernacchi bested Farinelli by surprising him with the plain style; published by Corrado Ricci in *I teatri di Bologna nei secoli XVII e XVIII*, reprint ed. (1888; Bologna: Forni, 1965), 435, and in Ludovico Frati, "Antonio Bernacchi e la sua scuola di canto," *Rivista musicale italiana* 29 (1922): 473–91, at 477. The sonnet refers to Bernacchi as a "capon," which, again, is the basis for competition.

5. Feldman, *Opera and Sovereignty: Transforming Myths in Eighteenth-Century Italy* (Chicago: University of Chicago Press, 2007), chapter 2, "Arias: Form, Feeling, Exchange."

6. The manuscript is A-Wn, MS 19111, part of which is transcribed in *Arie per Carlo Broschi Farinelli*, edited by Verdi and Jacoboni. Vitali's preface to the edition asserts, in accord with Haböck, that the ungendered form of the address used in the dedication does not make its dedicatee unambiguous, arguing instead that it is addressed to the Emperor Francis I, not to Empress Maria Teresia, as is usually said (xi and n. 10).

7. "What Is an Author?" is printed in many different editions in English, among which is *The Essential Foucault: Selections from Essential Works of Foucault, 1954–1984*, edited by Paul Rabinow and Nikolas Rose (New York: New Press, 2003), 377–91. Scott Burnham's

book title *Beethoven Hero* (Princeton, NJ: Princeton University Press, 1995) throws this new status of the nineteenth-century composer into relief.

8. Johann Friedrich Agricola, *Anleitung zur Singkunst* (Berlin, 1757), an expanded and revised translation of Pierfrancesco Tosi, *Opinioni dei cantori antichi, e moderni o sieno Osservazioni sopra il canto figurato* (Bologna: Lelio dalla Volpe, 1723); translated into English and edited as *Introduction to the Art of Singing* by Julianne C. Baird (Cambridge: Cambridge University Press, 1995), 138.

It is a bit puzzling why Burney reckoned that the divisions sung by Farinelli "would hardly be thought sufficiently brilliant in 1788" (Charles Burney, *A General History of Music, from the Earliest Ages to the Present Period*, 4 vols. [London, 1776–89], 4: 413), but there are many ways to read this—as a figment of myth, memory, or nostalgia, or a sense that a singer delivering written-out divisions was different from one who was improvising them. At these extremes compare Farinelli's aria with one sung by Marchesi, Ex. 23, famous in the late eighteenth century for his "torrente di variazioni" (and see chapter 5 below).

9. See Hilary Poriss, *Changing the Score: Arias, Prima Donnas, and the Authority of Performance*, AMS Studies in Music (New York: Oxford University Press, 2009).

10. On Ferri see Giovanni Andrea Angelini Bontempi, *Historia Musica* (Perugia: Costantini, 1695; Geneva: Minkoff Reprints, 1976), 110–11; and recently Biancamaria Brumana, *"Il pianto de' cigni in morte della fenice de' musici": Poesie per Baldassare Ferri e nuove ipotesi sulla carriera del cantante* (Perugia: Deputazione di storia patria per l'Umbria, 2010). Giancarlo Conestabile, *Notizie biografiche di Baldassarre Ferri: Musico celebratissimo* (Perugia: Bartelli, 1846), writes about him:

> Since, beyond the clarity of the voice, the radiance of the passaggi, the beating of trills, the agility in arriving sweetly on any note after the drawing out of a very long and very beautiful passaggio whose length was such as others would not have been able to hold their breath for, he would burst forth without taking a breath into a very long and very beautiful trill, from which he passed into another passaggio even longer and more vigorous than the first without any movement of the forehead, the mouth, nor any sign of life, immobile as a statue. He rose and fell again, as even Rousseau repeats, semitone by semitone without even the slightest break *[incisura]*, with the voice lightly reinforced by means of a continuous distinct trill over the span of two octaves, and that he performed with such precision, deprived as he was of an accompaniment, that on whichever note the instruments reached him, whether flat or sharp, they always found his voice perfectly tuned to the orchestra. (9)
>
> Poichè, oltre la chiarezza della voce, la felicità dei passaggi, il battimento dei trilli, l'agilità d'arrivar dolcemente a qualsivoglia corda, dopo la continuazione di un lunghissimo e bellissimo passaggio, sotto la qual misura altri non avrebbero potuto contenere la respirazione, Egli prorompea senza respiro in un lunghissimo e bellissimo trillo, che da quello passava ad un altro passaggio assai più lungo, e vigoroso del primo senza movimento alcuno nè di fronte, nè di bocca, nè di vita, immobile come una statua. Egli saliva e riscendeva, ripete anche Rousseau, di semituono in semituono senza alcuna incisura, con voce leggiadramente rinforzata due piene ottave con un trillo continuato distinto, e ciò

praticava in tanta giustezza, privo com'era d'Accompagnamento, che a qualunque nota gli strumenti il raggiugnessero, fosse pure *o diesis, o bemolle,* trovavano sempre la sua voce perfettamente accordata con l'orchestra. (10)

Should the reader not believe these possible, Conestabile adds, thinking Bontempi knew too little of physics or anatomy

so that the present anecdote is confabulated to contain things impossible to execute: for Ferri they were not only possible but very easy; since, not having a fold in his diaphragm like others, he had viscera that were that much more vigorous and natural than theirs; and his chest being in one piece and large, one is again persuaded perforce that he must have had uncommonly viscous lungs and a cooler temperament whereby, more than others, he could hold his breath and make miracles of art audible, which he turned into things greater than marvels and with which he almost exceeded that which is possible of the human. (10)

esser favoloso il presente raccontamento, per contener cose impossibili a praticarsi: al Ferri non solo erano possibili, ma facilissime; poichè Egli, per non aver come gli altri la piegatura nel Diafragma, tanto più vigorose degli altri aveva le viscere spirituali, e naturali. Ed avendo il petto intero, e grande, e da persuadersi necessariamente ancora, che avesse il polmone fangoso, e raro, e il temperamento più frigido; ond'era che più degli altri poteva contener lo spirito, e far sentire i miracoli dell'arte; coi quali si rendeva maggiore della meraviglia, e quasi eccedeva il possibile dell'umanità. (10-11)

Mancini seconds the praises of Matteuccio, calling his voice "sì florida" and saying that he sang "in every method with such flexibility and agility that every listener, not seeing him nor believing it, believed him to be in the flower of youth" ("in ogni metodo con tanta flessibilità, e agilità, che ogni ascoltante, non vedendolo, lo credeva un Giovane nel fior degli anni"). Giambattista Mancini, *Pensieri, e riflessioni prattiche sopra il canto figurato* (Vienna: Ghelen, 1774), 13. See also Ulisse Prota-Giurleo, "Matteo Sassano detto 'Matteuccio' (documenti napolitani)," *Rivista italiana di musicologia* (1966): 97–119; and Federico Marri, "Muratori, la musica e il melodramma negli anni milanesi (1695–1700)," *Muratoriana* 16 (1988): 19–124; on Siface, see Corrado Ricci, *Farinelli: Quattro storie di castrati e primedonne fra Sei e Settecento* (Lucca: LIM, 1995), "Siface e la sua tragica fine," 47–75, and the forthcoming work of Louise K. Stein.

11. Matteo Noris, Giovanni Legrenzi, Niccoló Beregan; in Corinna Herr, *Gesang gegen "Die Ordnung der Natur": Kastraten und Falsettisten in der Musikgeschichte* (Kassel: Bärenreiter, 2013), 134–54.

12. On the tradition of the bird aria, see Rudolfo Celletti, *A History of Bel Canto,* translated by Frederick Fuller (Oxford: Clarendon Press, 1991), 52. The late medieval tradition is the subject of Elizabeth Eva Leach, *Sung Birds: Music, Nature, and Poetry in the Later Middle Ages* (Ithaca, NY: Cornell University Press, 2007). On French Renaissance birdsong, see Kate van Orden, "Sexual Discourse in the Parisian Chanson: A Libidinous Aviary," *JAMS* 48 (1995): 1–41; and on treatments in the late madrigal, see Gary Tomlinson's analysis comparing Wert with Monteverdi in *Monteverdi and the End of the Renaissance* (Berkeley: Univer-

sity of California Press, 1987), 48–52. Mancini's generic praise of music, prefacing his *Pensieri, e riflessioni prattiche*, says the art "was born from the first men themselves, who from the charming and natural concert of birds learned to sweetly modulate their own voices" (3). A facsimile of the Sonata violino solo representativa by Heinrich Ignaz Franz von Biber (1644–1704) is published in the Denkmäler der Musik in Salzburg, Faksimileausgaben, vol. 5 (Munich, 1994), and a modern edition in *Instrumentalwerke handschriftlicher Überlieferung*, in Denkmäler der Tonkunst in Österreich vol. 127, edited by Jiri Sehnal (Graz: Akademische Druck- u. Verlagsanstalt, 1976). Johann Jakob Walther (ca. 1650–1717) continually imitated instruments, birds, and other animals (e.g., in his *Scherzi d'augelli con il cucci* [sic], *leuto harpeggiante e rossignuolo*, and *Galli e galline*, 2nd ed. (Mainz: Ludovico Borgeat, 1694).

13. In Alessandro Scarlatti's "Ma il ben mio," written for Matteuccio in his role as Appio in *La caduta de' Decemviri* (Venice: San Bartolomeo, 1697), the vocal line starts unaccompanied with long-held notes that were probably sung as messe di voce with some amount of decoration.

14. Tosi, *Opinioni dei cantori antichi*, 30: "Benché il passaggio non abbia in sé forza, che basti al produrre quella soavità, che s'interna, nè sia considerate per lo più, che per ammirar in un cantante la felicità d'una voca flessibile, nondimeno è di somma urgenza, che il maestro nè istruisca lo scolaro, acciò con facile velocità, e giusta intonazione lo possegga, che quando in sito proprio è ben eseguito esige il suo applauso, e fa il cantore universale, cioè capace di cantare in ogni stile" (translated by Galliard in *Observations on the Florid Song; or, Sentiments on the Ancient and Modern Singers*, 2nd ed. [London: J. Wilcox, 1743], chapter 4.1, "On Divisions," 51). Sergio Durante situates the treatise in the trends of rationalist thought and sees it as more innovative than conservative in breaking the guild-like traditional resistance to anything but oral tradition in conveying insider knowledge about singing traditions. He also understands it as an amphibious work, part treatise, part satire— hence its satirical register in Durante's view is often mistaken for conservatism. See his "Strutture mentali e vocabolario di un cantore antico/moderno: Preliminari per una lettura delle fonti didattiche settecentesche," in *Alessandro Scarlatti und seine Zeit*, edited by Max Lütolf (Bern: Paul Haupt, 1995). He delineates its relationship to the Bolognese school in "Theorie und Praxis der Gesangsschulen zur Zeit Händels: Bemerkungen zu Tosis 'Opinioni de' cantori antichi e moderni,'" in *Händel auf dem Theater: Bericht über die Symposien der Internationalen Händel-Akademie, Karlsruhe, 1986 und 1987*, edited by Hans Joachim Marx (Laaber: Laaber, 1988), 59–72.

15. "Questo è troppo difficile: / Questa è d'autore antico, / Senza tremuli, trilli e appoggiature, / Troppo contraria alla moderna scuola,/ Che adorna di passaggi ogni parola." From *L'impresario delle canarie, intermezzo per La Didone*, intermezzo primo, in Pietro Metastasio, *Tutte le opere*, 5 vols., edited by Bruno Brunelli (Milan: Mondadori, 1943–54), 1: 55.

16. Flying Childers is still regarded as the first truly great thoroughbred racehorse. See "Thoroughbred Heritage," www.tbheritage.com/Portraits/FlyingChilders.html (accessed April 9, 2010).

17. From Riccardo Broschi, *Idaspe. Dramma per musica da rappresentarsi nel famosissimo Teatro Grimani di S. Gio. Grisostomo nell carnevale dell'anno 1730. Dedicato al prencipe regente di Waldeck in viaggio come conte di Pirmont. Venezia, Carlo Buonarigo. Pag. 47. Dedica di Domenico Lalli. Scene dei fratelli Giuseppe e Domenico Valeriani, ingegnieri del teatro*

e pittori di S.A.S.E. di Baviera, 47; autograph manuscript, A-Wn MS 18281, act 1, scene 16. A piano-vocal reduction appears in Haböck, ed., *Carlo Broschi Farinelli,* 16-24.

18. Carlo Broschi Farinelli, *La solitudine amica: Lettere al conte Sicinio Pepoli,* edited by Carlo Vitali with Roberto Pagano and Francesca Boris (Palermo: Sellerio, 2000), 114, 123, 129. Farinelli denied the rumors.

19. Robert Freeman, "Farinello and His Repertory," in *Studies in Renaissance and Baroque Music in Honor of Arthur Mendel,* edited by Robert L. Marshall (Kassel: Bärenreiter, 1974), 301-30, at 324-30.

20. De Castris might be seen as a precedent for this, having done much the same from 1687 onward in the Florence of Ferdinando de' Medici, Grand Prince of Tuscany, though at that time public performance, and certainly public theatrical performance, were not default modalities for success. Cf. Carlo Vitali, "De Castris [De' Massimi], Francesco [Cecchino, Checchino]," *GMO.*

21. Natalie Zemon Davis, *The Gift in Sixteenth-Century France* (Madison: University of Wisconsin Press, 2000).

22. On the new cult and industry of celebrity in London, see William Weber, *Music and the Middle Class: The Social Structure of Concert Life in London, Paris, and Vienna* (London: Croom Helm, 1975). An important primary source for the phenomenon is Benedetto Frizzi, *Dissertazione di biografia musicale* ([Trieste]: ca. 1802), esp. the early sections "On musical celebrity," "On the same subject," and "On other celebrated singers"; cf. John Rice, "Benedetto Frizzi on Singers, Composers, and Opera in Late Eighteenth-Century Opera," *Studi musicali* 23 (1994): 367-93. Stephen Willier documents intimately how Pacchierotti was encountered, cultivated, and circulated as a star in London in 1779-80 in "Gasparo Pacchierotti in London: The 1779-80 Season in Susanna Burney's 'Letter Journal,'" *Studi musicali* 29 (2000): 251-91. Ethnomusicology and popular music studies have been working on star cults for some time, importantly in Konstanze Kriese, ed., *Zwischen Rausch und Ritual: Zum Phänomen des Starkults* (Berlin: Zyankrise Berlin, 1994); Tom Mole, "Hypertrophic Celebrity," *M/C Journal: A Journal of Media and Culture* 7, no. 5 (2004); Kenneth Sasis Habib, "The Superstar Singer Fairouz and the Ingenious Rahbani Composers: Lebanon Sounding," PhD diss., University of California at Santa Barbara, 1995; Martin Stokes, *The Arabesk Debate: Music and Musicians in Modern Turkey* (Oxford: Clarendon Press, 1992). Comparable in musicology is Dana Gooley, "Franz Liszt: The Virtuoso as Strategist," in *The Musician as Entrepreneur, 1700–1914: Managers, Charlatans, and Idealists,* edited by William Weber (Bloomington: Indiana University Press, 2004), 145-61.

23. In Hedy Law's canny reading of Beaumarchais and Salieri's opera *Tarare* (Paris, 1787), the castrato Calpigi (a tenor) is negatively aligned with Louis XVI on the eve of the French Revolution. Calpigi is a eunuch husband; and the figure who stands in for the monarch is a sultan named Atar, whose harem Calpigi guards in a quietly embattled state. See Law, "Gestural Rhetoric," chapter 4.

24. Burkhard Schnepel, *Twinned Beings: Kings and Effigies in Southern Sudan, East India, and Renaissance France* (Göteborg: IASSA, 1995).

25. Important to my notion of kingship (whether under the alias of monarchy or sovereignty) in the early modern era are Ralph E. Giesey, *The Royal Funeral Ceremony in Renaissance France* (Geneva: E. Droz, 1960), which deals with the central conundrum of royal continuity; Giesey, *Rulership in France, 15th–17th Centuries* (Aldershot: Ashgate, 2004), a

collection of reprints of essays printed earlier, esp. chapter 12, "The King Imagined," and chapter 14, "The Two Bodies of the French King"; Paolo Prodi, *The Papal Prince: One Body and Two Souls: The Papal Monarchy in Early Modern Europe,* translated by Susan Haskins (Cambridge: Cambridge University Press, 1987); and Gabriel Guarino, *Representing the King's Splendour: Communication and Reception of Symbolic Forms of Power in Viceregal Naples* (Manchester: Manchester University Press / Palgrave Macmillan, 2010). Classic anthropological works that inform my thinking include A. M. Hocart, *Kingship* (London: Humphrey Milford for Oxford University Press, 1927); Hocart, *Kings and Councillors: An Essay in the Comparative Anatomy of Human Society,* edited with an introduction by Rodney Needham, foreword by E. E. Evans-Pritchard (Chicago: University of Chicago Press, 1970), chapter 8, "The King"; E. E. Evans Pritchard, "The Divine Kingship of the Shilluk of the Nilotic Sudan," in *Social Anthropology and Other Essays* (New York: The Free Press of Glencoe, 1964), 192–212; Godfrey Lienhardt, *Divinity and Experience: The Religion of the Dinka* (Oxford: Clarendon Press, 1961); Valerio Valeri, *Kingship and Sacrifice: Ritual and Society in Ancient Hawaii,* translated by Paula Wissing (Chicago: University of Chicago Press, 1985); and Valerio Valeri, "Regalità," in *Enciclopedia Einaudi,* 16 vols., directed by Ruggiero Romano (Turin: G. Einaudi, 1977–1984), vol. 11 (1980), 742–71.

26. I am indebted here to Alfred Gell, *Art and Agency: An Anthropological Theory* (Oxford: Clarendon Press, 1998); Gell, "Technology and Magic," *Anthropology Today* 4 (1988): 6–9; and Gell, *Anthropology, Art, and Aesthetics,* edited by Jeremy Coote and Anthony Shelton (Oxford: Clarendon Press, 1992), 40–63.

27. Tosi, *Opinioni dei cantori antichi,* 30.

28. Tosi, *Observations on the Florid Song,* 52–53.

29. Tosi, *Opinioni dei cantori antichi,* 31.

30. Tosi, *Opinioni dei cantori antici,* 34: "Sappia l'istruttore che se una buona voce agiatamente sparsa si fa migliore, agitate poi dal moto velocissimo dei passaggi in cui non ha tempo d'organizzarsi si converte in mediocre, e talvolta per negligenza del maestro e con pregiudicio dello scolaro diventa pessima." In Galliard's translation of Tosi, *Observations on the Florid Song,* see chapter 4, "On Divisions," 4.3, 4.4, 4.11, 4.12, 4.13, and 4.17 (the last a translation of the quote here).

31. "Chi dunque non l'ha da natura, neppure deve perdere vanamente il tempo col tentar d'acquistarla, nè deve gettar la fatica, e il fiato col cercar d'eseguirla, così pure il prudente Maestro, ritrovato lo scolare senza disposizione naturale per cantar d'agilità, invece di condurlo per questa strada, egli deve additargliene un'altra." Mancini, *Riflessioni pratiche sul canto figurato* (Milan: Giuseppe Galeazzo, 1777), Article 12, "On the Agility of the Voice," paragraph 2 (added to 1774 edition). Until at least the 1790s there were not supposed to be any real glottal attacks in marked passaggi.

32. Precise technologies of breathing were not spelled out in ways that satisfy modern-day expectations until the nineteenth century, with Crescentini and especially Garcia. But from the more rhetorically oriented eighteenth-century singing manuals we can infer much about uses of breath and even theories of breath control.

33. John Potter has interesting comments on how Tosi advised combining *strascino* with portamento and messa di voce ("Vocal Performance in the 'Long Eighteenth Century,'" in *The Cambridge History of Performance,* edited by Colin Lawson and Robin Stilwell [Cambridge: Cambridge University Press, 2012] 512).

34. This was a tall order for the amateurs who bought Tenducci's printed solfeggi, not to mention much more difficult solfeggi or *vocalizzi* by Crescentini and others oriented to professional singers. That divisions would also be "perfectly in tune" went without saying. Richard Wistreich has written eloquently on the importance on the trill in Mancini in "'Il canto nobile': Vocal Technique and Sonic Identity in the Renaissance," paper given at the Renaissance Society of America Annual Meeting, 2006. On Mancini's dispute with Manfredini on the trill, which Manfredini thought could not be taught to untalented students, see Julianne Baird, "An Eighteenth-Century Controversy about the Trill: Mancini vs. Manfredini," *Early Music* 15 (1987): 36–45; and see Mancini, *Pensieri, e riflessioni prattiche*, 15 and passim.

35. Quantz, *Lebenslauf*, in facsimile in Willi Kahl, *Selbstbiographien deutscher Musiker des 18. Jahrhunderts* (Cologne: Staufen-Verlag, 1948; The Netherlands: Frits Knuf, 1972) on Senesino, 213; on Farinelli, 234; and on Orsini, 218.

36. Bontempi, *Historia musica*, 110. For Verri, see chapter 5 below.

37. Rosa Ponselle sings a continuous series of trills in a 1936 recording of Rossini's "Bel raggio lunsighier," discussed below, esp. at 4:42 through 5:00. Elvira de Hidalgo delivers a true trill at the end of the cabaletta of "Una voce poco fa" at 5:58 through 6:02. One can also hear a rich trill from Sigrid Onégin in Mozart's "Alleluja," from the *Exultate jubilate*, at 1:25, on the eponymous album (remastered and released by Pearl Records, October 1, 1999), catalog no. 9274, track 2. The radio broadcasts of Rosa Ponselle are remastered on *Rosa Ponselle on the Air, Vol. 1, 1934–1936* (52012-2 Marston, 1999), and *Rosa Ponselle on the Air, Vol. 2, 1936–1937* (52032-2 Marston, 2000), and discussed in Mary Jane Philipps-Matz, *Rosa Ponselle: American Diva* (Boston: Northeastern University Press, 1997); and James Drake, *Rosa Ponselle: A Centenary Biography* (Portland, OR: Amadeus Press, 1997). The young Maria Callas (1923–77) and de Hidalgo have been remastered together on the CD *The Pupil and Her Teacher: De Hidalgo, Callas* (CD Fono 1010, 2001). Later in life Callas disclaimed having listened to Ponselle's weekly radio broadcasts (on the documentary by John Ardoin with Franco Zeffirelli, *Callas: A Documentary Plus Bonus* [Bel Canto Society, 1978]), but it defies belief that a passionate young singer living in New York would never have heard any of them or known who Ponselle was.

38. I take the term "rocketing virtuosity" from Desmond Shawe-Taylor, quoted in Jürgen Kesting, *Maria Callas*, translated by John Hunt (Boston: Northeastern University Press, 1993), 161. We might assume that the greater the range, the further the rocket could move from its launching pad. Mancini said that in this respect only Ferri in the seventeenth century could match Farinelli in the eighteenth, though the assertion probably says more about singing as a form of myth and memory than about Ferri and how Mancini knew what exactly he did. Mancini, *Pensieri, e riflessioni pratiche*, 11–12, and see 105 for a direct comparison of the two.

39. On the fate of the trill in modern vocal history, see Will Crutchfield, "The Trill Is Gone . . . But It May Be Coming Back," *Opera News*, January 1999, 26–30; and Crutchfield, "Vocal Performance in the Nineteenth Century," in *The Cambridge History of Performance*, edited by Colin Lawson and Robin Stilwell (Cambridge: Cambridge University Press, 2012), 616–17.

40. Rossini's father Giuseppe Rossini wrote in a letter to his son that Colbran "does not remember when Crescentini gave her lessons out of charity, at the time when they were in

Madrit [sic]"; quoted in Herbert Weinstock, *Rossini: A Biography*. New York (Alfred A. Knopf, 1968), 175.

41. The version sung by Callas and almost all other late nineteenth- and twentieth-century singers comes from a late nineteenth-century source. See the different ornamentations in several sources contemporaneous with Rossini discussed by Will Crutchfield, "Early Vocal Ornamentation," Appendix V of *Il barbiere di Siviglia, Critical Commentary*, pp. 361–420, esp. pp. 393–409, in *Il barbiere di Siviglia: Almaviva o sia l'inutile precauzione, commedia in due atti di Cesare Sterbini dalla commedia di Pierre-Augustin Caron de Beaumarchais*, edited by Patricia B. Brauner, vol. 2 of *Works of Gioacchino Rossini*, general editor Philip Gossett (Kassel: Bärenreiter, 2008), 360–420.

42. Wistreich, "Il canto nobile."

43. Siface had been sent to England to entertain his patron Francesco's sister, Mary of Modena, queen of England and consort of James II.

44. Harold S. Powers, "Il Serse Trasformato," *Musical Quarterly* 47 (1961): 481–92 and 48 (1962): 73–92, shows the deep antecedents of the libretto and Handel's music in operatic versions of the story created by Minato and Cavalli (Venice, 1654) and Stampiglia and Bononcini (Rome, 1694). Winton Dean, "Handel's *Serse*," in *Opera and the Enlightenment*, edited by Thomas Bauman and Marita Petzoldt McClymonds (Cambridge: Cambridge University Press, 1995), 135–67, esp. 14–47, does much to straighten out the questions of genre and the music's relationship to Bononcini, though I think Dean failed to see the bathos in Serse's "Ma come, non sò" of "Se bramate" (140), nor do the singers figure there.

45. See James Davidson, "Versailles with Panthers," *London Review of Books* 25, no. 13 (July 10, 2003).

46. If Handel's Xerxes is part conquerer and part tragic clown, the pagan idol of a tree that he is first seen venerating after emerging from the parched deserts of central Asia does give shade and promise water, making "Ombra mai fu" less comical as an elegiac sostenuto. (Its ancient literary background is the subject of Frank H. Stubbings, "Xerxes and the Plane-Tree," *Greece & Rome* 15, no. 44 [May 1946]: 63–67.) The plane tree is mentioned by Herodotus, *Book VII*, translated and edited by Cyril E. Robinson (Oxford: Clarendon Press, 1922), 112, 115, and on 39, where he attributes the gift of the plane tree (which gives off a wonderful sap for honey) to the very rich father of Darius. An amusing and informative revisitation of Xerxes's plane tree occurs at the start of Davidson's "Versailles with Panthers," 7–10.

This was related comically by Goldoni in his memoirs. A similar polarity had applied in Monteverdi's time. He told Striggio that divinities should execute *tirate* (runs), *gorgheggi* (shakes), and trills, while mortal men and women (presumably including mythical ones like Orpheus and Ariadne) could execute the sustained style of *spianato*. With Metastasian opera seria, mortal men and women had replaced deities as the alpha to omega of dramatis personae, whether clearly historical or (less often) mythical. In the Metastasian incarnation following Corneille, all can be glossed as mytho-historical, which made some of them also quasi-divine.

47. Here we have a single sentence, distributed in four short verse lines and stated twice. The singing world has consistently recognized the weight of "Ombra mai fu" and the difficulty of executing it well. In 1989 Dmitri Hvorostovsky won the BBC Cardiff Singer of the World Competition over Welsh native Bryn Terfel with a combination of a Verdi aria and "Ombra mai fu." The expressions "mettere bene la voce" and "fermare la voce" were used by

Tosi (the *Opinioni* mentions "l'arte di mettere la voce" and "la bella messa di voce" [17]), and Mancini (*Pensieri, e riflessioni pratiche,* article VII, "Della maniera di cavare, modulare, e fermare la voce," 76; Article VIII, "Dell'unione de' due registri, portamento di voce, e dell'appoggiatura," which speaks of "l'arte di graduare, e sostenere la voce, proverà poi una dolce facilità nel perfezzionare la messa di voce," 95; and Article IX, "Della messa di voce," 99–107). Frati, "Antonio Bernacchi," 477, says Raaff's teaching used Bernacchi's methods, of which one of the three main goals was learning *mettere bene la voce*, from which ornamentation and much else proceeded.

48. Daston and Park, *Wonders and the Order of Nature*, 255.

49. Jean Grundy Fanelli, "A Sweet Bird of Youth: Caffarelli in Pistoia," *Early Music* 27 (1999): 55–63; Daniel Heartz, "Caffarelli's Caprices," in *Music Observed: Studies in Memory of William C. Holmes*, edited by Colleen Reardon and Susan Parisi (Warren, MI: Harmonie Park Press, 2004), chapter 11.

50. Burney, *General History*, 4: 419 note n.

51. "In tutto quello ch'egli canta regna sempre un tòno lagrimevole di lamentazioni da far venire l'accidia all'allegria." Metastasio, *Tutte le opere* 3: 395, letter of May 28, 1749. The criticism implied a disdain for the older singing styles of Nicolino and Sassani (Matteuccio).

52. In *Opera and Sovereignty,* chapter 6, I trace such contrasts through the errant Hadrian to the benevolent Titus, from the rather terrible Valentinian III to the proud and jealous Porus, or in one and the same being the errant but ultimately virtuous king Alexander the Great, who comes to conquer lands and a woman but relents in a moment of moral contrition.

53. In English as Georges Bataille, *The Accursed Share: An Essay on General Economy*, 3 vols. in 2, translated by Robert Hurley (New York: Zone Books, 1993) (and see my reading of Bataille vis-à-vis the world of eighteenth-century Italian opera in *Opera and Sovereignty,* 280–83).

54. Io mi trovo a spalla con spalla coll'Imperatore senza conoscerlo, figurandomi di doverlo distinguere dal vestimento, ma subito suggeritomi dal gentilissimo signor Principe mi buttai a piedi del Patrone, con dirli queste seguenti parole: "Il momento più fortunato di mia vita, è questo d'esser genuflesso ai Clementissimi Piedi della Sacra Cesarea Cattolica Maestrà Vostra." In ciò mi ripose senza ch'io potessi comprendere quello che dicesse, solo nell'ultimo intesi con distinzione: "Avremo piacere di sentire la vostra virtù con gran desiderio" ed ecco che mi fa mettere al cembalo e sonai e cantai da me un'aria. Assicuro a Vostra Eccellenza in che posi le mani sul cembalo non avevo più animo nè spirito, ma siccome la clemenza eccede, e dall'animo che mi faceva il signor Principe, quale era sempre appresso di me, cantai come Iddio volse, li feci tre messe di voce ed altre cose studiose, alle quali la Clemenza Sua si degnò animarle con dir "Bravo." Finito l'aria mi disse: "Voi siete Napoliello," ed io li risposi "Son di quei dei veri macaroni," e si attaccò a sorridere. Li baggiai di novo la mano, e lui me la strinse fortemente con dirmi un'altra volta bravo, e se n'andiede per andare in chiesa, e la Patrona l'accompagnò. (Farinelli, *La solitudine amica,* 99–100, letter of March 31, 1732)

The further quotations come from Farinelli's reception at court later that spring: "Dopo terminata la prima cantata, venne il gentilissimo signor Principe Pio da parte dei Patroni a dimandarmi che senso mi faceva tale notizia. Risposi allo stesso, che i trilli hanno guadagnati quelli [docati], e spero che i medesimi possano riguadagnarne de gl'altri; sentito questo, si attaccorono a ridere d'un gran gusto, e poi l'Imperatrice mi disse che non dubitasse che sarò pagato" (ibid., 101, letter of April 26, 1732).

55. "Vocabolario degli Accademia della Crusca," "grazia," online at http://vocabolario. biblio.cribecu.sns.it/cgi-bin/Vocabolario/search_co . . . (accessed May 11, 2007).

56. Dal signor Inviato di Genova ho avuto per regalo un servizio d'argento per cioccolata ben polito e grazioso, ed una borsa di cento unghari nuovi che paiono tante medaglie; dalla signora Marchesa Serra una gentilissima scattola d'oro; dal signor Conte Martiniz una superba scattola d'oro di Parigi, dal signor Principe di Cardona una pesantissima scatola [sic] d'oro d'Inghilterra; dal signor Conte Chinxi, un orologio d'Inghilterra d'oro senza ripetizione e per la sua gentilezza me lo mangiarei, da signor Conte Slich una scattola che non v'è oro che la paga, essendo tutta diaspro legata in Inghilterra, che chiunque la vede resta stordita, ed in verità io non ho visto in quel genere la compagna. Dalla signora Contessa di Coll'alto uno stucchio d'oro d'Inghilterra ascendendo la summa di 80 luigi, dal signor Marchese Perlas un servizio d'argento per viaggio di valore di 1000 fiorini, questo ultimo non è poco, tanto più essendo il Primo Ministro che comanda le teste. (Farinelli, *La solitudine amica,* 101–2)

The conflation of gifts and cash was long-standing. On Ferri receiving precious objects with money inside, see Baiocco, "Su Baldassare Ferri, cantante evirato del Seicento," *Esercizi, musica e spettacolo,* new series, 6, no. 15 (1996): 31.

57. See Thomas McGeary, "Farinelli's Progress to Albion: The Recruitment and Reception of Opera's 'Blazing Star,'" *British Journal for Eighteenth-Century Studies* 28 (2005): 339–60.

As usual for a newcomer, shortly after arriving in London and before appearing on stage in October 1734, Farinelli sang at court for the king and queen. He wrote, "All'improviso [sic] mi furono tirate arie d'Endel; con gran franchezza mi posi ad eseguir quelle e grazie al Cielo ne sortie con tutta la Gloria e tal cosa mi fa giungere a questa presente sorte." Farinelli thus scored as huge a success at court as on stage, even with Handel's arias, which were not in his stage repertory (Farinelli, *La solitudine amica,* 132, letter of November 30, 1734). He later complained to Pepoli, with some defensiveness, about the cost of living: "Le ghinee qui volano come mezzi pauli, e tutto è caro, e per la casa sola per un anno con tale denaro in Bologna comprerei molto terreno; io grazie a Dio spendo quello che solamente è necessario per il mio bisognevole, non buttando a male neanche un scelino per capriccio" (ibid., 133).

58. Cf. McGeary, "Farinelli's Progress to Albion," 340–41 and passim; and Farinelli, *La solitudine amica,* 132–33 (letter from London of November 11, 1734).

59. "Ho rimesso a Venezia tre mila zecchini alla macina, e l'anno venturo rimettere se non tanto, più; ed andando di questo passo presto presto presto lasciare il mestiere di canoro accento" (July 2, 1735). Farinelli, *La solitude amica,* 139.

60. Georg Simmel, *The Philosophy of Money,* edited by David Frisby, translated by Tom Bottomore and David Frisby, 2nd ed., revised and enlarged (1907; London: Routledge, 1990), 222–23.

61. Elisabetta Avanzati, "The Unpublished Senesino," in the catalog of the exhibition *Handel and the Castrati: The Story behind the 18th-Century Superstar Singers, 19 March–1 October 2006* (London: Handel House Museum, 2006), 5–9.

62. Jacques Derrida, *Given Time: 1. Counterfeit Money*, translated by Peggy Kamuf (Chicago: University of Chicago Press, 1992). The original title was *Donner le temps. 1. La fausse monnaie*.

63. A marvelous early account of the system of incommensurable exchange within patron-client relations in old-regime France is Sharon Kettering, *Patrons, Brokers, and Clients in Seventeenth-Century France* (New York: Oxford University Press, 1986).

64. "Mi bevo tutte le sante sere 8 in 9 arie in corpo, non v'è mai riposo" (palazzo del Pardo, February 16, 1738); Farinelli, *La solitudine amica*, 143–44.

65. Balatri wrote something similar—that on arriving at the khanate on the Lower Volga, he had nothing to feed on but arias, which he chewed up for the khan, one after another. See "Frutti del Mondo," 1: 31v: "(Sia maled[etto] . . . il Diavol, io hò fame / et altr'hò intasca che cantare Ariette, / e tantopiù che tuttequelle hò dette / che mi potea saper, son' un'infame.)" The episode extends from 1: 29v to 1: 41r.

66. On Siface see Carlo Nardini, *Il musico Siface e l'ambasciatore di Francia a Roma nel 1683* (Florence: Coppini e Bocconi, 1891).

67. I discuss the long-standing convention of public "gifts" from "ladies" as it relates to operatic dedications in *Opera and Sovereignty*, 348–56.

68. William C. Holmes, *Opera Observed: Views of a Florentine Impresario in the Early Eighteenth Century* (Chicago: University of Chicago Press, 1993), 136–39. Cf. David Hunter, "Senesino Disobliges Caroline, Princess of Wales, and Princess Violante of Florence," *Early Music* 30 (2002): 214–23. On Parma's plans for regaling Loreto Vittori, see Biancamaria Antolini, "La carriera di cantante e compositore di Loreto Vittori," *Studi musicali* 7 (1978): 141–88, at 148–50.

69. This was the nineteenth-century French lawyer, composer, poet, and critic François-Henri-Joseph Blaze, known simply as Castil-Blaze (1784–1857).

70. Heartz, "Caffarelli's Caprices," 204–7.

71. Caffarelli famously dueled with the poet Ballot de Sauvot over the merits of French versus Italian music. See Eugenio Faustini-Fasini, "Gli astri maggiori del 'bel canto' napoletano: Gaetano Majorano detto 'Caffarelli,'" *Note d'archivio per la storia musicale* 15 (1938): 121–28, 157–70, 258–70, at 264–65, who takes the story from Giorgio Cucuel, *La Pouplinière et la musique de chambre au XVIIIe siècle* (Paris: Fischbacher, 1913), 302–3.

72. Caffarelli debuted in Sarro's *Il Valdemarro* at the Teatro delle Dame (Rome, Carnival 1726). Playing male roles was normally a sign of ascent in a castrato's professional career and his place on the social ladder, though some by type were never suited to female roles. The only well-known castrati who seem to have been content to remain in female roles were a few who were renowned for them in the Papal States, primarily, it seems, because they fit the bill physically. Examples include Farfallino (Giacinto Fontana), appropriately nicknamed, and Marianino, earlier in his Roman career. Even those with extra-high voices, like Matteo Berselli and Egizziello (Gioacchino Conti, also called Gizziello), played female parts only at the beginning of their careers (if then).

73. The whole production is shadowed with irony. When the opera debuted in Vienna two years earlier, an apologetic *licenza* was appended disclaiming any likeness between

Hadrian and the emperor Karl VI, to whom it was dedicated, but within two years it hardly mattered.

74. The aria that ends act 1, "Lieto così tal volta," was embellished by Pergolesi with obbligato oboe throughout. The aria that ends act 2, "Torbido in volto e nero," was threaded with astounding coloratura and supported by a double orchestra. For a pointed discussion of these, see Daniel Heartz, *Music in European Capitals: The Galant Style, 1720–1780* (New York: Norton, 2003), 114–15. See Dale E. Monson," Drama in Pergolesi's Opere Serie: Expression and Tradition," in the issue entitled "Aspetti della vita, dell'opera e del contesto storico pergolesiani," *Studi pergolesiani* 4 (2000): 273–92.

75. See Giovanni Battista Pergolesi, *Adriano in Siria*, edited by Dale E. Monson, Pergolesi Complete Works, no. 1 (Stuyvesant, NY: Pendragon, 1986).

76. He may have been viewed as a grown-up boy wonder, a changed man, or, in later times, as a mutilated freak—a strangeness familiar to music histories but not made any less strange for that.

77. The images appear in Mercedes Viale Ferrero, *La scenografia del '700 e i fratelli Galliari* (Turin: Edizioni d'Arte Fratelli Pozzo, 1963), and plate 18 (p. 181), commentary on p. 69, and see Marini's young prince Euristeo in plate 16 (p. 157). Both are associated with performances at Turin's Regio Teatro.

78. Ernst Kantorowicz, *The King's Two Bodies: A Study in Mediaeval Political Theology* (Princeton, NJ: Princeton University Press, 1957).

79. Henri Hubert and Marcel Mauss, *Sacrifice: Its Nature and Functions*, translated by W. D. Halls, foreword by E. E. Evans-Pritchard (Chicago: University of Chicago Press, 1964), esp. chapter 3.

80. If the concept seems hard to grasp we need only consider that none of this would apply to modern Western monarchies, as epitomized by the royals of Britain, in that they are hidebound and honor-bound to uphold the norms of a bourgeois middle class, which they represent and mirror in ways that were not true before bourgeois rationalist codes took root—codes that had much to do with the demise of operatic castrati in the years around 1800.

81. Roger Freitas, *Portrait of a Castrato: Politics, Patronage, and Music in the Life of Atto Melani* (Cambridge: Cambridge University Press, 2009), 159–60 and 180.

82. On Loreto, see Antolini, "La carriera di cantante e compositore di Loreto Vittori." On Pellegrini, see Winton Dean and John Rosselli, "Pellegrini, Valeriano," in *GMO*. The score is available in modern edition as Agostino Steffani, *Tassilone, tragedia per musica (in 5 atti)*, edited by Gerhard Croll, Denkmäler rheinischer Musik, vol. 8 (Düsseldorf: Schwann, 1958).

83. Ferri had already been much honored in Vienna by Ferdinand III and then Leopold I in Vienna. Nicolini was much honored in Handel's London, as well as in Venice, Naples, and elsewhere.

84. The portrait is now in Stuttgart's Staatsgalerie. Other Amigoni portraits of Farinelli are listed in Ellen T. Harris, "Farinelli [Broschi, Carlo; Farinello]," *GMO*.

85. Some honorific titles awarded castrati were not unlike the courtier-styled titles bestowed on singers that often appear in libretto cast lists, though they seem to have been less usual and more marked. In 1702 Pistocchi was named *virtuoso di camera e di cappella* to Prince Ferdinando de' Medici of Tuscany, and Bernacchi was made *virtuoso* to Prince Antonio

Farnese of Parma in 1714. In 1730 Caffarelli was made *virtuoso da camera* to the Grand Duke of Tuscany (Winton Dean, "Caffarelli [Cafariello, Cafarellino, Gaffarello] [Majorano, Gaetano]," *GMO*); and in 1793 Bruni was made *virtuoso da camera* in Modena to Ercole III d'Este (Nicola Lucarelli, "Bruni, Domenico Luigi," *GMO*). The list goes on and on and includes all kinds of singers. These appointments were similar to modern job titles—closer to, say, Professor Mary Douglas than to Dame Mary Douglas—save the crucial fact that the honor conveyed by the old patronage systems of courts was still profoundly bound up with royalty and nobility in a world in which honor and obligation were motors of the universe. They defined loyalties on both sides while generally still allowing singers so "entitled" to travel, often for very substantial periods. It's nevertheless important to recognize that these titles encompass wide-ranging differences in levels of prestige and duty. The mutual obligations of singer and patron involved could be heavily burdened with entailments or hardly entailing at all.

86. Freitas, *Portrait of a Castrato*, chapter 2, esp. 46–47, about the Tuscans' wish to "obligate" the French. Mattias calls him "Atto mio castrato."

> 87. È così grande la premura, che tengo di servire a S.M. Christianissima et a V.E., che non ostante, che molti rispetti mi ritenessero in mandare Atto mio castrato a Francia, e particolarmente l'haver fatte molte negative a Principi Grandi ... nondimeno mi contento, che venga a servire S.M.tà in tutto quello li verrà comandato, e lo concedo all'E.V. per il tempo, che s'è compiaciuta ricercarmene, sperando, che doppo, mi farà favore di rimandarmelo, e di non trattenerlo d'avantaggio ... per poter servirmene in un'opera che già ho determinata di far recitare.

The letter dates from September 24, 1644, from Mattias in Siena to Mazarin. I quote here the translation into English and the original Italian as given in Roger Freitas, "Un atto d'ingegno: A Castrato in the Seventeenth Century," PhD diss., Yale University, 1998, 56 n. 21.

88. Malcolm Boyd and John Rosselli, "Tosi, Pier Francesco"; *GMO*; Colin Timms, "Cecchi, Domenico ['Il Cortona']"; Lawrence Bennett, "Vismarri [Vismari], Filippo"; Carlo Vitali, "De Castris [De' Massimi], Francesco [Cecchino, Checchino]," all in *GMO*.

89. See Freitas, *Portrait of a Castrato*, 186–91, on Rospigliosi's election.

90. Burney, *General History* 4: 490–91.

91. "He had a powerful, clear, equal and sweet contralto voice, with a perfect intonation and an excellent shake. His manner of singing was masterly and his elocution unrivalled. Though he never loaded Adagios with too many ornaments, he delivered the original and essential notes with the utmost refinement. He sang Allegros with great fire, and marked rapid divisions, from the chest, in an articulate and pleasing manner. His countenance was well adapted to the stage, and his action was natural and noble. To these qualities he joined a majestic figure."

92. See Feldman, *Opera and Sovereignty*, 318, fig. 7.9.

93. On the regality of Scalzi's pose, dress, and gesture, theatrically imitating a royal pose but pointing to music, see Daniel Heartz, "Portrait of a Primo Uomo: Carlo Scalzi in Venice ca. 1740," in *Musikalische Ikonographie*, edited by Harald Heckmann, Monika Holl, and Hans Joachim Marx (Laaber: Laaber-Verlag, 1994), 137–38.

94. Romualdo Sasso, *Un celebre musico fabrianese: Gaspare Pacchierotti* (Fabriano: Stab. di Arte Grafiche "Gentile," 1935); Giovanni Toffano, *Gaspare Pacchierotti: Il crepuscolo di un*

musico al tramonto della Serenissima ([Padova?]: Armelin Musica, 1999); and Stephen A. Willier, *The Life and Career of a Celebrated Eighteenth-Century Castrato, Gasparo Pacchierotti (1740–1821)*, in preparation. My sincere thanks to Stephen Willier for allowing me to read his book in typescript.

95. Cristoforo Arnaboldi bought former noble lands from the revolutionary government of the Cisalpine Republic, enabling his nephew to marry later into the restored Piemontese aristocracy. Carlo Antonio Vianello, *Teatri spettacoli musiche a Milano nei secoli scorsi* (Milan: Lombarda, 1941), 283–84.

96. Benedetto Croce, *I teatri di Napoli* (Naples: L. Pierro, 1891), 411n, collected eighteenth-century anecdotes told by Joseph Lalande and Stefano Arteaga relating that someone responded to the motto by writing on the house "Ille cum, tu sine!" Don Fastidio, "La Casa di Caffarello," *Napoli nobilissima* 8 (1898): 119–21, traces the origins of the motto without proposing to change its significance as a reflection of Caffarelli's self-image. The small palace is at vico Carminiello 15, near the central corridor of via Toledo in Naples. My thanks to photographer Matteo Piscitelli for taking several photographs of it for this book over a period of time.

97. The *OED* gives the following for "regalia" n.[1]:

"a. Chiefly Law. Rights belonging to a monarch or ruler; royal powers or privileges.

b. The right of a monarch to exercise control over the revenues of a vacant bishopric or abbey, and over appointments in its dependent benefices. Also: †the revenues so treated (obs.). Cf. REGALE n.[1] 1. Now *hist.* c. With pl. concord. Rights or privileges, esp. jurisdiction over property, granted by a sovereign to the Church. Cf. REGALITY n.[1] 2b. rare. Now *hist.*"

Under "regale," we read: "a. Church Hist. The right of the king of France to appropriate revenues from a vacant bishopric or abbey; (also) the right of the king to appoint to any benefice in a diocese with an episcopal vacancy. Now *hist.* and *rare*. The former right is sometimes known as *temporal regale,* and the latter as *spiritual regale;* cf. *Dict. de Trévoux* (1721)."

Under "regality": "2. b. In *pl.* A right or privilege granted by a monarch to the Church; = *regalia* n.[1] 1c. Obs. rare."

98. 1. Eccl. Hist.

99. Chambers *Cyclopedia* (1727–38) is copying the *Dictionnaire de Trévoux* here. *OED,* "regale, *n.*[1].

100. I-Bas, *Notarile,* Lorenzo Gambarini, "Inventario legale della eredità di Carlo Broschi detto Farinelli." Dated 1783, it is based on his own (now lost) inventory of 1778, as attested in his holograph will. My thanks to Francesca Boris of the Archivio di Stato di Bologna and the Centro Studi Farinelli for providing easy access to this and other materials. On paintings in the inventory, see Francesca Boris and Giampietro Cammarota, "La collezione di Carlo Broschi detto Farinelli," *Accademia Clementina: Atti e memorie* 27, new series (1990): 187–237, with a transcription of portions of the inventory pertaining to paintings on 209–19 and extensive notes including many identifiable paintings on 220–37. See also Francesca Boris, "Il Farinello: La villa perduta," *Il carrobbio: Tradizioni, problemi, immagini dell'Emilia Romagna* 24 (1998): 157–72; and Luigi Verdi, "Il Farinelli a Bologna: Dai primi successi alla fama internazionale del più celebre cantante italiano del Settecento," *Nuova rivista musicale italiana* 2 (2003): 197–237; and Verdi, "Farinelli in Bologna," *British Journal for Eighteenth-Century Studies* 28, no. 3 (2005): 411–20.

101. Boris and Cammarota, "La collezione di Carlo Broschi detto Farinelli," 189–91.

102. Ibid., 191.

103. It was for Karl VI and his wife Elisabeth Christine that Farinelli had sung privately in Vienna in 1732, aged twenty-seven, and from the emperor that he received the legendary advice reported by Burney and Sacchi to temper his powers of execution in favor of expressive singing, hence to please more than astonish.

The royal portraits did not include the Bourbons at Naples and Spain, from whom he kept a distance after being gently dismissed on Ferdinand's death from the new court of Carlo III. Bologna meant reconfirming ties not just to his adopted city but, by settling at last in Bolognese territory, to the land of his deceased father figure, Count Sicinio Pepoli, to whom in 1740 he had written, "I am Bolognese, and all happiness falls to me for that reason." (The fuller quote: "Son bolognese, tutte le contentezze mi cadono di ragione, e sono a parte di quell godimento che hanno goduto gli abitatori di sì degna città.") When he wrote those lines to Pepoli on September 8, 1740, it would still be nineteen years before he returned home (Farinelli, *La solitudine amica*, 163).

104. The genre paintings included hunting scenes, castles, servants, and artisans (an apple seller and a cook). Even the servants' quarters were adorned with artwork. In their little salon were architectural ovals, a sacred conception, groves, and bucolic scenes, and a San Francesco. Unlike Padre Martini's portraiture, which wanted to follow the life of musical Europe as a whole, Farinelli's followed its courts. As Boris and Cammarota stress, the collection traces a life story more than it does antiquarian collecting habits—"not meticulous collectionism, but ... the disordered accumulation of gifts received by a divo" (Boris and Cammarota, "La collezione di Carlo Broschi detto Farinelli," 192).

CHAPTER 5. COLD MAN, MONEY MAN, BIG MAN TOO

1. Debbo bensi alla verità una dichiarazione. Nel declamare contro i castrati, non intendere di togliere da qualcheduno di essi quei meriti di cultura, di onestà, di viver civile che in pochi d'essi si trovano ma che pure trovansi. Io mi scateno contra la lor professione, contro lo loro stato, e contro l'indegna massima mantenerlo, alimentarlo, fomentarlo, premiarlo.

    La sola Italia ha il bel vanto di produrre e coltivar sì bel frutto. E la sola Francia ha poi quello di abborirlo e di ricusarlo. Ognuno infatti è dispensato dal conoscere l'uomo in costoro. Pure i rari pregi di qualcheduno di essi fanno sì forte illusione che talvolta si giunge a scordarsi ancora della loro mostruosità.

    Ma tempo sarebbe ormai che si cessasse di sacrificare queste misere vittime. Non basta che la gola e il lusso espongano le vite di tante genti e tanti disastri sol per comporci e recarci alle labbra una tazza di cioccolata, che ancor si vuole ridur gli uomini in vili mostri scifosi solo per solleticarci le orecchie con un'arietta. (Francesco Albergati Capacelli, *Il ciarlator maldicente*, in *Scelta di commedie e novelle morali*, 2 vols., edited by Antonio Ravelli [London: Giuseppe Cooper, 1794?], 2: vii–viii; play on 10–123)

    A first edition of the play was published as part of a duodecimo vanity set (Venice: Carlo Palese, 1783–85), in vol. 12, and the last was evidently issued in Milan in 1828. Ravelli stressed in his preface the capacity of Albergati's plays to "instruct and delight," teaching Englishmen an "elegant," "natural style" of modern Italian while inculcating good morals (1: v–viii). Albergati translated numerous French plays, published his own plays, novellas, and letters, was the dedicatee of an edition of Petrarch's lyrics (Livorno, 1778), and carried on a correspondence with Goldoni, Voltaire, Alfieri, Baretti, Bettinelli, and Gozzi. He had a private theater built outside Bologna, where he acted and staged works that displayed the combination of satire and moralism that marked his own plays. See the *Dizionario enciclopedico della letteratura italiana*, 6 vols., edited by Giuseppe Petronio (Bari: Laterza, 1966–70), 1: 42, 44; and *Il Settecento: L'Arcadia e l'età delle riforme*, edited by Gaetano Campagnino, Guido Nicastro, and Giuseppe Savoca (Bari: Laterza, 1970–80), 6, no. 2: 483–84, which paints him as an "organizer and popularizer of culture" and collector of new literary attitudes.

2. "If fathers wish to allot some of their sons to the art of singing, let them allot only those who have good and beautiful voices." Giambattista Mancini, *Riflessioni pratiche sul canto figurato* (Vienna: Ghelen, 1774), n. 41, art. 5; facsimile edition, Bibliotheca musica Bononiensis, sezione II (1777; Bologna: Forni, 1970), n. 41, article 5; translated in *Practical Reflections on Figured Singing: The Editions of 1774 and 1777 Compared*, translated and edited by Edward V. Foreman, Masterworks on Singing, vol. 7 (Minneapolis: Pro Musica, 1996), 18.

3. See Gerhold K. Becker, "The Divinization of Nature in Early Modern Thought," in *The Invention of Nature*, edited by Thomas Bargatzky and Rolf Kuschel (Frankfurt: Peter Lang, 1994), 47–61. The literature exploring the moral underpinnings of nature is very large. In addition to the particularist studies of Rousseau, Hume, Kant, Adam Smith, Edmund Burke, Thomas Jefferson, and others, it includes many studies of early Romantic and idealist literatures (especially British, Scottish, French, and German). A good collected overview is David Williams, ed., *The Enlightenment* (Cambridge: Cambridge University Press, 1999). See also Lorraine Daston and Gianna Pomata, eds., *The Faces of Nature in Enlightenment Europe* (Berlin: Berliner Wissenschafts-Verlag, 2003); and Lorraine Daston and Fernando Vidal, eds., *The Moral Authority of Nature* (Chicago: University of Chicago Press, 2004).

4. I am grateful to Courtney Quaintance for this insight. The castrato Loreto Vittori's *La troia rapita* (1662) followed Tassoni's genre title as well; see chapter 2 above. Curiously, there was a castrato in early eighteenth-century Rome called Menecuccio, a member of the papal chapel who was drawn by Ghezzi, but there's no way to know whether Albergati knew the association.

5. Albergati Capacelli, *Il ciarlator maldicente*, 2:viii–ix.

> Ma tempo sarebbe ormai che si cessasse di sacrificare queste misere vittime. Non basta che la gola e il lusso espongano le vite di tante genti a tanti disastri sol per comporci e recarci alle labbre una tazza di cioccolata, che ancor si vuole ridur gli uomini in vili mostri schifosi solo per sollecitarci le orecchie con un' arietta?
>
> Facilmente si potrebbe dimostrare che dopo che la barbarie ha resi vili e deformi questi infelici destinati ad un canto sì snaturato, d'ordinario la pessima loro educazione, il non istudiare niente che il canto dover conversare sovente con altri lor simili, poi le carezze, poi gli applausi degl'ignoranti, poi l'oro dei pazzi e dei prodighi contribuiscono a renderli ognora più temarari e malvagi.

6. Ibid., 12. Emphasis mine.

7. See Gilbert Herdt's seminal "Introduction: Third Sexes and Third Genders," in *Third Sex, Third Gender: Beyond Sexual Dimorphism in Culture and History*, edited by Herdt (New York: Zone Books, 1994), 21–81.

8. Even a figure as venerated as Farinelli was satirized as an amphibious being, costly and corrupting of the proper sexual order, well before his flight to Spain. On this issue, see especially Thomas McGeary, "Farinelli and the English: 'One God' or the Devil?," *La revue LISA* 2 (2004): 29–50; McGeary, "Gendering Opera: Italian Opera as the Feminine Other in England, 1700–42," *Journal of Musicological Research* 14 (1994): 17–34; McGeary, "Farinelli in Madrid: Opera, Politics, and the War of Jenkins' Ear," *Musical Quarterly* 82 (1998): 383–421; and Todd S. Gilman, "The Italian (Castrato) in London," in *The Work of Opera: Genre, Nationhood, and Sexual Difference*, edited by Richard Dellamora and Daniel Fischlin (New York: Columbia University Press, 1997), 49–70, which traces such attacks to John Bulwer (1606–56), *Anthropometamorphosis: Man Transform'd, or the Artificial Changelin, Historically Presented, in the Mad and Cruel Gallantry, Foolish Bravery, Ridiculous Beauty, Filthy Fineness, and Loathesome Loveliness of Most Nations, Fashioning & Altering Their Bodies from the Mould Intended by Nature, with a Vindication of the Regular Beauty and Honesty of Nature, and an Appendix of the Pedigree of the English Gallant* (London: J. Hardesty, 1650; 2nd ed. 1653).

9. Cited from Charles Henri de Blainville, *Travels through Holland, Germany, Switzerland and Italy, Containing a Particular Description of the Antient and Present State of Those Countries*, 3 vols. (London, 1767), 1: 560; originally *Travels through Holland, Germany, Switzerland, and Other Parts of Europe; But Especially Italy*. Blainville, Monsieur de.; George Turnbull; William Guthrie; Daniel Soyer; John Lockman; Herman Moll, 3 vols. (London: Printed by W. Strahan for the Proprietor, 1743–45), reprinted as *Travels through Holland, Germany, Switzerland, but especially Italy: de Blainville*, 3 vols. (London: John Noon, 1757). See also his *Histoire générale, critique et philologique de la musique* (1767; Geneva: Minkoff Reprints, 1972).

10. Voltaire, *Candide, ou l'optimisme, traduit de l'allemand par M. de Volt**** (London [Netherlands], 1759), 131: "Se pâmera de plaisir qui voudra, ou qui pourra, en voyant un châtre fredonner le rôle de César & de Caton, & se promener d'un air gauche sur des planches. Pour moi il y a longtems [sic] qui j'ai renoncé à ces pauvretés, qui sont aujourdhui la gloire d'Italie, & que des Souverains payent si chérement. Candide disputa un peu, mais avec discrétion, Martin fut entiérement satisfait de l'avis du Sénateur." Cf. Voltaire's *The Ignorant Philosopher*, originally published in 1766:

> In the digest of Roman laws, we find a law of Adrian denouncing death to those physicians who should make eunuchs, either by taking out or bruising the *testes*. The possessions of those who underwent castration were forfeited by the same law. Origen ought certainly to have been punished, as he had submitted to this operation from having rigidly interpreted that passage of St. Matthew, which says, *There be eunuchs which have made themselves so for the kingdom of Heaven's sake*. Things changed under the succeeding emperors, who imitated the voluptuousness of Asia; especially in the empire of Constantinople, where eunuchs became patriarchs, and generals of armies. It is the

custom at Rome, even at these times, to castrate young children to qualify them for being musicians to the Pope; so that *castrato* and *musico del Papa* are synonymous. (Quoted from *The Ignorant Philosopher, Translated from the French of Mr. de Voltaire, by the Rev. David Williams*, translated by David Williams [London: Printed for Fielding and Walker, 1779])

Cf. *An Essay on* Crimes and Punishments, *Translated from the Italian; with a Commentary, Attributed to Mons. de Voltaire, Translated from the French* (Dublin: n.p., 1767).

11. D'Aumont, "Eunuque," *Encyclopédie* 6: 158.

12. Quoted from the *Appendix to Grassineau's Musical Dictionary, Selected from the Dictionnaire de musique of J J. Rousseau* (London, 1769), 8–9, under "Castrato." The passage continues in a paradoxically superstitious vein: "Beside, the other advantage of a voice is overbalanced by many other disadvantages. These men who sing so well, but without warmth or passion, are in the theatre the most awkward actors in the world, they moreover lose their voice very early, and become disagreeably gross. They pronounce a language worse than real men, and there are some letters, such as *r*, that they cannot even pronounce at all." Charles Burney, contra Rousseau, was deeply skeptical. See his A *General History of Music, from the Earliest Ages to the Present Period*, 4 vols. (London, 1776–89), 4: 42–43, esp. 42 n. x.

13. Peter Browe, S.J., *Zur Geschichte der Entmannung: Eine religions- und rechtsgeschichtliche Studie* (Breslau: Müller & Seiffert, 1936), 99–117.

14. Bologna, Museo e Biblioteca Internazionale della Musica, MS I.12.107, letter to composer and chapelmaster Girolamo Chiti dated February 18, 1750. Chiti tried to fudge the situation by claiming the young man was only partially a castrato, from "necessity," not for music (MS I.12.108 [February 24, 1750]). Martini had written a recommendation for a young man to enter the order. Elsewhere he declared that the alto castrato Giuseppe Poma, although rude, should be pitied because he had had to play female roles. Cf. Feldman, *Opera and Sovereignty: Transforming Myths in Eighteenth-Century Italy* (Chicago: University of Chicago Press, 2007), 366. The letters are now available online, thanks to librarian Alfredo Vitolo, at http://badigit.comune.bologna.it/cmbm/scripts/lettere/search.asp.

15. Giovanni Antonio Bianchi [Lauriso Tragiense], *De i vizi, e de i difetti del moderno teatro* (Rome: Pagliarini, 1753), 93–94.

16. "Italo Genitore . . . / Te non error ma vizio / Spinge all'orrido ufizio." Giuseppe Parini, "La musica," in *Il giorno e le odi* (Bologna: Zanichelli, 1817), 189.

17. Sara Goudar, *Relation historique des divertissements du Carnaval de Naples, ou Lettre de Madame Goudar sur ce sujet À Monsieur le Général Alexis Orlow* (Lucca, 1774), 9, on Tenducci's performance in *Telemaco nell'isola di Calipso* at the Teatro del Cocomero in Florence (autumn 1773): "Je ne sais si c'est parceque je suis femme, mais je n'aime point les Eunuques" (9). Tenducci's involvement in the marriage scandal discussed in chapter 2 made him a good target. Implied in Goudar's *Relation historique* was a comparison between the tastes of the author and those of Tenducci's ex-wife (see chapter 2, above).

18. Marquis de Sade, *Voyage d'Italie*, edited by Maurice Lever (Paris: Fayard, 1995), 68.

19. John Moore, *A View of Society and Manners in Italy*, 4th ed., 2 vols. (1779; London, 1787), 2: 89–90. Moore's attitude was shared by, among many others, Joseph Jérôme Le Français de Lalande, V*oyage d'un français en Italie, fait dans les années 1765 & 1766*, 8 vols., rev. and expanded (Yverdon, 1769–90), 5: 437–38.

20. See Philippe Ariès, *Centuries of Childhood: A Social History of Family Life*, translated by Robert Baldick (New York: Vintage Books, 1962), summarized on 411–15.

21. See Lorraine Daston and Katharine Park, *Wonders and the Order of Nature, 1150–1750* (New York: Zone Books, 1998), chapter 9, "The Enlightenment and the Anti-Marvelous"; Anne C. Vila, *Enlightenment and Pathology: Sensibility in the Literature and Medicine of Eighteenth-Century France* (Baltimore, MD: Johns Hopkins University Press, 1998).

22. Robert Holzer, "Music and Poetry in Seventeenth-Century Rome: Settings of the Canzonetta and Cantata Texts of Francesco Balducci, Domenico Benigni, Francesco Melosio, and Antonio Abati," PhD diss., University of Pennsylvania, 1990; Thomas McGeary, "Verse Epistles on Italian Opera Singers, 1724–1736," *RMA Research Chronicle* 33 (2000): 29–88; Antonio Bettagno, ed., *Caricature di Anton Maria Zanetti* (Venice: Neri Pozza, 1996); Giancarlo Rostirolla, with Stefano La Via and Anna Lo Bianco, *Il "mondo novo" musicale di Pier Leone Ghezzi* (Milan: Skira; Rome: Accademia Nazionale di Santa Cecilia, 2001); and Pierluigi Petrobelli, "On Reading Musical Caricatures: Some Italian Examples," *Imago musicae* 2 (1985): 135–42. An important instance of animal/musical caricature is Zaccaria Seriman's illustrated *I viaggi di Enrico Wanton: Alle terre incognite australi, ed al paese delle scimie ne'quale si spiegano il carattere li costumi, le scienze, e la polizia di quegli straordinari abitanti* (Venice: Giovanni Tagier, 1749), a literary satire involving an entire Swiftian world of simian creatures who (among other things) attend the opera in Venice (cf. Feldman, *Opera and Sovereignty*, 178–81).

23. Castorino was said to have had a vigorous singing style and imposing presence and to have played largely kings, tyrants, and barbaric hero types; see Carlo Vitali, "Castori (Antonio, Castorino)," *GMO*. Peter of Abano thought eunuchs and effeminate men had blocked pores and a cold nature; see Joan Cadden, *Meanings of Sex Difference in the Middle Ages: Medicine, Science, and Culture* (New York: Cambridge University Press, 1993), 214.

24. *The Remarkable Trial of the Queen of Quavers and Her Associates, for Sorcery, Witchcraft, and Enchantments at the Assizzes Held in the Moon, for The County of Gelding before the Rt. Hon. Sir Francis Lash, Lord Chief Baron of the Lunar Exchequer. Taken in Short Hand, by Joseph Democritus and William Diogenes* (London: Printed for J. Bew, No. 28, in Paternoster Row, [1778]), 6.

The *OED* defines "imp" thus: "imp n.": " 4 *spec.* A 'child' of the devil, or of hell. a. with parentage expressed: Applied to wicked men, and to petty fiends or evil spirits"; "4b. Hence, with omission of the qualification: A little devil or demon, an evil spirit; esp. in 17th c., one of those with which witches were supposed to be familiar; now chiefly in art and mythology."

25. *Remarkable Trial*, 6.

26. Ibid., 6–7. Note also: "I am . . . not inclined to yield unto their delusive conceit, who hold that pigs can afford the most exquisive [sic] music, nay that there is no good music without Italian pigs" (12).

27. Ibid., 4–5.

28. Ibid., 5.

29. Ian Woodfield, *Opera and Drama in Eighteenth-Century London: The King's Theatre, Garrick, and the Business of Performance* (Cambridge: Cambridge University Press, 2001), chapter 12.

30. *Remarkable Trial*, 31. See n. 87 below for both Leach and Stallybrass and White on these themes.

31. Meaning "named" or "called" in quaint and comical usage.

32. *Remarkable Trial*, 7–8. They stink because they are "Italian pigs" (ibid., 12), for which garlic is the olfactory symbol.

33. "This will be much more humane and honourable, than to squander away mountains of gold merely to encourage the wanton extravagance of a loathsome Castrato, who cannot live upon a clear income of three thousand pounds" (*Remarkable Trial*, 31).

34. Cf. Zanetti's depiction of Farinelli in traveling clothes in Fig. 25. Other protruding lips on the lesser-known castrati Menicuccio and Marchetti were drawn by Ghezzi in the 1720s; see Rostirolla, *Il "mondo novo,"* 141 and 341, = no. 134 (in Rome, Gabinetto Nazionale delle Stampe, and Vatican City, Biblioteca Apostolica Vaticana, Ottob. Lat. 3116, fol. 158). Compare Ghezzi's renditions of the soprano Cecchino Vendetta in 1729, pictured next to a tenor (Rostirolla, *Il "mondo novo,"* 141); and Giuseppe Guspelti, called "Giuseppino" (ibid., nos. 241–242 and 292–94). About Mommo, relatedly, see Fig. 30. Rostirolla notes characteristics shared with other castrati: large forehead, bleary eyes, large mouth, ample lower jaw, double chin ("ampie fronte, occhi cisposi, grande bocca, ampie mascelle cadenti, doppio mento").

35. Cf. the drawing of Carlo Scalzi (Carlino) by Ghezzi, which gives him a very long jaw and chin, March 29, 1729, I-Rvat, Ottob. Lat. 3116, fol. 147, reproduced in Rostirolla, *Il "mondo novo,"* no. 136, with commentary on 342–44. Zanetti's caricature of Scalzi (Bettagno, *Caricature di Zanetti*, no. 321, undated) resonates with Ghezzi's (Rostirolla, *Il "mondo novo,"* no. 136, pp. 142 and 242–44) in giving him a square, wide jaw, and very long chin.

36. Sander L. Gilman, *Difference and Pathology: Stereotypes of Sexuality, Race, and Madness* (Ithaca, NY: Cornell University Press, 1985), 18 and passim. The process of producing a stereotyped, negative castrato would operate in the "biosocial" subcategory of the biological by doing what Ian Hacking calls "making up people." Many head-scratching, scientistic explanations were attempted in the eighteenth century to rationalize why castrati were socially problematic.

37. Innocenzo Della Lena, *Dissertazione ragionata sul teatro moderno* (Venice: Giacomo Storti, 1791), 85. The text is written as a comparison between one castrato and the prima donna he supported; see Laura Spreti, "Venezia, carnevale 1791," in *Rassegna veneta di studi musicali* 9–10 (1993/1994): 185–200.

38. A critical modern text is Margaret Tallmadge May, *Galen on the Usefulness of the Parts of the Body*, 2 vols. (Ithaca, NY: Cornell University Press, 1968). See May on Galen's belief that testes did not produce semen at 1: 19 n. 67.

39. Owsei Temkin, *Galenism: Rise and Decline of a Medical Philosophy* (Ithaca, NY: Cornell University Press, 1973), chapter 4; on the survival of Galenism in medical practice, see 165 ff.

40. This was probably so for quite a long time, even into the nineteenth century, when belief in Galenic cures (for example, castration to cure gout) was at the very least a usable pretext for making church singers. One might call this, after Temkin, a "hidden afterlife," but it is probably hidden only to us, in a nontextual world, and even at that not entirely.

41. Juan Huarte, *Examen de ingenios: The Examination of Men's Wits in Which, by Discovering the Varietie of Natures, Is Shewed for Which Profession Each One Is Apt, and How Far He Shall Profit Therein*, translated into Italian by Camillo Camilli and into English by Richard Carew (London: Adam Islip, 1596), 278–81. Cf. Mary E. Frandsen, "Eunuchi conjugium: The Marriage of a Castrato in Early Modern Germany," *Early Music History: Studies*

in Medieval and Early Modern Music 24 (2005); Filippo Balatri, "Vita e viaggi di F. B., nativo di Pisa," RUS-Mrg. MS F. 218, no. 1247 (1–9), 1: 14–15. The business about pronouncing r's was an ancient belief; see Dario Cosi, "Comunicazione disturbata: Battos, il fondatore di Cirene, balbuziente e castrato," in *Le regioni del silenzio: Studi sui disagi della comunicazione*, edited by Maria Grazia Ciani (Padova: Bloom Edizioni, 1983), 123–54.

42. Quoted from the translation into English of 1718, Charles Ancillon, *Eunuchism Display'd*, translated by Robert Samber (London: Printed for E. Curll, 1718), 17. On the issues of humors, generation, and degeneration, see Valeria Finucci, "Introduction: Genealogical Pleasures, Genealogical Disruptions," in *Generation and Degeneration: Tropes of Reproduction in Literature and History*, edited by Valeria Finucci and Kevin Brownlee (Durham, NC: Duke University Press, 2001); and Finucci, *The Manly Masquerade: Masculinity, Paternity, and Castration in the Italian Renaissance* (Durham, NC: Duke University Press, 2003), chapter 6.

43. "I cantori oggidì si sono dimenticati affatto che l'obbligo loro è d'imitar la favella degl'uomini col numero e coll'armonia; anzi credono allora esser valent'uomini quanto più si dilungano dalla natura umana. I loro archetipi sono i rosignuoli, i flautini, i grilli e le cicale, non le persone e gli affetti loro: quando han suonata con la gola la loro sinfonia credono aver adempiti tutti i doveri dell'arte." (Singers nowadays have completely forgotten their obligation to imitate the language of men with number and sound [Ciceronian terms]. To the contrary, they think themselves better the more they stray from human nature. Their archetypes are nightingales, piccolos, crickets, and cicadas, not persons and their emotions. Once they have played their symphony with their throat they believe they have fulfilled all their obligations to art.) Letter no. 878 of August 9–28, 1755, to Francesco D'Argenvillières in Rome, in Pietro Metastasio, *Tutte le opere*, 5 vols., edited by Bruno Brunelli (Milan: Mondadori, 1943–54), 3: 1055.

44. The focus of Metastasio's rantings was a bit improbable since many people, including Francesco Algarotti and Count Vincenzio Martinelli, an Italian opera fan based in London, accused Bernacchi himself of sacrificing expression to mechanical coloratura. See chapter 3, above, and Vincenzio Martinelli's *Lettere familiari, e critiche* (London: G. Nourse, 1758), 358–61, from his "Letter to the Count of Buckingham" "on the origins of opera."

45. To Bernacchi: "You wisely deplore the lamentable state of our music, or better said, our castrati" (a pun on referring to castrati with the common euphemism "musici"). The quote about Gabrielli comes from a letter to Mattia Verazi, October 1, 1762, no. 1280 (Metastasio, *Tutte le opere*, 4: 272–74, at 273–74)—"not to blame the songs of the artists on the art." Cf. Metastasio's letter to Bernacchi in Bologna, September 15, 1755, in ibid. 3: 1065, no. 890, and letter of March 15, 1756, to abate N.N. in ibid., 1102, no. 928: "The *musici* instead of representing and speaking in music play symphonies with the voice." Planelli echoed these remarks in 1772 in his critique of Caterina Gabrielli and elsewhere. Antonio Planelli, *Dell'opera in musica* (Naples: Donato Campo, 1772); modern edition edited by Francesco Degrada (Fiesole: Discanto, 1981), 70.

46. Letter to his brother Leopoldo Trapassi, January 30, 1764, no. 1360, in Metastasio, *Tutte le opere*, 4: 337–38 (emphasis mine).

47. Letter to his brother, February 27, 1764, in ibid., 343–44, no. 1368, at 344.

48. Letter to Giuseppe Santoro of March 26, 1764, in ibid., 349–50, no. 1375, at 350. The word I translate as "radiator grills" *(calandre)* could be also rendered as "radiator covers" or

"calenders." There are innumerable other instances in the eighteenth century of singing being conceived as the basis of an ideal musical "humanity" while certain other sounds made by humans are deemed mechanical. This correspondence informs Horace Walpole's disdainful comment on encountering the aged Senesino in Naples in 1739: "We thought it a fat old woman; but it spoke in a shrill little pipe, and proved itself to be Senesini." Horace Walpole, *The Letters of Horace Walpole, Earl of Orford: Including Numerous Letters Now First Published from the Original Manuscript*, 6 vols, edited by John Wright (London: Richard Bentley, 1840).

49. "Il . . . principale studio [della massima parte de' musici] è di squartare la voce, saltellare di nota in nota, gorgheggiare, arpeggiare, e con passaggi, trilli, spezzature, e volate, infiorano, infrascano, sfigurano ogni bellezza. In questa guisa più non si canta, e tutte le *arie* si rassomigliano come le donne di Francia." Francesco Milizia, *Trattato completo, formale e materiale del teatro* (1772), in *Opere complete di Francesco Milizia risguardanti le belle arti*, 9 vols. (Bologna: Cardinali e Friuli, 1926), 1: 93.

50. "Sì, fuggirsene certamente di là, ove la poesia non è imperante, e dominatrice per ignoranza, e pecoraggine degli attori, che altrimenti attori, ma insensate macchine, o stolti, privati affatto d'azione, e d'espressione, adatta a manifestare i giusti sentimenti di quella" (Della Lena, *Dissertazione ragionata*, 22).

51. From William Tooke, ed., *Selections from the Most Celebrated Foreign Literary Journals and Other Periodical Publications*, 2 vols. (London: J. Debrett, 1798), 2: 175–76. In the section between the bits I quote the reviewer wrote about Marchesi, "However, at present, since his return from London, he has begun to sing more in the true taste, I mean with sentiment and emotion. Of this one cannot be better convinced, than by hearing him sing the airs in the opera *Olimpiade*, Se cerca, se dice &c." Cf. Stephen Willier, "Gasparo Pacchierotti in London: The 1779–80 Season in Susanna Burney's 'Letter Journal,'" *Studi musicali* 29 (2000): 251–91, at 252. Willier identifies the reviewer as being from the *Merkur*.

52. See Gerhard Croll, *Gluck-Schriften: Ausgewählte Aufsätze und Vorträge, 1967–2002*, edited by Irene Brandenburg, Elisabeth Richter, et al. (Kassel: Bärenreiter, 2003), 34, 292 (although there is nothing on the Parma performance that I could find).

53. *Carteggio di Pietro e Alessandro Verri dal 1766 al 1797*, edited by Alessandro Giulini et al. (Milan: L. F. Cogliati, 1923), vol. 8, no. CCXIX (969), Alessandro to Pietro, Rome, February 2, 1777, 251–52:

> L'ordinario scorso i tempi erano pessimi; il mio servitore non venne ed io non ebbi occasione di mandare lettera alla posta. Spero che, secondo i nostri patti, non sarai stato nella menoma agitazione. Giuseppe II è un vero Marco Aurelio. Egli è nato per comandare agli uomini. Io credo che se fosse anche un particolare, ne farebbe quello che ne volesse. L'educazione dei monarchi del nostro secolo, ed anche degli ultimi, era la maestà della rappresentanza ed un contegno di divinità. Ora i principi sono bravi di lor persona, si espongono alle cannonate e trattano i sudditi da amici. I nostri teatri sono al solito, vale a dire mostruosi. Non vi è di buono che Millico, musico di somma espressione e che canta sullo stile di Caffarello. Mi pare sorprendente. Per me, lo sai bene che non sono molto armonico. Ho lasciato da dieci anni il mio violino e mi ritrovo un nemico di meno. Se la musica non è eccellente mi annoia e non

posso reggere ad un'opera intera. I colpi di contrabasso, che accompagnano i recitativi, mi fanno positivamente male. Le arie delle ultime parti mi tormentano; ma un'aria cantabile veramente alla Sacchini, cantata da un valent'uomo mi rapisce. Vuol esser eccellente o mi turo le orecchie.

54. Millico then begged Rousseau to sing. Though he was embarrassed to do so, he was finally persuaded, trembling, to sing "some mediocre song," after which his "fat, ugly wife went to him in an animated, consoling manner, calling him 'mon petit ami.'" *Carteggio di Pietro e Alessandro Verri*, vol. 8, no. CCXXIX (974), Alessandro to Pietro, Rome, February 22, 1777, 267:

> Questo musico Vito Millico, che ha cantato nel passato carnevale all'opera di Roma, ha pure conosciuto a Parigi Gian-Giacomo Rousseau. Andò da lui col solito pretesto di copiar musica. Vedendo ch'era musico, si rasserenò e lo pregò di cantare. Cantò per compiacerlo, benché il cembalo, orribilmente scordato, fosse un tormento per accompagnarsi. Rousseau rimase attonito e trasportato, massimamente per il di lui canto delle ottave più belle di Ariosto e del Tasso, nelle quali egli ha inventata una musica di espressiva declamazione affatto nuova e che è mirabile. Gli disse Rousseau che, se il Tasso lo avesse inteso, avrebbe fatto per lui un nuovo poema. Millico pregò a Giangiacomo di cantare. Non voleva, s'imbarazzava, finalmente, tremando, fece qualche mediocre cantilena e la grossa e brutta moglie lo andava animando e consolando chiamandolo *mon petit ami*. Voltaire chiama quella donna *une sorcière* e non la può soffrire, ed io sono sempre stato un freddo conoscitore del merito di Rousseau, le di cui opere mi hanno quasi mai persuaso e spesso dispiaciuto e la di cui condotta mi ha risvegliato sentimenti anche di minor considerazione. Lo crederò un ottimo uomo, ma certamente strano quanto Diogene. Io credo che mi farebbe compassione di vederlo ed è certo che, per quanto sia ammiratore delle sue opere, nessuno troverebbe sensato di far la parte di anacoreta e misantropo in una capitale di seicentomila anime e di far il copista di musica per essere accessibile a tutti, sempre non volendo vedere alcuno. È un ciarlatano.

Millico may have sung Ariosto and Tasso in the centuries-old oral tradition of improvising epic stanzas on decorated melodic formulas, which was a great declamatory art, on which see James Haar, *Essays on Italian Poetry and Music in the Renaissance, 1350–1600* (Berkeley: University of California Press, 1986), chapter 4; Anthony Welch, *The Renaissance Epic and the Oral Past* (New Haven, CT: Yale University Press, 2012). My student Jessica Peritz has written an essay on the episode, "The Tale of the Cantimbanco and the Rhapsodist: Thoughts on Voice, Authenticity, and History at Rousseau's Harpsichord" (seminar paper for "Voice: Subjective, Material, Abstract," co-taught with David Levin, winter 2014).

55. *Carteggio di Pietro e Alessandro Verri*, vol. 8, no. CCIX (964), Alessandro to Pietro, Rome, January 15, 1777, 243:

> Ho conosciuto il Pacchiarotti quando passò da Roma, l'ho inteso cantare in camera, è musico di molta espressione e mi dicono che abbia in teatro molto

> sentimento nella azione. Quando abbiamo Millico, brutta figura, ma eccellente musico. Il Pacchiarotti ha avuta una avventura a Napoli. Un signore del paese, che serve nel militare, per gelosia gli diede in pubblico alcuni colpi di bastone; egli cavò la spada, ferì l'avversario, che parimenti cavò la sua e credo che Pacchiarotti lo disarmasse o gli rompesse in faccia la sua spada, insomma finì per lui molto onoratamente e fuor del costume degli eunuchi.

Clearly Alessandro wanted not just to report to his brother that he had heard Pacchierotti sing but to show that he had made his acquaintance and in was in on the local gossip about him.

56. *Carteggio di Pietro e Alessandro Verri*, vol. 8, no. XVII (1064), Pietro to Alessandro, Milan, February 19, 1780, 27–28:

> Il Marchesini è stato universalmente applaudito, ha cantato sempre con impegno e senza capricci. Se vuoi sapere quale sentimento io abbia provato nel suo canto, ti dirò, che la voce è bellissimo, sonora, eguale in ogni corda e che non ho ascoltato verun altro contralto che se le possa paragonare; è senza difetto nella intonazione, fa cose di somma difficoltà, e domina la sua voce come potrebbe se suonasse un violino. Egli anche ha l'abilità di fare un trillo granito e crescente per sei o sette toni di seguito senza interruzione come si fa negli stromenti d'arco scivolando la mano sulla corda. Egli sostiene la voce e ne riempie il teatro per vasto che sia, e a tutto ciò aggiungi che la bella sua voce è passionata, tenera, compassionevole, e io non l'ho trovato in alcuno fra i cantanti. Egli ha tutto adunque. Solamente gli manca, credo, il sentimento, che sa toccarti nell'anima, il qual talento da Giziello a lui superiore anche a lui per la forza e l'agilità. La mancanza del sentimento fa che sul più bello d'una musica tenera, mentre già provi un soave principio di raccapriccio, il Marchesini ti fa una voltata violenta, ti esce con un capriccio bizzarro e gajo, e così ti ammorza la nascente sensibilità. Se s'innamorerà una volta di cuore, diverrà un incantatore perfetto, *ma sinora è un non senso maraviglioso a pezzo a pezzo*. (emphasis mine)

Sergio Durante wondered whether the contradiction of something that is passionate yet dampens one's "nascent sensibility" might not be invested in a kind of ritual condemnation of virtuosity (private communication), but I am inclined to read it within the historical moment as intended to show how feeling can be ruined.

57. The remainder of the definition of "castrato" as given in Rousseau's *Appendix to Grassineau's Musical Dictionary, Selected from the Dictionnaire de Musique of J. J. Rousseau* (London, 1769): "Let us endeavour to make the voice of modesty and humanity heard, which cries out against this infamous practice; and let those princes who seek to encourage it, for once blush at a custom that is so injurious to the preservation of mankind. // Beside, the advantage of a voice is overbalanced by many other disadvantages. These men who sing so well, but without warmth or passion, are in the theatre the most awkward actors in the world" (9).

58. See Helen Berry, *The Castrato and His Wife* (Oxford: Oxford University Press, 2011), 147–52, on the Edinburgh years and 162–67 on the return to Tuscany. On Guadagni see most

recently the well-chronicled Patricia Howard, *The Modern Castrato: Gaetano Guadagni and the Coming of a New Operatic Age* (New York: Oxford University Press, 2014), chapters 4 and 6, which appeared when this book was in press.

59. An anonymous portrait of a beautiful young singer has been associated with Guadagni in *Handel and the Castrati* (London: Handel House Museum, 2006), but is apparently rejected by Howard, *The Modern Castrato*, 3.

60. Prominent among them was Giovanni Maria Rubinelli (1753–1829), whom Della Lena grouped with Marchesi as one of the three worst singers of his time (*Dissertazione ragionata*, 97).

61. Planelli, *Dell'opera in musica*, 1772 and 1982 editions.

62. Pacchierotti had had his Neapolitan debut in 1771 in a rather nonreformist revision (and failed performance) of Niccolò Jommelli and Mattia Verazi's *Ifigenia in Tauride* (originally done at Mannheim in 1764); see Nicole Edwina Ivy Baker, "Italian Opera at the Court of Mannheim, 1758–1770," PhD diss., University of California at Los Angeles, 1994. The original 1762 production of *Orfeo ed Euridice* was revived in Vienna in 1763. Thereafter the work lay dormant until 1769, when Gluck famously conducted it in an Italian production. Because *Orfeo ed Euridice* was one of three works that made up *Le feste d'Apollo* at Parma (printed as *Le feste d'Apollo: Celebrate sul teatro di corte nell'agosto del MDCCLXIX per le auguste seguite nozze tra il reale infante don Ferdinando e la r. arciduchessa infanta Maria Amalia* [Parma: Nella stamperia reale, 1769], it was performed without an intermission. The alto part shown in Ex. 22, originally written for Guadagni, was transposed for the soprano Millico. The French version of 1774, made for the Académie Royale de Musique (the "Opéra"), entailed a much more radical revision. Orfeo became Orphée, sung in French by Joseph Legros, an *haute-contre*, the vocal type who used the chest and an upward extension into the head and presumably into falsetto, which was standard for heroes and lovers in French opera, in which the castrato was not in use and was sometimes an object of ridicule. The opera also became both longer and grander by virtue of its instrumental forces and pieces. See Alessandra Martina, *Orfeo/Orphée di Gluck: Storia della trasmissione e della recezione* (Florence: Passigli, 1995). For a brief overview of some of Gluck's Orfei in the years after its premiere, see Jeremy Hayes, "Orfeo ed Euridice (i) [*Orphée et Eurydice* ('Orpheus and Eurydice')]," *GMO*, as well as Bruce Alan Brown, "Gluck, Christoph Willibald Ritter von, §4: Collaboration with Calzabigi," *GMO*; Renate Ulm, *Glucks Orpheus-Opern: Die Parma-Fassung von 1769 als wichtiges Bindeglied zwischen dem Wiener Orfeo von 1762 und dem Pariser Orphée von 1774* (Frankfurt am Main: Lang, 1991).

63. Ranieri de' Calzabigi, *Le feste d'Apollo*.

64. Giuseppe Millico, *La pietà d'amore, dramma messo in musica dal signor D. Giuseppe Millico* (Naples: Giuseppe-Maria Porcelli a S. Biaggio de' Librari, 1782), [iii]–[viii], copy in US-Cn. He proceeds, ideologically, "And since then I have noted that even among us [moderns] one can obtain the same effects as in Greek music by expressing the words with that naturalness that is necessary to the feeling of the opera."

65. Ibid.

66. Some arias that Marchesi sang had been sung by Pacchierotti and even Millico before him—a marked shift away from the older practice of arias being largely custom-made for one singer. To have different singers singing the same aria over time meant more opportunities for listeners to make direct comparisons, as in modern times. It certainly

happened in the early part of the eighteenth century, especially with the many pasticci done in London, but all in all it was less common then than it was to become later in the century and into the nineteenth.

67. Nancy Storace, who sang the aria, had learned as a teenager to imitate Marchesi's so-called "bomba." A full edition of it appears in Dorothea Link, ed., *Arias for Nancy Storace: Mozart's First Susanna* (Middleton, WI: A-R Editions, 2002), with historical discussion on viii, xi. On the aria and the musical relationship between Marchesi and Storace, see Dorothea Link, *The National Court Theatre in Mozart's Vienna: Sources and Documents, 1783–1792* (Oxford: Clarendon Press; New York: Oxford University Press, 1998), 250; and John A. Rice, *Antonio Salieri and Viennese Opera* (Chicago: University of Chicago Press, 1998), 371, 378–81, 394–95, and 383–84, which deal with Storace's parody of Marchesi. I thank Daniel Heartz for reminding me of this evidence.

68. *L'olimpiade. Dramma per musica da rappresentarsi nel Nuovo Teatro in Padova per la solita fiera di giugno 1763. Dedicato a Piero Vendramin proveditor di detta città.*

69. Susan Burney, *The Journals and Letters of Susan Burney: Music and Society in Late Eighteenth-Century England*, edited by Philip Olleson (Farnham, Surrey, England: Ashgate, 2012), 121–22.

70. Ibid., 124.

71. See two recent important works on the sentimental: James Chandler, *An Archaeology of Sympathy: The Sentimental Mode in Literature and Cinema* (Chicago: University of Chicago Press, 2013), esp. xvi–xx and part 2, "The Sentimental Mode"; and Stefano Castelvecchi, *Sentimental Opera: Questions of Genre in the Age of Bourgeois Drama* (Cambridge: Cambridge University Press, 2013).

72. Burney, *Letters*, 124; emphases in original.

73. Della Lena, *Dissertazione ragionata*, 104–5. The audiences had even started disappearing from the theater "per non aver trovato nulla di corrispondente, ma solo freddezza, e languore senz'anima, e sentimento: L'aria poi *se cerca se dice* confrontata dall'uno all'altro cantante, fu ravvisata tanto differente, quant'un corpo animato, da un ombra apparente, senza forme, e senza vita." Footnote 1 explains, "Il concorso al teatro si scemò da una sera all'altra in iscambio di accrescersi, specialmente nella seconda, e terza rappresentazione, che sono osservabili: si mantenne moderatamente massime nelle feste per le logge tutte affittate, ma senz' affollamento."

74. Tooke, ed., *Selections from the Most Celebrated Foreign Literary Journals*, 2: 175–76.

75. Modern edition in Franz Joseph Haydn, *Joseph Haydn: Werke*, edited by J. Haydn-Institut, Cologne, edited by Marianne Helms (Munich: Henle Verlag, 1990), vol. 29, pt. 2: 2–23, which follows a printed source the publication of which was supervised by Haydn following the London performances rather than earlier manuscript sources. For the textual and performance background of the cantata, see ibid., iii–v. In the Haydn catalogue, Anthony van Hoboken, ed., *Joseph Haydn: Thematisch-bibliographisches Werkverzeichnis* (Mainz, 1957–78), the work is listed as Hoboken XXVIb:2.

76. Jean Baptiste de Boyer Argens, *New Memoirs Establishing a True Knowledge of Mankind, by Discovering the Affections of the Heart, and the Operations of the Understanding*, 2 vols. (London: Printed for D. Brown, R. Hett, and A. Millar, 1747), 2: 44; original as *Nouveaux memoires pour servir à l'histoire de l'esprit et du coeur, par monsieur le marquis d' Argens, . . . et par mademoiselle Cochois*, 2 vols. (The Hague: Frederic-Henri Scheurleer, 1745–46).

77. A remarkable book on the evolution of a postrevolutionary self with emphases on the political and psychic but with far-reaching implications in all domains is Jan Goldstein, *The Post-Revolutionary Self: Politics and Psyche in France, 1750–1850* (Cambridge: Harvard University Press, 2005).
78. Della Lena, *Dissertazione ragionata*, 97.
79. Blainville, *Travels through Holland, Germany, Switzerland and Italy* (1767), 1: 560.
80. Cf. Biancamaria Brumana, "Il cantante Giacinto Fontana detto Farfallino e la sua carriera nei teatri di Roma," *Roma moderna e contemporanea* 4, no. 1 (January–April 1996): 75–112.
81. "The Roman abbots become impassioned for these Antinoi," he wrote, "and each castrato has his crowd of adulators, who court him in the morning":

> Tu sei in gran festa di ballo e noi abbiamo già finito con mio sommo piacere lo strepitoso e noioso carnevale romano, che non consiste in altro che nella corsa de' Barberi ed in musica di castrati vestiti da principesse. È veramente indecente il vedere come si scaglino per tutta l'Italia castrati belli e giovani, per imitare su queste sacre scene i vezzi della Gabrielli e delle più leggiadre attrici per mezzo di occhiate languide ed atti amorosi. Gli abati romani prendono delle passioni per questi Antinoi ed ognuno di essi ha il suo stuolo di adoratori, che li corteggia la mattina. (*Carteggio di Pietro e Alessandro Verri*, vol. 6, no. XXX [579], Rome, February 27, 1773, 25–26)

Verri's footnote on p. 26 calls a "favorito" of Hadrian an "Antinoi."
82. The octave attacked the inhumanity of parents: "Peasants in the Papal States / Are allowed to castrate their sons / With impunity, out in the open. / So that the boys can squeal up high when they sing. / Now if they were castrating cats or dogs, / A horse or a goat, I'd keep my mouth shut. / But their sons? Christ Almighty, / What cruel, inhuman thieves they are."

> Sarà dunque permesso alli villani
> Dello [nello?] Stato Papal publicamente
> Di castrare i suoi figli impunemente
> Perché strillin cantando in modi strani.
>
> Che si castrin i gatti, o pur i cani,
> Un cavallo, un capron, non dico niente;
> Ma i figliuoli? Per Cristo Onnipotente
> Che son padri crudeli, ed innumani.
>
> O Roma soffrirà, che ne' suoi Stati
> Un mutilato attor de' più briconi
> Serva spesso di Donna alli Prelati?
>
> Se i Romani a castrar son bravi, e buoni;
> Deh! Castrassero almeno i Porporati,
> Ché il Colleggio saria senza Coglioni.

The sonnet also appears in Anton Giulio Bragaglia, *Degli evirati cantori*, 35, redacted from a manuscript in Palermo, Biblioteca Nazionale, MS III.E.3, fol. 440. There are a few variants with a version in I-Vc: verse 3 reads "di castrare i lor figli empiamente"; verse 6 gives "un somar" in place of "un capron"; verses 11–13 read "finge la donna a spasso dei Prelati / Ma se i Prelati voglion esser buoni / castrin piuttosto gli altri Porporati." My thanks to Courtney Quaintance, who shared the poem with me in the redaction from I-Vmc. The poem is unsigned and must date from the nineteenth century (or perhaps the very late eighteenth century) given its implication that castrati were only being produced in the Papal States.

83. Blainville, *Travels through Holland*, 1: 560.

84. Della Lena, *Dissertazione ragionata*, 95 and passim. The matter of congruity between illusions had become vital to Enlightenment thinking in many domains. See, for example, Marian Hobson, *The Object of Art: The Theory of Illusion in Eighteenth-Century France* (Cambridge: Cambridge University Press, 1982).

85. Some of this and what follows appears in Feldman, "Strange Births and Surprising Kin: The Castrato's Tale," in *Italy's Eighteenth Century: Gender and Culture in the Age of the Grand Tour*, edited by Paula Findlen et al. (Stanford, CA: Stanford University Press, 2009), 175–202, 400–414.

86.

> Io non saprei dirvi altro sennon, chè un Forastiero, il qual dà poco tempo è venuto a stare in questa Città. Uh comee brutto (Agata mia) io tremo di spavento di sognarmelo. Lo consideravo ancor'io sorella, e per dirvela sinceramente mi son pentita della mia curiosità. . . . ; poiché hò l'istesso vostro timore. Et io Agata cara son capace di star tre dì senza mangiare, tanto mi fa stomaco; [. . .]
>
> [. . .] Sorella benedetta, non vedete che non hà ancor messo barba, nè viè segno di essergli mai stata fatta! La Malattia sarà stata lunga e penosa [. . .]. Ei non hà barba perché è Musico; altro che fichi secchi.
>
> Ah era musico eh? O s'è così, egli averà lasciato di gran denaro; Si sa nulla a chi habbia testato? (Filippo Balatri, "Testamento, o sia ultima volontà, di F. B., nativo Alfeo," G-Mbs, cod. It. 329, fols. 29–30)

I use brackets around ellipses when needed to indicate that they are not Balatri's, since his texts do use ellipses.

In fact Balatri's parents and brother were all dead by then.

87. See Edmund Leach, "Verbal Abuse and Animal Categories," in *New Directions in the Study of Language*, edited by Eric H. Lenneberg (Cambridge, MA: MIT Press, 1964), 23–63; Peter Stallybrass and Allon White, *The Politics and Poetics of Transgression* (Ithaca, NY: Cornell University Press, 1986), 44–59 and passim; and the brilliant analysis in connection with early modern anti-Semitism in Jud Newborn, "'Work Makes Free': The Hidden Cultural Meaning of the Holocaust," 4 vols., PhD diss., University of Chicago, 1994, 1: 72–78 and passim.

88. "Se io fossi stato un'uomo tenace, averei fatto la figura del Porco. Il Porco (finche vive) èstimato il più vile Animale; ogni buco, *è buono per il Porco;* tutte l'immondizzie *si diano al Porco*. Chi v'ha che lo carezzi, o sel tenga attorno? Morto però ch'eglè, tutti corrono al lardo; e, dal pelo inpoi, non v'è minuta parte che non s'apprezzi. Si loda, si sapora, et è delizzia d'ognuno; perchè si fa mangiare." Balatri, "Testamento," fol. 90.

89. Julia Kristeva, *Powers of Horror: An Essay on Abjection*, translated by Leon S. Roudiez (New York: Columbia University Press, 1982), 1. My thanks to David Levin for pressing me to think here about Kristeva's text.

90. Charles Burney, *The Present State of Music in France and Italy, or, the Journal of a Tour through Those Countries, Undertaken to Collect Materials* ... (London: T. Becket and Co., 1771), 215, where Farinelli is quoted as saying, "If you have a mind to compose a good work, never fill it with accounts of such despicable beings as I am."

CHAPTER 6. SHADOW VOICES, CASTRATO AND NON

1. See Patrick Barbier, *La maison des italiens: Les castrats a Versailles* (Paris: Bernard Grasset, 1998), 253–63, esp. 259–63. The two eunuchs were Josephini and Rossetti, who had arrived at the Chapel in 1774 and were paid 2,200 livres each. Critical to the archival history are the memoirs of the Bêche brothers, located in F-Pn, Départment de Musique, MS Res. F 1661.

2. At the time of his death, Louis XVI was trying to simplify his musical establishment. The number of singers had been reduced, though he still dispensed more than 200,000 livres a year for his music. See Barbier, *La maison des italiens*, 260.

3. My account of the conservatories in the period is largely based on Francesco Florimo, *La scuola musicale di Napoli e i suoi conservatorii, con uno sguardo sulla storia della musica in Italia* (Naples: Stabilimento tip. V. Morano, 1883); Salvatore Di Giacomo, *Il conservatorio di Sant'Onofrio a Capuana e quello di S.M. della Pietà dei Turchini* (Milan: Remo Sandron, 1924); and Michael F. Robinson, "The Governors' Minutes of the Conservatory S. Maria de Loreto, Naples," *RMA Research Chronicle* 10, no. 1 (1972): 1–97.

4. Carol Padgham Albrecht, "The Face of the Vienna Court Opera, 1804–1805," *Music in Art: International Journal for Music Iconography* 34, nos. 1–2 (Spring-Fall 2009): 191–202.

Arthur Schopenhauer was present for the Vienna performances, and reported that the audience so admired Crescentini that it always clapped for five minutes when he appeared and that he was a staple of conversation in society; in Schopenhauer, *Reisentagebücher aus dem Jahren 1803-1804*, edited by Charlotte von Gwinner (Leipzig: F.A. Brockhaus, 1723), 269.

5. David Charlton and M. Elizabeth C. Bartlet, "Napoleon I, Emperor of France," *GMO*, note that Napoleon's chapel originally had eight singers (including castrati) plus instrumentalists, with an annual budget of 90,000 francs, which rose by 1812 to fifty musicians and 153,800 francs. Numerous "private" concerts took place at Malmaison, more brilliant ones at the Tuileries. Napoleon opened theaters at Malmaison and Saint Cloud before Crescentini's arrival there and at the Tuileries, beginning in 1808, in addition to staging music and theater at Fontainebleau and Versailles. He also greatly strengthened the Conservatoire, expanded repertory and productions at the Opéra, and supported the new Théâtre Italien with the goal of, as he wrote, "perfecting the art of singing in France" (quoted in Charlton and Bartlet, "Napoleon I, Emperor of France"). See M. Elizabeth C. Bartlet, "Etienne Nicolas Méhul and Opera during the French Revolution, Consulate and Empire: A Source, Archival, and Stylistic Study," 5 vols., PhD diss., University of Chicago, 1982; and Bartlet, *Etienne-Nicolas Méhul and Opera: Source and Archival Studies of Lyric Theatre during the French Revolution, Consulate, and Empire*, 2 vols., Études sur l'opéra français du XIX siècle, vol. 4 (Heilbronn: Musik-Edition Galland, 1999). On opera at the Académie Imperiale de Musique under Napoleon, see Rachel R. Schneider, "The Administrative History of L'Académie Imperiale de Musique in the Age of Napoleon: Opera for *Gloire* and Indoctrination," Ph.D. diss., University of Akron, 1990.

6. See Janet Lynn Johnson, "The Théâtre Italien and Opera and Theatrical Life in Restoration Paris, 1818–1827," 3 vols., PhD diss., University of Chicago, 1988, 3: 516–17 for libretti of *Giulietta e Romeo* done at the Théâtre Italien and passim for context and aftermath. Crescentini played here opposite his long-standing partners Josephina Grassini (Giulietta) and Antonio Benelli (Everardo). I have benefited from Benjamin Walton, *Rossini in Restoration Paris: The Sound of Modern Life* (Cambridge: Cambridge University Press, 2007), and Jean Mongrédien, *French Music from the Enlightenment to Romanticism, 1789–1830*, translated from the French *La Musique en France, des lumières au romantisme* by Sylvain Frémaux, Reinhard G. Pauly, general editor (Portland: Amadeus Press, 1996), chapters 3 and 5.

7. Stendhal, *Vie de Rossini suivie des Notes d'un dilettante*, edited by Henri Prunières (Paris: E. Champion, 1922), 90.

8. Important on the shift of Italianate singing from Italy to France in the nineteenth century is Marco Beghelli, "I trattati di canto italiani dell'Ottocento: Bibliografia, caratteri generali, prassi esecutiva, lessico," Tesi di dottorato, Università degli Studi di Bologna, 1995.

9. Jean Starobinski, *Enchantment: The Seductress in Opera* (New York: Columbia University Press, 2008), chapter 14, "Ombra adorata," 177–230, 239–45. The book was originally published in French as *Les Enchantresses* (Paris: Éditions du Seuil, 2005), and the section of the chapter dealing with Stendhal was first published in English in *Opera Quarterly* 21, no. 4 (Autumn 2005): 612–30, in a translation by Robert S. Huddleston. *Enchantment* includes the entire essay as it appeared in the original Paris publication and is the one from which I cite below. Mademoiselle D'Avrillon says about the event, "As is known, it was after one of those performances [of *Giulietta e Romeo*] that the Emperor, ravished by the way Crescentini had sung the part of Romeo, gave him the Cross of the Iron Crown." Charles Maxime Catherinet de Villemarest *Mémoires de Mlle. Avrillon* [pseud.] . . . *sur Vie privée de Joséphine, sa famille et sa cour*, 2 vols., Bibliothèque des mémoires historiques et militaires sur la révolution, le consulat et l'empire (Paris: Garnier frères, 1896), 2: 85–86.

10. Cf. Alessandra Martina, *Orfeo-Orphée di Gluck: Storia della trasmissione e della recezione* (Florence: Passigli, 1995).

11. Niccolò Zingarelli, *Giulietta e Romeo*, 2 vols., I-Mr, MS (undated). The whole scena is transcribed in Andrea Malnati, "Drammaturgia musicale e filologia delle varianti: Il caso di 'Ombra adorata, aspetta' di Niccolò Zingarelli," Tesi di Laurea, Università degli Studi di Milano, 2008–9 (hereafter Malnati, "Il caso di 'Ombra adorata, aspetta'"), 100–114. See also Malnati's "Per una storia della prassi esecutiva dell'opera italiana: Il caso di 'Ombra adorata, aspetta' di Niccolò Zingarelli," *Bollettino del Centro Rossiniano di Studi* 50 (2010): 29–84. Alessandro De Bei discusses operatic settings of the subject in "Giulietta e Romeo di Nicola Zingarelli: Fortuna ed eredità di un soggetto shakespeariano," in *Aspetti dell'opera italiana fra Sette e Ottocento: Mayr e Zingarelli*, edited by Guido Salvetti (Lucca: LIM, 1993), 71–125, but not the compositional and performance history of "Ombra adorata, aspetta."

The reviewer in the *Allgemeine musikalische Zeitung* 6 (May 2, 1804) was disgusted by the liberties librettist Giuseppe Foppa took with Shakespeare: "Shakespeare's *Romeo and Juliet* has been impiously mistreated by the Italian librettist. Romeo's father, the coarse but courageous Tybalt, the venerable monk, and the loquacious nurse have all disappeared, and it is a friend of both houses who gives Juliet the fatal potion. The Italian poet has sought furthermore to improve Shakespeare, by having Juliet reawakened even before Romeo dies.

However, it is useless to dwell anymore on a plot in which the poet's only goal is to make a singer shine at all costs" (618).

12. The text comes from the original libretto by Giuseppe Foppa, *Giulietta e Romeo, tragedia per musica da rappresentarsi nel Teatro alla Scala il carnevale dell'anno 1796* (Milan: Gio. Batista Bianchi, 1796).

13. Starobinski, *Enchantment*, 179.

14. Villemarest, *Mémoires de Mlle. Avrillon*, 2: 85–86.

15. *Allgemeine musikalische Zeitung* 6 (May 2, 1804), 618.

16. Starobinski the literary critic left the pages of these musical sources virtually unturned. Will Crutchfield has been collecting numerous ornamented sources of the aria in connection with his much-anticipated book on eighteenth- and nineteenth-century operatic performance practice. I am deeply grateful to him for his generosity in sharing scores and discussing them with me.

17. Ex. 27 has been made from the undated version that survives in I-Vc, busta 8.2 (originally at the Museo e Biblioteca Correr). To my knowledge the aria has been recorded three times in modern recording history: 1) by an unnamed performer on an LP called *Obscure Italian Opera*, published privately in 1975; 2) by Martine Dupuy on *Concerto di altri tempi*, Rina Cellini, piano, LP recording in stereo (Bologna: Bongiovanni, 1981), GB 10, LCCN: 89-750419; 3) by Deborah Riedel with conductor Richard Bonynge leading the Arcadia Lane Orchestra on a CD called *Cherry Ripe: Vocal Treasures of the 18th & 19th Centuries* (Victoria, Australia: Elwood, 2008), MR 301118. A filmed performance is available at https://www.youtube.com/watch?v=8yeUn6OQWpU

18. Malnati, "Il caso di 'Ombra adorata, aspetta,'" 11; on matters of form and possibilities for performerly elaboration, see 51–56; on Zingarelli's first version, 45–46; and on Zingarelli's second version, 46–48 (cf. n. 20 below).

19. Maurice Bourges, "Crescentini, Girolamo," *Encyclopédie des gens du monde, répertoire universel des science, des lettres et des arts*, 22 vols. (Paris: Truettel & Würtz, 1833–44), vol. 7 (1836): 232–33, quoted in Malnati, "Il caso di 'Ombra adorata, aspetta,'" 55.

20. Malnati's edition of Zingarelli's original autograph of act 3, scene 1 is given in "Il caso di 'Ombra adorata, aspetta,'" 89–114, with "Idolo del mio cor" on 100–102, "Ma che vale il mio duol?" on 102–5, "Tranquillo sono" on 105–6, and "Ombra adorata, aspetta" in Zingarelli's initial version on 107–12. Malnati gives a transcription of a second "Ombra adorata" by Zingarelli (115–26), taken from an "appendix" to the autograph scores, plus editions of two further settings by Zingarelli (146–58), including one specifically written for Maria Malibran (153–58). He establishes that altogether there are five distinct settings of "Ombra adorata, aspetta" associated with Zingarelli's opera, four by Zingarelli and one by Crescentini. On top of those are almost innumerable copies with variant readings, different ornamentations, or different arrangements, almost all of Crescentini's setting.

21. This was done along with a number of other changes he made to the opera; see Francesco Florimo, *La scuola musicale di Napoli*, 2: 428; Alfred Loewenberg, *Annals of Opera, 1597–1940, Compiled from the Original Sources*, with an introduction by Edward J. Dent, 3rd ed. (Totowa, NJ: Rowman and Littlefield, 1978); and De Bei, "Giulietta e Romeo di Nicola Zingarelli," 83 and 83 n. 26; and see 86. According to RISM, a copy of Zingarelli's opera at US-Wfh marks all the parts composed by Crescentini with asterisks, but the staff of the library there has thus far not been unable to lay hands on the volume.

22. Catalani sang the aria in only two on-stage productions: one a production of the whole opera in Trieste in 1800, another a concert performance in Paris at the Académie Royale de Musique on August 15, 1815.

23. I cite from the edition of 1847, Manuel Garcia, *Traité complet de l'art du chant en deux parties*, part 1, 2nd ed., part 2, 1st ed. (Paris: E. Troupenas et cie., 1847), facsimile reprint in *Chant: Les grandes méthodes romantiques de chant*, 7 vols., edited by Jeanne Roudet, in *Méthodes et traités*, series 2, France, 1800–1860 (Courlay: Fuzeau, 2005), vol. 4. The first part was originally published in 1840. Many subsequent editions with variants were published during the author's long life (1805–1906).

24. For an excellent reading of Velluti's singing of it, see J.Q. Davies, *Romantic Anatomies of Performance* (Berkeley: University of California Press, 2014), chapter 1. Will Crutchfield has written an article on Velluti's ornamental style of singing and its impact on romantic melody in instrumental composers, including Chopin, based on a great many of newly discovered ornamented arias of Velluti's. See "Giovanni Battista Velluti e lo sviluppo della melodia romantica," *Bolletino del Centro Rossiniano di Studi* 54 (2014): 9–83.

25. Among other versions that attribute the aria to Crescentini are CZ-BER, Okresni archive, MS HU 505, a reduction for voice and keyboard titled "Romeo e Giulietta, Del Sigr. Crescentini" (Berna, Czech Republic); I-MC, MS 6-C-19e, MS (Montecassino), titled "Ombra adorata aspetta Rondo del Sig.r Girolamo Crescentini," with orchestral accompaniment by strings, two flutes, two oboes, two bassoons, and two horns, dated to the late eighteenth century; and a Neapolitan print by Girard (undated; copy at I-Mc).

26. "Rondò cantata [sic] da Girolamo Crescentini, e di sua composizione," Northwestern University, Music Library, MSS 1012. Also on the Northwestern manuscript is a designation of its owner—"Appartiene a [belongs to] Filippo Rolla." A pianist and composer who died sometime after 1842, Rolla was a son of the composer, violinist, and violist Alessandro Rolla. Malnati cites another MS copy marked as belonging to Filippo Rolla ("Il caso di 'Ombra adorata, aspetta,'" 11).

27. Garcia, *Traité complet*, 100.

28. *Variations pour deux violons sur l'air Ombra adorata aspetta de l'opéra Giuletta e Romeo, composées par J. Conti*, 2 parts (Vienna: Jean Cappi, [1810?]). The print was evidently published posthumously around 1809–10. A facsimile edition appears in the series Musica revindicata, no. 234 (Amsterdam: A.J. Heuwekemeijer, 1970). Conti (1754–1805) led the orchestra of the Italian opera in Vienna from 1793, was a member of the Hofkapelle from 1797, and was a violin teacher to Count Moritz von Fries, for whom he composed various violin duos.

29. This is no. 6 among transcriptions in Malnati, "Il caso di 'Ombra adorata, aspetta,'" 159–63 (original in I-Mc, Noseda P. 5.23). To my knowledge, it survives only in a Milanese manuscript. Eppinger (ca. 1776–1823) was a Jewish violin player who performed at private concerts and soirées and also a composer. He evidently first appeared at a charity concert in Vienna in 1789 and thereafter devoted himself entirely to music, supporting himself in Vienna mostly by independent means. Thayer calls him a violinist of the highest reputation who formed part of Beethoven's "circle of dilettanti." Alexander Wheelock Thayer, *Thayer's Life of Beethoven*, 3 vols., edited by Elliot Forbes (Princeton, NJ: Princeton University Press, 1967), 1: 225. J.F. von Schönfeld praises Eppinger's violin playing highly in his *Jahrbuch der Tonkunst von Wien und Prag*, Gesellschaft der Musikfreunde in Wien (Munich:

E. Katzbilder, 1796). See also Harry Peter Clive, *Beethoven and His World: A Biographical Dictionary* (New York: Oxford University Press, 2001), 100; and Malnati, "Il caso di 'Ombra adorata, aspetta,'" 53–56. On the lost second violin part see Robert Eitner, "Eppinger, Enrico," in his *Biographisch-Bibliographisches Quellen-Lexicon der Musiker und Musikgelehrten der christlichen Zeitrechnung bis zur Mitte des neunzehnten Jahrhunderts*, 10 vols. (Leipzig: Breitkopf & Härtel, 1900–1904), 3: 343.

30. Will Crutchfield's essay "Early Vocal Ornamentation" is revelatory on the matter: in Gioachino Rossini, *Il barbiere di Siviglia: Almaviva, o sia, L'inutile precauzione: commedia in due atti di Cesare Sterbini dalla commedia di Pierre-Augustin Caron de Beaumarchais*, edited by Patricia B. Brauner (Kassel: Bärenreiter, 2008), Appendix 5, 361–420. Also see Crutchfield, "Voices," chapter 15 in *Performance Practice: Music after 1600*, edited by Howard Mayer Brown and Stanley Sadie (New York: Norton, 1990), 442–58.

31. I quote from Stendhal, *Vie de Rossini*, 151. Chapter 35 is devoted to Pasta. Stendhal also writes often of Pasta in his autobiographical *Souvenirs d'égotisme*. Some manuscript letters to her are transcribed in Maria Giulini Ferranti, ed., *Giuditta Pasta e i suoi tempi: Memorie e lettere* (Milan: Cromotipia E. Sormani, 1935).

32. Cf. Philip Downes, "Musical Pleasures and Amorous Passions: Stendhal, the Crystallization Process, and Listening to Rossini and Beethoven," *19th-Century Music* 26, no. 3 (2003): 235–57, esp. 235–42. Starobinski's marvelous reading of Balzac's "treatise on love" is included with his interpretation of Balzac's musical short story *Massimilla Doni* (*Enchantment*, 207–30).

33. Stendhal heard Pasta a good deal both on stage and in her Parisian salon, from where he knew her personally. Although there is some slight evidence that he heard Crescentini, it is not definitive. The evidence is reviewed in Starobinski, *Enchantment*, 183–84.

34. The quote comes from Walton, *Rossini in Restoration Paris*, 28, whose point is made by many other writers on *Vie de Rossini*, for example Béatrice Didier, "Stendhal et la musique: De la biographie à l'autobiographie," in *Stendhal e Milano: Atti del 14º congresso internazionale stendhaliano, Milano, 19–23 marzo 1980*, 2 vols. (Florence: Leo S. Olschki, 1982), 2: 591–606. A fine work on Stendhal's *Vie* is Suzel Esquier, *Vie de Rossini par M. de Stendhal: Chronique parisienne, 1821–1823*, Collection "Stendhal Club" (Moncalieri: Centro Universitario di Ricerche sul "Viaggio in Italia," 1997).

35. Pierfrancesco Moliterni and Carmela Ferrandes, "Alle origine del 'bel canto': Stendhal e gli 'idéologues,'" in *Stendhal tra letteratura e musica: Atti del Convegno Internazionale, Martina Franca, 26–29 novembre 1992*, edited by Giovanni Dotoli (Fasano: Schena, 1993), 237–52, esp. 241–45 on Cabanis and melody; and Starobinski, *Enchantment*, 197–98 on Destrutt de Tracy. A treatment of the *idéologues* with respect to sensationalism and the development of a self *(moi)* in France is Jan Goldstein, *The Post-Revolutionary Self: Politics and Psyche in France, 1750–1850* (Cambridge, MA: Harvard University Press, 2005), esp. chapters 3 and 4.

The attention of Stendhal to melody in the way of the idéologues might stand as a philosophical and literary support to Crutchfield's musical thesis in "Giovanni Battista Velluti e lo sviluppo della melodia romantica," supported with exacting musical detail, that during Stendhal's active years Velluti was at the crux of widely transmitting this bel canto–based style of romantic melody to instrumental composers as well as other vocal ones and to performers.

36. "Les nuances pour tenues la voix, le chant de *portamento*, l'art de modérer la voix pour la faire monter également sur toutes les notes dans le chant *legato*, l'art de reprendre la respiration d'une manière insensible et sans rompre le long période vocal des airs de l'ancienne école, composaient autrefois la partie la plus difficile et la plus nécessaire de l'exécution." From Stendhal, *Vie de Rossini*, chapter 32.

37. Stendhal never says that Velluti's voice is "fluted," a word Richard N. Coe uses in his very free translation of Stendhal, *Life of Rossini*, rev. ed. (New York: Orion Press, 1970), 263, which generally makes little sense applied to castrato voices, especially ones used in large halls.

38. For Stendhal's strenuous objections to composers writing out all ornamentation, see *Vie de Rossini*, 115 and passim. The matter of Rossini's abundant ornamentation relates obliquely to the issue of Rossinian overabundance—of emotions, effects, stimulation, instruments, speeds, etc.—which was the focus of various critical tensions in Rossini's time. On this issue see recently Walton, *Rossini in Restoration Paris*, chapter 1 and passim; Melina Esse, "Rossini's Noisy Bodies," *Cambridge Opera Journal* 21, no. 1 (March 2009): 27–64; and Janet Johnson, "The Musical Environment in France," in *The Cambridge Companion to Berlioz*, edited by Peter Bloom (Cambridge: Cambridge University Press, 2000), 20–38.

39. Starobinski, *Enchantment*, 187.

40. "Paradox of the Actor," in Denis Diderot, *Selected Writings on Art and Literature*, translated and with introduction and notes by Geoffrey Bremner (Harmondsworth: Penguin Books, 1994), 154; Denis Diderot, *Le paradoxe sur le comédien; Le neveu de Rameau* (Strasbourg: J. H. E. Heitz, 1913), 97.

41. Davies traces this multi-voicedness in male voices of the third to fourth decades of the nineteenth century, especially in the so-called *bari-tenor* of Francesco Bennati and Domenico Donzelli and the *voix mixte* of Adolphe Nourrit (*Romantic Anatomies of Performance*, chapter 5). See also Joy Ratliff, "Women in Pants: Male Roles for the Mezzo-Soprano or Contralto Voice," DMA thesis, University of Maryland, College Park, 1997; Heather Hadlock, "On the Cusp between Past and Future: The Mezzo-Soprano Romeo of Bellini's *I Capuleti*," *Opera Quarterly* 17, no. 3 (2001): 299–322; Hadlock, "Women Playing Men in Italian Opera, 1810–1835," in *Women's Voices across Musical Worlds*, edited by Jane A. Bernstein (Boston: Northeastern University Press, 2004), 285–307; Naomi André, *Voicing Gender: Castrati, Travesti, and the Second Woman in Early-Nineteenth-Century Italian Opera* (Bloomington: Indiana University Press, 2006); and on the contralto voice Marco Beghelli and Raffaele Talmelli, *Ermafrodite armoniche: Il contralto nell'Ottocento* (Varese: Zecchini, 2011), which argues that the contralto voice had a kind of double register consisting of a large, mannish low voice and a lighter, higher one and that this doubleness indexes a sexual ambiguity both of the characters portrayed by contraltos and of the bodies that portrayed them.

42. A thoughtful explanation of the "castrato-tenor connection" is given by John Potter, *Tenor: History of a Voice* (New Haven, CT: Yale University Press, 2009), chapter 2.

43. See, for example, Herbert Weinstock, *Rossini: A Biography* (New York: Alfred A. Knopf, 1968), xvii. It would not be possible to try to name even a representative selection of secondary sources that uncover inaccuracies, inventions, borrowings, and the like in Stendhal's text, nor would it illuminate his philosophical aesthetics, which is my interest here. Readers who wish to pursue the former line might start with the excellent work of Stéphane Dado and Philippe

Vendrix, "Stendhal e Rossini: Uno studio documentario," translated by Reto Müller and Mauro Tosti-Croce, *Bolletino del Centro Rossiniano di Studi* 49 (1999): 21–60. Dado and Vendrix point out that despite the thin line between fiction and nonfiction that Stendhal walks, he did hear an astounding number of performances of Rossini's operas and had the advantage over Parisians of having heard them in Milan where he lived between 1814 and 1821.

44. "Cet art donne des regrets tendres en procurant la *vue du bonheur;* et faire voir le bonheur, quoique en songe, c'est presque donner de l'ésperance." From Stendhal, *Vie de Rossini,* chapter 33, "Excuses," 119.

45. One wonders whether Micheroux had in mind Lorenzo's speech to Jessica in Shakespeare's *Merchant of Venice,* act 5, scene 1: "How sweet the moonlight sleeps upon this bank. Here will we sit and let the sounds of music creep in our ears. Soft stillness and the night become the touches of sweet harmony."

46. The words are "éloge sublime du suicide" (Stendhal, *Vie de Rossini,* 405). Like Micheroux via Stendhal, a reviewer in the *Chronique musicale* of September 27, 1821 remarked that all that was needed never to forget Pasta in the role was to remember her "ultimo pianto" ("Sarebbe bastato a ciò sentire l'ultimo grido di Romeo nell'opera omonima"); quoted in Ferranti, ed., *Giuditta Pasta e i suoi tempi,* 39.

47. Micheroux to Pasta, quoted in Ferranti, ed., *Giuditta Pasta e i suoi tempi,* 92.

48. "Ce passage doit être executé par des mouvements souples de gosier."

49. *Souvenir à Pasta, et Rubini,* no. 5, *"Ombra adorata aspetta," cavatina de l'opéra Romeo e Giulietta, de Zingarelli,* arranged by Anton Diabelli and Johann Jean Sedlatzek (London: Wessel & Co, 1832).

50. Stendhal, *Vie de Rossini,* 142.

51. Ibid., 145 and passim.

52. Another amateur singer, Elizabeth Augusta Wrightson, probably added her own handwritten ornaments, as found on her copy of the same Birchall print, though she seems to have wanted to begin the first iteration of "Avrò contento il cor" rather simply and then build the ornamental surface over the course of the aria. In Elizabeth Augusta Wrightson Collection of Italian printed arias with ornamentation added by hand, ca. 1810–40, Northwestern University, Music Library (US-En), MSS 617: Zingarelli [attrib.], "Tranquillo io son/Ombra adorato [sic] aspetta . . . sung by Madame Catalani . . ." (London: Robert Birchall, [ca. 1823–24]), m. 11.

53. Crutchfield's book in preparation will attend to a great many ornamented sources of "Ombra adorata, aspetta" and passages in it that I have not.

54. Malnati, "Il caso di 'Ombra adorata aspetta,'" 58–60, which quotes Carpani's letters.

55. E. T. A. Hoffmann, "Ombra adorata," translated in *E. T. A. Hoffmann's Musical Writings:* Kreisleriana, The Poet and the Composer, *Music Criticism,* edited, annotated, and introduced by David Charlton, translated by Martyn Clarke (Cambridge: Cambridge University Press, 1989), 88–91, quote at 89–90 (emphasis mine). Hoffmann asterisks the title and gives this note: "Who does not know Crescentini's wonderful aria 'Ombra adorata' which he composed for Zingarelli's opera *Giulietta e Romeo* and sang with such characteristic delivery?" (88).

56. Stendhal, *Vie de Rossini,* 115.

57. Ibid. "Crescentini donnait sa voix et à ses inflexions une teinte vague et générale de contentement dans l'air: *ombra adorata, aspetta*; il lui semblait *au moment où il chantait que*

tel devait être le sentiment d'un amant passionné qui va rejoindre ce qu'il aime" (in chapter 32, titled "Détails de la révolution opérée par Rossini"). Stendhal clinches the point by adding, "Velluti, qui comprend la situation d'une manière différente, y met de la mélancholie et une réflexion triste sur le sort commun des deux amants" (115). (Velluti, who understands the situation differently, places some melancholy and sad meditation on the common fate of the two lovers.

58. *Raccolta di esercizi per il canto all'uso del vocalizzo, con discorso preliminare, del signor Girolamo Crescentini / Recueil d'exercices pour la vocalisation musicale, avec un discours préliminaire, par m. Jérôme Crescentini* (Paris: Imbault, [ca. 1810–11]); facsimile reprint in *Chant: Les grandes méthodes romantiques*, vol. 1. The *Raccolta* should be read in conjunction with Crescentini's *Vingt-cinq nouvelles vocalises* [ca. 1818–23] and his *Méthode complète de chant* (2nd ed.), both in vol. 2 of the series, as well as the *26 Solfeggi progressivi per mezzo-soprano con accompagnamento di pianoforte* (Naples: n.d.) and *Ultima e nuova raccolta di venti-quatro solfeggi all'uso del vocalizzo per voce di soprano* (Milan: Ricordi, 1835), both treated by Annarosa Vannoni, "'Ombra adorata, aspetta': Girolamo Crescentini, il cantante e il didatta," in *Martini docet: Atti delle Giornate di studio: Io la musica son . . . : Per il bicentenario del manifestazioni Conservatorio di Bologna; classi, regolamenti, musicisti e musicologi per due secoli: lo stato di attuazione della riforma e prospettive di sviluppo. Sala Bossi, 30 settembre–2 ottobre 2004*, edited by Piero Mioli, preface by Carmine Carrisi (Bologna: Conservatorio di musica Giovan Battista Martini, 2007), 159–63 and 163–64, respectively. On the French solfeggio tradition of Crescentini, see Sylvie Mamy, "L'importation des solfèges italiens en France à la fin du XVIII siècle," in *L'opera tra Venezia e Parigi*, edited by Maria Teresa Muraro (Venice: Fondazione Giorgio Cini, 1986), 67–90.

59. "Those who pretend they cannot sing with expression without their breathing being heard" were to his mind simply wrong, for only in the rarest of situations did a breath have to be "squeezed, heavy, or noisy." Crescentini, *Raccolta di esercizi*, 8-9.

60. Carolyn Abbate, *Unsung Voices: Opera and Musical Narrative in the Nineteenth Century* (Princeton, NJ: Princeton University Press, 1991), and more recently Carolyn Abbate and Roger Parker, *A History of Opera* (New York: Norton, 2012), chapter 6, "Speaking and Singing before 1800," esp. 156–59.

61. Berlioz, *Mémoires*, chapter 35 (emphasis mine): "Mais, au nom de Dieu, est-il donc décidé que l'amant de Juliette doit paraître dépourvu des attributs de la virilité? Est-il un enfant, celui qui, en trois passes, perce le cœur du *furieux Tybalt, le héros de l'escrime*, et qui, plus tard, après avoir brisé les portes du tombeau de sa maîtresse, d'un bras dédaigneux, étend mort sur les degrés du monument le comte Páris qui la provoqué ? Et son désespoir au moment de l'exil, sa sombre et terrible résignation en apprenant la mort de Juliette, son délire convulsif après avoir bu le poison, toutes ces passions volcaniques germent-elles d'ordinaire dans l'âme d'un eunuque?" Quoted in full from *Mémoires de Hector Berlioz membre de l'Institut de France comprenant ses voyages en Italie, en Allemagne, en Russie et en Angleterre, 1803–1865* (Paris: Éditions du Sandre, 2010), 160–61. Starobinski elaborates on the passage in *Enchantment*, 194–96.

62. See Hedy Law, "Gestural Rhetoric: In Search of Pantomime in the French Enlightenment, ca. 1750–1785," 3 vols., PhD diss., University of Chicago, 2007, chapter 4.

63. In 1807 the company of the Théâtre Italien got exclusive rights to perform Italian opera in Paris—staging operas by Cimarosa, Paisiello, then Paer, Mayr, Fioravanti, and the Mozart

/Da Ponte operas—and by 1810 *opere serie* by Zingarelli, then later on extending to Rossini and others. The operations were fraught with all the financial crises typical of Italian opera.

64. Starobinksi, *Enchantment*, 198-207 and 207-30. Useful on music in Balzac is Jean-Pierre Barricelli, *Balzac and Music: Its Place in His Life and Work* (New York: Garland, 1990).

65. From Vigny's "La Canne de jonc," the third story in his trilogy *Servitude et grandeur militaires*; see Maxwell Smith, "Alfred de Vigny, Founder of the French Historical Novel," *French Review* 13, no. 1 (October 1939): 5-13, at 11-13; and Starobinski, *Enchantment*, 180. The memory must date from when Vigny was quite young, as he was born in 1797; Crescentini sang Romeo for the last time, in Paris, when Vigny was just twelve, and the singer left France three years later. Vigny was educated by his Rousseau-influenced young mother, a noblewoman who had lost everything in the Revolution. He composed *Servitude et grandeur militaires* as a meditation on the soldier's condition when he was thirty-eight, having spent fourteen years as a soldier. His comment about Crescentini is cited without documentation in Heriot and repeated frequently.

66. See also the description in Barbier by an anonymous woman, published in 1835; Patrick Barbier, *The World of the Castrati: The History of an Extraordinary Operatic Phenomenon*, translated by Margaret Crosland (London: Souvenir Press, 1996), 231-32.

67. Roland Barthes, in *Image—Music—Text*, translated and edited by Stephen Heath (New York: Noonday Press, 1977), chapter 12, 179-89.

68. Michel Poizat, *The Angel's Cry: Beyond the Pleasure Principle in Opera*, translated by Arthur Denner (1986; Ithaca, NY: Cornell University Press, 1992), esp. 119; the original French had the more pointed title *L'opéra, ou Le cri de l'ange: Essai sur la jouissance de l'amateur d'opéra*, which lacks the Freudian common coin "Beyond the Pleasure Principle." For extreme variations on these themes, see Joke Dame, "Unveiled Voices: Sexual Difference and the Castrato," in *Queering the Pitch*, edited by Philip Brett, Elizabeth Wood, and Gary C. Thomas (New York: Routledge, 1994), 139-54, who draws on *Sarrasine* to assert a Freudian sublimated homoerotics as explanation for certain historical descriptions of castrati as feminine in body but masculine in voice; Beth Kowaleski-Wallace, "Shunning the Bearded Kiss: Castrati and the Definition of Female Sexuality," *Prose Studies* 15, no. 2 (1992): 153-70; and Margaret Reynolds, "Ruggiero's Deceptions, Cherubino's Distractions," in *En Travesti: Women, Gender Subversion, Opera*, edited by Corinne E. Blackmer and Julianna Smith (New York: Columbia University Press, 1995), 132-51, which picks up the Lacanian/Barthesian strain in saying that the castrato "pointed away from ordinary meanings of the voice ... and directed the listening ear to the particularities of the voice itself" (37). A thoroughly original development of some of these themes is Wayne Koestenbaum, *The Queen's Throat: Opera, Homosexuality, and the Mystery of Desire* (New York: Da Capo Press, 1993), which thinks about opera listeners in relation to homosexuality, desire, fetishism, queerness, and voice. Emily Wilbourne's "The Queer History of the Castrato," in *Oxford Handbook on Queerness and Music*, edited by Fred Maus and Sheila Whiteley (forthcoming), is a smart, canny exploration of the castrato.

69. Renata Salecl and Slavoj Žižek, eds., *Gaze and Voice as Love Objects* (Durham, NC: Duke University Press, 1996), 3 (emphasis mine).

70. Mladen Dolar, *A Voice and Nothing More* (Cambridge, MA: MIT Press, 2006), end of "Introduction: 'Che bella voce!,'" quote on p. 10, story and analysis on 3-4.

71. The feminine diminutive Zambinella does not accord with any moniker a historical castrato ever had.

72. See Thomas E. Crow, *Emulation: David, Drouais, and Girodet in the Art of Revolutionary France*, rev. ed. (1995; New Haven, CT: Yale University Press, in association with The Getty Research Institute, 2008), chapter 5, esp. 133–39. Crow speaks of "a body that gives back to narcissistic desire its primitive dream of bliss in death" (136) and the "pervasive effect of androgyny" caused by Endymion (139).

73. Of course in castrato lore, the wounds of wild boars often were said to have necessitated castrations; see chapter 1 above.

74. Cf. Armine Kotin Mortimer, *For Love or Money: Balzac's Rhetorical Realism* (Columbus: Ohio State University Press, 2011).

75. Honoré de Balzac, *Sarrasine*, in Roland Barthes, *S/Z: An Essay*, translated by Richard Miller, preface by Richard Howard (New York: Hill and Wang, 1974), 251.

76. "A hundred years old" may be inspired by the renowned Swiss castrato Antonio (Antoine) Bagniera (variously given as Bagnera, Baniera, and Bannieri), who was probably born in Rome in 1638 and died at Versailles in 1740. Son of a Swiss guard of the French kings, he spent many decades at the court of Versailles. See M.-F. Bêche: [Mémoires], F-Pn, Rés. F.1661, 92–106; and Benoit, *Versailles et les musiciens*, 133, 135, 270, 324–29, and Fig. 30, plate 32 for La maison des Italiens au Grand-Montreuil, country residence of the castrati of the royal music. See also Lionel Sawkins, "The Brothers Bêche: An Anecdotal History of Court Music," *Recherches sur la musique française classique* 24 (1986): 192–221. Bagniera was the eventual owner of the Maison des Italiens and composed a *Divertissement pour la cérémonie de la découverte de la statue du Roy* (Paris, 1704).

77. Balzac, *Sarrasine*, 229.

78. Boccaccio, *Decamerone*, Filomena 2, 9.42; and Nicolò Machiavelli's famously raunchy, misogynistic letter to Luigi Guicciardini of December 8, 1509, about going to an old prostitute (Machiavelli, *Lettere*, edited by Franco Gaeta [Milan: Feltrinelli, 1961]), 204–6. Machiavelli's *La clizia* tropes on the *vecchio innamorato*, the old man in love (note especially the canzone that forms the intermedio between acts 2 and 3), who was a persistent target of critique in Renaissance conduct books and may hover equally in the background of Balzac's Zambinella.

79. Balzac, *Sarrasine*, 226.

80. Ibid., 234.

81. Ibid., 230 and 235.

82. Its more literal meaning of "Genoese man" conjures up something like a self-made shipping magnate.

83. Balzac, *Sarrasine*, 253.

84. Ibid., 254.

85. Pierre Bourdieu, *Distinction: A Social Critique of the Judgment of Taste*, translated by Richard Nice (1979; Cambridge, MA: Harvard University Press, 1984).

86. Balzac, *Sarrasine*, 224.

87. Balzac heard Malibran in a salon in 1830; see *The Correspondence of Honoré de Balzac with a Memoir by His Sister Madame de Surville*, 2 vols., translated by C. Lamb Kennedy (London: Richard Bentley & Son, 1878), 1: 211, letter of April 14, 1830.

88. Balzac, *Sarrasine*, 251 (emphasis mine). One wonders if Stendhal was thinking of the relationship of La Zambinella and Marianina when he had his similarly named Marietta, in

The Charterhouse of Parma (1839), stop nearly every evening along with Fabrice to see Crescentini, "who felt that he was a little bit of a father to Marietta" (beginning of chapter 13).

89. Edmond Michotte, *Richard Wagner's Visit to Rossini (Paris 1860) and An Evening at Rossini's in Beau-Sejour (Passy) 1858*, translated from the French and annotated, with an introduction and appendix, by Herbert Weinstock (Chicago: University of Chicago Press, 1968), 109.

90. See Crutchfield, "Giovanni Battista Velluti e lo sviluppo della melodia romantica."

91. Cf. Velluti with moustache in Turin, 1821, reproduced in Naomi André, *Voicing Gender: Castrati, Travesti, and the Second Woman in Early-Nineteenth-Century Italian Opera* (Bloomington: Indiana University Press, 206), 58.

92. Cf. chapter 3 on Rossini's earlier use of the term "bel canto." The phrase in italics comes from Petrarch's sonnet no. 172.

93. The information is taken from Leopold M. Kantner and Angela Pachovsky, *La cappella musicale pontificia nell'Ottocento*, Storia della cappella musicale pontificia, vol. 6 (Rome: Hortus Musicus, 1998), and Salvatore De Salvo Fattor, *La cappella musicale pontificia nel Novecento*, Storia della cappella musicale pontificia, vol. 7, edited by Giancarlo Rostirolla (Rome: Fondazione Giovanni Pierluigi da Palestrina, 2005).

94. Michotte, *Richard Wagner's Visit to Rossini*, 73 and n. on 72-73.

95. The polemic with Berton is treated by Jean Mongrédien, "A propos de Rossini: Une polémique Stendhal-Berton," in *Stendhal e Milano*, 2: 673-93; and see Walton, *Rossini in Restoration Paris*, 54-57.

BIBLIOGRAPHY

SELECTED PRIMARY MUSICAL SOURCES

Balatri, Filippo. "Frutti del mondo, esperimentati da. F. B. nativo dell'Alfea, in Toscana," 2 vols. G-Mbs, cod. It. 39.
———. "Testamento, o sia ultima volontà, di F. B., nativo Alfeo." G-Mbs, cod. It. 329.
———. "Vita e viaggi di F. B., nativo di Pisa." RUS-Mrg, MS F. 218, no. 1247.
Bêche, M.-F. [Mémoires]. F-Pn, Rés. F. 1661.
Broschi, Carlo, detto Farinello. "Inventario legale della eredità di Carlo Broschi detto Farinelli." I-Bas, *Notarile*.
———. Letter to Anna Gatteschi, Sept. 12, 1769." I-Bas, Lorenzo Gambarini, *Notarile*, 22 Genn. 1769–23 Dic. 1770.
Burney, Susan. MS Egerton 3691, 2692. GB-Lb.
Crescentini, Girolamo. "Ombra adorata, aspetta." I-Vc.
"Italian Theater Collection." Shelf number 2003.M.33. Special Collections, Research Library, Getty Research Institute, Getty Center, Los Angeles.
"Lamento del castrato." Anonymous. I-Bc, MS Q 46.
Martini, Padre. "Carteggi." Museo Internazionale e Biblioteca della Musica di Bologna. http://badigit.comune.bologna.it/cmbm/scripts/lettere/search.asp.
MS D-MÜs, SANT Hs 458.
Tosi, Pierfrancesco. "Inventario e dimissione, Aug. 2, 1732, per Pierfrancesco Tosi." I-Bas, Gioacchino Roffeni, *Notarile* 5/11, vol. 29, fols. 151r–153r.
Wrightson, Elizabeth Augusta, Collection of Italian Printed Arias, with ornamentation added by hand, ca. 1810–1840. US-Eu, Music Library, MSS 617.

SELECTED ARTICLES, BOOKS, RECORDINGS, AND EDITIONS

Abbate, Carolyn. "Music—Drastic or Gnostic?" *Critical Inquiry* 30 (2004): 505-36.

———. "Opera; or the Envoicing of Women." In *Musicology and Difference: Gender and Sexuality in Music Scholarship*, edited by Ruth A. Solie, 225-58. Berkeley: University of California Press, 1993.

———. *Unsung Voices: Opera and Musical Narrative in the Nineteenth Century*. Princeton, NJ: Princeton University Press, 1991.

Abbate, Carolyn, and Roger Parker. *A History of Opera*. New York: Norton, 2012.

Acland, Robert D. *Acland's DVD Atlas of Human Anatomy*. 6 vols. Philadelphia: Lippincott Williams & Wilkins, 2004.

Agricola, Johann Friedrich. *Anleitung zur Singkunst*. Berlin, 1757.

Albergati Capacelli, Francesco. *Il ciarlator maldicente*, in *Scelta di commedie e novelle morali*. 2 vols. Edited by Antonio Ravelli. London: Giuseppe Cooper, [1794?], vol. 2.

Albrecht, Carol Padgham. "The Face of the Vienna Court Opera, 1804-1805." *Music in Art: International Journal for Music Iconography* 34, nos. 1-2 (Spring-Fall 2009): 191-202.

Alessandro Moreschi, soprano-castrato (1858-1922), Complete Gramophone Co. Recordings (Roma, 1902-1904). Remastered by Christian Zwarg from source material provided by Michael E. Gunrem, Michael Seil, Axel Weggen, and Christian Zwarg. Stutensee: True Transfers, TT-3040, 2004.

Alessandro Moreschi, The Last Castrato, Complete Vatican Recordings. Production notes by John Wolfson and liner notes by Elsa Scammell. Opal CD 9823, 1987.

Algarotti, Francesco. *An Essay on the Opera Written in Italian by Count Algarotti*. London, 1767.

———. *Saggio sopra l'opera in musica*. Livorno: Marco Coltellini, 1763.

———. *Saggio sopra l'opera in musica*. Venice: G. Pasquali, 1755.

———. *Saggio sopra l'opera in musica: Le edizioni del 1755 e del 1763*. Edited by Annalisa Bini. Lucca: Libreria Musicale Italiana, 1989.

Ancillon, Charles. *Eunuchism Display'd*. Translated by Robert Samber. London: Printed for E. Curll, 1718.

———. *Traité des eunuques* [1707]. Edited and introduced by Michela Gardini. Paris: L'Harmattan, 2007.

———. *Traité des eunuques dans lequel on explique toutes les différentes sortes d'eunuques, quel rang ils ont tenu, & quel cas on en a fait, &c. . . . Par M*** D****. Berlin, 1707.

Anderson, Benedict. "The Idea of Power in Javanese Culture." In Benedict Anderson, *Language and Power: Exploring Political Cultures in Indonesia*. Ithaca, NY: Cornell University Press, 1990.

Anderson, Perry. *Lineages of the Absolutist State* [1974]. London: Verso, 1979.

André, Naomi. *Voicing Gender: Castrati, Travesti, and the Second Woman in Early-Nineteenth-Century Italian Opera*. Bloomington: Indiana University Press, 2006.

Annibaldi, Claudio. *La cappella musicale pontificia nel Seicento*. Storia della cappella musicale pontificia, vol. 4. Palestrina [Rome]: Fondazione Giovanni Pierluigi da Palestrina, 2011.

Antolini, Bianca Maria. "La carriera di cantante e compositore di Loreto Vittori." *Studi musicali* 7 (1978): 141-88.

Aprile, Giuseppe. *The Modern Italian Method of Singing, with a Variety of Progressive Examples and Thirty-Six Solfeggi by Sigr. S. G. Aprile*. London: R. Birchall, [ca. 1795].
Argens, Jean-Baptiste de Boyer. *New Memoirs Establishing a True Knowledge of Mankind, by Discovering the Affections of the Heart, and the Operations of the Understanding*. 2 vols. London: Printed for D. Brown, R. Hett, and A. Millar, 1747.
Arie per Carlo Broschi Farinelli. Edited by Luigi Verdi and Maria Pia Jacoboni. Rome: Bardi, 2007.
Ariès, Philippe. *Centuries of Childhood: A Social History of Family Life*. Translated by Robert Baldick. New York: Vintage Books, 1962.
Arte e musica all'Ospedaletto: Schede d'archivio sull'attività musicale degli ospedali dei derelitti e dei mendicanti di Venezia (sec. XVI–XVIII). [Venice]: Stamperia di Venezia, 1978.
Avanzati, Elisabeth. "The Unpublished Senesino." In the catalog of the exhibition *Handel and the Castrati: The Story behind the 18th-Century Superstar Singers*, 19 March–1 October 2006, 5–9. London: Handel House Museum, 2006.
Baiocco, Monica. "Su Baldassare Ferri, cantante evirato del Seicento." *Esercizi, musica e spettacolo*, new series 6, no. 15 (1996): 19–46.
Baird, Julianne. "An Eighteenth-Century Controversy about the Trill: Mancini vs. Manfredini." *Early Music* 15 (1987): 36–45.
Bajada, Joseph. *Sexual Impotence: The Contribution of Paolo Zacchia, 1584–1650*. Rome: Ed. Pontificia Universitaria Gregoriana, 1988.
Baker, Nicole Edwina Ivy. "Italian Opera at the Court of Mannheim, 1758–1770." PhD diss., University of California at Los Angeles, 1994.
Balatri, Filippo. *"Frutti del mondo": L'autobiografia di Filippo Balatri*. Edited by Karl Vossler. Milan: Remo Sandron, 1924.
Balzac, Honoré de. *Sarrasine*. In Roland Barthes, *S/Z: An Essay*, translated by Richard Miller, preface by Richard Howard. New York: Hill and Wang, 1974.
Barbier, Patrick. *La maison des italiens: Les castrats a Versailles*. Paris: Bernard Grasset, 1998.
———. *The World of the Castrati: The History of an Extraordinary Operatic Phenomenon*. Translated by Margaret Crosland. London: Souvenir Press, 1996.
Barcham, William L. "Il teatro della moda." In *Tiepolo: Ironia e comico*, edited by Adriano Mariuz and Giuseppe Pavanello, 69–93. Venice: Marsilio Editori, 2004.
Barrett Collection [Letters of Susan Burney]. Published electronically in *The Journals and Letters of Susan Burney: Music and Society in Late Eighteenth-Century England*, edited by Philip Olleson. Farnham, Surrey, England: Ashgate, 2012.
Barricelli, Pierre. *Balzac and Music: Its Place in His Life and Work*. New York: Garland, 1990.
Barthes, Roland. "The Grain of the Voice." In Roland Barthes, *Image—Music—Text*, essays selected and translated by Stephen Heath. New York: Hill & Wang, 1977.
———. *S/Z: An Essay*. Translated by Richard Miller, preface by Richard Howard. New York: Hill and Wang, 1974.
Bartlet, M. Elizabeth C. "Etienne Nicolas Méhul and Opera during the French Revolution, Consulate and Empire: A Source, Archival, and Stylistic Study." 5 vols. PhD diss., University of Chicago, 1982.
———. *Etienne-Nicolas Méhul and Opera: Source and Archival Studies of Lyric Theatre during the French Revolution, Consulate, and Empire*. 2 vols. Études sur l'opéra français du XIX siècle, vol. 4. Heilbronn: Musik-Edition Galland, 1999.

Bauer, Robert. *The New Catalogue of Historical Records, 1898–1908/09.* 2nd ed. London: Sidgwick and Jackson, 1947.
Becker, Gerhold K. "The Divinization of Nature in Early Modern Thought." In *The Invention of Nature*, edited by Thomas Bargatzky and Rolf Kuschel. Frankfurt: Peter Lang, 1994.
Beghelli, Marco. "Il *do di petto*: Dissacrazione di un mito." *Il saggiatore musicale* 3, no. 1 (1996): 105–49.
———. "Per fedeltà di una nota." *Il saggiatore musicale* 8 (2001): 295–316.
———. "I trattati di canto italiani dell'Ottocento: Bibliografia, caratteri generali, prassi esecutiva, lessico." Tesi di dottorato, Università degli Studi di Bologna, 1995.
Beghelli, Marco, and Raffaele Talmelli. *Ermafrodite armoniche: Il contralto nell'Ottocento.* Varese: Zecchini, 2011.
Behl, Vinod. "The Eunuchs." In *Men of the Global South: A Reader*, edited by Adam Jones. London: Zed Books, 2006.
Belcastro, Maria Giovanna, et al. "Hyperostosis Frontalis Interna (HFI) and Castration: The Case of the Famous Singer Farinelli (1705–1782)." *Journal of Anatomy* 219 (2011): 632–37.
Bellucci La Salandra, Mario. "Vito Giuseppe Millico (Il terlizzese): Sopranista e compositore melodrammatico del Settecento (da nuovi documenti)." *Archivio storico pugliese* 3 (1950): 201–27.
Benelli, Antonio Peregrino [Pellegrino]. *Regole per il canto figurato, o siano Precetti ragionati per apprendere i principi di musica, con esercizi, lezioni et infine solfeggi, per imparare a cantare*, 2nd ed. Dresden: Arnoldische Buchhandlung, 1819.
Bennett, Lawrence E. "Vismarri [Vismari], Filippo." *Grove Music Online*. Edited by Deane Root. www.oxfordmusiconline.com.
Benoit, Marcelle. *Versailles et les musiciens du roi, 1661–1733: Étude institutionnelle et sociale.* Paris: A. et J. Picard, 1971.
Bergeron, Katherine. "The Castrato as History." *Cambridge Opera Journal* 8 (1996): 167–84.
Bergson, Henri-Louis. *Laughter: An Essay on the Meaning of the Comic.* Translated by Cloudesley Brereton and Fred Rothwell [1911]. Los Angeles: Consortium Books, 1999; repr. ed. New York: Dover Publications, 2005.
Berlioz, Hector. *Mémoires de Hector Berlioz comprenant ses voyages en Italie, en Allemagne, en Russie et en Angleterre, 1803–1865.* Edited by Michel M. Austin. Paris: Sandre, 2010.
———. *The Memoirs of Hector Berlioz.* Translated and edited by David Cairns. Everyman's Library. New York: Alfred A. Knopf, 2002.
Berni, Francesco. *Poesie e prose.* Edited by Ezio Chiòrboli. Geneva: Leo S. Olschki, 1934.
Berry, Helen. *The Castrato and His Wife.* Oxford: Oxford University Press, 2011.
Bertini, Argia, and J. Victor Crowther. "Erculeo [Ercoleo, Erculei], Marzio." *Grove Music Online.* Edited by Deane Root. www.oxfordmusiconline.com.
Bettagno, Antonio, ed. *Caricature di Anton Maria Zanetti.* Venice: Neri Pozza, 1996.
Bianchi, Giovanni Antonio. *De i vizi, e de i difetti del moderno teatro.* Rome: Pagliarini, 1753.
Blainville, Charles Henri de. *Histoire générale, critique et philologique de la musique* [1767]. Geneva: Minkoff Reprints, 1972.
———. *Travels through Holland, Germany, Switzerland and Italy, Containing a Particular Description of the Antient and Present State of Those Countries.* 3 vols. London, 1767.
———. *Travels through Holland, Germany, Switzerland, but Especially Italy.* 3 vols. London: John Noon, 1757.

Blainville, Monsieur de, et al. *Travels through Holland, Germany, Switzerland, and Other Parts of Europe, but Especially Italy*. 3 vols. London: Printed by W. Strahan for the Proprietor, 1743–45.
Bondin, Joseph Vella. "Who was Girolamo Abos?" *Sunday Times* (Malta), March 17, 1996.
Bontempi, Giovanni Andrea Angelini. *Historia musica* [1695]. Geneva: Minkoff Reprints, 1976.
———. *Historia musica* [1695]. Facsimile reprint. Bibliotheca Musica Bononiensis, II, 48. Bologna: Forni, 1971.
———. *Historia musica, nella quale si ha piena cognitione della teorica, e della pratica antica della musica harmonica; secondo la dottrina de' greci* . . . Perugia: Costantini, 1695.
Boris, Francesca. "Il Farinello: La villa perduta." *Il carrobbio: Tradizioni, problemi, immagini dell'Emilia Romagna* 24 (1998): 157–72.
Boris, Francesca, and Giampietro Cammarota. "La collezione di Carlo Broschi detto Farinelli." *Accademia Clementina: Atti e memorie* 27, new series (1990): 187–237.
Borris, Kenneth, and George Rousseau, eds. *The Sciences of Homosexuality in Early Modern Europe*. London: Routledge, 2008.
"Both Choirs Lack Vatican Sanction." *Sun Times*, September 6, 1919.
Bourges, Maurice. "Crescentini, Girolamo." *Encyclopédie des gens du monde, répertoire universel des science, des lettres et des arts*. 22 vols. Paris: Truettel & Würtz, 1833–44; vol. 7 (1836): 232–33.
Bowman, Horace Bushnell. "The Castrati Singers and Their Music." PhD diss., Indiana University, 1951.
Boyd, Malcolm, and John Rosselli. "Tosi, Pier Francesco." *Grove Music Online*. Edited by Deane Root. www.oxfordmusiconline.com.
Bragaglia, Anton Giulio. *Degli "evirati cantori": Contributo alla storia del teatro*. Florence: Sansoni Antiquariato, 1959.
Bray, Alan. *The Friend*. Chicago: University of Chicago Press, 2003.
———. *Homosexuality in Renaissance England*. London: Gay Men's Press, 1982.
———. *Homosexuality in Renaissance England*. Electronic edition. New York: Columbia University Press, 1995.
Browe, Peter, S.J. *Zur Geschichte der Entmannung: Eine religions- und rechtsgeschichtliche Studie*. Breslau: Verlag Müller & Seiffert, 1936.
Brown, Bruce Alan. "Gluck, Christoph Willibald Ritter von, §4: Collaboration with Calzabigi." *Grove Music Online*. Edited by Deane Root. www.oxfordmusiconline.com.
Brugnoli, Anna. "Ritratto di un libertino del '700: Il cavaliere Giovanni Verri (1745–1818)." In Cinzia Cremonini, ed., *Titolati, cadetti e parvenus: Il caso lombardo tra Antico regime e Rivoluzione francese*, 169–220. Rome: Bulzoni, 1999.
Brumana, Biancamaria. "Il cantante Giacinto Fontana detto Farfallino e la sua carriera nei teatri di Roma." *Roma moderna e contemporanea* 4, no. 1 (January–April 1996): 75–112.
———. *"Il pianto de' cigni in morte della fenice de' musici": Poesie per Baldassare Ferri e nuove ipotesi sulla carrier del cantante*. Perugia: Deputazione di storia patria per l'Umbria, 2010.
Bryson, H. Courtney. *The Gramophone Record*. London: E. Benn, 1935.
Bulwer, John. *Anthropometamorphosis: Man Transform'd, or the Artificial Changelin, Historically Presented, in the Mad and Cruel Gallantry, Foolish Bravery, Ridiculous Beauty,*

Filthy Fineness, and Loathesome Loveliness of Most Nations, Fashioning & Altering Their Bodies from the Mould Intended by Nature, with a Vindication of the Regular Beauty and Honesty of Nature, and an Appendix of the Pedigree of the English Gallant. London: J. Hardesty, 1650; 2nd ed. 1653.

Buning, Robert Anthony. "Alessandro Moreschi and the Castrato Voice." MA thesis, Boston University, School of Music of the School of the Arts, September 1990.

Burney, Charles. *An Eighteenth-Century Musical Tour in France and Italy.* Edited by Percy A. Scholes [1773]. London: Oxford University Press, 1959.

———. *A General History of Music, from the Earliest Ages to the Present Period,* 4 vols. London, 1776–89.

———. *Memoirs of the Life and Writings of the Abate Metastasio, in Which Are Incorporated Translations of His Principal Letters.* 3 vols. London, 1796.

———. *The Present State of Music in France and Italy, or, the Journal of a Tour through Those Countries, Undertaken to Collect Materials . . .* [London]: T. Becket and Co., 1771.

Burney, Susan. *The Journals and Letters of Susan Burney: Music and Society in Late Eighteenth-Century England.* Edited by Philip Olleson. Farnham, Surrey, England: Ashgate, 2012.

Burzio, Eugenia. *Verismo Soprano: Complete Recorded Operatic Repertoire.* 2 CDs. Produced by Ward Marston. Marston, 1999.

Caccini, Giulio. *Le nuove musiche.* Florence: Marescotti, 1601.

Cadden, Joan. *Meanings of Sex Difference in the Middle Ages: Medicine, Science, and Culture.* New York: Cambridge University Press, 1993.

Cafiero, Rosa. "Conservatories and the Neapolitan School: A European Model at the End of the Eighteenth Century?" In *Musical Education in Europe (1770–1914): Compositional, Institutional, and Political Challenges,* 2 vols., edited by Michael Fend and Michel Noiray, 1: 15–29. Berlin: Berliner Wissenschafts-Verlag, 2005.

Caldwell, Robert, and Joan Wall. *The Singer's Voice: Complete Set.* 5 DVDs. Redmond, WA: Caldwell Publishing, 1991–93.

Calvé, Emma. *Emma Calve, the Complete 1902 G&T, 1920 Pathé, and "Mapleson Cylinder" Recordings.* 2 CDs. Marston, 1998.

———. *My Life.* Translated by Rosamond Gilder. New York: D. Appleton, 1922; repr. New York: Arno Press, 1977.

———. *Sous tous les ciels j'ai chanté: . . . Souvenirs.* Paris: Librairie Plon, 1940.

Calzabigi, Ranieri de'. *La ragione dei "buffoni" (La Lulliade di Ranieri de' Calzabigi).* Edited by Gabriele Muresu. Rome: Bulzoni, 1977.

Camiz, Franca Trinchieri. "The Castrato Singer: From Informal to Formal Portraiture." *Artibus et Historiae: An Art Anthology* 18, no. 9 (1988): 171–86.

———. "Putti, eunuchi, bella cantatrice: L'iconographie des chanteurs en Italie." *Musique, images, instruments: Revue française d'organologie et d'iconologhie musicale* 2 (1996): 9–16.

Camporesi, Piero. *The Juice of Life: The Symbolic and Magic Significance of Blood.* Translated by Robert R. Barr. New York: Continuum, 1995.

———. *Il sugo della vita: Simbolismo e magia del sangue.* Milan: Mondadori, 1988.

Cappelletto, Sandro. *La voce perduta: Vita di Farinelli, evirato cantore.* Turin: Edizioni di Torino, 1995.

Caricature di Anton Maria Zanetti. Edited by Antonio Bettagno. Venice: Neri Pozza, 1996.
Carteggio di Pietro e Alessandro Verri dal 1766 al 1797. Edited by Alessandro Giulini et al. Milan: L. F. Cogliati, 1923.
Carter, Philip. *Men and the Emergence of Polite Society, 1660–1800.* Harlow: Longman, 2001.
Casanova. *Histoire de ma vie.* Edited by Gerard Lahouati and Marie-Françoise Luna, with Furio Lucchichenti and Helmut Watzlawick. Bibliothèque de la Pléiade, 132. 3 vols. Paris: Gallimard, 2013.
Castelvecchi, Stefano. *Sentimental Opera: Questions of Genre in the Age of Bourgeois Drama.* Cambridge: Cambridge University Press, 2013.
Castil-Blaze. *L'Opéra-Italien de 1548 à 1856.* Paris: Castil-Blaze, 1856.
Celani, Enrico. *I cantori della cappella pontificia nei secoli XVI a XVIII.* Turin: Bocca, 1909.
Celletti, Rodolfo. *A History of Bel Canto,* translated by Frederick Fuller. Oxford: Clarendon Press, 1991.
Celoni, Anna Maria Pellegrini. *Grammar, or, Rules for Singing Well.* Edited and translated by Edward V. Foreman. Masterworks on Singing, vol. 4. Minneapolis: Pro Musica Press, 2001.
———. *Grammatica, o siano, Regole per ben cantare.* Opera 6. Rome: P. Piale, 1810; Leipzig: Peters, 1810.
Cervantes, Xavier. "'Tuneful Monsters': The Castrati and the London Operatic Public, 1667–1737." *Restoration and Eighteenth-Century Theatre Research,* 2nd ser., 13 (1998): 1–24.
Cervantes, Xavier, and Thomas McGeary. "From Farinelli to Monticelli: An Opera Satire of 1742 Re-examined." *Burlington Magazine* 141, no. 1154 (May 1999): 287–89.
Chambers, Ephraim. *Cyclopaedia, or, An Universal Dictionary of Arts and Sciences Containing an Explication of the Terms, and an Account of the Things Signified Thereby, in the Several Arts both Liberal and Mechanical, and the Several Sciences, Human and Divine . . .* 4th ed. London: Printed for D. Midwinter, 1741.
Chandler, James. *An Archaeology of Sympathy: The Sentimental Mode in Literature and Cinema.* Chicago: University of Chicago Press, 2013.
Charvet, Jean-Loop. "Hautes-contre et castrats: La voix des anges, la voix du coeur." *Littérature classique* 12 (1990): 305–21.
Chénier, Marie-Joseph Blaise de. "Aux auteurs de la chronique de Paris." In Chénier, *Charles IX, ou L'école des rois, tragédie.* Paris: P. Fr. Didot jeune, 1790.
Cherry Ripe: Vocal Treasures of the 18th and 19th Centuries. Deborah Riedel, Richard Bonynge, Arcadia Lane Orchestra. Victoria, Australia: Elwood, 2008, MR 30111.
Claretta, Gaudenzio. "Un nobile piemontese musico al principio del XVII." *Estratto dalla Nuova rivista (pubblicazione settimanale di Scienze, Lettere ed Arti).* Turin: Angelo Baglione, 1883.
Clapton, Nicholas. *Moreschi: The Last Castrato.* London: Haus Books, 2004.
Clapton, Nicholas, et al. *Moreschi and the Voice of the Castrato.* London: Haus Books, 2008.
Commedie di Jacopo Angelo Nelli. 3 vols. Edited by Alcibiade Moretti, Biblioteca di scrittori italiani. Bologna: Nicola Zanichelli, 1883–99.
The Complete Adelina Patti and Victor Maurel. 2 CDs. [Swarthmore, PA]: Marston, 1998.
Complete Gramophone Company Recordings, Vol. 1. Nellie Melba, soprano, Landon Ronald, Herman Bemberg, piano, Landon Ronald, conductor, produced by Ward Marston. Naxos Historical, 2002.

The Complete Victor Recordings (1901–11). [London]: Romophone, 1993.

Concerto di altri tempi. Martine Dupuy, Rina Cellini. GB 10, LCCN: 89-750419. Bologna: Bongiovanni, 1981.

Conestabile, Giancarlo. *Notizie biografiche di Baldassarre Ferri: Musico celebratissimo*. Perugia: Bartelli, 1846.

Conti, J. *Variations pour deux violons sur l'air* Ombra adorata aspetta *de l'opéra Giuletta e Romeo, composées par J. Conti*. 2 parts. Vienna: Jean Cappi, [1810?].

———. *Variations pour deux violons sur l'air* Ombra adorata aspetta *de l'opéra Giuletta e Romeo*. Facsimile edition. Musica revindicata, no. 234. Amsterdam: A. J. Heuwekemeijer, 1970.

Corri, Domenico. *Domenico Corri's Treatises on Singing: A Select Collection of the Most Admired Songs, Duetts, &c. and The Singer's Preceptor: A Four-Volume Anthology*. 4 vols. Edited with introductions by Richard Maunder. New York: Garland, 1993–95.

Cosi, Dario. "Comunicazione disturbata: Battos, il fondatore di Cirene, balbuziente e castrato." In *Le regioni del silenzio: Studi sui disagi della comunicazione*, edited by Maria Grazia Ciani. Padova: Bloom Edizioni, 1983.

Costa, G. Andrea. *Considerations on the Art of Singing in General and Particularly on Several Errors into Which Singers Are Liable to Fall, Also on the Three Styles of Singing Prevalent in Europe, viz. the Popular, the Sacred, and the Theatrical and on the Four Fundamental Bases of Singing, viz. the Nature of the Vocal Organs—The Art of Employing Those Organs—Music, and Genius, to Which Are Added Some Opinions on the Elemental Instruction of the Art, . . .* London: G. Schulze, 1824.

Cremonini, Cinzia, ed. *Titolati, cadetti e parvenus: Il caso lombardo tra Antico regime e Rivoluzione francese*. Rome: Bulzoni, 1999.

Crescentini, Girolamo. *Méthode complète de chant*. 2nd ed. In *26 Solfeggi progressivi per mezzo-soprano con accompagnamento di pianoforte*. Naples: n.d.

———. *Raccolta di essercizi per il canto all'uso del vocalizzo, con discorso preliminare, del signor Girolamo Crescentini / Recueil d'exercises pour la vocalisation musicale, avec un discours préliminaire, par m. Jérôme Crescentini*. Paris: Imbault, [ca. 1810–11].

———. *Raccolta di essercizi per il canto all'uso del vocalizzo / Recueil d'exercises pour la vocalisation musicale*. Facsimile reprint in *Chant: les grandes méthodes romantiques de chant*. Vol. 2. Courlay: Fuzeau, 2005.

———. *Ultima e nuova raccolta di venti-quatro solfeggi all'uso del vocalizzo per voce di soprano*. Milan: Ricordi, 1835.

———. *Vingt-cinq nouvelles vocalises*. Facsimile reprint in *Chant: Les grandes méthodes romantiques de chant*. Vol. 4, edited by Jeanne Roudet. Méthodes et traités, series 2, France, 1800–1860. Courlay: Fuzeau, 2005.

Croce, Benedetto. *I teatri di Napoli, secolo VX–XVIII*. Naples: L. Pierro, 1891.

Croll, Gerhard. *Gluck-Schriften: Ausgewählte Aufsätze und Vorträge, 1967–2002*. Edited by Irene Brandenburg, Elisabeth Richter, et al. Kassel: Bärenreiter, 2003.

Crow, Thomas E. *Emulation: David, Drouais, and Girodet in the Art of Revolutionary France*. Rev. ed. New Haven, CT: Yale University Press, in association with The Getty Research Institute, 2008.

Crutchfield, Will. "The 19th Century: Voices." In *Performance Practice, 2: Music after 1600*, edited by Howard Mayer Brown and Stanley Sadie. London: Macmillan, 1989.

———. "The Bel Canto Connection." *Opera News*, July 1997, 30–35 and 51.
———. "Early Vocal Ornamentation." In *Il barbiere di Siviglia: Almaviva o sia l'inutile precauzione, commedia in due atti di Cesare Sterbini dalla commedia di Pierre-Augustin Caron de Beaumarchais*, edited by Patricia B. Brauner. *Works of Gioacchino Rossini*, vol. 2, general editor Philip Gossett. Kassel: Bärenreiter, 2008.
———. "Giovanni Battista Velluti e lo sviluppo della melodia romantica." *Bolletino del Centro Rossiniano di Studi* 54 (2014): 9–83.
———. "Some Thoughts on Reconstructing Singing Styles of the Past." *Journal of the Conductors' Guild*, 10, nos. 3–4 (1989): 111–20.
———. "The Trill Is Gone . . . But It May Be Coming Back." *Opera News*, January 1999, 26–30.
———. "Verdi Performance: Restoring the Color." *High Fidelity/Musical America* 33, no. 6 (1983): 64–66, 100–101.
———. "Vocal Ornamentation in Verdi: The Phonographic Evidence." *19th-Century Music* 7 (1983): 3–54.
———. "Vocal Performance in the Nineteenth Century." In *The Cambridge History of Performance*, edited by Colin Lawson and Robin Stilwell. Cambridge: Cambridge University Press, 2012.
———. "Voices." In *Performance Practice: Music after 1600*, edited by Howard Mayer Brown and Stanley Sadie. New York: Norton, 1990.
Cucuel, Giorgio. *La Pouplinière et la musique de chambre au XVIIIe siècle*. Paris: Fischbacher, 1913.
Dado, Stéphane, and Philippe Vendrix. "Stendhal e Rossini: Uno studio documentario." Translated by Reto Müller and Mauro Tosti-Croce. *Bolletino del Centro Rossiniano di Studi* 49 (1999): 21–60.
D'Ambrosio, Wilma. "Domenico Dal Pane e la tradizione della Messa nel Seicento." In *Tullio Cima, Domenico Massenzio e la musica del loro tempo*, edited by Fabio Carboni, Valeria De Luca, Agostino Ziino, and Manuela Farina. Collana dell'Istituto di Bibliografia Musicale, no. 2. Rome: IBIMUS, 2003.
———. "Le messe di Domenico dal Pane su mottetti palestriniani: Un capitolo emblematico della ricezione del Palestrina nel tardo Seicento." In *Palestrina e l'Europa: Atti del III Convegno Internazionale di Studi (Palestrina, 6–9 ottobre 1994)* ([Rome]: IBIMUS, 2003), edited by Giancarlo Rostirolla, Stefania Soldati, and Elena Zomparelli. Palestrina: Fondazione Giovanni Pierluigi da Palestrina, 2006.
Dame, Joke. "Unveiled Voices: Sexual Difference and the Castrato." In *Queering the Pitch*, edited by Philip Brett, Elizabeth Wood, and Gary C. Thomas. New York: Routledge, 1994.
D'Amico, F. "Evirato." In *Enciclopedia dello spettacolo*, 4: cols. 1719–23. Rome: Unione Editoriale, 1954–65.
Daston, Lorraine, and Katharine Park. *Wonders and the Order of Nature, 1150–1750*. New York: Zone Books, 1998.
Daston, Lorraine, and Gianna Pomata, eds. *The Faces of Nature in Enlightenment Europe*. Berlin: Berliner Wissenschafts-Verlag, 2003.
Daston, Lorraine, and Fernando Vidal, eds. *The Moral Authority of Nature*. Chicago: University of Chicago Press, 2004.

Davidson, James. *The Greeks and Greek Love: A Bold New Exploration of the Ancient World.* New York: Random House, 2007.

———. *The Greeks and Greek Love: A Radical Reappraisal of Homosexuality in Ancient Greece.* London: Weidenfeld & Nicolson, 2007.

———. "Mr. and Mr. and Mrs. and Mrs." *London Review of Books* 27, no. 11 (June 2, 2005).

———. "Versailles with Panthers." *London Review of Books* 25, no. 13 (July 10, 2003).

Davies, J. Q. *Romantic Anatomies of Performance.* Berkeley: University of California Press, 2014.

———. "'Veluti in speculum': The Twilight of the Castrato." *Cambridge Opera Journal* 17, no. 3 (2005): 271–301.

Davis, Natalie Zemon. *The Gift in Sixteenth-Century France.* Madison: University of Wisconsin Press, 2000.

Dean, Winton. "Andreoni, Giovanni Battista." *Grove Music Online.* Edited by Deane Root. www.oxfordmusiconline.com.

———. *Aufführungspraxis und Interpretation Händelscher Werke in Vergangenheit und Gegenwart*, edited by Walther Siegmund-Schultze, 32–37. Halle (Saale): Martin-Luther-Universität Halle-Wittenberg, 1980.

———. *Handel and the Opera Seria.* Berkeley: University of California Press, 1969.

———. "Handel's Serse." In *Opera and the Enlightenment*, edited by Thomas Bauman and Marita Petzoldt McClymonds. Cambridge: Cambridge University Press, 1995.

———. "Pacini, Andrea ['Il Lucchesini']." *Grove Music Online.* Edited by Deane Root. www.oxfordmusiconline.com.

———. "Senesino [Bernardi, Francesco]." *Grove Music Online.* Edited by Deane Root. www.oxfordmusiconline.com.

Dean, Winton, and John Rosselli. "Pellegrini, Valeriano." *Grove Music Online.* Edited by Deane Root. www.oxfordmusiconline.com.

De Angelis, Alberto. *Domenico Mustafà: La Cappella Sistina e la società musicale romana.* Bologna: Zanichelli, 1926.

De Bei, Alessandro. "Giulietta e Romeo di Nicola Zingarelli: Fortuna ed eredità di un soggetto shakespeariano." In *Aspetti dell'opera italiana fra Sette e Ottocento: Mayr e Zingarelli*, edited by Guido Salvetti. Lucca: LIM, 1993.

De Giorgio, Michela, and Christiane Klapisch-Zuber, eds. *Storia del matrimonio.* Bari: Laterza, 1996.

Delany, Mary Granville Pendarves. *The Autobiography and Correspondence of Mrs. Delaney, Rev. from Lady Llanover's Edition*, 2 vols. Edited by Sarah Chauncey Woolsey. Boston: Roberts Brothers, 1882.

Della Lena, Innocenzo. *Dissertazione ragionata sul teatro moderno.* Venice: Giacomo Storti, 1791.

Della Seta, Fabrizio. "Il relator sincero (Cronache teatrali romane, 1736–1756)." *Studi musicali* 9 (1980): 73–116.

De Martino, Ernesto. *Morte e pianto rituale nel mondo antico: Dal lamento pagano al pianto di Maria.* Turin: Edizioni Scientifiche Einaudi, 1958.

———. *Sud e magia.* Milan: Feltrinelli, 1959.

———. *La terra del rimorso.* Milan: Il Saggiatore, 1961.

Derksen, Jörg. "Der römische Sopranist Alessandro Moreschi: Ein Sängerleben zwischen der Tradierung einer Künstlervita und den Wirklichkeiten neuer Medien nach 1900." In

Professionalismus in der Musik: Arbeitstagung in der Verbindung mit dem Heinrich-Schütz-Haus Bad Köstritz vom 22. bis 25. August 1996, edited by Christian Kaden and Volker Kalisch. Essen: Die blaue Eule, 1999.
Derrida, Jacques. *Given Time: 1. Counterfeit Money.* Translated by Peggy Kamuf. Chicago: University of Chicago Press, 1992.
De Salvo Fattor, Salvatore. *La cappella musicale pontificia nel Novecento.* Storia della cappella musicale pontificia, vol. 7. Edited by Giancarlo Rostirolla. Rome: Fondazione Giovanni Pierluigi da Palestrina, 2005.
De Simone, Roberto, Annabella Rossi, et al. *Carnevale si chiamava Vincenzo: Rituali di carnevale in Campania.* Roma: De Luca Editore, 1977.
Diderot, Denis. *Le paradoxe sur le comédien; Le neveu de Rameau.* Strasbourg: J. H. E. Heitz, 1913.
———. "Paradox of the Actor." In *Denis Diderot, Selected Writings on Art and Literature*, translated and with introduction and notes by Geoffrey Bremner. Harmondsworth: Penguin Books, 1994.
Didier, Béatrice. "Stendhal et la musique: De la biographie à l'autobiographie." In *Stendhal e Milano: Atti del 14° congresso internazionale stendhaliano, Milano, 19–23 marzo 1980.* 2 vols. Florence: Leo S. Olschki, 1982.
Dietz, Hanns-Bertold. "Mele [Melle], Giovanni Battista [Juan Bautista]." *Grove Music Online.* Edited by Deane Root. www.oxfordmusiconline.com.
Di Giacomo, Salvatore. *Il conservatorio di Sant'Onofrio a Capuana e quello di S.M. della Pietà dei Turchini.* Milan: Remo Sandron, 1924.
Di Salvo, Maria. "The 'Italian' Nemetskaia Sloboda." In *Personality and Place in Russian Culture: Essays in Memory of Lindsey Hughes*, edited by Simon Dixon. London: Modern Humanities Research Association for the UCL School of Slavonic and East European Studies, 2010.
———. "*Vita e viaggi* di Filippo Balatri (preliminari all'edizione del testo)." *Russica romana* 6 (1999): 37–57.
Dizionario enciclopedico della letteratura italiana. 6 vols. Edited by Giuseppe Petronio. Bari: Laterza, 1966–70.
Dolar, Mladen. "The Object Voice." In *Gaze and Voice as Love Objects*, edited by Renata Salecl and Slavoj Žižek. Durham: Duke University Press, 1996.
———. *A Voice and Nothing More.* Cambridge, MA: MIT Press, 2006.
"Domenico Mancini." Translated by Flavio Ferri Benedetti. Simone Bartolini Official Website. web.tiscali.it/simone_bartolini/Intervista_Mancini_en.htm.
Doniger, Wendy. *The Woman Who Pretended to Be Who She Was: Myths of Self-Imitation.* New York: Oxford University Press, 2005.
Donington, Robert. *The Interpretation of Early Music*, rev. ed. 1963; New York: Norton, 1992.
———. *A Performer's Guide to Baroque Music.* London: Faber, 1973.
Douglas, Mary. *Purity and Danger: An Analysis of Concepts of Pollution and Taboo* [1966]. London: Routledge, 2002.
Downes, Philip. "Musical Pleasures and Amorous Passions: Stendhal, the Crystallization Process, and Listening to Rossini and Beethoven." *19th-Century Music* 26, no. 3 (2003): 235–57.
Drake, James. *Rosa Ponselle: A Centenary Biography.* Portland, OR: Amadeus Press, 1997.

Duey, Philip A. *Bel Canto in Its Golden Age: A Study of Its Teaching Concepts*. New York: King's Crown Press, 1951.
Duncan, Michelle. "The Operatic Scandal of the Singing Body: Voice, Presence, Performativity." *Cambridge Opera Journal* 16 (2004): 283–306.
Dunn, Thomas D., with Martin Morell, eds. *Loreto Vittori: La Galatea*. Recent Researches in the Music of the Baroque Era. Madison, WI: A-R Editions, 2002.
Durante, Sergio. "Il cantante." In *Storia dell'opera italiana*, edited by Lorenzo Bianconi and Giorgio Pestelli. Vol. 4 of 6, *Il sistema produttivo e le sue competenze*. Turin: Einaudi, 1987.
———. "Condizioni materiali et trasmissione del sapere nelle scuole di canto a Bologna a metà Settecento." In *Atti del XIV congresso della Società Internazionale di Musicologia, Bologna, 1987: Trasmissione e recezione delle forme di cultura musicale*, edited by Angelo Pompilio et al., 2: 175–89. 3 vols. Turin: Edizioni di Torino, 1990.
———. "'Dal dire al fare . . . ' Ossia osservazioni sull'esecuzione musicale in rapporto al 'Lessico italiano del canto.'" *Musica e storia* 10, no. 1 (2002): 139–50.
———. *Opera Production and Its Resources*. Edited by Lorenzo Bianconi and Giorgio Pestelli, translated by Lydia G. Cochrane. The History of Italian Opera, part 2, *Systems*, vol. 4. Chicago: University of Chicago Press, 1998.
———. "Strutture mentali e vocabolario di un cantore antico/moderno: Preliminari per una lettura delle fonti didattiche settecentesche." In *Alessandro Scarlatti und seine Zeit*, edited by Max Lütolf. Bern: Haupt, 1995.
———. "Theorie und Praxis der Gesangsschulen zur Zeit Händels: Bemerkungen zu Tosis 'Opinioni de' cantori antichi e moderni.'" In *Händel auf dem Theater: Bericht über die Symposien der Internationalen Händel-Akademie, Karlsruhe, 1986 und 1987*, vol. 2, edited by Hans Joachim Marx. Laaber: Laaber, 1988.
Durante, Sergio, Leonella Grasso Capiroli, and Roberta Ziosi. *Lessico italiano del canto*. Naples: Liguori, 2014.
Edelstein, Dan. *The Terror of Natural Right: Republicanism, the Cult of Nature, and the French Revolution*. Chicago: University of Chicago Press, 2009.
Edwards, Michael. "Hernia: Inguinal Child Herniotomy, A Pantogen Operation Script." WikiSurgery: The Free Surgical Encyclopedia. http://wikisurgery.com.
Encyclopedia of Recorded Sound, 2nd ed., 2 vols. Edited by Frank W. Hoffmann and Howard Ferstler, technical editor. New York: Routledge, 2005.
Engelstein, Laura. *Castration and the Heavenly Kingdom: A Russian Folktale*. Ithaca, NY: Cornell University Press, 1999.
Esquier, Suzel. *Vie de Rossini par M. de Stendhal: Chronique parisienne, 1821–1823*. Collection "Stendhal Club." Moncalieri: Centro Universitario di Ricerche sul "Viaggio in Italia," 1997.
Esse, Melina. "Rossini's Noisy Bodies." *Cambridge Opera Journal* 21, no. 1 (March 2009): 27–64.
Evans-Pritchard, E. E. "The Divine Kingship of the Shilluk of the Nilotic Sudan." In *Social Anthropology and Other Essays*. New York: The Free Press of Glencoe, 1964.
Evelyn, John. *The Diary of John Evelyn*. 2 vols. Edited by William Bray. London: George Bell & Sons, 1895.
Farinelli, Carlo Broschi. *La solitudine amica: Lettere al conte Sicinio Pepoli*. Edited by Carlo Vitali with Roberto Pagano and Francesca Boris. Palermo: Sellerio, 2000.

The Fashionable Tell-tale, Containing a Great Variety of Curious and Interesting Anecdotes of Emperors, Kings, Queens, Statesmen, Prelates, Divines, Generals, Admirals, Captains, Physicians, Poets, and Players. Vol. 2, 2nd ed. [London]: R. Baldwin, in Paternoster-Row, 1778.

Fastidio, Don. "La casa di Caffarello." *Napoli nobilissima* 8 (1898): 119–21.

Faustini-Fasini, Eugenio. "Gli astri maggiori del 'bel canto' napoletano: Il Cav. Nicola Grimaldi detto 'Nicolini.'" *Note d'archivio per la storia musicale* 12 (1935): 297–316.

———. "Gli astri maggiori del bel canto napoletano: Gaetano Majorano detto 'Caffarelli.'" *Note d'archivio per la storia musicale* 15 (1938): 121–28, 157–70, 258–70.

Feldman, Martha. "Castrato Acts." In *The Oxford Handbook of Opera*, edited by Helen M. Greenwald. New York: Oxford University Press, 2014. pp. 395–418.

———. *Opera and Sovereignty: Transforming Myths in Eighteenth-Century Italy*. Chicago: University of Chicago Press, 2007.

———. "Strange Births and Surprising Kin: The Castrato's Tale." In *Italy's Eighteenth Century: Gender and Culture in the Age of the Grand Tour*, edited by Paula Findlen et al. Stanford, CA: Stanford University Press, 2009.

Feldman, Martha, with Martina Piperno. "Moreschi and Fellini: Delineating the Vernacular Castrato in Post-Unification Italy." *voiceXchange* 5, no. 1 (2011): 1–34.

Fenlon, Iain. *Music and Patronage in Sixteenth-Century Mantua*. 2 vols. Cambridge: Cambridge University Press, 1980.

Ferranti, Maria Giulini, ed. *Giuditta Pasta e i suoi tempi: Memorie e lettere*. Milan: Cromotipia E. Sormani, 1935.

Fielding, Henry. *The Historical Register for the year 1736, as It Is acted at the New Theatre in the Hay-Market*. Dublin: A. Jones, 1737.

Finucci, Valeria. "Introduction: Genealogical Pleasures, Genealogical Disruptions." In *Generation and Degeneration: Tropes of Reproduction in Literature and History from Antiquity through Early Modern Europe*, edited by Valeria Finucci and Kevin Brownlee. Durham, NC: Duke University Press, 2001.

———. *The Manly Masquerade: Masculinity, Paternity, and Castration in the Italian Renaissance*. Durham, NC: Duke University Press, 2003.

Finucci, Valeria, and Kevin Brownlee, eds. *Generation and Degeneration: Tropes of Reproduction in Literature and History*. Durham, NC: Duke University Press, 2001.

Florimo, Francesco. *Breve metodo di canto*. Naples: Girard, [ca. 1840].

———. *La scuola musicale di Napoli e i suoi conservatorii, con uno sguardo sulla storia della musica in Italia*. 4 vols. in 3. Naples: Stabilimento tip. V. Morano, 1883.

Foppa, Giuseppe. *Giulietta e Romeo, tragedia per musica da rappresentarsi nel Teatro alla Scala il carnevale dell'anno 1796*. Milan: Gio. Batista Bianchi, 1796.

Foreman, Edward V. *The Art of Bel Canto in the Italian Baroque: A Study of the Original Sources*. Minneapolis: Pro Musica Press, 2006.

Frandsen, Mary E. "Eunuchi conjugium: The Marriage of a Castrato in Early Modern Germany." *Early Music History: Studies in Medieval and Early Modern Music* 24 (2005): 53–124.

Frati, Ludovico. "Antonio Bernacchi e la sua scuola di canto." *Rivista musicale italiana* 29 (1922): 473–91.

Frazer, James George. *The Golden Bough* [1922]. Abridged ed. New York: Macmillan, 1963.

Freeman, Robert. "Farinello and His Repertory." In *Studies in Renaissance and Baroque Music in Honor of Arthur Mendel*, edited by Robert Marshall. Kassel: Bärenreiter, 1974.
Freitas, Roger. "The Eroticism of Emasculation: Confronting the Baroque Body of the Castrato." *Journal of Musicology* 20 (2003): 196-249.
———. *Portrait of a Castrato: Politics, Patronage, and Music in the Life of Atto Melani.* Cambridge: Cambridge University Press, 2009.
———. "Un atto d'ingegno: A Castrato in the Seventeenth Century." PhD diss., Yale University, 1998.
Freud, Sigmund. "Humor." *International Journal of Psychoanalysis* 9 (1928): 1-6.
———. *Jokes and Their Relation to the Unconscious*. Translated and edited by James Strachey [1905]. New York: W. W. Norton, 1960.
———. *Moses and Monotheism*. Translated by Katherine Jones. New York: Vintage Books, 1967.
———. *Totem and Taboo: Some Points of Agreement between the Mental Lives of Savages and Neurotics*. Translated by James Strachey. New York: W. W. Norton, 1950.
Fritz, Hans. *Kastratengesang: Hormonelle, konstitutionelle und pädagogische Aspekte*. Tutzing: Hans Schneider, 1994.
Frizzi, Benedetto. *Dissertazione di biografia musicale*. [Trieste]: ca. 1802.
Frye, Northrup. *Anatomy of Criticism: Four Essays*. Princeton, NJ: Princeton University Press, 1957.
Gabrielli, Alessandro. "Il canto dei falsettisti romani." *Musica*, February 1918.
———. "Il canto dei falsettisti romani." Rome: Officina Poligrafica Italiana, 1918.
———. "Riassunto delle conversazioni sulla storia delle cappelle musicali romane (Cappella Giulia, Cappella Sistina, cappella Libertiana, Cappella Lateranense, contabelle cronologiche di cantori e maestri)." *Rassegna dorica: Cultura e cronaca musicale* 9 (1937-38).
———. "Ricordi d'un falsettista (continuazione)." *Rassegna dorica: Cultura e cronaca musicale* 13, no. 5 (May 1942): 58-61.
Garcia, Manuel Patricio Rodriguez. *Traité complet de l'art du chant en deux parties*. 1e partie, 2 éd; 2e partie, 1e éd. Paris: E. Troupenas et cie., 1847.
———. *Traité complet de l'art du chant en deux parties*. Paris: Eugène Duverger, 1847.
———. *Traité complet de l'art du chant en deux parties*. Facsimile reprint in *Chant: Les grandes méthodes romantiques de chant*. Vol. 4, edited by Jeanne Roudet. Méthodes et traités, series 2, France, 1800-1860. Courlay: Fuzeau, 2005.
Garzoni, Tommaso. "De' castradori. Et de' bracherari." In *La piazza universale de tutte le professioni del mondo*, revised ed. Venice: Gio. Battista Somasco, 1587.
Gealt, Adelheid M. "The Telling Line: Domenico Tiepolo as a Draftsman/Narrator." In *Domenico Tiepolo, Master Draftsman*, curated by Adelheid M. Gealt and George Knox. Catalog of an exhibition held at Castello di Udine, September 14-December 31, 1996, and at Indiana University Art Museum, Bloomington, January 15-March 9, 1997. Bloomington: Indiana University Press, 1996.
Geertz, Clifford. "Centers, Kings, and Charisma: Reflections on the Symbolics of Power." In *Local Knowledge: Further Essays in Interpretive Anthropology*, 121-46. New York: Basic Books, 1983.
———. "Deep Play: Notes on the Balinese Cockfight." In *The Interpretation of Cultures: Selected Essays*, 412-53. New York: Basic Books, 1973.

———. *Negara: The Theatre State in Nineteenth-Century Bali.* Princeton, NJ: Princeton University Press, 1980.
Gell, Alfred. *Art and Agency: An Anthropological Theory.* Oxford: Clarendon Press, 1998.
———. "Technology and Magic." *Anthropology Today* 4 (1988): 6–9.
Gentilcore, David. *Medical Charlatanism in Early Modern Italy.* New York: Oxford University Press, 2006.
Gerber, Ernst Ludwig. *Historisch-biographisches Lexikon der Tonkünstler (1790–1792) und Neues historisch-biographisches Lexikon der Tonkünstler (1812–1814).* 4 vols. Reprint edition. Edited by Othmar Wessely. Graz: Akademische Druck- u. Verlagsanstalt, 1966–77.
Gerbino, Giuseppe. "The Quest for the Soprano Voice: Castrati in Renaissance Italy." *Studi musicali* 33, no. 2 (2004): 303–57.
Gianturco, Carolyn. *Alessandro Stradella, 1639–1682: His Life and Music.* Oxford: Clarendon, 1994.
Giesey, Ralph E. *The Royal Funeral Ceremony in Renaissance France.* Geneva: E. Droz, 1960.
———. *Rulership in France, 15th–17th Centuries.* Aldershot: Ashgate, 2004.
Gilman, Sander L. *Difference and Pathology: Stereotypes of Sexuality, Race, and Madness.* Ithaca, NY: Cornell University Press, 1985.
Gilman, Todd S. "The Italian (Castrato) in London." In *The Work of Opera: Genre, Nationhood, and Sexual Difference,* edited by Richard Dellamora and Daniel Fischlin. New York: Columbia University Press, 1997.
Gjerdingen, Robert O. *Music in the Galant Style.* New York: Oxford University Press, 2007.
———. *Research into the History, Theory, and Cognition of Music.* Hosted by Northwestern University. http://faculty-web.at.northwestern.edu/music/gjerdingen/ index.htm.
Glixon, Beth L. "Private Lives of Public Women: Prima Donnas in Mid-Seventeenth-Century Venice." *Music & Letters* 76 (1995): 509–31.
Glixon, Beth L., and Jonathan Glixon. *Inventing the Business of Opera: The Impresario and His World in Seventeenth-Century Venice.* AMS Studies in Music. New York: Oxford University Press, 2006.
Gluck, Christoph Willibald. *Antigono: Rom 1756: Dramma per musica in drei Akten von Pietro Metastasio.* Edited by Irene Brandenburg. Sämtliche Werke. Abt. III, Bd. 20. Kassel: Bärenreiter, 2007.
Goldstein, Jan. *The Post-Revolutionary Self: Politics and Psyche in France, 1750–1850.* Cambridge, MA: Harvard University Press, 2005.
Gooley, Dana. "Franz Liszt: The Virtuoso as Strategist." In *The Musician as Entrepreneur, 1700–1914: Managers, Charlatans, and Idealists,* edited by William Weber, 145–61. Bloomington: Indiana University Press, 2004.
Goudar, Sara. *Relation historique des divertissements du Carnaval de Naples, ou Lettre de Madame Goudar sur ce sujet À Monsieur le Général Alexis Orlow.* Lucca, 1774.
———. *Supplement au supplement de la musique et de la danse ou lettres de M.r G. . . . a Milord Pembroke.* [Venice], 1774.
"Grazia." *Vocabolario degli Accademici della Crusca.* http://vocabolario.sns.it/html/ index.html.
Greated, Clive. "Frequency." *Grove Music Online.* Edited by Deane Root. www.oxfordmusiconline.com.

Greco, Franco Carmelo, ed. *Pulcinella, maschera del mondo: Pulcinella e le arti dal Cinquecento al Novecento.* Naples: Electa Napoli, 1990.

———. *Pulcinella: Una maschera tra gli specchi.* Naples: Edizioni Scientifiche Italiane, 1990.

Greenwood, Andrew. "Musical Ideas of Sympathy, Sensibility, and Improvement in the Scottish Enlightenment." PhD diss., University of Chicago, 2012.

Grundy Fanelli, Jean. "A Sweet Bird of Youth: Caffarelli in Pistoia." *Early Music* 27 (1999): 55–63.

Guarino, Gabriel. *Representing the King's Splendour: Communication and Reception of Symbolic Forms of Power in Viceregal Naples.* Manchester: Manchester University Press / Palgrave Macmillan, 2010.

Haar, James. *Essays on Italian Poetry and Music in the Renaissance, 1350–1600.* Berkeley: University of California Press, 1986.

Habermas, Jürgen. *The Structural Transformation of the Public Sphere: An Inquiry into a Category of Bourgeois Society*, 2nd ed. Translated by Thomas Burger with Frederick Lawrence. Cambridge, MA: MIT Press, 1991.

Habib, Kenneth Sasis. "The Superstar Singer Fairouz and the Ingenious Rahbani Composers: Lebanon Sounding." PhD diss., University of California at Santa Barbara, 1995.

Haböck, Franz. *Die Gesangskunst der Kastraten, Erster Notenband: A, Die Kunst des Cavaliere Carlo Broschi Farinelli. B, Farinellis berühmte Arien.* Vienna: Universal, 1923.

———. *Die Kastraten und ihre Gesangskunst: Eine gesangsphysiologische, kultur- und musikhistorische Studien.* Stuttgart: Deutsche Verlags-Anstalt, 1927.

Hadlock, Heather. "On the Cusp between Past and Future: The Mezzo-Soprano Romeo of Bellini's *I Capuleti*." *Opera Quarterly* 17, no. 3 (2001): 299–322.

———. "Women Playing Men in Italian Opera, 1810–1835." In *Women's Voices across Musical Worlds*, edited by Jane A. Bernstein. Boston: Northeastern University Press, 2004.

Hammond, Frederick. *Music and Spectacle in Baroque Rome: Barberini Patronage under Urban VIII.* New Haven, CT: Yale University Press, 1994.

Handel and the Castrati: The Story behind the 18th-Century Superstar Singers, 19 March–1 October 2006. London: Handel House Museum, 2006.

Harries, Meredydd, Sarah Hawkins, Jeremy Hacking, and Ieuan Hughes. "Changes in the Male Voice at Puberty: Vocal Fold Length and Its Relationship to the Fundamental Frequency of the Voice." *Journal of Laryngology and Otology* 112 (1998): 451–54.

Harris, Ellen T. "Farinelli [Broschi, Carlo; Farinello]." *Grove Music Online.* Edited by Deane Root. www.oxfordmusiconline.com.

———. "Messa di voce." *Grove Music Online.* Edited by Deane Root. www.oxfordmusiconline.com.

Harris, Ellen T., with Owen Jander, "Singing." *Grove Music Online.* Edited by Deane Root. www.oxfordmusiconline.com.

Hasse, Johann Adolf. *The Favourite Songs in the Opera Call'd Artaxerxes.* Bibliotheca musica Bononiensis. Sect. 4, n. 209. London: Walsh, 1735; Bologna: Arnaldo Forni, 1980.

Hatzinger, M., D. Vöge, M. Stastny, F. Moll, and M. Sohn. "Castrati Singers: All for Fame." *Journal of Sexual Medicine* 9, no. 9 (September 2012): 2233–37.

Hayes, Jeremy. "Orfeo ed Euridice (i) [*Orphée et Eurydice* ('Orpheus and Eurydice')]." *Grove Music Online.* Edited by Deane Root. www.oxfordmusiconline.com.

Heartz, Daniel. "Caffarelli's Caprices." In *Music Observed: Studies in Memory of William C. Holmes*, edited by Colleen Reardon and Susan Parisi. Warren, MI: Harmonie Park Press, 2004.

———. "Farinelli and Metastasio: Rival Twins of Public Favour." *Early Music* 12 (1984): 358–66.

———. "Farinelli Revisited." *Early Music* 18 (1990): 430–43.

———. *Music in European Capitals: The Galant Style, 1720–1780*. New York: Norton, 2003.

Hegermann-Lindencrone, Lillie de. *The Sunny Side of Diplomatic Life, 1875–1912*. New York: Harper & Brothers, 1914.

Heller, Wendy. "Varieties of Masculinity: Trajectories of the Castrato from the Seventeenth Century." *British Journal for Eighteenth-Century Studies* 28 (2005): 307–21.

Herdt, Gilbert. "Introduction: Third Sexes and Third Genders." In *Third Sex, Third Gender: Beyond Sexual Dimorphism in Culture and History*, edited by Herdt. New York: Zone Books, 1994.

Heriot, Angus. *The Castrati in Opera*. London: Calder and Boyars, 1956.

Herr, Corinna. "'Ad altro modo si canta nelle Chiese & nelle Capelle publiche': Zur Ästhetik des Kirchengesangs." In *Singstimmen: Ästhetik, Geschlecht, Vokaprofil*, edited by Anno Mungen, Stephan Mösch, and Saskia Woyke. Forthcoming.

———. *Gesang gegen die "Ordnung der Natur": Kastraten und Falsettisten in der Musikgeschichte*. Kassel: Bärenreiter, 2013.

Hill, John Walter. "Dreyer, Giovanni Filippo Maria ['Il Tedeschino']." *Grove Music Online*. Edited by Deane Root. www.oxfordmusiconline.com.

Hiller, Johann Adam. *Treatise on Vocal Performance and Ornamentation by Johann Adam Hiller*. Translated and edited by Suzanne J. Beicken. Cambridge: Cambridge University Press, 2001.

Hobson, Marian. *The Object of Art: The Theory of Illusion in Eighteenth-Century France*. Cambridge: Cambridge University Press, 1982.

Hocart, A. M. *Kings and Councillors: An Essay in the Comparative Anatomy of Human Society*. Edited and with an introduction by Rodney Needham and forward by E. E. Evans-Pritchard [1936]. Chicago: University of Chicago Press, 1970.

———. *Kingship*. London: Humphrey Milford for Oxford University Press, 1927.

Hoffmann, E. T. A. "Ombra adorata." Translated in *E. T. A. Hoffmann's Musical Writings: Kreisleriana, The Poet and the Composer, Music Criticism*. Edited, annotated, and introduced by David Charlton, translated by Martyn Clarke. Cambridge: Cambridge University Press, 1989.

Holmes, William C. *Opera Observed: Views of a Florentine Impresario in the Early Eighteenth Century*. Chicago: University of Chicago Press, 1993.

———. "Yet Another *Orontea*: Further Rapport between Venice and Vienna." In *Venezia e il melodramma nel Seicento*, edited by Maria Teresa Muraro, 199–225. Florence: Olschki, 1976.

Holub, Robert C. *Jürgen Habermas: Critic in the Public Sphere*. New York: Routledge, 1991.

Holzer, Robert. "Music and Poetry in Seventeenth-Century Rome: Settings of the Canzonetta and Cantata Texts of Francesco Balducci, Domenico Benigni, Francesco Melosio, and Antonio Abati." PhD diss., University of Pennsylvania, 1990.

Howard, David M. "Acoustics of the Castrato Voice." In Nicholas Clapton, *Moreschi and the Voice of the Castrato*. London: Haus Books, 2008.

Howard, David M., and Jamie Angus. *Acoustics and Psychoacoustics*. Amsterdam: Focal Press, 2006.

Howard, David M., and Damian T. Murphy. *Voice Science, Acoustics, and Recording*. San Diego: Plural Publishing, 2008.

Howard, Patricia. *The Modern Castrato: Gaetano Guadagni and the Coming of a New Operatic Age*. Oxford: Oxford University Press, 2014.

Huarte, Juan. *Examen de ingenios, para las sciencias, donde se muestra la differencia de habilidades que ay en los hombres, y el genero de letras que a cada uno responde en particular* . . . Baeca: Iuan Baptista de Montoya, 1575.

———. *Examen de ingenios: The Examination of Men's Wits in Which, by Discovering the Varietie of Natures, Is Shewed for Which Profession Each One Is Apt, and How Far He Shall Profit Therein*. Translated into Italian by Camillo Camilli and into English by Richard Carew. London: Adam Islip, 1596.

Hubert, Henri, and Marcel Mauss. "Essai sur la nature et la fonction du sacrifice." *L'Année sociologique* (1898): 29–138.

———. *Sacrifice: Its Nature and Functions*. Translated by W. D. Halls. Chicago: University of Chicago Press, 1964.

Hübscher, Arthur, ed. *Arthur Schopenhauer: Mensch und Philosoph in seinen Briefen*. Wiesbaden: F. A. Brockhaus, 1960.

Hunter, David. "Senesino Disobliges Caroline, Princess of Wales, and Princess Violante of Florence." *Early Music* 30 (2002): 214–23.

Jackman, James L. "Finazzi, Filippo." *Grove Music Online*. Edited by Deane Root. www.oxfordmusiconline.com.

Jankélévitch, Vladimir. *Music and the Ineffable*. Translated by Carolyn Abbate. Princeton, NJ: Princeton University Press, 2003.

Jenkins, J. S. "The Lost Voice: A History of the Castrato." *Journal of Pediatric Endicronological Metabolism* 13, supplement 6 (2000): 1503–8.

Johnson, Janet Lynn. "The Musical Environment in France." In *The Cambridge Companion to Berlioz*, edited by Peter Bloom. Cambridge: Cambridge University Press, 2000.

———. "The Théâtre Italien and Opera and Theatrical Life in Restoration Paris, 1818–1827." 3 vols., PhD diss., University of Chicago, 1988.

Jones, Ann Rosalind, and Peter Stallybrass. "Fetishizing Gender: Constructing the Hermaphrodite in Renaissance Europe." In *Body Guards: The Cultural Politics of Gender Ambiguity*, edited by Julia Epstein and Kristina Straub. New York: Routledge, 1991.

Kahl, Willi. "Herrn Johann Joachim Quantzens Lebenslauf, von ihm selbst entworfen." In Friedrich Wilhelm Marpurg, *Historisch-kritische Beyträge zur Aufnahme der Musik*, vol. 1, st. 5. Berlin: Schütz, 1755.

———. *Selbstbiographien deutscher Musiker des 18. Jahrhunderts*. Cologne: Staufen-Verlag, 1948; The Netherlands: Frits Knuf, 1972.

Kandler, Franz Sales. "Sur l'état actuel de la musique à Rome." *Revue musicale* 3 (1828): 49–102.

Kantner, Leopold M., and Angela Pachovsky. *La cappella musicale pontificia nell'Ottocento*. Storia della cappella musicale pontificia, vol. 6. Rome: Hortus Musicus, 1998.

Kantorowicz, Ernst. *The King's Two Bodies: A Study in Mediaeval Political Theology*. Princeton, NJ: Princeton University Press, 1957.

Kelbe, Dorit. "Effeminate Professional Musicians in Sources of Ottoman-Turkish Court Poetry and Music of the Eighteenth and Nineteenth Centuries." *Music in Art* 30 (2005): 97–116.

Kelly, Linda. *Susanna, the Captain, and the Castrato: Scenes from the Burney Salon, 1779–1780*. London: Starhaven, 2004.

Kelly, Michael. *Reminiscences . . . of the King's Theatre and Theatre Royal Drury Lane*. New York: Da Capo Press, 1968.

Kent, Francis William. *Household and Lineage in Renaissance Florence: The Family Life of the Capponi, Ginori, and Ruscellai*. Princeton, NJ: Princeton University Press, 1977.

Kesting, Jürgen. *Maria Callas*. Translated by John Hunt. Boston: Northeastern University Press, 1993.

Kettering, Sharon. *Patrons, Brokers, and Clients in Seventeenth-Century France*. New York: Oxford University Press, 1986.

Keyser, Dorothy. "Cross-Sexual Casting in Baroque Opera: Musical and Theatrical Conventions." *Opera Quarterly* 5 (1988): 46–57.

Kirnbauer, Martin. "Eunuch Flutes: Source Studies on a Still-forgotten Instrument." In *Festschrift Rainer Weber*, edited by Eszter Fontana. Halle an der Saale: Janos Stekovics, 1999.

Koestenbaum, Wayne. *The Queen's Throat: Opera, Homosexuality, and the Mystery of Desire*. New York: Da Capo Press, 1993.

Kowaleski-Wallace, Beth. "Shunning the Bearded Kiss: Castrati and the Definition of Female Sexuality." *Prose Studies* 15, no. 2 (1992): 153–70.

Kriese, Konstanze, ed. *Zwischen Rausch und Ritual: Zum Phänomen des Starkults*. Berlin: Zyankrise Berlin, 1994.

Kristeva, Julia. *Powers of Horror: An Essay on Abjection*. Translated by Leon S. Roudiez. New York: Columbia University Press, 1982.

Lalande, Joseph Jérôme Le Français de. *Voyage d'un français en Italie, fait dans les années 1765 & 1766*. 8 vols., rev. and expanded. Yverdon, 1769–90.

Lang, Paul Henry. "Performance Practice and the Voice." In *Musicology and Performance*, edited by Alfred Mann and George J. Buelow. New Haven, CT: Yale University Press, 1997.

Laqueur, Thomas. *Making Sex: Body and Gender from the Greeks to Freud*. Cambridge, MA: Harvard University Press, 1990.

Law, Hedy. "Gestural Rhetoric: in Search of Pantomime in the French Enlightenment, ca. 1750–1785." 3 vols. PhD diss., University of Chicago, 2007.

Law, Joe K. "Alessandro Moreschi Reconsidered: A Castrato on Records." *Opera Quarterly* 2, no. 2 (Summer 1984): 1–12.

Leach, Edmund. *Social Anthropology*. Oxford: Oxford University Press, 1982.

———. "Verbal Abuse and Animal Categories." In *New Directions in the Study of Language*, edited by Eric H. Lenneberg. Cambridge, MA: MIT Press, 1964.

Lebrun, Elisabeth Vigée. *Souvenirs*. 2 vols. Edited by Claudine Herrmann. Paris: Des Femmes, 1984.

Lehmann, Lilli. *How to Sing*. Translated by Richard Aldrich, rev. ed. translated by Clara Willenbücher [1902]. New York: Macmillan, 1924; repr. ed. New York: Dover, 1993.

Leopold, Silke. "Mannsbilder—Weibsbilder: Händels Personendarstellung im Kontext höfischer Sitten." *Händel-Jahrbuch* 49 (2003): 263–82.
Libby, Dennis. "Minelli, Giovanni Battista Minelli." *Grove Music Online*. Edited by Deane Root. www.oxfordmusiconline.com.
Liebscher, Julia. "Das Kastratentum im Diskurs von Thomas Laqueurs 'One-Sex Model.'" In *Frauen- und Männerbilder in der Musik: Festschrift für Eva Rieger zum 60. Geburtstag*, edited by Freia Hoffmann, Jane Bowers, and Ruth Heckmann. Oldenburg: Bibliotheks- und Informationssystem der Universität Oldenberg, 2000.
Lienhardt, Godfrey. *Divinity and Experience: The Religion of the Dinka*. Oxford: Clarendon Press, 1961.
Lindgren, Lowell E. "La carriera di Gaetano Berenstadt, contralto evirato (ca. 1690–1735)." *Rivista italiana di musicologia* 19 (1984): 36–112.
———. "An Intellectual Florentine Castrato at the End of the Medicean Era." In *"Lo stupor dell'invenzione": Firenze e la nascita dell'opera, Atti del Convegno Internazionale di Studi, Firenze, 5–6 ottobre, 2000*, edited by Piero Gargiulo. Florence: Leo S. Olschki, 2001.
Link, Dorothea. *The National Court Theatre in Mozart's Vienna: Sources and Documents, 1783–1792*. Oxford: Clarendon Press; New York: Oxford University Press, 1998.
———, ed. *Arias for Nancy Storace: Mozart's First Susanna*. Middleton, WI: A-R Editions, 2002.
Lucarelli, Nicola. "Bruni, Domenico Luigi." *Grove Music Online*. Edited by Deane Root. www.oxfordmusiconline.com.
———. *Domenico Bruni (1758–1821): Biografia di un cantante evirato*. Città di Castello: Grafiche 2GF and Comune di Umbertide, 1992.
Mado Robin. Lebendige Vergangenheit series. Austro Mechana Historic Recordings 89614, 2005.
Madock, David Carter. "A Study of the *Stile Antico* in the Masses and Motets of Antonio Lotti as Contained in the Codice Marciano Italiano IV, Venice." PhD diss., Catholic University of America, 1996.
Maffei, Giovanni Camillo. *Delle lettere . . . da Solofro . . . dove tra gli bellissimi pensieri di filosofia, e di medicina v'è un discorso della voce e del modo d'apparare di cantar di garganta, senza maestro*. 2 vols. Naples: Raymundo Amato, 1562.
Magrini, Tullia. "The Contribution of Ernesto De Martino to the Anthropology of Italian Music." *Yearbook of Traditional Music* 26 (1994): 66–80.
Malnati, Andrea. "Drammaturgia musicale e filologia delle varianti: Il caso di 'Ombra adorata, aspetta' di Niccolò Zingarelli." Tesi di Laurea, Università degli Studi di Milano, 2008–9.
———. "Per una storia della prassi esecutiva dell'opera italiana: Il caso di 'Ombra adorata, aspetta' di Niccolò Zingarelli." *Bollettino del Centro Rossiniano di Studi* 50 (2010): 29–84.
Mamone, Sara. *Serenissimi fratelli principi impresari: Notizie di spettacolo nei carteggi medicei: Carteggi di Giovan Carlo de' Medici e di Desiderio Montemagni suo segretario, 1628–1664*. Florence: Le lettere, 2003.
Mamy, Sylvie. *Les grands castrats napolitains à Venise au XVIIIe siècle*. Collection Musique, musicologie. Liège: Mardaga, 1994.
———. "L'importation des solfèges italiens en France à la fin du XVIII siècle." In *L'opera tra Venezia e Parigi*, edited by Maria Teresa Muraro. Venice: Fondazione Giorgio Cini, 1986.

———. "Tradizione pedagogica del canto a Napoli: Giuseppe Aprile." In *Musicisti nati in Puglia ed emigrazione musicale tra Seicento e Settecento: Atti del Convegno Internazionale di Studi, Lecce, 6-8 dicembre 1985*, edited by Detty Bozzi and Luisa Cosi. Rome: Edizioni Torre d'Orfeo, 1988.

"Managers Seeking Light on Visit of The Roman Singers." *Musical America*, September 6, 1919: 1 and 3.

Mancini, Giambattista. *Pensieri, e riflessioni prattiche sopra il canto figurato*. Vienna: Ghelen, 1774.

———. *Practical Reflections on Figured Singing: The Editions of 1774 and 1777 Compared*. Translated and edited by Edward V. Foreman. Masterworks on Singing, vol. 7. Champaign, IL: Pro Musica Press, 1967.

———. *Riflessioni pratiche sul canto figurato*. Milan: Giuseppe Galeazzo, 1777.

Manén, Lucie. *Bel Canto, the Teaching of the Classical Italian Song-Schools, Its Restoration and Decline*. Oxford: Oxford University Press, 1987.

Manfredini, Vincenzo. *Difesa della musica moderna e de' suoi celebri esecutori*. Reprint of the 1788 edition. Bibliotheca musica Bononiensis, sezione II, no. 73. Bologna: Forni, 1972.

Marcello, Benedetto. *Il teatro alla moda*. Edited by Giacomo Alessandro Caula [1720]. Turin: Giacomo A. Caula, n.d.

Mariuz, Adriano. *Giandomenico Tiepolo*. Venice: Alfieri, 1971.

Márquez, Gabriel Garcia. "A Very Old Man with Enormous Wings: A Tale for Children." Translated by Gregory Rabassa, in *Fictions*, edited by Joseph F. Trimmer and C. Wade Jennings. San Diego: Harcourt Brace Jovanovich, 1985.

Martina, Alessandra. *Orfeo-Orphée di Gluck: Storia della trasmissione e della recezione*. Florence: Passigli, 1995.

Martinelli, Vincenzio. *Lettere familiari, e critiche*. London: G. Nourse, 1758.

Martini, Giambattista. *Catalogo degli aggregati della Accademia Filarmonica di Bologna*. Pubblicazioni dell'Accademia filarmonica di Bologna. Monumenti 1. Bologna, 1973.

Martini, Giovanni Battista et al., eds. *Epistolario Giovanni Battista Martini e Girolamo Chiti (1745-1759): 472 lettere del Museo Internazionale e Biblioteca della Musica di Bologna*. Rome: IBIMUS, 2010.

May, Margaret Tallmadge. *Galen on the Usefulness of the Parts of the Body*. 2 vols. Ithaca, NY: Cornell University Press, 1968.

McCormick, John P. *Weber, Habermas, and Transformations of the European State: Constitutional, Social, and Supranational Democracy*. Cambridge: Cambridge University Press, 2007.

McGeary, Thomas. "Farinelli and the English: 'One God' or the Devil?" *La revue LISA* 2 (2004): 29-50.

———. "Farinelli in Madrid: Opera, Politics, and the War of Jenkins' Ear." *Musical Quarterly* 82 (1998): 383-421.

———. "Farinelli's Progress to Albion: The Recruitment and Reception of Opera's 'Blazing Star.'" *British Journal for Eighteenth-Century Studies* 28 (2005): 339-60.

———. "Gendering Opera: Italian Opera as the Feminine Other in England, 1700-42." *Journal of Musicological Research* 14 (1994): 17-34.

———. "Verse Epistles on Italian Opera Singers, 1724-1736." *RMA Research Chronicle* 33 (2000): 29-88.

McLaren, Angus. *Impotence: A Cultural History.* Chicago: University of Chicago Press, 2007.
Mecke, Ann-Christine. *Mutantenstadl: Der Stimmwechsel und die deutsche Chorpraxis im 18. und 19. Jahrhundert.* Berlin: Wissenschaftlicher Verlag Berlin, 2007.
Mecke, Ann-Christine, Johan Sundberg, and Bernhard Richter. "A Virtual Castrato?" *Logopedics, Phonatrics, Vocology* 35 (2010): 138–43.
Medina, Ángel. *Los atributos del capón: Imagen histórica de los cantores castrados en España.* Madrid: Instituto Complutense de Ciencias Musicales, 2001.
Melba, Nellie. *Melodies and Memories.* Freeport, NY: Books for Libraries Press, 1970.
Melicow, Meyer M. "Castrati Singers and the Lost 'Cords.'" *Bulletin of the New York Academy of Medicine* 59 (1983): 744–64.
Melicow, Meyer M., with Stanford Pulrang. "Castrati Choir and Opera Singers." *Urology* 3 (1974): 663-670.
Melosio, Francesco. *Poesie e prose di Francesco Melosio da città della Pieve, aggiuntovi in questa nova impressione altre spiritose, erudite, e bizarre compositioni dello stesso auttore, consacrate all'Illustriss. & Eccellentiss. Sig. Gio: Alberto di Ferschen.* Venice, 1695.
Mengozzi, Bernardo. "Singers." In *Opera Production and Its Resources.* Chicago: University of Chicago Press, 1988.
Merrick, Jeffrey, and Bryant T. Ragan Jr., eds. *Homosexuality in Early Modern France: A Documentary Collection.* New York: Oxford University Press, 2001.
Metastasio, Pietro. *Tutte le opere.* 5 vols. Edited by Bruno Brunelli. Milan: Mondadori, 1943–54.
Michotte, Edmond. *Richard Wagner's Visit to Rossini (Paris 1860) and An Evening at Rossini's in Beau-Sejour (Passy) 1858.* Translated and annotated, with an introduction and appendix, by Herbert Weinstock. Chicago: University of Chicago Press, 1968.
Miles-Kingston, Paul. "Training Boys to Sing." MA thesis, York University, Music, 2008.
Milizia, Francesco. *Trattato completo, formale e materiale del teatro.* In *Opere complete di Francesco Milizia risguardanti le belle arti.* 9 vols. Bologna: Cardinali e Friuli, 1926.
Miller, Felicia. "Farinelli's Electronic Hermaphrodite and the Contralto Tradition." In *The Work of Opera: Genre, Nationhood, and Sexual Difference*, edited by Richard Dellamora and Daniel Fischlin. New York: Columbia University Press, 1997.
Miller, Richard. *The Structure of Singing: System and Art in Vocal Technique.* Belmont, CA: Schirmer / The Wadsworth Group, 1996.
Millico, Giuseppe. *La pietà d'amore, dramma messo in musica dal signor D. Giuseppe Millico.* Naples: Giuseppe-Maria Porcelli a S. Biaggio de' Librari, 1782.
Milner, Anthony. "The Sacred Capons." *Musical Times* 114, no. 1561 (March 1973): 250–52.
Mojon, Benedetto. *Dissertazione sugli effetti della castratura nel corpo umano.* Milan: Giovanni Pirotta, 1822.
Mole, Tom. "Hypertrophic Celebrity." *M/C Journal: A Journal of Media and Culture* 7, no. 5 (2004).
Moliterni, Pierfrancesco, and Carmela Ferrandes. "Alle origine del 'bel canto': Stendhal e gli 'idéologues.'" In *Stendhal tra letteratura e musica: Atti del Convegno Internazionale, Martina Franca, 26–29 novembre 1992*, edited by Giovanni Dotoli. Fasano: Schena, 1993.
Monaldi, Gino. *Cantanti evirati del teatro italiano.* Rome: Ausonia, 1920.

Mongrédien, Jean. "A propos de Rossini: Une polémique Stendhal-Berton." In *Stendhal e Milano: Atti del 14° congresso internazionale stendhaliano, Milano, 19-23 marzo 1980*. 2 vols. Florence: Leo S. Olschki, 1982.

———. *French Music from the Enlightenment to Romanticism, 1789-1830*. Translated by Sylvain Frémaux; Reinhard G. Pauly, general editor. Portland: Amadeus Press, 1996.

Monson, Dale E. "Drama in Pergolesi's Opere Serie: Expression and Tradition." In "Aspetti della vita, dell'opera e del contesto storico pergolesiani." *Studi pergolesiani* 4 (2000): 273-92.

Monuments of Solfeggi. Edited by Robert O. Gjerdingen. Monuments series 2. Hosted by Northwestern University. http://faculty-web.at.northwestern.edu/music/gjerdingen/ Solfeggi/collections/index.htm.

Moore, Jerrold Northrup. *A Voice in Time: The Gramophone of Fred Gaisberg, 1873-1951*. London: Hamilton, 1976.

Moore, John. *A View of Society and Manners in Italy*. 4th ed., 2 vols. London, 1787.

Moran, Neil K. "Byzantine Castrati." *Plainsong and Medieval Music* 11 (2002): 99-112.

Mortimer, Armine Kotin. *For Love or Money: Balzac's Rhetorical Realism*. Columbus: Ohio State University Press, 2011.

Moses, Paul J. *The Psychology of the Castrato Voice*. Basel: Folia Phoniatrica, 1960.

Mozart: Briefe und Aufzeichnungen, Gesamtausgabe. Edited by Wilhelm A. Bauer and Otto Erich Deutsch with Ulrich Konrad, Internationalen Stiftung Mozarteum Salzburg 8 vols. Kassel: Bärenreiter, 1962-2005.

Müller, Walther. *Johann Adolphe Hasse als Kirchenkomponist: Ein Beitrag zur Geschichte der neapolitanischen Kirchenmusik mit thematischen Katalog der liturgischen Kirchenmusik J. A. Hasses*. Publikationen der Internationalen Musikgesellschaft, Beihefte, series 2, vol. 9. Leipzig: Breitkopf & Härtel, 1911.

Nardini, Carlo. *Il musico Siface e l'ambasciatore di Francia a Roma nel 1683*. Florence: Coppini e Bocconi, 1891.

Negus, V. E., Owen Jander, and Peter Giles. "Falsetto." *Grove Music Online*. Edited by Deane Root. www.oxfordmusiconline.com.

Newborn, Jud. "'Work Makes Free': The Hidden Cultural Meaning of the Holocaust." 4 vols. PhD diss., University of Chicago, 1994.

Newcomb, Anthony. *The Madrigal at Ferrara, 1579-1797*. 2 vols. Princeton, NJ: Princeton University Press, 1980.

"Ombra adorata aspetta," cavatina de l'opera Romeo e Giulietta, de Zingarelli. In *Souvenir à Pasta, et Rubini*, arranged by Diabelli and Sedlatzek. London: Wessel & Co, 1832.

"Online-Katalog der Hamburger Hasse-Handschriften." *Universität Hamburg Staats- und Universitätsbibliothek Fachbibliotheken*. www.sub.uni-hamburg.de/bibliotheken/ sammlungen /sondersammlungen/musiksammlung/hasse-katalog.htm.

Ortkemper, Hubert. *Engel wider Willen: Die Welt der Kastraten*. Berlin: Henschel Verlag, 1993.

Pacchierotti, Giuseppe Cecchini. *Ai cultori ed amatori della musica vocale: Cenni biografici intorno a Gaspare Pacchierotti*. Padova: Seminario, 1844.

Pacchioni, Antonio Maria. *Il canto ecclesiastico*. Modena, 1686.

———. *Cantus omnis ecclesiasticus*. Modena, 1688.

———. *Primi elementi di musica*. Modena, 1683.

Paglialunga, Arcangelo. *Lorenzo Perosi*. [Rome]: Paoline, 1952.
Pampaloni, Christina. "Giovani castrati nell'Assisi del Settecento." *Musica/Realtà* 8 (1987): 133–53.
Panzacchi, Enrico. *I miei racconti*. 1st ed. Milan: Treves, 1889.
———. *Racconti*. Edited by Valeria Giannantonio. Chieti Scalo: Vecchio Faggio, 1993.
Papa, Cristina. "Famiglia, residenza, patrimonio: Quali modelli?" *La ricerca folklorica* 27, "Forme di famiglia: Ricerche per un Atlante italiano," part 2 (April 1993): 13–33.
Parini, Giuseppe. "La musica." In *Il giorno e le odi*. Bologna: Zanichelli, 1817.
Park, Katharine. "Stones, Bones, and Hernias: Specialists in Fourteenth- and Fifteenth-Century Italy." In *Medicine from the Black Death to the French Disease*, edited by Roger French et al. Aldershot: Ashgate, 1998.
Parolari, Cornelio. "Giambattista Velluti, ultimo dei sopranisti sulle liriche scene." *Rivista musicale italiana* 39 (1932): 263–98.
Parvulescu, Anca. *Laughter: Notes on a Passion*. Cambridge, MA: MIT Press, 2010.
Pasqualigo, Zacharias. *Eunvchi, nati, facti, mystici: Ex sacra et humana literatura illustrati*. Divione: Apud Philibertum Chavance, 1655.
Pergolesi, Giovanni Battista. *Adriano in Siria*. Edited by Dale E. Monson, Pergolesi Complete Works, no. 1. Stuyvesant, NY: Pendragon, 1986.
Petersen, Scott. "What Are We Listening To? An Analysis of Early Sound Recordings and Early Recording Technology." Unpublished seminar paper, Eastman School of Music, University of Rochester, May 2006.
Petrobelli, Pierluigi. "On Reading Musical Caricatures: Some Italian Examples." *Imago musicae* 2 (1985): 135–42.
Philipps-Matz, Mary Jane. *Rosa Ponselle: American Diva*. Boston: Northeastern University Press, 1997.
Il pianto de' cigni in morte della fenice de' musici. Perugia, 1680.
Pilo, Giuseppe Maria, ed. *Marco Ricci: Catalogo della mostra . . . con un saggio di Rodolfo Pallucchini, sui caratteri di Marco Ricci, Bassano del Grappa, Palazzo Sturm, 1 settembre–10 novembre 1963*. Venice: Alfieri, [1963].
Planelli, Antonio. *Dell'opera in musica*. Naples: Donato Campo, 1772.
———. *Dell'opera in musica*. Edited by Francesco Degrada. Fiesole: Discanto, 1981.
Plato. *Sophist*.
Poizat, Michael. *The Angel's Cry: Beyond the Pleasure Principle in Opera*. Translated by Arthur Denner [1986]. Ithaca, NY: Cornell University Press, 1992.
Pomata, Gianna. "Family and Gender." In *Early Modern Italy*, edited by John A. Marino. Oxford: Oxford University Press, 2002.
Poriss, Hilary. *Changing the Score: Arias, Prima Donnas, and the Authority of Performance*. AMS Studies in Music. New York: Oxford University Press, 2009.
Potter, John. "Beggar at the Door: The Rise and Fall of Portamento in Singing." *Music & Letters* 87 (2006): 523–50.
———. *Tenor: History of a Voice*. New Haven, CT: Yale University Press, 2009.
———. "Vocal Performance in the 'Long Eighteenth Century.'" In *The Cambridge History of Performance*, edited by Colin Lawson and Robin Stilwell. Cambridge: Cambridge University Press, 2012.

Powers, Harold S. "Il Serse Trasformato." *Musical Quarterly* 47 (1961): 481–92 and 48 (1962): 73–92.
Price, Curtis, Judith Milhous, and Robert D. Hume. *Italian Opera in Late Eighteenth-Century London.* Oxford: Clarendon Press, 1995.
Prodi, Paolo. *The Papal Prince, One Body and Two Souls: The Papal Monarchy in Early Modern Europe*, translated by Susan Haskins. Cambridge: Cambridge University Press, 1987.
Prota-Giurleo, Ulisse. "Matteo Sassano detto 'Matteuccio' (documenti napolitani)." *Rivista italiana di musicologia* (1966): 97–119.
Pryer, Anthony. "Mozart's Operatic Audition: The Milan Concert, 12 March 1770, A Reappraisal and Revision." *Eighteenth-Century Music* 1 (2004): 265–88.
The Pupil and Her Teacher: De Hidalgo, Callas. CD Fono 1010, 2001.
Ratliff, Joy. "Women in Pants: Male Roles for the Mezzo-Soprano or Contralto Voice." DMA thesis, University of Maryland, College Park, 1997.
Rau, Carl August. *Loreto Vittori: Beiträge zur historisch-kritischen Würdigung seines Lebens, Wirkens und Schaffens.* Munich: Verlag für Moderne Musik, 1913.
Ravagli, Francesco. *Il Cortona, Domenico Cecchi.* Città di Castello: Scipione Lapi, 1896.
Ravelli, Antonio, ed. *Il ciarlator maldicente.* In *Scelta di commedie e novelle morali del marchese Albergati Capacelli*, 2 vols. London: Giuseppe Cooper, [1794], vol. 2.
Ravenni, Gabriella Biagi. "'Molti in Lucca si applicavano alla professione della musica': Storie di formazione e di emigrazione nella patria di Luigi Boccherini." *Chigiana: Rassegna annuale di studi musicologici* 43 (1993): 69–109.
The Remarkable Trial of the Queen of Quavers and Her Associates, for Sorcery, Witchcraft, and Enchantments at the Assizzes Held in the Moon, for The County of Gelding before the Rt. Hon. Sir Francis Lash, Lord Chief Baron of the Lunar Exchequer. Taken in Short Hand, by Joseph Democritus and William Diogenes. [London]: Printed for J. Bew, No. 28, in Paternoster Row, [1778].
Revathi, A. *The Truth about Me: A Hijra Life Story.* Translated by V. Geetha Rēvati. New Delhi: Penguin Books, 2010.
Reynolds, Margaret. "Ruggiero's Deceptions, Cherubino's Distractions." In *En Travesti: Women, Gender Subversion, Opera*, edited by Corinne E. Blackmer and Julianna Smith. New York: Columbia University Press, 1995.
Ricci, Corrado. *I teatri di Bologna nei secoli XVII e XVIII.* Reprint ed. 1888. Bologna: Forni, 1965.
Rice, John. *Antonio Salieri and Viennese Opera.* Chicago: University of Chicago Press, 1998.
———. "Benedetto Frizzi on Singers, Composers, and Opera in Late Eighteenth-Century Opera." *Studi musicali* 23 (1994): 367–93.
Rinaldi, Mario. *Lorenzo Perosi.* Rome: De Santis, 1967.
Roach, Joseph R. *The Player's Passion: Studies in the Science of Acting.* Ann Arbor: University of Michigan Press, 1993.
Robinson, David M. *Bandits, Eunuchs, and the Son of Heaven: Rebellion and the Economy of Violence in Mid-Ming China.* Honolulu: University of Hawai'i Press, 2001.
———, ed. *Culture, Courtiers, and Competition: The Ming Court (1368–1644).* Cambridge, MA: Harvard University Asia Center with Harvard University Press, 2008.
Robinson, Michael F. "The Governor's Minutes of the Conservatory S. Maria di Loreto, Naples." *RMA Research Chronicle* 10, no. 1 (1972): 1–97.

———. *Naples and Neapolitan Opera*. Oxford: Clarendon Press, 1972.
Rosa Ponselle on the Air, Vol. 1, 1934–1936. Marston, 1999, 52012-2.
Rosa Ponselle on the Air, Vol. 2, 1936–1937. Marston, 2000, 52032-2.
Rosa, Salvator. *Satire, liriche, lettere*. Edited by Anton Maria Salvini et al. Milan: Sonzogno, 1892.
———. *Satire, odi e lettere*. Florence: G. Barbèra, 1860.
Rosand, Ellen. "Barbara Strozzi, *virtuosissima cantatrice*: The Composer's Voice." *Journal of the American Musicological Society* 31 (1978): 241–81.
Rosselli, John. "L'apprendistato del cantante italiano: Rapporti contrattuali fra allievi e insegnanti dal Cinquecento al Novecento." *Rivista italiana di musicologia* 23 (1988): 157–81.
———. "The Castrati as a Professional Group and as a Social Phenomenon, 1550–1850." *Acta musicologica* 60 (1988): 143–79.
———. "Moreschi, Alessandro." *Grove Music Online*. Edited by Deane Root. www.oxfordmusiconline.com.
———. *Singers of Italian Opera: The History of a Profession*. Cambridge: Cambridge University Press, 1992.
Rossi Scotti, Giovanni Battista. *Della vita e delle opere del cavalier Francesco Morlacchi*. Perugia, 1860.
Rostirolla, Giancarlo, Stefano La Via, and Anna Lo Bianco. *Il "mondo novo" musicale di Pier Leone Ghezzi*. Milan: Skira; Rome: Accademia Nazionale di Santa Cecilia, 2001.
Roudet, Jeanne, ed. *Chant: Les grandes méthodes romantiques de chant*. 7 vols. Méthodes et traités, series 2, France, 1800–1860. Courlay: Fuzeau, 2005.
Rousseau, J. J. *Appendix to Grassineau's Musical Dictionary, Selected from the Dictionnaire de Musique of J. J. Rousseau*. London, 1769.
Ruggiero, Guido. *Binding Passions: Tales of Magic, Marriage, and Power from the End of the Renaissance*. New York: Oxford University Press, 1993.
———. *The Boundaries of Eros: Sex Crime and Sexuality in Renaissance Venice*. New York: Oxford University Press, 1985.
———. *Machiavelli in Love: Sex, Self, and Society in the Italian Renaissance*. Baltimore, MD: Johns Hopkins University Press, 2007.
Sacchi, Giovanale. *Vita del Cavaliere Don Carlo Broschi detto Il Farinello*. Edited by Alessandro Abbate [1784]. Naples: Pagano, 1994.
Sade, Marquis de. *Voyage d'Italie*. Edited by Maurice Lever. Paris: Fayard, 1995.
Salecl, Renata, and Slavoj Žižek, eds. *Gaze and Voice as Love Objects*. Durham, NC: Duke University Press, 1996.
Sartori, Claudio. *I libretti italiani a stampa dalle origini al 1800: Catalogo analitico con 16 indici*. Cuneo: Bertola & Locatelli, 1990.
Sassi, Romualdo. *Un celebre musico fabrianese: Gaspare Pacchierotti*. Fabriano: Stab. di Arte Grafiche "Gentile," 1935.
Sawkins, Lionel. "The Brothers Bêche: An Anecdotal History of Court Music." *Recherches sur la musique française classique* 24 (1986): 192–221.
Sayrus, Gregorius. *Clavis regia sacerdotum casuum conscientiae, sive Theologiae moralis thesauri locos omnes aperiens*. 2 vols. in 1. Venice: B. Baretium, 1607.
Scafoglio, Domenico. *La maschera della cuccagna: Spreco, rivolta e sacrificio nel carnevale napoletano del 1764*. Naples: Guida, 1994.

———. *Pulcinella.* Napoli Tascabile 30, edited by Romualdo Marrone. Rome: Tascabili Economici Newton, 1996.
Scafoglio, Domenico, and M. Luigi Lombardi Satriani. *Pulcinella: Il mito e la storia.* Milan: Leonardo, 1990.
Scammell, Elsa. "The Counter Tenor Phenomenon." *Opera-L* on *Opera-L Archives.* http://listserv.bccls.org/cgi-bin/wa?A2=indo111B&L=OPERA-L&P=R9920&m=120987.
Schafer, R. Murray. *The New Soundscape: A Handbook for the Modern Music Teacher.* Toronto: Don Mills, 1969.
Schlafly, Daniel L., Jr. "Filippo Balatri in Peter the Great's Russia." *Jahrbüchen für Geschichte ostereuropas* 45 (1997): 18–98.
———. "A Muscovite Boiarynia Faces Peter the Great's Reforms: Dar'ia Golitsyna between Two Worlds." *Canadian-American Slavic Studies* 31 (1997): 249–68.
Schleiner, Winfried. "Early Modern Controversies about the One-Sex Model." *Renaissance Quarterly* 53, no. 1 (Spring 2001): 180–91.
Schneider, Rachel R. "The Administrative History of L'Académie Imperiale de Musique in the Age of Napoleon: Opera for Gloire and Indoctrination." Ph.D. diss., University of Akron, 1990.
Schnepel, Burkhard. *Twinned Beings: Kings and Effigies in Southern Sudan, East India, and Renaissance France.* Göteborg: IASSA, 1995.
Schnoebelen, Anne. "Bernacchi, Antonio." *Grove Music Online.* Edited by Deane Root. www.oxfordmusiconline.com.
———. *Padre Martini's Collection of Letters in the Civico Museo Bibliografico Musicale in Bologna: An Annotated Index.* New York: Pendragon, 1979.
Schoenbaum, David. "Jascha Heifetz at 100: Both Thrilling and Chilling." *New York Times,* December 23, 2001.
Scholz, Piotr O. *Eunuchs and Castrati: A Cultural History.* Translated by John A. Broadwin and Shelley L. Frisch. Princeton, NJ: Markus Wiener Publishers, 2001.
Schönfeld, J. F. von. *Jahrbuch der Tonkunst von Wien und Prag.* Gesellschaft der Musikfreunde in Wien. Munich: E. Katzbilder, 1796.
Schütze, J. F. *Hamburgische Theater-Geschichte.* Hamburg: Treder, 1794.
Schwarz, Birthe. "Das Spiel mit den Geschlechterrollen: Kastraten und Primadonnen im Musiktheater des 18. Jahrhunderts." In *Gender Studies und Musik: Geschlechterrollen und ihre Bedeutung für die Musikwissenschaft,* edited by Stefan Fragner, Jan Hemming, and Beate Kutschke. Regensburg: Con Brio, 1998.
Seingalt, Jacques Casanova de. *Histoire de ma vie: Texte intégral du manuscrit original, suivi de textes inédits.* 12 vols. Edited by Francis Lacassin. Bouquins: Éditions Robert Laffont, 1993.
———. *History of My Life.* 12 vols. in 6. Translated by Willard R. Trask. Baltimore, MD: Johns Hopkins University Press, 1966.
Seriman, Zaccaria. *I viaggi di Enrico Wanton: Alle terre incognite australi, ed al paese delle scimie ne'quale si spiegano il carattere li costumi, le scienze, e la polizia di quegli straordinari abitanti.* Venice: Giovanni Tagier, 1749.
Il Settecento: L'Arcadia e l'età delle riforme. Edited by Gaetano Campagnino, Guido Nicastro, and Giuseppe Savoca. Bari: Laterza, 1970–80.
Shawe-Taylor, Desmond. "Melchior, Lauritz (Lebrecht Hommel)." *Grove Music Online.* Edited by Deane Root. www.oxfordmusiconline.com.

Shearon, Stephen. "Latin Sacred Music and Nicola Fago: The Career and Sources of an Early Eighteenth-Century Neapolitan *Maestro di cappella.*" PhD diss., University of North Carolina at Chapel Hill, 1992.
Sherr, Richard. "Competence and Incompetence in the Papal Choir in the Age of Palestrina." *Early Music* 22, no. 4 (1994): 606–29.
———. "Competence and Incompetence in the Papal Choir in the Age of Palestrina." In *Palestrina e l'Europa: Atti del III Convegno Internazionale di Studi (Palestrina, 6–9 ottobre 1994),* edited by Giancarlo Rostirolla, Stefania Soldati, and Elena Zomparelli. [Rome]: Fondazione Giovanni Pierluigi da Palestrina, 2006.
———. "Guglielmo Gonzaga and the Castrati." *Renaissance Quarterly* 33, no. 1 (Spring 1980): 33–56.
Simmel, Georg. *The Philosophy of Money.* Edited by David Frisby. Translated by Tom Bottomore and David Frisby. 2nd ed., rev. and enlarged. London: Routledge, 1990.
Sittard, Josef. *Geschichte des Musik- und Concertwesens in Hamburg vom 14. Jahrhundert bis auf die Gegenwart.* Altona and Leipzig: A. C. Reher, 1890.
———. *Zur Geschichte der Musik und des Theaters am württembergischen Hofe, nach Originalquellen.* 2 vols. in 1. Stuttgart: W. Kohlhammer, 1890–91.
Somerset-Ward, Richard. *Angels and Monsters: Male and Female Sopranos in the Story of Opera, 1600–1900.* New Haven, CT: Yale University Press, 2004.
Sonino, Annalisa Scarpa. *Marco Ricci.* Milan: Berenice, 1991.
Spitzer, John, and Neal Zaslaw, *The Birth of the Orchestra: History of an Institution, 1650–1815.* New York: Oxford University Press, 2004.
Spreti, Laura. "Venezia, carnevale 1791." *Rassegna veneta di studi musicali* 9–10 (1993/1994): 185–200.
Stallybrass, Peter, and Allon White. *The Politics and Poetics of Transgression.* Ithaca, NY: Cornell University Press, 1986.
Starobinski, Jean. *Enchantment: The Seductress in Opera.* Translated by Christopher Jon Delogu. New York: Columbia University Press, 2008.
Steane, J. B. *The Grand Tradition: Seventy Years of Singing on Record.* 2nd ed. Portland, OR: Amadeus Press, 1993.
Steffani, Agostino. *Tassilone, tragedia per musica (in 5 atti).* Edited by Gerhard Croll, Denkmäler rheinischer Musik, vol. 8. Düsseldorf: Schwann, 1958.
Stein, Louise K. "*Siface* (Giovanni Francesco Grossi), a Castrato Voice of Virility." Paper delivered at the American Musicological Society, San Francisco, November 10–13, 2011.
Stella, Pietro. "Strategie familiari e celibato sacro in Italia tra '600 e '700." *Salesianum* 41 (1979): 73–109.
Stendhal. *The Charterhouse of Parma.* Translated with an introduction and notes by John Sturrock. London: Penguin, 2006.
———. *Life of Rossini,* rev. ed. Translated by Richard N. Coe. New York: Orion Press, 1970.
———. *Souvenirs d'egotisme.* Edited by Henri Martineau. Paris: Divan, 1950.
———. *Vie de Rossini suivie des Notes d'un dilettante.* Edited by Henri Prunières. Oeuvres complètes de Stendhal, vol. 2. Paris: E. Champion, 1922.
Stokes, Martin. *The Arabesk Debate: Music and Musicians in Modern Turkey.* Oxford: Clarendon Press, 1992.

———. "The Tearful Public Sphere: Turkey's 'Sun of Art,' Zeki Mürin." In *Music and Gender: Perspectives from the Mediterranean*, edited by Tullia Magrini. Chicago: University of Chicago Press, 2003.

Strohm, Reinhard. "Who Is Farinelli?" Liner notes to *Arias for Farinelli*. Vivica Genaux with the Akademie für Alte Musik Berlin, dir. René Jacobs. Arles: Harmonia Mundi, HMC 901778, 2002.

Stromayr, Caspar. *Die Handschrift des Schnitt- und Augenarztes Caspar Stromayr in Linden im Bodensee in der Lindauer Handschrift (P.I. 46) vom 4. Juli 1559*. Edited by Walter von Brunn. Berlin: Idra, 1925.

Stubbings, Frank H. "Xerxes and the Plane-Tree." *Greece & Rome* 15, no. 44 (May 1946): 63–67.

Stuve, Lynn A., ed. and trans. *Voices from the Ming-Qing Cataclysm: China in Tigers' Jaws*. New Haven, CT: Yale University Press, 1993.

Sundberg, Johan. "Level and Centre Frequency of the Singer's Formant." *Journal of Voice* 15 (2001): 176–86.

———. *The Science of the Singing Voice*. DeKalb: Northern Illinois University Press, 1987.

———. "Where Does Sound Come From?" In *The Cambridge Companion to Singing*, edited by John Potter. Cambridge: Cambridge University Press, 2000.

Sundberg, Johan, Marianne Troven, and Bernhard Richter. "Sopranos with a Singer's Formant? Historical, Physiological, and Acoustical Aspects of Castrato Singing." *Speech, Music, and Hearing, KTH, CSC Computer Science and Communication*, Stockholm, Sweden TMH-QPSR, KTH 49 (2007): 1–6.

The Symposium and the Phaedrus: Plato's Erotic Dialogues. Translated with introduction and commentaries by William S. Cobb. Albany: State University of New York Press, 1993.

Taylor, Charles, with Murray Campbell. "Sound." *Grove Music Online*. Edited by Deane Root. www.oxfordmusiconline.com.

Taylor, Gary. *Castration: An Abbreviated History of Western Manhood*. New York: Routledge, 2000.

Temkin, Owsei. *Galenism: Rise and Decline of a Medical Philosophy*. Ithaca, NY: Pergamon Press, 1973.

Tenducci, Dora Maunsell. *A True and Genuine Narrative of Mr. and Mrs. Tenducci, in a Letter to a Friend at Bath, Giving a Full Account, from Their Marriage in Ireland, to the Present Time*. London: Printed for J. Pridden, 1768.

Tenducci, Giusto Ferdinando. *Orpheus and Eurydice, a Musical Drama, in Imitation of the Ancient Greek Theatrical Feasts, as Performed at the King's Theatre in the Haymarket*. London: J. Jarvis, 1785.

Tiberi, M. "Domenico Mancini." In notes to *Le voci di Roma*, vol. 1, TIMA 37. Roma: Edizioni del Timaclub, 198.

Tiepolo: Ironia e comico. Edited by Adriano Mariuz and Giuseppe Pavanello. Venice: Marsilio with the Fondazione Giorgio Cini, 2004.

Timms, Colin. "Cecchi, Domenico ['Il Cortona']." *Grove Music Online*. Edited by Deane Root. www.oxfordmusiconline.com.

———. *Polymath of the Baroque: Agostini Steffani and His Music*. Oxford: Oxford University Press, 2003.

Timpanaro, Maria Augusta Morelli. "Su Gaetano Berenstadt, contralto (Firenze, 1687–1734), e i suoi amici." *Studi italiani* 9 (1997): 147–211.
Titze, Ingo R. *Principles of Voice Production*. 1994; Iowa City: National Center for Voice and Speech, 2000.
Toffano, Giovanni. *Gaspare Pacchierotti: Il crepuscolo di un musico al tramonto della Serenissima*. Padova: Armelin Musica, 1999.
Tooke, William, ed. *Selections from the Most Celebrated Foreign Literary Journals and Other Periodical Publications*. 2 vols. London: J. Debrett, 1798.
Tosi, Pierfrancesco. *Introduction to the Art of Singing*. Edited by Julianne C. Baird. Cambridge: Cambridge University Press, 1995.

———. *Observations on the Florid Song; or, Sentiments on the Ancient and Modern Singers*. 2nd ed. Translated by Mr. Galliard. London: J. Wilcox, 1743.

———. *Opinioni de' cantori antichi, e moderni, o sieno Osservazioni sopra il canto figurato*. Bologna: Lelio dalla Volpe, 1723.

———. *Opinioni de' cantori antichi, e moderni*. Reprinted ed. Monuments of Music and Music Literature in Facsimile, 2nd series, Music Literature, no. 133. New York: Broude Brothers, 1968.
Tougher, Shaun. *The Eunuch in Byzantine History and Society*. London: Routledge, 2008.
Trials for Adultery, or, The History of Divorces: Being Select Trials at Doctors Commons, for Adultery, Fornication, Cruelty, Impotence, &c. from the Year 1760, to the Present Time, Including the Whole of the Evidence on Each Cause: Together with the Letters &c. That Have Been Intercepted between the Amorous Parties. London: Printed for S. Bladon, 1779–81; repr. ed. [Buffalo, NY]: William S. Hein & Co., [2007]; electronic resource at www.heinonline.org.
Ulm, Renate. *Glucks Orpheus-Opern: Die Parma-Fassung von 1769 als wichtiges Bindeglied zwischen dem Wiener Orfeo von 1762 und dem Pariser Orphée von 1774*. Frankfurt am Main: Lang, 1991.
Urban, Lina Padoan, ed. *Il carnevale veneziano nelle maschere incise da Francesco Bertelli*. Milan: Il Polifilo, 1986.
Valeri, Valerio. *The Forest of Taboos: Hunting, Morality, and Identity among the Huaulu of the Moluccas*. Madison: University of Wisconsin Press, 1999.

———. *Kingship and Sacrifice: Ritual and Society in Ancient Hawaii*. Translated by Paula Wissing. Chicago: University of Chicago Press, 1985.

———. "Regalità." In *Enciclopedia Einaudi*, 16 vols., directed by Ruggiero Romano. Turin: G. Einaudi, 1977–1984. Vol. 11 (1980), 742–71.
Vannoni, Annarosa. "'Ombra adorata, aspetta': Girolamo Crescentini, il cantante e il didatta." In *Martini docet: Atti delle Giornate di studio: Io la musica son . . . : Per il bicentenario del manifestazioni Conservatorio di Bologna; classi, regolamenti, musicisti e musicologi per due secoli: lo stato di attuazione della riforma e prospettive di sviluppo. Sala Bossi, 30 settembre–2 ottobre 2004*, edited by Piero Mioli, preface by Carmine Carrisi, 139–85. Bologna: Conservatorio di Musica Giovan Battista Martini, 2007.
Vennard, William. *Singing: The Mechanism and the Technic*. New York: Carl Fischer, 1968.
Venturi, Franco. *La caduta dell'Antico Regime: Corso di storia moderna per l'anno accademico, 1980–81*. Turin: Tirreni, 1981.

———. *Italy and the Enlightenment: Studies in a Cosmopolitan Century*. Edited by Stuart Woolf and translated by Susan Corsi. London: Longman, 1972.

Verdi, Luigi. "Il Farinelli a Bologna: Dai primi successi alla fama internazionale del più celebre cantante italiano del Settecento." *Nuova rivista musicale italiana* 2 (2003): 197–237.

———. "Farinelli in Bologna." *British Journal for Eighteenth-Century Studies* 28, no. 3 (2005): 411–20.

Vetrocq, Marcia E. *Domenico Tiepolo's Punchinella Drawings, September 2–October 6, 1979, Indiana Art Museum; November 13–December 30, 1979, Stanford University Museum of Art*. Introduction by Adelheid M. Gealt. Bloomington: Indiana University Art Museum, 1979.

Viale Ferrero, Mercedes. *La scenografia del '700 e i fratelli Galliari*. Turin: Edizioni d'Arte Fratelli Pozzo, 1963.

Vianello, C. A. *Teatri, spettacoli, musiche a Milano nei secoli scorsi*. Milan: Lombarda, 1941.

Vila, Anne C. *Enlightenment and Pathology: Sensibility in the Literature and Medicine of Eighteenth-Century France*. Baltimore, MD: Johns Hopkins University Press, 1998.

Villemarest, Charles Maxime Catherinet de. *Mémoires de Mlle. Avrillon . . . sur vie privée de Joséphine, sa famille et sa cour*. 2 vols. Bibliothèque des mémoires historiques et militaires sur la révolution, le consulat et l'empire. Paris: Garnier frères, 1896.

Vismarri, Filippo et al. *Cantatas*. Edited by Lawrence Bennett. The Italian Cantata in the Seventeenth Century, vol. 16. New York: Garland, 1985.

Vitali, Carlo. "Castori (Antonio, Castorino)." *Grove Music Online*. Edited by Deane Root. www.oxfordmusiconline.com.

———. "Da 'schiavottiello' a 'fedele amico': Lettere (1731–1749) di Carlo Broschi Farinelli al conte Sicinio Pepoli." *Rivista musicale italiana* 26 (1992): 1–36.

———. "De Castris [De' Massimi], Francesco [Cecchino, Checchino]." *Grove Music Online*. Edited by Deane Root. www.oxfordmusiconline.com.

Vitali, Carlo, with Juliane Riepe. "Cavalletti, Giulio Maria [Giulietto]." *Grove Music Online*. Edited by Deane Root. www.oxfordmusiconline.com.

Vittori, Loreto. *La troia rapita, poema giocoso del cavaliere Loreto Vittori da spoleto dedicato al Serenissimo Fran. Duca di Toscana Ferdinando II*. Macerata: Per li Grifei, e Giuseppe Piccini, 1662.

Voltaire. *Candide, ou l'optimisme, traduit de l'allemand par M. de Volt****. London [Netherlands], 1759.

———. *An Essay on Crimes and Punishments. Translated from the Italian, with a commentary, attributed to Mons. de Voltaire, translated from the French*. Dublin, 1767.

———. *The Ignorant Philosopher*. Translated by David Williams. London: Printed for Fielding and Walker, 1779.

Walpole, Horace. *The Letters of Horace Walpole, Earl of Orford: Including Numerous Letters Now First Published from the Original Manuscript*. 6 vols. Edited by John Wright. London: Richard Bentley, 1840.

Walton, Benjamin. *Rossini in Restoration Paris: The Sound of Modern Life*. Cambridge: Cambridge University Press, 2007.

Weaver, Robert Lamar, and Norma Wright Weaver. *A Chronology of Music in the Florentine Theater: Operas, Prologues, Finales, Intermezzos, and Plays with Incidental Music*. 2 vols. Detroit: Information Coordinators, 1978–93.

Weber, William. *Music and the Middle Class: The Social Structure of Concert Life in London, Paris, and Vienna*. London: Croom Helm, 1975.

Weinstock, Herbert. *Rossini: A Biography.* New York: Alfred A. Knopf, 1968.
Welch, Anthony. *The Renaissance Epic and the Oral Past.* New Haven, CT: Yale University Press, 2012.
Whenham, John. "Vittori [Vittorij], Loreto [Victorius, Lauretus; Rovitti, Olerto]." *Grove Music Online.* Edited by Deane Root. www.oxfordmusiconline.com.
Wigmore, Richard. "Singing." In A *Performer's Guide to Music of the Classical Period,* edited by Anthony Burton. London: Associated Board of the Royal Schools of Music, 2002.
Wilbourne, Emily. "The Queer History of the Castrato." In *Oxford Handbook on Queerness and Music,* edited by Fred Maus and Sheila Whiteley. Forthcoming.
Williams, David, ed. *The Enlightenment.* Cambridge: Cambridge University Press, 1999.
Willier, Stephen. "Gasparo Pacchierotti in London: The 1779–80 Season in Susanna Burney's 'Letter Journal.'" *Studi musicali* 29 (2000): 251–91.
———. *The Life and Career of a Celebrated Eighteenth-Century Castrato, Gasparo Pacchierotti (1740–1821).* In preparation.
Wistreich, Richard. "'Il canto nobile': Vocal Technique and Sonic Identity in the Renaissance." Paper given at the Renaissance Society of America Annual Meeting, 2006.
———. "Reconstructing Pre-Romantic Singing Technique." In *The Cambridge Companion to Singing,* edited by John Potter, 178–91, 258–61. Cambridge: Cambridge University Press, 2000.
Witzenmann, Wolfgang. "Dal Pane [Da'l Pane, Del Pane]." *Grove Music Online.* Edited by Deane Root. www.oxfordmusiconline.com.
———. "Mazzocchi, Virgilio." *Grove Music Online.* Edited by Deane Root. www.oxfordmusiconline.com.
Wood, Elizabeth. "On the Sapphonic Voice." In *Music, Culture, and Society: A Reader,* edited by Derek B. Scott. New York: Oxford University Press, 2000.
Woodfield, Ian. *Opera and Drama in Eighteenth-Century London: The King's Theatre, Garrick, and the Business of Performance.* Cambridge: Cambridge University Press, 2001.
Wunnicke, Christine. *Die Nachtigall des Zaren: Das Leben des Filippo Balatri.* Munich: Claassen, 2001.
Zacchia, Paolo. *Questiones medico-legales in quibus omnes eae materiae medicae, quae ad legales facultates videntur pertinere, proponuntur, pertractantur, resoluuntur.* 6 vols. Rome: Sumptibus Andreae Brugiotti apud Iacobum Mascardum, 1621–34.
Zacconi, Lodovico. *Prattica di musica utile e necesssario si al compositore per comporre i canti suoi regolatamente, si anco al cantare per assicurarsi in tutte le cose cantabili.* 4 vols. Venice: Girolamo Polo, 1592.
———. *Prattica di musica utile e necesssario si al compositore per comporre i canti suoi regolatamente, si anco al cantare per assicurarsi in tutte le cose cantabili.* Repr. ed. Bibliotheca musica Bononiensis, sezione 2, nos. 1–2. Bologna: Forni, 1967.
Zanetti, Dante E. *La demografia del patriziato milanese nei secoli XVII, XVIII, XIX.* Annales cisalpines d'histoire sociale, 2nd ser., no. 2. Pavia: Università, 1972.

ILLUSTRATIONS

MUSICAL EXAMPLES

1. Anonymous cantata "Lamento del castrato," excerpt from Bologna, MS Q46, recitative "E se dice talun" through arioso "gli rispondo che nel mond"   20
2. Anonymous cantata "Lamento del castrato," Bologna, MS Q46, excerpt from aria "Poco amate delle guancie" through arioso "ché nemica dell'età"   21
3. Johann Adolphe Hasse, "Per questo dolce amplesso"   41
4. Manuel Garcia, *Traité complet de l'art du chant*, registers   87
5. Charles Gounod, *Méditation sur le premier prélude de piano de S. Bach*   88
6. Hasse's melody line for his aria "Digli che io son fedele" compared with versions with the ornaments supposedly fashioned by soprano Faustina Bordoni (second system) and by the castrato Porporino (third system)   92
7. Sustained note and trill from George Frideric Handel, *Radamisto* (December 1720), "Perfido, di a quell'empio tiranno," mm. 80–92   94
8. Anton Maria Bernacchi, solfeggio in B♭ major marked Adagio, mm. 1–42   97
9. Christoph Willibald Gluck, aria from *Antigono*, "Contro il destin," mm. 16–49   111
10. First exercise from *Instruction of Mr. Tenducci to His Scholars*   114
11. Demonstration of a soprano singing a messa di voce, followed by exercises for practicing it. From Domenico Corri, *The Singer's Preceptor*   115
12. Four different sets of ornaments on the aria "Cara negli occhi tuoi" from Zingarelli's opera *Pirro, re di Epiro*   117
13. Exercises for practicing how to carry the voice ("portar la voce"), from Francesco Rognoni's *Selva di vari passaggi*   119

14. Garcia's exercises for practicing *port de voix* (portamento), from his *Traité complet*   120
15. Portamenti notated for singing Haydn's canzonetta "She Never Told Her Love"   121
16. Portamenti in Garcia's edition of Morlacchi's romanza "Caro suono lusinghier" from *Tebaldo ed Isolina*   123
17. Riccardo Broschi's aria "Qual guerriero in campo armato," excerpt   135
18. Riccardo Broschi, excerpts from "Son qual nave" as included in Farinelli's presentation manuscript   143
19. Handel, short score of "Se bramate, d'amar chi vi sdegna," from *Serse*, mm. 9-59   155
20. Handel, short score of "Ombra mai fu"   160
21. Christoph Willibald Gluck, *Paride ed Elena*, "O del mio dolce ardor," mm. 1-23   191
22. Gluck, *Orfeo ed Euridice*, recitative, "Smanio, fremo e deliro," act 3, scene 1   193
23. Aria by Giuseppe Sarti, "Non dubitar—Là tu vedrai," mm. 24-71   197
24. Antonio Sacchini / Domenico Cimarosa, *Se cerca se dice* sung by Sig.r Marchesi, in the opera *Olimpiade*, opening   201
25. Second recitative from Haydn, "Arianna a Nasso" (Hob.XXVIb:2), mm. 188-222   203
26. Nicola Zingarelli, "Idolo del mio cor," recitative transcribed from Zingarelli's *Giulietta e Romeo*   214
27. Zingarelli, "Tranquillo io son," recitative transcribed from Zingarelli's *Giulietta e Romeo*   216
28. Girolamo Crescentini, short score of "Ombra adorata, aspetta / Rondeau / inserito nel dramma serio di / Giulietta, e Romeo / del Sig. Girolamo Crescentini / in Reggio la Fiera dell'anno / 1796"   218
29. Crescentini's "Ombra adorata, aspetta" with ornaments, from Garcia's *Traité complet*   225
30. Three melody lines for Crescentini's "Ombra adorata, aspetta!"   230
31. *Souvenir à Pasta, et Rubini*, no. 5, "Ombra adorata aspetta," Cavatina de l'opera *Romeo et Giulietta, de Zingarelli*   241
32. *Tranquillo io son Recitative—Ombra adorata, aspetta! The Celebrated Air sung by Madame Pasta in the Opera Romeo e Giulietta composed by Zingarelli*   244
33. Facsimile from print of Crescentini's aria *Tranquillo io son / Ombra adorato [sic] aspetta . . . sung by Madame Catalani . .*, mm. 10-12   246

FIGURES

1. Surgical preparation for testicular castration, from Caspar Stromayr, *Practica copiosa*   Following page 76

2. Jacopo Amigoni, Farinelli crowned by Music
3. Corrado Giaquinto, Farinelli with King Ferdinand VI and Queen Maria Barbara
4. Anton Maria Zanetti, caricature of two castrati with their prime donne
5. Zanetti, castrato Filippo Balatri
6. John Faber Jr., mezzotint of Giovanni Carestini
7. Bartolomeo Nazari, young Farinelli
8. Photograph of Domenico Mustafà in 1898
9. Andrea Sacchi, Marc'Antonio Pasqualini crowned by Apollo
10. Pier Leone Ghezzi, caricature of Andrea Adami da Bolsena
11. Ghezzi, caricature of Valeriano Pellegrini
12. Ghezzi, caricature of Antonio Bernacchi
13. Zanetti, caricature of Bernacchi
14. Zanetti's depiction of the tenor Salvatici
15. Greek equerry following his master
16. Ludovico Ottavio Burnacini, *Pulcinella*, watercolor
17. Anonymous painting of Pulcinella birthing little Pulcinellini
18. C. Lindstrom, Pulcinella *cantastorie,* singing outdoors in the Largo del Castello
19. Giandomenico Tiepolo, drawing of Pulcinella hatching from the egg of a turkey
20. Anonymous painting of Pulcinella and the Bourbons
21. Zanetti, Bernacchi in street clothes watching a Pulcinella puppet show
22. Francesco Bertelli, "Maschera di Pulisinella"
23. Peter Jakob Horemans, *Court Concert at Schloß Ismaning*
24. Zanetti, Nicola Tricarico
25. Zanetti, Farinelli in traveling clothes
26. Zanetti, Senesino among friends
27. Jacopo Amigoni, *Farinelli e i suoi amici*
28. The lungs, larynx, and nasopharyngeal tract as drawn by David M. Howard   84
29. Zanetti, caricature of Bernacchi singing a cadenza   102
30. Pier Leone Ghezzi's sketch sheet of various singers, castrated and not   104
31. Poster announcing a performance by the Quartetto Vocale Romano Gabrielli-Gentili   131
32. Leonardo Marini's drawing of a castrato dressed to play the Maometto Gran Mogul   Following page 174
33. John Vanderbank, painting of Senesino as Bertarido in Handel's *Rodelinda*
34. Charles Joseph Flipart, painting of Carlo Scalzi
35. James Hutchinson, portrait of Venanzio Rauzzini
36. Portal over the front of the house of Caffarelli, bearing the inscription "AMPHYON THEBAS EGO DOMUM ANNO MDCCLIV"

37. G. Stuppi, lithograph of Caffarelli in neoclassical garb
38. Farinelli's villa
39. Zanetti, caricature of Andrea Pacini
40. Zanetti, caricature of Castorino
41. Zanetti, caricature of Nicolini, pointing to an alligator-like nobleman
42. Ghezzi, caricature of Domenico Annibali
43. Ghezzi, caricature of Farinelli in female dress at age nineteen
44. Ghezzi, drawing of Gaetano Berenstadt
45. Engraved woodcut by the alchemist Leonhard Thurneysser showing humors in relation to the human body
46. John Nixon, caricature of Luigi Marchesi in concert
47. Ghezzi, sketch of Farfallino of Urbino
48. Engraving of Girolamo Crescentini as the Cavaliere dell'Ordine di Croce di Ferro
49. Engraving of Giuditta Pasta as Romeo in Zingarelli's *Giulietta e Romeo*
50. Pacchierotti (attributed), *Modi generali del canto*, title page
51. Crescentini, title page of *Raccolta di essercizi*
52. Anne-Louis Girodet de Roussy-Trioson, *The Sleep of Endymion*
53. Alfred Edward Chalon, watercolor of Giambattista Velluti

INDEX

Abbate, Carolyn, 249, 308n1
Abrahams, Darren, 101
absolutism: across different kinds of polities, 270n15; castrati and, xvi, 9, 149, 150, 207; Della Lena's musical, 205; in refeudalization of Europe, 277n18
acciaccaturas, 127
Adami da Bolsena, Andrea, 11, 62, Fig. 10
Adonis myths, 252–54
Adriano in Siria (Metastasio and Pergolesi), 166, 340n73, 341n74
Agamemnon, xiii
Agatea, Mario, 62
agility singing, 80, 133, 134, 151–52, 177, 196
Agricola, Johann Friedrich, 86, 112, 142
Agujari, Lucrezia, 142
Albergati Capacelli, Francesco, 177–78, 207, 344n1
Albinoni, Tomaso, 57
Albizzi, Luca Casimiro degli, 165–66
Alboni, Marietta, 299n69
Albrecht V of Bavaria, Duke, 7
Algarotti, Francesco, 142, 179–80, 297n61, 298n63, 350n44
Allegri, Gregorio, 29
allegro, 133
Amadori (Giovanni Tedeschi; Giovanni Filippo Maria Dreyer; Il Tedeschino), 61, 62, 95, 180, 300n84

Amigoni, Jacopo, 9, 66, 75, 173, 302n98, Fig. 2, Fig. 27
Aminta (Albinoni), 57
Ancillon, Charles: on castrati voices, 308n2; on eunuch marriage, 14, 49–50; on Mommo, 126; on Nicolini's proposal of marriage, 49, 185; on Pauluccio, 46–47, 73, 280n42; on prophylactic value of castration, 279n36; treatise on eunuchs, 14, 274n6
Anderson, Benedict, 272n28
Andreoni, Giovanni Battista, 71
androgyny, 5, 22, 24, 251
Angelou, Maya, 125
animal myths, 4
Annibali, Domenico, 181, 183, Fig. 42
Ansani, Giovanni, 127, 235
Antigona (Zeno and Mysliveček), 167
Antigono (Gluck), 111
appoggiatura, 40, 118, 147
Aprile, Giuseppe: agility singing of, 133; in "la bonne école," 235; book of solfeggi of, 324n107; brother Raffaello, 65; as composer, 6; in flamboyant line, 189; freelances in secular world, 61; as Kelly's teacher, 305n114, 324n107; at Perugia theater reopening, 171; Quick Time audio files for, 275n8; returns to his native patria, 71–72; in Zeno and Mysliveček's *Antigona*, 167

405

Argens, Jean Baptiste de Boyer, Marquis d', 44, 200, 205, 288n5
"Arianna a Naxos" (Haydn), 200, 203–4
arias: increasing bravura in, 134, 147; increasing length of, 142
Ariès, Philippe, 60, 180
Aristotle, 48–49, 185
Arnabaldi, Cristoforo, 172, 343n95
Arne, Thomas, 51
arpeggiato, 152
Artaserse (Hasse), 40–43, 288n2
Artaxerxes (Arne), 51
Aumont, Arnulphe de, 179
Aureliano in Palmira (Rossini), 260
Avanzati, Elisabetta, 73
Avrillon, Mademoiselle d' (Charles-Maxime Villemarest), 215, 217

Babbini, Matteo, 235
Bach, Johann Christian, 6
Bach-Gounod *Ave Maria* (*Méditation sur le premier prélude de piano de S. Bach*), 82, 83, 86, 88
Bagniera, Antonio (Antoine), 367n76
Bagnolesi, Anna, 64, Fig. 25
Balatri, Ferrante, 65, 302n94
Balatri, Filippo: on being deprived of fatherhood, 73–74; on being the "baron of the piazza," 74; brother Ferrante, 65, 302n94; as capon, 11, 30, Fig. 5; on castrati and Pulcinella, xviii; on castration as victimization, 56; castration of, 55–56; on castrato myth of origin, 18, 30, 162; funeral plan of, 56–57; on his body's destiny after death, 208–9; on his coldness, 56, 185; on his singing voice, 55–56, 107, 108; in Horemans's *Court Concert at Schloß Ismaning*, 57, 101, Fig. 23; jaw of, Fig. 23; melancholy of, 74; as monk, 62; prose and verse autobiographies of, 18, 56, 282n57; in Russia, 18, 63, 301n89, 340n65; satirical nature of writings, xviii; self-mockery of, 50, 73, 181; on solo coloratura, 57–58, 298n63; surgeons named by, 12, 278n31; "Testamento," 57, 279n31; training of, 62; verses on falling in love with women, 50; on whether he was male or female, 18–19; will of, 73–74; Zanetti's depiction of, 11, Fig. 5
Balzac, Honoré de: on castrato legacy, 212; on Crescentini, 243; Malibran heard by, 367n87; *Massimilla Doni*, 250. See also *Sarrasine* (Balzac)

Banti, Brigida, 235
Barber, Patricia, 125
Il barbiere di Siviglia (Rossini), 152, 153, 337n41
Baroe, Charles, 53
Barthes, Roland, xxii, 79, 250–52, 271n18
"Basta, basta, o compagni" (*Orfeo ed Euridice*), 213
Bataille, Georges, 162, 167
battaglini, 29
Battistini, Mattia, 126
Beaumarchais, Pierre-Augustin-Caron de, 250
Beccaria, Cesare, 180
Beghelli, Marco, 105, 320n67, 363n41
bel canto: castrati and, xii, 128, 205–6, 269n1; Crescentini on, 248; as nostalgia, 109–10, 322n93, 323n94; origins of, xxii; Pasta aligned with, 243; portamento of, 122; revival of repertory, 153; shift in vocal production in, 153; in training of early-twentieth-century singers, 127
Belcastro, Maria Giovanna, 278n25
Bellini, Vincenzo, xii, xxii, 109, 238
Bellucci La Salandra, Mario, 288n5
Benedict XIV, Pope, 179
Benelli, Antonio, 110, 359n6
Bennati, Francesco, 59, 363n41
Beregan, Niccolò, 147
Berenstadt, Gaetano: in book trade, 65, 302n93; as first son, 13; Ghezzi's depiction of, 101, 183, Fig. 44; jokes made about, 73; moves to Naples, 65; returns to his hometown, 305n115
Bergson, Henri, 272n20
Berlioz, Hector, xxii, 238, 249, 250, 365n61
Bernacchi, Antonio Maria: agility singing, 133; Balatri appears on same stage as, 57, 96, 97–98; Bolognese school of, 95, 127; in "la bonne école," 235; contest with Farinelli, 134, 330n4; Farinelli influenced by, 257; Ghezzi's depiction of, 17, 101, Fig. 12; honorific title for, 341n85, Fig. 21; instrumental style of singing of, 57, 96, 298n63; jaw of, 101; on Martini's motet, 275n9; on "mettere bene la voce," 338n47; Quantz on Carestini and, 95; Quick Time audio files for, 275n8; returns to his native patria, 305n115; solfeggi of, 57, 96; students of, 58, 59; teacher Pistocchi, 72, 127, 257; upward extension of, 96; Zanetti's depictions of, 17, 26, 64, Fig. 13, Fig. 21, Fig. 29a, b, and c
Bernardi, Francesco. See Senesino (Francesco Bernardi)

Berni, Francesco, 279n32
Berry, Helen, 51, 53, 295n41, 295n42
Bertelli, Francesco, 47, Fig. 22
Bertini, Argia, 299n73
Berton, Henri-Montan, 261
Bianchi, Giovanni Antonio, 179
Biber, Heinrich Ignaz Anton von, 147
Bigelli, Antonio Girolamo (Memmo; Mommo; Girolamo di Rospiglioso), 101, 126, 349n34, Fig. 30
binary sexual regime, xxi, 183, 303n101
Birchall, Robert, 243, 246, 364n52
birdsong, 147, 332n12
Bjoerling, Jussi, 108
Blainville, Charles de, 179, 207
blood: in Adonis myths, 253; in Balzac's *Sarrasine*, 256–57; harm by wild animals checked by acts of bloodshed, 16; symbolism of, xiv–xv, xvii
Boccaccio, Giovanni, 256, 367n78
Bononcini, Giovanni, 105, 112, 159, 337n44
Bontempi, Giovanni Andrea Angelini: on Ferri, 112–13, 152, 281n46; *Historia musica*, 29; on Mazzocchi, 58–59, 298n68; on order and "divine singing," 29; on power of semen, 48
Bordoni, Faustina, 57, 65, 142, 151, 298n62, Fig. 4
Bori, Lucrezia, 127
Bourdieu, Pierre, 258
Brauner, Patricia B., 316n40
bravura, 133–47; of Caffarelli, 154, 159, 161; Milizia on, 186; Orphic versus bravura castrati, xxi, 206; otherness of bravura castrato, 150; Tosi on, xx
breath control: in agility singing, 151; of Caffarelli, 159; of castrati, 105; in eighteenth-century singing manuals, 335n32; of Farinelli, 43, 134; as marker of aesthetic and social difference, 154; *messa di voce* and, 116; Tosi on, xx; unwritten embellishments require, 112
Bristed, Grace, 128
Brodsky, Seth, 327n129
Brooke, Frances, 182
Broschi, Carlo. *See* Farinelli (Carlo Broschi)
Broschi, Matteo Pisani, 71, 73, 169
Broschi, Riccardo: death of, 71; follows his brother, 66; *Idaspe*, 10, 173; "Qual guerriero in campo armato," 10, 134, 135–41, 173, 330n2; "Son qual nave ch'agitata," 43, 142; on vocal coloration, 195
Broschi family, 271n17
Brownlee, Lawrence, 101

Bruni, Domenico: on his castration, 14; honorific title for, 342n85; returns to his native patria, 72, 169; teacher of, 60
Bryson, H. C., 312n14
Bulgarelli, Maria Benti, 69
Buning, Robert Anthony, 309n6, 314n30
Burnacini, Lodovico Ottavio, 22, Fig. 16
Burney, Charles: on Caffarelli, 161; on Carestini, 105; on Castellini, 303n100; on castrati voices, 308n2; on Conservatorio di Sant'Onofrio, 286n95; daughter Susanna, 50; on Egizziello, 301n84; on Farinelli, 43, 72, 73, 106, 134, 148, 210, 303n100, 330n2, 331n8, 358n90; on Guarducci, 170–71; on Manzuoli, 321n82; on Pistocchi, 297n61; on Rauzzini, 321n76; on Ricciarelli, 322n83; on Rubinelli, 94; on secrecy about castrations, 13; on Senesino, 43, 108
Burney, Susanna, 50, 106, 188, 196, 235, 294n36, 321n80
Burzio, Eugenia, 83, 84, 86, 89, 313n21
Bustamante, Hernando, 6

Cabanis, Pierre Jean George, 236
Caccini, Giulio, 90, 110, 314n34
cadetti, xv, 275n7
Caffarelli (Gaetano Majorano): agility singing of, 133; bravura of, 154, 159, 161; contests of, 26; as dependent on written-out form, 147; in duels, 161, 340n71; in economy of luxury, 162; as enfant terrible, 159, 161–62; freelances in secular world, 61; gifts for, 166; in Handel's *Serse*, 154–59; on his teacher, 59; honorific title for, 342n85; portal of Naples house of, Fig. 36; retirement of, 172, 343n96; roles of, 166, 340n72; as royal double, 153–62; Stich's depiction of, Fig. 37; sweet (ringing) voice of, 106, 107; timbre of, 105
Calcina, Giacomo, 298n66
Caldara, Antonio, 57
Caldwell, Robert, 124
Callas, Maria, 152, 153, 336n37, 337n41
Calvé, Emma, 122, 124, 125, 128, 153, 328n135
Calzabigi, Ranieri de', 26, 147, 187, 190, 213
La Campioli (Margherita Gualandi), 64–65
Camporesi, Piero, xiv, 270n6
Cancellieri, Felice, 302n95
Candide (Voltaire), 179
canon law, xiii, 14, 16
Canzonetta di Nice (Metastasio), 67
Capocci, Gaetano, 127, 128, 129–30

408 INDEX

capons: Balatri depicted as, 11, 30, Fig. 5; Balatri describes himself as, 73; Bernacchi described as, 330n4; castrati cast as, 3, 17, 18, 26, 27, 181, 285n72
"Cara negli occhi tuoi" (*Pirro, re di Epiro*), 117–18, 195–96
Carestini, Giovanni (Il Cusanino): agility singing, 133; in *Artaserse*, 288n2; chest voice of, 94–95; English make jokes about, 73; Faber's print of, 11, Fig. 6; timbre of, 105; vocal fold calcification in, 89; Zanetti's depiction of, 64
Carlino. *See* Scalzi, Carlo (Carlino)
Carlo II, Duke of Mantua, 50
Carlyle, Thomas, 108
Carnival, xix, 22, 24, 286n87
"Caro suono lusinghier" (*Tebaldo ed Isolina*), 224, 239–40
Carpani, Giuseppe, 246
Casanova, Giovanni Giacomo, 29, 30, 44–45, 72
Casimiri, Raffaele, 329n154
Castellini, Teresa, 66, 68, 302n98, Fig. 27
Castelvecchi, Stefano, 285n71
Castorino, 181, 348n23, Fig. 40
castrati: adaptive strategies of, xvii, xix; agility singing in, 80, 133; Ancillon's treatise on, 14, 274n6; angelic representational imagery for, 29–30; apprenticeship of, 6; as band of brothers, 63, 75; banned from papal chapel, 81, 129; beastly stereotypes of, 181–84; Berlioz on, 249, 250; boyishness of, xx, 11, 44, 50, 166–67; bravura versus Orphic, xxi, 206; break in male operatic tradition after, 109; as capons, 3, 17, 18, 26, 27, 181, 285n72; career options for, 60–64; caricatures of, 3–4, 10–11, 17–22, 43; during Carnival season, 24; as celibate, xv, 46; chest voice of, 90–96, 105; class background of, 15, 46; clergy and phenomenon of, 206–7; coldness associated with, 55–58, 184–88; as composers, 6, 275n8; contests of, 26–27, 133–34; countertenors contrasted with, 98; cultural capital gained by, xi; as cut, 56, 74; as decidedly male, xvii; decline in numbers of, xviii, 46, 207–8, 272n24, 275n10, 290n14; and delimitation of human body, 208; deluxe, 19, 159, 164, 167, 172, 179, 254, 257; diplomatic missions by, 170; disappearance of, xxii, 238, 254; earliest, 6, 276n11; 1830 as significant year for, 238, 252; electronic reconstruction of voice of, 101; Enlightenment disapproval of, xxi, 44, 177–81, 183–84, 207, 212, 289n6; erections in, 50, 54, 274n6, 292n27; as exaggeration of maleness, 25–26; factors contributing to becoming, xvi–xvii, 7; father figures for, 63; as figures of luxury, 148; in France, 211, 212, 250; friends of, 64–66; in Germany, 6–7; gifts for, 164–66; Greek phallic grotesques compared with, 22, Fig. 15; heirs of, 72–73; heroic physical characteristics of stars, 170–71; ideal type of, 11–12; as income sources, 29; as infertile, xii, xvii, xix, 44, 45, 48, 50, 253; journeymen, 5; last one's death, xi, 275n10; male elites representatives represented by, 25; maleness questioned, 43–45; marriage by, 14, 48, 49–55; *messa di voce* by, 113–14; metal terms to describe voices of, 107–12; as monarchs' representatives, xix–xx, 9, 149–50, 166–70; and money, 26–27, 29, 30, 49; as monks, 62; as musical elite, 5–6; myths regarding, 4–5; Napoleonic proscription of, 211, 212; natal family renounced by, 28; navigating between registers, 317n42; and new way of thinking about maleness, 206; as non-normative male, 25, 44; as object-encrusted, 259; passage-work by, 114; patriliny associated with, xvi–xvii, 45–46; pregnancy attributed to, 47–48, Fig. 22; as priests, 62, 301n86; Pulcinella associated with, xviii–xix, 22–26; purity of voice in, 321n79; recordings of last, xx, 81–82; and refeudalization of Europe, 8–9; reinventing "natural" order by, 66; as reproducers of other castrati, 292n23; retirements of, 171–73; return to their native patria, 71–72, 305n115; Rossini and, xii, xxii, 6, 110, 259–60, 261; as sacralized creature, xx, 29; selecting, 5; sexuality of, 5, 44, 274n6; siblings of, 65–66; singer's formant in, 99; sing in Catholic Church, xiii, 5, 7; social networks of, 63–64; as stars, 30, 170–71; survival of sound of, 126–32; as teachers, 59–60; terminology for, xi; as third kind, 44; titles for, xx, 168–69, 341n85; training of, 28–29, 58–59, 298n67; transactional, 162–66; transition from public arena to private luxury, 148–49; as uncles, 47, 174; as unnatural, 178, 180, 183, 210; variety of roles of, 24; vocal cords (folds) in, 100–101, 319n57; vocal fold calcification in, 89; vocal technology of, xx, 114; voice box (larynx) in, 100–101, 105; voices of, xi, xx–xxi, 5, 10, 44, 79–132; who they were, 5–6; wills of, 70; woman take over roles of, 212, 237–38, 260
castration (testicular): accident said to be cause of, xvii, 14–15, 47, 80; age of, 11, 278n28;

attainment through, xii–xiii, 16; Barthes on "axis of," 251; Catholic Church forbids, xiii, 5, 7, 8; Catholic Church instigates, 8; consent required for, 14; developmental problems result from, 10–11; as form of male reproduction, 47; Freud on, 75; hormonal effects of, xi; justifications and explanations for, xiii–xiv, 3, 12, 13, 14–15, 17, 47, 54; male authority sanctions, 47; for medical reasons, 13, 14, 271n16; obfuscations surrounding, 12; paradoxes regarding, 9–10; as perlocutionary, xiii, 16; political valence of, 180–81; preparing for, Fig. 1; prophylactic and therapeutic uses of, 14, 16; as renunciation, xii–xiii, 16, 28; as sacred donation to the Church, xiii, 7, 14, 47; as sacrifice, xii–xiii, xv–xvi, xvii–xviii, 7, 14–17, 27–29, 47, 53, 168; surgeons for, 12–13; symbolism of blood, xiv–xv, xvii; techniques of, 7–8; underground commerce in child, 60; vocal cords affected by, 10, 11; wounds compared with, 15–16, 54

"Il castrato" (*Lamento del castrato*) (cantata), 19–22, 31–34, 283n63

Catalani, Angelica, 224, 243, 246, 361n22

Catherine of Siena, Saint, xiv

Catholic Church: Benedict XIV on castrati, 179; canon law, xiii, 14, 16; castration as sacred donation to, xiii, 7, 14, 47; castration forbidden by, xiii, 5, 7; castrations instigated by, 8; castrati sing in, xiii, 5, 7; Enlightenment reformist incursions on church power, 207; Innocent XI on castrati marriage, 50; Sixtus V on castrati, 48; women not allowed to sing in, xiii, 5. *See also* Sistine Chapel

Cavalletti, Giulio Maria (Giulietto), 61, 300n80, 305n115

Cavalli, Pier Francesco, 6, 62, 106

Cecchi, Domenico (Il Cortona), 50, 170

Cecchini, Ezio, 130

celebrity, cult of, 149, 163

celibacy: castrati as celibate, xv, 46; decline in number of celibates, xviii, 272n24; patriliny and increase in, xvii; for younger sons, 45

Celoni, Anna Maria Pellegrini, 113

Cervantes, Xavier, 307n126

Cesari, Giovanni, 126, 127, 260, 310n8, 311n10

Chalon, Edward Alfred, 260, Fig. 53

Chappell & Co., 115, 240, 243, 244

charisma, 150

"Charmant oiseau" (David), 125, 328n135

Charterhouse of Parma, The (Stendhal), 367n88

chest voice: of castrati, 90–96, 105; of Duprez, 109; in early recordings, 116; forced, 116; Garcia on, 86, 89–90; Mancini on, 93; of Moreschi, 84–85; physiology of register, 96–100; of Senesino, 94; in speech pathology, 85; superseded by penchant for high notes, 110; unforced, 98, 126

chickens: in animal myths, 4; castrati glossed as, 30, 209; death associated with, 27; money associated with, 27; Pantalone and, 26; Pulcinella associated with, 24, 25. *See also* capons

child development, 60

Il ciarlator maldicente (Albergati), 177–78, 344n1

Cigna-Santi, Vittorio Amadeo, 167, Fig. 32

Cimarosa, Domenico: Sacchini's "Se cerca, se dice" rewritten for Marchesi by, 199–200, 201–2; Théâtre Italien stages works of, 365n63; writing for castrati as goal of, 6

Clapton, Nicholas, 101, 312n15

closed quotient, 98–99

Colbran, Isabella, 110, 127, 153, 336n40

Colonna, Giovanni Battista, 61

color, 85, 89, 195

coloratura: Balatri on solo, 57–58, 298n63; becomes ever more elaborate, 112; of Bernacchi, 350n44; of Caffarelli, 166; command of castrati over, 178; castrato-like, 153; in composed-out arias, 134; of Farinelli, 10, 134; of Gabrielli, 185; marked, 152–53; mechanistic, 147; Metastasio on, 185–86, 350n43; of Moreschi, 89, 196; pure head sound of older singers, 122; of Senesino, 94; of Storace, 196

comportamento, 116

composers: castrati as, 6; singers alter scores of, 205; singers' status compared with that of, 142

Conestabile, Giancarlo, 331n10

conservatories, Neapolitan, 28–29

Conservatorio dei Poveri di Gesù Cristo, 29

Conservatorio della Pietà dei Turchini, 28

Conservatorio di Santa Maria di Loreto, 286n92

Conservatorio di Sant'Onofrio, 286n95

Consoni, Don Giovanni Battista, 59

Conti, Giacomo, 229, 230–34, 240, 243, 361n28

Conti, Gioacchino (Egizziello; Gizziello), 59, 62, 110, 301n84

Corey, Jacquelynne, 96

Corri, Domenico, 113, 115, 118, 121, 133

Il Cortona (Domenico Cecchi), 50, 170

Costa, Andrea, 110

countertenors, 98, 105
Crescentini, Girolamo: agility singing of, 133; Balzac's *Sarrasine*'s Marianina and, 258–59; on bel canto, 110; in "la bonne école," 235; on breath control, 335n32; Colbran as student of, 110, 127, 153, 336n40; as composer, 6; Gibelli as teacher of, 127; knighting of, xx, 54, 212, Fig. 48; Maelzel on a mechanical, 261; melody line for "Ombra adorata, aspetta," 230–34; on *messa di voce*, 116; in Napoleonic court, 211–12, 250; "Ombra adorata, aspetta" sung by, 122, 217–24, 240, 243, 246–47; Pasta compared with, 240, 243; *Raccolta di esercizi per il canto all'uso del vocalizzo con discorso preliminare del signor Girolamo Crescentini*, 110, 247–48, Fig. 51; Schopenhauer on voice of, 107; solfeggi of, 336n34; Stendhal on, 212, 237, 247, 364n57; as teacher, 59; time difference between early recording and singing of, 153; Velluti compared with, 237; Vigny on, 250; in Zingarelli's *Giulietta e Romeo*, 211, 212, 213–17, 238, 251, 359n6, 366n65
Creus, Eugène de, 113
Crimes and Punishments (Beccaria), 180
cross-dressing, 44, 289n5
Crowther, J. Victor, 299n73
Crumb, George, 124, 327n129
Crutchfield, Will, 81, 90, 116, 153, 229, 313n19, 314n27, 315n37, 360n16, 361n24, 362n35, 364n53
Il Cusanino. *See* Carestini, Giovanni (Il Cusanino)
Cuzzoni, Francesca, 142

Dado, Stéphane, 363n43
Dame, Joke, 366n68
D'Amico, F., 274n6
Daniels, David, 325n111
Daston, Lorraine, 180–81, 330n3
David, Félicien, 125, 328n135
David, Giacomo, 235
Davidson, James, 69, 305n111
Davies, J. Q., 361n24, 363n41
Davis, Natalie Zemon, 149
De Amicis, Anna, 142, 235
Dean, Winston, 337n44
De Angelis, Alberto, 129
De Castris (De' Massimi), Francesco, 50, 170, 334n20
De l'amour (Stendhal), 235
Delany, Mary Granville Pendarves, 106
Delécluze, Étienne-Jean, 213, 215, 217

Della Lena, Innocenzo: on best and worst singers of his time, 206; on castrati, 207; on forbidding singers to alter composer's score, 205; on Marchesi, 184, 186, 188, 195, 199, 200
De Martino, Ernesto, 282n54
De' Massimi (De Castris), Francesco, 50, 170, 334n20
Derksen, Jörg Wilhelm Walter, 311n10
Derrida, Jacques, 164
De Simone, Roberto, 27
Destrutt de Tracy, Antoine Louis Claude, 236
Diabelli, Anton, 240, 241, 243
Diderot, Denis, 237, 253
Didone abbandonata (Metastasio), 147
Di Giacomo, Salvatore, 287n97
Di Lasso, Orlando, 7
Di Maio, Giuseppe, 142, 305n111
Dimitrescu, Giovanni, 108
Di Rospiglioso, Girolamo (Memmo; Mommo; Antonio Girolamo Bigelli), 101, 126, 349n34, Fig. 30
Dolar, Mladen, 251
Domingo, Placido, 101, 108
Doniger, Wendy, 55, 70, 304n109
Donington, Robert, 309n3, 311n11
Donizetti, Gaetano, xii, xxii, 89, 109
Donzelli, Domenico, 363n41
Dos Santos, Augusto, 130
Dreyer, Giovanni Filippo Maria (Giovanni Tedeschi; Il Tedeschino; Amadori), 61, 62, 95, 180, 300n84
Du bist mein Gluck (film), 127, 329n144
Duey, Philip A., 322n93
Duncan, Michelle, 308n1
Duprez, Gilbert-Louis, xxii, 109, 127, 153
Durante, Sergio, 91, 290n14, 297n60, 323n94, 333n14, 353n56
Durastanti, Margherita, 64, 114, 325n112, Fig. 26

Eames, Emma, 83, 84, 86, 152, 153, 313n21
Egizziello (Gioacchino Conti; Gizziello), 59, 62, 110, 301n84
Elisi, Filippo, 196
Elyot, Sir Thomas, 172
Émile (Rousseau), 60, 299n75
Eppinger, Heinrich, 229, 230–34, 240, 243, 361n29
Erculeo, Marzio, 59, 299n73
Evelyn, John, 106, 113, 154
Evening at Rossini's in Beau-Sejour (Passy) 1858, An (Michotte), 259–60, 323n96
"L'evirazione" (Verri), 180
Exsultate, jubilate (Mozart), 177

Faber, John, Jr., 11, Fig. 6
Facchinelli, Lucia (La Beccheretta), Fig. 4
Fago, Nicola, 306n123
Faix-Brown, Winifred, 159
falsettists: boys introduced to sing alongside, 310n7; castrati replace in papal chapel, 48; and castrati sing high parts, 6; castrato voice contrasted with that of, 44; falsetto as head voice, 85; female, 326n126, 327n127; Garcia on falsetto, 86; *haute-contres*, 179, 250, 354n62; Domenico Mancini as, 95; Giambattista Mancini on falsetto voice, 93, 112; physiology of falsetto mechanics, 314n33; physiology of register, 96, 318n52; *voci finte*, 90
Farfallino (Giacinto Fontana), 206, Fig. 47
Farinelli (Carlo Broschi): agility singing of, 133; Amigoni's portraits of, 9, 66, 75, 173, 302n98, Fig. 2, Fig. 27; Bernacchi as influence on, 257; in "la bonne école," 235; in bourgeois order, 9, 280n42; brother Riccardo, 10, 66, 71; brother Riccardo's "Qual guerriero in campo armato," 135–41, 173; brother Riccardo's "Son qual nave ch'agitata," 134, 142; Burney on, 148, 331n8; on Caffarelli, 161; castration of, 15, 75–76, 271n17, 279n36; childhood accident of, 15, 75–76; as composer, 6; contest with Bernacchi, 134, 330n4; contest with trumpeter, 26, 133–34, 330n2; on cost of living in London, 163, 339n57; Crudeli on voice of, 171; in economy of luxury, 162–63; English make jokes about, 73, 306n126; father figures of, 66; friendship with Metastasio, 50, 66–70; Ghezzi's caricatures of, 11, 25, 181, 183, Fig. 4, Fig. 43; Giaquinto's depiction of, 9, 171, 173, Fig. 3; gifts for, 164–65; grandniece of, 71, 72, 173; in Hasse's *Artaserse*, 40, 41, 148; heir of, 71, 72–73, 169, 257; on himself as "despicable creature," 73, 210, 358n90; in knighthood of Calatrava, xx, 66, 71, 169, Fig. 3; in love with a woman, 50; Mancini on Ferri and, 336n38; melancholy of, 74; Nazari's depiction of, 163, Fig. 7; *passaggio scivolato* of, 118, 151; patriarchal character of, 290n10; "Per questo dolce amplesso" sung by, 41; physical characteristics of, 278n25; portraits owned by, 173, 344n103; pregnancy attributed to, 48, 67, 291n22, 303n101; Quantz on Carestini and, 95; Quick Time audio files for, 275n8; range of, 95; retirement of, 71, 172–74, 343n100, Fig. 38; royal connections of, 9, 291n17; satirized as amphibious being, 346n8; seeks to secure a sister-in-law, 70–71; Senesino's embrace of, 43, 49; at Spanish court, xix, 9, 66, 148, 154, 164–65, Fig. 3; sweet voice of, 106, 320n76; timbre of, 105; trills by, 152; at Turin opera house, 1713, 10; variety of roles of, 148; vocal embellishments of, 308n2; Zanetti's depiction of, 64, 183, Fig. 25
La favorita (Donizetti), 89
Feldman, Martha: "Castrato Acts," 271n18, 285n46, 289n5; "Moreschi and Fellini," 294n36; "Strange Births and Surprising King," 357n85. See also *Opera and Sovereignty* (Feldman)
Ferri, Baldassare: "angelic" singing of, 29; castration of, 13; Conestabile on, 331n10; honorific title for, xx, 281n46; Kandler on clear, light singing of, 328n140; knighthood for, 169, 341n83; Mancini on Farinelli and, 336n38; *passaggio* of, 112–13, 147; returns to his native patria, 72; social climbing by, 291n17; sweet voice of, 106; time difference between early recording and singing of, 153; trills of, 152; virility said to be in his voice, 48
Fetonte (Jommelli), 142, 147
Fielding, Henry, 48, 291n22
Finazzi, Filippo, 51
Finucci, Valeria, 48, 285n76
Flipart, Charles Joseph, 171, 183, 342n93, Fig. 34
Florimo, Francesco, 110
flute tones, 124–26, 128
Fodor, Joséphine, 258
Fontana, Agostino, 151
Fontana, Giacinto (Farfallino), 206, Fig. 47
Fontana, Teresa Bolognini, 298n66
Foppa, Giuseppe, 249, 359n11, 360n12
Foreman, Edward V., 314n34
formants, 98, 99, 100, 101, 108
Foucault, Michel, 142
Frandsen, Mary, 53, 54, 55, 296n51
Frati, Ludovico, 338n47
Freitas, Roger, 25, 44, 50, 66, 166, 169, 289n5, 293n30, 311n11, 314n28
Freud, Sigmund, 75, 251, 271n20, 307n129
Frugoni, Carlo Innocenzo, 196
Frye, Northrop, xviii, 272n21, 272n22

Gabrielli, Alessandro, 130, 132, 309n5, 328n138
Gabrielli, Caterina, 142, 185, 186, 235, 350n45
Gagnidze, George, 322n84
Galen, 15, 48, 184–85, 282n52, 349n40
Galliard, Johann Ernst, 91, 150, 151, 315n34
Galli-Curci, Amelita, 122
Garcia, Manuel del Pópulo Vicente Rodriguez (father), 127

Garcia, Manuel Patricio Rodriguez (son): on breath control, 335n32; chart of ambitus and registers for different voice types, 87; on children's timbre, 108; on falsetto, 112, 313n26; on male and female students, 85–86; Marchesi as student of, 153; on *messa di voce*, 113; "Ombra adorata, aspetta" of, 224–29, 243, 247, 249; on portamento, 118, 120; on singing high in chest, 99; *Traité complet de l'art du chant*, 85, 87, 122, 225–28, 329n147; on Velluti's "Caro suono lusinghier" from Morlacchi's *Tebaldo ed Isolina*, 239–40; Viardot as sister of, 127

Garcia Márquez, Gabriel, 3–4, 29–30, 250

Garrick, David, 182

Gasparini, Francesco, 61

Geertz, Clifford, 4, 272n28

Gell, Alfred, xx, 335n26

Gentilcore, David, 12

Gentili, Luigi, 130, 322n85

Gerbino, Giuseppe, 276n13

Gherardini, Rinaldo, 14

Ghezzi, Pier Leone: Adami da Bolsena depicted by, 11, Fig. 10; Annibali depicted by, 181, 183, Fig. 42; Berenstadt depicted by, 101, 183, Fig. 44; Bernacchi depicted by, 17, 101, Fig. 12; Farfallino depicted by, 206, Fig. 47; Farinelli depicted by, 11, 25, 181, 183, Fig. 4, Fig. 43; Pellegrini depicted by, 11, 168, 183, Fig. 11; Scalzi depicted by, 349n35; sketch sheet of, Fig. 30; Vendetta depicted by, 349n34; works on, 278n26

Giacomelli, Geminiano, 134

Giaquinto, Corrado, 9, 171, 173, Fig. 3

Gibelli, Lorenzo, 58, 127, 298n66

gifts, 164–66; in castrati transactions, 162–64; gift register, 149; in patron-client relations, xvi; of song, 162

Gigli, Beniamino, 127

Gilman, Sander, 183–84

Giovinardi (Zanardi), Nicolò, 58, 298n66

Giovio, Paolo, 15

Girodet de Roussy-Trioson, Anne-Louis, 252, Fig. 52

Giulietta e Romeo (Zingarelli): Crescentini in, 211, 212, 213–17, 238, 251, 359n6, 366n65; debut of, 217; "Idolo de mio cor," 213, 214–15; Pasta in, 224, 235, 238–39, 240–43, 246, 364n46, Fig. 49; "Tranquillo io son," 215, 216, 240, 244, 246; Vienna production of 1811, 213, 359n11. *See also* "Ombra adorata, aspetta"

Giulietto (Giulio Maria Cavalletti), 61, 300n80, 305n115

Giulio Cesare (Handel), 25

Giulio Sabino (Sarti), 196, 197–99

Giuseppino (Giuseppe Guspelti), 349n34

Il Giustino (Beregan and Legrenzi), 147

Gizzi, 59, 61

Gizziello (Egizziello; Gioacchino Conti), 59, 62, 110, 301n84

Gjerdingen, Robert O., 96, 275n8

Glixon, Beth L., 299n71

Gluck, Christoph Willibald: *Antigono*, 111; Calzabigi as librettist of, 26, 147; *Le feste d'Apollo*, 187, 190, 354n62; Millico as favorite of, 180; *Paride ed Elena*, 189, 190, 191–92. *See also Orfeo ed Euridice* (Gluck)

Goldoni, Carlo, 172, 337n46

Gonzaga, Guglielmo, 271n16, 294n36

Gorr, Rita, 108

Goudar, Ange, 250

Goudar, Sara, 29, 180, 307n126

Gounod, Charles: *Faust*, 89; *Méditation sur le premier prélude de piano de S. Bach* (Bach-Gounod *Ave Maria*), 82, 83, 86, 88, 128

Grassini, Josephina, 246, 359n6

Grimaldi, Nicola. *See* Nicolini (Nicola Grimaldi)

Grimm, Baron Friedrich Melchior von, 106, 161

Grossi, Giovanni Francesco. *See* Siface (Giovanni Francesco Grossi)

Guadagni, Gaetano: freelances in secular world, 61; in Gluck's *Orfeo ed Euridice*, 65, 169, 188, 189, 213, 354n62; knighthood for, 169; returns to his native patria, 72; sisters of, 65, 302n94

Gualandi, Margherita (La Campioli), 64–65

Guarducci, Tommaso, 95, 106, 170–71, 321n76

Guglielmi, Pietro Alessandro, 142

Guillaume Tell (Rossini), xxii, 109

Guspelti, Giuseppe (Giuseppino), 349n34

Habermas, Jürgen, 8, 277n18

Haböck, Franz: on animal bites and castration, 15, 281n50; on Gabrielli, 130, 132; on Moreschi, 89, 107, 108; on papal singers touring, 80, 309n5; on "Son qual nave ch'agitata," 330n6

Hacking, Ian, 349n36

Handel, George Frideric: arias of, 142; *Giulio Cesare*, 25; and Metastasio's preference in voices, 112; "Ombra mai fu," 101; "Perfido, di a quell'empio tiranno," 94; *Radamisto*, 94, 113, 325n112; *Rodelinda*, 171, Fig. 33; roles written for Senesino by, 25, 94, 113–14, 164, 171, Fig. 33; *Serse*, 154–59, 160–61, 337n44, 337n46, 337n47; and upward expansion of range, 110;

"Voglio che sia," 105; writing for castrati as goal of, 6
Handel and the Castrati (BBC program), 101
Harris, Ellen T., 325n110
Harvey, William, 185
Hasse, Johann Adolph, 40–43, 64, 91, 92–93
haute-contres, 179, 250, 354n62
Haydn, Joseph: "Arianna a Naxos," 200, 203–4; Rauzzini visited by, 172; "She Never Told Her Love," 118, 121; writing for castrati as goal of, 6
head voice (*voce di testa*): in early recordings, 116; Garcia (Patricio Rodriguez, aka Jr.) on, 86, 108; Mancini on, 93, 112; new age of, 112; physiology of register, 96, 100; pure, 122; as register, 85, 89; of Rubinelli, 94; of sopranos, 99; Tosi on, 327n130
Heartz, Daniel, 66, 302n98
Hegermann-Lindencrone (Greenough; Moulton), Lillie de, 127–28
Heifetz, Jascha, 122
Heller, Wendy, 290n10
Heriot, Angus, 294n33
hermaphrodites, 43, 289n5
Herr, Corinna, 6, 147, 276n12, 276n13, 315n34
Hidalgo, Elvira de, 152–53
high notes, 122–26
Hiller, Johann Adam, 93
Historia musica (Bontempi), 29
Hitchcock, Robert, 206
Hocart, A. M., xix, 272n28
Hoffmann, E. T. A., xxii, 243, 246–47, 250, 364n55
Hogarth, William, 183
Holmes, William C., 165, 302n92
Horemans, Peter Jacob, 57, Fig. 23
Horne, Marilyn, 113
Howard, David M., 96, 101, 107, 311n14, 318n52, Fig. 28
Howell, David, 309n5
Huarte, Juan, 185, 289n6
Hubert, Henri, xv–xvi, 168, 270n10
humoral theory, 14, 15, 38, 184–85, 279n36, Fig. 45
Hutchinson, James, Fig. 35
Hvorostovsky, Dmitri, 337n47

Idaspe (Broschi), 10, 173
"Idolo de mio cor" (*Giulietta e Romeo*), 213, 214–15, 329n147, 360n20
Ignorant Philosopher, The (Voltaire), 346n10
L'incoronazione di Poppea (Monteverdi), 11
Innocent XI, Pope, 50
intersex relations, 69, 178

Jenkins, J. S., 10
Jerome of Moravia, 85
Jommelli, Niccolò, 110, 142, 147, 354n62
Jones, Ann Rosalind, 289n5
Jorden, James, 322n84
Josephini, 358n1
July Revolution (1830), 238, 254

Kandler, Franz Sales, 328n140
Kantorowicz, Ernst, 167
Kelly, Michael, 305n114, 324n107
Kingsley, Charles, 109
Koestenbaum, Wayne, 366n68
Kristeva, Julia, 209–10

Lacan, Jacques, xxii, 79, 250, 251, 253
Lalande, Joseph de, 13
"Lamento dei Castrati: I Madrigali" (Marcello?), 35–36
"Lamento Dell'Impotente (Parole del Signor Melosi)", 36–39
Lang, Paul Henry, 80, 81, 122, 128–29, 132
larynx (voice box): cartilages of, 90; of castrati, 10, 11, 100–101, 105; diagram of vocal anatomy, Fig. 28; physiology of register, 96, 98, 101; register and, 85
Law, Hedy, 250, 292n23, 334n23
legato singing: in bravura singing, 134; of Caffarelli, 174; in castrati, 10, 43; in early recording era, 126; Mancini on, 113; and *messa di voce*, 116; and portamento, 116; Tosi on, xx
Legrenzi, Giovanni, 147
Legros, Joseph, 354n62
Lehmann, Lilli, 124, 125, 326n126, 327n130
Leo, Leonardo, 112
Leoncavallo, Ruggero, 153
Leopold, Silke, 11
Lezhneva, Julia, 330n2
Lombardi Satriani, M. Luigi, 26, 283n65
Lotti, Antonio, 57, 297n59
Louis XVI, King of France, 211, 358n2
Il Lucchesino (Andrea Pacini), 181, 301n85, Fig. 39
Luciani, Luciano, 129
Lyric Records, 130, 329n151

Macaroni, The (Hitchcock), 206
Machiavelli, Nicolò, 256, 367n78
Madonna delle Galline, feast of, 27
Maelzel, Johann Nepomuk, 261
Maffei, Camillo, 315n34
Magrini, Tullia, 282n54

Majorano, Gaetano. *See* Caffarelli (Gaetano Majorano)
Malibran, Maria, 127, 224, 258, 367n87
Malnati, Andrea, 223, 360n20
Mancini, Domenico, 95–96, 99–100, 110, 125, 309n5, 318n49
Mancini, Giambattista: on agility singing, 151, 177; in Bernacchi's Bolognese school, 95; on differences in castrati voices, 308n2; on falsetto, 93, 112; on "fermare la voce," 338n47; Ferri and Farinelli compared by, 336n38; on Matteuccio, 332n10; on *messa di voce*, 113; on portamento, 116, 325n115; on register, 93, 316n42; on scivolo and strascino, 118; on soprano voice, 91, 93; on strength of voice, 101; on trills, 152, 336n34; on vocal coloration, 195; vocal technology added to by, xx; on *voce naturale*, 112; warning to fathers about castrating their sons, 177, 345n2
Mancini, Hortense, 50
Manén, Lucie, 127
Manfredini, Vincenzo, 112, 195
Manzuoli, Giovanni: in Cigna and Pugnani's *Tamas Kouli-Khan*, 167, Fig. 32; Neri as student of, 107, 321n82; returns to his native patria, 305n115; sweet voice of, 106; timbre of, 105; vocal fold calcification in, 89
Marcello, Benedetto, 14–15, 35, 279n36
Marchesi, Luigi: agility singing of, 133; in "la bonne école," 235; Della Lena's criticism of, 184, 186, 195; in flamboyant line, 189; Nixon's caricature of, 186, Fig. 46; Pacchierotti contrasted with, 186–88, 195, 353n56; physical characteristics of, 170; regular features of, 184; returns to his native patria, 305n115; Sacchini's "Se cerca, se dice" rewritten by Cimarosa for, 199, 201–2; Salieri's *Prima la musica, poi le parole* spoofs, 196; sings arias sung by other singers, 354n66; Storace parodies, 197, 355n67; textual evidence of singing style of, 195–96; time difference between early recording and singing of, 153; "torrente de variazioni," 331n8; trill of, 107–8, 152; vocal gymnastics of, 114; Zingarelli's "Cara negli occhi tuoi" sung by, 117–18
Marchesi, Mathilde, 84, 153
Marianino, 106
Marini, Biagio, 147
Marini, Leonardo, 167, Fig. 32
Mariuccio (Mario Pippi), Fig. 30
martellato, xx, 151–52
Martin, Daniel, 96

Martinelli, Vincenzio, 105, 298n63, 350n44
Martini, Andrea, 321n76
Martini, Padre, 58, 106, 179, 275n9, 298n65, 344n104, 347n14
Martoni, Alessandro, 301n91
Mascagni, Pietro, 128, 153
Massi, Pietro Antonio, 12
Massi, Tommaso, 12, 279n31
Massimilla Doni (Balzac), 250
Matteuccio (Matteo Sassano or Sassani): as church singer who occasionally sang in theaters, 61; Mancini on, 332n10; Metastasio on, 338n51; ornamental passage-work of, 147; returns to his native patria, 169; time difference between early recording and singing of, 153
Mauss, Marcel, xv–xvi, 168, 270n10
Maximilian Emanuel, Elector, 57
Mazzanti, Ferdinando, 111, 324n101, 324n102
Mazzocchi, Virgilio, 58–59, 298n68
McGeary, Thomas, 307n126
Mecke, Ann-Christine, 319n57
Medina, Ángel, 285n72
Méditation sur le premier prélude de piano de S. Bach (Bach-Gounod *Ave Maria*), 82, 83, 86, 88
Melani, Atto: circulation among monarchs, 169–70; as composer, 6; diplomatic mission by, 170; as family "padrone," 66; permanent appointments of, 61, 300n81; rank and privileges for, 53, 168; romantic overtures to Hortense Mancini, 50; satires about, 286n84; sex with men, 50, 293n30; social climbing, 291n17; voice of, 308n2
Melani, Filippo, 62, 300n83
Melani, Jacopo, 302n95
Melani family, 271n17, 275n7
Melba, Nellie, 83, 84, 86, 126, 152, 153, 313n21
Melchior, Lauritz, 108
Mele, Giovanni Battista, 305n111
Melicow, Meyer M., 292n27
Melosio, Francesco, 23–24, 36, 47, 74, 181, 285n71
Memmo (Mommo; Antonio Girolamo Bigelli; Girolamo di Rospiglioso), 101, 126, 349n34, Fig. 30
Mendelssohn, Felix, 328n133
Mengozzi, Bernardo, 323n94
Meniconi, Pasquale, 260
Menicuccio (Domenico Ricci), 183
Mersenne, Marin, 126
messa di voce, 112–16; of Caffarelli, 174; of Farinelli, 134; of Moreschi, 108; portamento

compared with, 118; of Siface, 106, 113, 154; soprano singing, 115
Metastasio, Pietro (Pietro Antonio Domenico Trapassi): *Adriano in Siria*, 166, 340n73, 341n74; in Amigoni's portrait of Farinelli, 66, 302n98, Fig. 27; *Artaserse*, 40, 288n2; on Caffarelli, 105, 107, 161, 338n51; *Canzonetta di Nice*, 67; on coloratura, 185–86, 350n43; *Didone abbandonata*, 147; on enlarged eighteenth-century range, 110–12; on Farinelli being pregnant, 67, 291n22; friendship with Farinelli, 50, 66–70; kings in librettos of, 162; *L'olimpiade*, 196, 199–200, 201–2; relationship with Bulgarelli, 69
Meyerbeer, Giacomo, 260, Fig. 53
mezzos: among castrati, xi; chest singing compared with, 105; in classification of voices, 79; females playing castrati roles, 212, 237–38, 260; females playing Romeo, xxii; Garcia on female voices, 85; Micheroux on Pasta's voice, 239; "Ombra adorata, aspetta" for, 224; in trouser roles, 94, 235
Micheroux, Alexandre, 238–39, 243, 364n45
Michotte, Edmond, 259–60, 299n69, 323n96
Miles-Kingston, Paul, 99–100
Milizia, Francesco, 186
Miller, Felicia, 289n5
Millico, Vito Giuseppe: in "la bonne école," 235; as composer, 6; death of, 72; in Gluck's *Orfeo ed Euridice*, 188, 190, 193–95, 213, 354n62; in Gluck's *Paride ed Elena*, 189, 191–92; Marchesi contrasted with, 187; Pacchierotti compared with, 187, 195, 196, 352n55; *La pietà d'amore*, 190, 354n64; on reformist agenda, 190; *The Remarkable Trial of the Queen of Quavers* on, 182; and Rousseau, 187, 352n54; Sade on, 180
Minato, Niccolò, 106
Minelli, Giovanni Battista, 62, 300n84
Minter, Drew, 319n64
mirlitons, 126
Miserere (Allegri), 29
Misse petite solennelle (Rossini), 89, 129
Modi generali del canto premessi alle maniere parziale onde adornare o rifiorire le nude o semplici melodie o cantilene giusta il metodo di Gasparo Pacchierotti (print), 235, Fig. 50
monarchs: as boundary figures, 168; eternal office of kingship, 167; increasing skepticism regarding, 154; physical characteristics attributed to, 170–71; twinning of, 149–50. *See also* absolutism

money: anxieties about, 208; in Balzac's *Sarrasine*, 256–58, 259; without blood relations, 209; castrati and, 26–27, 29, 30, 49, 163–64; pigs as mediators of, 209; Pulcinella and, 26
Moniglia, Giovanni Andrea, 302n95
Monteverdi, Claudio: *L'incoronazione di Poppea*, 11; on musical representation of divinities, 337n46; Orpheus of, xxi; writing for castrati as goal of, 6
Monticelli, Angelo Maria, 73, 106, 307n126, 321n76
Moore, John, 180
Moreschi, Alessandro: in Beethoven's *Christus am Ölberge*, 89, 310n6; Capocci as teacher of, 127; career at papal chapel, 310n7; continues singing until just before his death, 129; and flute tones, 126; and Gabrielli, 309n5; Hegermann-Lindencrone on, 128; as last known castrato, 80, 260, 275n10; Mancini studies with, 95, 99, 125; *messa di voce of*, 108; portamento of, 121; and Quartetto Vocale Romano, 129, 130; recordings of, 81–82, 83, 108, 126, 310n10; vibrato of, 122; vocal fold calcification in, 89; voice of, 80–82, 84–85, 86, 89, 107, 108, 311n11, 314n28
Morlacchi, Francesco, 122, 123, 224, 239–40
Mosè in Egitto (Meyerbeer), 260, Fig. 53
Mount-Edgcumbe, Lord, 106
"Mourning Grace" (Angelou), 125
Mozart, Wolfgang Amadeus: and Aprile, 305n114; *Exsultate, jubilate*, 177; technical virtuosity of singers of, 142; Théâtre Italien stages works of, 365n63; and upward expansion of range, 110; writing for castrati as goal of, 6
Murphy, Damian T., 96, 107, 318n52
Mustafà, Domenico: after ban of 1902, 81, 310n8; Calvé studies with, 122, 124, 125, 153, 328n135; castration of, 260; fourth voice of, 124, 125–26, 128; photograph of, 11, Fig. 8; returns to his native patria, 72
Mysliveček, Josef, 142, 167

Napoleon, 211–12, 213, 215, 217, 229, 250, 358n5
natural voice, 85, 89–90, 91, 93, 112
Nature: castrati seen as unnatural, 178, 180, 183, 210; D'Argens on "smothering" of, 44, 200, 205; restoring "natural" order by castrati, 66; as sacrosanct, 180–81; truth to, 207
Nazari, Bartolomeo, 163, Fig. 7
Neri, Michele Angiolo, 107, 321n82

Nicolini (Nicola Grimaldi): bequests of, 306n123; knighthood for, 169, 341n83; Metastasio on, 338n51; proposal to a woman, 49, 185; returns to his native patria, 305n115; time difference between early recording and singing of, 153; voice seen as otherworldly, 171; Zanetti's depictions of, 17–18, 181, Fig. 4, Fig. 41
Nixon, John, 186, Fig. 46
Norcia (Italy), 12–13, 19, 279n32
norcino surgeons, 12–13, 283n60
Noris, Matteo, 147

Oedipal complex, 75
L'olimpiade (Metastasio), 196, 199–200, 201–2
"Ombra adorata" (Hoffmann), 246–47, 250, 364n55
"Ombra adorata, aspetta," 217–34; in Balzac's *Massimilla Doni*, 250; Berlioz on, 249, 250, 365n61; Conti's variations on, 229, 230–34, 361n28; Crescentini sings, 122, 217–24, 240, 243, 246–47; Eppinger's score of, 229, 230–34, 361n29; Garcia's version of, 224–29, 243, 247, 249; location in Zingarelli's *Giulietta e Romeo*, 213; as metasong, 248–49; Pasta sings, 238–39, 240–43, 244–45; portamento indications in, 122; printed versions of, 223–24; three melody lines for, 230–34; Zingarelli's versions of, 223, 360n20
"Ombra mai fu" (*Serse*), 101, 159, 160, 337n46, 337n47
Onégin, Sigrid, 152
Opera and Sovereignty (Feldman), 134, 271n15, 272n23, 285n74, 285n75, 291n15, 330n5, 338n52, 338n53, 340n67, 347n14, 348n22
opera seria, 25, 46, 154, 196, 255n74, 337n46, 366n63
Opinioni de' cantori antichi, e moderni (Tosi), xx
Orfeo ed Euridice (Gluck): "Basta, basta, o compagni," 213; Guadagni as Orpheus, 65, 169, 188; nature of virtuosity changed by, 147, 188–90; production history of, 354n62; "Smanio, fremo e deliro," 190, 193–95; Tenducci as Orpheus, 188, 295n41
Orlandini, Giuseppe Maria, 61
Orleans, Susan, 273n3
Orsini, Gaetano, 89, 95, 152
Osasco, Ottavio Cacherano d', 17
Ottoboni, Pietro, Cardinal, 62

Pacchierotti, Gasparo: biographies of, 306n122; in "la bonne école," 235; Susan Burney on, 188, 196, 235; downward tenor extension of, 100; in Gluck's *Orfeo ed Euridice*, 188, 213; Haydn's "Arianna a Naxos" sung by, 200, 203–4; in Jommelli and Verazi's *Ifigenia in Tauride*, 354n62; Marchesi contrasted with, 186–88, 195, 353n56; in Metastasio's *L'olimpiade*, 199–200; Millico compared with, 187, 195, 196, 352n55; *Modi generali del canto premessi alle maniere parziale onde adornare o rifiorire le nude o semplici melodie o cantilene giusta il metodo di Gasparo Pacchierotti* print, 235, Fig. 50; nephew of, 73, 298n68; retirement of, 171–72; romantic attachment to Susanna Burney, 50, 294n36; Stendhal, 243; sweet voice of, 106, 321n80; in Traetta's *Ippolito ed Aricia*, 196
Pacchioni, Antonio Maria, 299n73
Pacini, Andrea (Il Lucchesino), 181, 301n85, Fig. 39
Padroni, Don Mariano, 301n86
Pantalone, 26
Panzacchi, Enrico, 126, 328n138
papal chapel. *See* Sistine Chapel
Paride ed Elena (Gluck), 189, 190, 191–92
Parini, Giuseppe, 180
Park, Katharine, 180–81, 330n3
parlante singing, 189
Pasi, Antonio, 95, 151
Pasqualigo, Zaccaria, 292n25
Pasqualini, Marc'Antonio, 11, 278n29, Fig. 9
Pasquin (Fielding), 48, 291n22
passaggio: of Balatri, 56; *battuto* versus *scivolato*, 150–51, 153, 229; defined, 85; of Ferri, 112–13; in funeral music, 57; glottal attacks in, 335n31; of Mancini, 96; as marker of aesthetic and social difference, 154; Milizia on castrato, 186; in Millico's *La pietà d'amore*, 190; ornamental, 142, 147; of Orsini, 95; public desire for virtuosic, 110–11; smoothing, 112–16; Tosi on, 147, 150–51, 229, 333n14; universal, 98
Pasta, Giuditta: affiliation with eighteenth century, 235; in "la bonne école," 235; Susan Burney on, 235; castrato-like fluctuations of register of, 240; as castrato-like mezzo, xxii; Crescentini compared with, 240, 243; Micheroux as teacher of, 238, 239; "Ombra adorata, aspetta" sung by, 238–39, 240–43, 244–45; Stendhal on, 234–35, 243, 247, 362n31; in Zingarelli's *Giulietta e Romeo*, 224, 235, 238–39, 240–43, 246, 364n46, Fig. 49
patriarchy, 45
patriliny, xvi–xvii, 45–46, 58, 72, 164
patronage: versus cash nexus, xvi, 149; and castrato careers, 60, 61, 63; castrations mobilized by, 3;

castrati remain within system of, 8; larger fraternal group cared for, 65; versus new bourgeois order, 9, 30; paternal role of, 27–28, 75
Patti, Adelina, 83, 84, 86, 89, 108, 126, 313n21
Pauluccio, 46–47, 73, 280n42, 291n18
Pavarotti, Luciano, 108
Pellegrini, Valeriano: Ghezzi's depiction of, 11, 168, 183, Fig. 11; honorific title for, xx, 168; as monk, 62; in Steffani's *Tassilone*, 168
Pepoli, Sicinio, 66, 69, 70, 71, 163, 164, 339n57
"Perfido, di a quell'empio tiranno" (*Radamisto*), 94, 114
Pergolesi, Giovanni Battista, 112, 128, 166, 275n8, 340n73, 341n74
Peritz, Jessica, 314n29
Perosi, Lorenzo, 81, 318n49
"Per questo dolce amplesso" (*Artaserse*), 43
Perti, Giacomo Antonio, 61
Petersen, Scott, 312n14
Piccinni, Niccolò, 65
Pichl, Václav, 114, 195
La pietà d'amore (Millico), 190, 354n64
pigs, 15, 209
Piperno, Martina, 294n36
Pippi, Mario (Mariuccio), Fig. 30
Pirro, re di Epiro (Zingarelli), 117–18, 195
Pistocchi, Francesco Antonio Massimiliano: Balatri as student of, 57, 297n61; Bernacchi as student of, 72, 127, 257; in "la bonne école," 235; Cavalletti as student of, 61; as composer, 6; heirs of, 72; honorific title for, 341n85; time difference between early recording and singing of, 153
Planelli, Antonio, 189–90, 350n45
Plato, 67, 182–83
Poizat, Michel, 251, 271n18, 366n66
Poma, Giuseppe, 347n14
Pons, Lily, 122
Ponselle, Rosa, 152, 153, 336n37
Porpora, Nicola: on Caffarelli, 161; Corri as student of, 113, 115; as father figure of Farinelli, 66; Gabrielli as student of, 142; librettist Rolli, 26; as teacher, 59
Porporino, 91
portamento, 116–22; in agility singing, 151; in early twentieth-century sopranos, 84; in Moreschi's inheritance, 127; in "Ombra adorata, aspetta," 229; of Pasta, 243; Tosi on, xx
Potter, John, 116, 325n109, 335n33
Powers, Harold S., 159
Prima la musica, poi le parole (Salieri), 196, 197–99

primogeniture, xvii, 7, 16, 45
Prisco, Giulia (Perrini), Fig. 30
Prittoni, Silvestro, 14
property devolution, 45
Puccini, Giacomo, 116, 128, 153
Pugnani, Gaetano, 167, Fig. 32
Pulcinella, xviii; androgynous sexuality of, 22–23; animal affinities of, 22–23, 284n67; as anti-castrato, xviii–xix, 22–26; birth given by, 22, 47, Fig. 17; Burnacini's depiction of, 22, Fig. 16; as busker, 23, Fig. 18; fraternizes with aristocrats and royals, 25, Fig. 20; as liminal, 22, 24; Melosio on, 23–24, 74; and money, 26; myths of origin of, 23–24; as nonnormative or hyponormative male, 25; pregnancy attributed to, 47, Fig. 22; reversibility of, 25; Tiepolo's drawings of, 23, 47, 284n70, Fig. 19; voice of, 23

"Qual guerriero in campo armato" (*Idaspe*), 10, 134, 135–41, 173, 330n2
Quantz, Johann Joachim, 89, 94–95, 106, 152, 171, 317n45
Quartetto Vocale Romano, 129–31, Fig. 31

Raaff, Anton, 59, 338n47
Raccolta di esercizi per il canto all'uso del vocalizzo con discorso preliminare del signor Girolamo Crescentini, 110, 247–48, Fig. 51
Race, Gianni, 275n8
Radamisto (Handel), 94, 113, 325n112
Raffaellino, 183
La ragione dei "buffoni" (*La Lulliade di Ranieri de' Calzabigi*) (Calzabigi), 26, 286n81
Rauzzini, Venanzio: as composer, 6; in flamboyant line, 189; Hutchinson's portrait of, Fig. 35; Mozart writes *Exsultate, jubilate* for, 177; retirement of, 172; sweet voice of, 321n76
recordings: early recorded sopranos, 82–89; limitations of early technology, 82, 313n23; of Moreschi, 81–82, 83, 108, 126, 310n10; of Quartetto Vocale Romano, 130; time difference between late operatic castrati and early, 153
Red and the Black, The (Stendhal), 238, 258
Redi, Francesco, 322n83
register, 84–86; castrati navigating between, 317n42; continuity between, xx, 90, 91, 116; conundrum of, 89–90; dictionary definition, 313n22; Mancini on, 93, 316n42; multiple, 112; Pasta as master of, 240, 243; physiology and, 96–105; Tosi on vocal production and, 91

Remarkable Trial of the Queen of Quavers, The (anonymous), 181–83
reproduction: castrati as infertile, xii, xvii, xix, 44, 45, 48, 50, 253; castrati as reproducers of other castrati, 292n23; castration as form of male, 47; the egg as symbol of, 285n73; Galen and Aristotle on generative man, 48–49; Italian contradictions regarding, 16; twinship as metaphor for, 69
resonance, 80, 82, 151
Reynolds, Margaret, 366n68
Ricci, Domenico (Menicuccio), 183
Ricci, Marco, 183, 282n56
Ricciarelli, Giuseppe, 322n83
Richter, Bernhard, 318n56, 319n5
ringing (sweet; *squillante*) voices, 105–6, 107
Ritarossi, Giuseppe, 127, 260, 310n8
Rivani, Antonio, 62, 172, 302n95, 308n2, 322n83
Rivani, Giulio, 62, 302n95
Robin, Mado, 327n132
Robinson, Anastasia, 298n63
Rocchini, Don Evangelista, 301n86
Rodelinda (Handel), 171, Fig. 33
Rognoni, Francesco, 116, 119
Rolla, Filippo, 224, 361n26
Rolli, Paolo, 26, 64, 181, Fig. 26
Romeo (character): Crescentini in Zingarelli's *Giulietta e Romeo*, 211, 212, 213–17, 238, 251, 359n6, 366n65; mezzos take over the role from castrati, xxii; Pasta in Zingarelli's *Giulietta e Romeo*, 224, 235, 238–39, 240–43, 246, 364n46, Fig. 49
Roncaglia, Francesco, 59, 182
Rosa, Salvatore, 181
Rosenfeld, Robert, 101, 320n66, 328n138
Rosselli, John, 7, 13, 14, 207, 274n5, 274n6, 280n40, 290n14, 299n74, 300n78, 300n79, 314n31
Rossetti (castrato), 358n1
Rossi, Carlo Antonio, 58, 298n66
Rossini, Gioacchino: and advent of heavier, more muscular way of singing, 109; on art of his day, 260–61; *Aureliano in Palmira*, 260; *Il barbiere di Siviglia*, 152, 153, 337n41; on bel canto, 109–10, 205–6, 269n1, 323n96; and castrati, xii, xxii, 6, 110, 259–60, 261; Crucifixus from *Misse petite solennelle*, 89, 129; *Guillaume Tell*, xxii, 109; Michotte's *An Evening at Rossini's in Beau-Sejour (Passy) 1858*, 259–60, 323n96; Pacchierotti visited by, 172; *Semiramide*, 152; *Stabat Mater*, 128; Stendhal on, 236, 363n38, 364n43; *Tancredi*, 259; on Velluti's voice, 321n79; and Viardot, 127; wife Isabella Colbran, 110, 127, 153, 336n40
Rostirolla, Giancarlo, 129, 349n34
Rousseau, Jean-Jacques: on castrati, 179, 180, 188, 347n12; on child development, 60, 299n75; *Émile*, 60, 299n75; Millico meets, 187, 352n54; on smothering Nature, 200
Rubinelli, Giovanni Maria, 94, 305n115
Rubini, Giovanni Battista, 250
Ruggiero, Guido, 69

Sacchi, Andrea, 11, 75–76, 278n29, Fig. 9
Sacchi, Giovenale, 15
Sacchini, Antonio, 196, 199–200, 201–2
sacrifice: castration as, xii–xiii, xv–xvi, xvii–xviii, 7, 14–17, 27–29, 47, 53, 168; by monarchs, 168; sacrificial cycle, 27–29; and therapy, 16
Sade, Marquis de, 180
Saggio sopra l'opera (Algarotti), 142, 179–80, 297n61
Salecl, Renata, 251
Salieri, Antonio, 196, 197–99, 250
Salimbeni, 30
Salvatici, Fig. 14
Salvatori, Domenico, 260, 310n8
same-sex relationships, 68–69, 178
Sanguinetti, Giorgio, 275n8
Sarrasine (Balzac), 250–61; Adonis image in, 252–54; antitheses in, 255–56; blood in, 256–57; castrato in, 250, 251–52, 254, 257, 258; genealogies in, 252, 253, 254, 255; Girodet's *The Sleep of Endymion* in, 252, Fig. 52; grandniece Marianina, 258–59; laughter in, 254–55; money in, 256–58, 259; new reading of, xxii; plot, 252; publication of, 238
Sarti, Giuseppe, 196, 197–99
Sassano (Sassani), Matteo. *See* Matteuccio (Matteo Sassano or Sassani)
Saussure, Ferdinand de, 251
Sayão, Bidú, 126
Sayrus, Gregorius (Gregory Robert Sayer), 48
sbalzar, 152
Scafoglio, Domenico, 26, 283n65, 285n74
scaletta, 151
Scalzi, Carlo (Carlino): Flipart's depiction of, 171, 183, 342n93, Fig. 34; Ghezzi's depiction of, 349n35; Gualandi defended by, 64–65
Scammell, Elsa, 309n5
Scarlatti, Alessandro, 61, 110
Schafer, R. Murray, 312n18
Schiassi, Gaetano Maria, 58, 298n66
Schipa, Tito, 113, 116, 126

Schnepel, Burkhard, 149
Schoenbaum, David, 122
Schopenhauer, Arthur, 107, 358n4
scivolo, 118, 151, 153, 229
Sebastianelli, Vincenzo, 129, 260, 310n8
La secchia rapita (Tassoni), 178, 293n29, 345n4
"Se cerca, se dice" (Sacchini), 199–200, 201–2
Sedlatzek, Johann Jean, 240, 241, 243
Selva di vari passaggi (Rognoni), 119
Semiramide (Rossini), 152
Semiramide in Ascalona (Caldara), 57
Seneca, 164
Senesino (Francesco Bernardi): agility singing of, 133; brother, 66; English make jokes about, 73; family had first sons castrated, 13; on Farinelli's "Per questo dolce amplesso," 43, 49; gifts for, 165–66; in Handel operas, 25, 94, 113–14, 164, 171, Fig. 33; heir of, 73, 164, 257; physical presence of, 171, 342n91; retirement of, 154, 172, 305n115; sweet voice of, 106; timbre of, 105, 320n71; trills by, 152; Vanderbank's depiction of, 171, Fig. 33; voice of, 94, 108, 322n88; Walpole on, 322n88, 351n48; Zanetti's depictions of, 17–18, 25, 64, Fig. 4, Fig. 26
Serafin, Tullio, 152, 153
Serse (Handel), 154–59, 160–61, 337n44, 337n46, 337n47
sexuality: androgyny, 5, 22, 24, 251; binary sexual regime, xxi, 183, 303n101; of castrati, 5, 44, 274n6; hermaphrodites, 43, 289n5; intersex relations, 69, 178; same-sex relationships, 68–69, 178. *See also* celibacy
Shawe-Taylor, Desmond, 108, 336n38
"She Never Told Her Love" (Haydn), 118, 121
Sievers, Georg Ludwig Peter, 106
Siface (Giovanni Francesco Grossi): gifts for, 165; *messa di voce* of, 106, 113, 154; ornamental passage-work of, 147; permanent appointments of, 61, 300n81; runs off with marquise, 50, 154; sweet voice of, 106; time difference between early recording and singing of, 153
silvery voice, xxi, 107, 108–9
Simmel, Georg, 163–64
Sistine Chapel: account of castrati in early twentieth century, 80; castrati banned at, 81, 129; castrati officially recognized at, 48; data on castrati at, 276n12, 276n13; first castrato at, 6; groups touring under name of, 81; Hegermann-Lindencrone on vocal performances at, 128; last castrati at, 260; Quartetto Vocale Romano linked to, 129, 130
Sixtus V, Pope, 48

"Smanio, fremo e deliro" (*Orfeo ed Euridice*), 190, 193–95
Società Polifonica Romana, 329n154
"Son qual nave ch'agitata" (Broschi), 43, 142
Sontag, Henriette, 108, 258
sopranos: desire for exceptional male, xvi; dramatic, 105; early recorded, 82–89; female, 91, 99, 100, 151, 212, 319n57, 327n127; head voice of, 99; Mancini on, 91, 93; singing *messa di voce*, 115; Tosi on male and female, 91; *voci finte*, 90; women take over castrato roles, 212
Sorlisi, Bartolomeo, 53–55, 185, 280n36
squillante, 105–6, 107
Stallybrass, Peter, 4, 55, 289n5
Starobinski, Jean, 213, 215, 237, 249, 250, 359n9, 360n16, 362n32
Steffani, Agostino, 168
Stein, Louise K., 106
Steinbeck, John, 108
Stendhal: on amateur listeners, 234, 249; on "la bonne école," 235, 236–37; *The Charterhouse of Parma*, 367n88; on Crescentini, 212, 237, 247, 364n57; *De l'amour*, 235; on dying castrato vocal tradition, xxii, 236, 238; on melody, 236, 362n35; on Micheroux on Pasta, 238–39; Pacchierotti visited by, 172; on Pasta, 234–35, 243, 247, 362n31; *The Red and the Black*, 238, 258; on Rossini, 236, 363n38, 364n43; on Velluti, 237, 247, 362n35, 363n37; *Vie de Rossini*, 234–36, 237, 238, 247; on writing out ornamentation, 237, 363n38
Stokes, Martin, 285n76
Storace, Nancy, 114–15, 196, 197, 355n67
strascino, 118, 151
Strohm, Reinhard, 290n10, 330n2
Stromayr, Caspar, 8, Fig. 1
subglottal pressure, 101, 108, 152
Sundberg, Johan, 99, 318n56, 319n57
suprafalsetto (whistle tone), 124–25
Sutherland, Joan, 108
sweet voices, 105–6, 107
Symposium (Plato), 67
S/Z (Barthes), xxii, 250–51

Talmelli, Raffaele, 320n67, 363n41
Tamburini, Tommaso, xiii
Tancredi (Rossini), 259
Tarare (Beaumarchais and Salieri), 250
Tassi, Nicolò, 53
Tassoni, Alessandro, 178, 293n29, 345n4
Taylor, Gary, 30, 274n6
Il Teatro alla moda (Marcello), 14–15

Tebaldo ed Isolina (Morlacchi), 122, 123, 224, 239–40
Tedeschi, Giovanni (Giovanni Filippo Maria Dreyer; Il Tedeschino; Amadori), 61, 62, 95, 180, 300n84
Temkin, Owsei, 184, 349n40
Tenducci, Dora Maunsell, 51–53
Tenducci, Giusto Ferdinando: on being deprived of fatherhood, 73; castration of, 295n42; as composer, 6; Gainsborough portrait of, 294n38; in Gluck's *Orfeo ed Euridice*, 188, 213, 295n41; marriage of, 51–53, 307n126, 347n17; printed solfeggi of, 336n34; singing manual of, 113, 114; surgeon of, 12
tenorini, 250
Terfel, Bryn, 337n47
Tesi, Vittoria, 59, 64, 142, 165–66, Fig. 25
tessituras, 80, 95, 217
"Testamento" (Balatri), 57, 279n31
testosterone, 10, 11, 100–101
Tetrazzini, Luisa, 122
Thayer, Alexander Wheelock, 361n29
Théâtre Italien (Paris), 358n5, 365n63
Thurneysser, Leonhard, Fig. 45
Tiepolo, Giandomenico, 23, 47, 284n70, Fig. 19
timbre, 105, 107, 108, 236, 243
Todi, Luigia, 235, 243
Tosi, Pierfrancesco: on agility singing, 151, 177; and Balatri's voice, 56; on Bernacchi's new instrumental style of singing, 57; on combining *strascino*, portamento, and *messa di voce*, 335n33; diplomatic mission by, 170; estate of, 72, 305n116, 306n118; on feigned voice, 327n130; heir of, 72–73; on *messa di voce*, 113; on "mettere la voce" and "fermare la voce," 337n47; *Opinioni de' cantori antichi, e moderni*, xx; on *passaggi*, 147, 150–51, 229, 333n14; as priest, 62; on register in relation to vocal production, 90–91; on scivolo and strascino, 118; on trills, 152; on *voce naturale*, 89–90, 91, 112; writes in era of chest singing, 110
Totila (Noris and Legrenzi), 147
Traetta, Tommaso, 147, 196
Traité complet de l'art du chant (Garcia), 85, 87, 122, 225–28, 329n147
"Tranquillo io son" (*Giulietta e Romeo*), 215, 216, 240, 244, 246
transsexuals, voice breaks in, 313n24
Tricarico, Nicola, 60, Fig. 24
trills: in agility singing, 151, 152, 336n34; Agricola on writing down of, 142; of Balatri, 56; Bontempi on, 152; Crescentini on, 248; as dead in big opera houses, 153; in deluxe singing, 148; of Farinelli, 163; of Ferri, 112–13; in funeral music, 57; of Marchesi, 107–8, 152, 188; Metastasio on, 111, 147; Milizia on castrato, 186; Moore on castrato, 180; in "Ombra adorata, aspetta," 229; Mancini on, 152; of Orsini, 95; in "Perfido, di a quell'empio tiranno," 94, 114; in portamento development, 116; Quantz on, 152; Tosi on, xx; Verri (Pietro) on, 152; in Zanetti's caricature of Bernacchi, 101, Fig. 29c
La troia rapita (Vittori), 15, 50, 293n29
trouser roles, xxii, 64, 94, 235, 237–38
Troven, Marianne, 318n56
True and Genuine Narrative of Mr. and Mrs. Tenducci, 51
twinship, 67–70, 149–50

Uccelli, Don Giovanni Battista, 301n86
Urbani, Valentino (Valentini), 64, Fig. 25

Vaccai, Nicola, 109
Valentini (Valentino Urbani), 64, Fig. 25
Vallisnieri, Antonio, 118, 151
Vanderbank, John, 171, Fig. 33
Velluti, Giambattista: agility singing of, 133; anecdote about birth of, 296n48; in "la bonne école," 235; "Caro suono lusinghier" from Morlacchi's *Tebaldo ed Isolina*, 224, 239–40; Chalon's depiction of, 260, Fig. 53; as last major castrato star, 238; in Meyerbeer's *Mosè in Egitto*, 260, Fig. 53; portamento of, 122; purity of voice of, 321n79; Rossini writes Armando in *Aureliano in Palmira* for, 260; singing style of, 361n24; Stendhal on, 237, 247, 362n35, 363n37; time difference between early recording and singing of, 153; on verge of castrati's demise, 251
Vendetta, Cecchino, 349n34
Vendrix, Philippe, 363n43
Verazi, Mattia, 354n62
Verdi, Giuseppe, 81, 109, 127, 153
Verri, Alessandro, 187, 206, 356n81, Fig. 47
Verri, Pietro, 107–8, 152, 187–88, 195
"Very Old Man with Enormous Wings, A: A Tale for Children" (Garcia Márquez), 3–4
Viardot, Pauline, 127
vibrato, 122
Vidal, Melchiorre, 152–53
Vie de Rossini (Stendhal), 234–36, 237, 238, 247
Vigée-Lebrun, Madame, 29
vigils, castrati in, 29
Vigny, Alfred de, 250, 366n65

INDEX   421

Villemarest, Charles-Maxime de, 215, 217
Vinci, Leonardo, 112, 288n2, Fig. 43
Visconti, Caterina (La Visconti), 152
Vismarri, Filippo, 65, 170, 300n82
Vissani, Giosafat Anselmo, 127, 260
Vitali, Carol, 301n87
Vittori, Loreto: on castrati as "musical swans," 15; as composer, 6; elopement with married woman, 50; gifts for, 165; knighthood for, 168; as priest, 62; *La troia rapita*, 15, 50, 293n29, 345n4
Vivaldi, Antonio: and Metastasio's preference in voices, 112; *Stabat mater*, 10, 278n24; writing for castrati as goal of, 6
vocal cords (folds): of castrati, 10, 11, 89, 100–101, 319n57; diagram of vocal anatomy, Fig. 28; physiology of register, 96, 318n51; and power, 108; and register, 85
voce di testa. *See* head voice (*voce di testa*)
voci bianche (white voices), 122, 326n123
voci finte, 90
voice: of Balatri, 55–56, 107, 108; of castrati, xi, xx–xxi, 5, 10, 44, 79–132; Garcia on male, 85–86; grain of the, 79; historical jargon about, 313n22; as medium, 237, 251; of Moreschi, 80–82, 84–85, 86, 89, 107, 108, 311n11, 314n28; of Pulcinella, 23; virility and, 48–49; vocal anatomy, 85, Fig. 28. *See also* register
voice box. *See* larynx (voice box)
volatina, 151
Voltaire, 179, 207, 346n10

Wagner, Richard, 105, 109, 261
Wall, Joan, 124

Walpole, Horace, 322n88, 351n48
Walsh, John, 43
Walther, Johann Jakob, 147
Walton, Benjamin, 235, 362n34
Weber, Max, 150
whistle tone (suprafalsetto), 124–25
White, Allon, 4, 55
white voices (*voci bianche*), 122, 326n123
Wigmore, Richard, 326n127
Willier, Stephen, 294n35, 306n122
Wistreich, Richard, 153, 336n34
Woodfield, Ian, 182
Wrightson, Elizabeth Augusta, 364n52

Yates, Mary Ann, 182

Zacchia, Paolo, 276n15
Zacconi, Lodovico, 315n34, 324n103
Zanetti, Anton Maria: Balatri depicted by, 11, Fig. 5; Bernacchi depicted by, 17, 26, Fig. 13, Fig. 21, Fig. 29a, b, and c; caricatures of castrati, 10–11, 64, 278n26; Castorino depicted by, 181, Fig. 40; Farinelli depicted by, 64, 183, Fig. 25; Nicolini depicted by, 17–18, 181, Fig. 4, Fig. 41; Pacini depicted by, 181, Fig. 39; Salvatici depicted by, Fig. 14; Senesino depicted by, 17–18, 25, 64, Fig. 4, Fig. 26; Tricarico depicted by, 60, Fig. 24
Zeno, Apostolo, 57, 167
Zingarelli, Nicola: *Pirro, re di Epiro*, 117–18, 195; Théâtre Italien stages works of, 366n63. *See also Giulietta e Romeo* (Zingarelli)
Žižek, Slavoj, 251

www.ingramcontent.com/pod-product-compliance
Lightning Source LLC
Chambersburg PA
CBHW030514230426
43665CB00010B/611